500 POTATO RECIPES

500 POTATO RECIPES

IRRESISTIBLE RECIPES FOR EVERY OCCASION, INCLUDING APPETIZERS, SNACKS, SALADS
AND MAIN COURSES, SHOWN IN 500 TEMPTING PHOTOGRAPHS   ELIZABETH WOODLAND

greene&golden

This edition is published by greene&golden,
an imprint of Anness Publishing Ltd
Blaby Road, Wigston
Leicestershire LE18 4SE
info@anness.com

www.annesspublishing.com

If you like the images in this book and would like to
investigate using them for publishing, promotions or
advertising, please visit our website www.practicalpictures.com
for more information.

Publisher: Joanna Lorenz
Project Editors: Elizabeth Woodland and Dan Hurst
Desk Editor: Barbara Toft
Production Controller: Don Campaniello

© Anness Publishing Ltd 2012

NOTES

Bracketed terms are intended for American readers.

For all recipes, quantities are given in both metric and imperial
measures and, where appropriate, in standard cups and spoons.
Follow one set of measures, but not a mixture, because they
are not interchangeable.

Standard spoon and cup measures are level. 1 tsp = 5ml,
1 tbsp = 15ml, 1 cup = 250ml/8fl oz.

Australian standard tablespoons are 20ml. Australian
readers should use 3 tsp in place of 1 tbsp for measuring
small quantities.

American pints are 16fl oz/2 cups. American readers should use
20fl oz/2.5 cups in place of 1 pint when measuring liquids.

Electric oven temperatures in this book are for conventional
ovens. When using a fan oven, the temperature will probably
need to be reduced by about 10–20°C/20–40°F. Since ovens
vary, you should check with your manufacturer's instruction
book for guidance.

The nutritional analysis given for each recipe is calculated per
portion (i.e. serving or item), unless otherwise stated. If the
recipe gives a range, such as Serves 4–6, then the nutritional
analysis will be for the smaller portion size, i.e. 6 servings.
The analysis does not include optional ingredients, such as
salt added to taste.

Medium (US large) eggs are used unless otherwise stated.

Front cover shows Potatoes in Chilli Tamarind Sauce
– for recipe, see page 233.

PUBLISHER'S NOTE

Contents

Introduction

There are few more important foods in the world than the potato. Its history goes back to the early days of man and has a past spanning feast and famine and it has long

played a vital role as one of the best all-round sources of nutrition for mankind.

The potato was discovered by pre-Inca inhabitants in the foothills of the Andes Mountains in South America. Archaeological remains have been found dating from 400BC on the shores of Lake Titicaca, in ruins near Bolivia, and on the coast of Peru.

The first recorded information about the potato was written in 1553 by the Spanish conquistador Pedro Cieza de Leon, and soon potatoes joined the treasures carried away by Spanish invaders. Its cultivation spread quickly throughout Europe via explorers such as Sir Francis Drake, who is reputed to have brought potatoes back to Britain. During Charles II's reign, the Royal Society recognized the potato as being nutritional and inexpensive and tried to persuade their farmers to start growing this valuable crop in abundance.

The United States, one of the world's largest producers of potatoes, was introduced to the potato by early European immigrants, but it was not until the Irish took the potato to Londonderry, New Hampshire, in 1719, that it began to be grown in any quantity.

Today the potato is the staple food for two-thirds of the world's population and our third most important food crop. It is one of the best complete sources of nutrition known to man, second only to eggs for protein. Growing potatoes is also the world's most efficient means of converting land, water and labour into an edible product – a field of potatoes produces more energy per acre per day than a field of any other crop.

This book explores the infinite adaptability of the potato and is the ultimate resource for the potato-loving cook. As you'd expect, it includes all the classic potato dishes, such as Potato Rösti, Shepherd's Pie and Leek and Potato Soup, but we've also investigated every conceivable way of introducing our favourite ingredient into some familiar and much-loved dishes. There are delicious and deceptively healthy Thai Potato Samosas, a rich and luxurious Fish Pie with Saffron Mash, an exotic and delicately spiced Beef Tagine with Sweet Potatoes and an unusual, and truly decadent, Chocolate Potato Cake.

Other tempting and surprising recipes include a flavoursome Potato, Smoked Mozzarella and Garlic Pizza, an impressive Spicy Potato Strudel, and a delightfully piquant Potato Curry with Yoghurt. There are countless distinctive variations of classic and mouthwatering potato dishes as well as a seemingly endless array of new and exciting recipes that will be sure to broaden your potato repertoire and have you cooking delectable potato dishes every day of the week.

The recipes are neatly split into eight easy-to-use sections which divide the book between Soups; Appetizers and Snacks; Salads; Fish and Shellfish; Meat and Poultry; Vegetable Dishes; Side Dishes; and finally Desserts, Bakes and Breads, making it easy to find the perfect potato dish, whatever the occasion. Whether you are looking for a sensational potato recipe for an elaborate formal dinner party, a simple and nutritious dish for a mid-week family meal, or a light and tasty snack to keep you going through the afternoon, the plethora of wonderful potato recipes on display here will be sure to deliver the perfect dish time and time again.

This book is the ultimate celebration of an underrated staple of the vegetable kingdom and clearly illustrates the many delicious uses of the potato, whatever the variety – whether you are using large maincrop potatoes, small new potatoes or candied sweet potatoes. So go on – expand your culinary horizons and unlock the potential of the nutritional powerhouse of the vegetable world, the humble potato, today.

Potato and Leek Vichyssoise

This classic, chilled potato soup was first created in the 1920s by Louis Diat, chef at the New York Ritz-Carlton. He named it after Vichy, near his home in France.

Serves 4–6
50g/2oz/¼ cup unsalted (sweet) butter
450g/1lb leeks, white parts only, thinly sliced
3 large shallots, sliced
250g/9oz floury potatoes (such as King Edward or Maris Piper), peeled and cut into chunks
1 litre/1¾ pints/4 cups light chicken stock or water
300ml/½ pint/1¼ cups double (heavy) cream
iced water (optional)
a little lemon juice (optional)
salt and ground black pepper
chopped fresh chives, to garnish

1 Melt the butter in a heavy pan and cook the leeks and shallots gently, covered, for about 15–20 minutes, until soft but not browned.

2 Add the potatoes and cook, uncovered, for a few minutes. Stir in the stock or water with 5ml/1 tsp salt and pepper to taste. Bring to the boil, then reduce the heat and partly cover the pan. Simmer for 15 minutes, or until the potatoes are soft.

3 Cool, then process the mixture until smooth in a blender or food processor. Strain the soup into a bowl and stir in the cream. Taste and adjust the seasoning and add a little iced water if the consistency of the soup seems too thick.

4 Chill the soup for at least 4 hours or until very cold. Before serving, taste the chilled soup for seasoning and add a squeeze of lemon juice, if required. Pour the soup into bowls and sprinkle with chopped chives. Serve immediately.

> **Variation**
> Add about 50g/2oz/1 cup shredded sorrel to the soup at the end of cooking. Finish and chill as in the main recipe, then serve the soup garnished with a little pile of finely shredded sorrel. The same quantity of watercress can be used in the same way.

Spicy Chilled Cardamom, Leek and Potato Soup

This subtly spiced version of the classic potato vichyssoise is enhanced with fragrant cardamom and topped with the refreshing tang of yogurt.

Serves 4
8 green cardamom pods
25g/1oz/2 tbsp butter
15ml/1 tbsp vegetable oil
1 small onion, chopped
3 leeks, sliced
2 floury potatoes, diced
600ml/1 pint/2½ cups vegetable stock
300ml/½ pint/1¼ cups milk
45ml/3 tbsp single (light) cream
a little extra milk (optional)
grated zest of 1 small lemon
60ml/4 tbsp natural (plain) yogurt and fried leeks, to serve
salt and ground black pepper

1 Scrape out the seeds from the cardamom pods and grind them to a fine powder in a mortar and pestle.

2 Heat the butter and oil in a large pan and add the onion, leeks, ground cardamom and potatoes. Cover and cook for 15 minutes, stirring occasionally, until the leeks have wilted and given up their juices. Bring to the boil, reduce the heat to a gentle simmer and cook for 10 minutes.

3 Stir in the stock and milk and heat until simmering. Cover again and cook for a further 15 minutes, until the vegetables are completely tender.

4 Ladle the vegetables and liquid into a blender or a food processor in batches and purée until smooth. Pour into a bowl or jug (pitcher) for chilling. Stir in the cream and grated lemon zest and season.

5 Leave the soup to cool, and then refrigerate for 3–4 hours, or longer until chilled and ready to serve. You may need to add a little extra milk to thin down the soup, as it will thicken up slightly as it cools.

6 Ladle the soup into soup bowls and serve topped with a spoonful of natural yogurt and a sprinkling of leeks.

Vichyssoise Energy 547kcal/2260kJ; Protein 4.6g; Carbohydrate 17.7g, of which sugars 6.8g; Fat 51.4g, of which saturates 31.7g; Cholesterol 129mg; Calcium 79mg; Fibre 3.6g; Sodium 103mg.
Spicy Cardamom Energy 410kcal/1695kJ; Protein 3.5g; Carbohydrate 13.2g, of which sugars 5.1g; Fat 38.5g, of which saturates 23.8g; Cholesterol 97mg; Calcium 59mg; Fibre 2.7g; Sodium 77mg.

Chunky Leek, Onion and Potato Soup

The nutritious combination of leek, onion and potato makes for a really tasty and substantial soup. It is incredibly simple to make and the ingredients are fresh, inexpensive and readily available to buy throughout the year, which makes this an essential addition to any home cook's repertoire.

Serves 4
50g/2oz/¼ cup butter
2 leeks, chopped
1 small onion, finely chopped
350g/12oz floury
    potatoes, chopped
900ml/1½ pints/3¾ cups
    chicken or vegetable stock
salt and ground black pepper
crusty bread, to serve

1 Heat 25g/1oz/2 tbsp of the butter in a large heavy pan, add the chopped leeks and onion and cook gently, stirring occasionally so that they do not stick to the bottom of the pan. Cook for about 6–8 minutes until the vegetables have softened but not browned.

2 Add the chopped potatoes to the pan and cook, stirring occasionally, for 2–3 minutes.

3 Pour in the stock and slowly bring to the boil, then reduce the heat, cover and simmer gently for 30–35 minutes until the vegetables are cooked through and very tender.

4 Season to taste with salt and black pepper, remove the pan from the heat and stir in the remaining butter in small pieces.

5 Ladle the soup into warmed soup bowls and serve hot with slices of thick crusty bread.

> **Cook's Tip**
> If you prefer your soup to have a smoother consistency, simply press the mixture through a sieve (strainer) or pass through a food mill once it is cooked. Don't use a food processor as it can give the potatoes a gluey texture.

Creamy Leek, Potato and Rocket Soup

Rocket adds its distinctive, peppery taste to this wonderfully creamy potato and leek soup. Serve this soup hot, garnished with a generous sprinkling of tasty ciabatta croûtons flavoured with garlic.

Serves 4–6
50g/2oz/¼ cup butter
1 onion, chopped
3 leeks, chopped
2 medium floury potatoes, diced
900ml/1½ pints/3¾ cups light
    chicken stock or water
2 large handfuls rocket (arugula),
    roughly chopped
150ml/¼ pint/⅔ cup double
    (heavy) cream
salt and ground black pepper
garlic-flavoured ciabatta croûtons,
    to garnish

1 Melt the butter in a large heavy pan, then add the chopped onion, leeks and diced potatoes and stir until the vegetables are coated in butter. Heat until the ingredients are sizzling, then reduce the heat to low.

2 Cover and sweat the vegetables for 15 minutes. Pour in the chicken stock or water and bring to the boil. Reduce the heat, cover again and simmer for about 20 minutes until all the vegetables are tender.

3 Press the soup through a sieve (strainer) using a wooden spoon, or pass it through a food mill, and return the mixture to the rinsed-out pan. (When puréeing the soup, don't use a blender or food processor, as these will cause the soup to develop a gluey texture.)

4 Add the chopped rocket to the pan and continue to cook the soup gently, uncovered, for 5 minutes.

5 Stir in the double cream, then season to taste with salt and black pepper and reheat gently. Ladle the soup into warmed soup bowls and serve with a sprinkling of garlic-flavoured ciabatta croûtons in each.

Creamy Leek Soup Energy 235kcal/972kJ; Protein 2.8g; Carbohydrate 9.4g, of which sugars 3.2g; Fat 20.9g, of which saturates 12.8g; Cholesterol 52mg; Calcium 75mg; Fibre 2.3g; Sodium 97mg.
Chunky Leek Soup Energy 178kcal/744kJ; Protein 3.4g; Carbohydrate 17.8g, of which sugars 3.9g; Fat 11.1g, of which saturates 7g; Cholesterol 29mg; Calcium 33mg; Fibre 3g; Sodium 288mg.

Irish Potato Soup

This most Irish of all soups is not only excellent as it is, but versatile too, as it can be used as an ideal base for numerous other delicious soups.

Serves 6–8
50g/2oz/¼ cup butter
2 large onions, peeled and
  finely chopped

675g/1½lb floury potatoes, diced
about 1.75 litres/3 pints/7½ cups
  hot chicken stock
sea salt and ground black pepper
a little milk, if necessary
chopped fresh chives, to garnish

1 Melt the butter in a large heavy pan and add the onions, turning them in the butter until well coated. Cover and leave to sweat over a very low heat for about 10 minutes.

2 Add the potatoes to the pan, and mix well with the butter and onions. Season with salt and pepper, cover and cook without browning over a gentle heat for about 10 minutes.

3 Add the stock, bring to the boil and simmer for 25 minutes, or until the vegetables are tender.

4 Remove the pan from the heat and allow the soup to cool slightly. Press the soup through a sieve (strainer) or pass it through a food mill, and return to the rinsed-out pan.

5 Reheat the soup over a low heat and adjust the seasoning. If the soup seems too thick, add a little extra stock or milk to achieve the right consistency.

6 Ladle the soup into warmed bowls. Sprinkle each serving with chopped chives and serve immediately.

Cook's Tip
The best potatoes to use in soups are the floury ones, because they cook more quickly and disintegrate easily. Choose varieties such as Golden Wonder, Estima and King Edward.

Leek and Potato with Heart of Palm Soup

This delicate soup has a luxurious, creamy, almost velvety texture. The subtle yet distinctive flavour of the hearts of palm complements the delicate traditional tastes of leek and potato. Serve with fresh bread for a really satisfying lunch.

Serves 4
25g/1oz/2 tbsp butter
10ml/2 tsp olive oil
1 onion, finely chopped
1 large leek, finely sliced

15ml/1 tbsp plain
  (all-purpose) flour
1 litre/1¾ pints/4 cups well-
  flavoured chicken stock
350g/12oz potatoes, peeled
  and cubed
2 x 400g/14oz cans hearts of
  palm, drained and sliced
250ml/8fl oz/1 cup double
  (heavy) cream
salt and ground black pepper
cayenne pepper and chopped
  fresh chives, to garnish

1 Heat the butter and oil in a large pan over a low heat. Add the onion and leek and stir well until coated in butter. Cover and cook for 5 minutes until softened and translucent.

2 Sprinkle the flour into the pan over the vegetables. Stir and cook, still stirring, for 1 minute.

3 Pour in the stock and add the potatoes. Bring to the boil, stirring, then lower the heat and simmer for 10 minutes. Stir in the hearts of palm and the cream, and simmer gently for a further 10 minutes.

4 Process the soup in a food processor or blender until smooth. Pour it back into the rinsed-out pan and heat gently, adding a little water if necessary. The consistency should be thick but not too heavy. Do not allow to boil. Season with salt and ground black pepper.

5 Ladle the soup into warm bowls and garnish each portion with a pinch of cayenne pepper and a sprinkling of fresh chives. Serve immediately.

Irish Potato Soup Energy 167kcal/699kJ; Protein 2.9g; Carbohydrate 23.5g, of which sugars 5.3g; Fat 7.5g, of which saturates 4.5g; Cholesterol 18mg; Calcium 26mg; Fibre 2.1g; Sodium 201mg.
Leek and Potato Energy 486kcal/2013kJ; Protein 5.2g; Carbohydrate 25.1g, of which sugars 7.9g; Fat 41.2g, of which saturates 24.5g; Cholesterol 99mg; Calcium 147mg; Fibre 4.9g; Sodium 184mg.

Potato and Mushroom Soup

Using a mixture of mushrooms in this soup adds character and the flavour mingles well with the earthy potatoes. Serve with fresh crusty bread.

**Serves 4–6 as a light meal
or 6–8 as a soup course**
20g/¾oz/1½ tbsp butter
15ml/1 tbsp oil
1 onion, roughly chopped
4 potatoes, about 250–350g/
9–12oz, roughly chopped

350g/12oz mixed mushrooms,
  such as brown cap (cremini),
  field (portabello) and button
  (white), roughly chopped
1 or 2 garlic cloves, crushed
150ml/¼ pint/⅔ cup white wine
  or dry (hard) cider
1.2 litres/2 pints/5 cups
  vegetable stock
bunch of fresh parsley, chopped
salt and ground black pepper
whipped or sour cream, to garnish

1 Heat the butter and oil in a large pan, over medium heat. Add the onion and potatoes. Cover and sweat over a low heat for 5–10 minutes until softened but not browned.

2 Add the mushrooms, garlic and white wine or cider and stock. Season, bring to the boil and cook for 15 minutes, until all the ingredients are tender.

3 Put the mixture through a food mill, using the coarse blade, or purée in a food processor or blender.

4 Return the soup to the rinsed-out pan, and add three-quarters of the parsley. Reheat and taste for seasoning, adding more salt or pepper if necessary. Serve garnished with cream and the remaining parsley.

Variation
Mustard and tarragon are a delicious combination together with mushrooms: try adding 15ml/1 tbsp wholegrain mustard to the onions and potatoes before stirring in the stock. For a hint of sweetness, use a medium sherry instead of the wine or cider, and add the leaves from a large sprig of fresh tarragon.

Cabbage and Potato Soup with Caraway

Earthy floury potatoes are essential to the texture of this soup, so it is best not to use waxy salad potatoes. Caraway seeds come from a plant in the parsley family. They are aromatic and nutty, with a delicate anise flavour, adding a subtle accent to this smooth and satisfying dish.

Serves 4
30ml/2 tbsp olive oil
2 small onions, sliced
6 garlic cloves, halved
350g/12oz green
  cabbage, shredded
4 potatoes, unpeeled
5ml/1 tsp caraway seeds
5ml/1 tsp sea salt
1.2 litres/2 pints/5 cups
  boiling water

1 Pour the olive oil into a large pan and add the onions. Cook, stirring occasionally, for 10 minutes, until the onions are softened, but not browned.

2 Add the garlic and the cabbage and continue to cook over a low heat for 10 minutes, stirring occasionally to prevent the cabbage from sticking.

3 Add the potatoes, caraway seeds, sea salt and water. Bring to the boil. Reduce the heat and cover the pan, then simmer until all the vegetables are cooked through, about 20–30 minutes.

4 Remove the pan from the heat and allow the soup to cool slightly before mashing it into a purée or processing in a food processor. Pass the soup through a sieve (strainer), if you like.

5 Return the soup to the rinsed-out pan and reheat gently, stirring, until almost boiling before serving.

Cook's Tip
Use floury potatoes to achieve the correct texture for this soup. King Edward or Maris Piper (US russet or Idaho) are excellent choices. Peel the potatoes if preferred or if they are old.

Mushroom Soup Energy 155kcal/648kJ; Protein 3.3g; Carbohydrate 13.6g, of which sugars 3.4g; Fat 7.6g, of which saturates 3.1g; Cholesterol 11mg; Calcium 23mg; Fibre 2.1g; Sodium 117mg.
Cabbage and Potato Energy 144kcal/601kJ; Protein 3.1g; Carbohydrate 20.4g, of which sugars 8.1g; Fat 6g, of which saturates 0.9g; Cholesterol 0mg; Calcium 60mg; Fibre 3.3g; Sodium 507mg.

Creamed Spinach and Potato Soup

This is a delicious low-fat potato soup that is both quick and simple to make. This recipe uses spinach but other vegetables would work just as well, such as cabbage or Swiss chard.

Serves 4
1.2 litres/2 pints/5 cups
  vegetable stock
1 large onion, finely chopped
1 garlic clove, crushed

900g/2lb floury potatoes, diced
2 celery sticks, chopped
250g/9oz fresh spinach leaves
200g/7oz/scant 1 cup low-fat
  soft (farmer's) cheese
300ml/½ pint/1¼ cups milk
dash of dry sherry
salt and ground black pepper

For the garnish
croûtons
a few baby spinach leaves or
  chopped fresh parsley

1 Place the stock, onion, garlic, potatoes and celery in a large pan. Bring to the boil, reduce the heat and cover the pan. Simmer the soup for 20 minutes.

2 Season the soup and add the spinach leaves, then bring back to the boil. Reduce the heat to a gentle simmer and cook for a further 10 minutes. Remove from the heat and cool slightly.

3 Process the soup in a food processor or blender until smooth and return it to the rinsed-out pan.

4 Stir in the soft cheese and milk. Reheat gently without boiling and taste for seasoning. Add a dash of sherry.

5 Ladle the soup into bowls and serve topped with croûtons and a few baby spinach leaves or chopped fresh parsley.

Cook's Tip
A hand-held blender is excellent for quickly puréeing soups in the pan. Remove the pan from the heat and let it cool slighlty first. Take care to keep the blender well down in the pan, otherwise the soup will spray everywhere. Start on a low setting to break up some of the ingredients, then increase the speed.

Summer Herb Soup with Potato

The sweetness of shallots and leeks in this soup is balanced beautifully by the potatoes and slightly acidic sorrel, with its hint of lemon, and a bouquet of summer herbs.

Serves 4–6
30ml/2 tbsp dry white wine
2 shallots, finely chopped
1 garlic clove, crushed
2 leeks, sliced
1 potato, about 225g/8oz,
  roughly chopped

2 courgettes (zucchini), chopped
600ml/1 pint/2½ cups
  boiling water
115g/4oz sorrel, torn
large handful of fresh chervil
large handful of fresh flat
  leaf parsley
large handful of fresh mint
1 round or butterhead lettuce,
  separated into leaves
600ml/1 pint/2½ cups
  vegetable stock
1 small head radicchio
5ml/1 tsp groundnut (peanut) oil
salt and ground black pepper

1 Put the wine, shallots and garlic into a heavy pan and bring to the boil. Cook for 2–3 minutes, until softened. Add the leeks, potato and courgette with enough of the water to come about halfway up the vegetables. Lay a wetted piece of baking parchment over the vegetables and put a lid on the pan, then cook gently for 10–15 minutes, until softened. Remove the paper and add the fresh herbs and lettuce. Cook for 1–2 minutes, or until wilted.

2 Pour in the remaining water and vegetable stock and simmer for 10–12 minutes. Cool the soup slightly, then process it in a food processor or blender until smooth. Return the soup to the rinsed-out pan and season well.

3 Cut the radicchio into thin wedges that hold together, then brush the cut sides with the oil. Heat a ridged griddle or frying pan until very hot and add the radicchio wedges. Cook the radicchio wedges for about 1 minute on each side until very well browned and slightly charred in places.

4 Reheat the soup over a low heat, stirring occasionally, then ladle it into warmed shallow bowls. Serve a wedge of charred radicchio on top of each portion.

Creamed Spinach Soup Energy 274kcal/1157kJ; Protein 15.3g; Carbohydrate 46.2g, of which sugars 11.6g; Fat 5g, of which saturates 2.7g; Cholesterol 13mg; Calcium 281mg; Fibre 4.4g; Sodium 348mg.
Summer Herb Energy 199kcal/837kJ; Protein 10.2g; Carbohydrate 29.2g, of which sugars 12.6g; Fat 4.4g, of which saturates 0.9g; Cholesterol 0mg; Calcium 227mg; Fibre 8.6g; Sodium 94mg.

Potato and Fennel Soup

This light potato and fennel soup is delicious served with moreish rosemary scones.

Serves 4
75g/3oz/6 tbsp butter
2 onions, chopped
5ml/1 tsp fennel seeds, crushed
3 bulbs fennel, coarsely chopped
900g/2lb potatoes, thinly sliced
1.2 litres/2 pints/5 cups
   chicken stock
150ml/¼ pint/²⁄₃ cup double
   (heavy) cream

salt and ground black pepper
handful of fresh herb flowers and
   15ml/1 tbsp chopped fresh
   chives, to garnish

For the rosemary scones
225g/8oz/2 cups self-raising
   (self-rising) flour
2.5ml/½ tsp salt
5ml/1 tsp baking powder
10ml/2 tsp chopped fresh rosemary
50g/2oz/¼ cup butter
150ml/¼ pint/²⁄₃ cup milk
1 egg, beaten, to glaze

1 Melt the butter in a pan. Add the onions and cook gently for 10 minutes, stirring occasionally, until very soft. Add the fennel seeds and cook for 2–3 minutes. Stir in the fennel and potatoes. Cover with wet baking parchment. Cover and simmer gently for 10 minutes, until very soft. Remove the parchment. Pour in the stock, bring to the boil, cover and simmer for 35 minutes.

2 Meanwhile, make the scones. Preheat the oven to 230°C/450°F/Gas 8 and grease a baking tray. Sift the flour, salt and baking powder into a bowl. Stir in the rosemary, then rub in the butter. Add the milk and mix to form a soft dough.

3 Knead very lightly on a floured surface. Roll out to 2cm/¾in thick. Stamp out 12 rounds with a cutter and place on the baking tray. Brush with egg and bake for 8–10 minutes, until risen and golden. Cool on a wire rack until warm.

4 Purée the soup in a food processor or blender until smooth. Press through a sieve (strainer) into the rinsed-out pan. Stir in the cream with seasoning to taste. Reheat gently but do not boil.

5 Ladle the soup into bowls, and sprinkle over a few herb flowers and some chopped chives. Serve with the warm rosemary scones.

Broad Bean and Potato Soup

Coriander provides a refreshing twist to this creamy soup of fresh beans and hearty potatoes.

Serves 4
30ml/2 tbsp olive oil
2 onions, chopped
3 large floury
   potatoes, diced

450g/1lb fresh shelled broad
   (fava) beans
1.75 litres/3 pints/7½ cups
   vegetable stock
1 bunch fresh coriander (cilantro),
   roughly chopped
150ml/¼ pint/²⁄₃ cup single
   (light) cream, plus a little extra,
   to garnish
salt and ground black pepper

1 Heat the oil in a large pan and fry the onions, stirring, for about 5 minutes, until they are soft.

2 Add the potatoes. Reserve a few of the broad beans for garnish, then add the rest to the pan. Pour over the stock, and bring it to the boil. Simmer the soup for 5 minutes, then add the coriander and simmer for a further 10 minutes.

3 Blend the soup in batches in a food processor or blender until smooth, then return it to the rinsed-out pan.

4 Reheat the soup until almost boiling, stirring to prevent it from sticking to the pan. Stir in the cream and heat for a few seconds, but do not allow the soup to simmer or boil.

5 Blanch the reserved beans in boiling water for 1 minute, then drain them and remove their skins.

6 Taste and season the soup, then ladle it into bowls and garnish with beans, cream and chopped coriander.

Variation
Instead of the broad (fava) beans, try a combination of peas – shelled fresh or frozen – and a bunch of watercress in this recipe. The peas and watercress are delicious with the coriander (cilantro).

Potato and Fennel Energy 797kcal/3332kJ; Protein 12.3g; Carbohydrate 84.1g, of which sugars 8.8g; Fat 48.1g, of which saturates 29.6g; Cholesterol 120mg; Calcium 316mg; Fibre 7.6g; Sodium 703mg.
Broad Bean and Potato Energy 236kcal/990kJ; Protein 9.3g; Carbohydrate 30.3g, of which sugars 4.6g; Fat 9.4g, of which saturates 3.8g; Cholesterol 14mg; Calcium 94mg; Fibre 6.8g; Sodium 30mg.

Creamy Corn, Cannellini Bean and Potato Chowder

This creamy, yet chunky, potato soup is filled with the sweet taste of corn. Punchy Cheddar cheese rounds off the fabulous flavour.

Serves 4
1 onion, chopped
1 garlic clove, crushed
1 baking potato, chopped
2 celery sticks, sliced
1 small green (bell) pepper, seeded, halved and sliced
30ml/2 tbsp sunflower oil
25g/1oz/2 tbsp butter
600ml/1 pint/2½ cups vegetable stock or water
300ml/½ pint/1¼ cups milk
200g/7oz can flageolet (small cannellini) beans
300g/11oz can corn
good pinch of dried sage or a few small fresh sage leaves
salt and ground black pepper
Cheddar cheese or Monterey Jack, grated, to serve

1 Put the onion, garlic, potato, celery and green pepper into a large heavy pan with the oil and butter.

2 Heat until the ingredients are sizzling, then reduce the heat to low. Cover and cook for 10 minutes, shaking the pan occasionally.

3 Pour in the stock or water, season with salt and pepper and bring to the boil. Reduce the heat, cover again and simmer gently for about 15 minutes or until the vegetables are tender.

4 Add the milk, beans and corn, including the liquor from the cans. Stir in the sage. Heat until simmering, then cook gently, uncovered, for 5 minutes. Check the seasoning before ladling the chowder into bowls. Sprinkle with cheese and serve immediately.

> **Variations**
> • Chickpeas are delicious with corn – add a can as well as the flageolet (small cannellini) beans.
> • For refreshingly spicy, zesty flavour, peel and chop a large chunk of fresh root ginger and cook it with the vegetables. Then add the grated rind of one lemon with the sage.

Country Vegetable Soup

Soup-making is a good way to make the most of seasonal vegetables. It is also a great way of making healthy meals from the best selection of frozen foods – plain frozen vegetables that cook fast and taste terrific. Serve this classic mixed vegetable soup with crusty bread and perhaps a wedge of cheese as a light meal.

Serves 6
15ml/1 tbsp oil
25g/1oz/2 tbsp butter
2 onions, finely chopped
4 carrots, sliced
2 celery sticks, sliced
2 leeks, sliced
1 potato, cut into small cubes
1 small parsnip, cut into small cubes
1 garlic clove, crushed
900ml/1½ pints/3¾ cups vegetable stock
300ml/½ pint/1¼ cups milk
25g/1oz/4 tbsp cornflour (cornstarch)
handful of frozen peas
30ml/2 tbsp chopped fresh parsley
salt and ground black pepper

1 Heat the oil and butter in a large pan and add the onions, carrots and celery. Cook over a medium heat for 5–10 minutes, stirring occasionally, until soft and just beginning to turn golden brown. Stir in the leeks, potato, parsnip and garlic.

2 Add the stock to the pan and stir into the vegetables. Bring the mixture slowly to the boil, reduce the heat if necessary and cover the pan. Simmer gently for 20–30 minutes until all the vegetables are soft.

3 Stir the milk into the cornflour to make a smooth paste. Stir into the vegetables. Add the frozen peas. Bring to the boil and simmer for 5 minutes, season to taste, add the parsley, and serve.

> **Variation**
> For a freezer soup, use onion as the base, with whatever other fresh vegetables you have. From a typical freezer stock, add any of the following: mixed vegetables, broccoli, broad (fava) and runner (green) beans, corn, peas, baby Brussels sprouts and cauliflower.

Country Vegetable Energy 160kcal/665kJ; Protein 3.6g; Carbohydrate 11.5g, of which sugars 10g; Fat 11.4g, of which saturates 6.8g; Cholesterol 27mg; Calcium 72mg; Fibre 5.4g; Sodium 106mg.
Corn and Potato Energy 320kcal/1347kJ; Protein 9.4g; Carbohydrate 43.2g, of which sugars 15.7g; Fat 13.5g, of which saturates 5g; Cholesterol 18mg; Calcium 119mg; Fibre 5g; Sodium 500mg.

Jerusalem Artichoke and Potato Soup with Anchovy Bruschetta

Jerusalem artichokes are a nutty and delicious addition to this potato soup.

Serves 6

squeeze of lemon juice
450g/1lb Jerusalem artichokes, peeled and diced
65g/2¹/₂oz/5 tbsp butter
175g/6oz potatoes, roughly diced
1 small onion, chopped
1 garlic clove, chopped
1 celery stick, chopped
1 small fennel bulb, chopped
1.2 litres/2 pints/5 cups vegetable stock
300ml/¹/₂ pint/1¹/₄ cups double (heavy) cream
pinch of freshly grated nutmeg
salt and ground black pepper
basil leaves, to garnish

For the bruschetta

6 thick slices French bread
1 garlic clove, halved
50g/2oz/¹/₄ cup unsalted (sweet) butter
400g/14oz can artichoke hearts, drained and halved
45ml/3 tbsp tapenade
9 salted anchovy fillets, halved lengthways

1 Prepare a bowl of water with lemon juice. Add the artichokes to the water to prevent discoloration.

2 Melt the butter in a large pan. Drain the artichokes and add to the pan with the potatoes, onion, garlic, celery and fennel. Cook for 10 minutes, stirring occasionally, until softening.

3 Add the stock, bring to the boil, and simmer for around 10–15 minutes, until all the vegetables are soft. Cool slightly, then purée until smooth. Add the cream and nutmeg, and season well.

4 For the bruschetta, lightly toast the French bread on both sides. Rub with the cut side of the garlic. Melt the butter in a small pan. Add the artichoke hearts and cook for 3–4 minutes, turning once.

5 Spread the tapenade on the toast and arrange the artichoke hearts on top. Top with anchovy fillets and garnish with basil.

6 Reheat the soup without boiling, then ladle it into shallow bowls. Serve the bruschetta with the soup.

Celeriac, Potato and Bacon Soup

Versatile, yet often overlooked, celeriac is a winter vegetable that makes excellent soup and is the perfect companion to potatoes.

Serves 4

50g/2oz/¹/₄ cup butter
2 onions, chopped
675g/1¹/₂lb celeriac, roughly diced
450g/1lb potatoes, roughly diced
1.2 litres/2 pints/5 cups vegetable stock
150ml/¹/₄ pint/²/₃ cup single (light) cream
salt and ground black pepper
sprigs of fresh thyme, to garnish

For the topping

1 small Savoy cabbage
50g/2oz/¹/₄ cup butter
175g/6oz rindless streaky (fatty) bacon, roughly chopped
15ml/1 tbsp roughly chopped fresh thyme
15ml/1 tbsp roughly chopped fresh rosemary

1 Melt the butter in a pan. Add the onions and cook for 4–5 minutes, until softened, then add the celeriac. Put a lid on the pan and cook gently for 10 minutes.

2 Stir in the potatoes and stock. Bring to the boil, reduce the heat and simmer for 20 minutes or until the vegetables are tender. Leave to cool slightly. Using a slotted spoon, remove about half the celeriac and potatoes and set them aside.

3 Purée the soup in a food processor or blender. Return it to the rinsed-out pan with the reserved celeriac and potatoes.

4 Prepare the topping. Discard the tough outer leaves from the cabbage. Roughly tear the remaining leaves, discarding any hard stalks, and blanch them in boiling salted water for 2–3 minutes. Refresh under cold running water and drain.

5 Melt the butter in a large frying pan and cook the bacon for 3–4 minutes. Add the cabbage, thyme and rosemary, and stir-fry for 5–6 minutes, until tender. Season well.

6 Add the cream to the soup and season it well, then reheat gently. Ladle the soup into bowls and pile the cabbage mixture in the middle. Garnish with sprigs of fresh thyme.

Artichoke Soup Energy 533kcal/2212kJ; Protein 7.2g; Carbohydrate 25.9g, of which sugars 4.3g; Fat 45.3g, of which saturates 27.1g; Cholesterol 114mg; Calcium 167mg; Fibre 3.4g; Sodium 787mg.
Celeriac and Potato Energy 462kcal/1919kJ; Protein 12.3g; Carbohydrate 24.3g, of which sugars 7.3g; Fat 35.8g, of which saturates 20.4g; Cholesterol 97mg; Calcium 144mg; Fibre 4.3g; Sodium 954mg.

Spinach and Root Vegetable Soup

This is a slow-cooker version of a typical Russian soup, which is traditionally prepared when the first vegetables of spring appear. You will need to use a large slow cooker in order to accommodate the spinach.

Serves 4
1 small turnip, cut into chunks
2 carrots, diced
1 small parsnip, cut into large dice
1 potato, peeled and diced
1 onion, chopped

1 garlic clove, finely chopped
1/4 celeriac bulb, diced
750ml/1 1/4 pints/3 cups boiling vegetable or chicken stock
175g/6oz fresh spinach, roughly chopped
1 small bunch fresh dill, chopped
salt and ground black pepper

For the garnish
2 hard-boiled eggs, sliced lengthways
1 lemon, sliced
30ml/2 tbsp fresh parsley and dill

1 Put the turnip, carrots, parsnip, potato, onion, garlic, celeriac and vegetable or chicken stock into the ceramic cooking pot of the slow cooker.

2 Set the cooker to the high or auto setting and cook for 1 hour, then either leave on auto or switch to low and cook for a further 5–6 hours, until the vegetables are soft and tender.

3 Stir the spinach into the cooking pot and cook on high for 45 minutes, or until the spinach is tender but still green and leafy. Season with salt and pepper.

4 Stir in the dill, then ladle the soup into warmed bowls and serve garnished with egg, lemon slices and a sprinkling of fresh parsley and dill.

Cook's Tip
For best results, use a really good-quality vegetable or chicken stock in this soup – either home-made or bought fresh from a delicatessen or supermarket.

Roast Vegetable Medley

Winter meets summer in this soup recipe for chunky roasted vegetables. Serve it with bread baked with a hint of added summer flavour in the form of sun-dried tomatoes.

Serves 4
4 parsnips, quartered lengthways
2 red onions, cut into thin wedges
4 carrots, thickly sliced
2 leeks, thickly sliced
1 small swede (rutabaga), cut into chunks
4 potatoes, cut into chunks
60ml/4 tbsp olive oil

few sprigs of fresh thyme
1 bulb garlic, broken into cloves, unpeeled
1 litre/1 3/4 pints/4 cups vegetable stock
salt and ground black pepper
fresh thyme sprigs, to garnish

For the sun-dried tomato bread
1 ciabatta loaf
75g/3oz/6 tbsp butter, softened
1 garlic clove, crushed
4 sun-dried tomatoes, finely chopped
30ml/2 tbsp chopped fresh parsley

1 Preheat the oven to 200°C/400°F/Gas 6. Cut the thick ends of the parsnip quarters into four, then place them in a large roasting pan. Add the onions, carrots, leeks, swede and potatoes, and spread them in an even layer.

2 Drizzle the olive oil over the vegetables. Add the thyme and unpeeled garlic cloves. Toss well and roast for 45 minutes, until all the vegetables are tender and slightly charred.

3 To make the sun-dried tomato bread, slice the loaf without cutting right through. Mix the butter, garlic, sun-dried tomatoes and parsley. Spread the butter between the slices. Wrap in foil. Bake for 15 minutes, opening the foil for the last 4–5 minutes.

4 Discard the thyme from the vegetables. Squeeze the garlic from its skins over the vegetables and purée half the mixture with the stock. Pour into a pan. Add the remaining vegetables. Bring to the boil and season well.

5 Ladle the soup into bowls and garnish with fresh thyme leaves. Serve the hot bread with the soup.

Spinach Soup Energy 229kcal/952kJ; Protein 7.8g; Carbohydrate 14.3g, of which sugars 9.2g; Fat 16.2g, of which saturates 8.7g; Cholesterol 133mg; Calcium 197mg; Fibre 4.1g; Sodium 148mg.
Vegetable Medley Energy 511kcal/2146kJ; Protein 13.9g; Carbohydrate 72.6g, of which sugars 18.9g; Fat 20.4g, of which saturates 10.6g; Cholesterol 40mg; Calcium 218mg; Fibre 12.1g; Sodium 521mg.

Potato and Spring Onion Soup

The sumptuously spring onion flavour of this creamy chilled soup is surprisingly delicate, thanks to the potatoes, quantity of stock and the addition of tangy lemon juice.

Serves 4–6
25g/1oz/2 tbsp butter
1 small onion, chopped
150g/5oz/1¾ cups spring onions (scallions), chopped
225g/8oz potatoes, peeled and chopped
600ml/1 pint/2½ cups vegetable stock
350ml/12fl oz/1½ cups single (light) cream
30ml/2 tbsp freshly squeezed lemon juice
salt and ground white pepper
chopped spring onions (scallions) or fresh chives, to garnish

1 Melt the butter in a pan and add all the onions. Cover and cook over a very low heat for about 10 minutes or until soft.

2 Add the potatoes and the stock. Bring to the boil, then cover the pan again and simmer over a moderately low heat for about 30 minutes. Cool slightly.

3 Purée the soup until smooth in a food processor or blender.

4 If serving the soup hot, pour it back into the pan. Add the cream and season with salt and pepper. Reheat gently, stirring occasionally. Add the lemon juice.

5 If serving the soup cold, pour it into a bowl. Stir in the cream and lemon juice and season with salt and pepper. Cover the bowl and cool, then chill for at least 1 hour.

6 Serve sprinkled with the chopped spring onions or chives.

Variation
For a lighter version that is still satisfyingly creamy, use olive oil instead of butter and plain (natural) yogurt instead of cream and omit the lemon juice.

Pasta-free Potato Minestrone

Minestrone is the famous Italian soup that can be made with almost any combination of seasonal vegetables. Many recipes are bulked out with pasta, but the combination of vegetables used here and the addition of pesto ensures that the soup is both substantial and flavoursome.

Serves 6
1.75 litres/3 pints/7½ cups vegetable stock
1 large onion, chopped
3 celery sticks, chopped
2 carrots, finely diced
2 large floury potatoes, finely diced
½ head of cabbage, very finely diced
225g/8oz runner (green) beans, sliced diagonally
2 x 400g/14oz cans cannellini beans, drained
60ml/4 tbsp ready-made pesto sauce
salt and ground freshly ground black pepper
crusty bread, to serve
freshly grated Parmesan cheese, to serve

1 Pour the stock into a large pan. Add the onion, celery and carrots. Bring to the boil, reduce the heat and cover the pan. Then simmer for 10 minutes.

2 Add the potatoes, cabbage and beans to the soup and simmer for 10–12 minutes or until the potatoes are tender.

3 Stir in the cannellini beans and pesto, and bring the soup to the boil, stirring frequently.

4 Season the soup to taste and serve hot, with crusty bread and plenty of freshly grated Parmesan cheese for adding to individual portions as required.

Variation
This already substantial soup can be made a real feast by adding a handful of either rice or barley with the vegetables in step 1 above. Instead of floury potatoes, dice small, waxy salad potatoes that will hold their shape and stay firm but tender during cooking to complement the grains.

Spring Onion Soup Energy 179kcal/744kJ; Protein 3.2g; Carbohydrate 8.9g, of which sugars 3.1g; Fat 14.8g, of which saturates 9.3g; Cholesterol 41mg; Calcium 67mg; Fibre 0.9g; Sodium 48mg.
Pasta-free Minestrone Energy 241kcal/1007kJ; Protein 9.7g; Carbohydrate 21.7g, of which sugars 9.3g; Fat 13.4g, of which saturates 4g; Cholesterol 13mg; Calcium 204mg; Fibre 3.6g; Sodium 165mg.

Winter Potato Soup

Simmer a selection of
popular winter root
vegetables together for a
warming and satisfying soup.
Its delicious creamy taste
comes from adding crème
fraîche, fromage frais or
yogurt just before serving.

Serves 6
3 medium carrots, chopped
1 large potato, chopped
1 large parsnip, chopped
1 large turnip or small swede
  (rutabaga), chopped

1 onion, chopped
30ml/2 tbsp sunflower oil
25g/1oz/2 tbsp butter
1.5 litres/2½ pints/6 cups water
1 piece fresh root ginger, peeled
  and grated
300ml/½ pint/1¼ cups milk
45ml/3 tbsp crème fraîche,
  fromage frais or natural
  (plain) yogurt
30ml/2 tbsp fresh dill, chopped
salt and ground black pepper

1 Put the carrots, potato, parsnip, turnip or swede and onion
into a large pan with the oil and butter. Fry lightly, then cover
and sweat the vegetables on a very low heat for 15 minutes,
shaking the pan occasionally.

2 Pour in the water, bring to the boil and season well with salt
and black pepper. Cover and simmer for 20 minutes until the
vegetables are soft.

3 Strain the vegetables, reserving the stock, add the grated
ginger and purée the vegetables in a food processor or blender
until smooth.

4 Return the purée and stock to the pan. Add the milk and stir
while the soup gently reheats.

5 Remove from the heat, stir in the crème fraîche, fromage
frais or natural yogurt plus the dill, lemon juice and extra
seasoning, if necessary.

6 Reheat the soup, if you wish, but do not allow it to boil as
you do so, or it may curdle. Ladle into warmed soup bowls and
serve immediately.

Baby Carrot and Potato Soup

Tender carrots and new
potatoes find their moment
of glory in this sweet and
delicately spiced soup.
The fennel provides a very
subtle aniseed flavour, which
does not overpower the
taste of the carrots.

Serves 4
50g/2oz/¼ cup butter
1 small bunch spring onions
  (scallions), chopped
150g/5oz fennel bulb, chopped

1 celery stick, chopped
450g/1lb baby carrots, grated
2.5ml/½ tsp ground cumin
150g/5oz new potatoes, peeled
  and diced
1.2 litres/2 pints/5 cups chicken
  or vegetable stock
60ml/4 tbsp double (heavy)
  cream, plus extra for garnish
salt and ground black pepper
60ml/4 tbsp chopped fresh
  parsley, to garnish

1 Melt the butter in a large heavy pan and add the spring
onions, fennel, celery, carrots and cumin. Cover the pan and
cook, stirring occasionally, for about 5 minutes, or until soft.

2 Add the diced potatoes to the pan and pour in the chicken
or vegetable stock. Bring the mixture to the boil, then reduce
the heat and simmer the mixture for a further 10–15 minutes
until the vegetables are just tender.

3 Purée the soup in the pan with a hand-held blender.
Alternatively, let it cool slightly and then pour it into a food
processor or blender and process until smooth.

4 Stir in the cream and season to taste with salt and ground
black pepper. Serve in individual soup bowls and garnish with a
swirl of cream and chopped parsley.

Cook's Tip
*For convenience, you can freeze the soup in portions before
adding the cream, seasoning and parsley. When required, simply
remove from the freezer and defrost the soup. Then reheat in a
pan and continue from step 4 before serving.*

Winter Potato Energy 106kcal/441kJ; Protein 3.4g; Carbohydrate 15.4g, of which sugars 8.3g; Fat 3.7g, of which saturates 0.6g; Cholesterol 0mg; Calcium 56mg; Fibre 3.9g; Sodium 23mg.
Baby Carrot Soup Energy 244kcal/1010kJ; Protein 2.5g; Carbohydrate 16.8g, of which sugars 10.6g; Fat 19g, of which saturates 11.7g; Cholesterol 47mg; Calcium 62mg; Fibre 4.4g; Sodium 122mg.

Potato Succotash Soup

Succotash is a popular and traditional American dish made with potatoes, corn and butter beans. Originally enriched with bear fat, modern day succotash is finished with milk or cream. This soup version of the dish makes an appetizing and filling main course, served with plenty of fresh crusty bread.

Serves 4
50g/2oz/¼ cup butter
1 large onion, chopped

2 large carrots, peeled and cut into short batons
900ml/1½ pints/3¾ cups milk
1 vegetable stock (bouillon) cube
2 medium waxy potatoes, peeled and diced
1 thyme sprig
225g/8oz/1⅓ cups frozen corn
225g/8oz/1½ cups frozen butter (wax) beans or broad (fava) beans
30ml/2 tbsp chopped fresh parsley, to garnish

1 Heat the butter in a large heavy pan. Add the onion and carrots and cook over a gentle heat, stirring occasionally, for about 3–4 minutes, until the vegetables begin to soften but not turn brown.

2 Add the milk, stock cube, potatoes, thyme, corn and butter beans or broad beans to the pan and bring gently to near-boiling point. Reduce the heat and simmer the mixture for about 10–15 minutes until the potatoes are cooked through and tender.

3 Season to taste with salt and ground black pepper. Ladle the soup into warmed bowls and garnish each serving with chopped fresh parsley.

Cook's Tip
Frozen corn and butter (wax) beans are used for convenience in this soup. Fresh corn and beans can be used if they are readily available, although canned corn and butter (lima) beans are also convenient options, if you prefer.

Potato, Broccoli and Brie Soup

The combination of broccoli and potatoes makes a delicious soup with an appetizing deep green colour. The addition of blue Brie cheese just before serving adds a tasty tang.

Serves 6
1 onion, chopped
450g/1lb broccoli spears, chopped
1 large courgette (zucchini), chopped

1 large carrot, chopped
1 medium potato, chopped
25g/1oz/2 tbsp butter
30ml/2 tbsp sunflower oil
2 litres/3½ pints/8 cups stock or water
about 75g/3oz blue Brie (or Dolcelatte) cheese, cubed
salt and ground black pepper
flaked (sliced) almonds, to garnish (optional)

1 Put all the vegetables into a large pan, together with the butter and oil plus about 45ml/3 tbsp stock or water.

2 Heat the ingredients until sizzling and stir well. Cover and cook gently for 15 minutes, shaking the pan occasionally, until all the vegetables have softened but not browned.

3 Add the rest of the stock or water, season to taste and bring to the boil, then cover and simmer gently for about 25–30 minutes.

4 Strain the vegetables and reserve the liquid. Purée the vegetables in a food processor or blender, then return them to the pan with the reserved liquid.

5 Bring the soup back to a gentle boil and stir in the cheese until it melts. (Be careful to avoid the soup boiling too rapidly or the cheese will become stringy.) Check the seasoning, then ladle into soup bowls. Garnish with a sprinkling of almond flakes.

Variation
Try using cauliflower instead of broccoli in this recipe. Stilton is a tasty and richer alternative to the blue Brie.

Succotash Soup Energy 398kcal/1676kJ; Protein 15.9g; Carbohydrate 52.8g, of which sugars 24.4g; Fat 15.5g, of which saturates 9.3g; Cholesterol 42mg; Calcium 335mg; Fibre 6.9g; Sodium 391mg.
Broccoli and Brie Energy 312kcal/1297kJ; Protein 14.5g; Carbohydrate 11.3g, of which sugars 6.8g; Fat 23.3g, of which saturates 14.7g; Cholesterol 61mg; Calcium 251mg; Fibre 3.3g; Sodium 310mg.

Vegetable Noodle Soup

Potatoes and noodles are a good soup combination, especially on cold winter days. This tasty and warming soup, served with warm crusty bread, is both substantial and delicious, making it the perfect lunchtime energy boost.

Serves 4
1 large onion, finely sliced
25g/1oz/2 tbsp butter
350g/12oz potatoes, peeled and diced
900ml/1½ pints/3¾ cups vegetable stock
1 bay leaf
salt and ground black pepper

For the drop noodles
75g/3oz/⅔ cup self-raising (self-rising) flour
pinch of salt
15g/½oz/1 tbsp butter
15ml/1 tbsp chopped fresh parsley, plus a little extra to garnish
1 egg, beaten
crusty bread, to serve

1 In a wide, heavy pan, cook the onion in the butter gently for 10 minutes, or until it begins to brown.

2 Add the diced potatoes and cook for 2–3 minutes, then pour in the vegetable stock. Add the bay leaf, salt and pepper. Slowly bring to the boil, then reduce the heat, cover and simmer gently for 10 minutes.

3 Meanwhile, make the noodles. Sift the flour and salt into a bowl and rub in the butter. Stir in the parsley, then add the egg to the flour mixture and mix to a soft dough.

4 Drop half-teaspoonfuls of the noodle dough into the gently simmering soup. Cover the pan and simmer gently for a further 10 minutes.

5 To serve, ladle the soup into warmed deep bowls, sprinkle over a little parsley, and serve immediately with generous chunks of warm crusty bread.

Cook's Tip
Use old potatoes, of a floury texture, such as King Edwards or Maris Pipers, so that they break down slightly in the soup.

Potato, Cabbage, Beetroot and Tomato Borscht

There are numerous versions of this classic soup, which originates in Eastern Europe. Beetroot and sour cream are the traditional ingredients in every borscht, but other ingredients tend to be many and varied. This slow-cooker version featuring potatoes and cabbage has a deliciously sweet and sour taste and can be served piping hot or refreshingly chilled.

Serves 6
1 onion, chopped
1 carrot, chopped
6 raw or vacuum-packed (cooked, not pickled) beetroot (beets), 4 diced and 2 coarsely grated
400g/14oz can chopped tomatoes
6 new potatoes, cut into bitesize pieces
1 small white cabbage, thinly sliced
600ml/1 pint/2½ cups vegetable stock
45ml/3 tbsp sugar
30–45ml/2–3 tbsp white wine vinegar or cider vinegar
45ml/3 tbsp chopped fresh dill
salt and ground black pepper
sour cream and dill, to garnish
buttered rye bread, to serve

1 Put the onion, carrot, diced beetroot, tomatoes, potatoes and cabbage into the ceramic cooking pot of a slow cooker and pour over the vegetable stock. Cover the cooking pot with the lid and cook in the slow cooker on high for about 4 hours, or until the vegetables are just tender.

2 Add the grated beetroot, sugar and vinegar to the slow cooker and stir to combine. Cook for a further hour until the beetroot is cooked through.

3 Taste the soup, checking for a good sweet/sour balance, and add more sugar and/or vinegar if necessary. Season to taste with plenty of salt and ground black pepper.

4 Just before serving, stir the chopped dill into the soup and ladle into warmed soup bowls. Garnish each serving with a generous spoonful of sour cream and plenty more fresh dill, then serve with thick slices of buttered rye bread.

Vegetable Noodle Energy 241kcal/1010kJ; Protein 5.7g; Carbohydrate 33.6g, of which sugars 4.9g; Fat 10.3g, of which saturates 5.7g; Cholesterol 69mg; Calcium 63mg; Fibre 2.5g; Sodium 91mg.
Cabbage Borscht Energy 125kcal/531kJ; Protein 3.5g; Carbohydrate 27.8g, of which sugars 7g; Fat 0.7g, of which saturates 0.1g; Cholesterol 0mg; Calcium 58mg; Fibre 3.2g; Sodium 357mg.

Creamy Cauliflower and Potato Soup

This soup is light in flavour, yet the potatoes add volume and make it silky, thick and satisfying enough for a lunchtime snack.

Serves 6
30ml/2 tbsp olive oil
2 large onions, finely diced
1 garlic clove, crushed
3 large floury potatoes, finely diced
3 celery sticks, finely diced
1.75 litres/3 pints/7½ cups vegetable stock
2 carrots, finely diced
1 medium cauliflower, chopped
15ml/1 tbsp chopped fresh dill
15ml/1 tbsp lemon juice
5ml/1 tsp mustard powder
1.5ml/¼ tsp caraway seeds
300ml/½ pint/1¼ cups single (light) cream
salt and ground black pepper
shredded spring onions (scallions), to garnish

1 Heat the oil in a large heavy pan, add the onions and garlic and fry them for a few minutes until they soften.

2 Add the diced potatoes and celery to the pan. Pour in the stock and simmer for 10 minutes.

3 Stir the carrots into the pan and simmer the vegetables for a further 10 minutes.

4 Mix in the cauliflower, fresh dill, lemon juice, mustard powder and caraway seeds and simmer for 20 minutes.

5 Press the soup through a sieve (strainer) by pressing it with a wooden spoon, or pass it through a food mill, and return the mixture to the rinsed-out pan.

6 Stir in the cream, season to taste and serve, garnished with shredded spring onions.

Cook's Tip
Fresh vegetable stock can be made simply by simmering vegetables in water for around an hour and then straining. For the best flavour avoid bitter vegetables such as cabbage.

Cauliflower and Potato Soup with Broccoli and Bacon

Creamy cauliflower soup is given real bite by adding garlic, potato and broccoli florets. This is delicious generously topped with melting Cheddar cheese and served with crusty bread.

Serves 4
1 onion, chopped
1 garlic clove, chopped
50g/2oz/¼ cup butter
2 cauliflowers, broken into florets
1 large potato, cut into chunks
900ml/1½ pints/3¾ cups chicken stock
225g/8oz broccoli, cut into florets
150ml/¼ pint/⅔ cup single (light) cream
6 rindless streaky (fatty) bacon rashers (strips)
1 small baguette, cut into 4 pieces
225g/8oz/2 cups medium-mature Cheddar cheese, grated
salt and ground black pepper
chopped fresh parsley, to garnish

1 Cook the onion and garlic in the butter for 4–5 minutes. Add half the cauliflower, all the potato and the stock. Bring to the boil, reduce the heat and simmer for 20 minutes.

2 Boil the remaining cauliflower for about 6 minutes, or until just tender. Use a draining spoon to remove the florets and rinse under cold running water, then drain well. Cook the broccoli in the water for 3–4 minutes, until just tender. Drain, refresh under cold water, then add to the cauliflower.

3 Cool the soup slightly, then purée it until smooth and return it to the rinsed pan. Add the cream and seasoning, then heat gently. Add the cauliflower and broccoli and heat through.

4 Preheat the grill (broiler) to high. Grill (broil) the bacon until crisp, then cool slightly. Ladle the soup into flameproof bowls.

5 Place a piece of baguette in each bowl. Sprinkle grated cheese over the top and grill for 2–3 minutes, until the cheese is melted and bubbling. Take care when serving the hot bowls.

6 Crumble the bacon and sprinkle it over the melted cheese, then scatter the parsley over the top and serve immediately.

Creamy Cauliflower Energy 169kcal/711kJ; Protein 7.4g; Carbohydrate 27.7g, of which sugars 10.8g; Fat 4g, of which saturates 1.1g; Cholesterol 3mg; Calcium 111mg; Fibre 4g; Sodium 55mg.
Cauliflower Soup Energy 737kcal/3071kJ; Protein 34.8g; Carbohydrate 45.5g, of which sugars 9.2g; Fat 46.2g, of which saturates 26.4g; Cholesterol 121mg; Calcium 589mg; Fibre 6.6g; Sodium 1206mg.

Spicy Potato and Red Lentil Soup

Red lentils and vegetables are cooked and puréed, then sharpened with lots of lemon juice. In hot weather, this soup is also good served cold, adding even more lemon. It is also known as 'Esau's soup' and it is sometimes served as part of a Sabbath meal in Jewish households.

Serves 4
45ml/3 tbsp olive oil
1 onion, chopped
2 celery sticks, chopped
1–2 carrots, sliced

8 garlic cloves, chopped
1 potato, peeled and diced
250g/9oz/generous 1 cup
    red lentils
1 litre/1¾ pints/4 cups
    vegetable stock
2 bay leaves
1–2 lemons, halved
2.5ml/½ tsp ground cumin, or
    to taste
cayenne pepper or Tabasco sauce,
    to taste
salt and ground black pepper
lemon slices and chopped
    fresh flat leaf parsley leaves,
    to serve

1 Heat the oil in a large pan. Add the onion and cook for about 5 minutes, or until softened. Stir in the celery, carrots, half the garlic and all the potato. Cook for a few minutes until beginning to soften.

2 Add the lentils and stock to the pan and slowly bring to the boil. Reduce the heat, cover and simmer for about 30 minutes, until the potato and lentils are tender.

3 Add the bay leaves, remaining garlic and half the lemons to the pan and cook the soup for a further 10 minutes. Remove the bay leaves. Squeeze the juice from the remaining lemons, then stir into the soup, to taste.

4 Pour the soup into a food processor or blender and process until smooth. (You may need to do this in batches.) Transfer the soup back into the pan and heat through, stir in the cumin, cayenne pepper or Tabasco sauce, and season.

5 Ladle the soup into warmed bowls and top each portion with lemon slices and a sprinkling of chopped fresh flat leaf parsley.

Chunky Potato, Split Pea, Mushroom and Barley Soup

This hearty vegetable soup from Eastern Europe is perfect on a freezing cold day. Serve it in warmed bowls, with plenty of rye (pumpernickel) bread. This is a vegetarian version that is bulked out with slow-cooked pulses and potatoes. For a meat version, use meat stock instead of vegetable and add chunks of tender, long-simmered beef to the soup.

Serves 6–8
30–45ml/2–3 tbsp small haricot
    (navy) beans, soaked overnight
45–60ml/3–4 tbsp green
    split peas

45–60ml/3–4 tbsp yellow
    split peas
90–105ml/6–7 tbsp pearl barley
1 onion, chopped
2 carrots, sliced
3 celery sticks, diced or sliced
½ baking potato, peeled and cut
    into chunks
10g/¼oz or 45ml/3 tbsp mixed
    dried mushrooms
5 garlic cloves, sliced
2 litres/3½ pints/8 cups water
2 vegetable stock (bouillon) cubes
salt and ground black pepper
30–45ml/2–3 tbsp chopped fresh
    parsley, to garnish

1 Put the beans, pearl barley, green and yellow split peas, onion, carrots, celery, potato, mushrooms, garlic and water into a large pan.

2 Bring the mixture to the boil, then reduce the heat, cover and simmer gently for about 1½ hours, or until the beans are completely tender.

3 Crumble the stock cubes into the soup, stir well and taste for seasoning. Ladle into warmed bowls, garnish with parsley and serve with rye or pumpernickel bread.

Cook's Tip
Do not add the stock cubes until the end of cooking, as the salt they contain will prevent the beans from becoming tender.

Hot Red Lentil Soup Energy 235kcal/991kJ; Protein 13g; Carbohydrate 28.4g, of which sugars 3.7g; Fat 8.9g, of which saturates 2.2g; Cholesterol 0mg; Calcium 66mg; Fibre 2.9g; Sodium 40mg.
Chunky Split Pea Energy 162kcal/689kJ; Protein 6.8g; Carbohydrate 34.1g, of which sugars 4.3g; Fat 0.8g, of which saturates 0.1g; Cholesterol 0mg; Calcium 34mg; Fibre 2.9g; Sodium 30mg.

Chunky Courgette and Potato Soup with Pasta

This is a delicious chunky
vegetable soup from Nice in
the south of France, served
with tomato pesto and fresh
Parmesan cheese. Serve in
small portions as an
appetizer, or in larger bowls
with crusty bread as
a filling lunch.

Serves 4–6
1 courgette (zucchini), diced
1 small potato, diced
1 shallot, chopped
1 carrot, diced

400g/14oz can chopped tomatoes
1.2 litres/2 pints/5 cups
  vegetable stock
50g/2oz French (green) beans, cut
  into 1cm/½in lengths
50g/2oz/½ cup frozen petits pois
  (baby peas)
50g/2oz/½ cup small
  pasta shapes
60–90ml/4–6 tbsp pesto
15ml/1 tbsp tomato
  purée (paste)
salt and ground black pepper
freshly grated Parmesan or
  Pecorino cheese, to serve

1 Place the courgette, potato, shallot, carrot and tomatoes, with the can juices, in a large pan. Add the stock and season well. Bring to the boil over a medium to high heat, then lower the heat, cover the pan and simmer for 20 minutes.

2 Bring the soup back to the boil and add the green beans and petits pois. Cook the mixture briefly, for about a minute. Add the pasta. Cook for a further 10 minutes, until the pasta is tender. Taste and adjust the seasoning.

3 Ladle the soup into bowls. Mix together the pesto and tomato purée, and stir a spoonful into each serving. Sprinkle with freshly grated Parmesan or Pecorino cheese.

Variation
To strengthen the tomato flavour, try using tomato-flavoured spaghetti, broken into small lengths, instead of the small pasta shapes. Sun-dried tomato purée (paste) can also be used instead of regular tomato purée.

Tuscan Bean and Potato Soup

There are lots of versions of
this wonderful and very
substantial soup, which
makes a meal in itself.
This one uses cannellini
beans, potatoes, cabbage and
good olive oil. It's a good
idea to make it in advance
of the meal, as it tastes even
better when reheated.

Serves 4
45ml/3 tbsp extra virgin olive oil
1 onion, roughly chopped
2 leeks, roughly chopped
1 large potato, peeled and diced
2 garlic cloves, finely chopped
1.2 litres/2 pints/5 cups
  vegetable stock

400g/14oz can cannellini beans,
  drained, liquid reserved
175g/6oz Savoy cabbage,
  finely shredded
45ml/3 tbsp chopped fresh flat
  leaf parsley
30ml/2 tbsp chopped
  fresh oregano
75g/3oz/1 cup Parmesan
  cheese, shaved
salt and ground black pepper

For the garlic toasts
30–45ml/2–3 tbsp extra virgin
  olive oil
6 thick slices country bread
1 garlic clove, peeled
  and bruised

1 Heat the oil in a large pan and gently cook the onion, leeks, potato and garlic for 4–5 minutes.

2 Pour on the stock and liquid from the beans. Cover and simmer for 15 minutes.

3 Stir in the cabbage and beans with half the herbs, season and cook for 10 minutes more. Spoon about one-third of the soup into a food processor or blender and process until fairly smooth. Return to the soup in the pan, taste for seasoning and heat through for 5 minutes.

4 Meanwhile make the garlic toasts. Drizzle a little oil over the slices of bread, then rub both sides of each slice with the garlic. Toast until browned on both sides.

5 Ladle the soup into bowls. Sprinkle with the remaining herbs and the Parmesan shavings. Add a drizzle of olive oil and serve with the toasts.

Chunky Vegetable Energy 204kcal/857kJ; Protein 10.6g; Carbohydrate 23.6g, of which sugars 8.8g; Fat 8.1g, of which saturates 1.9g; Cholesterol 4mg; Calcium 150mg; Fibre 9.3g; Sodium 451mg.
Tuscan Bean Soup Energy 445kcal/1863kJ; Protein 18.9g; Carbohydrate 45.8g, of which sugars 9.3g; Fat 21.8g, of which saturates 6g; Cholesterol 19mg; Calcium 391mg; Fibre 9.1g; Sodium 707mg.

Peanut and Potato Soup

In this rich Latin-American soup, the peanuts and potatoes are used as a thickening agent, with unexpectedly delicious results.

Serves 6
60ml/4 tbsp groundnut
  (peanut) oil
I onion, finely chopped
2 garlic cloves, crushed
I red (bell) pepper, seeded
  and chopped
250g/9oz potatoes, peeled
  and diced
2 fresh red chillies, seeded
  and chopped
200g/7oz canned
  chopped tomatoes
150g/5oz/1¼ cups
  unsalted peanuts
1.5 litres/2½ pints/6¼ cups
  vegetable stock
salt and ground black pepper
30ml/2 tbsp chopped fresh
  coriander (cilantro), to garnish

I Heat the oil in a large heavy pan over a low heat. Stir in the onion and cook for around 5 minutes, until soft. Add the garlic, pepper, potatoes, chillies and tomatoes. Stir well, cover and cook for 5 minutes.

2 Meanwhile, toast the peanuts by gently cooking them in a large dry frying pan. Turn and stir the peanuts until they are evenly golden. Take care not to burn them.

3 Set 30ml/2 tbsp of the peanuts aside for garnish. Grind the remaining nuts to a fine powder in a blender or food processor. Add the vegetables to the food processor and process until smooth. Return the mixture to the pan and stir in the vegetable stock. Bring to the boil, then lower the heat and simmer for 10 minutes.

4 Pour the soup into heated bowls. Garnish with a generous sprinkling of coriander and the remaining peanuts.

Cook's Tip
Replace the unsalted peanuts with peanut butter, if you like. Use equal quantities of chunky and smooth peanut butter for the ideal texture.

Spanish Potato and Garlic Soup

This classic Spanish potato and tomato soup is given a deliciously rich, tangy flavour by the addition of garlic and paprika.

Serves 6
30ml/2 tbsp olive oil
I large onion, finely sliced
I large potato, halved and cut
  into thin slices
4 garlic cloves, crushed
5ml/1 tsp paprika
400g/14oz can chopped
  tomatoes, drained
5ml/1 tsp thyme leaves
900ml/1½ pints/3¾ cups
  vegetable stock
5ml/1 tsp cornflour
  (cornstarch)
salt and ground black pepper
chopped thyme leaves, to garnish

I Heat the oil in a large heavy pan and gently fry the onions, potato, garlic, and paprika for 5 minutes, until the onions have softened, but not browned.

2 Add the chopped tomatoes, thyme leaves and vegetable stock to the pan and bring the mixture slowly to the boil.

3 Reduce the heat and simmer the soup for 15–20 minutes until the potatoes have cooked through.

4 Mix the cornflour with a little water in a bowl to form a paste. Stir into the soup, then simmer for a further 5 minutes until the soup has thickened.

5 Using a wooden spoon, break the potatoes up slightly. Season to taste with salt and ground black pepper, then serve garnished with the chopped thyme leaves.

Cook's Tip
Making your own vegetable stock for this soup will result in a much better flavour. Simply add a selection of vegetables, such as onions, celery, leeks and carrots, and a few bay leaves to a large pan. Cover with water and bring to the boil, then simmer for about 30–45 minutes until the vegetables are soft and the water has taken on their flavours. Strain the stock.

Peanut and Potato Energy 260kcal/1079kJ; Protein 8g; Carbohydrate 14.7g, of which sugars 6.2g; Fat 19.2g, of which saturates 3.6g; Cholesterol 0mg; Calcium 30mg; Fibre 3g; Sodium 20mg.
Spanish Potato Energy 86kcal/359kJ; Protein 1.5g; Carbohydrate 11.5g, of which sugars 4.4g; Fat 4.1g, of which saturates 0.6g; Cholesterol 0mg; Calcium 15mg; Fibre 1.5g; Sodium 12mg.

Potato, Corn and Chilli Chowder

Corn, potatoes and chillies are traditional buddies, and here the cooling combination of creamed corn and milk is the perfect foil for the raging heat of the chillies.

Serves 6

2 tomatoes, skinned
1 onion, roughly chopped
375g/13oz can creamed corn
2 red (bell) peppers, halved
  and seeded
15ml/1 tbsp olive oil, plus extra
  for brushing
3 fresh red chillies, seeded
  and chopped
2 garlic cloves, chopped
5ml/1 tsp ground cumin
5ml/1 tsp ground coriander
600ml/1 pint/2½ cups milk
350ml/12fl oz/1½ cups
  vegetable stock
3 cobs of corn, kernels removed
450g/1lb potatoes, finely diced
60ml/4 tbsp double
  (heavy) cream
60ml/4 tbsp chopped
  fresh parsley
salt and ground black pepper

1 Process the tomatoes and onion in a food processor or blender to a smooth purée. Add the creamed corn and process again, then set aside. Preheat the grill to high.

2 Put the peppers, skin side up, on a grill (broiler) rack and brush with oil. Grill (broil) for 8–10 minutes, until the skins blacken and blister. Transfer to a bowl and cover with clear film (plastic wrap), then leave to cool. Peel and dice the peppers, then set aside.

3 Heat the oil in a large pan and add the chopped chillies and garlic. Cook, stirring, for 2–3 minutes, until softened.

4 Add the ground cumin and coriander, and cook for a further 1 minute. Stir in the corn purée and cook for about 8 minutes, stirring occasionally.

5 Pour in the milk and stock, then stir in the corn kernels, potatoes, red pepper and seasoning to taste. Cook for about 15–20 minutes, until the corn and potatoes are tender.

6 Pour the soup into deep bowls and add the cream, pouring it slowly into the middle of the bowls. Sprinkle with the chopped parsley and serve immediately.

Potato and Garlic Broth

Although there is plenty of garlic in this fragrant potato soup, it is not overpowering. Serve it piping hot with plenty of wholemeal bread, as the perfect winter warmer, or with one of the suggested accompaniments below.

Serves 4

2 small or 1 large head of garlic
  (about 20 cloves)
4 potatoes, diced
1.75 litres/3 pints/7½ cups
  vegetable stock
salt and ground black pepper
flat leaf parsley, to garnish

1 Preheat the oven to 190°C/375°F/Gas 5. Place the unpeeled garlic bulbs or bulb in a small roasting pan and bake for about 30 minutes until they are soft in the centre.

2 Meanwhile, place the potatoes in a large pan and pour in water to cover. Add a little salt, if needed. Bring to the boil, then reduce the heat, part-cover the pan and simmer for 10 minutes.

3 Meanwhile, simmer the stock for 5 minutes. Drain the potatoes and add them to the stock.

4 Squeeze the garlic pulp from the skins into the soup, reserving a few cloves to garnish. Stir and add seasoning to taste. Simmer the soup for a further 15 minutes before serving, garnished with whole garlic cloves and parsley.

Variations
- *Make the soup more substantial by toasting slices of French bread on one side, then topping the second sides with cheese and toasting until golden. Place a slice or two of toasted cheese in each bowl before ladling in the soup.*
- *Hot herb bread, with lots of chopped fresh parsley and plenty of grated lemon rind, is delicious with the broth. Mix the parsley and lemon rind with butter, and spread it between slices of French bread. Reshape the slices into a loaf and wrap in foil, then heat in the oven.*
- *You could roast shallots with the garlic, or sauté some celery to add to the simmering soup about 10 minutes before serving.*

Potato and Garlic Energy 115kcal/488kJ; Protein 4.3g; Carbohydrate 24.3g, of which sugars 2.1g; Fat 0.7g, of which saturates 0.2g; Cholesterol 0mg; Calcium 14mg; Fibre 2.3g; Sodium 219mg.
Corn and Chilli Energy 294kcal/1241kJ; Protein 8.9g; Carbohydrate 47.8g, of which sugars 20.8g; Fat 8.9g, of which saturates 4.8g; Cholesterol 20mg; Calcium 168mg; Fibre 4.2g; Sodium 299mg.

Goan Potato Soup with Samosas

Soup and vegetable samosas are ideal partners. Bought samosas are given an easy, but clever, flavour lift in this simple recipe.

Serves 4

60ml/4 tbsp sunflower oil
10ml/2 tsp black mustard seeds
1 large onion, chopped
1 fresh red chilli, seeded
   and chopped
2.5ml/½ tsp ground turmeric
1.5ml/¼ tsp cayenne pepper
900g/2lb potatoes, cut into cubes

4 fresh curry leaves
750ml/1¼ pint/3 cups
   vegetable stock
225g/8oz spinach leaves,
   torn if large
400ml/14fl oz/1⅔ cups
   coconut milk
handful of fresh coriander
   leaves (cilantro)
salt and black pepper

For the garlic samosas

1 large garlic clove, crushed
25g/1oz/2 tbsp butter
6 vegetable samosas

1 Heat the oil in a large pan. Add the mustard seeds, cover and cook until they begin to pop. Stir in the onion and chilli and cook for 5–6 minutes, until softened.

2 Stir in the turmeric, cayenne pepper, potatoes, curry leaves and stock. Bring to the boil, reduce the heat and cover the pan. Simmer for 15 minutes, stirring occasionally, until the potatoes are tender.

3 Meanwhile, prepare the samosas. Preheat the oven to 180°C/350°F/Gas 4. Melt the butter in a small pan with the garlic, stirring and crushing the garlic into the butter.

4 Place the samosas in an ovenproof dish – a gratin dish or quiche dish is ideal. Brush them lightly with the butter, turn them over and brush with the remaining butter. Heat through in the oven for about 5 minutes, until piping hot.

5 Add the spinach to the soup and cook for 5 minutes. Stir in the coconut milk and cook for a further 5 minutes.

6 Season and add the coriander leaves before ladling the soup into bowls. Serve with the garlic samosas.

Cinnamon-spiced Chickpea and Vegetable Soup

Cinnamon, ginger and turmeric are a warming mix of spices to perfectly complement earthy potatoes and nutty chickpeas.

Serves 6

1 large onion, chopped
1.2 litres/2 pints/5 cups
   vegetable stock
5ml/1 tsp ground cinnamon
5ml/1 tsp turmeric
15ml/1 tbsp grated fresh
   root ginger

pinch of cayenne pepper
2 carrots, diced
2 celery sticks, diced
400g/14oz can
   chopped tomatoes
450g/1lb floury potatoes, diced
pinch of saffron strands
400g/14oz can
   chickpeas, drained
30ml/2 tbsp chopped fresh
   coriander (cilantro)
15ml/1 tbsp lemon juice
salt and ground black pepper
fried wedges of lemon, to serve

1 Place the onion in a large pot with 300ml/½ pint/1¼ cups of the vegetable stock. Bring to the boil, reduce the heat and simmer gently for about 10 minutes.

2 Meanwhile, mix the cinnamon, turmeric, ginger, cayenne pepper and 30ml/2 tbsp of stock to form a paste. Stir into the onion mixture with the carrots, celery and remaining stock.

3 Bring to the boil, stirring constantly, and reduce the heat. Cover and simmer gently for 5 minutes.

4 Add the tomatoes and potatoes and heat until simmering gently again, then cover and cook for 20 minutes.

5 Add the saffron, chickpeas, coriander and lemon juice. Season to taste and heat briefly, then serve with fried wedges of lemon.

Cook's Tip
Shallow frying lemon wedges – or halves, if the fruit are small – caramelizes them, giving the juice a particularly rich flavour.

Goan Soup Energy 836kcal/3503kJ; Protein 16.7g; Carbohydrate 112g, of which sugars 8.6g; Fat 38.7g, of which saturates 4.9g; Cholesterol 0mg; Calcium 227mg; Fibre 8.9g; Sodium 117mg.
Chickpea Soup Energy 399kcal/1685kJ; Protein 20.6g; Carbohydrate 58.1g, of which sugars 4.1g; Fat 11g, of which saturates 1.4g; Cholesterol 0mg; Calcium 209mg; Fibre 10.8g; Sodium 101mg.

Sweet Potato and Parsnip Soup

The delicious combination of honeyed sweet potatoes and parsnips, two of the most popular root vegetables, is used in both the soup itself and, when roasted, also serves as a tasty garnish.

Serves 6
15ml/1 tbsp sunflower oil
1 large leek, sliced

2 celery sticks, chopped
450g/1lb sweet potatoes, diced
225g/8oz parsnips, diced
900ml/1½ pints/3¾ cups
   vegetable stock
salt and ground black pepper

For the garnish
15ml/1 tbsp chopped
   fresh parsley
roasted strips of sweet potatoes
   and parsnips

1 Heat the sunflower oil in a large pan and add the chopped leek, celery, sweet potatoes and parsnips. Cook gently for about 5 minutes, stirring to prevent them from browning or sticking to the pan.

2 Stir in the vegetable stock and slowly bring to the boil, then cover and simmer gently for about 25 minutes, or until the vegetables are tender, stirring occasionally. Season with salt and pepper to taste. Remove the pan from the heat and allow the soup to cool slightly.

3 Purée the soup in a food processor or blender until smooth, then return the soup to the pan and reheat gently.

4 Ladle the soup into warmed soup bowls to serve, and sprinkle over the chopped parsley and roasted strips of sweet potatoes and parsnips.

Cook's Tip
Making and freezing soup is a practical way of preserving a glut of root vegetables that are unlikely to keep well. Not only can excess raw vegetables be used this way, but leftover boiled, mashed or roasted root vegetables, can all be added to soup puréed, cooled or frozen.

Tangy Sweet Potato and Red Pepper Soup

This delicious soup has a sweet and tangy flavour, as well as a wonderful colour thanks to the sweet potato and red pepper. The bonus is that it also tastes as good as it looks.

Serves 6
500g/1¼lb sweet potato
1 onion, roughly chopped

2 red (bell) peppers, about
   225g/8oz, seeded and cubed
2 large garlic cloves,
   roughly chopped
300ml/½ pint/1¼ cups dry
   white wine
1.2 litres/2 pints/5 cups vegetable
   or light chicken stock
Tabasco sauce (optional)
sea salt and ground black pepper
country bread, to serve

1 Peel the sweet potato and cut it into cubes. Place the pieces in a large heavy pan with the red pepper, onion, garlic, white wine and vegetable or chicken stock.

2 Bring the mixture to the boil, then lower the heat and simmer the soup for about 25–30 minutes or until all the vegetables are quite soft.

3 Remove the pan from the heat and leave the soup to cool. Transfer the mixture to a blender and process until smooth.

4 Return the blended soup to the pan and reheat gently, if serving hot. Season to taste with salt, ground black pepper and a generous dash of Tabasco, if you like.

5 Pour the soup into a tureen or serving bowl and cool slightly. Serve warm or at room temperature, with plenty of thick, country-style bread.

Cook's Tip
For an attractive finish to this soup, try garnishing it with a sprinkling of finely diced bell pepper, if you like. Any colour will work well, whether red, green or yellow.

Sweet Potato and Parsnip Energy 113kcal/479kJ; Protein 2.1g; Carbohydrate 21.6g, of which sugars 7.2g; Fat 2.6g, of which saturates 0.4g; Cholesterol 0mg; Calcium 45mg; Fibre 4.3g; Sodium 40mg.
Sweet Potato and Pepper Energy 121kcal/513kJ; Protein 1.6g; Carbohydrate 21.2g, of which sugars 7.9g; Fat 0.4g, of which saturates 0.1g; Cholesterol 0mg; Calcium 30mg; Fibre 2.7g; Sodium 37mg.

Chunky Corn, Pepper and Sweet Potato Soup

The combination of corn kernels and sweet potato gives this soup a flavour that is deep and delicious.

Serves 6

15ml/1 tbsp olive oil
1 onion, finely chopped
2 garlic cloves, crushed
1 small red chilli, seeded and
    finely chopped
1.75 litres/3 pints/7½ cups
    vegetable stock
10ml/2 tsp ground cumin
1 medium sweet potato, diced
½ red (bell) pepper,
    finely chopped
450g/1lb corn kernels
salt and ground black pepper
lime wedges, to serve

1 Heat the oil in a large heavy pan and fry the onion for about 5 minutes until softened. Add the garlic and chilli and fry for a further 2 minutes.

2 In the same pan, add 300ml/½ pint/1¼ cups of the stock, and simmer for 10 minutes.

3 Mix the cumin with a little stock to form a paste and then stir into the soup. Add the diced sweet potato, stir and simmer for 10 minutes. Season to taste with salt and black pepper and stir again.

4 Add the chopped pepper, corn kernels and the remaining stock to the pan and simmer for 10 minutes.

5 Process half of the soup in a blender or food processor until smooth and then stir into the chunky soup. Check the seasoning and serve with lime wedges for squeezing over.

Cook's Tip
You may need to wear rubber gloves when chopping fresh chillies as the oils from the chilli may cause irritation to the skin, or inflammation to the eyes if touched after handling.

Creamy Chicken and Potato Soup

A flavoursome creamy chicken soup thickened with potatoes makes a fabulous lunch served with crispy bread. It is essential to use a really strong, home-made chicken stock for this recipe to give the soup a full flavour.

Serves 6

50g/2oz/¼ cup butter
2 onions, chopped
2 medium potatoes, chopped
1 large carrot, diced
1 celery stick, diced
750ml/1¼ pints/3 cups
    chicken stock
25g/1oz/¼ cup plain
    (all-purpose) flour
150ml/¼ pint/⅔ cup milk
175g/6oz cooked chicken
300ml/½ pint/1¼ cups single
    (light) cream
salt and ground black pepper
parsley leaves, to garnish

1 Melt the butter in a large pan and cook the onions, potatoes, carrot and celery gently for 5 minutes. Do not allow the vegetables to brown.

2 Add the stock and simmer gently for 30 minutes. Season with salt and pepper to taste. Purée the soup in a food processor or blender until smooth and then return to the pan. Blend the flour with the milk and stir into the soup. Cook over a low heat, stirring, until the soup thickens.

3 Meanwhile, chop the chicken finely. Add to the soup and heat through for 5 minutes. Add 75ml/2½fl oz/⅓ cup of the cream and simmer for 5 minutes more.

4 Serve in individual bowls topped with a swirl of the remaining cream and garnished with ground black pepper and parsley leaves.

Cook's Tip
Fresh parsley is simple to grow yourself. Buy a plant and keep it on a sunny windowsill in your kitchen. Ensure it is kept moist but don't over-water it and pull off the leaves as and when you need them. They will regrow in a matter of days.

Corn and Sweet Potato Energy 146kcal/618kJ; Protein 2.9g; Carbohydrate 28.9g, of which sugars 10.7g; Fat 2.9g, of which saturates 0.5g; Cholesterol 0mg; Calcium 15mg; Fibre 2.3g; Sodium 217mg.
Creamy Chicken Soup Energy 295kcal/1231kJ; Protein 11g; Carbohydrate 23.6g, of which sugars 8.9g; Fat 18.2g, of which saturates 11.1g; Cholesterol 61mg; Calcium 111mg; Fibre 2.1g; Sodium 137mg.

Chicken, Pork and Sweet Potato Soup with Aubergine Sauce

A garlicky aubergine sauce mingles well with chicken, pork and sweet potatoes.

Serve 6–8
225g/8oz/generous 1 cup
  chickpeas, soaked overnight
1.3kg/3lb chicken, cut into eight
350g/12oz belly of pork, rind
  removed or pork fillet, cubed
2 chorizo, thickly sliced
2 onions, chopped
60ml/4 tbsp vegetable oil
2 garlic cloves, crushed
3 large tomatoes, peeled, seeded
  and chopped

15ml/1 tbsp tomato purée (paste)
1–2 sweet potatoes, cut into
  1cm/½in cubes
2 plantains, sliced (optional)
salt and ground black pepper
chives or chopped spring onions
  (scallions), to garnish
½ head Chinese leaves (Chinese
  cabbage), shredded, to serve

For the aubergine sauce
1 large aubergine (eggplant), skin
  pricked in places
3 garlic cloves, crushed
60–90ml/4–6 tbsp wine vinegar
  or cider vinegar

1 Put the drained chickpeas in a pan with water to cover; boil rapidly for 10 minutes. Reduce the heat and simmer for 30 minutes until the chickpeas are half-tender. Drain.

2 Put the chickpeas, chicken, pork, chorizo and half of the onions in a pan with 2.5 litres/4 pints/10 cups water. Boil, lower the heat, cover and simmer for 1 hour until the meat is tender.

3 Preheat the oven to 200°C/400°F/Gas 6. Bake the aubergine for 30 minutes. Cool, peel and mash with the garlic, seasoning and vinegar to sharpen the sauce.

4 Heat the oil in a pan and fry the remaining onion and garlic for 5 minutes. Add the tomatoes and tomato purée and cook for 2 minutes. Add the sweet potato and plantains, if using. Simmer for 20 minutes until the sweet potato is cooked. Add the Chinese leaves for the last minute or two.

5 Serve the soup and vegetables separately, garnished with chives or spring onions. Serve with the aubergine sauce.

Chicken, Leek and Potato Soup

This chicken and potato soup makes a substantial main course when served with fresh crusty bread.

Serves 4–6
1.4kg/3lb whole chicken
1 small head of celery, trimmed
1 onion, coarsely chopped
1 bouquet garni

3 large leeks
65g/2½oz/5 tbsp butter
2 potatoes, cut into chunks
150ml/¼ pint/⅔ cup dry
  white wine
30–45ml/2–3 tbsp single (light)
  cream (optional)
salt and ground black pepper
90g/3½oz pancetta, grilled until
  crisp, to garnish

1 Cut the breasts from the chicken and set aside. Chop the rest of the chicken carcass into eight or ten pieces and place in a large pan. Chop four or five of the celery sticks and add them to the pan with the onion and bouquet garni. Pour in about 2.4 litres/4 pints/10 cups water to cover and bring to the boil. Reduce the heat and cover the pan, then simmer for 1½ hours.

2 Remove the chicken and cut off and reserve the meat. Strain the stock, then return it to the pan and boil rapidly until it has reduced to about 1.5 litres/2½ pints/6¼ cups.

3 Set about 150g/5oz of the leeks aside. Slice the remaining leeks and the remaining celery, reserving any celery leaves. Melt half the butter in a pan. Add the sliced leeks and celery, cover and cook over a low heat for 10 minutes, until soft but not brown. Add the potatoes, wine and 1.2 litres/2 pints/5 cups of the stock. Season, bring to the boil and reduce the heat. Part-cover and simmer for 15–20 minutes, or until the potatoes are cooked.

4 Dice the reserved uncooked chicken. Melt the remaining butter in a pan and fry the chicken for 5–7 minutes, until cooked. Slice the remaining leeks, add to the chicken and cook, stirring occasionally, for a further 3–4 minutes, until just cooked.

5 Purée the soup and diced chicken from the stock. Season and add more stock if the soup is thick. Stir in the cream and chicken and leek mixture. Reheat gently and serve topped with pancetta and the chopped reserved celery leaves.

Chicken and Pork Energy 290kcal/1219kJ; Protein 46.4g; Carbohydrate 9.8g, of which sugars 8.7g; Fat 7.5g, of which saturates 1.5g; Cholesterol 169mg; Calcium 40mg; Fibre 2.2g; Sodium 150mg.
Chicken and Leek Energy 294kcal/1246kJ; Protein 40.5g; Carbohydrate 22.1g, of which sugars 5.9g; Fat 2.8g, of which saturates 0.7g; Cholesterol 105mg; Calcium 69mg; Fibre 4.8g; Sodium 124mg.

Spicy Chicken and Potato Broth

This colourful South-east Asian chicken and potato soup can be served as an appetizer or as a dish on its own.

Serves 4–6

30ml/2 tbsp palm, groundnut (peanut) or corn oil
25g/1oz fresh root ginger, finely chopped
5ml/1 tsp ground turmeric
1 lemon grass stalk, finely chopped
4–5 kaffir lime leaves, crushed
4 candlenuts, coarsely ground
2 garlic cloves, crushed
5ml/1 tsp coriander seeds
5ml/1 tsp shrimp paste
2 litres/3½ pints chicken stock
corn or vegetable oil, for deep-frying
2 waxy potatoes, finely sliced
350g/12oz skinless chicken breast fillets, thinly sliced widthways
150g/5oz leafy green cabbage, finely sliced
150g/5oz mung beansprouts
3 hard-boiled eggs, thinly sliced
salt and ground black pepper

To serve

1 bunch fresh coriander (cilantro) leaves, roughly chopped
2–3 spring onions (scallions), finely sliced
2–3 hot red or green chillies, seeded and finely sliced
2 limes, cut into wedges
kecap manis (Indonesian soy sauce)

1 Prepare the ingredients for serving by putting the coriander, spring onions, chillies and lime wedges into a serving bowl.

2 Heat the oil in a pan, stir in the ginger, turmeric, lemon grass, kaffir lime leaves, candlenuts, garlic, coriander seeds and shrimp paste. Fry until the mixture darkens and becomes fragrant. Pour in the stock, bring to the boil, then simmer for about 20 minutes.

3 Meanwhile, heat the oil for deep-frying in a wok. Fry the potato slices until crisp. Remove with a slotted spoon, drain on kitchen paper and put aside. Strain the chicken stock and reserve. Pour back into the pan and season. Return to the boil, reduce the heat and add the chicken. Simmer for 2–3 minutes.

4 Sprinkle the finely sliced cabbage and beansprouts into the base of the serving bowls. Ladle over the broth and top with the thinly sliced boiled eggs and potatoes, and serve. Diners help themselves to the ingredients for serving, and drizzle the kecap manis over the top.

Rich Chicken, Bacon and Potato Minestrone Soup

This special minestrone made with succulent chicken and potatoes makes a hearty meal served with crusty bread.

Serves 4–6

15ml/1 tbsp olive oil
2 chicken thighs
3 rindless streaky (fatty) bacon rashers (strips), chopped
1 onion, finely chopped
a few fresh basil leaves, shredded
a few fresh rosemary leaves, finely chopped
15ml/1 tbsp chopped fresh parsley
2 potatoes, cut into 1cm/½in cubes
1 large carrot, cut into 1cm/½in cubes
2 small courgettes (zucchini), cut into 1cm/½in cubes
1–2 celery sticks, cut into 1cm/½in cubes
1 litre/1¾ pints/4 cups chicken stock
200g/7oz/1¾ cups frozen peas
90g/3½oz/scant 1 cup stellette or other dried tiny soup pasta
salt and ground black pepper
coarsely shaved Parmesan cheese
fresh basil leaves, to garnish

1 Heat the oil in a large frying pan, add the chicken and fry for about 5 minutes on each side. Remove and set aside.

2 Lower the heat, add the bacon, onion and herbs to the pan and stir well. Cook gently, stirring constantly, for 5–7 minutes. Add all the vegetables, except the frozen peas, to the pan and cook for 5–7 minutes more, stirring frequently.

3 Return the chicken thighs to the pan, add the stock and bring to the boil. Cover and cook over a low heat for about 35–40 minutes, stirring the soup occasionally.

4 Remove the chicken thighs with a slotted spoon and place them on a board. Stir the peas and pasta into the soup and bring back to the boil. Simmer, stirring frequently until the pasta is al dente: 7–8 minutes or according to the packet instructions.

5 Meanwhile, remove and discard the chicken skin, then cut the meat from the bones and chop into 1cm/½in pieces. Add the chicken to the soup, season with salt and pepper, and heat through. Serve garnished with Parmesan shavings and basil leaves.

Spicy Broth Energy 296kcal/1238kJ; Protein 21.1g; Carbohydrate 14.8g, of which sugars 3g; Fat 17.5g, of which saturates 2.8g; Cholesterol 136mg; Calcium 63mg; Fibre 2.7g; Sodium 96mg.
Minestrone Energy 226kcal/948kJ; Protein 15.7g; Carbohydrate 25.1g, of which sugars 11.4g; Fat 7.7g, of which saturates 3.2g; Cholesterol 43mg; Calcium 75mg; Fibre 5.2g; Sodium 102mg.

Clear Chickpea and Potato Broth with Sausage

Chickpeas are very versatile and are a terrific addition to soups, providing a boost of flavour and bulk, and transforming a light broth into a substantial meal. Here, the distinctive nutty flavour of the chickpeas is used to enhance the flavours of potato and salami. The flavour can be varied according to the herbs and spices used.

Serves 4–6
500g/1¼lb/3½ cups chickpeas, rinsed and drained
2 litres/3½ pints/8 cups vegetable stock
3 garlic cloves, sliced
3 large waxy potatoes, peeled and cut into bitesize chunks
50ml/2fl oz/¼ cup olive oil
50g/2oz salami, sliced
225g/8oz spinach leaves, washed and drained well
a little freshly grated nutmeg
salt and ground black pepper

1 Place the chickpeas in a large bowl of cold water and leave to soak overnight. The next day, drain them well and place in a large pan with the stock.

2 Bring to the boil, then reduce the heat and cook gently for about 1 hour. Add the garlic, potatoes, olive oil, salami and seasoning and cook for a further 15 minutes, until the potatoes are tender but not broken.

3 Add the spinach leaves to the soup and bring it back to simmering point, then cook for a further 5 minutes, until the spinach has wilted.

4 Season the soup with a little freshly grated nutmeg and taste, adding salt and pepper, if necessary. Ladle into bowls to serve.

Variation
Instead of salami, slice Polish sausage, ham sausage or garlic sausage to add to the soup with the potatoes. Grilled (broiled) fresh sausages can be sliced and added, if you like.

Kale, Chorizo and Potato Soup

This hearty winter soup with delicious earthy chunks of potato and shredded iron-rich kale is given a spicy kick from the addition of chorizo sausage. The soup becomes more potent if chilled overnight. It is worth buying the best possible chorizo sausage to achieve superior flavour.

Serves 6–8
225g/8oz kale, stems removed
225g/8oz chorizo sausage
675g/1½lb potatoes, cut into chunks
1.75 litres/3 pints/7½ cups vegetable stock
5ml/1 tsp ground black pepper
pinch of cayenne pepper (optional)
12 slices French bread, toasted on both sides
salt and ground black pepper

1 Place the kale in a food processor or blender and process for a few seconds to chop it finely. Alternatively, shred it finely by hand.

2 Prick the sausages and place in a pan with enough water to cover. Bring just to boiling point, then reduce the heat immediately before the water boils too rapidly and simmer for 15 minutes. Drain and cut into thin slices.

3 Boil the potatoes for about 15 minutes or until the slices are just tender. Drain, and place in a bowl, then mash, adding a little of the cooking liquid to form a thick paste.

4 Bring the vegetable stock to the boil and add the kale. Bring back to the boil. Reduce the heat to a simmer and add the chorizo, then cook for 5 minutes. Gradually add the potato paste, stirring it into the soup, then simmer for 20 minutes. Season with black pepper and cayenne pepper.

5 Divide the freshly-made toast among serving bowls. Pour the soup over and serve immediately, sprinkled with black pepper.

Cook's Tip
Select maincrop, floury potatoes for this soup rather than new potatoes or waxy salad potatoes.

Chickpea Broth Energy 399Kcal/1681kJ; Protein 20.5g; Carbohydrate 58g, of which sugars 4g; Fat 10.9g, of which saturates 1.4g; Cholesterol 0mg; Calcium 203mg; Fibre 10.7g; Sodium 96mg.
Kale and Chorizo Energy 411kcal/1740kJ; Protein 13.2g; Carbohydrate 69.3g, of which sugars 6.2g; Fat 11g, of which saturates 4.1g; Cholesterol 15mg; Calcium 140mg; Fibre 4g; Sodium 812mg.

Tamarind, Pork and Vegetable Soup

This sweet-and-sour soup, flavoured with tamarind, has its roots in South-east Asian cooking. The punchy combination of sweet potato, fish sauce and ginger gives this robust lunchtime dish a delightful piquancy, but despite the exotic sounding ingredients this impressive soup is quick and easy to make.

Serves 4–6
2 litres/3½ pints/8 cups pork or
  chicken stock, or a mixture of
  stock and water
15–30ml/1–2 tbsp tamarind
  paste (see Cook's Tip)
30ml/2 tbsp patis (fish sauce)
25g/1oz fresh root ginger,
  finely grated
1 sweet potato, cut into
  bitesize chunks
8–10 snake beans
  (yard-long beans)
225g/8oz kangkong (water
  spinach) or ordinary spinach,
  well rinsed
350g/12oz pork tenderloin,
  sliced widthways
2–3 spring onions (scallions),
  white parts only, finely sliced
salt and ground black pepper

1 Bring the stock to the boil in a wok or deep pan. Stir in the tamarind paste, patis and ginger, reduce the heat and simmer for about 20 minutes. Season with salt and lots of pepper.

2 Add the sweet potato and snake beans to the pan and bring back to the boil, then immediately reduce the heat and cook gently for 3–4 minutes, until the sweet potato is tender.

3 Stir in the kangkong or spinach and the sliced pork tenderloin and simmer gently for 2–3 minutes, until the pork is just cooked and turns opaque.

4 Ladle the soup into individual warmed bowls and sprinkle the sliced spring onions over the top.

Cook's Tip
Fresh tamarind pods, packaged tamarind pulp and pots of tamarind paste are all available in Middle Eastern, Indian, African and South-east Asian food stores.

Hearty Gammon, Potato and Bean Broth

In this hearty soup, the potatoes cook in the gammon stock, absorbing its flavour and saltiness. Take care not to add too much salt and spoil the soup.

Serves 4
450g/1lb gammon (smoked or
  cured ham), in one piece
2 bay leaves
2 onions, sliced
10ml/2 tsp paprika
675g/1½lb baking potatoes, cut
  into large chunks
225g/8oz spring greens (collards)
425g/15oz can haricot (navy) or
  cannellini beans, drained
salt and ground black pepper

1 Soak the gammon overnight in cold water. Drain and put in a large pan with the bay leaves and onions. Pour in 1.5 litres/2½ pints/6¼ cups cold water. Bring to the boil, reduce the heat and simmer very gently for 1½ hours or until the meat is deliciously tender.

2 Remove the meat from the cooking liquid and leave to cool slightly. Discard the skin and any excess fat and cut the meat into small even chunks. Return to the pan with the paprika and potatoes. Bring back to the boil, then reduce the heat, cover and simmer for 20 minutes until the potatoes are cooked through, but not falling apart.

3 Trim the greens. Roll up the leaves and cut into thin shreds. Add to the pan with the beans and simmer, uncovered, for about 10 minutes. Remove the bay leaves. Season with salt and pepper to taste and serve hot.

Variations
• Bacon knuckle can be used instead of the gammon (smoked or cured ham) – they are economical and the bones will give the stock a delicious flavour. Freeze any stock you don't use.
• Peel the potatoes if you prefer, but the flavour is best when the skins are left on.

Sweet-and-sour Pork, Prawn and Sweet Potato Soup

This hearty and delicious soup is ideal as a main course, served with crusty bread or even some plain boiled rice. The complex sweet and sour flavours, as well as the stunning appearance of the soup, make it a great centrepiece for a special occasion.

Serves 4–6

350g/12oz lean pork
225g/8oz raw or cooked prawn (shrimp) tails
30ml/2 tbsp tamarind sauce
juice of 2 limes
1 small green guava, peeled, seeded and chopped
1 small, under-ripe mango, peeled, seeded and chopped
1.4 litres/2½ pints/6¼ cups chicken stock
15ml/1 tbsp fish or soy sauce
285g/10oz sweet potato, peeled and cut into even pieces
225g/8oz unripe tomatoes, quartered
115g/4oz green beans, trimmed and halved
1 star fruit (carambola), thickly sliced widthways
85g/3oz green cabbage, shredded
5ml/1 tsp crushed black pepper
salt
2 spring onions (scallions), shredded, to garnish
lime wedges, to serve

1 Trim any fat from the pork and finely dice the meat. Peel the prawns and set aside.

2 Gently heat the tamarind sauce and lime juice in a large heavy pan and add the pork pieces. Add the guava, mango, chicken stock, and fish or soy sauce to the pan and stir until well combined.

3 Bring the mixture to the boil, then reduce the heat and simmer, uncovered, for about 30 minutes, stirring occasionally.

4 Stir the prawns into the pan, then add all the remaining fruit and vegetables. Simmer the soup for a further 10–15 minutes until all the vegetables are tender.

5 Add the black pepper, and salt to taste. Garnish with the spring onions and serve immediately with lime wedges.

Country Lamb and Potato Soup

Traditionally, Irish soda bread would be served with this hearty one-pot meal based on classic Irish lamb and potato stew.

Serves 4

15ml/1 tbsp vegetable oil
675g/1½lb boneless lamb chump chops, trimmed and cut into small cubes
2 small onions, quartered
2 leeks, thickly sliced
1 litre/1¾ pints/4 cups lamb stock or water
2 large potatoes, cut into chunks
2 carrots, thickly sliced
sprig of fresh thyme, plus extra to garnish
15g/½oz/1 tbsp butter
30ml/2 tbsp chopped fresh parsley
salt and ground black pepper
Irish soda bread, to serve

1 Heat the oil in a pan. Add the lamb and brown in batches. Use a slotted spoon to remove the lamb from the pan.

2 Add the onions and cook for 4–5 minutes, until browned. Return the meat to the pan and add the leeks. Pour in the stock or water, then bring to the boil. Reduce the heat, cover and simmer gently for about 1 hour.

3 Add the potatoes, carrots and thyme, and continue cooking for a further 40 minutes, until the lamb is tender. Remove from the heat and leave to stand for 5 minutes to allow the fat to settle on the surface of the soup.

4 Skim off the fat. Pour off the stock from the soup into a clean pan and whisk in the butter. Stir in the parsley and season well, then pour the liquid back over the soup ingredients.

5 Ladle the soup into warmed bowls and garnish with sprigs of fresh thyme. Serve with chunks of brown or Irish soda bread.

> **Variation**
> The vegetables in this rustic soup can be varied according to the season. Swede (rutabaga), turnip, celeriac and even cabbage could be added in place of some of the listed vegetables.

Sweet-and-sour Soup Energy 234kcal/981kJ; Protein 26.2g; Carbohydrate 24.8g, of which sugars 1.6g; Fat 3.3g, of which saturates 1g; Cholesterol 137mg; Calcium 84mg; Fibre 1.1g; Sodium 681mg.
Country Lamb Soup Energy 500kcal/2092kJ; Protein 38.2g; Carbohydrate 30.2g, of which sugars 12.2g; Fat 26g, of which saturates 11.3g; Cholesterol 136mg; Calcium 104mg; Fibre 6.1g; Sodium 197mg.

Lamb Meatball and Vegetable Soup

A variety of vegetables creates a tasty base for meatballs in this substantial soup, which will make a hearty meal served with crusty bread.

Serves 4

1 litre/1¾ pints/4 cups lamb stock
1 onion, finely chopped
2 carrots, finely sliced
½ celeriac, finely diced
75g/3oz/¾ cup frozen peas
50g/2oz green beans, cut into 2.5cm/1in pieces
3 tomatoes, seeded and chopped
1 red (bell) pepper, seeded and diced
1 potato, coarsely diced
2 lemons, sliced
salt and ground black pepper
crusty bread, to serve

For the meatballs

225g/8oz/1 cup very lean minced (ground) lamb
40g/1½oz/¼ cup short grain rice
30ml/2 tbsp chopped fresh parsley
plain (all-purpose) flour, for coating

1 Pour the stock into a large pan and place over medium heat. Stir in the onion, carrot, celeriac and peas.

2 Add the beans, tomatoes, red pepper and potato with the slices of lemon. Stir in a little salt and ground black pepper and bring the mixture to the boil. Reduce the heat, cover the pan and simmer for 15–20 minutes.

3 Meanwhile, prepare the meatballs. Mix the meat, rice and parsley together in a bowl and season well. The best way of mixing meat for meatballs is by hand, squeezing and kneading the mixture so that the meat mixes with the rice.

4 Take out a rounded teaspoon of the meat mixture and roll it into a small ball, roughly the size of a walnut. Toss it in the flour. Repeat with the remaining mixture.

5 Add the meatballs to the soup and simmer gently for 25–30 minutes, stirring occasionally, to prevent the meatballs from sticking. The rice should be plumped up and cooked in the meat. Adjust the seasoning and serve in warm bowls, accompanied by crusty bread.

Lamb and Vegetable Stew with Rice

This is based on a traditional Jewish dish of baked meats, potatoes and beans. A parcel of rice is often added to the broth part way through cooking, to produce pressed, chewy rice.

Serves 8

250g/9oz/1 cup chickpeas, soaked overnight
45ml/3 tbsp olive oil
1 onion, chopped
10 garlic cloves, chopped
1 parsnip, sliced
3 carrots, sliced
5–10ml/1–2 tsp ground cumin
2.5ml/½ tsp ground turmeric
15ml/1 tbsp chopped fresh root ginger
2 litres/3½ pints/8 cups beef stock
1 potato, cut into chunks
½ vegetable marrow, sliced
400g/14oz fresh or canned tomatoes, diced
45–60ml/3–4 tbsp brown or green lentils
2 bay leaves
250g/9oz salted meat such as salt beef
250g/9oz piece of lamb
½ large bunch fresh coriander (cilantro), chopped
200g/7oz/1 cup long grain rice

For serving

chopped fresh chillies
1 lemon, cut into wedges

1 Preheat the oven to 120°C/250°F/Gas ½. Drain the chickpeas. Heat the oil in a deep flameproof casserole, add the onion, garlic, parsnip, carrots, cumin, turmeric and ginger and cook for 2–3 minutes. Add the chickpeas, stock, potato, marrow, tomatoes, lentils, bay leaves, salted meat, lamb and coriander. Cover and cook in the oven for 1 hour.

2 Tie the rice in a double thickness of muslin (cheesecloth), allowing enough room for it to expand while it is cooking. Place the rice parcel in the casserole, anchoring the edge of the muslin parcel under the lid so it is held above the soup and allowed to steam. Return the casserole to the oven and continue cooking for a further 2 hours.

3 Carefully remove the lid and the rice. Skim any fat off the top of the soup. Ladle the soup into bowls. Open the rice parcel and add a scoop to each bowl with one or two pieces of meat. Sprinkle with chopped fresh chillies and serve with lemon.

Lamb Meatball Soup Energy 226kcal/948kJ; Protein 15.7g; Carbohydrate 25.1g, of which sugars 11.4g; Fat 7.7g, of which saturates 3.2g; Cholesterol 43mg; Calcium 75mg; Fibre 5.2g; Sodium 102mg.
Lamb Stew Energy 463kcal/1941kJ; Protein 28.5g; Carbohydrate 60.5g, of which sugars 17g; Fat 12.7g, of which saturates 3.5g; Cholesterol 47mg; Calcium 130mg; Fibre 9.4g; Sodium 409mg.

Hearty Beef and Vegetable Soup

This substantial meat and vegetable soup has a deliciously rustic flavour and is great for using the less expensive cuts of beef.

Serves 6

225g/8oz braising steak, cut into 1.5cm/½in cubes
225g/8oz lean boned pork shoulder, cut into 1.5cm/½in cubes
2 litres/3½ pints/8 cups beef stock
1 bay leaf
350g/12oz tomatoes, skinned, seeded and chopped
1 small red (bell) pepper, seeded and chopped
1 small onion, chopped
2 carrots, chopped
1 large boiling potato, peeled and diced
175g/6oz fresh or thawed frozen corn kernels
15ml/1 tbsp Worcestershire sauce
salt and ground black pepper

1 Put the beef and pork in a large heavy pan and add the stock. Bring to the boil, skimming off all the froth that rises to the surface.

2 When you have removed all of the froth from the liquid, add the bay leaf. Partially cover the pan and gently simmer over a very low heat for about 1 hour.

3 Add the tomatoes, red pepper, onion, carrots and potato. Bring back to the boil, then reduce the heat and continue simmering, partly covered, for about 45 minutes. Stir the soup from time to time.

4 Add the corn and simmer for a further 20–30 minutes or until all the vegetables and meat are tender.

5 Discard the bay leaf. Stir in the Worcestershire sauce. Taste and adjust the seasoning before serving.

Cook's Tip
This soup is ideal to make two or three days before you plan to serve it as the flavours will continue to develop and improve over time.

Fisherman's Potato Stew

This substantial one-pot soup of fish and potatoes makes a rewarding supper after a hard day's fishing.

Serves 6

500g/1¼lb mussels
3 onions
2 garlic cloves, sliced
300ml/½ pint/1¼ cups fish stock
12 scallops, shelled
450g/1lb cod fillet, cut into cubes
30ml/2 tbsp olive oil
1 potato, cut into 1cm/½in slices
few sprigs of fresh thyme, chopped
1 red and 1 green (bell) pepper, seeded and cut into chunks
120ml/4fl oz/½ cup dry white wine
250ml/8fl oz/1 cup crème fraîche
275g/10oz peeled prawns (shrimp)
salt and ground black pepper
fresh thyme sprigs, to garnish
75g/3oz/¾ cup grated mature (sharp) Cheddar cheese, to serve

1 Clean the mussel shells, removing any beards. Discard any that stay open when tapped. Rinse in cold water.

2 Pour water to a depth of 2.5cm/1in into a large, deep frying pan. Chop one onion and add it to the pan, with the garlic. Bring to the boil, then add the mussels and cook, covered, for 5–6 minutes, shaking the pan occasionally. Remove the mussels as they open, discarding any that remain shut. Set aside.

3 Strain the cooking liquid from the mussels through muslin (cheesecloth) to remove any remaining sand. Make up the liquid with fish stock to 300ml/½ pint/1¼ cups.

4 Cut the remaining onions into wedges. Heat the oil in a large pan and fry the wedges for 3 minutes. Add the potato and thyme, cover and cook for 15 minutes, until the potato has softened.

5 Add the peppers to the pan and cook for a few minutes. Stir in the mixed mussel and fish stock, the wine and crème fraîche. Bring to near-boiling point, then add the cod and scallops.

6 Reduce the heat and simmer for 5 minutes, then add the prawns. Simmer for 3–4 minutes more, until the seafood is cooked. Add the mussels for 1–2 minutes. Season if necessary, then spoon into bowls, garnish with thyme sprigs. Serve with the cheese on the side so diners can help themselves.

Hearty Beef Soup Energy 226kcal/948kJ; Protein 15.7g; Carbohydrate 25.1g, of which sugars 11.4g; Fat 7.7g, of which saturates 3.2g; Cholesterol 43mg; Calcium 75mg; Fibre 5.2g; Sodium 102mg.
Fisherman's Stew Energy 450kcal/1880kJ; Protein 42.7g; Carbohydrate 14.9g, of which sugars 5.7g; Fat 23.1g, of which saturates 14.4g; Cholesterol 220mg; Calcium 208mg; Fibre 1.4g; Sodium 408mg.

Mediterranean Potato and Fish Soup

This chunky fish and potato soup makes a robust and wonderfully aromatic dish, perfect for a lingering al fresco summer lunch or a light supper with friends. Serve it with fresh crusty bread dunked in warm olive oil.

Serves 6

2 large thick leeks
15ml/1 tbsp olive oil
5ml/1 tsp crushed coriander seeds
pinch of dried red chilli flakes
300g/11oz small salad potatoes, peeled and thickly sliced
400g/14oz can chopped tomatoes
600ml/1 pint/2½ cups fish stock
150ml/¼ pint/⅔ cup white wine
1 fresh bay leaf
1 star anise
strip of pared orange rind
good pinch of saffron threads
450g/1lb white fish fillets, such as monkfish, sea bass, cod or haddock
450g/1lb small squid, cleaned
250g/9oz fresh raw peeled prawns (shrimp)
30–45ml/2–3 tbsp chopped fresh flat leaf parsley
salt and ground black pepper

1 Slice the leeks, keeping the green and white parts separate. Wash both sets of leek slices thoroughly and drain them well. Set the white slices aside for later.

2 Heat the oil in a heavy pan and add the green leek slices, crushed coriander seeds and dried red chilli flakes. Cook gently, stirring occasionally, for 5 minutes.

3 Add the potatoes and tomatoes, and pour in the stock and wine. Add the bay leaf, star anise, orange rind and saffron. Bring to the boil, then reduce the heat and partially cover the pan. Simmer for 20 minutes, or until the potatoes are tender. Taste and adjust the seasoning.

4 Cut the white fish into chunks. Cut the squid sacs into rectangles and score in a criss-cross pattern. Add the fish to the soup and cook gently for 4 minutes.

5 Add the prawns and cook for 1 minute. Add the squid and the reserved white parts of the leeks and cook for 2 minutes. Finally, stir in the chopped parsley and serve immediately.

Salmon and Potato Chowder

Dill is the perfect partner for salmon in this classic, full-flavoured dish. Use the best possible boneless fish.

Serves 4

20g/¾oz/1½ tbsp butter
1 onion, finely chopped
1 leek, finely chopped
1 small fennel bulb, finely chopped
25g/1oz/¼ cup plain (all-purpose) flour
1.75 litres/3 pints/7½ cups fish stock
2 potatoes, cut into 1cm/½in cubes
450g/1lb boneless, skinless salmon, cut in 2cm/¾in cubes
175ml/6fl oz/¾ cup milk
120ml/4fl oz/½ cup whipping cream
30ml/2 tbsp chopped fresh dill
salt and ground black pepper

1 Melt the butter in a large pan. Add the onion, leek and chopped fennel and cook over a medium heat for 5–8 minutes until softened, stirring from time to time.

2 Stir in the flour. Reduce the heat to low and cook for 3 minutes, stirring occasionally.

3 Add the fish stock and potatoes. Season with salt and ground black pepper. Bring to the boil, then reduce the heat, cover and simmer for about 20 minutes or until the potatoes are just tender.

4 Add the salmon to the pan and simmer gently for about 3–5 minutes until it is just cooked.

5 Stir in the milk, cream, and dill. Cook until just warmed through, but do not boil. Adjust the seasoning and then serve.

> **Variation**
> Fresh young mackerel fillets are delicious in soup. They are particularly good in this recipe, which has lots of vegetables. Add a crushed garlic clove, if you like, and use tarragon instead of dill. For a zesty flavour to cut the oily fish, add the grated rind of 1 lemon and season with a hint of cayenne pepper.

Fish Soup Energy 249kcal/1051kJ; Protein 35.2g; Carbohydrate 13.3g, of which sugars 4.5g; Fat 4.7g, of which saturates 0.9g, Cholesterol 285mg; Calcium 90mg; Fibre 3g; Sodium 223mg.
Salmon Chowder Energy 301kcal/1254kJ; Protein 18.3g; Carbohydrate 13g, of which sugars 3.8g; Fat 19.9g, of which saturates 8.6g; Cholesterol 67mg; Calcium 83mg; Fibre 1.5g; Sodium 78mg.

Fish and Sweet Potato Cream Soup

The subtle honeyed taste of sweet potato combines with the stronger flavours of fish and oregano to make this appetizing soup, popular throughout the Caribbean.

Serves 4

175g/6oz white fish fillet, skinned
½ onion, chopped
1 sweet potato, about 175g/6oz, peeled and diced
1 small carrot, about 50g/2oz, chopped
5ml/1 tsp chopped fresh oregano or 2.5ml/½ tsp dried oregano
2.5ml/½ tsp ground cinnamon
1.35 litres/2¼ pints/5½ cups fish stock
75ml/5 tbsp single (light) cream
chopped fresh parsley, to garnish

1 Remove any bones from the white fish and put it in a pan. Add the onion, sweet potato, carrot, oregano, cinnamon and half the stock. Bring to the boil, then simmer for around 20 minutes or until the potatoes are cooked through.

2 Leave to cool, then pour into a food processor or blender and blend until smooth. Return the soup to the pan, stir in the remaining fish stock and gently bring to the boil. Reduce the heat.

3 Stir the cream into the soup, then gently heat it through without allowing it to boil. If the soup boils the cream will curdle. Serve hot, garnished with the chopped parsley.

Variations
• Omit the fish and use ham or chicken stock. Serve the soup topped with crisp fried bacon or pancetta.
• Use ordinary potato instead of sweet potato and omit the cinnamon. Add a pinch of ground mace.
• For a chicken and sweet potato soup, use 2 diced, skinless chicken breast fillets instead of the fish, and chicken stock instead of the fish stock.
• For a ham and sweet potato soup, use 1 trimmed, diced gammon steak (cured or smoked ham) instead of the fish, and ham or chicken stock.

Smoked Haddock and Potato Soup

This is a classic Scottish dish, known as Cullen Skink, which uses one of the country's tastiest fish, the haddock. The result is a thick, creamy potato soup with a deliciously rich, smoky fish flavour. Serve with plenty of fresh crusty bread for a substantial meal.

Serves 6

350g/12oz smoked haddock fillet
1 onion, chopped
bouquet garni
900ml/1½ pints/3¾ cups water
500g/1¼lb floury potatoes, quartered
600ml/1 pint/2½ cups milk
40g/1½oz/3 tbsp butter
salt and ground black pepper
chopped chives, to garnish
crusty bread, to serve

1 Put the haddock, onion, bouquet garni and water into a large heavy pan and bring to the boil. Skim off any foam that rises to the surface, then cover the pan and reduce the heat. Gently poach the fillets for about 10–15 minutes until the haddock flakes easily when tested with a fork.

2 Lift the haddock from the pan and leave to cool slightly, then remove the skin and bones, but do not discard. Flake the fish flesh and put to one side. Return the skin and bones to the pan and simmer for about 30 minutes.

3 Strain the fish stock and return it to the pan, then add the potatoes and simmer for about 25 minutes. Using a slotted spoon, remove the potatoes from the pan. Add the milk to the pan and bring to the boil briefly.

4 Mash the potatoes with the butter, then whisk into the soup. Add the flaked fish and heat through. Season to taste, then ladle into soup bowls, sprinkle with chives and serve with crusty bread.

Cook's Tip
This soup works best if you use naturally smoked fish fillets, which will be off-white, rather than those that are dyed yellow.

Fish and Sweet Potato Energy 119kcal/501kJ; Protein 9.4g; Carbohydrate 11.9g, of which sugars 4.7g; Fat 4.1g, of which saturates 2.4g; Cholesterol 30mg; Calcium 38mg; Fibre 1.6g; Sodium 53mg.
Smoked Haddock Energy 205kcal/864kJ; Protein 16.1g; Carbohydrate 19g, of which sugars 6.4g; Fat 7.8g, of which saturates 4.7g; Cholesterol 41mg; Calcium 142mg; Fibre 1g; Sodium 536mg.

Spiced Mussel and Potato Soup

Chunky and colourful, this Turkish fish and potato soup is like a chowder in its consistency. It is flavoured with harissa sauce, which is a spicy red paste made from dried chillies and garlic.

Serves 6

1.3–1.6kg/3–3¹/₂lb fresh mussels
900ml/1¹/₂ pints/3³/₄ cups
   vegetable stock
150ml/¹/₄ pint/²/₃ cup white wine
2 bay leaves
30ml/2 tbsp olive oil
1 onion, finely chopped
2 garlic cloves, crushed
2 celery sticks, finely sliced
bunch of spring onions (scallions),
   finely sliced
1 potato, diced
7.5ml/1¹/₂ tsp harissa sauce
3 tomatoes, peeled and diced
45ml/3 tbsp chopped
   fresh parsley
ground black pepper
thick natural (plain) yogurt, to
   serve (optional)

1 Scrub the mussels under cold running water and remove their beards. Discard any mussels that are damaged or do not close with a sharp tap of a knife. Leave in a basin of cold water until they are needed.

2 Bring the stock and wine to the boil in a large pan with the bay leaves. Add the mussels and cover with a lid. Cook for 4–5 minutes until the mussels have opened wide. Discard any mussels that remain closed. Drain the mussels, reserving the cooking liquid. Reserve a few mussels in their shells to use as a garnish and shell the rest.

3 Heat the oil in a pan and fry the onion, garlic, celery and spring onions for 5 minutes.

4 Add the reserved liquid from the shelled mussels, along with the potato, harissa sauce and tomatoes. Bring to the boil, reduce the heat and cover. Simmer gently for 25 minutes or until the potatoes are breaking up.

5 Stir in the parsley and pepper and add the shelled mussels. Heat through for 1–2 minutes. Ladle into bowls and garnish with the unshelled mussels. Serve hot with a spoonful of yogurt, if you like.

Clam, Mushroom and Potato Chowder

The delicate, sweet shellfish taste of clams and the soft earthiness of wild mushrooms combine with potatoes to make this a great meal on its own – fit for any occasion.

Serves 4

48 clams, scrubbed
50g/2oz/¹/₄ cup unsalted
   (sweet) butter
1 large onion, chopped
1 celery stick, sliced
1 carrot, sliced
225g/8oz assorted wild
   mushrooms, such as
   chanterelles, ceps, porcini or field
   (portabello) mushrooms, sliced
225g/8oz floury potatoes,
   thickly sliced
1.2 litres/2 pints/5 cups light
   chicken or vegetable stock
1 thyme sprig
4 parsley stalks
salt and ground black pepper
fresh thyme, to garnish

1 Place the clams in a large pan, making sure to discard any that are open. Put 1cm/¹/₂in of water in the pan, cover, bring to the boil and steam the clams over a medium heat for between 6–8 minutes until they have opened (be sure to discard any clams that do not open).

2 Drain the clams over a bowl, remove the shells, reserving a few clams in their shells for the garnish. Chop the shelled clams into quarters. Strain the cooking juices into the bowl, add the chopped clams and set aside.

3 Add the butter, onion, celery and carrot to the pan and cook gently for about 10 minutes, until the vegetables are softened but not coloured.

4 Add the mushrooms to the pan and cook for 3–4 minutes until their juices begin to seep out. Add the thickly sliced potatoes, the clams and their juices, the chicken or vegetable stock, thyme and parsley stalks.

5 Bring the soup to the boil, then reduce the heat, cover the pan and simmer for about 25 minutes, stirring occasionally. Check the chowder for seasoning, ladle into bowls and garnish with the reserved clams and fresh thyme.

Spiced Mussel Soup Energy 153kcal/644kJ; Protein 14.5g; Carbohydrate 7.8g, of which sugars 3.2g; Fat 5.6g, of which saturates 0.9g; Cholesterol 30mg; Calcium 178mg; Fibre 1.5g; Sodium 175mg.
Clam Chowder Energy 203kcal/848kJ; Protein 10.8g; Carbohydrate 15.8g, of which sugars 5.2g; Fat 11.2g, of which saturates 6.8g; Cholesterol 60mg; Calcium 66mg; Fibre 2.4g; Sodium 696mg.

Potato, Corn and Scallop Chowder

Fresh corn is ideal for this potato and scallop chowder, although canned corn also works well. This soup makes a perfect lunch dish.

Serves 4–6

2 corn on the cob or 200g/7oz
   frozen or canned corn
600ml/1pint/2½ cups milk
15g/½oz butter or margarine
1 small leek or onion, chopped
1 small garlic clove, crushed
40g/1½oz smoked lean bacon,
   finely chopped
1 small green (bell) pepper,
   seeded and diced
1 celery stick, chopped
1 medium potato, diced
15ml/1 tbsp plain
   (all-purpose) flour
300ml/½ pint/1¼ cups chicken
   or vegetable stock
4 scallops
115g/4oz cooked fresh mussels
pinch of paprika
150ml/¼ pint/⅔ cup single
   cream (optional)
salt and ground black pepper

1 If using corn on the cob, slice down the corn cobs with a sharp knife to remove the kernels. Place half of the kernels in a food processor or blender and process with a little of the milk.

2 Melt the butter or margarine in a large pan and gently fry the leek or onion, garlic and bacon for 4–5 minutes until the leek is soft but not browned. Add the green pepper, chopped celery and diced potato and cook over low heat for a further 3–4 minutes, stirring frequently.

3 Stir in the flour and cook for 1–2 minutes until the mixture is golden and frothy. Gradually stir in the milk and corn mixture, stock, the remaining milk, reserved corn kernels and seasoning.

4 Bring to the boil, then reduce the heat and simmer, partially covered, for about 15–20 minutes or until the vegetables are tender.

5 Pull the pink corals away from the scallops and carefully slice the white flesh into 5mm/¼in slices. Stir the scallops into the soup, cook for 4 minutes and then stir in the corals, mussels and paprika. Heat through for a few minutes and then stir in the cream, if using. Adjust the seasoning to taste and serve.

Chunky Prawn and Potato Chupe

South American chupes are a substantial meal in themselves. Potatoes are always included, but the other ingredients vary. This chupe uses annatto oil, which is olive oil infused with annatto seeds: if unavailable, use chilli, or olive oil.

Serves 6

500g/1¼lb raw king prawns
   (jumbo shrimp)
750ml/1¼ pints/3 cups fish stock
1 carrot, finely chopped
2 celery sticks, thinly sliced
45ml/3 tbsp annatto (achiote) oil
1 large onion, finely chopped
1 red (bell) pepper, seeded
   and diced
2 garlic cloves, crushed
2 fresh red chillies, seeded
   and chopped
5ml/1 tsp ground turmeric
1 large tomato, peeled
   and chopped
675g/1½lb potatoes, peeled and
   cut into 2.5cm/1in cubes
115g/4oz/1 cup fresh or
   frozen peas
15ml/1 tbsp chopped fresh mint
15ml/1 tbsp chopped fresh
   coriander (cilantro)
salt

1 Peel the prawns and set them aside. Place the shells in a large pan with the fish stock, carrot and celery. Bring to the boil, then simmer over a low heat for 20 minutes. Strain into a bowl or jug (pitcher) and set the stock aside.

2 Heat the oil in a large pan over a low heat. Stir in the onion and red pepper and sauté for 5 minutes. Stir in the garlic, chillies and turmeric and cook for a further 2 minutes.

3 Add the chopped tomato and potatoes to the pan, season to taste with salt and cook for about 10 minutes, allowing the tomato to break down slightly and the potatoes to absorb the flavours of the other ingredients.

4 Pour in the strained stock and bring to the boil. Lower the heat and simmer for 15 minutes, or until the potatoes are cooked through.

5 Stir the prawns and peas into the soup and simmer for 4–5 minutes, or until the prawns become opaque. Finally, stir in the mint and coriander, and serve in warmed bowls.

Corn and Scallop Energy 200kcal/845kJ; Protein 13g; Carbohydrate 23.6g, of which sugars 10.5g; Fat 6.7g, of which saturates 3.2g; Cholesterol 31mg; Calcium 150mg; Fibre 1.9g; Sodium 326mg.
Prawn Chupe Energy 175kcal/742kJ; Protein 18.9g; Carbohydrate 23.2g, of which sugars 4.3g; Fat 1.4g, of which saturates 0.3g; Cholesterol 163mg; Calcium 100mg; Fibre 2.7g; Sodium 175mg.

Mini Baked Potatoes with Blue Cheese

These little oven-baked potatoes are perfect as finger food for a party, especially as you can prepare them in advance.

coarse salt
120ml/4fl oz/½ cup sour cream
25g/1oz blue cheese, crumbled
30ml/2 tbsp chopped fresh chives, for sprinkling

Makes 20

20 small new or salad potatoes
60ml/4 tbsp vegetable oil

1 Preheat the oven to 180°C/350°F/Gas 4. Wash and dry the potatoes. Pour the oil into a bowl. Add the potatoes and toss to coat well with oil.

2 Dip the potatoes in the coarse salt to coat lightly. Spread out the potatoes on a baking sheet. Bake in the oven for about 45–50 minutes until tender.

3 In a small bowl, mix together the sour cream and blue cheese until well combined.

4 Cut a cross in the top of each potato. Pinch gently with your fingers to open up the cross.

5 Top each potato with a dollop of the cheese mixture. It will melt down into the potato gently.

6 Sprinkle the potatoes with chives on a serving dish and serve them hot. Alternatively, leave them to cool and serve at room temperature.

> **Cook's Tip**
> This dish works just as well as a light snack; if you don't want to be bothered with lots of fiddly small potatoes, simply bake an ordinary baking potato.

Mini Filled Jacket Potatoes

Jacket potatoes are always delicious, and the toppings can easily be varied: choose from luxurious and extravagant ingredients, such as caviar and smoked salmon, to equally satisfying, but more everyday fare, such as grated cheese and baked beans.

Makes 36

36 potatoes, about 4cm/1½in in diameter, well scrubbed
250ml/8fl oz/1 cup thick sour cream
45–60ml/3–4 tbsp chopped fresh chives
coarse salt, for sprinkling

1 Preheat the oven to 180°C/350°F/Gas 4. Place the potatoes on a baking sheet and bake in the oven for 30–35 minutes, or until the potatoes are tender when pierced with the tip of a sharp kitchen knife.

2 Cut a cross in the top of each potato and squeeze the sides gently to open up the cross. Make a small hole in the centre of each potato.

3 Fill each hole with a dollop of sour cream, then sprinkle with a little salt and top with some chopped chives. Serve the filled potatoes immediately.

> **Cook's Tip**
> For convenience, the potatoes can be baked in advance in the oven, then reheated in a hot oven for 10 minutes, or reheat in the microwave on the highest setting for 3–4 minutes.

> **Variation**
> If your guests are likely to be hungry, use larger potatoes and bake at the same temperature until tender. When cooked, cut each one in half, scoop out the flesh, mash with the other ingredients and spoon the mixture back into the potato skins. Serve the potatoes while still hot.

Mini Baked Potatoes Energy 63kcal/262kJ; Protein 1.1g; Carbohydrate 6.3g, of which sugars 0.7g; Fat 3.9g, of which saturates 1.3g; Cholesterol 5mg; Calcium 14mg; Fibre 0.4g; Sodium 22mg.
Mini Jacket Potatoes Energy 73kcal/309kJ; Protein 1.7g; Carbohydrate 13.7g, of which sugars 1.4g; Fat 1.6g, of which saturates 1g; Cholesterol 4mg; Calcium 14mg; Fibre 0.9g; Sodium 12mg.

Spicy Jacket Potatoes

Potatoes baked in their jackets are the ultimate comfort food and enjoyed by everyone. This twist on the traditional baked potato sees the flesh being scooped out and mixed with a blend of delicate spices before being put back in its shell. The result is a deliciously fragrant, spiced alternative to a traditional classic.

Serves 2–4
2 large baking potatoes
5ml/1 tsp sunflower oil
1 small onion, finely chopped
2.5cm/1in piece fresh root ginger, peeled and grated
5ml/1 tsp ground cumin
5ml/1 tsp ground coriander
2.5ml/½ tsp ground turmeric
garlic salt
natural (plain) yogurt and fresh coriander (cilantro) sprigs, to garnish

1 Preheat the oven to 190°C/375°F/Gas 5. Prick the potatoes all over with a fork. Bake in the oven for about 35–40 minutes, or until tender.

2 Cut the potatoes in half and scoop out the flesh with a spoon. Heat the oil in a non-stick frying pan and cook the onion for a few minutes to soften. Stir in the ginger, cumin, coriander and turmeric.

3 Cook over a low heat for about 2 minutes, stirring frequently until the spices release their fragrances. Add the potato flesh to the pan, and season to taste with garlic salt.

4 Cook the spiced potato mixture for a further 2 minutes, stirring occasionally. Spoon the filling back into the potato shells and top each with a spoonful of natural yogurt and a sprig or two of fresh coriander. Serve immediately.

Cook's Tip
Ensure that the potatoes are completely cooked by inserting a sharp knife or a metal skewer all the way through the potato. You will be able to tell if they need cooking a bit longer because there will be a little resistance.

New Potatoes with Mock Caviar and Cream Cheese

These mini stuffed potatoes are pretty to look at and make an impressive one-bite snack for a party or decadent buffet. They make the most of tender new potatoes with their waxy texture. If you are feeling especially extravagant authentic caviar finishes these treats off perfectly, but they are almost as delicious with Danish black mock caviar.

Makes 30
30 small new potatoes
200g/7oz/scant 1 cup full-fat cream cheese
15ml/1 tbsp chopped fresh parsley
1 jar Danish black mock caviar (lumpfish roe)
1 jar salmon roe
salt and ground black pepper
dill sprigs, to garnish

1 Cook the potatoes in a large pan of boiling water for about 10–15 minutes or until tender. Drain through a colander and then trim off both ends of each potato, creating a flat base so they will stand up on a serving plate.

2 Sit the potatoes on one of their cut ends. Beat the cream cheese and chopped parsley together and season with salt and pepper to taste. Spoon the mixture on to the potatoes and top with a little mock caviar and salmon roe. Garnish with sprigs of dill and serve immediately.

Cook's Tip
Fresh parsley is simple to grow yourself. Buy a plant and keep it on a sunny windowsill in your kitchen. Ensure it is kept moist but don't over-water it, and pull off the leaves as and when you need them. They will regrow in a matter of days.

Variation
If you can't get hold of any mock caviar, then top the new potatoes with thin slices of smoked salmon.

Spicy Jacket Potatoes Energy 85kcal/361kJ; Protein 2g; Carbohydrate 17.6g, of which sugars 2.2g; Fat 1.2g, of which saturates 0.2g; Cholesterol 0mg; Calcium 18mg; Fibre 1.5g; Sodium 17mg.
New Potatoes Energy 83kcal/348kJ; Protein 2.8g; Carbohydrate 10.7g, of which sugars 0.9g; Fat 3.5g, of which saturates 2.1g; Cholesterol 28mg; Calcium 11mg; Fibre 0.7g; Sodium 35mg.

Curry-spiced Potato Pakoras

These delicious potato bites make a wonderful snack, drizzled with fragrant chutney.

Makes 25
15ml/1 tbsp sunflower oil
20ml/4 tsp cumin seeds
5ml/1 tsp black mustard seeds
1 small onion, finely chopped
10ml/2 tsp grated fresh
    root ginger
2 fresh green chillies, seeded
    and chopped
600g/1lb 5oz potatoes, cooked
200g/7oz fresh peas
juice of 1 lemon
90ml/6 tbsp chopped fresh
    coriander (cilantro) leaves
115g/4oz/1 cup gram flour

25g/1oz/¼ cup self-raising
    (self-rising) flour
40g/1½oz/⅓ cup rice flour
large pinch of turmeric
10ml/2 tsp coriander seeds,
    finely crushed
350ml/12fl oz/1½ cups water
vegetable oil, for frying
salt and ground black pepper

For the chutney
105ml/7 tbsp coconut cream
200ml/7fl oz/scant 1 cup natural
    (plain) yogurt
50g/2oz mint leaves,
    finely chopped
5ml/1 tsp golden caster
    (superfine) sugar
juice of 1 lime

1 Heat a wok over a medium heat and add the sunflower oil. When hot, fry the cumin and mustard seeds for 1–2 minutes. Add the onion, ginger and chillies and cook for 3–4 minutes more. Add the cooked potatoes and peas and stir-fry for a further 5–6 minutes. Season, then stir in the lemon juice and coriander leaves. Leave the mixture to cool slightly, then divide into 25 portions. Shape each portion into a ball and chill.

2 To make the chutney, place all the ingredients in a blender and process until smooth. Season, then chill.

3 To make the batter, put the gram flour, self-raising flour and rice flour in a bowl. Season and add the turmeric and coriander seeds. Gradually whisk in the water to make a smooth batter.

4 Fill a wok one-third full of oil and heat to 180°C/350°F. Working in batches, dip the chilled balls in the batter, then drop into the oil and fry for 1–2 minutes, or until golden. Drain on kitchen paper, and serve immediately with the chutney.

Spiced Sweet Potato Turnovers

The subtle flavour of sweet potato makes a great filling when enhanced with spices.

Serves 4
1 sweet potato, about 225g/8oz
30ml/2 tbsp vegetable oil
2 shallots, finely chopped
10ml/2 tsp coriander seeds, crushed
5ml/1 tsp ground cumin
5ml/1 tsp garam masala
115g/4oz/1 cup frozen peas
15ml/1 tbsp chopped fresh mint
salt and ground black pepper
mint sprigs, to garnish

For the pastry
15ml/1 tbsp olive oil
1 small egg
150ml/¼ pint/⅔ cup natural
    (plain) yogurt
115g/4oz/8 tbsp
    butter, melted
275g/10oz/2½ cups plain
    (all-purpose) flour
1.5ml/¼ tsp bicarbonate of soda
    (baking soda)
10ml/2 tsp paprika
5ml/1 tsp salt
beaten egg, to glaze

1 Cook the sweet potato in boiling salted water for 15–20 minutes, until tender. Drain well and leave to cool. When cool enough to handle, peel the potato and cut into 1cm/½in cubes.

2 Heat the oil in a frying pan, add the shallots and cook until soft. Add the sweet potato cubes and fry until brown at the edges. Mix in the spices and fry for a few seconds. Remove from the heat and add the peas, mint and seasoning. Leave to cool.

3 Preheat the oven to 200°C/400°F/Gas 6. To make the pastry, whisk together the oil and egg, stir in the yogurt, then add the melted butter. Sift the flour, bicarbonate of soda, paprika and salt into a bowl, then stir into the yogurt mixture to form a soft dough. Knead gently, then roll it out and stamp into rounds with a 7.5cm/3in pastry (cookie) cutter.

4 Spoon about 10ml/2 tsp of the filling on to one side of each round, then fold over and seal the edges. Re-roll the trimmings and stamp out more rounds until the filling is used up.

5 Arrange the turnovers on a greased baking sheet and brush the tops with beaten egg. Bake for about 20 minutes until crisp and golden brown. Serve hot, garnished with mint.

Spiced Turnovers Energy 660kcal/2760kJ; Protein 13.9g; Carbohydrate 75.8g, of which sugars 9.3g; Fat 35.9g, of which saturates 17g; Cholesterol 105mg; Calcium 216mg; Fibre 5.2g; Sodium 740mg.
Curry-spiced Pakoras Energy 126kcal/525kJ; Protein 4.1g; Carbohydrate 8.3g, of which sugars 2.6g; Fat 8.8g, of which saturates 5.2g; Cholesterol 0mg; Calcium 35mg; Fibre 1.3g; Sodium 16mg.

Spiced Beef and Potato Puffs

These crisp, golden pillows of pastry filled with spiced beef and potatoes are delicious served straight from the wok. The light pastry puffs up in the hot oil and contrasts enticingly with the fragrant spiced beef.

Serves 4
15ml/1 tbsp sunflower oil
½ small onion, finely chopped
3 garlic cloves, crushed
5ml/1 tsp fresh root ginger, grated
1 red chilli, seeded and chopped
30ml/2 tbsp hot curry powder
75g/3oz minced (ground) beef
115g/4oz mashed potato
60ml/4 tbsp chopped fresh
  coriander (cilantro)
2 sheets ready-rolled, fresh
  puff pastry
1 egg, lightly beaten
vegetable oil, for frying
salt and ground black pepper
fresh coriander (cilantro) leaves,
  to garnish
tomato ketchup, to serve

1 Heat the oil in a wok, then add the onion, garlic, ginger and chilli. Stir-fry over a medium heat for 2–3 minutes. Add the curry powder and beef and stir-fry over a high heat for a further 4–5 minutes, or until the beef is browned and just cooked through, then remove from the heat.

2 Transfer the beef mixture to a large bowl and add the mashed potato and chopped fresh coriander. Stir well, then season and set aside.

3 Lay the pastry sheets on a clean, dry surface and cut out eight rounds, using a 7.5cm/3in pastry (cookie) cutter. Place a large spoonful of the beef mixture in the centre of each pastry round. Brush the edges of the pastry with the beaten egg and fold each round in half to enclose the filling. Press and crimp the edges with the tines of a fork to seal.

4 Fill a wok one-third full of oil and heat to 180°C/350°F (or until a cube of bread, dropped into the oil, browns in 15 seconds).

5 Deep-fry the puffs, in batches, for about 2–3 minutes until they turn a golden brown colour. Drain on kitchen paper and serve garnished with fresh coriander leaves. Offer tomato ketchup to diners for dipping.

Potato Samosas

Throughout the East, these tasty potato snacks are sold by street vendors, and eaten at any time of day.

Makes about 20
1 packet 25cm/10in square spring
  roll wrappers, thawed if frozen
30ml/2 tbsp plain (all-purpose)
  flour, mixed to a paste
  with water
vegetable oil, for deep frying
coriander (cilantro) leaves,
  to garnish

For the filling
25g/1oz/2 tbsp ghee or
  unsalted (sweet) butter
1 small onion, finely chopped
1cm/½in piece fresh root ginger,
  peeled and chopped
1 garlic glove, crushed
2.5ml/½ tsp chilli powder
1 large potato, about 225g/8oz,
  cooked until just tender and
  finely diced
50g/2oz/½ cup cauliflower
  florets, lightly cooked, chopped
  into small pieces
50g/2oz/½ cup frozen
  peas, thawed
5–10ml/1–2 tsp garam masala
15ml/1 tbsp chopped fresh
  coriander (leaves and stems)
squeeze of lemon juice
salt

1 Heat the ghee or butter in a large frying pan and fry the onion, ginger and garlic for 5 minutes until the onion has softened but not browned.

2 Add the chilli powder to the pan and cook for 1 minute, then stir in the potato, cauliflower and peas. Sprinkle with garam masala and set aside to cool. Stir in the chopped coriander, lemon juice and salt.

3 Cut the spring roll wrappers into three strips (or two for larger samosas). Brush the edges with a little of the flour paste. Place a small spoonful of filling about 2cm/¾in in from the edge of one strip. Fold one corner over the filling to make a triangle and continue this folding until the entire strip has been used and a triangular package has been formed. Seal any open edges with more flour and water paste.

4 Heat the oil for deep frying to 190°C/375°F and fry the samosas, a few at a time, until golden and crisp. Drain well on kitchen paper and serve hot, garnished with coriander leaves.

Beef and Potato Puffs Energy 408kcal/1695kJ; Protein 9g; Carbohydrate 24.2g, of which sugars 1.8g; Fat 31.8g, of which saturates 4.2g; Cholesterol 67mg; Calcium 46mg; Fibre 0.5g; Sodium 202mg.
Samosas Energy 56kcal/235kJ; Protein 1.3g; Carbohydrate 10g, of which sugars 0.8g; Fat 1.4g, of which saturates 0.2g; Cholesterol 0mg; Calcium 16mg; Fibre 0.7g; Sodium 8mg.

Thai Potato Samosas

Most samosas are deep-fried, but these are baked, making them a healthier option. They are also perfect for parties as no deep-frying is involved.

Makes 25

1 large potato, about
  250g/9oz, diced
15ml/1 tbsp groundnut
  (peanut) oil
2 shallots, finely chopped
1 garlic clove, finely chopped
60ml/4 tbsp coconut milk
5ml/1 tsp Thai red or green
  curry paste
75g/3oz/¾ cup peas
juice of ½ lime
25 samosa wrappers or
  10cm/4in x 5cm/2in strips
  of filo pastry
salt and ground black pepper
oil, for brushing

1 Preheat the oven to 220°C/425°F/Gas 7. Bring a small pan of water to the boil, add the diced potato, cover and cook for 10–15 minutes, until tender. Drain and set aside.

2 Meanwhile, heat the groundnut oil in a large frying pan and cook the shallots and garlic over a medium heat, stirring occasionally, for 4–5 minutes, until softened and golden.

3 Add the drained potato, coconut milk, red or green curry paste, peas and lime juice to the frying pan. Mash coarsely with a wooden spoon. Season to taste with salt and pepper and cook over a low heat for 2–3 minutes, then remove the pan from the heat and set aside until the mixture has cooled a little.

4 Lay a samosa wrapper or filo strip flat on the work surface. Brush with a little oil, then place a generous teaspoonful of the mixture in the middle of one end. Turn one corner diagonally over the filling to meet the long edge.

5 Continue folding over the filling, keeping the triangular shape as you work down the strip. Brush with a little more oil if necessary and place on a baking sheet. Prepare all the other samosas in the same way.

6 Bake for 15 minutes, or until the pastry is golden and crisp. Leave to cool slightly before serving.

Rosemary Potato Wedges with Salmon Dip

This creamy dip with spiced herby potato wedges can be served as an appetizer or as part of a buffet lunch.

Serves 4

115g/4oz smoked salmon
250g/9oz/generous 1 cup
  mascarpone cheese
60ml/4 tbsp chopped fresh chives
grated rind and juice of 1 lemon
1 red (bell) pepper, seeded and
  cut into strips
1 yellow (bell) pepper, seeded and
  cut into strips
sea salt and ground black pepper

For the potato wedges
675g/1½lb large potatoes
60ml/4 tbsp olive oil
30ml/2 tbsp chopped
  fresh rosemary
1 fresh red chilli, seeded and
  finely chopped

1 Preheat the oven to 200°C/400°F/Gas 6. To make the wedges, cut the potatoes into thick pieces. Pour the oil into a roasting pan and heat it in the oven for 10 minutes. Toss the wedges in the pan, then sprinkle over the rosemary and the chilli.

2 Shake the pan gently to coat the potatoes in the oil, rosemary and chilli. Season with salt and black pepper. Bake for 50–60 minutes or until tender, turning occasionally.

3 Cut the smoked salmon into small pieces, using kitchen scissors or a sharp filleting knife. Put the mascarpone cheese, chives and lemon rind in a bowl and mix with a fork until thoroughly blended.

4 Add the lemon juice, a little at a time, mixing constantly, so that the mixture is thinned and is given a lemony tang, but does not curdle.

5 Add the salmon to the cheese mixture and season with pepper. Place into a serving bowl, cover and chill until required.

6 To serve, arrange the pepper strips and wedges around the edge of a serving platter and place the dip in the centre.

Thai Samosas Energy 42kcal/178kJ; Protein 1.2g; Carbohydrate 8.5g, of which sugars 0.6g; Fat 0.6g, of which saturates 0.1g; Cholesterol 0mg; Calcium 14mg; Fibre 0.5g; Sodium 4mg.
Rosemary Wedges Energy 487kcal/2030kJ; Protein 16.9g; Carbohydrate 33.2g, of which sugars 7.9g; Fat 32.7g, of which saturates 14.2g; Cholesterol 71mg; Calcium 124mg; Fibre 3.9g; Sodium 774mg.

Spicy Potato Wedges with Chilli Dip

For a healthy snack with a superb flavour, try these roasted potato wedges. The crisp spice crust makes them taste irresistible, especially when they are served with a vibrant chilli dip.

Serves 2

2 baking potatoes, about 225g/
   8oz each
30ml/2 tbsp olive oil
2 garlic cloves, crushed
5ml/1 tsp ground allspice
5ml/1 tsp ground coriander
15ml/1 tbsp paprika
salt and ground black pepper

For the chilli dip

15ml/1 tbsp olive oil
1 small onion, finely chopped
1 garlic clove, crushed
200g/7oz can chopped tomatoes
1 fresh red chilli, seeded and
   finely chopped
15ml/1 tbsp balsamic vinegar
15ml/1 tbsp chopped fresh
   coriander (cilantro), plus extra
   to garnish

1 Preheat the oven to 200°C/400°F/Gas 6. Cut the potatoes in half, then cut each half lengthways into eight wedges.

2 Place the wedges in a pan of cold water. Bring to the boil, then lower the heat and simmer gently for 10 minutes or until the potatoes have softened slightly. Drain well and pat dry on kitchen paper.

3 Mix the oil, garlic, allspice, coriander and paprika in a roasting pan and add salt and pepper to taste. Add the potatoes to the pan and shake to coat them thoroughly in the spicy oil. Roast for 20 minutes, turning the potato wedges occasionally, or until they are browned, crisp and fully cooked.

4 Meanwhile, to make the chilli dip, heat the oil in a pan and add the onion and garlic. Cook over a medium heat for 5–10 minutes until softened. Add the tomatoes, with their juice. Stir in the chilli and vinegar.

5 Cook gently for 10 minutes until the mixture has reduced and thickened, then check the seasoning. Stir in the fresh coriander and serve hot, with the potato wedges, garnished with salt and fresh coriander sprigs.

Tangy Potato Wedges with Garlic Tofu Dip

Tofu makes a fabulous dip that is cool and creamy – the perfect foil for these deliciously crispy and piquant potato wedges.

Serves 4

6 potatoes, scrubbed
15ml/1 tbsp cumin seeds, ground
2.5–5ml/½–1 tsp cayenne pepper
grated rind of 2 limes or 1 lemon
45ml/3 tbsp olive oil
sea salt and ground black pepper

For the garlic tofu dip

1 garlic clove, crushed
175g/6oz silken tofu
dash of lemon juice
25ml/1½ tbsp olive oil
10g/¼oz fresh mint, stalks
   removed (optional)

1 Cut the potatoes lengthways in half, then cut each half lengthways into thirds or quarters to make wedges. Place them in a shallow dish and sprinkle over the spices, citrus rind, oil and seasoning. Toss together and leave to marinate for at least 30 minutes. Meanwhile, preheat the oven to 220°C/425°F/Gas 7.

2 Place the potato wedges in a roasting pan and bake for 30–35 minutes, until golden and tender, turning occasionally.

3 Meanwhile, make the garlic tofu dip by placing all the ingredients, except the oil, in a blender or food processor and processing until smooth.

4 With the machine running, gradually add the olive oil in a slow, steady stream until the dip is smooth and thickened. Season with salt and pepper to taste, then pour into a serving bowl. Transfer the potato wedges to a warm dish and serve with the dip.

Cook's Tips
• Garlic tofu dip is good with any roasted root vegetables, such as carrots, swede (rutabaga), celeriac and parsnips.
• If covered, the dip will keep in the refrigerator for up to 1 week.

Spicy Potato Wedges Energy 239kcal/1001kJ; Protein 4g; Carbohydrate 30.8g, of which sugars 4.9g; Fat 11.9g, of which saturates 1.9g; Cholesterol 0mg; Calcium 23mg; Fibre 2.6g; Sodium 28mg.
Tangy Potato Wedges Energy 320kcal/1340kJ; Protein 8.2g; Carbohydrate 38.5g, of which sugars 3.1g; Fat 15.9g, of which saturates 2.3g; Cholesterol 0mg; Calcium 246mg; Fibre 2.3g; Sodium 28mg.

Simple Potato Wedges

These potato wedges are so easy to make, and can be served on their own with a garlic mayonnaise dip, or as an accompaniment to meat or fish dishes. To make extra-spicy potato wedges, use chilli powder instead of paprika.

Serves 4
675g/1½lb floury potatoes, such
   as Maris Piper
45ml/3 tbsp olive oil
10ml/2 tsp paprika
5ml/1 tsp ground cumin
salt and ground black pepper

1 Preheat the oven to 190°C/375°F/Gas 5. Using a sharp knife, cut the potatoes into chunky wedges and place them in a roasting pan.

2 In a small bowl, combine the olive oil with the paprika and cumin and season with plenty of salt and ground black pepper.

3 Pour the spiced oil mixture over the potatoes and toss well to coat all the wedges thoroughly.

4 Spread the potatoes in a single layer in the roasting pan and bake in the preheated oven for about 30–40 minutes, or until golden brown and tender. Turn them once or twice during cooking to ensure they are evenly browned all over. Serve immediately.

Variation
If you prefer less spice in your food, substitute the paprika and cumin for finely chopped rosemary.

Cook's Tip
To make a garlic mayonnaise dip for the wedges, place 45ml–3 tbsp of good-quality mayonnaise in a bowl and stir in a crushed or finely chopped garlic clove. Season with a little salt and ground black pepper.

Potato Skins with Cajun Dip

Divinely crisp and decadent, these potato skins are great on their own, or served with this piquant dip as a garnish or to the side. They are delicious as a snack, or as an accompaniment to a barbecued feast.

Serves 2
2 large baking potatoes
vegetable oil, for deep frying

For the dip
120ml/4fl oz/½ cup natural
   (plain) yogurt
1 garlic clove, crushed
5ml/1 tsp tomato purée (paste)
2.5ml/½ tsp green chilli purée or
   ½ small green chilli, chopped
1.5ml/¼ tsp celery salt
salt and ground black pepper

1 Preheat the oven to 180°C/350°F/Gas 4. Bake the potatoes for 45–50 minutes until tender. Remove from the oven and set aside to cool slightly.

2 When the potatoes have cooled down enough to handle, cut them in half and scoop out the flesh, leaving a thin layer on the skins. Keep the flesh for another meal.

3 To make the dip, mix together all the ingredients and chill in the refrigerator until the skins are ready.

4 Heat a 1cm/½in layer of oil in a large pan or deep-fat fryer. Cut each potato half in half again, then fry them until crisp and golden on both sides.

5 Drain on kitchen paper, sprinkle with salt and black pepper and serve with a bowl of dip or a dollop of dip in each skin.

Cook's Tip
• If you prefer, you can microwave the potatoes to save time. This will take about 10 minutes.
• The scooped-out flesh from the potatoes is delicious if mixed with leftover vegetables such as peas or cabbage, then formed into small cakes and fried in a little oil until golden.

Potato Wedges Energy 200kcal/838kJ; Protein 3.3g; Carbohydrate 28.1g, of which sugars 2.2g; Fat 9.1g, of which saturates 1.4g; Cholesterol 0mg; Calcium 15mg; Fibre 1.7g; Sodium 20mg.
Potato Skins Energy 211kcal/873kJ; Protein 2.7g; Carbohydrate 12.5g, of which sugars 3.3g; Fat 17g, of which saturates 2.2g; Cholesterol 0mg; Calcium 62mg; Fibre 0.7g; Sodium 35mg.

Sweet Potato Crisps

You can use these sweet pink potatoes to make sweet or savoury crisps, and they have a lovely colour and a unique, almost fruity flavour. They are ideal as snacks at a party, or enjoy as a comforting supper treat.

Serves 4

2 medium sweet potatoes
vegetable oil, for deep-frying
salt

1 Using a vegetable peeler or knife, peel the sweet potatoes under cold running water.

2 Cut each sweet potato into 3mm/⅛in thick slices with a sharp knife or vegetable slicer and place in a bowl of salted cold water.

3 Heat a 1cm/½in layer of oil in a large pan or deep-fat fryer. While the oil is heating, remove the slices from the water and pat dry on kitchen paper.

4 When the oil is hot enough, fry a few potato slices at a time until crisp. Remove the slices from the pan with a slotted spoon and drain thoroughly on kitchen paper. Sprinkle with salt and serve warm.

Variation
For a sweet version, sprinkle with cinnamon and caster (superfine) sugar, and toss well, before cooling. You can prepare yams in just the same way.

Cook's Tip
These sweet potato crisps (chips) are delicious served warm, but if you don't manage to finish them in one sitting then they are equally good as a cold snack. Serve with a home-made dip, either sweet or savoury.

Potato Skewers with Mustard Dip

These potatoes are cooked on the barbecue and have a great flavour and a deliciously crisp skin. Try these tasty kebabs served with a thick, garlic-rich dip.

Serves 4
For the dip
4 garlic cloves, crushed
2 egg yolks

30ml/2 tbsp lemon juice
300ml/½ pint/1¼ cups extra virgin olive oil
10ml/2 tsp wholegrain mustard
salt and ground black pepper

For the skewers
1kg/2¼lb small new potatoes
200g/7oz shallots, halved
30ml/2 tbsp olive oil
15ml/1 tbsp sea salt

1 Prepare the barbecue for cooking the skewers before you begin. To make the dip, place the garlic, egg yolks and lemon juice in a blender or a food processor fitted with the metal blade and process for a few seconds until the mixture is throughly combined and smooth.

2 Keep the blender motor running and add the oil very gradually, pouring it in a thin stream, until the mixture forms a thick, glossy cream. Add the mustard and stir the ingredients together, then season with salt and black pepper. Chill until ready to use.

3 Par-boil the potatoes in their skins in boiling water for about 5 minutes. Drain well and then thread them on to metal skewers alternating with the shallots.

4 Brush the skewers with oil and sprinkle with salt. Cook over a barbecue for 10–12 minutes, turning occasionally. Serve immediately, accompanied by the dip.

Cook's Tips
• *New potatoes have a firmness necessary to stay on the skewer. Don't be tempted to use other types of small potato.*
• *These are just as delicious prepared under the grill (broiler): preheat the grill and continue as per step one above.*

Sweet Potato Crisps Energy 285kcal/1185kJ; Protein 1.2g; Carbohydrate 21.3g, of which sugars 5.7g; Fat 22.3g, of which saturates 2.4g; Cholesterol 0mg; Calcium 24mg; Fibre 2.4g; Sodium 40mg.
Potato Skewers Energy 488kcal/2024kJ; Protein 4.3g; Carbohydrate 29.5g, of which sugars 4.1g; Fat 40g, of which saturates 6.1g; Cholesterol 65mg; Calcium 28mg; Fibre 2.2g; Sodium 49mg.

Artichokes with New Potatoes

Among the first spring vegetables, artichokes appear in the middle of March. Together with new potatoes and other spring vegetables they make a delicious, healthy and unusual appetizer or snack.

Serves 4 as a first course

4 globe artichokes
juice of 1½ lemons
150ml/¼ pint/⅔ cup extra virgin
  olive oil
1 large onion, thinly sliced
3 carrots, peeled and sliced
  into long batons
300ml/½ pint/1¼ cups
  hot water
400g/14oz small new potatoes,
  scrubbed or peeled
4 or 5 spring onions (scallions),
  finely chopped
60–75ml/4–5 tbsp chopped
  fresh dill
salt and ground black pepper

1 Remove and discard the outer leaves of the artichoke until you reach the tender ones. Cut off the top, at around halfway down. Scoop out the hairy choke. Trim the stalk, leaving 4cm/1½in, and peel away its outer surface. Drop the artichokes into a bowl of cold water acidulated with about one-third of the lemon juice, which is about half a lemon. Add enough hot water to just about cover the artichokes.

2 Heat the extra virgin olive oil in a large, deep frying pan and gently cook the onion slices over a low to medium heat, stirring frequently, until they become translucent but not brown.

3 Add the carrots to the pan and cook for about 2–3 minutes. Stir in the remaining lemon juice and the hot water and bring the mixture to the boil.

4 Drain the artichokes and add them to the pan, followed by the potatoes, spring onions and seasoning. The vegetables should be almost covered with the sauce, so add a little more hot water if needed.

5 Cover and cook gently for about 45 minutes. Sprinkle over the dill and cook for 2–3 minutes more. Serve immediately.

Jerusalem Artichoke and Potato Rösti

A traditional potato dish, rösti is originally from Switzerland where it is often combined with other ingredients such as onion and bacon. Here it has the addition of Jerusalem artichokes to create an unusual and tasty version, which works great as a snack or as a side dish.

Serves 4–6

450g/1lb Jerusalem artichokes
juice of 1 lemon
450g/1lb potatoes
about 50g/2oz/4 tbsp butter
salt

1 Peel the Jerusalem artichokes and place in a pan of water together with the lemon juice and a pinch of salt. Bring to the boil and cook for about 5 minutes until barely tender.

2 Peel the potatoes and place in a separate pan of salted water. Bring to the boil and cook until barely tender – the potatoes will take slightly longer than the artichokes.

3 Drain and cool the artichokes and potatoes, and then grate them into a bowl. Mix well, without breaking them up too much.

4 Melt the butter in a large heavy frying pan. Add the artichoke mixture, spreading it out with the back of a spoon. Cook gently for about 10 minutes.

5 Invert the 'cake' on to a plate and slide back into the pan. Cook for about 10 minutes until golden. Serve immediately.

Cook's Tip
Jerusalem artichokes are not a true artichoke but the root of a variety of sunflower. They may be labelled as sunroot or sunchoke.

Variation
Make individual rösti and serve topped with a mixed julienne of vegetables for an unusual first course.

Artichokes Energy 373kcal/1552kJ; Protein 5.6g; Carbohydrate 30.2g, of which sugars 13.7g; Fat 26.5g, of which saturates 3.9g; Cholesterol 0mg; Calcium 142mg; Fibre 6.7g; Sodium 103mg.
Artichoke Rösti Energy 119kcal/500kJ; Protein 1.7g; Carbohydrate 12.8g, of which sugars 1.7g; Fat 7.2g, of which saturates 4.6g; Cholesterol 19mg; Calcium 37mg; Fibre 1.6g; Sodium 116mg.

Wild Rice and Potato Rösti

This version of the Swiss potato dish features wild rice and a bright simple sauce.

Serves 6
90g/3½oz/½ cup wild rice
900g/2lb large potatoes
45ml/3 tbsp walnut oil
5ml/1 tsp yellow mustard seeds
1 onion, coarsely grated
  and drained
30ml/2 tbsp fresh thyme leaves
salt and ground black pepper
vegetables, to serve

For the purée
350g/12oz carrots, peeled and
  roughly chopped
pared rind and juice of
  1 large orange

1 For the purée, place the chopped carrots in a pan, cover with cold water and add two pieces of orange rind. Bring to the boil and cook for around 10 minutes, until the carrots are tender. Drain and discard the rind.

2 Purée the mixture in a food processor or blender with 60ml/4 tbsp of the orange juice. Return to the pan.

3 Place the wild rice in a clean pan and cover with water. Bring to the boil and cook for about 30–40 minutes, until the rice is just starting to split, but is still crunchy. Drain the rice.

4 Place the potatoes in a large pan and cover with cold water. Bring to the boil and cook for 10–15 minutes until just tender. Drain well and leave to cool slightly. Peel and coarsely grate them into a large bowl. Add the cooked rice.

5 Heat 30ml/2 tbsp of the oil in a frying pan and add the mustard seeds. When they start to pop, add the onion and cook gently for 5–7 minutes until soft. Add to the potato mixture, with the thyme, and mix thoroughly. Season to taste.

6 Heat the remaining oil and add the grated potato and rice mixture. Press down firmly to form a pancake and cook for 10 minutes or until golden brown. Cover the pan with a plate and flip over, then slide the rösti back in for another 10 minutes. Serve with the reheated carrot purée.

Gruyère and Potato Soufflés

This potato recipe can be prepared in advance if you are entertaining and given its second baking just before you serve it up.

Serves 4
225g/8oz floury potatoes
2 eggs, separated
175g/6oz/1½ cups Gruyère
  cheese, grated
50g/2oz/½ cup self-raising
  (self-rising) flour
50g/2oz spinach leaves
butter, for greasing
salt and freshly ground black
  pepper
salad leaves, to serve

1 Preheat the oven to 200°C/400°F/Gas 6. Cook the potatoes in lightly salted boiling water for around 20 minutes until very tender. Drain the potatoes and mash thoroughly before adding the two egg yolks and mixing to combine.

2 Stir in half of the Gruyère cheese and all of the flour. Season to taste with salt and pepper.

3 Finely chop the spinach leaves and gently fold into the potato and egg yolk mixture.

4 Whip the egg whites until they form soft peaks. Fold a little of the egg white into the mixture to loosen it slightly. Using a large metal spoon, fold the remaining egg white into the mixture.

5 Butter four large ramekin dishes. Pour the mixture in, place on a baking sheet and bake for 20 minutes. Remove from the oven and leave to cool.

6 Turn the soufflés out on to a baking sheet and sprinkle with the remaining cheese. Bake again for 5 minutes and serve immediately with salad leaves.

Variation
For a different flavouring, try replacing the Gruyère with a crumbled blue cheese, such as Stilton or Shropshire Blue cheeses, which have a more intense taste than the Gruyère.

Wild Rice Rösti Energy 235kcal/989kJ; Protein 4.2g; Carbohydrate 42.3g, of which sugars 7.6g; Fat 6.2g, of which saturates 0.7g; Cholesterol 0mg; Calcium 30mg; Fibre 3.1g; Sodium 32mg.
Gruyère Soufflés Energy 304kcal/1270kJ; Protein 16.7g; Carbohydrate 19g, of which sugars 1.2g; Fat 17.5g, of which saturates 10.4g; Cholesterol 138mg; Calcium 380mg; Fibre 1.2g; Sodium 376mg.

Potato Pizza

This 'pizza' is made with mashed potatoes, and contains a tasty filling of anchovies, capers and tomatoes. It is a speciality from Puglia in northern Italy.

2 garlic cloves, finely chopped
350g/12oz tomatoes, chopped
3 anchovy fillets, chopped
30ml/2 tbsp capers, rinsed
salt and ground black pepper

Serves 4
1kg/2¼lb floury potatoes
120ml/4fl oz/½ cup extra virgin
   olive oil

1 Cook the potatoes in their skins in boiling water until tender. Drain well and leave to cool slightly. When they are cool enough to handle, peel them and mash or pass through a food mill. Beat in 45ml/3 tbsp of the oil and season to taste with salt and pepper. Set aside.

2 Heat another 45ml/3 tbsp of the oil in a medium pan. Add the garlic and the chopped tomatoes and cook over a medium heat for 12–15 minutes, stirring a little to cook evenly, until the tomatoes soften and begin to dry out a little. Meanwhile, preheat the oven to 200°C/400°F/Gas 6.

3 Oil a round, shallow baking dish. Spread half the mashed potatoes in the dish in an even layer. Cover with the chopped tomatoes, and dot with the chopped anchovies and capers.

4 Spread over the rest of the potatoes in an even layer. Brush the top with the remaining oil and bake for 20–25 minutes until the top is golden brown. Sprinkle with black pepper and serve immediately.

> **Variation**
> For a vegetarian version of this dish, simply omit the anchovies. A few pitted and chopped olives may be added to the filling instead. Add them in step 3, on top of the tomatoes.

Idaho Potato Slices

This unusual and tasty dish is made from a layered ring of potatoes, cheese and herbs. Cooking the ingredients together gives them a very rich flavour.

Serves 4
3 large potatoes
butter, for greasing
1 small onion, finely sliced
   into rings
200g/7oz/1¾ cups red Leicester
   or mature (sharp) Cheddar
   cheese, grated
fresh thyme sprigs
150ml/¼ pint/⅔ cup single
   (light) cream
salt and ground black pepper
salad leaves, to serve

1 Preheat the oven to 200°C/400°F/Gas 6. Peel the potatoes and cook in boiling water for 10 minutes until they are just starting to soften. Remove from the water and pat dry with kitchen paper.

2 Finely slice the potatoes, using the straight edge of a grater or a mandoline. Grease the base and sides of an 18cm/7in cake tin (pan) with butter and lay some of the potatoes on the base to cover it completely. Season with salt and pepper.

3 Sprinkle some of the onion rings over the potatoes and top with a little of the cheese. Sprinkle over some of the thyme and then continue to layer the ingredients, finishing with a layer of cheese and a little more seasoning.

4 Press the potato layers right down. (The mixture may seem quite high at this point but it will cook down.)

5 Pour over the cream and bake in the oven for between 35–45 minutes. Remove from the oven and cool. Invert on to a plate and cut into wedges. Serve immediately with a few salad leaves.

> **Variation**
> If you want to make this dish more substantial, top the potato wedges with slices of crispy bacon, or strips of roasted red or yellow (bell) peppers.

Idaho Potato Slices Energy 408kcal/1706kJ; Protein 17.1g; Carbohydrate 30.2g, of which sugars 4g; Fat 24.1g, of which saturates 15.6g; Cholesterol 69mg; Calcium 417mg; Fibre 2g; Sodium 392mg.
Potato Pizza Energy 356kcal/1492kJ; Protein 5.6g; Carbohydrate 43.4g, of which sugars 6g; Fat 19g, of which saturates 2.8g; Cholesterol 0mg; Calcium 28mg; Fibre 3.5g; Sodium 124mg.

Boxty Potato Pancakes

Said to have originated during the Irish famine, these delicious pancakes use blended potatoes in the batter mix and can be made as thin or thick as you like. They are delicious served rolled around a hot savoury filling, such as cooked cabbage and chopped bacon bound together in a light mustard sauce.

Makes 4 pancakes

450g/1lb potatoes, peeled and chopped
50–75g/2–3oz/½–⅔ cup plain (all-purpose) flour
about 150ml/¼ pint/⅔ cup milk
salt and ground black pepper
knob (pat) of butter

1 Place the peeled and chopped potatoes in a blender or in the bowl of a food processor and process until the potato is thoroughly blended and smooth.

2 Add the flour and enough milk to the processed potato to give a dropping consistency, about the thickness of double (heavy) cream. Season to taste with salt and ground black pepper. The milk and flour can be adjusted, depending on how thin you like your pancake. Heat a little butter on a griddle or cast-iron frying pan.

3 Pour about a quarter of the mixture into the pan – if the consistency is right it will spread evenly over the base. Cook over a medium heat for about 5 minutes on each side, depending on the thickness of the cake. Serve rolled, with the hot filling of your choice.

Cook's Tip
To prepare a mustardy cabbage and bacon filling: Chop half a large Savoy cabbage, discarding the tough veins, and dice 4–6 rashers (strips) of bacon. Fry these together in a large frying pan until the bacon is cooked through and the cabbage has softened and wilted a little. Stir 30ml/2 tbsp of wholegrain mustard into the cabbage and bacon.

Potato Pancakes

These little potato snacks are popular street food in the Czech Republic, and they are available at roadside stalls and cafés. Quick and easy to make, they are a tasty adaptation of the classic flour-based pancake.

Serves 6–8
6 large waxy potatoes, peeled
2 eggs, beaten

1–2 garlic cloves, crushed
115g/4oz/1 cup plain (all-purpose) flour
5ml/1 tsp chopped fresh marjoram
50g/2oz/¼ cup butter
60ml/4 tbsp oil
salt and ground black pepper
sour cream, chopped fresh parsley and a tomato salad, to serve

1 Grate the potatoes and squeeze thoroughly dry, using a clean dish towel.

2 Put the potatoes in a bowl with the eggs, garlic, flour, marjoram and seasoning and mix well.

3 Heat half the butter and oil together in a large frying pan, then add large spoonfuls of the potato mixture to form rounds. Carefully flatten the 'pancakes' well with the back of a dampened spoon.

4 Fry the pancakes until crisp and golden brown, then turn them over and cook on the other side. Drain on kitchen paper and keep warm while cooking the rest of the pancakes, adding the remaining butter and oil to the frying pan as necessary.

5 Serve the pancakes topped with sour cream, sprinkled with chopped fresh parsley, and accompanied by a fresh, juicy tomato salad.

Cook's Tip
Put the peeled potatoes in water with a few drops of lemon juice, to prevent them turning brown.

Potato Pancakes Energy 291kcal/1221kJ; Protein 6g; Carbohydrate 35.4g, of which sugars 2.9g; Fat 15g, of which saturates 2.2g; Cholesterol 63mg; Calcium 36mg; Fibre 2.1g; Sodium 42mg.
Boxty Pancakes Energy 163kcal/689kJ; Protein 4.8g; Carbohydrate 30.9g, of which sugars 2.7g; Fat 3.1g, of which saturates 1.7g; Cholesterol 8mg; Calcium 69mg; Fibre 1.9g; Sodium 236mg.

Indian Potato Pancakes

Although called a pancake, these crispy spiced potato cakes are more like a bhaji. They make a great appetizer before an Indian main course of curry and rice, as well as being ideal for a party buffet.

Makes 10

300g/11oz potatoes
25ml/1½ tsp garam masala or curry powder
4 spring onions (scallions), finely chopped
1 large egg white, lightly beaten
30ml/2 tbsp vegetable oil
salt and ground black pepper
selection of chutney and relishes, to serve

1 Peel the potatoes, then coarsely grate the flesh. Using your hands, squeeze the excess liquid from the grated potatoes and pat dry with kitchen paper.

2 Place the dry, grated potatoes in a separate bowl and add the spices, spring onions, egg white and seasoning. Stir the mixture until all the ingredients are well combined.

3 Heat a large, non-stick frying pan over a medium heat and add the vegetable oil.

4 Drop tablespoonfuls of the potato into the pan and flatten out with the back of a spoon (you will need to cook the pancakes in batches).

5 Cook for a few minutes and then flip the pancakes and continue cooking for a further 3 minutes until golden brown.

6 Drain the pancakes on kitchen paper and serve with a selection of chutney and relishes.

> **Cook's Tip**
> Wait until the last moment before grating the potatoes. If you prepare them too early before use, the flesh will quickly turn brown due to contact with the air.

Potato and Peanut Butter Fingers

Children will love these crispy, tasty peanut and potato croquettes. Make up a batch and freeze some ready for a quick midweek meal.

Makes 12

1kg/2¼lb potatoes
1 large onion, chopped
2 large (bell) peppers, red or green, chopped
3 carrots, coarsely grated
45ml/3 tbsp sunflower oil
2 courgettes (zucchini), coarsely grated
115g/4oz mushrooms, chopped
15ml/1 tbsp dried mixed herbs
115g/4oz mature (sharp) Cheddar cheese, grated
75g/3oz/⅓ cup crunchy peanut butter
salt and ground black pepper
2 eggs, beaten
about 50g/2oz/1 cup dried breadcrumbs
45ml/3 tbsp Parmesan cheese
oil, for deep frying

1 Cook the potatoes in plenty of boiling water until tender, then drain well and mash. Set aside.

2 Fry the onion, peppers and carrots gently in the sunflower oil for about 5 minutes, then add the courgettes and mushrooms. Cook for a further 5 minutes.

3 Mix the potato with the dried mixed herbs, grated cheese and peanut butter. Season with salt and ground black pepper to taste. Leave the mixture to cool for 30 minutes, then stir in one of the eggs.

4 Spread out on a large plate, cool and chill, then divide into 12 portions and shape. Dip your hands in cold water if the mixture sticks.

5 Put the second egg in a bowl and dip the potato fingers into it first, then into the crumbs and Parmesan cheese until coated evenly. Return the fingers to the refrigerator until set.

6 Heat oil in a deep fat fryer to 190°C/375°F/Gas 5, then fry the fingers in batches for about 3 minutes until golden. Drain well on kitchen paper. Serve immediately.

Indian Pancakes Energy 50kcal/210kJ; Protein 1.3g; Carbohydrate 5.8g, of which sugars 0.5g; Fat 2.6g, of which saturates 0.3g; Cholesterol 0mg; Calcium 8mg; Fibre 0.4g; Sodium 11mg.
Peanut Fingers Energy 269kcal/1120kJ; Protein 8.3g; Carbohydrate 23.3g, of which sugars 6.6g; Fat 16.3g, of which saturates 4.2g; Cholesterol 41mg; Calcium 110mg; Fibre 2.9g; Sodium 151mg.

Potato Cakes with Stuffing

Only a few communities in India make these unusual potato cakes. Serve them as a tasty appetizer, or they can also be served as a main meal, accompanied by a fresh tomato salad.

Makes 8–10
15ml/1 tbsp vegetable oil
1 large onion, finely chopped
2 garlic cloves, finely crushed
5cm/2in piece fresh root ginger, finely crushed
5ml/1 tsp ground coriander
5ml/1 tsp ground cumin
2 fresh green chillies, finely chopped
30ml/2 tbsp each chopped fresh coriander (cilantro) and mint
225g/8oz lean minced (ground) beef or lamb
50g/2oz/⅓ cup frozen peas, thawed
juice of 1 lemon
900g/2lb potatoes, boiled and mashed
2 eggs, beaten
dry breadcrumbs, for coating
vegetable oil, for shallow-frying
salt
lemon wedges and salad leaves, to serve

1 Heat the oil and fry the onion, garlic, ginger, coriander, cumin, chillies and fresh coriander until the onion is translucent.

2 Add the meat and peas and fry well until the meat is cooked, then season to taste with salt and lemon juice. The mixture should be very dry.

3 Divide the mashed potato into 8–10 portions, take one portion at a time and flatten into a pancake in the palm of your hand. Place a spoonful of the meat in the centre and gather the sides together to enclose the meat. Flatten it slightly to make a round.

4 Dip the cakes in beaten egg and then coat in breadcrumbs. Set aside to chill in the refrigerator for about 1 hour until they have firmed up slightly.

5 Heat the oil in a frying pan and shallow-fry the cakes until brown and crisp all over. Serve them hot with lemon wedges on a bed of salad leaves.

Potato Cakes with Feta Cheese

Yummy little fried mouthfuls of potato and tangy-sharp Greek feta cheese, flavoured with dill and lemon juice. Serve as an appetizer or party bite.

Serves 4
500g/1¼lb floury potatoes
115g/4oz/1 cup feta cheese
4 spring onions (scallions), finely chopped
45ml/3 tbsp chopped fresh dill
1 egg, beaten
15ml/1 tbsp lemon juice
salt and ground black pepper
plain (all-purpose) flour, for dredging
45ml/3 tbsp olive oil
dill sprigs, to garnish
shredded spring onions (scallions), to garnish
lemon wedges, to serve

1 Cook the potatoes in their skins in boiling, lightly salted water until soft. Drain and leave to cool slightly, then chop them in half and peel while still warm.

2 Place the potatoes in a bowl and mash. Crumble the feta cheese into the potatoes, add the spring onions, dill, egg and lemon juice and season with salt and pepper. (The cheese is salty, so taste before you add salt.) Stir well.

3 Cover the bowl and chill in the refrigerator until the mixture is firm. Divide the mixture into walnut-size balls, then flatten them slightly. Dredge with flour, shaking off the excess.

4 Heat the oil in a heavy frying pan and fry the cakes in batches until golden brown, about 3–5 minutes on both sides. Keep the cooked cakes warm while you use up the mixture. Drain well on kitchen paper and serve hot, garnished with spring onions, dill and lemon wedges.

Cook's Tip
Ensure that you use floury varieties of potato for this dish rather than waxy potatoes, such as new or salad potatoes. Look out for varieties such as Golden Wonder, Maris Piper, Estima and King Edward.

Stuffed Potato Cakes Energy 260kcal/1086kJ; Protein 10.6g; Carbohydrate 21.3g, of which sugars 3.4g; Fat 15.4g, of which saturates 3.6g; Cholesterol 88mg; Calcium 29mg; Fibre 1.9g; Sodium 62mg.
Feta Potato Cakes Energy 263kcal/1098kJ; Protein 8.6g; Carbohydrate 22.8g, of which sugars 2.4g; Fat 15.9g, of which saturates 5.6g; Cholesterol 68mg; Calcium 126mg; Fibre 1.5g; Sodium 446mg.

Rice and Potato Tortitas

Like miniature tortillas, these little rice and potato pancakes are great served hot, either plain or with tomato sauce for dipping. They make an excellent scoop for any soft vegetable mixture or dip.

Serves 4
30ml/2 tbsp olive oil
115g/4oz/1 cup cooked long
 grain white rice
1 potato, grated
4 spring onions (scallions),
 thinly sliced
1 garlic clove, finely chopped
15ml/1 tbsp chopped
 fresh parsley
3 large (US extra large)
 eggs, beaten
2.5ml/¹⁄₂ tsp paprika
salt and ground black pepper

1 Heat half the olive oil in a large frying pan and stir-fry the rice, with the potato, spring onions and garlic, over a high heat for 3 minutes until golden.

2 Transfer the rice and vegetable mixture into a bowl and stir in the parsley and eggs, with the paprika and plenty of salt and pepper. Mix well.

3 Heat the remaining oil in the frying pan and drop in large spoonfuls of the rice mixture, leaving enough room for the mixture to spread. Cook the tortitas for about 1–2 minutes on each side.

4 Drain the tortitas on kitchen paper and keep hot in a warm oven while cooking the remaining mixture. Pile the cooked tortitas on a large serving platter or on individual plates and serve immediately.

Cook's Tip
These tortitas can be used as a base for a variety of dishes. Try using them in place of plain boiled rice or mashed potatoes for a change. Children love them just as they are, with a large dollop of tomato ketchup for dipping.

Potato Cakes with Spicy Chickpeas and Green Chillies

These spicy potato cakes and the accompanying chickpeas are typical of tasty Indian cuisine. They make a delicious and substantial appetizer or light lunch.

Makes 10 to 12
30ml/2 tbsp vegetable oil
30ml/2 tbsp ground coriander
30ml/2 tbsp ground cumin
2.5ml/¹⁄₂ tsp ground turmeric
2.5ml/¹⁄₂ tsp salt
2.5ml/¹⁄₂ tsp sugar
30ml/2 tbsp flour paste
450g/1lb cooked
 chickpeas, drained
2 fresh green chillies, chopped
5cm/2in piece fresh root ginger,
 finely crushed
75g/3oz fresh coriander (cilantro)
 leaves, chopped
2 firm tomatoes, chopped

For the potato cakes
450g/1lb potatoes, boiled and
 coarsely mashed
4 green chillies, finely chopped
50g/2oz fresh coriander (cilantro)
 leaves, finely chopped
7.5ml/1¹⁄₂ tsp ground cumin
5ml/1 tsp amchur (dry
 mango powder)
salt, to taste
vegetable oil, for shallow-frying

1 Make the spicy chickpeas. Heat the oil in a heavy pan and fry the coriander, cumin, turmeric, salt, sugar and flour paste, stirring frequently, until the oil has separated and the water evaporated.

2 Add the chickpeas to the spicy paste, then stir in the chillies, ginger, fresh coriander and tomatoes. Mix well and simmer for 5 minutes. Transfer to a serving dish and keep warm while you prepare the potato cakes.

3 To make the potato cakes, mix the mashed potato in a large bowl with the green chillies, coriander, ground cumin and amchur. Season with salt to taste. Mix well until all the ingredients are thoroughly combined.

4 Using your hands, shape the potato mixture into little cakes. Heat the oil in a shallow frying pan or griddle and fry the cakes on both sides until golden brown. Transfer to a serving dish and serve with the spicy chickpeas.

Potato Cakes with Black Pudding and Apple

This dish makes a deliciously rustic treat. The combination of crisp potato cake, tasty black pudding topped with apples and mushrooms is a real winner. Serve as an appetizer or as a light lunch.

Serves 4
4 large potatoes, peeled
45ml/3 tbsp olive oil
8 slices of black pudding (blood sausage)
115g/4oz cultivated mushrooms, such as oyster or shiitake
2 eating apples, peeled, cored and cut into wedges
15ml/1 tbsp sherry vinegar or wine vinegar
15g/1oz/2 tbsp butter
salt and ground black pepper

1 Grate the potatoes, putting them into a bowl of water as you grate them, drain and squeeze out the excess moisture.

2 Heat 30ml/2 tbsp olive oil in a large non-stick frying pan, add the grated potatoes and seasoning. Press the potatoes into the pan with your hands.

3 Cook the potatoes until golden brown on the underside, then turn over and cook the other side. When cooked, slide on to a warm plate.

4 Heat the remaining oil and fry the black pudding and mushrooms together for a few minutes. Remove from the pan and keep warm.

5 Add the apple wedges to the frying pan and gently cook until golden brown. Add the sherry or wine vinegar to the apples, and boil up the juices. Add the butter, stir with a wooden spatula until it has melted and season to taste with salt and ground black pepper.

6 Cut the potato cake into wedges and divide among four warmed plates. Arrange the black pudding and cooked mushrooms over the bed of potato cake, pour over the apples and the warm juices, and serve immediately.

Irish Potato Cakes

This is the traditional Irish method of making potato cakes on a griddle or heavy frying pan. Commercially made versions are available throughout Ireland as thin, pre-cooked potato cakes, which are fried for breakfast or occasionally, in the north of the country, for high tea. Griddle-cooked potato cakes were traditionally buttered and eaten hot topped with sugar, rather like pancakes.

Makes about 12
675g/1½lb potatoes, peeled
25g/1oz/2 tbsp unsalted (sweet) butter
about 175g/6oz/1½ cups plain (all-purpose) flour
salt

1 Boil the potatoes in a large pan until tender, then drain well and mash thoroughly. Salt the mash well, then mix in the butter and leave to cool a little.

2 Turn the mashed potatoes out on to a lightly floured work surface and knead in about one-third of their volume in flour, or as much as is needed to make a pliable dough. It will become easier to handle as the flour is incorporated, but try to avoid overworking it.

3 Roll out the dough to a thickness of about 1cm/½in and cut it into even triangles.

4 Heat a dry griddle pan or heavy frying pan over a low heat and cook the potato cakes for about 3 minutes on each side until browned. You will probably need to do this in batches; keep the cooked ones warm in a low oven. Serve hot with butter, or sugar, if you prefer.

Cook's Tip
For authenticity look out for these Irish varieties of potato: Avalanche, a white-skinned early maincrop potato; Avondale, a beige-skinned maincrop; and Barna, an excellent red-skinned late maincrop.

Black Pudding Energy 247kcal/1034kJ; Protein 4.2g; Carbohydrate 28.8g, of which sugars 5.4g; Fat 13.6g, of which saturates 4g; Cholesterol 13mg; Calcium 16mg; Fibre 2.4g; Sodium 132mg.
Irish Potato Cakes Energy 1276kcal/5392kJ; Protein 30.4g; Carbohydrate 249.1g, of which sugars 6.7g; Fat 24.1g, of which saturates 13.4g; Cholesterol 53mg; Calcium 282mg; Fibre 14g; Sodium 203mg.

Bacon and Potato Cakes

Golden and crisp, but soft when you bite into them, these potato cakes are wonderful for breakfast or supper, with or without anything else.

Serves 4

450g/1lb waxy potatoes, peeled
1 small onion, grated

4 slices streaky (fatty) bacon,
   finely chopped
30ml/2 tbsp self-raising
   (self-rising) flour
2 eggs, beaten
vegetable oil, for deep-frying
salt and ground black pepper
fresh parsley sprigs, to garnish

1 Coarsely grate the potatoes, rinse, drain and pat dry on kitchen paper, then mix with the onion, half the bacon, flour and eggs, and season with salt and black pepper.

2 Heat a 1cm/½in layer of oil in a frying pan until really hot, then add about 15ml/1 tbsp of the potato mixture and quickly spread the mixture out with the back of the spoon, taking care that it does not break up.

3 Add a few more spoonfuls of the mixture to the pan in the same way, leaving space between each one so they do not stick together, and fry them for 4–5 minutes until golden brown on the undersides.

4 Carefully turn the cakes over using a metal spatula and fry the other side until golden brown. Drain on kitchen paper, transfer to an ovenproof dish and keep warm in a low oven while frying the remainder.

5 Fry the remaining bacon pieces in the pan. Serve the cakes on individual plates and top with the fried bacon. Serve immediately, sprinkled with the parsley sprigs.

Variation
For a vegetarian alternative to this dish, omit the bacon and replace it with a seeded and chopped red (bell) pepper.

Gateshead Bacon and Potato Floddies

From Tyneside in northern England, floddies are traditionally cooked for breakfast in bacon fat, served with eggs and sausages. A kind of potato cake, floddies are said to have originated with canal workers, who cooked them over an open fire. They should be served crisp and golden brown, and are great as a snack or as part of a bigger breakfast feast.

Serves 4–6

250g/9oz potatoes, weighed
   after peeling
1 large onion
175g/6oz rindless streaky (fatty)
   bacon, finely chopped
50g/2oz/½ cup self-raising
   (self-rising) flour
2 eggs
oil, for frying
salt and ground black pepper

1 Grate the potatoes on to a clean dish towel, and then gather up the edges to make a pouch. Squeeze and twist the towel to remove the liquid.

2 Grate or finely chop the onion into a mixing bowl and add the grated potato, chopped bacon and flour. Season with salt and black pepper. Mix well with your hands until all the ingredients are thoroughly combined.

3 Beat the eggs in a separate bowl and stir them into the potato mixture. Heat some oil in a large frying pan.

4 Add generous tablespoonfuls of the potato mixture to the hot oil and flatten them slightly to make thin cakes. Cook over a medium heat for 3–4 minutes on each side until golden brown. Lift out, drain on kitchen paper and serve immediately.

Cook's Tips
• Push the floddies into oiled metal rings before frying if you wish, for a neat circular shape.
• Serve with grilled (broiled) sausages and fried eggs for a hearty and substantial breakfast treat.

Bacon and Potato Cakes Energy 363kcal/1512kJ; Protein 9.8g; Carbohydrate 25g, of which sugars 2.4g; Fat 25.6g, of which saturates 4.7g; Cholesterol 111mg; Calcium 53mg; Fibre 1.6g; Sodium 390mg.
Bacon Floddies Energy 214kcal/891kJ; Protein 8.8g; Carbohydrate 17.1g, of which sugars 3.5g; Fat 12.7g, of which saturates 3.4g; Cholesterol 82mg; Calcium 38mg; Fibre 1.4g; Sodium 397mg.

Curried Lamb and Potato Cakes

An unusual variation on burgers, these little lamb and potato triangles are easy and quick to make. They are really good served hot as part of a buffet, but they can also be eaten cold as a snack or taken on picnics.

Makes 12–15
450g/1lb new or small,
  firm potatoes
3 eggs
1 onion, grated
30ml/2 tbsp chopped
  fresh parsley
450g/1lb finely minced (ground)
  lean lamb
115g/4oz/2 cups fresh
  breadcrumbs
vegetable oil, for frying
salt and ground black pepper
sprigs of fresh mint,
  to garnish
pitta bread and herby green
  salad, to serve

1 Cook the potatoes in a large pan of boiling salted water for 20 minutes or until tender, then drain and leave to cool.

2 Beat the eggs in a large bowl. Add the onion, parsley and seasoning and beat together.

3 When the potatoes are cold, grate them coarsely and stir into the egg mixture, together with the minced lamb. Knead the mixture well for 3–4 minutes until all the ingredients are thoroughly blended.

4 Take a handful of the lamb mixture and roll it into a ball. Repeat this process until all the meat is used.

5 Roll the balls in the breadcrumbs and then mould them into fairly flat triangular shapes, about 13cm/5in long. Coat them in the breadcrumbs again.

6 Heat a 1cm/½in layer of oil in a frying pan over a medium heat. When the oil is hot, fry the potato cakes for 8–12 minutes until golden brown on both sides, turning occasionally. Drain on kitchen paper.

7 Serve immediately, garnished with mint and accompanied by pitta bread and salad.

Potato Blinis with Smoked Salmon

These crisp, light potato pancakes originated in Russia, where they are served with the finest caviar, but they are also good with salmon roe. They make great canapés to serve at a party.

**Serves 6 as part of
a buffet**
1 potato, about 115g/4oz, boiled
  and mashed
15ml/1 tbsp easy-blend (rapid-
  rise) dried yeast
175g/6oz/1½ cups plain
  (all-purpose) flour
300ml/½ pint/1¼ cups
  lukewarm water
oil, for greasing
90ml/6 tbsp sour cream
6 slices smoked salmon
salt and ground black pepper
lemon slices, to garnish

1 Mix the mashed potato, yeast, flour, salt and pepper with the water to make a smooth dough. Cover with clear film (plastic wrap) and leave to rise in a warm place for 30 minutes or until doubled in bulk.

2 Heat a non-stick frying pan and add a little oil. Drop small spoonfuls of the blini dough on to the pan. Each blini should measure about 5cm/2in in diameter.

3 Cook the blinis for 2 minutes until lightly golden on the underside. Turn over using a metal spatula and cook the second side. Remove each batch as it cooks and keep them warm while you cook the remaining blinis.

4 To serve, top each blini with a little sour cream and a small folded slice of smoked salmon. Garnish with black pepper and a small slice of lemon.

> **Variation**
> *For an alternative topping for the blinis, mix 200g/7oz/ scant 1 cup cream cheese with 15ml/1 tbsp chopped fresh parsley or dill. Spread over the blinis and top with the salmon. Add slivers of sweet pickled cherry chillies or a spoonful of salmon roe.*

Lamb and Potato Cakes Energy 181kcal/760kJ; Protein 10.8g; Carbohydrate 13.9g, of which sugars 1.1g; Fat 9.6g, of which saturates 2.8g; Cholesterol 76mg; Calcium 31mg; Fibre 0.8g; Sodium 128mg.
Potato Blinis Energy 220kcal/930kJ; Protein 17.2g; Carbohydrate 26.3g, of which sugars 1.3g; Fat 5.9g, of which saturates 2.4g; Cholesterol 34mg; Calcium 66mg; Fibre 1.1g; Sodium 1024mg.

Smoked Salmon with Warm Potato Cakes

Although the ingredients are timeless, this combination makes an excellent modern dish, which is deservedly popular as a first course or as a substantial canapé to serve with drinks. It also makes a perfect brunch dish, served with lightly scrambled eggs and freshly squeezed orange juice. Choose wild fish if possible.

Serves 6
450g/1lb potatoes, cooked
   and mashed

75g/3oz/²⁄₃ cup plain
   (all-purpose) flour
2 eggs, beaten
2 spring onions
   (scallions), chopped
a little freshly grated nutmeg
50g/2oz/¼ cup butter, melted
150ml/¼ pint/²⁄₃ cup sour cream
12 slices of smoked salmon
salt and ground black pepper
chopped fresh chives, to garnish

1 Put the potatoes, flour, eggs and spring onions into a large bowl. Season with salt, black pepper and a little nutmeg, and add half the butter. Mix thoroughly and shape into 12 small potato cakes.

2 Heat the remaining butter in a non-stick frying pan and cook the potato cakes until browned on both sides.

3 To serve, mix the sour cream with some salt and pepper. Fold a piece of smoked salmon and place on top of each potato cake. Top the salmon with the cream and then the chives, and serve immediately.

Cook's Tip
If it is more convenient, you can make the potato cakes in advance and keep them overnight in the refrigerator. When required, warm them through in a hot oven 15 minutes before assembling and serving.

Herbed Plaice and Potato Croquettes

These tasty croquettes are made with a mixture of mashed potato and flaked fish. They are great as an appetizer and are very popular with children.

Serves 4–6
450g/1lb plaice fillets
300ml/½ pint/1¼ cups milk
450g/1lb cooked potatoes

1 fennel bulb, finely chopped
45ml/3 tbsp chopped
   fresh parsley
2 eggs
15g/½ oz/1 tbsp unsalted
   (sweet) butter
115g/4oz/2 cups white
   breadcrumbs
25g/1oz/2 tbsp sesame seeds
oil, for deep-frying
salt and ground black pepper

1 Gently poach the plaice fillets in the milk for approximately 15 minutes until the fish flakes. Drain and reserve the milk.

2 Peel the skin off the fish and remove any bones. In a food processor or blender, process the fish, potatoes, fennel, parsley, eggs and butter.

3 Add 30ml/2 tbsp of the reserved cooking milk and season with salt and ground black pepper. Mix well. Chill for 30 minutes, then shape into 20 croquettes with your hands.

4 Mix together the breadcrumbs and sesame seeds, then roll the croquettes in this mixture to form a good coating. Heat the oil in a large, heavy pan until it is hot enough to brown a cube of stale bread in 30 seconds.

5 Deep-fry the croquettes in batches for about 4 minutes until they are golden brown all over. Drain well on kitchen paper and serve the croquettes hot.

Cook's Tip
Serve these baby croquettes with a tartare sauce, if you like. Simply chop some capers and gherkins, and stir into home-made or good quality store-bought mayonnaise. Season to taste with salt and pepper.

Smoked Salmon Energy 326kcal/1365kJ; Protein 21.9g; Carbohydrate 22.9g, of which sugars 2.3g; Fat 17g, of which saturates 8.6g; Cholesterol 119mg; Calcium 70mg; Fibre 1.2g; Sodium 1315mg.
Croquettes Energy 397kcal/1673kJ; Protein 21.8g; Carbohydrate 45g, of which sugars 2.7g; Fat 15.8g, of which saturates 3.3g; Cholesterol 100mg; Calcium 138mg; Fibre 2.8g; Sodium 458mg.

Potato and Salt Cod Fritters

These bitesize fish and potato cakes, dipped into creamy aioli, are irresistible as an appetizer.

Serves 6
300ml/¹⁄₂ pint/1¹⁄₄ cups milk
6 spring onions (scallions), finely chopped
450g/1lb salt cod, soaked for 24 hours in three changes of water
500g/1¹⁄₄lb floury potatoes, cooked and mashed
30ml/2 tbsp extra virgin olive oil
30ml/2 tbsp chopped fresh parsley
juice of ¹⁄₂ lemon
2 eggs, beaten
plain (all-purpose) flour, for dusting
90g/3¹⁄₂oz/1¹⁄₄ cups dried white breadcrumbs
olive oil, for shallow frying
lemon wedges and salad leaves, to serve
salt and ground black pepper

For the aioli
2 large garlic cloves, finely chopped
2 egg yolks
300ml/¹⁄₂ pint/1¹⁄₄ cups olive oil
juice of ¹⁄₂ lemon, to taste

1 Simmer the milk in a pan with half the spring onions. Add the cod and poach gently for 10–15 minutes. Remove the cod and flake it with a fork into a bowl, discarding bones and skin.

2 Add 60ml/4 tbsp potato to the cod and mix well. Add the oil, then the remaining potato. Beat in the remaining spring onions and the parsley. Season with lemon juice and salt and pepper to taste. Beat one egg into the mixture, then chill until firm.

3 Shape the mixture into 12–18 balls, then flatten into small round cakes. Coat each one in flour, then dip in the remaining egg and coat with breadcrumbs. Chill until ready to fry.

4 Meanwhile, make the aioli. Pound the garlic with a little salt in a mortar and pestle. Whisk in the egg yolks. Beat in half the olive oil, a drop at a time. When the sauce is as thick as soft butter, beat in 5–10ml/1–2 tsp lemon juice. Continue adding oil until the aioli is thick. Season to taste.

5 Heat about 2cm/³⁄₄in oil in a large, heavy frying pan. Add the fritters and cook over a medium-hot heat for about 4 minutes on each side, until crisp and golden. Drain on kitchen paper, then serve with the aioli, lemon wedges and salad leaves.

Potato and Chive Pancakes with Pickled Herring and Onion Rings

Serve these moreish potato pancakes as an appetizer or as a light main course with salad.

Serves 6
275g/10oz potatoes, cooked and mashed
2 eggs, beaten
150ml/¹⁄₄ pint/²⁄₃ cup milk
40g/1¹⁄₂oz plain (all-purpose) flour
30ml/2 tbsp chopped fresh chives
vegetable oil or butter, for greasing
salt and ground black pepper

For the topping
2 small red or yellow onions, thinly sliced into rings
60ml/4 tbsp sour cream or crème fraîche
5ml/1 tsp wholegrain mustard
15ml/1 tbsp chopped fresh dill
6 pickled herring fillets

To garnish
fresh dill sprigs
fresh chives or chive flowers

1 Prepare the topping. Place the onions in a bowl and cover with boiling water. Set aside for 2–3 minutes, then drain and dry on kitchen paper. Mix the onions with the sour cream or crème fraîche, mustard and chopped dill. Season to taste. Cut the pickled herring fillets into 12–18 pieces. Set them aside.

2 Put the mashed potato in a bowl and beat in the eggs, milk and flour with a wooden spoon to make a batter. Season to taste with salt and pepper and whisk in the chopped chives.

3 Heat a frying pan over a medium heat and grease it with a little oil or butter. Spoon about 30ml/2 tbsp of batter into the pan to make a pancake, measuring about 7.5cm/3in across. Cook for 3–4 minutes, until the underside is set and brown.

4 Turn the pancake over and cook the other side for 3–4 minutes, until golden brown. Transfer to a plate and keep warm while you make the remaining pancakes.

5 Place two pancakes on each of six warmed plates and distribute the pickled herring fillets and onions equally among them. Garnish with dill sprigs, fresh chives and/or chive flowers. Season with black pepper and serve immediately.

Potato Pancakes Energy 164kcal/686kJ; Protein 5.8g; Carbohydrate 15.3g, of which sugars 3.1g; Fat 9.4g, of which saturates 2.5g; Cholesterol 75mg; Calcium 67mg; Fibre 0.8g; Sodium 78mg.
Salt Cod Fritters Energy 718kcal/2980kJ; Protein 21.1g; Carbohydrate 33.1g, of which sugars 1.9g; Fat 56.5g, of which saturates 8.3g; Cholesterol 165mg; Calcium 67mg; Fibre 1.6g; Sodium 196mg.

Salmon Fish Cakes

The secret of a good fish cake is to make it with freshly prepared fish and potatoes, home-made breadcrumbs and plenty of fresh herbs, such as dill and parsley or tarragon.

Serves 4
450g/1lb cooked salmon fillet
450g/1lb freshly cooked
 potatoes, mashed
25g/1oz/2 tbsp butter, melted or
 30ml/2 tbsp olive oil
10ml/2 tsp wholegrain mustard
15ml/1 tbsp each chopped fresh
 dill and chopped fresh parsley
 or tarragon
grated rind and juice of ½ lemon
15g/½oz/2 tbsp wholemeal
 (whole-wheat) flour
1 egg, lightly beaten
150g/5oz/2 cups dried
 breadcrumbs
60ml/4 tbsp sunflower oil
sea salt and ground black pepper
rocket (arugula) leaves and
 chives, to garnish
lemon wedges, to serve

1 Flake the cooked salmon, discarding any skin and bones. Put it in a bowl with the mashed potato, melted butter or oil and wholegrain mustard, and mix well.

2 Stir the herbs and the lemon rind and juice into the fish and potato mixture. Season to taste with plenty of sea salt and ground black pepper.

3 Divide the mixture into eight portions and shape each into a ball, then flatten into a thick disc. Dip the fish cakes first in flour, then in egg and finally in breadcrumbs, making sure that they are evenly coated with crumbs.

4 Heat the oil in a frying pan until it is very hot. Fry the fish cakes in batches until golden brown and crisp all over. As each batch is ready, drain on kitchen paper and keep hot. Garnish with rocket and chives and serve with lemon wedges.

Cook's Tip
Any fresh white or hot-smoked fish is suitable. Always buy organically farmed fish, or sustainably caught wild fish.

Haddock and Potato Fish Cakes

These tasty fish and potato cakes can be made slightly larger and served as substantial fish burgers, or made into smaller balls and served as tasty finger food at a party or buffet lunch.

Makes 20
450g/1lb skinned haddock,
 pollock or cod
2 medium potatoes, peeled
4 green chillies, finely chopped
5cm/2in piece fresh root ginger,
 finely crushed
a few fresh coriander (cilantro)
 and mint leaves, chopped
4 spring onions (scallions),
 finely chopped
2 eggs
breadcrumbs, for coating
vegetable oil, for shallow-frying
salt and ground black pepper
chilli sauce or sweet chutney,
 to serve

1 Place the fish in a lightly greased steamer and steam until cooked. The flesh should flake easily when tested with a fork or the tip of a knife. Remove from the heat but leave on the steaming tray to cool.

2 Meanwhile, cut the potatoes into chunks and cook in a pan with plenty of boiling water for 10–15 minutes until tender, then drain well and mash. Set aside.

3 When the fish is cool, flake it coarsely into a large bowl and add the potatoes, spices, coriander and mint, spring onions, seasonings and one of the eggs. Mix with a wooden spoon or your hands until the ingredients are thoroughly combined.

4 Shape into cakes. Beat the remaining egg and dip the cakes in it, then coat with the breadcrumbs. Heat the oil in a frying pan and cook the fish cakes until brown on all sides. Serve hot.

Cook's Tip
Any firm, white-fleshed fish can be used for making this dish. Haddock and pollock are cheaper than cod and they also tend to come from more sustainable stocks, making them the ideal choice for this recipe.

Fish Cakes Energy 586kcal/2453kJ; Protein 29.8g; Carbohydrate 49.9g, of which sugars 3.2g; Fat 31g, of which saturates 7.2g; Cholesterol 117mg; Calcium 79mg; Fibre 1.3g; Sodium 266mg.
Haddock Fish Cakes Energy 67kcal/284kJ; Protein 5.5g; Carbohydrate 6.9g, of which sugars 1.5g; Fat 2.2g, of which saturates 1.1g; Cholesterol 14mg; Calcium 30mg; Fibre 0.7g; Sodium 116mg.

Coquilles St Jacques

A classic French appetizer that calls for the best quality scallops and rich piped potato to ensure a wonderful result. You will need four scallop shells to serve these.

Serves 4
450g/1lb potatoes, chopped
50g/2oz/4 tbsp butter
4 large or 8 small scallops
120ml/4fl oz/¹/₂ cup fish stock

For the sauce
25g/1oz/2 tbsp butter
25g/1oz/¹/₄ cup plain
   (all-purpose) flour
300ml/¹/₂ pint/1¹/₄ cups milk
30ml/2 tbsp single (light) cream
115g/4oz/1 cup mature (sharp)
   Cheddar cheese, grated
salt and ground black pepper
dill sprigs, to garnish
grilled lemon wedges, to serve

1 Preheat oven to 200°C/400°F/Gas 6. Place the chopped potatoes in a large pan, cover with plenty of water and boil for about 10–15 minutes or until tender. Drain and mash well with the butter.

2 Spoon the mixture into a piping (pastry) bag fitted with a star nozzle. Pipe the potatoes around the outside of a cleaned scallop shell. Repeat the process, making four in total.

3 Simmer the scallops in a little fish stock for 3 minutes or until they are just firm. Drain well and slice the scallops finely. Set them aside.

4 To make the sauce, melt the butter in a small pan, add the flour and cook over a low heat for a couple of minutes, then gradually add the milk and cream, stirring constantly, and cook until thickened.

5 Stir in the cheese and cook until melted. Season to taste. Spoon a little sauce in the base of each shell. Divide the scallops between the shells and then pour the remaining sauce over the scallops.

6 Bake the scallops in the preheated oven for about 10 minutes, or until golden. Garnish with the dill sprigs. Serve with grilled lemon wedges.

Sweet Potato and Prawn Patties

You can make these delicious prawn and sweet potato patties any size: small for a snack or appetizer, or large for a main course; simply adjust the amount you spoon on to the spatula before frying. Traditionally, the patties are served with herb and lettuce leaves for wrapping and a sauce for dipping.

Serves 4
50g/2oz/¹/₂ cup plain
   (all-purpose) flour
50g/2oz/¹/₂ cup rice flour

scant 5ml/1 tsp baking powder
10ml/2 tsp sugar
2.5cm/1in fresh root ginger,
   peeled and grated
2 spring onions (scallions),
   finely sliced
175g/6oz small fresh prawns
   (shrimp), peeled and deveined
1 slim sweet potato, about
   225g/8oz, peeled and cut into
   fine matchsticks
vegetable oil, for deep-frying
salt and ground black pepper
chopped fresh coriander (cilantro),
   to garnish
nuoc cham or other dipping
   sauce, to serve

1 Sift the flours and baking powder into a bowl. Add the sugar and about 2.5ml/¹/₂ tsp each of salt and pepper. Gradually stir in 250ml/8fl oz/1 cup water, until thoroughly combined. Add the ginger and spring onions and leave to stand for 30 minutes.

2 Add the prepared prawns and sweet potato matchsticks to the batter and gently fold them in, making sure they are well coated. Heat enough vegetable oil for deep-frying in a wok or heavy pan.

3 Place a heaped tablespoon of the mixture on to a metal spatula and pat it down a little. Lower it into the oil, pushing it off the spatula so that it floats in the oil. Fry the patty for 2–3 minutes, turning it over so that it is evenly browned. Drain on kitchen paper. Continue with the rest of the batter, frying the patties in small batches.

4 Arrange the patties on a serving dish, or on lettuce leaves, garnish with coriander, and serve immediately with nuoc cham or another dipping sauce of your choice.

Coquilles St Jacques Energy 466kcal/1948kJ; Protein 24.2g; Carbohydrate 28.8g, of which sugars 5.7g; Fat 28.6g, of which saturates 18.3g; Cholesterol 103mg; Calcium 342mg; Fibre 1.3g; Sodium 496mg.
Sweet Potato Patties Energy 276kcal/1159kJ; Protein 11g; Carbohydrate 35g, of which sugars 6g; Fat 11g, of which saturates 1g; Cholesterol 85mg; Calcium 83mg; Fibre 81g; Sodium 0.2g.

Potatoes with Egg and Lemon Dressing

This potato favourite takes on a new lease of life when mixed with hard-boiled eggs and lemon juice. With its tangy flavour, this is the ideal salad to accompany a summer barbecue.

Serves 4
900g/2lb new potatoes
1 small onion, finely chopped
2 hard-boiled eggs, shelled
300ml/½ pint/1¼ cups mayonnaise
1 garlic clove, crushed
finely grated rind and juice of 1 lemon
60ml/4 tbsp chopped fresh parsley, plus extra for garnishing
salt and ground black pepper

1 Scrub or scrape the potatoes. Put them in a pan, cover with cold water and add a pinch of salt. Bring to the boil, then simmer for 15 minutes, or until tender.

2 Drain and leave to cool. Cut the potatoes into large dice, season with salt and pepper and combine with the onion.

3 Halve the eggs and set aside the yolk. Roughly chop the whites and place in a mixing bowl. Stir in the mayonnaise. Mix the garlic, lemon rind and lemon juice in a small bowl and stir into the mayonnaise mixture, combining thoroughly.

4 Stir the mayonnaise mixture into the potatoes, coating them well, then fold in the chopped parsley. Press the egg yolk through a sieve (strainer) and sprinkle on top. Serve cold or chilled, garnished with parsley.

> **Variation**
> *For a change, replace the potato with cooked beetroot (beets). The mayonnaise will turn bright pink, which may surprise your guests, but the flavour is excellent. Alternatively, use a mixture of potatoes and beetroot.*

The Simplest Potato Salad

The secret of this potato salad is to mix the potatoes with the dressing while they are still hot so that they absorb its flavours. This is perfect with grilled pork, lamb chops or juicy roast chicken or for a vegetarian version, serve with a colourful selection of roasted vegetables.

Serves 4–6
675g/1½lb small new or salad potatoes
4 spring onions (scallions)
45ml/3 tbsp olive oil
15ml/1 tbsp white wine vinegar
175ml/6fl oz/¾ cup good mayonnaise, preferably home-made
45ml/3 tbsp chopped chives
salt and ground black pepper

1 Cook the potatoes in their skins in a large pan of boiling salted water until tender.

2 Meanwhile, wash the spring onions, then finely chop the white parts along with a little of the green parts; they look more attractive cut on the diagonal. Set aside the chopped onions until ready to use.

3 Whisk together the olive oil and wine vinegar. Drain the potatoes well and place them in a large bowl, then immediately toss lightly with the prepared dressing and the spring onions. Put the bowl to one side to cool.

4 Gently stir the mayonnaise and chopped chives into the potatoes, season well with salt and ground black pepper and chill thoroughly until ready to serve. Adjust the seasoning before serving, if necessary.

> **Cook's Tips**
> • *When making dressings, instead of whisking the ingredients in a bowl, simply place them in a screw-top jar and give it a good shake to combine.*
> • *This is the perfect dish for a picnic or barbecue, as it can be made well ahead and is served chilled. If you want to do this, add the mayonnaise and chives just before serving.*

Deli Potato Salad with Egg, Mayonnaise and Olives

Potato salad is synonymous with deli food and there are many varieties, some with sour cream, some with vinaigrette and others with vegetables. This tasty version includes a piquant mustard mayonnaise, chopped eggs and green olives.

Serves 6–8

1kg/2¼lb waxy salad potatoes, scrubbed
1 red, brown or white onion, finely chopped
2–3 celery sticks, finely chopped
60–90ml/4–6 tbsp chopped fresh parsley
15–20 pimiento-stuffed olives, halved
3 hard-boiled eggs, chopped
60ml/4 tbsp extra virgin olive oil
60ml/4 tbsp white wine vinegar
15–30ml/1–2 tbsp mild or wholegrain mustard
celery seeds, to taste (optional)
175–250ml/6–8fl oz/¾–1 cup mayonnaise
salt and ground black pepper
paprika, to garnish

1 Put the potatoes in a pan, pour in water to cover and add a pinch of salt. Bring to the boil, then reduce the heat and cook gently for about 10 minutes, or until the potatoes are just tender. Drain well and return to the pan. Leave for 2–3 minutes to cool and dry a little.

2 When the potatoes are cool enough to handle but still very warm, cut them with a sharp knife into chunks or slices and place in a salad bowl.

3 Sprinkle the potatoes with salt and ground black pepper, then add the onion, celery, parsley, olives and the chopped eggs.

4 Place the olive oil in a small bowl, then whisk in the vinegar, mustard and celery seeds, if using. Pour the dressing over the salad and toss to combine.

5 Stir in enough mayonnaise to bind the salad together. Chill in the refrigerator before serving. Sprinkle with a little paprika when you are ready to serve.

Potato and Olive Salad

This delicious salad is simple and zesty – the perfect choice for lunch, as an accompaniment, or as an appetizer. Similar in appearance to flat leaf parsley, fresh coriander has a distinctive pungent, almost spicy flavour. It is widely used in India, the Middle and Far East and in eastern Mediterranean countries. This unusual potato salad is particularly good served as part of a decadent brunch.

Serves 4

8 large new potatoes
45–60ml/3–4 tbsp garlic-flavoured oil and vinegar dressing
60–90ml/4–6 tbsp chopped fresh herbs, such as coriander (cilantro) and chives
10–15 dry-fleshed black Mediterranean olives

1 Cut the new potatoes into chunks. Put them in a pan, pour in water to cover and add a pinch of salt. Bring to the boil, then reduce the heat and cook gently for about 10 minutes.

2 When the potatoes are just tender, drain well and leave in a colander to dry thoroughly and cool slightly.

3 When the potatoes are cool enough to handle, chop them into bitesize chunks and place them in a serving bowl.

4 Drizzle the garlic dressing over the potatoes. Toss well until the pieces are evenly coated and sprinkle with the chopped fresh coriander, chives, and black olives. Mix well until all the ingredients are well combined. Chill in the refrigerator for at least 1 hour before serving.

Variations

• If you like your food a little spicier, add a pinch of ground cumin or a sprinkling of roasted whole cumin seeds to the salad before serving.
• Try different flavoured dressings, if you like, in place of the garlic version. Those flavoured with mustard, chilli or herbs, will work equally well.

Deli Potato Salad Energy 323kcal/1343kJ; Protein 5.2g; Carbohydrate 21.5g, of which sugars 2.7g; Fat 24.7g, of which saturates 4g; Cholesterol 88mg; Calcium 49mg; Fibre 2g; Sodium 149mg.
Potato and Olive Salad Energy 132kcal/548kJ; Protein 1.9g; Carbohydrate 12.4g, of which sugars 1.2g; Fat 8.6g, of which saturates 1.3g; Cholesterol 0mg; Calcium 42mg; Fibre 2g; Sodium 575mg.

Potato Salad with Capers and Black Olives

This dish from southern Italy is quick and easy to make. The combination of potatoes, olives, capers and anchovies is quite perfect.

Serves 4–6
900g/2lb large white potatoes
50ml/2fl oz/¼ cup white
   wine vinegar
75ml/5 tbsp olive oil
30ml/2 tbsp chopped flat
   leaf parsley
30ml/2 tbsp capers,
   finely chopped
50g/2oz/½ cup pitted black
   olives, chopped in half
3 garlic cloves, finely chopped
50g/2oz marinated
   anchovies (unsalted)
salt and ground black pepper

1 Boil the potatoes in their skins in a large pan of water for about 15–20 minutes or until they are just tender. Remove from the pan using a slotted spoon and place them in a separate bowl.

2 When the potatoes are cool enough to handle, carefully peel off the skins.

3 Cut the peeled potatoes into even chunks and place in a large, flat earthenware dish.

4 Mix together the white wine vinegar and olive oil, season to taste with salt and pepper and add the parsley, capers, olives and garlic. Toss carefully to combine and then pour over the potato chunks.

5 Lay the anchovies on top of the salad. Cover with a cloth and leave to settle for 30 minutes or so before serving to allow the flavours to permeate.

Variation
If you want to serve this dish to vegetarians, simply omit the anchovies; it tastes delicious even without them.

Tangy Potato Salad

If you like a good kick of mustard and the distinctive flavour of tarragon, you'll love the piquant dressing in this potato salad.

Serves 8
1.3kg/3lb small new or
   salad potatoes
30ml/2 tbsp white wine vinegar
15ml/1 tbsp Dijon mustard
45ml/3 tbsp vegetable or olive oil
75g/3oz/6 tbsp chopped
   red onion
120ml/4fl oz/½ cup mayonnaise
30ml/2 tbsp chopped fresh
   tarragon, or 7.5ml/1½ tsp
   dried tarragon
1 celery stick, thinly sliced
salt and ground black pepper
celery leaves and tarragon leaves,
   to garnish

1 Cook the potatoes in their skins in boiling salted water for about 10–15 minutes until tender. Drain well.

2 Mix together the vinegar and Dijon mustard, then slowly whisk in the oil.

3 When the potatoes are cool enough to handle, cut them into even slices and place them into a large bowl. Add the onion to the potatoes, then pour the dressing over them. Season with salt and pepper to taste, then toss gently to combine. Leave to stand for at least 30 minutes.

4 Mix together the mayonnaise and tarragon. Gently stir into the potatoes, together with the celery. Serve garnished with celery leaves and tarragon.

Cook's Tip
The delicious, distinctive tarragon flavour in this dish makes it the perfect partner to roast or grilled (broiled) chicken.

Variation
When available, use small red or even blue potatoes to give an interesting colour to the salad.

Olive Potato Salad Energy 282kcal/1174kJ; Protein 5g; Carbohydrate 24.4g, of which sugars 2.2g; Fat 18.9g, of which saturates 2.8g; Cholesterol 5mg; Calcium 54mg; Fibre 2g; Sodium 347mg.
Tangy Potato Salad Energy 283kcal/1182kJ; Protein 3.7g; Carbohydrate 32.4g, of which sugars 3.4g; Fat 16.2g, of which saturates 2.5g; Cholesterol 11mg; Calcium 18mg; Fibre 2.1g; Sodium 147mg.

Potato, Caraway Seed and Parsley Salad

This highly fragrant potato salad is enhanced with the distinctive flavours of garlic and caraway. Adding the garlic infused oil and the caraway seeds while the potatoes are still hot will help the potatoes to soak up the delicious flavours of the dressing.

Serves 4–6
675g/1½lb new potatoes, scrubbed
45ml/3 tbsp garlic-infused olive oil
15ml/1 tbsp caraway seeds, lightly crushed
45ml/3 tbsp chopped fresh parsley
salt and ground black pepper

1 Cook the potatoes in salted, boiling water for about 10 minutes, or until just tender. Drain thoroughly and transfer to a large bowl.

2 Add the garlic-infused oil, caraway seeds and some salt and ground black pepper to the hot potatoes, then mix until all of the ingredients are well combined. Set the bowl aside to allow the potatoes to cool a little.

3 When the potatoes are almost cold, stir in the chopped parsley and serve.

Cook's Tip
If the salad has stood for a while, give it a thorough mix before serving to ensure the dressing is evenly distributed. It will tend to settle to the bottom of the bowl over time.

Variation
This recipe is also delicious if made with the same quantity of sweet potatoes instead of new potatoes. Peel and roughly chop the sweet potatoes into chunks about the same size as new potatoes, then follow the recipe as before.

Potato and Radish Salad

Crunchy radishes add a splash of peppery flavour and an appealing hint of colour to this subtle honey-scented salad. Unlike many potato salads, which are dressed in thick creamy sauces, this is quite light and cleanly flavoured with a truly tasty yet delicate dressing.

Serves 4–6
450g/1lb new or salad potatoes
45ml/3 tbsp olive oil
15ml/1 tbsp walnut or hazelnut oil (optional)
30ml/2 tbsp wine vinegar
10ml/2 tsp coarse-grain mustard
5ml/1 tsp honey
about 6–8 radishes, thinly sliced
30ml/2 tbsp chopped chives
salt and ground black pepper

1 Cook the potatoes in their skins in a large pan of boiling salted water for about 10–15 minutes until just tender. Drain well and leave to cool slightly. When cool enough to handle, cut the potatoes in half, but leave any small ones whole. Place in a large bowl and set aside.

2 To make the dressing, place the oils, vinegar, mustard and honey in a bowl and season to taste with salt and pepper. Whisk together until thoroughly combined.

3 Toss the dressing into the potatoes in the bowl while they are still cooling and leave to stand for 1–2 hours to allow the flavours to penetrate.

4 Finally, mix in the sliced radishes and chopped chives and chill in the refrigerator until ready to serve.

5 Just before serving, toss the salad mixture together again, as some of the dressing may have drained to the bottom, and adjust the seasoning.

Variation
Sliced celery stick, diced red onion and/or chopped walnuts would make good alternatives to the radishes if you are unable to obtain any.

Potato and Radish Salad Energy 108kcal/451kJ; Protein 1.5g; Carbohydrate 13g, of which sugars 1.9g; Fat 5.9g, of which saturates 0.9g; Cholesterol 0mg; Calcium 8mg; Fibre 0.9g; Sodium 36mg.
Potato and Parsley Salad Energy 131kcal/549kJ; Protein 2.1g; Carbohydrate 18.3g, of which sugars 1.6g; Fat 5.9g, of which saturates 0.9g; Cholesterol 0mg; Calcium 22mg; Fibre 1.5g; Sodium 15mg.

Warm Hazelnut and Pistachio Salad

Two kinds of crunchy nuts turn ordinary potato salad into a really special accompaniment. This would be lovely with cold sliced roast beef, tongue or ham, but you can also serve it on its own as a healthy snack.

Serves 4
900g/2lb small new or
    salad potatoes

30ml/2 tbsp hazelnut or
    walnut oil
60ml/4 tbsp sunflower oil
juice of 1 lemon
25g/1oz/¼ cup hazelnuts,
    shells removed
15 pistachio nuts, shells removed
salt and ground black pepper
flat leaf parsley sprig, to garnish

1 Cook the potatoes in their skins in boiling salted water for about 10–15 minutes until tender.

2 Drain the potatoes well in a colander and leave them to cool slightly.

3 Meanwhile, mix together the hazelnut or walnut oil with the sunflower oil and lemon juice. Season well with salt and ground black pepper.

4 Using a sharp knife, roughly chop the shelled hazelnuts and the pistachio nuts.

5 Put the cooled potatoes into a large bowl and pour the dressing over. Toss to combine.

6 Sprinkle the salad with the chopped nuts. Serve immediately, garnished with flat leaf parsley.

Variation
Use chopped walnuts in place of the hazelnuts, if you like. Try to buy the broken pieces of nut, which are less expensive than walnut halves, but chop them into smaller pieces before adding them to the salad.

Ensaladilla

A Spanish version of what is commonly known as Russian salad, this potato dish is a meal in itself.

Serves 4
8 new potatoes, scrubbed
    and quartered
1 large carrot, diced
115g/4oz fine green beans,
    cut into 2cm/¾in lengths
75g/3oz/¾ cup peas
½ Spanish onion, chopped
4 cornichons or small
    gherkins, sliced
1 small red (bell) pepper, seeded
    and diced

50g/2oz/½ cup pitted
    black olives
15ml/1 tbsp drained
    pickled capers
15ml/1 tbsp freshly squeezed
    lemon juice
30ml/2 tbsp chopped fresh fennel
    or parsley
salt and ground black pepper

For the aioli
2 garlic cloves, finely chopped
2.5ml/½ tsp salt
150ml/¼ pint/⅔ cup
    mayonnaise

1 To make the aioli, crush the garlic with the salt in a mortar with a pestle, then whisk or stir into the mayonnaise.

2 Cook the potatoes and diced carrot in a pan of boiling, lightly salted water for 5–8 minutes until almost tender. Add the beans and peas to the pan and cook for 2 minutes, or until all the vegetables are tender. Drain well.

3 Transfer the vegetables to a large bowl. Add the onion, cornichons or gherkins, red pepper, olives and capers. Stir in the aioli and season to taste with pepper and lemon juice.

4 Toss the vegetables and aioli together, adjust the seasoning and chill well. Serve garnished with fennel or parsley.

Variation
This salad is delicious using any combination of chopped, cooked vegetables. Work with the calendar and use fresh seasonal ingredients.

Warm Hazelnut Salad Energy 369kcal/1541kJ; Protein 5.4g; Carbohydrate 36.9g, of which sugars 3.4g; Fat 23.2g, of which saturates 2.6g; Cholesterol 0mg; Calcium 27mg; Fibre 2.9g; Sodium 45mg.
Ensaladilla Energy 397kcal/1645kJ; Protein 4.9g; Carbohydrate 25.3g, of which sugars 7.8g; Fat 31.4g, of which saturates 4.9g; Cholesterol 28mg; Calcium 47mg; Fibre 4.4g; Sodium 609mg.

New Potato and Quail's Egg Salad

Freshly cooked quail's eggs and tender waxy potatoes mix perfectly in this salad with the flavours of celery salt and the peppery-tasting rocket leaves. If you prefer your salad a little spicier, then replace the paprika with chilli powder.

Serves 6
900g/2lb new potatoes
50g/2oz/¼ cup butter
15ml/1 tbsp chopped chives
a pinch of celery salt
a pinch of paprika
12 quail's eggs
a few rocket (arugula) leaves
salt and ground black pepper
chopped chives, to garnish

1 Boil the potatoes in a large pan of salted water for about 20 minutes or until tender.

2 Meanwhile, beat the butter and chives together with the celery salt and the paprika.

3 While the potatoes are cooking, boil the eggs for 3 minutes, then drain and plunge into a bowl of cold water. Peel the eggs under running water.

4 Arrange the rocket leaves on individual plates or a serving platter and top with the eggs.

5 Drain the potatoes and add the seasoned butter. Toss well to melt the butter and carefully spoon the potatoes on to the plates of rocket and egg. Garnish the salad with a few of the remaining chopped chives and serve immediately.

Cook's Tips
• *You can buy bags of distinctive peppery rocket (arugula), on its own, or mixed with other leaves, in many supermarkets. It is also easy to grow from seed and makes a worthwhile and versatile addition to a herb patch.*
• *Tiny quail's eggs are available from larger supermarkets and butchers. They make an attractive addition to any salad. If unavailable, use hen's eggs, quartered.*

Beetroot and Potato Salad

A brightly coloured potato salad with a lovely texture. The sweetness of the beetroot contrasts perfectly with the tangy dressing. It is the ideal salad to serve with a selection of cold meats.

Serves 4
4 medium beetroot (beets)
4 potatoes, peeled and diced

1 red onion, finely chopped
150ml/¼ pint/⅔ cup natural (plain) yogurt
10ml/2 tsp cider vinegar
2 small sweet and sour cucumbers, finely chopped
10ml/2 tsp creamed horseradish
salt and ground black pepper
parsley sprigs, to garnish

1 Trim the leafy stalks of the beetroot down to about 2.5cm/1in of the root. Wash, but do not peel, the beetroot. Boil the unpeeled beetroot in a large pan of water for 40 minutes or until tender.

2 Meanwhile, boil the diced potatoes in a separate pan for 20 minutes until just tender.

3 When the beetroot are cooked, rinse and remove the skins. Chop into rough pieces and place in a bowl. Drain the potatoes and add to the bowl, together with the onions.

4 Mix the yogurt, vinegar, cucumbers and horseradish. Reserve a little for a garnish and pour the remainder over the salad. Toss and serve with parsley sprigs and the remaining dressing.

Cook's Tip
If you are short of time, buy vacuum-packed, ready-cooked and peeled beetroot, available in most supermarkets.

Variation
Add a few toasted chopped hazelnuts or walnuts to the yogurt dressing, if you like.

Potato and Egg Salad Energy 204kcal/855kJ; Protein 5.7g; Carbohydrate 24.2g, of which sugars 2g; Fat 10.1g, of which saturates 5.3g; Cholesterol 113mg; Calcium 25mg; Fibre 1.5g; Sodium 102mg.
Beetroot and Potato Energy 141kcal/597kJ; Protein 5.8g; Carbohydrate 28.8g, of which sugars 12.9g; Fat 1.2g, of which saturates 0.3g; Cholesterol 1mg; Calcium 107mg; Fibre 3.4g; Sodium 144mg.

Italian Potato Salad

A combination of antipasto ingredients and potatoes makes this a very substantial and delicious dish. It is a great side dish to grilled meats, or is hearty enough to serve on its own as a vegetarian treat.

Serves 6
1 aubergine (eggplant), sliced
75ml/5 tbsp olive oil

2 garlic cloves, cut into slivers
4 sun-dried tomatoes in oil, halved
2 red (bell) peppers, halved, seeded and cut into large chunks
2 large baking potatoes, cut into wedges
10ml/2 tsp mixed dried Italian herbs
30–45ml/2–3 tbsp balsamic vinegar
salt and ground black pepper

1 Preheat the oven to 200°C/400°F/Gas 6. Place the aubergine slices in a medium roasting pan with the olive oil, garlic and sun-dried tomatoes. Lay the pepper chunks over the top of the aubergine slices.

2 Arrange the potato wedges on top of the other ingredients in the roasting pan. Sprinkle the mixed herbs over the vegetables and season with salt and plenty of ground black pepper. Tightly cover the pan with foil and bake in the oven for about 45 minutes.

3 Remove the pan from the oven and turn the vegetables over. Then return to the oven and cook, with the foil removed, for about 30 minutes, until the vegetables are tender and browned.

4 Transfer the vegetables to a serving dish with a slotted spoon. Add the vinegar and seasoning to the pan, whisk and pour over the vegetables. Garnish with salt and black pepper.

Variation
This is a versatile recipe and it is worth experimenting with other vegetables to accompany the potato wedges. Try using slices of courgettes (zucchini), red onion wedges, green (bell) peppers or slices of fennel bulb.

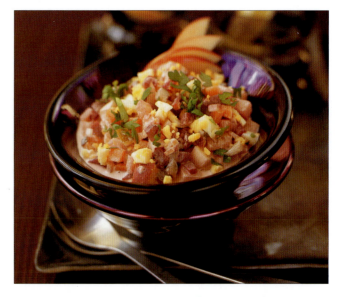

Beetroot, Apple and Potato Salad

This salad is from Finland, where it is known as rosolli. It is served on Christmas Eve, just as the festive excitement mounts. The sweet apple and beetroot are the perfect partner for potatoes, pickled gherkins and eggs.

Serves 4
1 apple
3 cooked potatoes, finely diced

2 large gherkins, finely diced
3 cooked beetroots (beet), finely diced
3 cooked carrots, finely diced
1 onion, finely chopped
500ml/17fl oz/generous 2 cups double (heavy) cream
3 hard-boiled eggs, roughly chopped
15ml/1 tbsp chopped fresh parsley
salt and ground white pepper

1 Cut the apple into small dice. Place the pieces into a large bowl and add the diced potatoes, gherkins, beetroot, carrots and onion. Season the ingredients with plenty of salt and ground black pepper.

2 Carefully mix together all the ingredients in the bowl until they are well combined. Spoon the mixture into individual serving bowls.

3 Place the double cream into a separate bowl. Add any juice from the diced beetroot into the cream to give it additional flavour and an attractive pinkish colour. Stir well until the juice and cream are thoroughly combined.

4 Spoon the beetroot cream over the chopped vegetables and apple. Sprinkle the chopped eggs and parsley over the top of each portion before serving.

Variation
Stir in ½ finely chopped salted herring fillet or 2 finely chopped anchovy fillets to the mixture with the parsley to add an extra dimension to the dish. Omit the added salt if you add the fish, as they will be salty themselves.

Italian Salad Energy 154kcal/644kJ; Protein 2.2g; Carbohydrate 15.6g, of which sugars 3.1g; Fat 9.7g, of which saturates 1.5g; Cholesterol 0mg; Calcium 12mg; Fibre 2.2g; Sodium 17mg.
Beetroot Potato Salad Energy 717kcal/2959kJ; Protein 8.5g; Carbohydrate 11g, of which sugars 10.2g; Fat 71.5g, of which saturates 42.9g; Cholesterol 314mg; Calcium 114mg; Fibre 2.3g; Sodium 132mg.

Potato and Feta Salad

This flavourful potato salad is quick and simple to assemble, making it ideal for a lunch or dinner dish on a busy day.

Serves 4
115g/4oz feta cheese
500g/1¼lb small new potatoes
5 spring onions (scallions), green and white parts finely chopped
15ml/1 tbsp rinsed bottled capers
8–10 black olives
45ml/3 tbsp finely chopped fresh flat leaf parsley
30ml/2 tbsp finely chopped mint
salt and ground black pepper

For the dressing
90–120ml/6–8 tbsp extra virgin olive oil
juice of 1 lemon, or to taste
45ml/3 tbsp Greek (US strained plain) yogurt
45ml/3 tbsp finely chopped fresh dill, plus a few sprigs, to garnish
5ml/1 tsp French mustard

1 Chop the feta cheese into small, even cubes and crumble slightly into a bowl. Set aside.

2 Bring a pan of lightly salted water to the boil and cook the potatoes in their skins for 25–30 minutes, or until tender. Take care not to let them become soggy and disintegrate. Drain them thoroughly and let them cool a little.

3 When the potatoes are cool enough to handle, peel them with your fingers and place them in a large bowl. If they are very small, keep them whole; otherwise cut them into large, even cubes. Add the chopped spring onions, capers, olives, feta cheese and fresh herbs, then toss gently with salad tongs to mix thoroughly.

4 To make the dressing, place the extra virgin olive oil in a bowl with the lemon juice. Whisk thoroughly for a few minutes until the dressing emulsifies and thickens; you may need to add a little more olive oil if it does not thicken.

5 Whisk in the yogurt, dill and mustard, with salt and pepper to taste. Dress the salad while the potatoes are still warm, tossing lightly to coat them.

Feta and Mint Potato Salad

The oddly named pink fir apple potatoes are perfect for this salad, and taste great with feta cheese, yogurt and fresh mint. This dish goes very well with salmon and roasted chicken.

Serves 4
500g/1¼ lb pink fir apple potatoes
90g/3½ oz feta cheese, crumbled

For the dressing
225g/8oz/1 cup natural (plain) yogurt
15g/½oz/½ cup fresh mint leaves
30ml/2 tbsp mayonnaise
salt and ground black pepper

1 Steam the potatoes over a pan of boiling water for about 20 minutes, until tender.

2 Meanwhile, make the dressing. Mix together the yogurt and mint, place in a food processor and pulse until the mint leaves are finely chopped. Scrape the blended mixture into a small bowl, stir in the mayonnaise and season to taste with salt and pepper.

3 Drain the potatoes well and transfer them to a large bowl. Spoon the dressing over the potatoes and scatter the feta cheese on top. Serve immediately.

Cook's Tip
Pink fir apple potatoes have a smooth waxy texture and retain their shape when cooked. Charlotte, Belle de Fontenay and other special salad potatoes could be used instead.

Variations
• Crumbled Kefalotiri or young Manchego could be used instead of the feta.
• For a richer dressing, use Greek (US strained plain) yogurt.

Potato and Feta Salad Energy 138kcal/566kJ; Protein 1.3g; Carbohydrate 1.2g, of which sugars 1.1g; Fat 14.2g, of which saturates 2g; Cholesterol 0mg; Calcium 75mg; Fibre 1.4g; Sodium 40mg.
Feta and Mint Potato Salad Energy 229kcal/959kJ; Protein 8.7g; Carbohydrate 25g, of which sugars 6.3g; Fat 11.2g, of which saturates 4.4g; Cholesterol 22mg; Calcium 204mg; Fibre 1.3g; Sodium 419mg.

Potato and Curry Plant Salad

This tasty and unusual potato salad is heightened by the distinctive and delicious aroma of curry plant leaves. This salad can be prepared well in advance and is therefore a useful dish to make for a buffet or picnic.

Serves 6
1kg/2lb new potatoes, in skins
300ml/½ pint/1¼ cups
   store-bought mayonnaise
6 curry plant leaves,
   roughly chopped
salt and ground black pepper
mixed lettuce or other salad
   greens, to serve

1 Place the potatoes in a pan of salted water and boil for about 15 minutes or until tender. Drain in a colander and place in a large bowl to cool slightly.

2 Meanwhile, make the dressing. In a separate bowl, mix together the mayonnaise with the curry plant leaves and ground black pepper.

3 Add the dressing to the potatoes while they are still warm. Stir until the ingredients are well combined and the potatoes are evenly coated. Season to taste with a little salt and some more ground black pepper, if necessary.

4 Leave the salad to cool to room temperature, then serve on a bed of mixed lettuce or other assorted salad leaves.

> **Cook's Tips**
> • The curry plant is a shrub of the daisy family from southern Europe. It is so called because its silvery needle-like leaves have a mild curry flavour. The leaves can be used in a similar way to other woody herbs such as rosemary. It should not be confused with curry leaves.
> • The quality of the mayonnaise is important to this recipe. Buy the best version you can find.
> • Curry plant leaves can lose their potency when dried; to make the most of their distinctive aroma, always try and find fresh leaves. They have a short shelf-life but freeze well.

Pasta, Asparagus and Potato Salad

This delicious wholewheat pasta and potato salad is a real treat, especially when made with fresh asparagus that is just in season.

60ml/4 tbsp extra virgin olive oil
350g/12oz baby new potatoes
225g/8oz asparagus
115g/4oz piece Parmesan cheese
salt and ground black pepper

Serves 4
225g/8oz wholewheat pasta
   shapes, such as fusilli

1 Cook the pasta in a pan of salted, boiling water for about 10–12 minutes, or according to the instructions on the packet, until it is al dente.

2 Drain well and toss with the olive oil while the pasta is still warm. Season with salt and ground black pepper.

3 Scrub the potatoes and cook in boiling salted water for about 15 minutes, or until tender. Drain the potatoes and toss together with the pasta.

4 Trim any woody ends off the asparagus and halve the stalks if very long. Blanch in boiling salted water for 6 minutes, until bright green and still crunchy. Drain well. Plunge into cold water to stop the asparagus cooking and allow to cool. Drain and dry on kitchen paper.

5 Toss the asparagus with the potatoes and pasta, adjust the seasoning to taste and transfer to a serving bowl. Using a vegetable peeler, shave the Parmesan over the salad and serve.

> **Cook's Tip**
> Asparagus only has a short season in most areas, usually for one or two months in spring and early summer – although greenhouse-grown asparagus may be available longer in some regions. It is grown in sandy soil, so wash thoroughly before use to ensure there is no grit in the spearheads.

Potato and Curry Leaf Salad Energy 342kcal/1421kJ; Protein 2.9g; Carbohydrate 21g, of which sugars 3.1g; Fat 28g, of which saturates 4.3g; Cholesterol 27mg; Calcium 27mg; Fibre 1.8g; Sodium 178mg.
Pasta and Potato Salad Energy 487kcal/2042kJ; Protein 22g; Carbohydrate 52.5g, of which sugars 4.3g; Fat 22.4g, of which saturates 7.8g; Cholesterol 29mg; Calcium 383mg; Fibre 6.6g; Sodium 397mg.

New Potato Spring Salad

This potato salad makes a satisfying meal. You could also use other spring vegetables, if you like.

Serves 4
675g/1½lb small new potatoes, halved
400g/14oz can broad (fava) beans, drained
115g/4oz cherry tomatoes
50g/2oz/⅓ cup walnut halves
30ml/2 tbsp white wine vinegar
15ml/1 tbsp wholegrain mustard
60ml/4 tbsp olive oil
pinch of sugar
225g/8oz young asparagus spears, trimmed
6 spring onions (scallions), trimmed
salt and ground black pepper
baby spinach leaves, to serve

1 Put the potatoes in a pan. Cover with cold water and bring to the boil. Cook for 10–12 minutes, until tender.

2 Meanwhile, put the broad beans into a bowl. Cut the tomatoes in half and add them to the bowl with the walnuts.

3 Put the white wine vinegar, mustard, olive oil and sugar into a jar. Add salt and pepper to taste. Close the jar tightly and shake well until combined.

4 Add the asparagus to the potatoes and cook for 3 minutes more. Drain the cooked vegetables well, cool under cold running water and drain again. Thickly slice the potatoes. Cut the spring onions into halves.

5 Add the asparagus, potatoes and spring onions to the bowl containing the broad bean mixture. Pour the dressing over the salad and mix until the ingredients are well combined. Serve on a bed of baby spinach leaves.

> **Variations**
> • Use other nuts such as hazelnuts or pecans in place of the walnuts, if you like.
> • Other beans will also work well in this recipe. Try cannellini, butter (lima) or haricot beans instead of the broad beans.

Coronation Salad

The famous salad dressing used in this dish was created especially for the coronation dinner of Queen Elizabeth II. It makes a truly wonderful accompaniment to hard-boiled eggs and potatoes.

Serves 6
450g/1lb new potatoes
45ml/3 tbsp French dressing
3 spring onions (scallions), chopped
6 eggs, hard-boiled and halved
frilly lettuce leaves
¼ cucumber, cut into thin strips
6 large radishes, sliced
1 carton salad cress
salt and ground black pepper

For the coronation dressing
30ml/2 tbsp olive oil
1 small onion, chopped
15ml/1 tbsp mild curry powder or korma spice mix
10ml/2 tsp tomato purée (paste)
30ml/2 tbsp lemon juice
30ml/2 tbsp sherry
300ml/½ pint/1¼ cups mayonnaise
150ml/¼ pint/⅔ cup natural (plain) yogurt

1 Boil the potatoes in salted water until tender. Drain, then transfer to a large bowl and toss them in the French dressing while they are still warm.

2 Stir in the spring onions and the salt and pepper to taste, and allow to cool thoroughly.

3 Meanwhile, make the coronation dressing. Heat the oil in a small pan and fry the onion for 3 minutes, until soft. Stir in the curry powder or spice mix and fry for a further 1 minute. Remove from the heat and mix in the tomato purée, lemon juice, sherry, mayonnaise and yogurt.

4 Stir the dressing into the potatoes, add the eggs, then chill. Line a serving platter with lettuce leaves and pile the salad in the centre. Sprinkle over the cucumber, radishes and cress.

> **Cook's Tip**
> Try making your own mayonnaise and French dressing for this dish, if time allows.

New Spring Salad Energy 323kcal/1343kJ; Protein 5.2g; Carbohydrate 21.5g, of which sugars 2.7g; Fat 24.7g, of which saturates 4g; Cholesterol 88mg; Calcium 49mg; Fibre 2g; Sodium 149mg.
Coronation Salad Energy 587kcal/2429kJ; Protein 10.1g; Carbohydrate 17.1g, of which sugars 4.7g; Fat 51.6g, of which saturates 8.8g; Cholesterol 228mg; Calcium 97mg; Fibre 1.1g; Sodium 401mg.

Chef's Potato Salad

This delicious and flexible potato salad can be adapted to contain all of your favourite ingredients. It is also a good opportunity to use up any leftover vegetables and small pieces of cheese from the refrigerator. For these reasons, the quantities given are approximate.

Serves 6
450g/1lb cooked new potatoes, halved if large
2 carrots, grated coarsely
½ small fennel bulb or 2 sticks celery, sliced thinly
50g/2oz sliced button mushrooms
¼ cucumber, sliced or chopped
small green or red (bell) pepper, sliced
200g/7oz/1 cup cooked pulses, such as red kidney beans or green lentils
1 Little Gem (Bibb) or baby lettuce, or 1 head chicory (endive)
2–3 hard-boiled eggs, quartered and/or grated cheese, to serve
½ carton salad cress, chopped

For the dressing
60ml/4 tbsp mayonnaise
45ml/3 tbsp natural (plain) yogurt
30ml/2 tbsp milk
30ml/2 tbsp chopped fresh chives or spring onion (scallion) tops
salt and ground black pepper

1 Place all the vegetables and beans or lentils (except the lettuce or chicory) into a large mixing bowl.

2 Line a large serving platter or individual plates with the lettuce or chicory leaves – creating a nest for the other salad ingredients to sit in.

3 In a separate bowl, mix all the dressing ingredients together until well combined. Pour over the vegetables and beans or lentils in the mixing bowl.

4 Toss the salad thoroughly in the dressing, season well with salt and ground black pepper, then pile into the centre of the lettuce nest on the serving platter.

5 Top the salad with the hard-boiled egg quarters, cheese or both, and then sprinkle over the chopped cress. Serve the salad lightly chilled.

Watercress and Potato Salad

New potatoes are equally good hot or cold, and this colourful, nutritious salad is an ideal way of making the most of them. This recipe is for making in the microwave but it can easily be made on the stove by boiling the potatoes in a pan of water.

Serves 4
450g/1lb small new or salad potatoes, skin on
45ml/3 tbsp water
1 bunch watercress
200g/7oz/1½ cups cherry tomatoes, halved
30ml/2 tbsp pumpkin seeds
45ml/3 tbsp low-fat fromage frais or low-fat cream cheese
15ml/1 tbsp cider vinegar
5ml/1 tsp soft light brown sugar
salt and ground black pepper
pinch of paprika

1 Place the potatoes and water in a microwave-proof bowl. Cover and microwave on the high setting for 7–10 minutes, stirring halfway through cooking. Leave to stand, covered, for 3 minutes, then drain and leave to cool.

2 Put the potatoes in a large mixing bowl. Add the watercress, tomatoes and pumpkin seeds and mix together until the ingredients are well combined.

3 Place the fromage frais or cream cheese, vinegar, sugar, salt, pepper and paprika to taste in a screw-top jar and shake well to mix. Pour over the salad just before serving.

> **Variation**
> To make a spinach and potato salad, substitute about 225g/8oz fresh baby spinach leaves for the watercress.

> **Cook's Tip**
> If you are preparing this salad in advance, mix the dressing in the jar and set aside until needed. Shake the dressing again and toss it into the salad just before serving.

Chef's Salad Energy 229kcal/956kJ; Protein 9g; Carbohydrate 24.1g, of which sugars 7.1g; Fat 11.5g, of which saturates 2.2g; Cholesterol 103mg; Calcium 93mg; Fibre 5.2g; Sodium 240mg.
Watercress Salad Energy 152kcal/644kJ; Protein 6.1g; Carbohydrate 23.1g, of which sugars 5.2g; Fat 4.6g, of which saturates 0.7g; Cholesterol 0mg; Calcium 114mg; Fibre 2.8g; Sodium 45mg.

Russian Potato Salad

This potato salad became fashionable in the hotel dining rooms of the 1920s and 1930s. Originally it consisted of lightly cooked vegetables, eggs, shellfish and mayonnaise. Today we find it diced in plastic pots in supermarkets. This version recalls better days and plays on the theme of the Fabergé egg.

Serves 4

115g/4oz large button
   (white) mushrooms
350g/12oz cooked peeled
   prawns (shrimp)
120ml/4fl oz/¹/₂ cup mayonnaise
15ml/1 tbsp lemon juice
1 large gherkin, chopped, or
   30ml/2 tbsp capers
115g/4oz broad (fava)
   beans, shelled
115g/4oz small new potatoes,
   scrubbed or scraped
115g/4oz young carrots, trimmed
   and peeled
115g/4oz baby corn
115g/4oz baby turnips, trimmed
15ml/1 tbsp olive oil, preferably
   French or Italian
4 eggs, hard-boiled and shelled
25g/1oz canned anchovy fillets,
   cut into fine strips
salt and ground black pepper
paprika, to garnish

1 Slice the mushrooms, then cut into matchsticks. Mix with the prawns. Combine the mayonnaise and lemon juice and fold half into the mushrooms and prawns, add the gherkin or capers and season with salt and pepper.

2 Bring a large pan of salted water to the boil, add the broad beans and cook for 3 minutes. Drain and cool under cold running water, then pinch the beans between thumb and forefinger to release them from their tough skins.

3 Boil the potatoes in a pan of water for about 20 minutes, and the remaining vegetables for 6 minutes. Drain and cool under running water.

4 Moisten the vegetables with olive oil and divide between four shallow serving bowls. Spoon the dressed prawns into the centre of each serving and place a hard-boiled egg in the centre. Decorate the egg with strips of anchovy and sprinkle with paprika. Serve the remaining mayonnaise separately so diners can help themselves.

Japanese-style Potato Salad

In this Asian salad, the potatoes are stir-fried with carrots and onion, then cooked in stock before the egg is added.

Serves 4

4 medium potatoes
2 carrots
1 large mild onion
20ml/4 tsp oil
1 vegetable stock (bouillon) cube
20ml/4 tsp rice vinegar
10ml/2 tsp sugar
2.5ml/¹/₂ tsp salt, plus extra
   for the cucumber
2 eggs, beaten
¹/₂ cucumber

1 Cut the potatoes lengthways into four, then slice the pieces across into thick chunks. Soak the potatoes in cold water for 2 minutes and drain well.

2 Halve the carrots vertically, then slice them across into chunks. Cut the onion into thick wedges.

3 Heat the oil in a deep frying pan or pan. Stir-fry the potatoes, carrots and onion for 1 minute. Dissolve the vegetable stock cube in 200ml/7fl oz/scant 1 cup boiling water and pour it into the pan. Add the rice vinegar, sugar and salt. Cover and simmer for 5 minutes.

4 Uncover the pan and cook over a moderate heat until all the liquid has evaporated. Shake the pan gently occasionally to prevent the vegetables from sticking to the base of the pan as the liquid dries up.

5 Remove from the heat and allow to cool for 30 seconds, then add the beaten egg, stirring quickly until the egg sets. Transfer to a dish and leave to cool, then chill.

6 Meanwhile halve the cucumber vertically and cut it into thin slices. Place the cucumber in a colander or sieve (strainer) over a bowl. Sprinkle with a little salt and leave to stand for 10 minutes. Gently squeeze out the liquid from the cucumber.

7 Add the cucumber to the potato mixture and check the seasoning, adding more salt, if necessary. Serve chilled.

Russian Salad Energy 455kcal/1890kJ; Protein 28.1g; Carbohydrate 12.8g, of which sugars 5g; Fat 32.8g, of which saturates 5.7g; Cholesterol 387mg; Calcium 162mg; Fibre 4.3g; Sodium 963mg.
Japanese-style Salad Energy 206kcal/868kJ; Protein 6.3g; Carbohydrate 31.3g, of which sugars 8.5g; Fat 7.2g, of which saturates 1.4g; Cholesterol 95mg; Calcium 42mg; Fibre 2.8g; Sodium 62mg.

Curried Potato Salad with Mango Dressing

This sweet and spicy potato salad is a wonderful partner to roasted meats.

Serves 4–6
900g/2lb new potatoes
15ml/1 tbsp olive oil
1 onion, sliced into rings
1 garlic clove, crushed
5ml/1 tsp ground cumin
5ml/1 tsp ground coriander
1 mango, peeled, stoned (pitted) and diced
30ml/2 tbsp demerara (raw) sugar
30ml/2 tbsp lime juice
15ml/1 tbsp sesame seeds
salt and ground black pepper
deep fried coriander (cilantro) leaves, to garnish

1 Cut the potatoes in half, then cook them in their skins in boiling salted water until tender. Drain well.

2 Heat the oil in a frying pan (skillet) and fry the onion and garlic over a low heat for 10 minutes until they start to brown.

3 Stir in the ground cumin and coriander and fry for a few seconds. Stir in the mango and sugar and fry for 5 minutes, until soft. Remove the pan from the heat and squeeze in the lime juice. Season with salt and pepper.

4 Place the potatoes in a large bowl and spoon over the mango dressing. Sprinkle with sesame seeds and serve while the dressing is still warm. Garnish the salad with the deep fried coriander leaves.

Cook's Tip
To prepare the mango, cut through the mango lengthwise on either side of the stone (pit) to slice off two sections. Leaving the skin on each section, cross hatch the flesh, then bend it back so that the cubes stand proud of the skin. Slice them off with a small knife. Peel the remaining central section of the mango, then cut off the remaining flesh in chunks and dice.

Hot Cajun Potato Salad

In Cajun country in Louisiana, where Tabasco sauce originates, hot means really hot, so you can go to town with this potato salad if you think you can take it.

Serves 6–8
8 waxy potatoes
1 green (bell) pepper, diced
1 large gherkin, chopped
4 spring onions (scallions), shredded
3 hard-boiled eggs, shelled and chopped
250ml/8fl oz/1 cup mayonnaise
15ml/1 tbsp Dijon mustard
salt and ground black pepper
Tabasco sauce, to taste
pinch or two of cayenne
sliced gherkin, to garnish
mayonnaise, to serve

1 Cook the potatoes in their skins in boiling salted water until tender. Drain and leave to cool.

2 When the potatoes are cool enough to handle, but while they are still warm, peel them and cut into coarse chunks. Place them in a large bowl.

3 Add the green pepper, gherkin, spring onions and hard-boiled eggs to the potatoes and toss gently to combine.

4 In a separate bowl, mix the mayonnaise with the mustard and season with salt, black pepper and Tabasco sauce to taste.

5 Pour the dressing over the potato mixture and toss gently so that the potatoes are well coated. Sprinkle with a pinch or two of cayenne pepper and garnish with a few slices of gherkin. Serve with extra mayonnaise.

Cook's Tips
• *The salad is good to eat immediately, when the potatoes are just cool. If you make it in advance and chill it, let it come back to room temperature before serving.*
• *Tabasco is one of thousands of commercial hot pepper sauces on the market, of varying intensity: use your favourite brand to make this salad.*

Cajun Potato Salad Energy 289kcal/1197kJ; Protein 4g; Carbohydrate 10.3g, of which sugars 2.7g; Fat 26.1g, of which saturates 4.2g; Cholesterol 95mg; Calcium 21mg; Fibre 0.9g; Sodium 229mg.
Curried Potato Salad Energy 174kcal/737kJ; Protein 3.3g; Carbohydrate 33.7g, of which sugars 11.2g; Fat 3.8g, of which saturates 0.7g; Cholesterol 0mg; Calcium 34mg; Fibre 2.5g; Sodium 18mg.

Gado Gado Salad with Peanut Sambal

This Indonesian potato salad combines lightly steamed vegetables and hard-boiled eggs with a richly flavoured dressing made from peanut butter and soy sauce.

Serves 6
225g/8oz new potatoes, halved
2 carrots, cut into sticks
115g/4oz green beans
1/2 small cauliflower, broken into florets
1/4 firm white cabbage, shredded
200g/7oz bean or lentil sprouts

4 eggs, hard-boiled and quartered
bunch of watercress (optional)

For the sauce
90ml/6 tbsp crunchy peanut butter
300ml/1/2 pint/1 1/4 cups cold water
1 garlic clove, crushed
30ml/2 tbsp dark soy sauce
15ml/1 tbsp dry sherry
10ml/2 tsp caster (superfine) sugar
15ml/1 tbsp fresh lemon juice
5ml/1 tsp anchovy essence (paste)

1 Place the halved potatoes in a metal colander or steamer and set over a pan of gently boiling water. Cover the pan or steamer with a lid and cook the potatoes for 10 minutes.

2 Add the rest of the vegetables to the steamer and steam for a further 10 minutes, until tender. Cool and arrange on a platter with the egg quarters and the watercress, if using.

3 Beat together all the ingredients for the sauce in a large mixing bowl until smooth. Drizzle a little sauce over each salad then pour the rest into a small bowl and serve separately.

Variation
There are a whole range of nut butters available in supermarkets and health-food stores. Try using hazelnut, almond or cashew nut butter in place of peanut butter to create a slightly milder flavoured sauce. Alternatively, make your own peanut butter by blending 225g/8oz/2 cups peanuts with 120ml/4fl oz/1/2 cup oil in a food processor.

Caribbean Potato Salad

Colourful vegetables in a creamy smooth dressing make this piquant potato salad ideal to serve on its own or with a vegetable flan.

Serves 6
900g/2lb small waxy or salad potatoes
2 red (bell) peppers, seeded and diced
2 celery sticks, finely chopped
1 shallot, finely chopped
2 or 3 spring onions (scallions), finely chopped
1 mild fresh green chilli, seeded and finely chopped
1 garlic clove, crushed
10ml/2 tsp finely chopped chives
10ml/2 tsp finely chopped basil
15ml/1 tbsp finely chopped fresh parsley
15ml/1 tbsp single (light) cream
30ml/2 tbsp salad cream
15ml/1 tbsp mayonnaise
5ml/1 tsp Dijon mustard
7.5ml/1/2 tbsp sugar
chopped chives and chopped red chilli, to garnish

1 Cook the potatoes in a large pan of boiling water until tender but still firm. Drain and set aside. When cool enough to handle, cut the potatoes into 2.5cm/1in cubes and place in a large salad bowl.

2 Add the peppers, celery, shallot and spring onions to the potatoes in the salad bowl, together with the chilli, garlic and all the chopped herbs.

3 Mix together the cream, salad cream, mayonnaise, mustard and sugar in a small bowl. Stir well until the mixture is thoroughly combined and forms a smooth dressing.

4 Pour the dressing over the potatoes and stir gently to coat. Serve garnished with chives and chopped red chilli.

Variation
To transform this light salad into a more substantial and complete meal, add quartered hard-boiled eggs and cooked green beans, serve on a bed of lettuce and top with sliced black olives.

Caribbean Potato Salad Energy 176kcal/742kJ; Protein 3.8g; Carbohydrate 31.3g, of which sugars 8.7g; Fat 4.8g, of which saturates 1g; Cholesterol 5mg; Calcium 42mg; Fibre 3.2g; Sodium 92mg.
Gado Gado Salad Energy 199kcal/831kJ; Protein 10.5g; Carbohydrate 14g, of which sugars 6.6g; Fat 11.3g, of which saturates 2.9g; Cholesterol 127mg; Calcium 58mg; Fibre 3.1g; Sodium 819mg.

Baked Sweet Potato Salad

This sweet potato salad has a truly tropical taste and is ideal served with Asian or Caribbean dishes.

Serves 4–6
1kg/2¼lb sweet potatoes
1 red (bell) pepper, seeded and finely diced
3 celery sticks, finely diced
¼ red onion, finely chopped
1 fresh red chilli, finely chopped

salt and ground black pepper
coriander (cilantro) leaves, to garnish

For the dressing
45ml/3 tbsp chopped fresh coriander (cilantro)
juice of 1 lime
150ml/¼ pint/⅔ cup natural (plain) yogurt

1 Preheat the oven to 200°C/400°F/Gas 6. Wash the potatoes, and pierce them all over with a fork. Place in the oven and bake for about 40 minutes, or until tender.

2 Meanwhile, make the dressing. Whisk together the coriander, lime juice and yogurt in a small bowl and season to taste with salt and pepper. Chill in the refrigerator while you prepare the remaining salad ingredients.

3 In a large bowl, mix the diced red pepper, celery, chopped onion and chilli together.

4 Remove the potatoes from the oven. As soon as they are cool enough to handle, peel and cut them into cubes. Add them to the bowl. Drizzle the dressing over and toss carefully. Taste and adjust the seasoning, if necessary. Serve, garnished with coriander leaves.

Cook's Tip
It is generally thought that the seeds are the hottest part of a chilli. In fact, the seeds contain no capsaicin – the hot element in chillies – but it is intensely concentrated in the membrane surrounding them. Removing the seeds from the chilli usually removes this extra-hot flesh.

Spicy Potato Salad

This tasty potato salad is quick to prepare, and makes a satisfying accompaniment to plainly cooked meat or fish.

Serves 6
900g/2lb potatoes
2 red (bell) peppers, seeded and diced
1 shallot, finely chopped
2 or 3 spring onions (scallions), finely chopped
1 green chilli, seeded and finely chopped

2 celery sticks, finely chopped
1 garlic clove, crushed
10ml/2 tsp finely chopped fresh chives
10ml/2 tsp finely chopped fresh basil
15ml/1 tbsp finely chopped fresh parsley
15ml/1 tbsp single (light) cream
30ml/2 tbsp salad cream
15ml/1 tbsp mayonnaise
5ml/1 tsp prepared mild mustard
7.5ml/1½ tsp sugar
salt
chopped fresh chives, to garnish

1 Peel the potatoes. Boil in salted water for 10–12 minutes, until tender. Drain and cool, then cut into cubes and place in a large mixing bowl.

2 Add the chopped red peppers, shallot, spring onions, green chilli and celery to the potatoes, together with the crushed garlic and chopped herbs. Stir gently until the ingredients are thoroughly combined.

3 To make the dressing, blend the cream, salad cream, mayonnaise, mustard and sugar in a small bowl, stirring until the mixture is well combined.

4 Pour the dressing over the salad and toss gently to coat evenly. Serve garnished with the chopped chives.

Variation
If you prefer, leave out the salad cream and increase the amount of mayonnaise by 30ml/2 tbsp. To turn the salad into a light lunch dish, add some diced ham and a handful of cooked green beans that have been refreshed under cold running water.

Sweet Potato Salad Energy 176kcal/750kJ; Protein 4g; Carbohydrate 40.4g, of which sugars 14.1g; Fat 1g, of which saturates 0.3g; Cholesterol 0mg; Calcium 116mg; Fibre 5.2g; Sodium 103mg.
Spicy Potato Salad Energy 178kcal/749kJ; Protein 3.9g; Carbohydrate 31.4g, of which sugars 8.7g; Fat 4.9g, of which saturates 1g; Cholesterol 5mg; Calcium 48mg; Fibre 3.3g; Sodium 118mg.

Chicken and Potato Salmagundi

Salads, with the ingredients elaborately arranged, were fashionable in 16th-century England, containing chopped meat, anchovies, potatoes and eggs, garnished with onions, lemon juice, oil and other condiments. This variation of the dish is thought to come from Northumbria.

Serves 4–6

1 large chicken, weighing
   about 2kg/4¹/₂lb
1 onion
1 carrot
1 celery stick
2 bay leaves
large sprig of thyme
10 black peppercorns
500g/1¹/₄lb new or baby potatoes
225g/8oz carrots, cut into
   small sticks
225g/8oz sugar snap peas
4 eggs
¹/₂ cucumber, thinly sliced
8–12 cherry tomatoes
8–12 green olives stuffed
   with pimento

For the dressing

75ml/5 tbsp olive oil
30ml/2 tbsp lemon juice
2.5ml/¹/₂ tsp sugar
1.5ml/¹/₄ tsp ready-made English
   (hot) mustard
salt and ground black pepper

1 Put the chicken in a deep pan with the onion, carrot, celery, bay leaves, thyme and peppercorns. Add water to cover by at least 2.5cm/1in. Bring to the boil and simmer gently for 45 minutes or until the chicken is cooked, then leave to cool in the stock for several hours to keep it moist.

2 Whisk together the ingredients for the dressing. Set aside.

3 Using a separate pan for each, cook the potatoes, carrots and peas in lightly salted boiling water until just tender, drain and then rinse under cold water. Halve the potatoes. Hard-boil the eggs, cool, shell and cut into quarters.

4 Lift the chicken out of the stock, remove the meat and cut or tear into bitesize pieces.

5 Arrange the vegetables, chicken and eggs on a large platter, or in a large bowl, and add the tomatoes and olives. Just before serving, drizzle the salad dressing over the top.

Bacon Potato Salad

Use either new or other waxy potatoes for this classic East European salad. They will hold their shape better than the floury variety when cooked.

Serves 6

675g/1¹/₂lb potatoes, scrubbed
45ml/3 tbsp olive oil
4 smoked streaky (fatty) bacon
   rashers (strips), rinded
   and chopped
10ml/2 tsp lemon juice
2 celery sticks, chopped
2 pickled sour cucumbers, diced
5ml/1 tsp Dusseldorf or
   German mustard
45ml/3 tbsp mayonnaise
30ml/2 tbsp chopped fresh chives
15ml/1 tbsp chopped fresh dill
salt and ground black pepper
chopped fresh chives and dill,
   to garnish
lettuce leaves, to serve

1 Cook the potatoes in a pan of boiling salted water for 15 minutes, until just tender. Drain, allow to cool for 5 minutes, then slice thickly and set aside in a bowl.

2 Meanwhile, heat 15ml/1 tbsp of the oil in a frying pan and fry the bacon for about 5 minutes, until crispy. Remove the bacon and set aside.

3 Stir the remaining oil and lemon juice into the pan, then pour over the sliced warm potatoes. Add the chopped celery, cucumber and half the crispy bacon and mix until all the ingredients are well combined. Leave to cool.

4 Blend the mustard in a small bowl with the mayonnaise, herbs and a little seasoning. Add to the potatoes and toss well to coat. Spoon the potatoes into a serving dish and sprinkle with the remaining bacon. Garnish with the fresh herbs and serve with lettuce leaves.

Cook's Tip
German mustard is typically dark with a medium heat and a slightly sweet flavour; it is an ideal accompaniment for sausages, ham and bacon.

Salmagundi Energy 397kcal/1664kJ; Protein 41.2g; Carbohydrate 24.9g, of which sugars 8.7g; Fat 15.5g, of which saturates 3g; Cholesterol 220mg; Calcium 63mg; Fibre 4.6g; Sodium 155mg.
Bacon Potato Salad Energy 206kcal/863kJ; Protein 2.8g; Carbohydrate 24.3g, of which sugars 2.1g; Fat 11.5g, of which saturates 1.7g; Cholesterol 0mg; Calcium 22mg; Fibre 1.8g; Sodium 19mg.

Warm Potato Salad with Bacon and Shallot Dressing

This warm potato salad with bacon makes a fine accompaniment for grilled sausages or delicious smoked mackerel. Vinegar, mustard and finely chopped herbs make a punchy dressing.

Serves 6
900g/2lb small new or
 salad potatoes
90ml/6 tbsp olive oil
200g/7oz dry-cure streaky (fatty)
 bacon, smoked or unsmoked,
 cut into strips

3 shallots, chopped
1 small garlic clove,
 finely chopped
30ml/2 tbsp white wine vinegar
30ml/2 tbsp dry white vermouth
 or white wine
5ml/1 tsp French mustard
45–60ml/3–4 tbsp chopped fresh
 herbs, such as chervil, parsley
 and tarragon
15ml/1 tbsp chopped fresh chives
salt and ground black pepper
whole chives, to garnish

1 Cook the potatoes in boiling, salted water for between 15–20 minutes until tender. Drain, leave to cool a little, then peel. Slice the potatoes directly into a bowl and add 45ml/3 tbsp of the olive oil. Season with ground black pepper to taste. Stir the potatoes to coat, then set aside.

2 Heat a further 30ml/2 tbsp of the olive oil in a heavy frying pan. Fry the bacon until crisp and lightly browned, then add the shallots and cook, stirring constantly, for 2–3 minutes. Add the garlic and cook for a further 1 minute. Scrape the contents of the pan over the potatoes and stir to mix.

3 Return the pan to the heat. Add the vinegar and vermouth or wine and reduce a little, then stir in the mustard. Immediately pour this mixture over the potatoes. Add most of the mixed herbs and stir to mix.

4 Spoon the salad into a large serving bowl or individual bowls. Drizzle the remaining oil over the top and sprinkle with the remaining herbs and the chives. Garnish with whole chives, then serve immediately.

Sweet Potato, Egg, Pork and Beetroot Salad

This dish is a delicious way to use up any leftover roast pork. The flavour of the sweet potato balances well with the bitterness of the salad leaves.

Serve 4
900g/2lb sweet potatoes
4 chicory (Belgian endive) heads
5 hard-boiled eggs, shelled

450g/1lb pickled young
 beetroot (beets)
175g/6oz cold roast pork
salt

For the dressing
75ml/5 tbsp groundnut (peanut)
 or sunflower oil
30ml/2 tbsp white wine vinegar
10ml/2 tsp Dijon mustard
5ml/1 tsp fennel seeds, crushed

1 Peel the sweet potatoes and dice into equal pieces. Add the diced sweet potatoes to a pan of boiling salted water. Bring back to the boil, then simmer for 10–15 minutes, or until the potatoes are soft. Drain and allow to cool.

2 To make the dressing, combine the groundnut or sunflower oil, vinegar, mustard and fennel seeds in a screw-top jar and shake vigorously to mix.

3 Separate the chicory leaves and arrange them around the edge of four individual plates.

4 Pour two-thirds of the dressing over the sweet potatoes, then stir to coat well. Spoon on top of the chicory leaves.

5 Slice the eggs and beetroot, and arrange in a circle on top of the sweet potato. Slice the pork, then cut into 4cm/1½in strips and moisten with the rest of the dressing. Pile the pork into the centre of each salad. Season with salt and serve.

> **Cook's Tip**
> To crush the fennel seeds, grind using a mortar and pestle. If you don't have these, use two dessertspoons instead.

Bacon Potato Salad Energy 318kcal/1319kJ; Protein 12.4g; Carbohydrate 10.9g, of which sugars 2.2g; Fat 25.4g, of which saturates 4g; Cholesterol 198mg; Calcium 106mg; Fibre 2.3g; Sodium 268mg.
Sweet Potato Salad Energy 507kcal/2132kJ; Protein 21.9g; Carbohydrate 56.7g, of which sugars 20.9g; Fat 23.3g, of which saturates 4.4g; Cholesterol 265mg; Calcium 119mg; Fibre 7.7g; Sodium 283mg.

Frankfurter and Potato Salad with Mustard Dressing

This is a last-minute potato salad that is ideal for serving as a midweek meal.

Serves 4
675g/1½lb small new potatoes, scrubbed or scraped
2 eggs
350g/12oz frankfurters
1 round (butterhead) or frisée lettuce

225g/8oz young spinach leaves, stems removed
salt and ground black pepper

For the dressing
45ml/3 tbsp safflower oil
30ml/2 tbsp olive oil
15ml/1 tbsp white wine vinegar
10ml/2 tsp mustard
5ml/1 tsp caraway seeds, crushed

1 Bring the potatoes to the boil in salted water and simmer for about 15 minutes, or until just tender. Drain, cover and keep warm. Hard-boil the eggs for 12 minutes. Refresh in cold water, shell and cut into quarters.

2 Score the frankfurter skins corkscrew fashion with a small knife, then cover with boiling water and simmer for about 5 minutes to heat through. Drain well, cover and keep warm.

3 To make the dressing, place all the ingredients in a screw-top jar and shake vigorously to combine.

4 Moisten the salad leaves with half the dressing and divide between four large serving plates. Moisten the warm potatoes and frankfurters with the remainder of the dressing and scatter over the salad.

5 Finish the salad with sections of hard-boiled egg, season with salt and black pepper and serve warm.

> **Cook's Tip**
> This salad has a German slant to it and calls for a sweet-and-sour German-style mustard. American mustard is similar.

Warm Salad of Bayonne Ham and New Potatoes

With a lightly spiced nutty dressing, this warm potato salad is as delicious as it is fashionable, and it will make an excellent choice for informal entertaining.

Serves 4
225g/8oz new potatoes, halved if large
50g/2oz green beans
115g/4oz young spinach leaves

2 spring onions (scallions), sliced
4 eggs, hard-boiled and quartered
50g/2oz Bayonne ham, cut into strips
juice of ½ lemon
salt and ground black pepper

For the dressing
60ml/4 tbsp olive oil
5ml/1 tsp ground turmeric
5ml/1 tsp ground cumin
50g/2oz/⅓ cup shelled hazelnuts

1 Cook the potatoes in boiling salted water for 10–15 minutes, or until tender, then drain well.

2 Cook the green beans in boiling water for 2 minutes or until just tender, then drain.

3 Toss the potatoes and beans with the spinach and spring onions in a bowl.

4 Arrange the hard-boiled egg quarters on the salad and sprinkle the strips of ham over the top. Sprinkle with the lemon juice and season with plenty of salt and pepper.

5 To make the dressing, heat all the ingredients in a large frying pan and continue to cook, stirring frequently, until the nuts have just turned golden. Pour the hot, nutty dressing over the salad. Serve immediately.

> **Variation**
> Replace the potatoes with a 400g/14oz can mixed beans and pulses. Drain and rinse the beans and pulses, then drain again. Toss lightly with the green beans and spring onions.

Frankfurter Salad Energy 561kcal/2336kJ; Protein 20.5g; Carbohydrate 31g, of which sugars 5.9g; Fat 40.4g, of which saturates 11g; Cholesterol 162mg; Calcium 160mg; Fibre 3.9g; Sodium 1014mg.
Bayonne Ham and Potatoes Energy 323kcal/1341kJ; Protein 12.4g; Carbohydrate 10.9g, of which sugars 2.2g; Fat 25.8g, of which saturates 4.2g; Cholesterol 199mg; Calcium 105mg; Fibre 2.3g; Sodium 270mg.

Bacon and New Potato Salad

A rich mustard sauce gives the new potatoes added flavour and colour.

Serves 4–6
5 eggs
30–45ml/2–3 tbsp Dijon mustard
200g/7oz mayonnaise
3 celery sticks, finely chopped
115g/4oz bacon lardons
900g/2lb small new potatoes
30ml/2 tbsp chopped fresh flat
    leaf parsley
salt and ground black pepper

1 Place the eggs carefully into a pan of water and bring to the boil. Simmer for 5–8 minutes, drain and plunge the eggs straight into a bowl containing cold water.

2 Peel the eggs and mash three in a large bowl with a fork. Stir in the mustard, mayonnaise and celery. Season with salt and pepper. Thin down the dressing with a little water, if you wish.

3 Fry the bacon pieces in a dry frying pan until crisp and golden brown. Toss half of the bacon into the mayonnaise dressing. Reserve the remainder.

4 Cook the potatoes in boiling water for 20 minutes until tender. Drain and leave to cool.

5 Toss the cooled potatoes into the mayonnaise dressing and spoon on to a serving platter. Slice the remaining eggs and sprinkle over the salad with the reserved bacon pieces. Scatter the chopped parsley over the top and serve immediately.

Cook's Tip
Use firm salad potatoes, cut into even pieces, or use whole baby new potatoes. Cook with mint sprigs for extra flavour.

Variation
Experiment with flavour and texture by replacing the bacon with cooked peeled prawns (shrimp).

Potato Salad with Garlic Sausage

In this delicious and hearty salad, the potatoes are moistened with a little white wine before adding the vinaigrette. Great served as part of a cold spread.

Serves 4
450g/1lb small waxy potatoes
30–45ml/2–3 tbsp dry
    white wine
2 shallots, finely chopped
15ml/1 tbsp chopped
    fresh parsley
15ml/1 tbsp chopped
    fresh tarragon
175g/6oz cooked garlic sausage
fresh flat leaf parsley sprig,
    to garnish

For the vinaigrette
10ml/2 tsp Dijon mustard
15ml/1 tbsp tarragon vinegar or
    white wine vinegar
75ml/5 tbsp extra virgin olive oil
salt and ground black pepper

1 Scrub the potatoes. Boil in salted water for 10–15 minutes, until tender. Drain and refresh under cold running water.

2 Peel the potatoes if you like, or leave in their skins, and cut into 5mm/¼in slices. Sprinkle with the wine and shallots.

3 To make the vinaigrette, mix the mustard and vinegar in a small bowl, then whisk in the oil, 15ml/1 tbsp at a time. Season with salt and pepper and pour over the potatoes.

4 Add the chopped parsley and tarragon to the potatoes and toss until well mixed.

5 Slice the garlic sausage thinly and toss with the potatoes to combine. Season the salad with salt and pepper to taste.

6 Serve at room temperature, garnished with a sprig of parsley.

Variation
The potatoes are also delicious served on their own, simply dressed with vinaigrette, and perhaps accompanied by marinated herrings.

Bacon and Potato Salad Energy 446kcal/1854kJ; Protein 11.7g; Carbohydrate 25.3g, of which sugars 2.9g; Fat 33.9g, of which saturates 6.5g; Cholesterol 194mg; Calcium 46mg; Fibre 1.7g; Sodium 677mg.
Potato with Garlic Sausage Energy 315kcal/1313kJ; Protein 8.3g; Carbohydrate 22.3g, of which sugars 3.1g; Fat 21.6g, of which saturates 4.4g; Cholesterol 50mg; Calcium 45mg; Fibre 2.3g; Sodium 372mg.

Hake and Potato Salad

Hake is excellent served cold, and is delicious with potatoes in a piquant dressing.

Serves 4
450g/1lb hake fillets
150ml/¼ pint/⅔ cup fish stock
1 onion, thinly sliced
1 bay leaf
450g/1lb cooked baby potatoes
1 red (bell) pepper, seeded and diced
115g/4oz/1 cup petits pois (baby peas), cooked
2 spring onions (scallions), sliced
½ cucumber, unpeeled and diced
4 large red lettuce leaves
salt and ground black pepper

For the dressing
150ml/¼ pint/⅔ cup Greek (US strained plain) yogurt
30ml/2 tbsp olive oil
juice of ½ lemon
15–30ml/1–2 tbsp capers

For the garnish
2 hard-boiled eggs, finely chopped
15ml/1 tbsp finely chopped fresh flat leaf parsley
15ml/1 tbsp finely chopped chives

1 Put the hake in a shallow pan with the fish stock, onion slices and bay leaf. Bring to the boil over a medium heat. Lower the heat and poach the fish gently for about 10 minutes, until it flakes easily when tested with the tip of a sharp knife. Leave it to cool, then remove and discard the skin and any remaining bones, and separate the flesh into large flakes.

2 Halve the potatoes, unless they are tiny, and place in a large bowl with the diced red pepper, petits pois, sliced spring onions and diced cucumber. Stir in the flaked hake and season to taste with salt and pepper.

3 Stir all the dressing ingredients together in a mixing bowl. Season with salt and pepper and toss gently into the salad. Place a lettuce leaf on each plate and spoon the salad over it. Mix the hard-boiled eggs with the parsley and chives. Sprinkle the mixture over each salad.

> **Variation**
> This is equally good made with halibut, monkfish or cod.

Fresh Tuna Salade Niçoise

Fresh tuna transforms this famous salad from the south of France into something really special.

Serves 4
4 tuna steaks, about 150g/5oz each
30ml/2 tbsp olive oil
225g/8oz fine green beans
1 small cos or romaine lettuce or 2 Little Gem (Bibb) lettuces
4 new potatoes, boiled
4 ripe tomatoes or 12 cherry tomatoes
2 red (bell) peppers, seeded and cut into thin strips
4 hard-boiled eggs, sliced
8 drained anchovy fillets in oil, halved lengthwise
16 large black olives
salt and ground black pepper
12 fresh basil leaves, to garnish

For the dressing
15ml/1 tbsp red wine vinegar
90ml/6 tbsp olive oil
1 fat garlic clove, crushed

1 Brush the tuna on both sides with a little olive oil and season with salt and pepper. Heat a ridged griddle or the grill (broiler) until very hot, then grill (broil) the tuna steaks for 1–2 minutes on each side; they should still be pink and juicy in the middle. Set aside.

2 Cook the beans in a pan of lightly salted boiling water for 4–5 minutes or until just tender. Drain, refresh under cold water and drain again.

3 Separate the lettuce leaves and arrange them on four individual serving plates. Slice the potatoes and tomatoes, if large (leave cherry tomatoes whole) and divide them among the plates. Arrange the fine green beans and red pepper strips on top of them.

4 Shell the eggs and cut into thick slices. Place two slices on each plate with an anchovy fillet draped over. Scatter four olives on to each plate.

5 To make the dressing, whisk together the vinegar, olive oil and garlic and season to taste. Drizzle over the salads. Arrange the tuna steaks on top, scatter over the basil and serve.

Salade Niçoise Energy 542kcal/2260kJ; Protein 46.8g; Carbohydrate 14.3g, of which sugars 9.8g; Fat 33.7g, of which saturates 6.5g; Cholesterol 236mg; Calcium 132mg; Fibre 4.4g; Sodium 671mg.
Hake Salad Energy 373kcal/1561kJ; Protein 31.2g; Carbohydrate 29.1g, of which sugars 8.8g; fat 15.8g, of which saturates 4.2g; Cholesterol 121mg; Calcium 129mg; Fibre 4.3g; Sodium 192mg.

Genoese Squid and Potato Salad

This Italian-style salad is good for summer days, when green beans and new potatoes are at their best.

Serves 4–6
450g/1lb prepared squid,
  cut into rings
4 garlic cloves, roughly chopped
300ml/½ pint/1¼ cups Italian
  red wine
450g/1lb Charlotte or new
  potatoes, scrubbed
225g/8oz green beans, trimmed
  and cut into short lengths
2–3 sun-dried tomatoes in oil,
  drained and thinly
  sliced lengthwise
60ml/4 tbsp extra virgin
  olive oil
15ml/1 tbsp red wine vinegar
salt and ground black pepper

1 Preheat the oven to 180°C/350°F/Gas 4. Put the squid rings in an earthenware dish with half the garlic, the wine and pepper to taste. Cover and cook for 45 minutes, or until the squid is tender.

2 Meanwhile, put the potatoes in a pan, cover with cold water and add a good pinch of salt. Bring to the boil, cover and simmer for about 15 minutes, until tender. Using a slotted spoon, lift out the potatoes and set aside. Add the beans to the boiling water and cook for 3 minutes. Drain.

3 When the potatoes are cool enough to handle, slice them thickly on the diagonal and place them in a bowl with the warm beans and sun-dried tomatoes. Whisk the oil, vinegar and the remaining garlic in a bowl and add salt and pepper to taste. Pour over the potato mixture.

4 Drain the squid and discard the liquid. Add the squid to the potato mixture and mix very gently until all the ingredients are well combined. Arrange on individual plates and season liberally with pepper before serving.

Cook's Tip
The French potato called Charlotte is perfect for this salad because it retains its shape when boiled.

Spiced Trout and Potato Salad

In this make-ahead salad, the trout is marinated in a mixture of coriander, ginger and chilli and served with cold baby roast potatoes.

Serves 4
2.5cm/1in piece fresh root
  ginger, peeled and finely
  grated (shredded)
1 garlic clove, crushed
5ml/1 tsp hot chilli powder
15ml/1 tbsp coriander seeds,
  lightly crushed
grated rind and juice of 2 lemons
60ml/4 tbsp olive oil
450g/1lb trout fillet, skinned
900g/2lb new potatoes
5–10ml/1–2 tsp sea salt
ground black pepper
15ml/1 tbsp whole or chopped
  fresh chives, to garnish

1 Mix the ginger, garlic, chilli powder, coriander seeds and lemon rind in a bowl. Whisk in the lemon juice with 15ml/1 tbsp of the olive oil to make a marinade.

2 Place the trout in a shallow, non-metallic dish and cover with the marinade. Turn the fish to make sure they are well coated, cover with clear film (plastic wrap) and chill.

3 Preheat the oven to 200°C/400°F/Gas 6. Place the potatoes in a roasting pan, toss them in 30ml/2 tbsp olive oil and season with salt and ground black pepper. Roast in the oven for about 45 minutes or until golden brown and tender. Remove from the oven and leave to cool for at least 2 hours.

4 Reduce the oven to 190°C/375°F/Gas 5. Remove the trout from the marinade and place in a roasting pan. Bake for 20 minutes until cooked. Remove from the oven and leave to cool.

5 Cut the potatoes into chunks, flake the trout into bitesize pieces and toss them together in a serving dish with the remaining olive oil. Sprinkle with the chives and serve.

Cook's Tip
Look for firm pieces of fresh root ginger, with smooth skin. If it is really fresh, it will keep for up to 2 weeks in a cool place.

Lobster and Potato Salad

When you're in a decadent mood, this salad of potatoes and lobster will satisfy your every whim.

Serves 4

1 medium lobster, cooked
675g/1½lb new potatoes, scrubbed
½ frisée lettuce
175g/6oz lamb's lettuce (corn salad) leaves
60ml/4 tbsp extra virgin olive oil
200g/7oz can young artichokes in brine, quartered
4 oranges, peeled and divided into segments
2 ripe tomatoes, peeled, seeded and diced
1 small bunch fresh tarragon, chervil or flat leaf parsley
salt

For the dressing

30ml/2 tbsp frozen concentrated orange juice, thawed
75g/3oz/6 tbsp unsalted butter, diced
salt and cayenne pepper

1 Twist off the legs and claws of the lobster, and separate the tail from the body. Break the claws with a hammer and remove the meat. Cut the tail piece open from the underside, slice the meat and set aside.

2 Bring the scrubbed new potatoes to the boil in salted water and simmer for about 15 minutes, until just tender. Drain, cover and keep warm.

3 To make the dressing, measure the orange juice into a heatproof bowl and set it over a pan containing 2.5cm/1in simmering water. Heat the juice for 1 minute, turn off the heat, then whisk in the butter a little at a time until the dressing reaches a coating consistency.

4 Season to taste with salt and a pinch of cayenne pepper, cover and keep warm.

5 Dress the salad leaves with olive oil, then divide between four large serving plates. Moisten the potatoes, artichokes and orange segments with olive oil and distribute among the leaves. Lay the sliced lobster over the salad, spoon on the warm dressing, add the diced tomato and decorate with the fresh herbs. Serve at room temperature.

Potato, Mussel and Watercress Salad

The creamy, well-flavoured dressing enhances all the ingredients in this tasty potato salad.

Serves 4

675g/1½lb salad potatoes
1kg/2¼lb mussels, scrubbed and beards removed
200ml/7fl oz/scant 1 cup dry white wine
15g/½oz fresh flat leaf parsley, chopped
1 bunch of watercress or rocket (arugula)
salt and ground black pepper
chopped fresh chives or spring onion (scallion) tops, to garnish

For the dressing

105ml/7 tbsp olive oil
15–30ml/1–2 tbsp white wine vinegar
5ml/1 tsp strong Dijon mustard
1 large shallot, finely chopped
15ml/1 tbsp chopped fresh chives
45ml/3 tbsp double (heavy) cream
pinch of caster (superfine) sugar (optional)

1 Boil the potatoes in salted water for 15–20 minutes, or until tender. Drain, cool, then peel. Slice the potatoes into a bowl and toss with 30ml/2 tbsp of the oil for the dressing.

2 Discard any open mussels. Bring the white wine to the boil in a large, heavy pan. Add the mussels, cover and boil vigorously, shaking the pan occasionally, for 3–4 minutes, until the mussels have opened. Discard any that do not open. Drain and shell the mussels, reserving the cooking liquid.

3 Boil the reserved mussel cooking liquid until reduced to about 45ml/3 tbsp. Pour through a fine sieve (strainer) over the potatoes and toss to mix.

4 To make the dressing, whisk together the remaining oil with 15ml/1 tbsp of the vinegar, the mustard, shallot and chives. Add the cream and whisk again to form a thick dressing. Adjust the seasoning, adding more vinegar and/or a pinch of sugar to taste.

5 Toss the mussels with the potatoes, then gently mix in the dressing and chopped parsley. Arrange the watercress or rocket on a serving platter and top with the salad. Serve sprinkled with extra chives or a little spring onion.

Lobster Salad Energy 662kcal/2775kJ; Protein 51.5g; Carbohydrate 47.7g, of which sugars 22.7g; Fat 30.7g, of which saturates 12g; Cholesterol 260mg; Calcium 325mg; Fibre 6.9g; Sodium 900mg.
Potato and Mussel Salad Energy 459kcal/1918kJ; Protein 17.2g; Carbohydrate 29.2g, of which sugars 3.8g; Fat 27.7g, of which saturates 7g; Cholesterol 45mg; Calcium 222mg; Fibre 2.5g; Sodium 231mg.

Classic Fish Pie

Originally a fish pie was based on the 'catch of the day'. Now we can choose either the fish we like best, or the variety that offers best value for money.

Serves 4
butter, for greasing
450g/1lb mixed fish, such as
  cod or salmon fillets and
  peeled prawns (shrimp)

finely grated rind of 1 lemon
450g/1lb floury potatoes
25g/1oz/2 tbsp butter
salt and ground black pepper
1 egg, beaten

For the sauce
15g/½oz/1 tbsp butter
15ml/1 tbsp plain
  (all-purpose) flour
150ml/¼ pint/⅔ cup milk
45ml/3 tbsp chopped fresh parsley

1 Preheat the oven to 220°C/425°F/Gas 7. Grease an ovenproof dish and set aside. Cut the fish into bitesize pieces. Season the fish, sprinkle over the lemon rind and place in the base of the prepared dish. Set aside while you make the topping.

2 Cook the potatoes in a pan of boiling salted water for about 10–15 minutes until tender.

3 Meanwhile, make the sauce. Melt the butter in a pan, add the flour and cook, stirring, for a few minutes. Remove from the heat and gradually whisk in the milk. Return to the heat and bring to the boil, then reduce the heat to a simmer, whisking constantly, until the sauce has thickened and achieved a smooth consistency. Add the parsley and season to taste. Pour over the fish mixture.

4 Drain the potatoes well and then mash with the butter. Pipe or spoon the potatoes on top of the fish mixture. Brush the beaten egg over the potatoes. Bake for 45 minutes until the top is golden brown. Serve hot.

> **Cook's Tip**
> If using frozen fish defrost it thoroughly first, as lots of water from the fish will ruin your pie.

Fish Pie with Saffron Mash

This is the ultimate fish pie. Breaking through the golden potato crust reveals prawns and chunks of cod swathed in a creamy parsley sauce.

Serves 6
750ml/1¼ pints/3 cups milk
1 onion, chopped
1 bay leaf
2–3 peppercorns
450g/1lb each of fresh cod fillet
  and smoked haddock fillet

350g/12oz cooked tiger prawns
  (jumbo shrimp), shelled, with tails
75g/3oz/6 tbsp butter
75g/3oz/¾ cup plain
  (all-purpose) flour
60ml/4 tbsp chopped fresh parsley
1.3kg/3lb floury potatoes, peeled
large pinch saffron threads, soaked
  in 45ml/3 tbsp hot water
75g/3oz/6 tbsp butter
250ml/8fl oz/1 cup milk
45ml/3 tbsp chopped fresh dill
salt and ground black pepper

1 Put the milk, onion, bay leaf and peppercorns into a pan. Bring to the boil, simmer for about 10 minutes, and set aside. Lay the cod and haddock fillets, skin side up, in a large pan. Strain over the milk, place over a gentle heat and simmer for 5–7 minutes until just opaque. Lift the fish out of the milk and transfer to a plate. Reserve the milk.

2 When the fish is cool enough to handle, pull off the skin and flake the flesh into large pieces, removing any bones as you go. Transfer to a large bowl and add the shelled prawns.

3 Melt the butter in a small pan. Stir in the flour and cook for a minute or so, then gradually stir in the flavoured milk from the pan until you achieve a smooth consistency. Whisk well and simmer gently for 15 minutes until thick and a little reduced, then taste and season with salt and pepper. Stir in the parsley. Pour the sauce over the fish. Carefully mix together, transfer the mixture to a pie dish and leave to cool.

4 Preheat the oven to 180°C/350°F/Gas 4. Boil the potatoes in salted water until tender, drain and mash until smooth. Using an electric whisk, beat in the saffron and its soaking water, then the butter, milk and dill to make light, fluffy mashed potato. When the fish mixture has cooled and set, pile the mash on top. Bake for 30–40 minutes, or until the potato is golden and crisp.

Classic Fish Pie Energy 301kcal/1262kJ; Protein 26.5g; Carbohydrate 24.1g, of which sugars 2.6g; Fat 11.6g, of which saturates 6.2g; Cholesterol 132mg; Calcium 76mg; Fibre 1.6g; Sodium 173mg.
Fish Pie with Saffron Energy 458kcal/1921kJ; Protein 29.4g; Carbohydrate 32.8g, of which sugars 5.8g; Fat 25g, of which saturates 3.7g; Cholesterol 74mg; Calcium 216mg; Fibre 1g; Sodium 867mg.

Creamy Fish and Mushroom Pie

Fish pie is a healthy dish for a hungry family. To eke out the fish, mushrooms and potatoes provide both flavour and nourishment.

Serves 4

225g/8oz assorted wild and
   cultivated mushrooms, such as
   oyster, button (white), chanterelle
   or field (porcini) mushrooms,
   trimmed and quartered
675g/1½lb cod or haddock fillet,
   skinned and diced
600ml/1 pint/2½ cups milk, boiling

For the topping
900g/2lb floury potatoes, quartered
25g/1oz/2 tbsp butter
150ml/¼ pint/⅔ cup milk
salt and ground black pepper
grated nutmeg

For the sauce
50g/2oz unsalted butter
1 medium onion, chopped
½ celery stick, chopped
50g/2oz/½ cup plain
   (all-purpose) flour
10ml/2 tsp lemon juice
45ml/3 tbsp chopped fresh parsley

1 Preheat the oven to 200°C/400°F/Gas 6. Butter an ovenproof dish, sprinkle the mushrooms over the base, add the fish and season with salt and pepper to taste. Pour on the boiling milk, cover the dish and bake in the oven for 20 minutes.

2 Using a slotted spoon, transfer the fish and mushrooms to a 1.5 litre/2½ pint/6¼ cup baking dish. Pour the poaching liquid into a jug (pitcher) and set aside.

3 Meanwhile, cook the potatoes in lightly salted boiling water for 20 minutes. Drain and mash with the butter and milk. Season well with salt, pepper and nutmeg.

4 To make the sauce, melt the butter in a pan, add the chopped onion and celery and fry until soft, but not coloured. Stir in the flour, then remove from the heat.

5 Gradually add the reserved liquid, stirring until absorbed. Return to the heat, stir and simmer to thicken. Add the lemon juice and parsley, season, then add to the baking dish.

6 Top with the mashed potato and return to the oven for 30–40 minutes until the topping is golden brown.

Fish Pie with Sweet Potato Topping

This unusual fish pie is crowned with a subtly sweet topping of mashed potato and sweet potato.

Serves 4

175g/6oz/ 1 cup basmati rice
   450ml/¾ pint/scant 2 cups
   well-flavoured stock
175g/6oz/1½ cups podded
   broad (fava) beans
675g/1½lb cod fillets, skinned
450ml/¾ pint/scant 2 cups milk

For the sauce
40g/1½oz/3 tbsp butter

30–45ml/2–3 tbsp plain
   (all-purpose) flour
15ml/1 tbsp chopped fresh parsley
salt and ground black pepper

For the topping
450g/1lb sweet potatoes, peeled
   and cut in large chunks
450g/1lb floury white potatoes,
   peeled and cut in large chunks
milk and butter, for mashing
10ml/2 tsp freshly chopped parsley
5ml/1 tsp freshly chopped dill
15ml/1 tbsp single (light)
   cream (optional)

1 Preheat the oven to 190°C/375°F/Gas 5. Put the rice in a pan with the stock. Bring to the boil, then cover and simmer for 10 minutes until tender. Cook the beans in lightly salted water until tender. Drain thoroughly. When cool, remove their skins.

2 For the topping, cook the sweet and white potatoes separately in boiling salted water until tender. Drain, then mash with milk and butter and spoon into separate bowls. Beat the parsley and dill into the sweet potatoes, with the cream, if using.

3 Place the fish in a pan and pour in milk to cover. Dot with 15g/½oz/1 tbsp of the butter and season. Simmer for 5 minutes until tender. Remove from the pan. Make up the cooking liquid to 450ml/¾ pint/scant 2 cups with the remaining milk.

4 Make a white sauce. Melt the butter in a pan, stir in the flour and cook for 1 minute. Gradually add the milk mixture, stirring, until a white sauce forms. Stir in the parsley, taste and season.

5 Spread the rice on the bottom of a gratin dish. Add the beans and fish and pour over the sauce. Top with the potatoes in a pattern. Dot with butter and bake for 15 minutes until browned.

Creamy Fish Pie Energy 574kcal/2414kJ; Protein 41.3g; Carbohydrate 59.6g, of which sugars 15.5g; Fat 20.8g, of which saturates 12.5g; Cholesterol 115mg; Calcium 308mg; Fibre 4.1g; Sodium 480mg.
Fish Pie with Sweet Potato Energy 604kcal/2545kJ; Protein 41.6g; Carbohydrate 88g, of which sugars 8.6g; Fat 10.7g, of which saturates 5.7g; Cholesterol 99mg; Calcium 94mg; Fibre 6.9g; Sodium 223mg.

Fish Stew and Herby Mash

Herby mashed potato is the perfect partner to this flavoursome stew. It is delicious with a mix of sea bream, turbot and tuna.

Serves 4

45ml/3 tbsp olive oil
1 onion, finely chopped
2 garlic cloves, crushed
30ml/2 tbsp tomato purée (paste)
3 plum tomatoes, seeded
  and chopped
15ml/1 tbsp vinegar
1 bay leaf
15ml/1 tbsp chopped fresh flat
  leaf parsley
600ml/1 pint/2½ cups good
  fish stock
675–900g/1½–2lb mixed fish
  fillets, cut into 10cm/4in cubes
675g/1½lb old potatoes, peeled
  and cut into chunks
30ml/2 tbsp sour cream
salt and ground black pepper
chopped fresh flat leaf parsley,
  bay leaves and grated lemon
  rind, to garnish

1 Heat the oil in a large pan, and cook the onion and garlic for 2–3 minutes or until just soft. Add the tomato purée, tomatoes, vinegar, bay leaf and parsley. Stir in the fish stock. Bring to the boil.

2 Add the fish to the pan. Bring back to the boil, then reduce the heat and cook for about 30 minutes, stirring occasionally.

3 Meanwhile, place the potatoes in a large pan of lightly salted water. Bring to the boil and cook for 20 minutes. Drain well. Return to the pan, add the sour cream and a little pepper. Mash well with a fork.

4 Season the fish to taste. Serve with the mashed potato on individual plates or in bowls. Garnish with the parsley and bay leaves, and sprinkle grated lemon rind over the mash.

> **Cook's Tip**
> *To make fish stock, place all the bones, trimmings, head and any leftover fish pieces in a pan. Add 1–2 carrots, 1 onion, sprigs of fennel or dill, a few peppercorns and a dash of dry white wine. Cover with cold water, bring to the boil then simmer for 20 minutes. Pour through a fine sieve (strainer).*

Fisherman's Potato Casserole

This delicious seafood casserole combines fish fillets with shellfish and new potatoes in a creamy sauce.

Serves 4

500g/1¼lb mixed fish fillets, such
  as haddock, bass, red mullet
  or salmon
500g/1¼lb mixed shellfish, such
  as squid strips, mussels, cockles
  and prawns (shrimp)
15ml/1 tbsp oil
25g/1oz/2 tbsp butter
1 medium onion, finely chopped
1 carrot, finely chopped
3 celery sticks, finely chopped
30ml/2 tbsp plain
  (all-purpose) flour
600ml/1 pint/2½ cups fish stock
300ml/½ pint/1¼ cups dry
  (hard) cider
350g/12oz small new
  potatoes, halved
150ml/¼ pint/⅔ cup double
  (heavy) cream
small handful of chopped mixed
  herbs, such as parsley, chives
  and dill
salt and ground black pepper

1 Wash the fish fillets and dry on kitchen paper. Remove the skin and any bones. Cut the fish into large, even chunks.

2 Shell the prawns if necessary. Scrub the mussels and cockles, discarding any with broken shells or that do not close when given a sharp tap. Pull off the black beards on the mussels.

3 Heat the oil and butter in a large pan, add the onion, carrot and celery and cook over a medium heat, stirring occasionally, until beginning to soften. Add the flour, and cook for 1 minute.

4 Remove the pan from the heat and gradually stir in the fish stock and cider. Return the pan to the heat and cook, stirring constantly, until the mixture comes to the boil and thickens.

5 Add the potatoes. Bring the sauce back to the boil, then cover and simmer gently for 10–15 minutes until the potatoes are nearly tender. Add all the fish and shellfish and stir in gently.

6 Stir in the cream. Bring back to a gentle simmer, then cover and cook gently for 5–10 minutes or until the fish is cooked through and all the shells have opened. Adjust the seasoning to taste and gently stir in the herbs. Serve immediately.

Fish Stew Energy 466kcal/1949kJ; Protein 35.3g; Carbohydrate 32.4g, of which sugars 7.1g; Fat 22.4g, of which saturates 9.3g; Cholesterol 111mg; Calcium 53mg; Fibre 2.9g; Sodium 219mg.
Casserole Energy 583kcal/2439kJ; Protein 49.3g; Carbohydrate 25.3g, of which sugars 6.1g; Fat 30.2g, of which saturates 16.5g; Cholesterol 354mg; Calcium 199mg; Fibre 2.5g; Sodium 404mg.

Salmon with Potatoes and Dill

Creamy potatoes and dill are the ideal partners for the salty salmon in this dish.

Serves 6–8

200g/7oz/2 cups sea salt
50g/2oz/¼ cup caster (superfine) sugar
1kg/2¼lb salmon, scaled, filleted and boned
1 litre/1¾ pints/4 cups water
675–900g/1½–2lb new potatoes

For the béchamel and dill sauce

25g/1oz/2 tbsp butter
45ml/3 tbsp plain (all-purpose) flour
750ml/1¼ pints/3 cups milk
120ml/4fl oz/½ cup double (heavy) cream
a little freshly grated nutmeg (optional)
25g/1oz/¼ cup chopped fresh dill
salt and ground black pepper

1 Mix together 100g/4oz/1 cup of the salt and the sugar. Cover the salmon fillets all over with the mixture and place them in a plastic bag. Seal the bag and put the fish on a plate in the refrigerator overnight.

2 The next day, make a brine by mixing the remaining salt and the water in a bowl. Place the salmon in the brine and leave in the refrigerator for another night.

3 Remove the salmon from the brine and cut into 5mm/¼in slices. If large, cut the potatoes in half then cook in boiling water for about 20 minutes until tender.

4 Meanwhile, make the béchamel sauce. Melt the butter in a pan, add the flour and cook over a low heat for 1 minute, stirring constantly to make a roux. Remove from the heat and slowly add the milk, stirring constantly, to form a smooth sauce. Return to the heat and cook, stirring constantly, for between 2–3 minutes until the sauce has thickened and is just starting to boil. Stir in the double cream and the grated nutmeg, if you are using. Season with salt and pepper to taste and heat gently.

5 Drain the cooked potatoes and add to the sauce with the chopped dill. Serve the salted salmon with the potatoes in béchamel and dill sauce.

Smoked Salmon and Potato Pudding

This mouthwateringly rich winter warmer – a classic dish from Sweden – is an excellent way to use up any leftover smoked salmon or gravlax. This is a good alternative to fish pie, with similar ingredients, but prepared very differently, with the potatoes sliced and layered at the base of the dish rather than as a mashed topping.

Serves 8

250g/9oz new potatoes
25g/1oz/2 tbsp butter
1 leek, sliced
200g/7oz gravlax, about 8 slices
a little chopped fresh dill
2 eggs
250ml/8fl oz/1 cup milk
30ml/2 tbsp double (heavy) cream
salt and ground black pepper

1 Cook the potatoes in boiling salted water for 15–20 minutes until tender. Drain and leave to cool.

2 Meanwhile, melt the butter in a pan. Add the sliced leek and cook gently for about 5–7 minutes, stirring occasionally, until softened but not browned.

3 Preheat the oven to 180°C/350°F/Gas 4. Thinly slice the cooled potatoes and place in a layer in the bottom of a terrine. Add one to three slices of gravlax and then add a layer of the cooked leeks. Repeat these layers, using all the ingredients, finishing with a neat layer of potatoes. Sprinkle over the chopped dill.

4 Beat the eggs in a jug (pitcher) or bowl. Add the milk and cream and beat together, then season with salt and pepper. Pour the egg mixture into the terrine. Bake in the oven for about 30 minutes until golden brown. Serve in slices.

Variation
If you like, the terrine can be finished with a garnish of 25g/1oz melted butter to which 30ml/2 tbsp chopped fresh parsley has been added.

Salmon Dill Energy 407kcal/1699kJ; Protein 26.4g; Carbohydrate 22.6g, of which sugars 5.9g; Fat 24g, of which saturates 9.7g; Cholesterol 85mg; Calcium 155mg; Fibre 1g; Sodium 118mg.
Salmon Pudding Energy 137kcal/573kJ; Protein 9.9g; Carbohydrate 7.2g, of which sugars 2.4g; Fat 7.8g, of which saturates 3.9g; Cholesterol 70mg; Calcium 59mg; Fibre 0.8g; Sodium 525mg.

Salmon Baked with Potatoes and Thyme

This is a very simple and absolutely delicious dish. Pepper-crusted salmon fillets are baked on a bed of potatoes and onions braised in thyme-flavoured vegetable or fish stock. It is ideal as a quick and easy midweek meal, or special enough for a dinner party.

Serves 4
675g/1½lb waxy potatoes, thinly sliced
1 onion, thinly sliced
10ml/2 tsp fresh thyme leaves
450ml/¾ pint/scant 2 cups vegetable or fish stock
40g/1½oz/3 tbsp butter, finely diced
4 salmon fillets, each about 150g/5oz, skinned
30ml/2 tbsp olive oil
15ml/1 tbsp black peppercorns, roughly crushed
salt and ground black pepper
fresh thyme, to garnish
mangetouts (snow peas) or sugar snap peas, to serve

1 Preheat the oven to 190°C/375°F/Gas 5. Layer the potato and onion slices in a shallow baking dish, such as a lasagne dish, seasoning each layer and sprinkling with thyme.

2 Pour the stock over the potato and onion slices to just cover. Scatter the surface liberally with cubes of butter, cover with foil and place in the oven.

3 Bake the potatoes and onions for about 40 minutes, then remove the foil and bake for a further 20 minutes, or until they are almost cooked.

4 Meanwhile, brush the salmon fillets with olive oil and coat with crushed black peppercorns, pressing them into the fish, if necessary, with the back of a spoon.

5 Place the salmon on top of the potatoes, cover with foil and bake for a further 15 minutes, or until the salmon is opaque, removing the foil for the last 5 minutes of cooking. Garnish the fish with the fresh thyme sprigs and serve with mangetouts or sugar snap peas.

Salmon and Potato Bake

Subtly flavoured with fresh dill and onion, this warming fish and potato bake from Finland uses graavilohi – salmon that has been pressed with salt, dill and brandy for 24 hours.

Serves 4
25g/1oz/2 tbsp unsalted (sweet) butter, softened
8 potatoes, thinly sliced
300g/11oz Pressed Salmon with Dill, sliced (see below)
1 onion, finely chopped
30ml/2 tbsp chopped fresh dill
3 eggs, beaten
400ml/14fl oz/1⅔ cups milk
5ml/1 tsp salt
2.5ml/½ tsp ground white pepper

For the pressed salmon with dill (graavilohi)
90ml/6 tbsp coarse sea salt
90ml/6 tbsp sugar
90ml/6 tbsp chopped fresh dill
30ml/2 tbsp brandy
5ml/1 tsp ground black pepper
1 small or ½ large fresh salmon, filleted

1 To make the pressed salmon with dill, put the salt, sugar, dill, brandy and pepper in a bowl and mix together. Rub the mixture over both sides of the salmon fillets. Place the flesh sides of the fillets together, so that the skin sides are on the outside, to form a whole fish and wrap in foil.

2 Place the wrapped fish in a deep dish or roasting pan and place a heavy weight or weights, such as cans, on the top. Put in the refrigerator and leave for 12 hours. Turn the fish over, replace the weights and leave for a further 12 hours. Scrape off the marinade and pat the fish dry with kitchen paper.

3 To prepare the salmon bake, preheat the oven to 200°C/400°F/Gas 6. Grease a deep, ovenproof dish with a little of the butter.

4 Arrange half the potato slices over the base of the dish, then add a layer of salmon and a layer of onion. Sprinkle over the dill and end with a layer of the remaining potato slices.

5 Mix the eggs, milk, salt and pepper together and pour over the dish. Dot the remaining butter on top. Bake in the oven for 1 hour, until the potatoes are tender. Serve immediately.

Salmon and Thyme Energy 517kcal/2160kJ; Protein 33.4g; Carbohydrate 28.4g, of which sugars 3.1g; Fat 30.8g, of which saturates 9g; Cholesterol 96mg; Calcium 47mg; Fibre 1.9g; Sodium 147mg.
Salmon Bake Energy 338kcal/1413kJ; Protein 24.3g; Carbohydrate 17.9g, of which sugars 10.2g; Fat 19.4g, of which saturates 7g; Cholesterol 199mg; Calcium 167mg; Fibre 0.7g; Sodium 665mg.

Salmon with Warm Potato Salad

The salmon's savoury taste shines through this dish, enriched by the wine and lemon juice flavours in the poaching liquid. This is perfect served, as here, with a warm potato salad.

Serves 6
3 bunches fresh dill
6 salmon steaks, each 2.5cm/1in thick (1.3kg/3lb total weight)
475ml/16fl oz/2 cups water
250ml/8fl oz/1 cup dry white wine
15ml/1 tbsp white vinegar or lemon juice
5ml/1 tsp salt
5 whole allspice berries
2 bay leaves
6 small dill sprigs, to garnish
6 lemon slices, to garnish

For the warm potato salad
1.2kg/2½lb potatoes, peeled
175g/6oz chopped onion
175ml/6fl oz/¾ cup water
45ml/3 tbsp cider vinegar
10ml/2 tsp caster (superfine) sugar
5ml/1 tsp mustard powder
salt and ground white pepper
25g/1oz/2 tbsp butter
45ml/3 tbsp chopped parsley

1 Place the dill sprigs in the bottom of a large, heavy pan and arrange the salmon on top. Combine the water with the wine, vinegar or lemon juice and salt and add the allspice berries and bay leaves. Pour over the salmon. Bring the liquid to a simmer, then lower the heat, cover and cook for around 10–15 minutes.

2 Boil the potatoes in lightly salted water for 20–25 minutes, until tender. To make the dressing, place the chopped onion in a pan with the water. Bring to the boil, and then simmer for 5 minutes, until the onion is transparent. Stir in the vinegar, sugar and mustard and season to taste, adding a little more water if necessary. Stir in the butter until melted and keep warm.

3 Drain the potatoes. While they are still warm, cut them into 1cm/½in slices and layer them in a large bowl. Pour over the dressing, add the parsley and mix to coat the potatoes evenly.

4 When the fish is opaque and flakes easily with a fork, skim off any scum and lift out the fish, drain and allow to cool slightly. Remove the skin from the salmon before placing on a serving platter or on individual plates. Garnish with dill sprigs and lemon slice twists, and serve with the warm potato salad.

Flaky Smoked Salmon with Warm New Potatoes

A type of smoked salmon that has remained true to itself down the ages while retaining its distinctive flavour is Salar, made on the island of South Uist in the Outer Hebrides of Scotland. It is a flaky smoked salmon and this is achieved by smoking the fish closer to the heat source. The result is a delicious, moist, full-flavoured smoked fish, perfect in this dish.

Serves 4
12 small new potatoes
4 x Salar flaky salmon steaks, about 75g/3oz each
mixed salad leaves
a little olive oil
a few fresh basil leaves, torn, to garnish

For the dressing
10ml/2 tsp balsamic vinegar
20ml/4 tsp virgin olive oil

1 Cook the potatoes until just done, about 15 minutes, then drain and leave to cool until you can handle them.

2 Meanwhile, for the dressing, mix the balsamic vinegar and olive oil together. Toss the mixed salad leaves in the dressing then divide between four individual serving plates.

3 Cut the potatoes in two and mix with a little olive oil. The warmth of the potatoes will create a great smell and bring out the flavour.

4 Arrange the potatoes over the salad leaves and place the smoked salmon on top. Garnish with a few torn fresh basil leaves and serve with crusty bread.

Cook's Tip
Choose small, tasty new potatoes, such as baby Maris Piper or King Edwards. Make sure that they are not overcooked as they need to retain some crispness.

Salmon with Salad Energy 578kcal/2420kJ; Protein 47.6g; Carbohydrate 36.3g, of which sugars 6g; Fat 27.9g, of which saturates 6.5g; Cholesterol 117mg; Calcium 67mg; Fibre 2.4g; Sodium 146mg.
Flaky Salmon Energy 651kcal/2,710kJ; Protein 35.8g; Carbohydrate 23.2g, of which sugars 3.3g; Fat 46.8g, of which saturates 23.2g; Cholesterol 159mg; Calcium 222mg; Fibre 2g; Sodium 359mg.

Smoked Salmon Quiche with Potato Pastry

The ingredients in this light quiche perfectly complement the melt-in-the-mouth pastry made with potatoes.

Serves 6

For the pastry
115g/4oz floury maincrop
    potatoes, diced
225g/8oz/2 cups plain
    (all-purpose) flour, sifted
115g/4oz/¹/₂ cup butter, diced
¹/₂ egg, beaten
10ml/2 tsp chilled water

For the filling
275g/10oz smoked salmon
6 eggs, beaten
150ml/¹/₄ pint/²/₃ cup full-cream
    (whole) milk
300ml/¹/₂ pint/1¹/₄ cups double
    (heavy) cream
30–45ml/2–3 tbsp chopped
    fresh dill
30ml/2 tbsp capers, chopped
salt and ground black pepper
salad leaves and chopped fresh
    dill, to serve

1 Boil the potatoes in a pan of salted water for 15 minutes or until tender. Drain well and return to the pan. Mash the potatoes until smooth and set aside to cool completely.

2 Place the flour in a bowl and rub in the butter to form fine crumbs. Beat in the potatoes and egg. Bring the mixture together, adding chilled water if needed.

3 Roll the pastry out on a floured surface and use to line a deep 23cm/9in round, loose-based, fluted flan tin (pan). Chill for 1 hour.

4 Preheat the oven to 200°C/400°F/Gas 6. Place a baking sheet in the oven to preheat it. Chop the salmon into bitesize pieces and set aside.

5 For the filling, beat the eggs, milk and cream together, then stir in the dill and capers and season with pepper. Add in the salmon and stir to combine.

6 Prick the base of the pastry case (pie shell) well and pour the mixture into it. Bake on a baking sheet for 35–45 minutes until cooked through. Serve warm with salad leaves and dill.

Grilled Salmon and Spring Vegetable Salad

Spring is the time to enjoy sweet, young vegetables. To make the most of their fresh flavour, toss in a simple dressing and serve with a lightly grilled salmon topped with sorrel and quail's eggs.

Serves 4
350g/12oz small new potatoes,
    scrubbed or scraped
4 quail's eggs
115g/4oz young carrots
115g/4oz baby corn on the cob
115g/4oz sugar snap peas
115g/4oz fine green (French) beans
115g/4oz young
    courgettes (zucchini)
115g/4oz patty-pan
    squash (optional)
120ml/4fl oz/¹/₂ cup
    French dressing
4 salmon fillets, about
    150g/5oz each, skinned
115g/4oz sorrel, stems removed
salt and ground black pepper

1 Bring the potatoes to the boil in salted water and cook for about 15 minutes, until tender. Drain, cover and keep warm.

2 Cover the quail's eggs with boiling water and cook for 8 minutes. Refresh under cold running water, shell and cut in half.

3 Bring a pan of salted water to the boil, add the carrots, corn, sugar snap peas, beans, courgettes and squash, if using, and cook for 2–3 minutes. Drain well. Place the hot vegetables with the potatoes in a bowl, moisten with a little French dressing and allow to cool. Preheat the grill (broiler).

4 Brush the salmon fillets with some of the French dressing and grill (broil) for 6 minutes, turning once.

5 Place the sorrel in a stainless-steel or enamel pan with 30ml/2 tbsp French dressing. Cover and soften over a gentle heat for 2 minutes. Strain and cool to room temperature.

6 Divide the potatoes and vegetables among four large serving plates. Add a piece of salmon to each plate and top with a spoonful of sorrel and two pieces of quail's egg. Season with salt and pepper to taste before serving.

Salmon Quiche Energy 338kcal/1413kJ; Protein 24.3g; Carbohydrate 17.9g, of which sugars 10.2g; Fat 19.4g, of which saturates 7g; Cholesterol 199mg; Calcium 167mg; Fibre 0.7g; Sodium 665mg.
Grilled Salmon Salad Energy 545kcal/2264kJ; Protein 32.3g; Carbohydrate 20.1g, of which sugars 6.3g; Fat 31g, of which saturates 6g; Cholesterol 110mg; Calcium 131mg; Fibre 4.2g; Sodium 739mg.

Cod Ceviche with Red Onion, Avocado and Sweet Potato

Ceviche is a South American dish of fish marinated in citrus juice and onion, which has a similar effect to cooking, served here with sweet potato for a truly exotic meal.

Serves 6 as an appetizer or 4 as a main course
500–675g/1¼–1½lb cod fillets, skinned
1 red onion, thinly sliced
pinch of dried red chilli flakes
grated rind of 1 small lime and juice of 5 limes
450–500g/1–1¼lb sweet potatoes

75ml/5 tbsp mild olive oil
15–25ml/3–5 tsp rice vinegar
2.5–5ml/½–1 tsp caster (superfine) sugar
2.5ml/½ tsp ground toasted cumin seeds
½–1 fresh red or green chilli, seeded and finely chopped
1 large or 2 small avocados, peeled, stoned (pitted) and sliced
225g/8oz peeled cooked prawns (shrimp)
45ml/3 tbsp chopped fresh coriander (cilantro)
30ml/2 tbsp roasted peanuts, chopped
salt and ground black pepper

1 Cut the fish into strips or chunks. Sprinkle half the onion over the base of a glass dish and lay the fish on top. Sprinkle on the dried red chilli flakes and pour in the lime juice. Cover and chill for 2–3 hours, spooning the lime juice over the fish once or twice. Drain, and discard the onion.

2 Steam or boil the sweet potatoes for 20–25 minutes, or until just tender. Peel and slice, or cut into wedges.

3 Place the oil in a bowl and whisk in the rice vinegar and sugar to taste, then add the cumin, season, and whisk in the fresh chilli and grated lime rind.

4 In a glass bowl, mix together the fish, sweet potatoes, avocado, prawns and most of the coriander, and the dressing.

5 Toss in the remaining half of the red onion slices and then sprinkle with the remaining chopped coriander and the peanuts. Serve immediately.

Cod Fillet Baked with Sliced Potatoes

Cod fillet bakes perfectly, its mild flavour enhanced by the herbs and its juices giving flavour to the sliced potatoes underneath.

Serves 4
2 large potatoes, sliced
600ml/1 pint/2½ cups water or fish stock
900g/2lb cod fillet, skinned and cut into 4 pieces

1 small bunch dill
1 small leek, shredded
50g/2oz/¼ cup butter
olive oil, to drizzle
salt and ground black pepper

For the sauce
150ml/¼ pint/⅔ cup single (light) cream
shredded leek, to garnish
chopped dill, to garnish

1 Preheat the oven to 200°C/400°F/Gas 6. Cook the potatoes in the water or fish stock for 7–10 minutes or until tender. Drain and reserve the stock.

2 Season the cod pieces. Divide the potatoes into four portions. Arrange each one in an overlapping fan shape on a greased non-stick roasting pan.

3 Season the potatoes and cut some of the dill over each fan, reserving a little for the sauce. Sprinkle over the leeks, reserving some for the sauce, and add a knob of the butter.

4 Lay the fish over the potatoes. Sprinkle the remaining leeks and sliced potatoes on top of the fish and drizzle with the olive oil. Bake, uncovered, for 15–20 minutes.

5 Meanwhile, to make the sauce, rapidly boil the reserved stock in a pan for 10 minutes or until reduced by two-thirds. Stir in the cream and the remaining dill. Boil for 5 minutes to thicken slightly.

6 Remove the fish from the oven and garnish with the shredded leek and chopped dill. Place the individual portions on plates and serve with the sauce.

Ceviche Energy 309kcal/1292kJ; Protein 24.7g; Carbohydrate 17.9g, of which sugars 5.4g; Fat 15.8g, of which saturates 2.6g; Cholesterol 111mg; Calcium 78mg; Fibre 3.2g; Sodium 155mg.
Cod Fillet Energy 428kcal/1788kJ; Protein 44.7g; Carbohydrate 19.1g, of which sugars 4g; Fat 19.5g, of which saturates 11.6g; Cholesterol 153mg; Calcium 74mg; Fibre 2.1g; Sodium 259mg.

Sweet Potato Cod Rolls

The flavour of the sweet potatoes is offset perfectly by the tartness of the lemon butter sauce served over these fish rolls.

Serves 4
2 large sweet potatoes
450g/1lb cod fillet
300ml/½ pint/1¼ cups milk
300ml/½ pint/1¼ cups water
30ml/2 tbsp chopped parsley
rind and juice of 1 lemon
2 eggs, beaten

For the coating
175g/6oz/3 cups fresh
   white breadcrumbs
5ml/1 tsp Thai 7-spice seasoning
vegetable oil, for frying

For the sauce
50g/2oz/¼ cup butter
150ml/¼ pint/⅔ cup single
   (light) cream
15ml/1 tbsp chopped fresh dill
lemon zest, to serve

1 Scrub the sweet potatoes and cook them in their skins in lightly salted boiling water for 45 minutes or until very tender. Drain and cool. When cool, peel the skins and mash the flesh.

2 Place the cod in a frying pan and pour over the milk and water. Cover and poach for 10 minutes or until the fish starts to flake.

3 Drain and discard the milk, and then remove the skin and the bones from the fish. Flake the fish into the potatoes in a large bowl, stir in the parsley, the rind and juice of half of the lemon and one egg. Chill for 30 minutes.

4 Divide and shape the mixture into eight sausages. Dip each in the remaining egg. Mix the breadcrumbs with the seasoning. Roll the dipped fish rolls in the breadcrumbs.

5 Heat the oil and shallow-fry in batches for 7 minutes, until evenly browned. Remove and drain on kitchen paper. Keep hot.

6 To make the sauce, melt the butter in a small pan and add the remaining lemon juice and rind. Cook for a few seconds.

7 Remove from the heat and add the cream and chopped dill. Whisk to prevent the sauce curdling and serve with the fish rolls.

Cod with Chilli and Potato

White-fleshed fish, such as cod and haddock, and potatoes, are the perfect foil for the flavours of robust spices, as is the case with the chilli and mustard seeds in this delicious dish.

Serves 4
30ml/2 tbsp olive oil
5ml/1 tsp mustard seeds
1 large potato, cubed

2 slices of Serrano ham, shredded
1 onion, thinly sliced
2 garlic cloves, thinly sliced
1 red chilli, seeded and sliced
115g/4oz skinless, boneless
   cod, cubed
120ml/4fl oz/½ cup
   vegetable stock
50g/2oz/½ cup grated tasty
   cheese, such as Manchego
   or Cheddar
salt and ground black pepper

1 Heat the oil in a heavy frying pan. Add the mustard seeds. Cook for 1–2 minutes, until the seeds begin to pop and splutter, then add the potato, ham and onion.

2 Cook the mixture, stirring regularly, for about 10–15 minutes, until the cubes of potato are brown and almost tender.

3 Add the garlic and chilli to the pan and cook for a further 2 minutes, stirring frequently.

4 Stir the cod cubes into the pan and cook for 2–3 minutes, until the fish turns white, then add the stock and plenty of salt and ground black pepper. Cover the pan and cook for a further 5 minutes, until the fish is just cooked and the potatoes are tender. The fish should be opaque and flake easily when tested with a knife.

5 Transfer the fish and potato mixture to a flameproof baking dish. Sprinkle over the grated cheese and place under a hot grill (broiler) for about 2–3 minutes, until the cheese is golden.

Cook's Tip
If you prefer a crisp topping, replace half the cheese with wholemeal (whole-wheat) breadcrumbs.

Sweet Potato Rolls Energy 613kcal/2568kJ; Protein 29.7g; Carbohydrate 56.1g, of which sugars 7.7g; Fat 31.5g, of which saturates 12.9g; Cholesterol 146mg; Calcium 133mg; Fibre 3.4g; Sodium 544mg.
Cod with Chilli Energy 178kcal/744kJ; Protein 11.8g; Carbohydrate 9.4g, of which sugars 1.6g; Fat 10.4g, of which saturates 3.7g; Cholesterol 33mg; Calcium 103mg; Fibre 0.7g; Sodium 264mg.

Indian Cod and Potato Stew

A spicy fish stew made with potatoes, peppers and traditional Indian spices.

Serves 4

30ml/2 tbsp oil
5ml/1 tsp cumin seeds
1 onion, chopped
1 red (bell) pepper, thinly sliced
1 garlic clove, crushed
2 red chillies, finely chopped
2 bay leaves
2.5ml/½ tsp salt
5ml/1 tsp ground cumin
5ml/1 tsp ground coriander
5ml/1 tsp chilli powder
400g/14oz can
  chopped tomatoes
2 large potatoes, cut into
  2.5cm/1in chunks
300ml/½ pint/1¼ cups
  fish stock
4 cod fillets
chapatis, to serve

1 Heat the oil in a large, deep-sided frying pan and fry the cumin seeds for about 2 minutes until they begin to splutter. Add the onion, pepper, garlic, chillies and bay leaves and fry for 5–7 minutes until the onions have browned.

2 Add the salt, ground cumin, ground coriander and chilli powder and cook for 3–4 minutes. Stir in the tomatoes, potatoes and fish stock. Bring to the boil and simmer for a further 10 minutes.

3 Add the fish, then cover and simmer for 10 minutes, or until the fish is tender. Serve with chapatis.

Variations
• *In place of chapatis, serve this fish curry with pilau or plain rice with a few chopped herbs added.*
• *If you prefer another fish, try haddock or another firm fish such as monkfish or hake.*
• *For a change, use 450ml/¾ pint/scant 2 cups coconut milk in place of the chopped tomatoes.*
• *To vary the flavours, replace the red chillies with green chillies. Deseed and finely chop them.*
• *Add another vegetable or replace the potatoes with two bulbs of fennel, sliced.*

Classic Cod and Chips

Quintessentially English, this is fish and chips as it should be cooked, with tender flakes of fish in a crisp batter, and home-made chips.

Serves 4

450g/1lb potatoes
groundnut (peanut) oil, for
  deep-frying
4 x 175g/6oz cod fillets, skinned
  and any tiny bones removed

For the batter
75g/3oz/⅔ cup plain
  (all-purpose) flour
1 egg yolk
10ml/2 tsp oil
175ml/6fl oz/¾ cup water
salt

1 To make the chips (French fries), cut the potatoes into slices about 5mm/¼in thick. Then cut the slices into 5mm/¼in fingers or chips. Rinse the slices thoroughly, drain well and then dry in a clean dish towel.

2 Heat the oil in a deep fat fryer to 180°C/350°F. Add the chips in the basket to the fryer and cook for 3 minutes. Lift out and shake off excess fat.

3 To make the batter, sift the flour into a bowl. Add a pinch of salt. Make a well in the middle of the flour and add the egg yolk, oil and a little of the water. Mix the yolk with the liquid, then add the remaining water and incorporate the surrounding flour to make a smooth batter. Cover and set aside.

4 Reheat the oil in the fryer and cook the chips again for about 5 minutes, until they are golden and crisp. Drain on kitchen paper and season with salt. Keep hot in a low oven.

5 Dip the pieces of fish fillet into the batter and turn them to make sure they are evenly coated. Allow any excess batter to drip off before carefully lowering the fish into the hot oil.

6 Cook the fish for 5 minutes, turning once, if necessary, so that the batter browns evenly all over. The batter should be crisp and golden. Remove with a slotted spoon and drain well on kitchen paper. Serve immediately, with lemon wedges and the chips.

Indian Stew Energy 332kcal/1396kJ; Protein 36.9g; Carbohydrate 27.6g, of which sugars 7.9g; Fat 9.2g, of which saturates 1.3g; Cholesterol 81mg; Calcium 59mg; Fibre 2.9g; Sodium 132mg.
Cod and Chips Energy 645kcal/2700kJ; Protein 32.6g; Carbohydrate 54.3g, of which sugars 0.7g; Fat 34.5g, of which saturates 4.2g; Cholesterol 0mg; Calcium 130mg; Fibre 3.4g; Sodium 294mg.

Cod, Basil, Tomato and Potato Pie

Natural and smoked fish make a great combination and are served here with potatoes and a subtle hint of tasty tomato and basil. Served with a green salad, this makes an ideal dish for lunch or a family supper.

Serves 8

1kg/2¼lb smoked cod
1kg/2¼lb white cod
900ml/1½ pints/3¾ cups milk
1.2litres/2 pints/5 cups water
2 basil sprigs
1 lemon thyme sprig
150g/5oz/10 tbsp butter
1 onion, chopped
75g/3oz/⅔ cup plain
    (all-purpose) flour
30ml/2 tbsp chopped fresh basil
4 firm plum tomatoes, peeled
    and chopped
12 medium floury potatoes
salt and ground black pepper
crushed black peppercorns,
    to garnish
lettuce leaves, to serve

1 Place both kinds of fish in a roasting pan with 600ml/1 pint/ 2½ cups of the milk, the water and the herb sprigs. Bring to a simmer and cook gently for about 3–4 minutes. Leave the fish to cool in the liquid for about 20 minutes. Drain the fish, reserving the cooking liquid for use in the sauce. Flake the fish, removing any skin and bone.

2 Melt 75g/3oz/6 tbsp of the butter in a large pan, add the onion and cook for about 5 minutes until softened and tender but not browned. Sprinkle over the flour and half the chopped basil. Gradually add the reserved fish cooking liquid, adding a little more milk if necessary to make a fairly thin sauce, stirring constantly to make a smooth consistency. Bring to the boil, season with salt and pepper, and add the remaining basil.

3 Remove the pan from the heat, then add the fish and tomatoes and stir gently to combine. Pour into an ovenproof dish. Preheat the oven to 180°C/350°F/Gas 4.

4 Cook the potatoes in boiling water until tender. Drain, then add the remaining butter and milk, and mash. Season to taste and spoon over the fish mixture, using a fork to create a pattern. Bake for 30 minutes until the top is golden. Sprinkle with the crushed peppercorns and serve hot with lettuce.

Cod, Tomato and Potato Bake

The wonderful sun-drenched flavours of the Mediterranean are brought together in this appetizing, potato-topped bake. Lightly cooked courgettes make a tasty accompaniment to this dish.

Serves 4

450g/1lb potatoes, cut into
    thin slices
30ml/2 tbsp olive oil
1 red onion, chopped
1 garlic clove, crushed
1 red (bell) pepper, seeded
    and diced
1 yellow (bell) pepper, seeded
    and diced
225g/8oz mushrooms, sliced
400g/14oz and 225g/8oz cans
    chopped tomatoes
150ml/¼ pint/⅔ cup dry
    white wine
450g/1lb skinless, boneless cod
    fillet, cut into 2cm/¾in cubes
50g/2oz/½ cup pitted black
    olives, chopped
15ml/1 tbsp chopped fresh basil
15ml/1 tbsp chopped
    fresh oregano
salt and ground black pepper
fresh oregano sprigs, to garnish
cooked courgettes (zucchini),
    to serve

1 Preheat the oven to 200°C/400°F/ Gas 6. Par-boil the potatoes in a pan of lightly salted, boiling water for 4 minutes. Drain thoroughly, then add 15ml/1 tbsp of the oil and toss together to mix. Set aside.

2 Heat the remaining oil in a heavy pan, add the onion, garlic and red and yellow peppers and cook for about 5 minutes, stirring occasionally.

3 Stir in the mushrooms, tomatoes and wine, bring to the boil and boil for a few minutes until the sauce has reduced slightly. Add the fish, olives, herbs and seasoning to the tomato mixture.

4 Spoon the mixture into a lightly greased casserole and arrange the potato slices over the top, covering the fish mixture completely.

5 Bake, uncovered, for about 45 minutes until the fish is cooked and tender and the potato topping is browned. Garnish with fresh oregano sprigs and serve with courgettes.

Cod and Pepper Bake Energy 318kcal/1334kJ; Protein 25.8g; Carbohydrate 28.8g, of which sugars 11.4g; Fat 9.1g, of which saturates 1.5g; Cholesterol 52mg; Calcium 74mg; Fibre 5.4g; Sodium 383mg.
Cod and Potato Pie Energy 474kcal/1989kJ; Protein 49.6g; Carbohydrate 30.7g, of which sugars 4.6g; Fat 17.8g, of which saturates 10.2g; Cholesterol 155mg; Calcium 62mg; Fibre 2.5g; Sodium 1672mg.

Salt Cod with Potato Mash Gratin

This recipe is reminiscent of the well-known French salt cod purée, brandade. Many similar dishes are produced around the Mediterranean, using salt or dried cod, which is also known as stockfish. Served with potatoes, garlic and cream, this traditional ingredient is transformed into a sophisticated main course or, in smaller portions, an elegant appetizer.

Serves 8
1kg/2¼lb potatoes, unpeeled
800g/1¾lb salt cod, soaked
105ml/7 tbsp olive oil
200ml/7fl oz/scant 1 cup single (light) cream
2 garlic cloves, chopped
1 small bunch of parsley, chopped
pinch of freshly grated nutmeg
salt

1 Cook the potatoes in a large pan of lightly salted boiling water for 20–30 minutes, until tender.

2 Drain the potatoes thoroughly, then peel and mash with a fork. Meanwhile, preheat the oven to 200°C/400°F/Gas 6.

3 Bring another large pan of water to the boil. Add the fish and bring the water back to the boil, then immediately remove the pan from the heat. Leave to stand for 5 minutes.

4 Remove the fish from the pan with a slotted spoon and leave to cool slightly. When cool enough to handle, remove and discard the skin and bones from the fish.

5 Mix the fish with the potatoes, then blend in the olive oil, cream and garlic. Stir in the parsley and nutmeg and season with salt, if necessary. Spoon the mixture into an ovenproof dish and bake for about 20 minutes. Serve hot.

Variation
This dish could also be made with sweet potatoes, if you like. Simply replace the white potatoes with the same quantity of sweet potatoes and prepare in the same way.

Salt Cod and Potato Casserole

Nowadays there is no longer any need to salt cod to preserve it, but the distinctive flavour of salted cod means that it is still an essential ingredient in many traditional recipes. This succulent Norwegian casserole recipe is made with salt cod layered with potatoes and onions in a delicate tomato and chilli sauce.

Serves 4
1kg/2¼lb salt cod
about 500g/1¼lb potatoes, sliced
1 onion, sliced
100ml/3½fl oz/scant ½ cup water
100ml/3½fl oz/scant ½ cup olive oil
75ml/2½fl oz/⅓ cup strained tomatoes
a little chopped red chilli

1 Soak the salt cod in cold water for two days, changing the water at least three times a day.

2 Drain the cod thoroughly and remove the skin and bones, then cut the fish into pieces, each measuring approximately 5cm/2in square.

3 Layer the fish, potatoes and finally the onion in a lightly oiled flameproof casserole.

4 Put the water, oil, strained tomatoes and the chilli in a separate pan and bring the mixture to the boil. Pour into the casserole, over the fish, potatoes and onions.

5 Return the liquid to the boil, reduce the heat, cover and simmer for about 1½–2 hours, until the potatoes are tender. Serve immediately.

Cook's Tip
It helps to have two sharp knives for preparing the salt cod; a small one to cut away the flesh from the bones, and a larger, flexible-bladed one to slide, in a sawing motion, between the flesh and the skin. A little salt on the fingers will help to get a firm grip on the skin.

Salt Cod Gratin Energy 366kcal/1535kJ; Protein 35.9g; Carbohydrate 21.4g, of which sugars 2.4g; Fat 15.8g, of which saturates 4.7g; Cholesterol 73mg; Calcium 65mg; Fibre 1.7g; Sodium 423mg.
Cod Casserole Energy 55kcal/231kJ; Protein 7.8g; Carbohydrate 2g, of which sugars 0.3g; Fat 1.8g, of which saturates 0.3g; Cholesterol 14mg; Calcium 6mg; Fibre 0.2g; Sodium 95mg.

Salt Cod with Scrambled Eggs, Onion and Potatoes

Salt cod is a traditional ingredient in Mediterranean and north European countries. This succulent salt cod recipe is a classic Portuguese dish: thin strips of cod are combined with onions, alongside a mixture of thin strips of potatoes and scrambled eggs.

Serves 4

400g/14oz salt cod, soaked
50ml/2fl oz/¼ cup olive oil
3 onions, thinly sliced
500g/1¼lb potatoes, cut into
    thin matchsticks (julienne)
    and deep-fried
8 eggs, lightly beaten
1 small bunch of parsley, chopped
12 black olives

1 Bring a pan of water to the boil. Add the fish and bring back to the boil, then immediately remove the pan from the heat. Leave to stand for 5 minutes.

2 Remove the fish from the pan with a slotted spatula and leave to cool slightly. When cool enough to handle, remove and discard the skin and bones.

3 Heat the olive oil in a large pan. Add the onions and cook over a low heat, stirring occasionally, for 5 minutes, until softened but not browned.

4 Add the fish, then the potatoes and, finally, the beaten eggs to the pan. Stir gently until all the ingredients are thoroughly combined but the eggs are still soft. Serve the dish straight away, sprinkled with the chopped parsley and black olives.

Variation
Another recipe called Bacalhau à Gomes de Sá originates in Porto (Oporto), and has the same ingredients but a different preparation technique. In this dish, the onions are cooked in olive oil, and mixed with cooked potatoes and salt cod marinated in milk. The dish is then served with parsley, cooked eggs and black olives.

Baked Salt Cod with Potatoes and Olives

This quintessentially Greek recipe, with its delicious mingling of salt cod, potatoes, tomatoes and olives, is resonant of afternoons spent languishing in the warm sun and the cool sea breeze. A true taste of the Mediterranean.

Serves 4

675g/1½lb salt cod
800g/1¾lb potatoes, cut
    into wedges
1 large onion, finely chopped
2 or 3 garlic cloves, chopped
leaves from 1 fresh
    rosemary sprig
30ml/2 tbsp chopped
    fresh parsley
120ml/4fl oz/½ cup olive oil
400g/14oz can
    chopped tomatoes
15ml/1 tbsp tomato purée (paste)
300ml/½ pint/1¼ cups hot water
5ml/1 tsp dried oregano
12 black olives
ground black pepper

1 Soak the cod in cold water overnight, changing the water as often as possible during the evening and morning. The cod does not have to be skinned for this dish, but you may prefer to remove the skin, especially if there is a lot of it on the fish. You should also remove any obvious fins or bones. After soaking, drain the cod and cut it into 7.5cm/3in squares.

2 Preheat the oven to 180°C/350°F/Gas 4. Mix the potatoes, onion, garlic, rosemary and parsley in a large roasting pan with plenty of black pepper. Add the olive oil and toss until coated.

3 Arrange the pieces of salt cod between the oil coated vegetables and spread the tomatoes evenly over the surface. Stir the tomato purée into the hot water until dissolved, then pour the mixture over the contents of the pan. Sprinkle the oregano on top. Bake for 1 hour, basting the fish and potatoes occasionally with the pan juices.

4 Remove the roasting pan from the oven, sprinkle the olives on top, and then cook for 30 minutes more, adding a little more hot water if the mixture seems to be drying out. Garnish with fresh parsley. Serve hot or cold.

Salt Cod with Eggs Energy 484kcal/2032kJ; Protein 49.1g; Carbohydrate 30.4g, of which sugars 8.9g; Fat 19.7g, of which saturates 4.4g; Cholesterol 440mg; Calcium 151mg; Fibre 4g; Sodium 843mg.
Baked Salt Cod Energy 624kcal/2,624kJ; Protein 61g; Carbohydrate 45.6g, of which sugars 12.9g; Fat 23.3g, of which saturates 3.5g; Cholesterol 100mg; Calcium 98mg; Fibre 4.8g; Sodium 918mg.

Baked Monkfish with Potatoes and Garlic

Firm-fleshed monkfish and crispy, golden potatoes are the perfect canvas for the complex flavours in this dish.

Serves 4
1kg/2¼lb potatoes, cut into chunks
50g/2oz/¼ cup butter
2 onions, thickly sliced
4 garlic cloves
few fresh thyme sprigs

2–3 fresh bay leaves
450ml/¾ pint/scant 2 cups fish stock, plus 45ml/3 tbsp
900g/2lb monkfish tail, skin and membrane removed
30–45ml/2–3 tbsp white wine
50g/2oz/1 cup fresh white breadcrumbs
15g/½oz fresh parsley, chopped
15ml/1 tbsp olive oil
salt and ground black pepper

1 Preheat the oven to 190°C/375°F/Gas 5. Put the chunks of potato in an ovenproof dish. Melt half the butter in a large frying pan and cook the onions gently for 5–6 minutes. Add the onions to the potatoes and mix.

2 Slice 2–3 of the garlic cloves and add to the potatoes with the thyme and bay leaves, and season with salt and pepper.

3 Pour in the main batch of stock over the potatoes and bake, stirring once or twice, for 50–60 minutes, until the potatoes are just tender.

4 Push the monkfish into the potatoes and season. Bake for 10–15 minutes. Mix the 45ml/3 tbsp stock with the wine and use to baste the monkfish a couple of times during cooking.

5 Finely chop the remaining garlic. Melt the remaining butter and toss it with the breadcrumbs, chopped garlic, most of the chopped parsley and seasoning. Spoon over the monkfish, pressing it down gently with the back of a spoon.

6 Drizzle the olive oil over the fish, return the dish to the oven and bake for a final 10–15 minutes, until the breadcrumbs are crisp and golden and the liquid has been absorbed. Sprinkle the remaining parsley on to the potatoes and serve immediately.

Hake with Turnip Tops and Sautéed Potatoes

Hake is highly prized in many regions of Europe and is served in numerous different ways. Here, sautéed potatoes and leafy turnip tops are paired with this delicate fish for a truly stunning result. Serve with spinach or broccoli for an elegant supper.

Serves 4
105ml/7 tbsp olive oil

2 small onions, chopped
2 garlic cloves, chopped
5ml/1 tsp sweet paprika
1 bay leaf
15ml/1 tbsp white wine vinegar
150ml/¼ pint/⅔ cup fish stock or water
4 hake steaks, about 225g/8oz each
200g/7oz turnip tops (the green part of the turnip)
8 potatoes, boiled without peeling
4 hard-boiled eggs, halved

1 Preheat the oven to 180°C/350°F/Gas 4. Heat 30ml/2 tbsp of the olive oil in a flameproof casserole. Add the onions, garlic, paprika and bay leaf and cook over a low heat, stirring occasionally, for 5 minutes, until the onions have softened.

2 Add the vinegar and the stock or water, then place the hake in the casserole and season with salt. Cover and cook in the oven for 15 minutes.

3 Meanwhile, steam the turnip tops or cook in a little boiling water for 3–5 minutes, then drain if necessary. Press them through a sieve (strainer) into a bowl, mix with 15ml/1 tbsp of the remaining olive oil and keep warm.

4 Peel the potatoes and cut into quarters. Heat the remaining olive oil in a sauté pan or frying pan, add the potatoes and cook, turning occasionally, over a medium-low heat for around 7–8 minutes until light golden brown.

5 Using a slotted spatula, transfer the fish to a large serving plate. Add the potatoes, turnip tops and eggs and spoon over the onion sauce. Serve immediately.

Hake with Potatoes Energy 614kcal/2571kJ; Protein 51g; Carbohydrate 36.2g, of which sugars 5.7g; Fat 30.7g, of which saturates 5.2g; Cholesterol 242mg; Calcium 102mg; Fibre 3.4g; Sodium 326mg.
Baked Monkfish Energy 529kcal/2230kJ; Protein 45.8g; Carbohydrate 54g, of which sugars 6.5g; Fat 15g, of which saturates 7.4g; Cholesterol 63mg; Calcium 67mg; Fibre 3.5g; Sodium 245mg.

Sea Bream and Potato Parcels

Each of these little fish and potato parcels is a meal in itself and can be prepared several hours in advance, which makes the recipe ideal for entertaining. Serve the parcels with a mixed leaf salad.

Serves 4
8 small waxy salad potatoes, preferably red-skinned
200g/7oz sorrel, stalks removed

30ml/2 tbsp extra virgin olive oil
16 filo pastry sheets, thawed if frozen
4 sea bream fillets, about 175g/6oz each, scaled but not skinned
50g/2oz/¼ cup butter, melted
120ml/4fl oz/½ cup fish stock
250ml/8fl oz/1 cup whipping cream
salt and ground black pepper
finely diced red (bell) pepper, to garnish

1 Preheat the oven to 200°C/400°F/Gas 6. Cook the potatoes in a pan of lightly salted boiling water for about 15–20 minutes, or until just tender. Drain and leave to cool. Set about half the sorrel leaves aside. Shred the remaining leaves by piling up six or eight at a time, rolling them up like a fat cigar and slicing them with a sharp knife. Thinly slice the potatoes lengthways.

2 Brush a baking sheet with a little of the oil. Lay a sheet of filo pastry on the sheet, brush it with oil, then lay a second sheet crossways over the first. Repeat with two more sheets. Arrange a quarter of the sliced potatoes in the centre, season and add a quarter of the shredded sorrel. Lay a bream fillet on top, skin side up. Season with salt and ground black pepper.

3 Loosely fold the filo pastry up and over to make a neat parcel, then repeat to make three more. Place the parcels on the baking sheet and brush with half the butter. Bake for about 20 minutes, or until the filo is puffed up and golden brown.

4 Meanwhile, make the sorrel sauce. Heat the remaining butter in a pan, add the reserved sorrel and cook gently for 3 minutes, stirring, until it wilts. Stir in the stock and cream. Heat almost to boiling point, stirring continuously so that the sorrel breaks down. Season to taste and keep hot until the fish parcels are ready. Serve garnished with red pepper. Pass round the sauce separately.

Smoked Haddock and Potato Flan

The classic combination of potatoes and smoked fish is here reworked in pastry for this delicious flan.

Serves 4
For the pastry
225g/8oz/2 cups plain (all-purpose) flour
pinch of salt
115g/4oz/1½ cup cold butter, cut into chunks
cold water, to mix

For the filling
2 undyed smoked haddock fillets, approximately 200g/7oz
600ml/1 pint/2½ cups full-fat (whole) milk
3–4 black peppercorns
sprig of fresh thyme
150ml/¼ pint/⅔ cup double (heavy) cream
2 eggs
200g/7oz potatoes, peeled and diced
ground black pepper

1 Preheat the oven to 200°C/400°F/Gas 6. Use a food processor to make the pastry. Put the flour, salt and butter into the food processor bowl and process until the mixture resembles fine breadcrumbs. Pour in a little cold water (you will need about 40ml/8 tsp) and continue to process until the mixture forms a ball. If this takes longer than 30 seconds, add a dash or two more water. Take the pastry ball out of the food processor, wrap in clear film (plastic wrap) and leave to rest in a cool place for about 30 minutes.

2 Roll out the dough and use to line a 20cm/8in flan tin (pan). Prick the base of the pastry all over with a fork, then bake blind in the preheated oven for 20 minutes.

3 Put the haddock in a pan with the milk, peppercorns and thyme. Poach for 10 minutes. Remove the fish from the pan and flake into small chunks. Allow the poaching liquor to cool.

4 Whisk the cream and eggs together thoroughly, then whisk in the cooled poaching liquid.

5 Layer the pastry case (pie shell) with the flaked fish and diced potato, seasoning with black pepper. Pour the cream mixture over the top. Put the flan in the oven and bake for 40 minutes, until lightly browned on top and set. Serve hot.

Sea Bream Energy 651kcal/2,710kJ; Protein 35.8g; Carbohydrate 23.2g, of which sugars 3.3g; Fat 46.8g, of which saturates 23.2g; Cholesterol 159mg; Calcium 222mg; Fibre 2g; Sodium 359mg.
Haddock Flan Energy 734kcal/3064kJ; Protein 23.8g; Carbohydrate 58.4g, of which sugars 8.2g; Fat 46.8g, of which saturates 27.9g; Cholesterol 225mg; Calcium 280mg; Fibre 2.3g; Sodium 636mg.

Smoked Haddock and Potato Pie

Smoked haddock has a salty flavour and can be bought either dyed or undyed. The dyed fish has a strong yellow colour while the undyed is almost creamy in colour.

Serves 4
450g/1lb smoked haddock fillet
475ml/16fl oz/2 cups
  semi-skimmed (low-fat) milk
2 bay leaves
1 onion, quartered
4 cloves
450g/1lb new potatoes
butter, for greasing
30ml/2 tbsp cornflour (cornstarch)
60ml/4 tbsp double (heavy) cream
30ml/2 tbsp chopped fresh chervil
salt and ground black pepper
mixed vegetables, to serve

1 Preheat the oven to 200°C/400°F/Gas 6. Place the haddock in a deep-sided frying pan. Pour the milk over and add the bay leaves. Stud the onion with the cloves and place it in the pan with the fish and milk. Cover the top and leave to simmer for about 10 minutes or until the fish starts to flake.

2 Remove the fish with a slotted spoon and set aside to cool. Strain the liquid from the pan into a separate pan and set aside.

3 Cut the potatoes into fine even slices, leaving the skins on. Blanch in a pan of lightly salted water for 5 minutes, then drain.

4 Grease the base and sides of a 1.2 litre/2 pint/5 cup ovenproof dish. Then, using a knife and fork, flake the fish.

5 Reheat the milk in the pan. Mix the cornflour with a little water to form a paste and stir in the cream and the chervil. Add to the milk in the pan and cook until thickened.

6 Arrange one-third of the potatoes over the base of the dish and season with pepper. Lay half of the fish over. Repeat the layering, finishing with a layer of potatoes on top.

7 Pour the sauce over the top, making sure that it sinks down through the mixture. Cover with foil and cook for 30 minutes. Remove the foil and cook for a further 10 minutes to brown the surface. Serve with a selection of mixed vegetables.

Trout with Fennel and Potatoes

Cooking trout, fennel and potatoes together in one pan makes for an easy supper. Add your favourite steamed green vegetables to complete the meal.

Serves 2
1 small fennel bulb, about
  175g/6oz, with fronds
25g/1oz/2 tbsp butter, plus extra
  for greasing
350g/12oz potatoes, peeled and
  thinly sliced
1 bay leaf
60ml/4 tbsp dry vermouth
60ml/4 tbsp water
2 trout, about 225g/8oz
  each, cleaned
lemon and lime slices, to garnish
steamed green vegetables,
  to serve

1 Preheat the oven to 180°C/350°F/Gas 4. Cut the feathery green fronds from the fennel, chop very finely and set aside. Slice the fennel bulb thinly. Grease a shallow baking dish with butter and spread out the fennel bulb slices to cover the base of the dish.

2 Spread out the potato slices on top of the fennel and top with the bay leaf. Pour the vermouth and water over the vegetables. Season to taste. Cover the dish tightly with foil and bake in the oven for 35–40 minutes.

3 Remove the dish from the oven and lift off the foil. Place the trout on top of the vegetables and dot generously with butter. Replace the foil and bake for 20–25 minutes more, until the trout are cooked and the vegetables are tender.

4 Remove the foil and sprinkle the remaining chopped fennel over the fish. Garnish with the lemon and lime slices. Serve immediately, with the steamed green vegetables.

> **Cook's Tip**
> *Dry vermouth has a concentrated flavour that works well in this recipe, and the herbs that are an intrinsic part of it are more than a match for the robust flavour of the fennel.*

Smoked Haddock Pie Energy 300kcal/1266kJ; Protein 23.9g; Carbohydrate 32.4g, of which sugars 1.9g; Fat 9.3g, of which saturates 5.3g; Cholesterol 61mg; Calcium 56mg; Fibre 1.5g; Sodium 881mg.
Trout with Fennel Energy 461kcal/1937kJ; Protein 38.8g; Carbohydrate 31.4g, of which sugars 5.4g; Fat 17.7g, of which saturates 8.5g; Cholesterol 173mg; Calcium 90mg; Fibre 3.9g; Sodium 259mg.

Burbot and Potato Chowder

Burbot is a large freshwater fish with soft, well-flavoured flesh. This fish and potato chowder can be served on its own as a tasty appetizer or with fresh crusty bread for a sustaining main meal.

Serves 4

1kg/2¼lb burbot or monkfish, with their bones, if filleted
20g/¾oz/1½ tbsp unsalted butter
1 onion, chopped
1 small celery stick, chopped
1 small leek, chopped
1 bay leaf
10 whole allspice
5 white peppercorns
1.5 litres/2½ pints/6¼ cups water
1 carrot, finely diced
500g/1¼lb potatoes, cubed
5ml/1 tsp plain white (all-purpose) flour
200ml/7fl oz/scant 1 cup double (heavy) cream
salt and ground white pepper
dill sprigs, to garnish

1 Fillet the fish or, if the fishmonger fillets it for you, ask him to reserve the bones and head. Cut the fish into large chunks.

2 Heat the butter in a pan, add the onion, celery, leek, fish bones, fish head and any fish trimmings. Fry for 5 minutes until the vegetables soften. Add the bay leaf, allspice, peppercorns, 15ml/1 tbsp salt and 1 litre/1¾ pints/4 cups of the water. Bring to the boil, then simmer very gently for 30 minutes.

3 Strain the stock through a sieve (strainer) into a clean pan. (There should still be about 1 litre/1¾ pints/4 cups of liquid. Add extra water, if necessary, to make up the correct amount.)

4 Add the carrot and potato to the stock and bring to the boil. Lower the heat and simmer until the potato is nearly cooked. The timing will depend on the size of the potato cubes.

5 Add the fish to the pan and return to simmering point, then sprinkle over the flour and continue to simmer for a further 5 minutes, or until the fish is just cooked.

6 Stir in the cream, then taste and add salt and pepper according to taste. Pour into individual serving dishes and serve hot, garnished with a sprig of dill.

Mediterranean Fish and Potato Bake

This fish and potato bake uses the delicious combination of potatoes, wine, garlic, tomatoes and fresh fish to produce a fragrant and elegant main course dish, perfect for alfresco dining on long summer evenings.

Serves 4

3 potatoes
2 onions, halved and sliced
30ml/2 tbsp olive oil, plus extra for greasing and drizzling
2 garlic cloves, very finely chopped
675g/1½ lb thick skinless fish fillets, such as turbot or sea bass
1 bay leaf
1 thyme sprig
3 tomatoes, peeled and thinly sliced
30ml/2 tbsp orange juice
60ml/4 tbsp dry white wine
2.5ml/½ tsp saffron strands, steeped in 60ml/4 tbsp boiling water
salt and ground black pepper

1 Cook the potatoes in boiling salted water for 15 minutes, then drain. When the potatoes are cool enough to handle, peel off the skins and slice the potatoes thinly.

2 Meanwhile, in a heavy frying pan, fry the onions in the oil over a medium-low heat for about 10 minutes, stirring frequently. Add the garlic and continue cooking for a few minutes until the onions are soft and golden.

3 Preheat the oven to 190°C/375°F/Gas 5. Oil a 2 litre/3½ pint/8 cup baking dish and cover the base with a layer of half of the cooked potato slices. Cover with half the onions and season well with salt and black pepper.

4 Place the fish fillets on top of the vegetables and tuck the herbs in between them. Top with the tomato slices and then the remaining onions. Finish with a second layer of potatoes, arranging them neatly.

5 Pour over the orange juice, white wine and saffron liquid, season with salt and black pepper and drizzle a little extra olive oil on top. Bake the fish uncovered for about 30 minutes, until the potatoes are tender and the fish is cooked. Serve hot.

Burbot Chowder Energy 582kcal/2431kJ; Protein 47.6g; Carbohydrate 25.8g, of which sugars 6.4g; Fat 32.6g, of which saturates 19.7g; Cholesterol 119mg; Calcium 77mg; Fibre 2.8g; Sodium 117mg.
Fish Bake Energy 342kcal/1440kJ; Protein 35.1g; Carbohydrate 33.1g, of which sugars 11.7g; Fat 7.5g, of which saturates 1.2g; Cholesterol 78mg; Calcium 61mg; Fibre 3.8g; Sodium 127mg.

Potato and Mackerel Pilaki

Pilaki are popular dishes from Turkey, where the most common dishes are made with firm-fleshed fish. The classic one is made with bonito, but mackerel and sea bass are equally good. Potatoes are always used.

Serves 4–6

2 good-sized fresh mackerel, gutted and rinsed
120ml/4fl oz/½ cup good quality olive oil
2 onions, chopped
3–4 garlic cloves, chopped
1 mild fresh green chilli, seeded and chopped
2–3 carrots, diced
2–3 potatoes, diced
1 medium celeriac, weighing about 450g/1lb, peeled, trimmed and diced
2 large tomatoes, skinned and chopped, or 400g/14oz can chopped tomatoes, drained
5ml/1 tsp sugar
2–3 bay leaves
juice of 2 lemons
1 small bunch of fresh flat leaf parsley
salt and ground black pepper

1 Preheat the oven to 160°C/325°F/Gas 3. Cut the fish crossways into 2cm/¾in slices, keeping it intact at the backbone.

2 Heat the oil in a heavy pan. Stir in the onions, garlic and chilli and cook until soft. Add the carrots, potatoes and celeriac and cook for 2 minutes, then add the tomatoes, sugar and bay leaves.

3 Pour in 600ml/1 pint/2½ cups water and bring to the boil. Cover the pan, then simmer for 5–10 minutes, until the vegetables are just tender. Season with salt and pepper.

4 Spoon half the vegetables over the bottom of an ovenproof dish, place the fish on top and spoon the remaining vegetables over them. Sprinkle with the lemon juice and lay a few sprigs of parsley on top.

5 Cover with baking parchment that has been soaked in water and squeezed out. Bake for 20 minutes until the fish is cooked.

6 Remove the paper and parsley sprigs and serve hot, garnished with a little chopped parsley. Alternatively, leave the pilaki to cool in the dish and serve at room temperature.

Halibut and Sweet Potato Curry

Although the rice is simply boiled, it is an integral part of this dish and takes on the delicious and complex flavours of the fragrant sweet potato sauce with which it is served.

Serves 4

2 halibut steaks, total weight about 500–675g/1¼–1½lb
30ml/2 tbsp groundnut (peanut) oil
2 cardamom pods
1 cinnamon stick
6 allspice berries
4 cloves
1 large onion, chopped
3 garlic cloves, crushed
10–15ml/2–3 tsp grated fresh root ginger
10ml/2 tsp ground cumin
5ml/1 tsp ground coriander
2.5ml/½ tsp cayenne pepper or to taste
4 tomatoes, peeled, seeded and chopped
1 sweet potato, about 225g/8oz, cut into 2cm/¾in cubes
475ml/16fl oz/2 cups fish stock
115g/4oz piece of creamed coconut or 120ml/4 fl oz/½ cup coconut cream
1 bay leaf
225g/8oz/generous 1 cup white long grain rice
salt

1 Rub the halibut steaks well with salt and set aside. Heat the oil in a flameproof casserole and stir-fry the cardamom pods, cinnamon stick, allspice berries and cloves for 3 minutes.

2 Add the onion, garlic and ginger. Continue cooking for 4–5 minutes over a gentle heat, until the onion is fairly soft, stirring frequently, then add the cumin, coriander and cayenne pepper and cook briefly, stirring constantly.

3 Stir in the tomatoes, sweet potato, stock or water, coconut and bay leaf. Season with salt. Bring to the boil, then cover and simmer for 15–18 minutes, until the sweet potato is tender.

4 Cook the rice according to your preferred method. Meanwhile, add the fish steaks to the pan of sauce and spoon the sauce over them. Cover the pan with a lid and simmer for about 10 minutes, until the fish is just tender and flakes easily.

5 Spoon the rice into a warmed serving dish, spoon over the sauce and arrange the steaks on top. Serve immediately.

Mackerel Pilaki Energy 270kcal/1127kJ; Protein 17.3g; Carbohydrate 22.9g, of which sugars 11.2g; Fat 12.7g, of which saturates 2.7g; Cholesterol 40mg; Calcium 76mg; Fibre 4.1g; Sodium 115mg.
Halibut Curry Energy 639kcal/2669kJ; Protein 34.1g; Carbohydrate 62g, of which sugars 8.3g; Fat 28.4g, of which saturates 18.7g; Cholesterol 44mg; Calcium 74mg; Fibre 2.4g; Sodium 115mg.

Basque-style Tuna and Potatoes

This traditional Spanish stew is made in a slow cooker and is packed with robust, fiery flavours which are soaked up by tasty chunks of potato and meaty tuna.

Serves 4

30ml/2 tbsp olive oil
1 onion, finely chopped
1 garlic clove, finely chopped
75ml/2½ fl oz/⅓ cup white wine, preferably Spanish
200g/7oz can chopped tomatoes
150ml/¼ pint/⅔ cup boiling fish or vegetable stock
5ml/1 tsp paprika
2.5ml/½ tsp dried crushed chillies
450g/1lb waxy new potatoes, cut into 1cm/½ in chunks
1 red and 1 yellow (bell) pepper, seeded and chopped
1 small sprig of fresh rosemary
1 bay leaf
450g/1lb fresh tuna, cut into 2.5cm/1in chunks
salt and ground black pepper
crusty bread, to serve

1 Heat the oil in a large frying pan, add the onion and fry gently for 10 minutes until soft and translucent. Stir in the garlic, followed by the wine, stock, tomatoes, paprika and chillies. Bring to just below boiling point, then carefully pour the mixture into the ceramic cooking pot of a slow cooker.

2 Add the chunks of potato, red and yellow pepper, rosemary and bay leaf to the pot and stir to combine. Cover the slow cooker with the lid and cook on high for 2–2½ hours, or until the potatoes are just tender, then season the sauce to taste with salt and a little ground black pepper.

3 Stir the chunks of tuna into the sauce. Cover and cook for 15–20 minutes until the fish is firm and opaque.

4 Remove the rosemary and bay leaf, then ladle the stew into warmed dishes, grind over a little more black pepper and serve with crusty bread.

Cook's Tip
For a more economical store cupboard dish, use a drained 200g/7oz can of tuna in place of the fresh fish.

Tuna and Potato Marmitako

This traditional Spanish fisherman's stew, of tuna and potatoes, is wonderfully balanced by the flavours of sweet peppers and cider. It takes its name from the French cooking pot known as a 'marmite'.

Serves 4

60ml/4 tbsp olive oil
1 onion, chopped
2 garlic cloves, finely chopped
3 green (bell) peppers, seeded and chopped
½ dried hot chilli, seeded and chopped
4 light tuna or bonito steaks about 150g/5oz each
400g/14oz can tomatoes with juice
10ml/2 tsp paprika
3 potatoes, diced
350ml/12 fl oz/1½ cups dry (hard) cider
salt and ground black pepper
30ml/2 tbsp chopped fresh parsley, to garnish

1 Heat half the oil in a shallow flameproof casserole big enough to take the fish. Fry the onion gently until softened, then add the garlic. Add the peppers and chilli and stir-fry gently.

2 Season the fish steaks. Heat the remaining oil in a frying pan and fry the fish steaks for 2 minutes on each side over a high heat.

3 Add the tomatoes to the casserole and stir briefly. Add the paprika, then season with salt and pepper to taste.

4 Slip the fish steaks into the sauce, moving the peppers into the spaces between them. Cover with the potatoes, pushing them as flat as possible. Add the cider and bring to a simmer. Cover and cook very gently for about 45 minutes, or until the potatoes are done.

5 Check the seasoning, sprinkle with the chopped parsley and serve immediately, straight from the casserole.

Variation
Veal chops can be used in the same way. Fry for 5 minutes on each side in step 2, then continue as with the fish.

Basque Tuna Energy 862kcal/3634kJ; Protein 55.2g; Carbohydrate 95.5g, of which sugars 0.6g; Fat 31.6g, of which saturates 12.3g; Cholesterol 209mg; Calcium 126mg; Fibre 13.6g; Sodium 1711mg.
Tuna Marmitako: Energy 393kcal/1648kJ; Protein 42.8g; Carbohydrate 13.8g, of which sugars 12.4g; Fat 16.8g, of which saturates 3.4g; Cholesterol 47mg; Calcium 64mg; Fibre 3.4g; Sodium 121mg.

Baked Tuna with Golden Potatoes

This delicious dish makes the most of tender, succulent tuna. Crisp, golden potatoes, which are baked alongside the fish, are the perfect accompaniment.

Serves 4

105ml/7 tbsp extra virgin
    olive oil
juice of 1 large lemon
3 garlic cloves, crushed
4 medium-thick tuna steaks, total
    weight about 800g/1¾lb
45ml/3 tbsp chopped fresh parsley
15ml/1 tbsp fresh oregano
500g/1¼lb potatoes, peeled and
    cut into small cubes
450g/1lb ripe tomatoes, peeled
    and chopped
150ml/¼ pint/⅔ cup hot water
salt and ground black pepper
fresh green salad tossed in olive
    oil, to serve

1 Mix the oil with the lemon juice and garlic, in a shallow dish that will hold all the tuna steaks snugly in a single layer. Stir in salt and pepper, then add the tuna steaks. Sprinkle over the herbs and turn the steaks to thoroughly coat in the marinade. Leave to marinate for 1–2 hours. Lift the steaks out and lay them in a roasting pan.

2 Preheat the oven to 180°C/350°F/Gas 4. Drop the cubes of potato into the marinating dish and turn to coat them thoroughly in the oil and lemon mixture.

3 Arrange the coated potatoes around the tuna steaks, drizzle over any remaining marinade and sprinkle the peeled and chopped tomatoes over the top. Pour the hot water into the roasting pan.

4 Bake the tuna for 40 minutes, turning it over halfway through and stirring the potatoes and other ingredients.

5 Lift the tuna out of the pan. Place on a warmed plate and cover with foil to keep warm. Increase the oven to 200°C/400°F/Gas 6 and add a little more hot water to the pan.

6 Cook the potatoes for about 15 minutes more to brown them and make them crisp. Serve the tuna and potato mixture with a green salad.

Tuna, Mascarpone and Potato Bake

This substantial one-dish meal, ideal for informal midweek entertaining, embraces the smoky flavour of seared tuna. The sweet and herby Italian sauce, a combination of mascarpone, tomatoes, basil and garlic, is a wonderful foil for the deliciously robust chunks of meaty fish and grated potato.

Serves 4

4 x 175g/6oz tuna steaks
400g/14oz can chopped
    tomatoes, drained
2 garlic cloves, crushed
30ml/2 tbsp chopped fresh basil
250g/9oz/generous 1 cup
    mascarpone cheese
3 large potatoes
25g/1oz/2 tbsp butter, diced
salt and ground black pepper

1 Preheat the oven to 200°C/400°F/Gas 6. Heat a griddle pan on the hob and sear the fish steaks for 2 minutes on each side, seasoning with a little black pepper. Set aside while you prepare the sauce.

2 Mix the chopped tomatoes, garlic, basil and cheese together in a bowl and season to taste with salt and plenty of ground black pepper.

3 Peel the potatoes, then grate half of them and dice the other half. Blanch them in separate pans of lightly salted water for about 3 minutes. Drain thoroughly and set aside to cool slightly. When the grated potato is cool enough to handle, squeeze out any excess moisture.

4 Lightly grease a 1.75 litre/3 pint/7½ cup ovenproof dish. Spoon over a little of the sauce and some of the grated potato. Lay the tuna over with more sauce and the remaining grated potato. Sprinkle the diced butter and the diced potatoes over the top. Bake for 30 minutes until cooked through and brown on top.

> **Variation**
> *This dish can easily be made into a side dish, simply leave out the tuna and prepare the other ingredients as above.*

Baked Tuna Energy 556kcal/2330kJ; Protein 50.7g; Carbohydrate 24g, of which sugars 5.4g; Fat 29.3g, of which saturates 5.4g; Cholesterol 56mg; Calcium 73mg; Fibre 3g; Sodium 122mg.
Tuna Bake Energy 520kcal/2185kJ; Protein 51g; Carbohydrate 29.3g, of which sugars 6.9g; Fat 22.9g, of which saturates 11.2g; Cholesterol 89mg; Calcium 65mg; Fibre 2.6g; Sodium 178mg.

Jansson's Temptation

Named after a well-known Swedish opera singer who liked to serve it to his guests after a performance, this warming baked dish of grated potatoes, cream and canned anchovies is the perfect antidote to the mid-winter blues.

Serves 6
6 large potatoes
1 Spanish (Bermuda) onion, thinly sliced
120ml/4fl oz/½ cup milk
250ml/8fl oz/1 cup double (heavy) cream
100g/3½oz can Swedish anchovies
salt and ground black pepper

1 Preheat the oven to 180°C/350°F/Gas 4. Peel and grate the potatoes. Put in a sieve (strainer) and wash under cold running water to remove any excess starch. Drain well and put in a bowl.

2 Add a sliced onion to the potatoes and mix together, then put in a greased, shallow, ovenproof dish.

3 Mix together the milk and cream. Put both the liquid and the fish from the can of anchovies into the milk mixture and stir together.

4 Pour the mixture over the potatoes and season with salt and pepper. Bake in the oven for 50 minutes until golden brown and bubbling.

Cook's Tips
• Swedish anchovies can be found at well-stocked delicatessens. If they are not readily available you can use ordinary salted anchovies and soak them in milk for a couple of hours to remove the saltiness.
• To make this recipe in individual portions, divide the ingredients on to large squares of buttered foil. Gather up the foil around the ingredients and bring the edges together. Bake for 40 minutes.
• This dish is delicious served on its own or with a salad and is also perfect when eaten with cold sliced ham.

Creamy Anchovy and Potato Bake

This tasty dish of potatoes, onions and anchovies cooked with cream makes a hearty winter lunch or simple supper, served with a refreshing salad. It could also be served as a hot appetizer.

Serves 4
1kg/2¼lb maincrop potatoes
2 onions

25g/1oz/2 tbsp butter
2 x 50g/2oz cans anchovy fillets
150ml/¼ pint/⅔ cup single (light) cream
150ml/¼ pint/⅔ cup double (heavy) cream
15ml/1 tbsp chopped fresh parsley
freshly ground black pepper
fresh crusty bread, to serve

1 Peel the potatoes and cut into slices slightly thicker than 1cm/½in. Cut the slices into strips slightly more than 1cm/½in wide. Peel the onions and cut into very thin rings.

2 Use half of the butter to grease the base and sides of the ceramic cooking pot, and layer half the potatoes and onions in the base of the dish.

3 Drain the anchovies, reserving 15ml/1 tbsp of the oil. Cut the anchovies into thin strips and lay these over the potatoes and onions, then layer the remaining potatoes and onions on the top.

4 Combine the single cream and anchovy oil in a small jug (pitcher) and season with a little ground black pepper. Pour the mixture over the potatoes and dot the surface with butter.

5 Cover and cook on high for 3½ hours, or until the potatoes and onions are tender. Brown under a hot grill (broiler), if you like, then drizzle over the double cream and sprinkle with parsley and pepper. Serve with fresh crusty bread.

Cook's Tip
This recipe can also be served as an appetizer for six, or as a side dish to accompany a main meal.

Jansson's Temptation Energy 400kcal/1669kJ; Protein 9.4g; Carbohydrate 36.5g, of which sugars 6.1g; Fat 25.1g, of which saturates 14.6g; Cholesterol 69mg; Calcium 115mg; Fibre 2.5g; Sodium 696mg.
Creamy Bake Energy 378kcal/1580kJ; Protein 11.3g; Carbohydrate 37.9g, of which sugars 6.4g; Fat 21.2g, of which saturates 11.4g; Cholesterol 54mg; Calcium 1460mg; Fibre 11.5g; Sodium 133mg.

Potatoes with Leeks and Herring

Potatoes and bread may seem like an unlikely combination, but this delicious open sandwich from Denmark proves that the two can be paired with triumphant results. Potatoes are an essential and valued part of the traditional Danish diet, and almost no meal is served without them.

Makes 4
40g/1½ oz/3 tbsp salted
   butter, softened
90g/3½oz leek, sliced
2 slices rye bread
2 round (butterhead)
   lettuce leaves
4–5 small new potatoes, peeled,
   boiled and thinly sliced
12–16 pieces pickled herring,
   about 2.5cm/1in square
10ml/2 tsp chopped chives

1 Melt 15g/½ oz/1 tbsp of the butter in a heavy frying pan. Stir in the leeks and cook over a medium heat, stirring constantly, for about 5 minutes, until wilted and softened slightly. Remove the pan from the heat and leave aside to cool.

2 Spread the slices of rye bread with the remaining butter, making sure to cover one side of each slice right up to the edge. Top the buttered rye bread with the lettuce leaves and cut each slice evenly in half.

3 Transfer each half slice of bread to a serving plate and layer between four to six slices of potato over the lettuce on each sandwich, making sure to cover the bread evenly.

4 Arrange three or four herring pieces down the centre of the potatoes and spoon 30ml/2 tbsp of the cooled fried leeks over the herring on each sandwich.

5 Generously sprinkle over the chopped chives and serve the sandwiches immediately.

Cook's Tip
After the bread has been sliced, move the slices to a serving plate or individual plates before arranging the toppings and garnish.

Pilchard and Leek Potato Cakes

This is a simple supper using a selection of basic store-cupboard ingredients, which makes it ideal for a quick and easy midweek meal. Using canned pilchards that come in tomato sauce gives a greater depth of flavour to the finished dish.

Serves 6
225g/8oz potatoes, diced
425g/15oz can pilchards
   in tomato sauce, boned
   and flaked
1 small leek, very finely chopped
5ml/1 tsp lemon juice
salt and ground black pepper

For the coating
1 egg, beaten
75g/3oz/1½ cups fresh
   white breadcrumbs
vegetable oil for frying
salad leaves, cucumber ribbons
   and lemon wedges, to garnish
mayonnaise, to serve

1 Cook the potatoes in a pan of lightly salted boiling water for about 10–15 minutes or until tender. Drain thoroughly, then mash, and set aside to cool.

2 Add the pilchards and their tomato sauce, the leek and lemon juice to the cooled mashed potato. Season with salt and ground black pepper and then beat well with a wooden spoon until you have formed a smooth paste. Chill in the refrigerator for 30 minutes.

3 Divide the mixture into six pieces and shape into cakes. Dip each cake in the egg and then the breadcrumbs.

4 Heat the oil and shallow fry the fish cakes on each side for 5 minutes until golden brown. Drain on kitchen paper and garnish with salad leaves, cucumber ribbons and lemon wedges. Serve with mayonnaise.

Cook's Tip
Chilling the mixture in the refrigerator before shaping makes it easier to form into cakes prior to coating and frying.

Pilchard Cakes Energy 294kcal/1229kJ; Protein 16.9g; Carbohydrate 17.1g, of which sugars 1.9g; Fat 18.1g, of which saturates 2.4g; Cholesterol 71mg; Calcium 243mg; Fibre 1.3g; Sodium 374mg.
Herring and Leeks Energy 196kcal/819kJ; Protein 6.6g; Carbohydrate 17.2g, of which sugars 4.2g; Fat 11.5g, of which saturates 5.3g; Cholesterol 32mg; Calcium 27mg; Fibre 1.7g; Sodium 347mg.

Eel and Potato Stew

This hearty eel and potato stew is both filling and full of flavour. The firm-fleshed eel and slices of potato soak up all the delicious flavours of the fragrant broth. This can also be made with a variety of other fish. One delicious variation is to combine several types of fish, such as sardines, skate or conger eel.

Serves 4

1kg/2½lb eel fillets, cut into
   4cm/1½in slices
500g/1¼lb potatoes, cut into
   5mm/¼in slices
2 onions, very thinly sliced
2 bay leaves, torn into pieces
2 garlic cloves, chopped
50ml/2fl oz/¼ cup white wine
105ml/7 tbsp olive oil
1 bunch of parsley, chopped
5–7.5ml/1–1½ tsp ground ginger
salt
bread, to serve

1 If you haven't asked your fishmonger to prepare the eels, prepare them yourself by cutting off the heads and sprinkling the skin with salt so you can pull it off. Then rinse them well in cold running water.

2 Make a layer of potatoes in a large pan, then make a layer of onions, followed by a layer of fish. Season with pieces of bay leaf, some garlic, a little wine and olive oil and a sprinkling of parsley, ginger and salt. Continue making layers in this way until all the ingredients have been used up.

3 Sprinkle in 100ml/3½fl oz/scant ½ cup water, cover and cook on a low heat for about 30 minutes, until the fish is cooked through and the vegetables are tender. Serve with fresh bread.

> **Variations**
> • You can add some green and red (bell) pepper between the layers, if you like.
> • The eels can also be cooked in 4cm/1½in boned pieces, in which case make the potato slices thicker as the eel will take longer to cook.

Eel with Potatoes in Cream Sauce

This dish is a great way to enjoy fried eel. Served with these delicious potatoes and accompanied by a cold beer, this seasonal dish is a summer speciality.

Serves 4

1kg/2¼lb eel, skinned and cleaned
1 egg
5ml/1 tsp water
25g/1oz/½ cup fine
   breadcrumbs, toasted
10ml/2 tsp salt
2.5ml/½ tsp white pepper
40g/1½oz/3 tbsp butter
2 lemons, sliced into wedges,
   to garnish

For the potatoes
800g/1¾lb potatoes, peeled
5ml/1 tsp salt
40g/1½oz/3 tbsp butter
20g/¾oz/4 tbsp plain
   (all-purpose) flour
475ml/16fl oz/2 cups single
   (light) cream
salt and white pepper, to taste
45ml/3 tbsp chopped fresh
   parsley, to garnish

1 Using a sharp knife, cut the skinned eel into 10cm/4in lengths. Whisk together the egg and water in a shallow dish. Place the breadcrumbs in a second shallow dish. Dip the eel first into the egg mixture, then into the breadcrumbs to coat both sides evenly. Sprinkle with salt and pepper. Leave the fish aside to rest for at least 10 minutes.

2 Melt the butter in a large pan over a medium-high heat. Add the eel pieces and cook, turning once, for around 10 minutes on each side, depending on thickness, until the coating is golden brown and the eel is tender. Remove from the pan and drain on kitchen paper. Keep warm.

3 Meanwhile, boil the potatoes in salted water for about 20 minutes. Drain, slice and keep warm. Melt the butter in a pan and stir in the flour. Cook, stirring, for 5 minutes until the roux is pale beige. Slowly stir in the cream and cook for about 5 minutes, stirring constantly, until the sauce has thickened. Season to taste.

4 Stir the potato slices into the cream sauce. Serve with the fried eel on warmed plates, sprinkled with parsley and garnished with lemon wedges.

Fried Eel Energy 978kcal/4074kJ; Protein 50.2g; Carbohydrate 43.7g, of which sugars 5.6g; Fat 68.2g, of which saturates 32.3g; Cholesterol 483mg; Calcium 184mg; Fibre 2.3g; Sodium 448mg.
Eel Stew Energy 738kcal/3074kJ; Protein 45.5g; Carbohydrate 30.4g, of which sugars 9g; Fat 48.3g, of which saturates 10.1g; Cholesterol 375mg; Calcium 113mg; Fibre 3.6g; Sodium 245mg.

Cuttlefish with Potatoes

Sautéed cuttlefish is sweeter and more tender than squid, provided you buy small or medium specimens. If the only ones available are very large, cook them for a little longer than stated in the recipe below. Serve as a sumptuous main course or a tasty meze dish.

Serves 4 as a main course; 6 as a first course

1kg/2¼lb fresh
  cuttlefish, cleaned
150ml/¼ pint/⅔ cup extra virgin
  olive oil
1 large onion, about
  225g/8oz, chopped
175ml/6fl oz/¾ cup white wine
300ml/½ pint/1¼ cups
  hot water
500g/1¼lb potatoes, peeled
  and cubed
4–5 spring onions
  (scallions), chopped
juice of 1 lemon
60ml/4 tbsp chopped fresh dill
salt and ground black pepper

1 Rinse and drain the cleaned cuttlefish well, then slice them into 2cm/¾in wide ribbons.

2 Heat the oil in a heavy pan, add the onion and cook for about 5 minutes until light golden.

3 Add the cuttlefish to the onions and cook, stirring occasionally, until all the water they exude has evaporated and the flesh starts to change colour. This will take approximately 10–15 minutes.

4 Pour the white wine into the pan and allow to simmer briskly. When it has evaporated, add the water. Cover the pan and simmer gently for 10 minutes.

5 Add the potatoes, spring onions and lemon juice to the pan. Season with salt and ground black pepper. There should be enough water in the pan almost to cover the ingredients; top up if necessary.

6 Cover and cook gently for 40 minutes, or until the cuttlefish is tender. Add the dill and cook for 5 minutes. Serve the cuttlefish immediately on oven warmed plates.

Squid and Potato Casserole

This hearty stew is ideal on a cold evening. The potatoes disintegrate to thicken and enrich the sauce, making a warming, comforting main course packed with taste.

Serves 6

800g/1¾lb squid
45ml/3 tbsp olive oil
5 garlic cloves, crushed
4 fresh jalapeño chillies, seeded
  and finely chopped
2 celery sticks, diced
500g/1¼lb small new potatoes
  or baby salad potatoes,
  scrubbed, scraped or peeled
  and quartered
400ml/14fl oz/1⅔ cups dry
  white wine
400ml/14fl oz/1⅔ cups fish stock
4 tomatoes, diced
30ml/2 tbsp chopped fresh flat
  leaf parsley
salt
white rice or corn bread,
  to serve

1 Clean the squid under cold water. Pull the tentacles away from the body. The squid's entrails should come out easily. Remove the cartilage from inside the body cavity and discard it. Wash the body thoroughly.

2 Pull away the membrane that covers the body. Cut between the tentacles and head, discarding both the head and entrails. Leave the tentacles whole but discard the hard beak in the middle. Cut the body into thin rounds.

3 Heat the oil, add the garlic, chillies and celery and cook for 5 minutes. Stir in the potatoes, then add the wine and stock. Bring to the boil, then simmer, covered, for 25 minutes.

4 Remove from the heat and stir in the squid, tomatoes and parsley. Cover the pan and leave to stand until the squid is cooked. Serve immediately with boiled white rice or cornbread.

> **Cook's Tip**
> Adding the tomatoes and parsley at the end of cooking gives a real freshness to the sauce. If you want an even heartier dish, add these ingredients to the pan with the potatoes.

Cuttlefish Energy 540kcal/2254kJ; Protein 43.3g; Carbohydrate 24.7g, of which sugars 5.1g; Fat 27.3g, of which saturates 4.2g; Cholesterol 275mg; Calcium 176mg; Fibre 2.2g; Sodium 943mg.
Squid Casserole Energy 273kcal/1150kJ; Protein 22.7g; Carbohydrate 17.5g, of which sugars 3.6g; Fat 8.3g, of which saturates 1.5g; Cholesterol 300mg; Calcium 53mg; Fibre 2g; Sodium 173mg.

Indonesian Prawns with Sliced Potatoes

With a fresh-tasting combination of prawns and potatoes, cooked Indonesian style with satay sauce, this dish makes a deliciously rich and filling main course.

Serves 4

2 large waxy potatoes, peeled
   and cut in half
120ml/4fl oz/½ cup vegetable oil
1 bunch spring onions (scallions),
   finely sliced
2 red chillies, seeded and diced
450g/1lb peeled cooked
   prawns (shrimp)
45ml/3 tbsp crunchy peanut butter
200ml/7fl oz/scant 1 cup
   coconut cream
15ml/1 tbsp dark soy sauce
1 bunch chopped fresh
   coriander (cilantro)
salt

1 Boil the potatoes in lightly salted water for 15 minutes until tender. Drain, and when cool enough to handle, cut into 3mm/⅛in slices. Heat the oil in a frying pan and fry the potatoes for 10 minutes, turning occasionally until browned. Drain on kitchen paper and keep hot.

2 Drain off almost all of the oil from the pan and fry the spring onions and half the chillies in the pan for 1 minute. Add the peeled prawns and toss for a few seconds.

3 Beat together the peanut butter, coconut cream, soy sauce and remaining chilli. Add this sauce to the prawns and cook for a further minute or two until heated through.

4 Lightly grease a large serving platter and arrange the potatoes evenly around the base. Spoon the prawn mixture over until the potatoes are mostly covered. Top with the coriander.

> **Cook's Tip**
> For a more luxurious version, replace the prawns (shrimp) with fresh raw, shelled king prawns (jumbo shrimp).

Prawn and New Potato Stew

New potatoes with plenty of flavour, such as Jersey Royals, Maris Piper or Nicola, are essential for this effortless stew. Use a good quality jar of tomato and chilli sauce; there are now plenty available in the supermarkets. For a really easy supper dish, serve with warm, crusty bread to mop up the delicious sauce, and a mixed green salad.

Serves 4

675g/1½lb small new or salad
   potatoes, scrubbed
15g/½oz/½ cup fresh
   coriander (cilantro)
350g/12oz jar tomato and
   chilli sauce
300g/11oz cooked peeled prawns
   (shrimp), thawed and drained
   if frozen

1 Cook the potatoes in lightly salted, boiling water for 15 minutes, until tender. Drain and return to the pan.

2 Finely chop half the fresh coriander and add to the pan along with the tomato and chilli sauce and about 90ml/6 tbsp water. Bring the mixture to the boil, reduce the heat, cover and simmer gently for 5 minutes.

3 Stir the prawns into the potatoes and sauce and heat briefly until they are warmed through. Do not overheat the prawns or they will quickly shrivel, becoming tough and tasteless.

4 Spoon the stew into shallow bowls and serve sprinkled with the remaining coriander, torn into pieces.

> **Cook's Tip**
> If you prefer, you can make your own tomato and chilli sauce for this dish. Gently fry some finely chopped onion in a little oil for 10 minutes until soft. Add 2 red chillies, that have been seeded and finely chopped, to the pan and cook for a further 3–5 minutes. Pour in a 400g/14oz can of chopped tomatoes and season with salt and pepper. Simmer for 10–15 minutes then use as specified in the recipe above.

Indonesian Prawns Energy 577kcal/2396kJ; Protein 26.7g; Carbohydrate 20.5g, of which sugars 4.6g; Fat 43.4g, of which saturates 18.4g; Cholesterol 219mg; Calcium 119mg; Fibre 2g; Sodium 489mg.
Prawn Stew Energy 218kcal/924kJ; Protein 16.9g; Carbohydrate 30.4g, of which sugars 5.4g; Fat 4.1g, of which saturates 0.7g; Cholesterol 146mg; Calcium 84mg; Fibre 2.9g; Sodium 171mg.

Sweet Potato, Pumpkin and Prawn Cakes

This unusual Asian combination of sweet potato, pumpkin and prawn makes a delicious dish which needs only a salty fish or soy sauce to dip into as an accompaniment. Serve with noodles or fried rice for a more substantial meal.

Serves 4

200g/7oz/1¾ cups strong white
  bread flour
2.5ml/½ tsp salt
2.5ml/½ tsp dried yeast
175ml/6fl oz/¾ cup warm water
1 egg, beaten
200g/7oz raw prawns (shrimp)
225g/8oz pumpkin, peeled,
  seeded and grated
150g/5oz sweet potato, grated
2 spring onions
  (scallions), chopped
50g/2oz water
  chestnuts, chopped
2.5ml/½ tsp chilli sauce
1 garlic clove, crushed
juice of ½ lime
vegetable oil, for deep-frying
lime wedges, to serve

1 Sift together the flour and salt into a large bowl and make a well in the centre. In a separate container, dissolve the yeast in the water until creamy, then pour into the centre of the flour and salt mixture. Pour in the egg and set aside for a few minutes until bubbles appear. Mix to form a smooth batter.

2 Peel the prawns, if necessary, then place in a pan with just enough boiling water to cover. Simmer for about 2 minutes or until the prawns have turned pink. Drain, rinse in cold water and drain again well. Coarsely chop the prawns, then place in a bowl with the pumpkin and sweet potato.

3 Add the spring onions, water chestnuts, chilli sauce, garlic and lime juice and mix well. Fold into the batter mixture carefully until evenly mixed.

4 Heat a 1cm/½ in layer of oil in a large frying pan until really hot. Spoon in the batter in heaps, leaving space between each one, and cook until golden brown on both sides. Drain well on kitchen paper and keep warm as you cook the rest. Serve hot with the lime wedges.

Prawn and Potato Omelette

Similar to a Spanish tortilla, this potato dish makes a delicious and filling lunch when served with a fresh leafy green salad. The sweet prawns are cooked gently inside the omelette, staying tender and succulent.

Serves 6

200g/7oz potatoes, peeled
  and diced
30ml/2 tbsp olive oil
1 onion, finely sliced
2.5ml/½ tsp paprika
2 large tomatoes, peeled, seeded
  and chopped
200g/7oz peeled raw
  prawns (shrimp)
6 eggs
2.5ml/½ tsp baking powder
salt

1 Cook the potatoes in a pan of salted boiling water for about 10 minutes or until tender.

2 Meanwhile, pour the oil into a 23cm/9in frying pan which can safely be used under the grill (broiler). Place the pan over a medium heat.

3 Add the onion slices and stir well to coat evenly in the oil. Cook for 5 minutes until the onions begin to soften but not turn brown. Sprinkle over the paprika and cook for a further 1 minute, stirring constantly.

4 Stir in the tomatoes. Drain the cooked potatoes thoroughly, then add them to the pan. Stir gently to mix. Increase the heat and cook for 10 minutes, or until the mixture has thickened and the potatoes have absorbed the flavour of the tomatoes.

5 Remove the pan from the heat. Add the prawns and stir gently to combine with the other ingredients.

6 Preheat the grill. Beat the eggs in a separate bowl, stir in the baking powder and salt. Pour the egg mixture into the pan and mix thoroughly.

7 Cover the pan and cook for 8–10 minutes until the omelette has almost set, then finish under the grill. Serve hot in wedges.

Prawn Cakes Energy 317kcal/1346kJ; Protein 18.2g; Carbohydrate 57.6g, of which sugars 9.1g; Fat 3.2g, of which saturates 0.9g; Cholesterol 145mg; Calcium 216mg; Fibre 6g; Sodium 383mg.
Prawn Omelette Energy 247kcal/1031kJ; Protein 19.6g; Carbohydrate 10.8g, of which sugars 3g; Fat 14.5g, of which saturates 3.3g; Cholesterol 383mg; Calcium 93mg; Fibre 1.2g; Sodium 211mg.

Chilli Crab and Potato Cakes

Crab meat makes wonderful fish and potato cakes, as shown by these gutsy morsels. Served with a rich tomato dip, they make great party food.

Makes about 15

225g/8oz white crab meat (fresh, frozen or canned)
115g/4oz cooked potatoes, mashed
30ml/2 tbsp fresh herb seasoning
2.5ml/½ tsp mild mustard
2.5ml/½ tsp ground black pepper
½ fresh hot chilli, finely chopped
5ml/1 tsp fresh oregano
1 egg, beaten
plain (all-purpose) flour, for dredging

vegetable oil, for frying
lime wedges and coriander (cilantro) sprigs, to garnish
fresh whole chilli peppers, to garnish

For the tomato dip
15g/½oz/1 tbsp butter or margarine
½ onion, finely chopped
2 canned plum tomatoes, chopped
1 garlic clove, crushed
150ml/¼ pint/⅔ cup water
5–10ml/1–2 tsp malt vinegar
15ml/1 tbsp chopped fresh coriander (cilantro)
½ hot fresh chilli, chopped

1 Mix together the crab meat, potatoes, herb seasoning, mustard, pepper, chilli, oregano and egg in a large bowl. Chill the mixture for at least 30 minutes.

2 Meanwhile, make the tomato dip. Melt the butter or margarine in a small pan over a medium heat. Add the onion, tomatoes and garlic and cook for about 5 minutes until the onion is tender. Add the water, vinegar, coriander and fresh chilli.

3 Bring to the boil, reduce the heat and simmer for about 10 minutes. Transfer the mixture to a food processor or blender and blend to a smooth purée.

4 Shape the chilled crab mixture into rounds and dredge with flour, shaking off the excess. Heat a little oil in a frying pan and fry, a few cakes at a time, for 2–3 minutes on each side. Drain on kitchen paper and keep warm in a low oven while cooking the remainder. Garnish with lime wedges, coriander sprigs and whole chillies and serve immediately with the tomato dip.

Baked Mussels and Potatoes

This imaginative shellfish and potato casserole uses some of the best Italian flavours – tomatoes, garlic, basil and, of course, plump, juicy mussels.

Serves 2–3
800g/1¾lb large mussels, in their shells

225g/8oz small firm potatoes
75ml/5 tbsp olive oil
2 garlic cloves, finely chopped
8 fresh basil leaves, torn into pieces
2 medium tomatoes, peeled and thinly sliced
45ml/3 tbsp breadcrumbs
ground black pepper
basil leaves, to garnish

1 Cut off the 'beards' from the mussels. Scrub and soak in several changes of cold water. Discard any with broken shells or ones that are open.

2 Place the mussels with a cupful of water in a large pan over a medium heat. As soon as the mussel shells open, lift them out of the water. Remove and discard the empty half shells, leaving the mussels in the other half. (Discard any mussels that do not open at this stage.) Strain any cooking liquid remaining in the pan through a layer of kitchen paper, and reserve to add at the final stage.

3 Cook the potatoes in a large pan of boiling water for about 10–12 minutes or until they are almost tender. Drain well and leave to cool. When they have cooled enough to handle, peel and slice them.

4 Preheat the oven to 180°C/350°F/Gas 4. Spread 30ml/2 tbsp of the olive oil in the bottom of a shallow ovenproof dish. Cover the base of the dish with the potato slices in one layer. Add the mussels in their half shells in a single layer on top of the potato slices. Sprinkle with the garlic and basil. Cover with a layer of sliced tomato.

5 Sprinkle with breadcrumbs and black pepper, the reserved mussel cooking liquid and the remaining olive oil. Bake for about 20 minutes until the tomatoes are soft and the breadcrumbs are golden brown. Serve hot directly from the baking dish, and garnish with basil.

Chilli Crab Cakes Energy 70kcal/290kJ; Protein 3.5g; Carbohydrate 2.9g, of which sugars 0.7g; Fat 5g, of which saturates 1.1g; Cholesterol 26mg; Calcium 24mg; Fibre 0.3g; Sodium 95mg.
Baked Mussels Energy 348kcal/1457kJ; Protein 16.7g; Carbohydrate 25.8g, of which sugars 3.4g; Fat 20.5g, of which saturates 3g; Cholesterol 30mg; Calcium 178mg; Fibre 1.7g; Sodium 288mg.

Potato and Smoked Mussel Bake

This recipe uses smoked mussels, which have a creamy texture and rich flavour, delicious with sour cream, chives and potatoes. You can easily substitute smoked oysters for the mussels.

Serves 4

2 large maincrop potatoes, cut in half

butter, for greasing
2 shallots, finely diced
2 x 85g/3¼oz cans smoked mussels
1 bunch chives, chopped
300ml/½ pint/1¼ cups sour cream
175g/6oz/1½ cups mature (sharp) Cheddar cheese, grated
salt and ground black pepper
mixed vegetables, to serve

1 Preheat the oven to 180°C/350°F/Gas 4. Cook the potatoes in a large pan of lightly salted boiling water for 15 minutes until they are just tender. Drain and leave to cool slightly. When cool enough to handle, cut the potatoes into even 3mm/⅛in slices.

2 Grease the base and sides of a 1.2 litre/2 pint/5 cup casserole dish. Lay a few potato slices over the base of the dish. Sprinkle a few shallots over and season well.

3 Drain the oil from the mussels into a bowl. Slice the mussels and add them again to the reserved oil. Stir in the chives and sour cream with half of the cheese. Spoon a little of the sauce over the layer of potatoes.

4 Continue to layer the sliced potatoes, shallots and the sauce. Finish with a layer of potatoes and sprinkle over the remainder of the grated cheese.

5 Bake in the oven for 30–45 minutes. Remove from the oven and serve while hot with a selection of mixed vegetables.

Cook's Tip
To serve this dish for a dinner party, rather than serve it in a large dish, once it has cooked, stamp out rounds using a 5cm/2in cutter and serve on a bed of salad leaves.

Clam and Potato Stovies

Clams are now harvested in the lochs of Scotland, especially in Loch Fyne where some of the best Scottish clams are grown on ropes. Here, they are layered with sliced potatoes and slow-cooked in a delicious and hearty baked dish.

Serves 4

2.5 litres/4 pints/10 cups clams
potatoes (see step 3)
oil, for greasing
chopped fresh flat leaf parsley, to garnish
50g/2oz/¼ cup butter
salt and ground black pepper

1 Wash the clams and soak them overnight in fresh cold water. This will clean them out and get rid of any grains of sand and other detritus.

2 Preheat the oven to 190°C/375°F/Gas 5. Put the clams into a large pan, cover with water and bring to the boil. Add a little salt, then simmer until the shells open. Reserve the cooking liquor. Shell the clams, reserving a few whole.

3 Weigh the shelled clams. You will need approximately three times the weight of the clams in unpeeled potatoes.

4 Peel and slice the potatoes thinly. Lightly oil the base and sides of a flameproof, ovenproof dish. Arrange a layer of sliced potatoes in the base of the dish, then add a layer of the clams and season with a little salt and ground black pepper. Repeat the layering process until the ingredients are all used, finishing with a layer of potatoes on top. Finally, season lightly with more salt and black pepper.

5 Pour in some of the reserved cooking liquor to come about halfway up the dish. Dot the top with the butter, then cover the dish tightly with foil. Bring to the boil on top of the stove over a medium-high heat, then transfer to the preheated oven and bake for about 2 hours until the potatoes are tender and the top is golden brown.

6 Serve the bake immediately, garnished with chopped fresh flat leaf parsley.

Mussel Bake Energy 454kcal/1890kJ; Protein 23.1g; Carbohydrate 20.7g, of which sugars 4.5g; Fat 30.6g, of which saturates 19.2g; Cholesterol 115mg; Calcium 424mg; Fibre 1.1g; Sodium 577mg.
Clam Stovies Energy 320kcal/1348kJ; Protein 17.3g; Carbohydrate 36.7g, of which sugars 3.3g; Fat 12.6g, of which saturates 7g; Cholesterol 57mg; Calcium 188mg; Fibre 2.9g; Sodium 262mg.

Smoked Venison with Garlic Potatoes

Smoked venison makes a delicious change from the more common meats. This warming dish makes an ideal supper or lunch, accompanied by creamy potatoes flavoured with plenty of garlic.

Serves 4
675g/1½lb peeled potatoes

175ml/6fl oz/¾ cup milk
1 garlic clove
10ml/2 tsp sea salt
olive oil, for greasing and
   to serve
75ml/2½fl oz/⅓ cup double
   (heavy) cream
115g/4oz sliced smoked venison
salad leaves, such as rocket
   (arugula) to garnish

1 Preheat the oven to 180°C/350°F/Gas 4. Thinly slice the potatoes and place in a pan. Pour in the milk. Using the side of a knife, crush the garlic with the sea salt. Stir the mixture into the potatoes. Bring to the boil over a gentle heat, stirring occasionally, until the milk begins to thicken.

2 Grease the inside of a large gratin dish with a little olive oil. Add the cream to the potatoes and, stirring gently so the potatoes don't break up, combine well. Allow to just come to the boil again, then pour the mixture carefully into the ovenproof gratin dish.

3 Place the dish in the preheated oven for about 1 hour or until the potatoes are lightly browned and tender. To serve, place a scoop of the potato on to a warmed plate and put a pile of smoked venison on top, adding a splash of olive oil over each serving. Garnish with salad leaves.

Cook's Tips
• Use good tasty potatoes, such as King Edward or Maris Piper, for this dish.
• If you cannot find smoked venison in your local supermarket or delicatessen, many smokehouses have websites that offer a mail order delivery service.
• If you are feeling generous, you could use more smoked venison.

Rack of Lamb with Vegetables

Gathering with family members and sharing a feast featuring a magnificent rack of lamb, is one of the real pleasures in life. The red potatoes make an exciting change from the usual white variety.

Serves 8–10
1.8–2kg/4–4½lb rack of lamb,
   fat trimmed from bones

900g/2lb red potatoes, peeled
   and halved
3 medium onions, quartered
900g/2lb carrots, halved
   lengthways
40g/1½oz/⅓ cup plain
   (all-purpose) flour
250ml/8fl oz/1 cup good
   lamb stock
salt and ground black pepper
chopped parsley, to garnish

1 Preheat the oven to 220°C/425°F/Gas 7. To prepare the meat, make a slit in the membrane on each rib and arrange the racks in a circle with the bone ends curving outward.

2 Tie the ribs with fine string to secure them in the crown position. (You can ask your butcher to prepare the crown roast for you.) Wrap the bone ends with foil to prevent them from burning. Rub the meat with salt and pepper, and place the crown on a rack in a roasting pan.

3 Place the lamb in the preheated oven and immediately lower the temperature to 180°C/350°F/Gas 4. Roast for 1½ hours. Do not cover or baste while cooking.

4 Remove the pan from the oven and arrange the potatoes, onions and carrots around the base of the crown. Cook for about 30 minutes more, or until the meat is done to your liking and the vegetables are tender.

5 Transfer the lamb and vegetables to a serving dish and keep warm. Skim the fat from the pan juices. To make the gravy, pour 45ml/3 tbsp pan juices into a pan over a medium heat. Whisk the flour into the pan juices and cook for 3–4 minutes until all of the flour is absorbed. Slowly stir in the remaining pan juices and the stock; cook until thickened. Season to taste with salt and ground black pepper. Serve alongside the lamb and vegetables.

Smoked Venison Energy 281kcal/1180kJ; Protein 15.6g; Carbohydrate 29.5g, of which sugars 4.5g; Fat 12g, of which saturates 6.1g; Cholesterol 25mg; Calcium 80mg; Fibre 1.7g; Sodium 1050mg.
Rack of Lamb Energy 493kcal/2050kJ; Protein 25.6g; Carbohydrate 28.7g, of which sugars 10.7g; Fat 31.5g, of which saturates 15.1g; Cholesterol 97mg; Calcium 62mg; Fibre 3.9g; Sodium 113mg.

Roast Lamb with Potatoes

This simple roast with potatoes owes its wonderful flavour to the addition of fresh rosemary and garlic. Serve with one or two lightly cooked fresh vegetables, such as broccoli, spinach or carrots.

Serves 4
1/2 leg of lamb, about 1.3kg/3lb
2 garlic cloves, cut lengthways into
  thin slivers
105ml/7 tbsp olive oil
leaves from 4 sprigs of fresh
  rosemary, finely chopped
about 250ml/8fl oz/1 cup lamb
  or vegetable stock
675g/1 1/2 lb potatoes, cut into
  2.5cm/1in cubes
a few fresh sage leaves, chopped
salt and ground black pepper

1 Preheat the oven to 230°C/450°F/Gas 8. Using the point of a sharp knife, make several deep incisions in the lamb, especially near the bone, and insert a sliver of garlic into each.

2 Place the lamb in a roasting pan and rub it all over with 45ml/3 tbsp of the oil. Sprinkle over about half of the chopped rosemary, patting it on firmly, and season with plenty of salt and pepper. Roast for 30 minutes, turning once.

3 Lower the temperature to 190°C/375°F/Gas 5. Turn the lamb over again. Pour in 125ml/4fl oz/1/2 cup of the stock.

4 Roast for a further 1 1/4–1 1/2 hours until the lamb is tender, turning the joint two or three times more and adding the rest of the stock in two or three batches. Baste the lamb each time it is turned.

5 Meanwhile, put the potatoes in a separate roasting pan and toss with the remaining oil and rosemary and the sage. Roast the potatoes on the same shelf as the lamb, if possible, for 45 minutes, turning the potatoes several times until golden and tender.

6 Transfer the lamb to a carving board, cover with foil and leave for 10 minutes before carving. Serve with the roast potatoes and accompany with green vegetables, baby carrots or roasted Mediterranean vegetables.

Gigot Boulangère

A delicious pairing of lamb, garlic and potatoes, this is a trouble-free choice for Sunday lunch.

Serves 6
50g/2oz/1/4 cup butter, plus extra
  for greasing
4–6 garlic cloves
2 yellow onions, thinly sliced
12–18 thyme or rosemary sprigs
2 fresh bay leaves
1.8kg/4lb red potatoes, thinly sliced
450ml/3/4 pint/scant 2 cups hot
  lamb or vegetable stock
2kg/4 1/2lb leg of lamb
30ml/2 tbsp olive oil
salt and ground black pepper

1 Preheat the oven to 190°C/375°F/Gas 5. Use a little butter to grease a large ovenproof dish, about 6cm/2 1/2in deep. Finely chop half the garlic and sprinkle a little over the prepared dish.

2 Fry the onions in 25g/1oz/2 tbsp of the butter for 5–8 minutes, until softened. Roughly chop half the thyme or rosemary and crush the bay leaves.

3 Arrange a layer of potatoes in the dish, season and sprinkle with half the remaining garlic, rosemary or thyme, one bay leaf and the onions. Add the remaining potatoes, garlic and herbs.

4 Pour in the stock and add a little hot water to bring the liquid to just below the level of the potatoes. Dot with the remaining butter, cover with foil and cook in the oven for 40 minutes. Increase the temperature to 200°C/400°F/Gas 6.

5 Meanwhile, cut the rest of the garlic into slivers. Make slits all over the lamb with a narrow, sharp knife and insert slivers of garlic and sprigs of thyme or rosemary into the slits. Season the lamb well with salt and pepper.

6 Uncover the potatoes and sprinkle a few rosemary or thyme sprigs over them. Rest a roasting rack or ovenproof cooling rack over the dish and place the lamb on it. Rub the olive oil over the meat, then return the dish to the oven. Cook, turning the lamb once or twice, for 1 1/2–1 3/4 hours, depending on how well done you prefer lamb. Leave the lamb to rest for 20 minutes in a warm place before carving.

Roast Lamb Energy 493kcal/2050kJ; Protein 25.6g; Carbohydrate 28.7g, of which sugars 10.7g; Fat 31.5g, of which saturates 15.1g; Cholesterol 97mg; Calcium 62mg; Fibre 3.9g; Sodium 113mg.
Gigot Boulangère Energy 980kcal/4114kJ; Protein 101.8g; Carbohydrate 52.3g, of which sugars 6.8g; Fat 41.9g, of which saturates 19.3g; Cholesterol 384mg; Calcium 82mg; Fibre 3.7g; Sodium 358mg.

Garlic-spiked Lamb with Potatoes

This is the Greek equivalent of the Sunday roast, but everything is cooked in a single dish so that all the flavours meld together. The fragrant lemon and garlic lamb is deliciously tender and the beautifully crisp potatoes, roasted in with the lamb, take on all the delicious flavours and aromas of the traditional Mediterranean ingredients.

Serves 6–8

1 leg of lamb, about 2kg/4¹/₂lb
3 garlic cloves, quartered
lengthways, plus 6–8 whole,
  unpeeled garlic cloves, or
  1–2 heads of garlic, halved
900g/2lb potatoes, peeled and
  quartered lengthways
juice of 1 lemon
45ml/3 tbsp extra virgin
  olive oil
450ml/³/₄ pint/scant 2 cups
  hot water
5ml/1 tsp dried
  Greek oregano
2.5ml/¹/₂ tsp dried Greek thyme
  or 5ml/1 tsp chopped
  fresh thyme
salt and ground black pepper

1 Preheat the oven to 220°C/425°F/Gas 7. Place the meat in a large roasting pan. Make several incisions in it and insert one or two quarters of garlic into each one.

2 Arrange the potatoes and whole garlic cloves or halved heads of garlic around the meat, pour the lemon juice and olive oil over, and add half the water to the dish. Sprinkle over half the herbs, and some seasoning.

3 Roast the lamb for 15 minutes, then reduce the oven temperature to 190°C/375°F/Gas 5. Roast for 1 hour.

4 Turn the meat over to brown the other side, sprinkle over the rest of the herbs and seasoning, and turn the potatoes over gently. Add the remaining hot water to the pan and cook for another 25–30 minutes, basting occasionally with the pan juices.

5 Cover the meat with a clean dish towel and let it rest for 10 minutes before serving. The cloves of garlic can be popped out of their skins and eaten with the meat; they will be deliciously creamy.

Middle Eastern Roast Lamb and Potatoes

When the aroma of garlic and saffron come wafting out of the oven, this deliciously garlicky lamb served with potatoes and onions won't last very long. It makes a welcome change from the traditional roast on a Sunday afternoon.

Serves 6–8

2.75kg/6lb leg of lamb
4 garlic cloves, halved
60ml/4 tbsp olive oil
juice of 1 lemon
2–3 saffron strands, soaked in
  15ml/1 tbsp boiling water
5ml/1 tsp mixed dried herbs
450g/1lb baking potatoes,
  thickly sliced
2 large onions, thickly sliced
salt and ground black pepper
fresh thyme, to garnish

1 Make eight incisions in the skin of the leg of lamb with a sharp knife, press the garlic cloves into the slits and place the lamb in a non-metallic dish.

2 In a bowl, mix together the olive oil, lemon juice, saffron mixture and dried herbs. Rub this mixture over the lamb and marinate for 2 hours. Turn the lamb in the marinade a couple of times, rubbing the marinade all over.

3 Preheat the oven to 180°C/350°F/Gas 4. Layer the potatoes and onions in a large roasting pan.

4 Lift the lamb out of the marinade and place the lamb on top of the potatoes and onions, fat side up, and season well with plenty of salt and ground black pepper.

5 Pour any remaining marinade over the lamb and roast in the preheated oven for about 2 hours. Baste the lamb with the juices that gather two or three times during the cooking process to keep the lamb moist.

6 Remove the pan from the oven, cover with foil and leave to rest for 10–15 minutes before carving. Garnish with fresh thyme and serve.

Garlic Lamb Energy 750kcal/3132kJ; Protein 73.4g; Carbohydrate 24.3g, of which sugars 2.1g; Fat 40.4g, of which saturates 17.3g; Cholesterol 273mg; Calcium 37mg; Fibre 1.8g; Sodium 175mg.
Roast Lamb Energy 270kcal/1124kJ; Protein 27.9g; Carbohydrate 4.9g, of which sugars 1.3g; Fat 15.4g, of which saturates 6.6g; Cholesterol 106mg; Calcium 12mg; Fibre 0.5g; Sodium 64mg.

Traditional Lancashire Lamb and Potato Hotpot

This famous lamb and potato hotpot was traditionally cooked in a farmhouse or communal bread oven, in time for supper at the end of the day. The ingredients would have been layered straight into the pot, but here the meat is first browned to add colour and flavour to the dish.

Serves 4

15–30ml/1–2 tbsp oil

8–12 lean best end of neck (cross rib) lamb chops
about 175g/6oz lamb's kidneys, skin and core removed and cut into pieces
2 medium onions, thinly sliced
few sprigs of fresh thyme or rosemary
900g/2lb potatoes, thinly sliced
600ml/1 pint/2½ cups lamb or vegetable stock
25g/1oz/2 tbsp butter, cubed
salt and ground black pepper

1 Preheat the oven to 180°C/350°F/Gas 4. Heat the oil in a large frying pan and brown the lamb chops quickly on all sides. Remove the meat from the pan and set aside.

2 Add the pieces of kidney to the hot pan and brown lightly over a high heat. Lift out.

3 In a casserole, layer the chops and kidneys with the onions, herbs and potatoes, seasoning each layer.

4 Finish off with a layer of potatoes. Pour over the stock, sprinkle with herbs and dot the top with butter. Cover, put into the preheated oven and cook for 2 hours. Remove the lid, increase the oven temperature to 220°C/425°F/Gas 7 and cook, uncovered, for a further 30 minutes until the potatoes on top are crisp.

Variation
Add sliced carrots or mushrooms to the layers of meat and potato. Replace 150ml/¼ pint/⅔ cup of the stock with dry (hard) cider or dry white wine.

Mutton and Potato Hotpot

Another traditional cottage favourite, this mutton and potato hotpot would have been a Sunday treat in days gone by. Mutton is hard to find today but it really is worth looking out for. Try your local farmers' market or ask your butcher if they could get it for you. It often has a far superior flavour to traditional lamb, although it does require much longer, slower cooking.

Serves 6

6 mutton chops
6 lamb's kidneys
1 large onion, sliced
450g/1lb potatoes, sliced
600ml/1 pint/2½ cups dark stock
salt and ground black pepper

1 Preheat the oven to 180°C/350°F/Gas 4. Trim the mutton chops, leaving a little fat but no bone. Slice the lamb's kidneys in two horizontally, and remove the fat and core with a pair of sharp scissors.

2 Place three of the chops in a deep casserole and season well with salt and ground black pepper.

3 Add a layer of half the kidneys, then half the onion and finally half the potatoes. Season lightly.

4 Repeat the process, seasoning as you go and making sure that you finish with an even layer of potatoes.

5 Heat the stock and pour it into the casserole, just about covering everything but leaving the potatoes just showing at the top. Cover and cook in the preheated oven for 1½ hours.

6 Remove the lid from the casserole and cook for 30 minutes more to allow the potatoes to brown. Serve immediately.

Variation
If you prefer, you can use lamb chops instead. Use two chops per person and reduce the cooking time by 30 minutes as lamb does not need 2 hours.

Hotpot Energy 810kcal/3400kJ; Protein 76.7g; Carbohydrate 43.7g, of which sugars 9.3g; Fat 37.8g, of which saturates 13.2g; Cholesterol 363mg; Calcium 140mg; Fibre 6.2g; Sodium 285mg.
Mutton Hotpot Energy 626kcal/2629kJ; Protein 76.9g; Carbohydrate 23.1g, of which sugars 5g; Fat 25.8g, of which saturates 11.6g; Cholesterol 374mg; Calcium 76mg; Fibre 2g; Sodium 269mg.

Lamb with Shallots and Potatoes

This lamb and potato casserole is finished with a topping of garlic, parsley and lemon rind.

Serves 6

1kg/2¼lb boneless shoulder
   of lamb, cut into 5cm/2in cubes
1 garlic clove, finely chopped
finely grated rind of ½ lemon and
   juice of 1 lemon
90ml/6 tbsp olive oil
45ml/3 tbsp plain (all-purpose)
   flour, seasoned
1 large onion, sliced
5 anchovy fillets in olive oil, drained
2.5ml/½ tsp caster (superfine) sugar

300ml/½ pint/1¼ cups white wine
475ml/16fl oz/2 cups lamb stock
   or half stock and half water
1 bouquet garni, made from
   1 fresh bay leaf, 1 fresh thyme
   sprig and 1 fresh parsley sprig
500g/1¼lb small new potatoes
250g/9oz shallots, peeled but whole
45ml/3 tbsp double (heavy)
   cream (optional)
salt and ground black pepper

For the topping

shredded rind of ½ lemon
45ml/3 tbsp chopped fresh flat
   leaf parsley
1 garlic clove, chopped

1 Mix the lamb, garlic, rind and half the lemon juice. Season, then add 15ml/1 tbsp olive oil and marinate for between 12–24 hours. When ready to cook, chop the topping ingredients together.

2 Drain the lamb, reserving the marinade. Preheat the oven to 180°C/350°F/Gas 4. Heat the oil in a frying pan, toss the lamb in the seasoned flour, then brown in the pan. Transfer to a flameproof casserole. Fry the onion for 10 minutes. Add the anchovies and sugar, mashing the fish well. Add the marinade, wine and stock. Bring to the boil, then simmer for 5 minutes. Pour over the lamb.

3 Add the bouquet garni to the casserole and season. Cover and cook in the oven for 1 hour. Add the potatoes, re-cover, and cook for 20 minutes. Brown the shallots in the frying pan and add to the casserole. Cover and cook for 30–40 minutes. Transfer the lamb and vegetables to a serving dish. Discard the herbs.

4 Boil the cooking juices on the stove to reduce them. Add the cream, if using, and heat through. Season and add lemon juice to taste. Pour over the lamb, sprinkle on the topping and serve.

Irish Lamb and Potato Stew

Simple yet delicious, this potato and lamb main course is quintessentially Irish. Traditionally mutton chops are used, but as they can be hard to find you can use lamb chops instead. The results will still be wonderful.

Serves 4

1.2kg/2½lb boneless lamb chops
15ml/1 tbsp vegetable oil

3 large onions, quartered
4 large carrots, thickly sliced
900ml/1½ pints/3¾ cups water
4 large firm potatoes, cut
   into chunks
1 large thyme sprig
15g/½oz/1 tbsp butter
15ml/1 tbsp chopped
   fresh parsley
salt and ground black pepper
Savoy cabbage, to serve
   (optional)

1 Trim any excess fat from the lamb chops. Heat the vegetable oil in a large flameproof casserole, add the lamb and brown on both sides. Remove from the pan.

2 Add the onions and carrots to the casserole and cook for 5 minutes until the onions are browned. Return the lamb to the pan with the water. Season with salt and pepper. Bring to a boil, then reduce the heat, cover and simmer for 1 hour.

3 Add the potatoes to the pan with the thyme, cover again, and simmer for a further hour.

4 Leave the stew to settle for a few minutes. Remove the fat from the liquid with a ladle, then pour off the liquid into a clean pan. Bring to a simmer and stir in the butter, then the parsley.

5 Season well with salt and pepper and pour back into the casserole. Serve with cabbage, boiled or steamed, if you like.

> **Cook's Tip**
> If you can't find boneless chops, use the same weight of middle neck (US shoulder or breast) of lamb. Ask the butcher to chop the meat into cutlets, which should then be trimmed of any excess fat before cooking.

Lamb with Shallots Energy 553kcal/2311kJ; Protein 37g; Carbohydrate 26.2g, of which sugars 5.3g; Fat 30.6g, of which saturates 10.4g; Cholesterol 128mg; Calcium 79mg; Fibre 2.7g; Sodium 261mg.
Irish Stew Energy 823kcal/3453kJ; Protein 80g; Carbohydrate 50.3g, of which sugars 10.4g; Fat 34.9g, of which saturates 14.8g; Cholesterol 266mg; Calcium 137mg; Fibre 4.4g; Sodium 540mg.

Minty Lamb, Leek and Potato Bake

This is especially good with new season's lamb and organically grown leeks, and the deliciously crisp potato crust hides a treasure trove of exciting flavours. If you have some home-made chicken stock it boosts the flavour tremendously; if not, use a good quality ready-made stock rather than a dried bouillon cube.

Serves 6

30ml/2 tbsp sunflower oil
2kg/4½lb fillet or boned leg of
  lamb, cubed
10 spring onions (scallions),
  thickly sliced
3 leeks, thickly sliced
15ml/1 tbsp flour
150ml/¼ pint/⅔ cup white wine
300ml/½ pint/1¼ cups
  chicken stock
15ml/1 tbsp tomato purée (paste)
15ml/1 tbsp sugar
30ml/2 tbsp fresh mint leaves,
  finely chopped, plus a few more
  to garnish
115g/4oz/⅔ cup dried
  pears, chopped
1kg/2¼lb potatoes, peeled
  and sliced
25g/1oz/2 tbsp melted butter
salt and ground black pepper

1 Preheat the oven to 180°C/350°F/Gas 4. Heat the oil in a large heavy frying pan and cook the cubed lamb fillet or leg for a few minutes, turning occasionally, to seal it. Transfer to a large casserole dish.

2 Add the sliced onions and leeks and cook for 3–5 minutes. Stir in the flour and cook for another minute. Add the wine and stock and bring to the boil.

3 Add the tomato purée and sugar, and season with salt and ground pepper. Stir in the chopped mint leaves and pears and then pour into the casserole. Stir the mixture well to combine the ingredients. Arrange the sliced potatoes on top and brush with the melted butter.

4 Cover the casserole with a tight-fitting lid and bake in the preheated oven for 1½ hours. Then increase the oven temperature to 200°C/400°F/Gas 6, and cook for a further 30 minutes, uncovered, to brown the potatoes. Garnish with mint leaves and serve immediately.

Moussaka

This classic Greek dish with lamb, potatoes and aubergine (eggplant) is layered through with a rich, cheesy topping to make a substantial meal.

Serves 6

30ml/2 tbsp olive oil
30ml/2 tbsp chopped
  fresh oregano
1 large onion, finely chopped
675g/1½lb lamb, minced (ground)
1 large aubergine (eggplant), sliced
2 x 400g/14oz cans
  chopped tomatoes
45ml/3 tbsp tomato purée (paste)
1 lamb stock cube, crumbled
2 floury main crop
  potatoes, halved
115g/4oz/1 cup Cheddar
  cheese, grated
150 ml/½ pint/⅔ cup single
  (light) cream
salt and ground black pepper
fresh bread, to serve

1 Preheat the oven to 180°C/350°F/Gas 4. Heat the olive oil in a large deep-sided frying pan. Fry the oregano and onions over a low heat, stirring frequently, for about 5 minutes or until the onions have softened.

2 Stir in the lamb and cook for 10 minutes until browned. Meanwhile, grill the aubergine slices for 5 minutes until browned, turning once.

3 Stir the tomatoes and purée into the mince mixture, and crumble the stock cube over it, stir well, season with salt and pepper and simmer uncovered for a further 15 minutes.

4 Meanwhile, cook the potatoes in lightly salted boiling water for 5–10 minutes until just tender. Drain, and when cool enough to handle, cut into thin slices.

5 Layer the aubergine, mince and potatoes in a 1.75 litre/3 pint/7½ cup oval ovenproof dish, finishing with a layer of potatoes.

6 Mix the cheese and cream together in a bowl and pour over the top of the other ingredients in the dish. Cook for around 45–50 minutes until the moussaka is bubbling and golden on the top. Serve straight from the dish, while hot, with plenty of fresh, crusty bread.

Minty Lamb Energy 846kcal/3542kJ; Protein 70.3g; Carbohydrate 37.3g, of which sugars 10.1g; Fat 45.5g, of which saturates 20.3g; Cholesterol 263mg; Calcium 75mg; Fibre 4.5g; Sodium 347mg.
Moussaka Energy 588Kcal/2444kJ; Protein 37.9g; Carbohydrate 14.8g, of which sugars 3.7g; Fat 40.9g, of which saturates 18.2g; Cholesterol 206mg; Calcium 379mg; Fibre 2.4g; Sodium 506mg.

Mutton and Potato Pies

These meat and potato pies make a nutritious portable meal and are ideal for family picnics.

Makes 6 small pies
450g/1lb boneless mutton or lamb
1 large onion, diced
2 carrots, diced
1 potato, diced
2 celery sticks, diced

1 egg, beaten
salt and ground black pepper

For the shortcrust pastry
500g/1¼lb/5 cups plain
 (all-purpose) flour
250g/9oz/generous 1 cup butter,
 or half butter and half white
 vegetable fat (shortening)
120ml/4fl oz/½ cup very
 cold water

1 To make the pastry, sift the flour into a large bowl and add the butter. Rub the butter into the flour with the fingertips or a pastry blender, lifting the mixture as much as possible to aerate. Add the chilled water. Mix with a knife or fork until the mixture clings together. Turn it on to a floured surface and knead lightly once or twice until smooth. Wrap in baking parchment or foil and leave in the refrigerator to relax for 20 minutes before using.

2 Trim any fat or gristle from the meat and cut it up into very small pieces. Place in a large bowl and add the diced onion, carrots, potato and celery. Mix well and season with salt and ground black pepper.

3 Preheat the oven to 180°C/350°F/Gas 4. Cut a third off the ball of pastry and reserve to make the lids of the pies. Roll out the rest and, using a small plate as a guide and re-rolling the pastry as necessary, cut out six circles. Divide the meat and vegetable mixture between the circles, piling it in the middle of each.

4 Roll out the remaining pastry and cut out six smaller circles, about 10cm/4in across. Lay these on top. Dampen the edges of the pastry bases, bring the pastry up around the meat, pleat it to fit the lid and pinch the edges together.

5 Make a small hole in the top of each pie to let out the steam. Brush with beaten egg and slide the pies on to baking sheets. Bake in the oven for an hour. Serve hot or cold.

Shepherd's Pie

This potato topped dish was developed during Victorian days as an economical way of making the most of leftover meat. By the 1930s it had become a regular part of the British eating pattern, and was made with meat from the Sunday roast and served to the family on Monday or Tuesday. When it is made with beef it is known as cottage pie.

Serves 4
1kg/2¼lb potatoes, peeled
60ml/4 tbsp milk
about 25g/1oz/2 tbsp butter
15ml/1 tbsp oil
1 large onion, finely chopped
1 medium carrot, finely chopped
450g/1lb cold cooked lamb,
 minced (ground)
150ml/¼ pint/⅔ cup lamb or
 beef stock
30ml/2 tbsp chopped parsley
salt and ground black pepper

1 Preheat the oven to 190°C/375°F/Gas 5. Boil the potatoes in salted water for about 20 minutes or until soft. Drain, and mash with the milk, adding butter, salt and ground black pepper to taste.

2 Heat the oil in a heavy frying pan and add the onion and carrot. Cook over medium heat for about 5–10 minutes, stirring occasionally, until softened. Stir in the minced meat, lamb or beef stock and parsley.

3 Spread the meat mixture in an ovenproof dish and spoon the mashed potato evenly over the top, creating an attractive pattern with a fork, if you like. Cook in the hot oven for about 30 minutes until the potatoes are crisped and browned.

Variations
• Add extra ingredients to the meat base, if you like, such as a clove or two of chopped garlic, a few wild mushrooms, a spoonful of tomato purée (paste) or ketchup, or a splash of Worcestershire sauce.
• You could also mix the potatoes with other vegetables, such as mashed parsnip, squash or swede (rutabaga), and grate over a layer of mature cheddar before cooking.

Mutton Pies Energy 784kcal/3275kJ; Protein 25.1g; Carbohydrate 74.6g, of which sugars 5.2g; Fat 44.9g, of which saturates 26.1g; Cholesterol 178mg; Calcium 155mg; Fibre 4g; Sodium 345mg.
Shepherd's Pie Energy 487kcal/2045kJ; Protein 29.4g; Carbohydrate 50.1g, of which sugars 15.2g; Fat 20.2g, of which saturates 8.4g; Cholesterol 69mg; Calcium 54mg; Fibre 5.3g; Sodium 379mg.

Lamb Pie with Mustard Potatoes

Shepherd's pie with a twist, the mustard gives a real tang to the potato topping.

Serves 4
800g/1¾lb floury potatoes, diced
60ml/4 tbsp milk
15ml/1 tbsp wholegrain or
 French mustard
a little butter
450g/1lb lamb, minced (ground)

1 onion, chopped
2 celery sticks, thinly sliced
2 carrots, diced
30ml/2 tbsp cornflour (cornstarch)
 blended into 150ml/¼ pint/⅔
 cup lamb stock
15ml/1 tbsp Worcestershire sauce
30ml/2 tbsp chopped fresh
 rosemary, or 10ml/2 tsp dried
salt and ground black pepper
fresh vegetables, to serve

1 Cook the potatoes in a large pan of boiling, lightly salted water until tender. Drain well and mash until smooth, then stir in the milk, mustard, butter and seasoning to taste. Meanwhile, preheat the oven to 200°C/400°F/Gas 6.

2 Fry the lamb in a non-stick pan, breaking it up with a fork, until lightly browned all over. Add the onion, celery and carrots to the pan and cook for 2–3 minutes, stirring, to stop the mixture sticking to the base.

3 Stir in the stock and cornflour mixture. Bring to the boil, stirring all the while, then remove from the heat. Stir in the Worcestershire sauce and rosemary and season with salt and pepper to taste.

4 Turn the lamb mixture into a 1.75 litre/3 pint/7 cup ovenproof dish and spread over the potato topping evenly, swirling with the edge of a palette knife. Bake for 30–35 minutes until golden on the top. Serve hot with a selection of fresh vegetables.

Variations
• This recipe can be adapted to make a cottage pie, simply follow the method above substituting lamb with minced (ground) beef.
• To vary the potato topping slightly, try adding horseradish – either creamed or for an even stronger flavour, freshly grated.

Lamb Pie with a Potato Crust

This tasty pie, topped with mashed potato, is cooked entirely in the microwave, making a quick and easy meal to prepare for all the family.

Serves 4
675g/1½lb potatoes, diced
45ml/3 tbsp water
30ml/2 tbsp skimmed milk
15ml/1 tbsp wholegrain or
 French mustard

1 onion, chopped
2 celery sticks, sliced
2 carrots, diced
450g/1lb lean minced
 (ground) lamb
150ml/¼ pint/⅔ cup beef stock
60ml/4 tbsp rolled oats
15ml/1 tbsp Worcestershire sauce
30ml/2 tbsp chopped
 fresh rosemary
salt and ground black pepper

1 Place the potatoes in a microwave-proof bowl with the water. Cover and microwave on HIGH for 8–10 minutes, until tender, stirring once. Drain and mash until smooth, then stir in the milk and mustard.

2 Place the onion, celery and carrots in a large microwave-proof bowl. Cover and microwave on HIGH for 5 minutes, stirring once. Add the minced lamb, mixing well. Microwave on HIGH for 2 minutes, stirring once.

3 Stir in the stock, oats, Worcestershire sauce and rosemary, and season to taste. Cover loosely and microwave on HIGH for 20–25 minutes, until cooked, stirring twice.

4 Turn the meat mixture into a 1.75 litre/3 pint/7½ cup microwave-proof dish that is suitable for grilling (broiling). Swirl the potato evenly over the top. Microwave, uncovered, on HIGH for 4–5 minutes until hot. Brown under a grill (broiler), if liked. Serve with freshly cooked vegetables.

Cook's Tip
This recipe is suitable for cooking in a combination microwave. Follow the oven manufacturer's timing guide for good results.

Lamb and Mustard Pie Energy 371kcal/1561kJ; Protein 26.5g; Carbohydrate 37.9g, of which sugars 7.7g; Fat 13.7g, of which saturates 6.2g; Cholesterol 86mg; Calcium 68mg; Fibre 3.3g; Sodium 194mg.
Lamb Pie Energy 408kcal/1716kJ; Protein 27.6g; Carbohydrate 44.1g, of which sugars 7.7g; Fat 14.7g, of which saturates 6.1g; Cholesterol 86mg; Calcium 65mg; Fibre 4.3g; Sodium 191mg.

Lamb, New Potato and Chilli Curry

This dish makes the most of an economical cut of meat by cooking it slowly until the meat is falling from the bone. Chillies, potatoes and coconut cream give it lots of flavour.

Serves 4

25g/1oz/2 tbsp butter

4 garlic cloves, crushed

2 onions, sliced into rings

2.5ml/½ tsp each ground cumin, ground coriander, turmeric and cayenne pepper

2–3 red chillies, seeded and finely chopped

300ml/½ pint/1¼ cups hot chicken stock

200ml/7fl oz/scant 1 cup coconut cream

4 lamb shanks, all excess fat removed

450g/1lb new potatoes, chopped into halves

6 ripe tomatoes, quartered

salt and ground black pepper

coriander (cilantro) leaves, to garnish

spicy rice, to serve

1 Preheat the oven to 160°C/325°F/Gas 3. Melt the butter in a large flameproof casserole dish, add the garlic and onions and cook over a low heat for 15 minutes, until soft and golden. Stir in the ground spices and chopped chillies, then cook for a further 2 minutes.

2 Stir in the hot stock and coconut cream. Place the lamb shanks in the liquid and cover the casserole dish with foil. Cook in the hot oven for around 2 hours, turning the shanks twice, first after about an hour or so and again about half an hour later. The meat should be beautifully tender and falling off the bone.

3 Par-boil the potatoes for 10 minutes, drain and add to the casserole dish with the tomatoes, then cook uncovered in the oven for a further 35 minutes. Season to taste and garnish with coriander leaves. Serve with the spicy rice.

> **Cook's Tip**
> *Make this dish a day in advance if possible. Cool and chill overnight, then skim off the excess fat that has risen to the surface. Reheat thoroughly before you serve it.*

Spicy Lamb and Potato Stew

Indian spices transform this simple lamb and potato stew into a mouthwatering dish fit for princes. Serve with a spicy dhal and some naan bread.

Serves 6

675g/1½lb lean lamb fillet

15ml/1 tbsp oil

1 onion, finely chopped

2 bay leaves

1 fresh green chilli, seeded and finely chopped

2 garlic cloves, finely chopped

10ml/2 tsp ground coriander

5ml/1 tsp ground cumin

2.5ml/½ tsp ground turmeric

2.5ml/½ tsp chilli powder

2.5ml/½ tsp salt

2 tomatoes, peeled and chopped

600ml/1 pint/2½ cups chicken stock

2 large potatoes, cut into bitesize chunks

chopped fresh coriander (cilantro), to garnish

1 Remove any visible fat from the lamb and cut the meat into neat 2.5cm/1in cubes.

2 Heat the oil in a large, heavy pan and fry the onion, bay leaves, chilli and garlic for 5 minutes.

3 Add the cubed meat and cook for about 6–8 minutes until lightly browned all over.

4 Add the ground coriander, ground cumin, ground turmeric, chilli powder and salt and cook the spices for 3–4 minutes, stirring constantly to prevent them from sticking to the bottom of the pan.

5 Add the tomatoes and stock to the pan. Bring the mixture to the boil, then reduce the heat, cover the pan and simmer for about 1 hour.

6 Add the bitesize chunks of potato to the simmering mixture, stir in well, and simmer gently for a further 30–40 minutes, or until the meat is tender, the potatoes are cooked and most of the excess juices have been absorbed, leaving a thick but minimal sauce. Garnish with the chopped fresh coriander and serve piping hot.

Lamb and Potato Curry Energy 364kcal/1528kJ; Protein 23.5g; Carbohydrate 30.5g, of which sugars 12.1g; Fat 17.4g, of which saturates 8.8g; Cholesterol 89mg; Calcium 58mg; Fibre 3.5g; Sodium 205mg.
Spicy Lamb Stew Energy 284kcal/1192kJ; Protein 24g; Carbohydrate 14.1g, of which sugars 3.1g; Fat 15.1g, of which saturates 6.3g; Cholesterol 86mg; Calcium 23mg; Fibre 1.3g; Sodium 109mg.

Lamb and Potato Parsi

This highly fragrant, delicately spiced lamb and potato dish is sure to impress.

Serves 6

900g/2lb lamb fillet, cubed
60ml/4 tbsp ghee or butter
2 onions, sliced
450g/1lb floury potatoes, cut into chunks
chicken stock or water (see method)
450g/1lb/2⅓ cups basmati rice, soaked

pinch of saffron threads, dissolved in 30ml/2 tbsp warm milk
fresh coriander (cilantro) sprigs, to garnish

For the marinade

475ml/16fl oz/2 cups natural (plain) yogurt
3–4 garlic cloves, crushed
10ml/2 tsp cayenne pepper
20ml/4 tsp garam masala
10ml/2 tsp ground cumin
5ml/1 tsp ground coriander

1 Make the marinade by mixing all the ingredients in a large bowl. Add the meat, stir to coat, then cover and leave for 3–4 hours in a cool place or overnight in the refrigerator.

2 Melt 30ml/2 tbsp of the ghee or butter in a large pan and cook the onions for 6–8 minutes. Transfer to a plate.

3 Melt a further 25ml/1½ tbsp of the ghee or butter in the pan. Cook the lamb, in batches, until brown. When all the lamb is browned, return it to the pan and add the remaining marinade.

4 Stir in the potatoes and add three-quarters of the cooked onions. Pour in stock or water to cover. Bring to the boil, then cover and simmer gently for 40–50 minutes, until the potatoes are cooked. Preheat the oven to 160°C/325°F/Gas 3.

5 Drain the rice. Cook it in a pan of boiling stock or water for 5 minutes. Meanwhile, spoon the lamb mixture into a casserole. Drain the rice and mound it on top of the lamb, then make a hole down the centre. Top with the leftover onions, pour the saffron milk over and dot with the remaining ghee or butter.

6 Cover the pan with a double layer of foil and a lid. Cook in the oven for 30–35 minutes, or until the rice is completely tender. Garnish with fresh coriander sprigs and serve.

Lamb Stew with Chilli Sauce

The chillies in this Mexican stew add depth and richness to the sauce, while the potato slices ensure that it is substantial enough to serve on its own.

Serves 6

6 dried guajillo chillies, seeded
2 dried pasilla chillies, seeded
250ml/8fl oz/1 cup hot water
3 garlic cloves, peeled

5ml/1 tsp ground cinnamon
2.5ml/½ tsp ground cloves
2.5ml/½ tsp ground black pepper
15ml/1 tbsp vegetable oil
1kg/2¼lb lean boneless lamb shoulder, cut into 2cm/¾in cubes
400g/14oz potatoes, scrubbed and cut into 1cm/½in thick slices
salt
strips of red pepper and fresh oregano, to garnish

1 Snap or tear the dried chillies into large pieces, put them in a bowl and pour over the hot water. Leave to soak for 30 minutes, then tip the contents of the bowl into a food processor or blender. Add the garlic and spices. Process until smooth.

2 Heat the oil in a large pan. Add the lamb cubes, in batches and stir-fry over a high heat until the cubes are evenly browned on all sides.

3 Return all the lamb cubes to the pan, spread them out, then cover them with a layer of potato slices. Add salt to taste. Put a lid on the pan and cook over a medium heat for 10 minutes.

4 Pour the chilli mixture over the lamb and mix thoroughly. Replace the lid and simmer over a low heat for about 1 hour or until both the meat and potato are tender. Serve with a rice dish, and garnish with strips of red pepper and fresh oregano.

Cook's Tips
• When frying the lamb do not be tempted to cook too many cubes at one time, as the meat will steam rather than fry.
• Both guajillo and pasilla chillies are dried at the time of harvest and it is important to wash them before use. They are available to buy from well-stocked supermarkets or online.

Lamb Parsi Energy 764kcal/3193kJ; Protein 41g; Carbohydrate 81.9g, of which sugars 9.8g; Fat 30.6g, of which saturates 16.1g; Cholesterol 147mg; Calcium 196mg; Fibre 1.5g; Sodium 295mg.
Lamb with Chilli Sauce Energy 367kcal/1536kJ; Protein 34g; Carbohydrate 11.8g, of which sugars 1.9g; Fat 20.8g, of which saturates 9g; Cholesterol 127mg; Calcium 19mg; Fibre 0.9g; Sodium 151mg.

Steak with Stout and Potatoes

The Irish way to braise beef is in stout, of course, and topped with thickly sliced potatoes. Bake it in a moderate oven for long, slow tenderizing if you prefer.

Serves 4
675g/1½lb stewing beef
15ml/1 tbsp vegetable oil
25g/1oz/2 tbsp butter
225g/8oz tiny white onions
175ml/6fl oz/¾ cup stout or dark beer

300ml/½ pint/1¼ cups beef stock
bouquet garni
675g/1½lb firm, waxy potatoes, cut into thick slices
225g/8oz/3 cups large mushrooms, sliced
15ml/1 tbsp plain (all-purpose) flour
2.5ml/½ tsp mild mustard
salt and ground black pepper
chopped thyme sprigs, to garnish

1 Trim any excess fat from the steak and cut into four pieces. Season the meat all over. Heat the oil and 10g/¼oz/1½ tsp of the butter in a large heavy pan. Add the steak and brown on both sides, taking care not to burn the butter. Remove from the pan and set aside.

2 Add the onions to the pan and cook for 3–4 minutes until lightly browned. Return the steak to the pan with the onions. Pour on the stout or beer and stock and season to taste.

3 Next add the bouquet garni and top with the potato slices, distributing them evenly over the surface to cover the steak. Bring to a boil, then cover and simmer gently for 1 hour.

4 Add the sliced mushrooms over the potatoes. Cover again and simmer for a further 30 minutes or so. Remove the steak and vegetables with a slotted spoon and arrange on a platter.

5 Mix the remaining butter with the flour. Whisk a little at a time into the cooking liquid in the pan. Stir in the mustard. Cook over a medium heat for 3 minutes, stirring, until thickened.

6 Season the sauce and pour over the steak. Garnish with plenty of thyme sprigs and serve the dish immediately.

Pot-roasted Brisket with Vegetables

This pot-roasted beef and potato dish includes a large, sausage-shaped dumpling, which is added to the pot and cooked with the meat.

Serves 6–8
5 onions, sliced
3 bay leaves
1–1.6kg/2¼–3½lb beef brisket
1 garlic head, broken into cloves
4 carrots, thickly sliced
5–10ml/1–2 tsp paprika
500ml/17fl oz/generous 2 cups beef stock
3–4 potatoes, peeled and quartered
salt and ground black pepper

For the dumpling
about 90cm/36in sausage casing
250g/9oz/2¼ cups plain (all-purpose) flour
120ml/4fl oz/½ cup semolina or couscous
10–15ml/2–3 tsp paprika
1 carrot, grated and 2 carrots, diced (optional)
250ml/8fl oz/1 cup rendered chicken fat
30ml/2 tbsp crisp, fried onions
½ onion, grated and 3 onions, thinly sliced
3 garlic cloves, finely chopped
salt and ground black pepper

1 Preheat the oven to 180°C/350°F/Gas 4. Put one-third of the onions and a bay leaf in an ovenproof dish, then top with the beef. Sprinkle over the garlic, carrots and the remaining bay leaves. Add salt, pepper and paprika, then top with the remaining onions. Pour in enough stock to fill the dish to about 5–7.5cm/2–3in and cover with foil. Cook in the oven for 2 hours.

2 Meanwhile, make the dumpling. In a bowl, combine all the ingredients and stuff the mixture into the casing, leaving enough space for the mixture to expand. Tie into sausage-shaped lengths.

3 When the meat has cooked for about 2 hours, add the dumpling and potatoes to the pan, re-cover and cook for a further 1 hour, or until the meat and potatoes are tender.

4 Remove the foil from the dish and increase the oven temperature to 190–200°C/375–400°F/Gas 5–6. Move the onions away from the top of the meat to the side of the dish and return to the oven for a further 30 minutes, or until the meat, onions and potatoes are beginning to brown and become crisp. Serve hot or cold.

Steak with Stout Energy 538kcal/2253kJ; Protein 43.4g; Carbohydrate 35.5g, of which sugars 6.2g; Fat 24.5g, of which saturates 10.2g; Cholesterol 111mg; Calcium 44mg; Fibre 3.2g; Sodium 172mg.
Pot-roasted Brisket Energy 586kcal/2453kJ; Protein 33.2g; Carbohydrate 55.5g, of which sugars 9.6g; Fat 27.3g, of which saturates 10.8g; Cholesterol 85mg; Calcium 93mg; Fibre 3.8g; Sodium 93mg.

Beef and Root Vegetable Stew

This slow-cooker dish features beans, grains, meat and root vegetables. The tasty addition of whole boiled eggs is a classic feature.

Serves 4

250g/9oz/1⅓ cups dried haricot
  (navy) beans
30ml/2 tbsp olive oil
1 onion, chopped
4 garlic cloves, finely chopped
50g/2oz pearl barley
15ml/1 tbsp ground paprika
pinch of cayenne pepper
1 celery stick, chopped
400g/14oz can chopped tomatoes
3 carrots, sliced
1 small turnip, diced
2 baking potatoes, peeled and
  cut into chunks
675g/1½lb mixture of beef
  brisket, stewing beef and
  smoked beef, cut into cubes
1 litre/1¾ pints/4 cups boiling
  beef stock
30ml/2 tbsp easy-cook
  (converted) white rice
4 eggs, at room temperature
salt and ground black pepper

1 Place the beans in a large bowl. Pour over cold water to cover and leave to soak for 8 hours, or overnight, if you like.

2 Drain the beans and place in a large pan, cover with fresh cold water and bring to the boil. Boil for 10 minutes, skimming off any froth from the surface, then drain well and set aside.

3 Meanwhile, heat the oil in a pan, add the onion and cook gently for about 10 minutes, or until soft. Transfer the onions to the ceramic cooking pot.

4 Add the garlic, beans, barley, paprika, cayenne pepper, celery, tomatoes, carrots, turnip, potatoes, beef and stock to the onions and stir to combine.

5 Cover the pot with the lid and cook on low for 5–6 hours, or until the meat and vegetables are tender. Add the rice, stir, and season with salt and pepper.

6 Rinse the eggs in tepid water, then lower them, one at a time, into the hot stock. Cover and cook for a further 45 minutes, or until the rice is cooked. Serve hot, making sure each portion contains a whole egg.

All-in-the-pot Beef Stew

This one-pot recipe of beef, potatoes, carrots and celery harks back to the idea of cooking everything in one pot over a fire in the hearth, the traditional way of preparing food in days gone by. It makes a superb alternative to a Sunday roast and is more forgiving as the beef, being boiled, can sit and wait while you have that extra glass of wine before lunch.

Serves 8

25g/1oz/2 tbsp butter, softened
25g/1oz/¼ cup plain
  (all-purpose) flour
1.6kg/3½lb silverside (pot roast),
  boned and rolled
450g/1lb small whole
  onions, peeled
450g/1lb small carrots, peeled
  and cut in two
8 celery sticks, peeled and cut
  into four pieces
12 small potatoes
30ml/2 tbsp chopped fresh parsley

1 Make a beurre manié by combining the butter and flour thoroughly. This will be used to thicken the sauce.

2 Put the beef in a large pan, pour in cold water to cover and put on the lid. Bring to the boil and simmer for 2 hours, topping up with boiling water.

3 After about 2 hours add the prepared vegetables to the pan and simmer for a further 30 minutes, until the vegetables are just cooked.

4 Remove the cooked beef and vegetables from the pan, arrange on a serving dish and keep warm. Ladle about 350ml/12fl oz/1½ cups of the cooking liquor into a clean pan and bring to the boil.

5 When the cooking liquor has come to the boil, whisk in the prepared beurre manié to thicken it and add the chopped fresh parsley.

6 When ready to eat, pour the sauce over the beef and vegetables, retaining some to pass round at the table. Serve the meat in thick slices, accompanied by a healthy serving of the cooked vegetables.

Root Veg Stew Energy 860kcal/3607kJ; Protein 58.9g; Carbohydrate 74.2g, of which sugars 13.7g; Fat 38.8g, of which saturates 12.7g; Cholesterol 341mg; Calcium 164mg; Fibre 10.9g; Sodium 639mg.
Beef Stew Energy 875kcal/3656kJ; Protein 89.8g; Carbohydrate 38.5g, of which sugars 16.7g; Fat 41.1g, of which saturates 17.7g; Cholesterol 231mg; Calcium 121mg; Fibre 6.3g; Sodium 358mg.

Traditional Beef Stew

A traditional casserole of beef cooked with potatoes and root vegetables makes this a complete meal in a pot. Cooking the vegetables separately from the meat for part of the time is an interesting technique, which allows them to keep more of their own flavour than would be possible if added to the meat at the beginning of the cooking.

Serves 4–6

1.2kg/2½lb stewing beef, cut into
   large cubes
1.2 litres/2 pints/5 cups
   beef stock
450g/1lb carrots, cut into
   bitesize pieces
1 small swede (rutabaga)
   or turnip
675g/1½lb potatoes, cut into
   bitesize pieces
1 onion, finely chopped
salt and ground black pepper

1 Put the beef in a large pan, add enough water to cover, season with salt and pepper and bring slowly to the boil. Lower the heat, cover and simmer for 1 hour.

2 When the beef has been cooking for 30 minutes, bring the stock to the boil in a flameproof casserole. Add the carrots and swede or turnip and simmer for 15 minutes. Add the potatoes and simmer for a further 15 minutes.

3 When the beef has been cooking for about 1 hour, strain the cubes, reserving the stock for a soup or another dish at a later date. Add the beef to the vegetables with the onion. Check the seasoning, adding salt and ground black pepper only if necessary.

4 Gently simmer the casserole for a further 15–30 minutes, depending on the quality of the meat, until the meat and vegetables are tender. Serve hot.

Cook's Tip
Try to select beef with a good marbling of fat running through it as this will give a moister, more tender result than a very lean cut of meat.

Braised Beef with Vegetables

Traditional stews like this were once the mainstay of many kitchens, when everything was left to cook gently all day in one large pot on the range or (in earlier times) the edge of the fire. Gentle simmering in a modern oven produces an equally delicious dish.

Serves 4–6

1kg/2¼lb lean stewing steak, cut
   into 5cm/2in cubes

45ml/3 tbsp plain
   (all-purpose) flour
45ml/3 tbsp oil
1 large onion, thinly sliced
1 large carrot, thickly sliced
2 celery sticks, finely chopped
300ml/½ pint/¼ cup beef stock
30ml/2 tbsp tomato purée (paste)
5ml/1 tsp dried mixed herbs
15ml/1 tbsp dark muscovado
   (molasses) sugar
225g/8oz baby potatoes, halved
2 leeks, thinly sliced
salt and ground black pepper

1 Preheat the oven to 150°C/300°F/Gas 2. Season the flour and use to coat the beef cubes.

2 Heat the oil in a large, flameproof casserole. Add a small batch of the cubed beef, cook quickly until browned on all sides and, with a slotted spoon, lift out. Repeat with the remaining beef, making sure not to cook too many cubes at once as the meat will steam rather than fry.

3 Add the onion, carrot and celery to the casserole. Cook over a medium heat for about 10 minutes, stirring frequently, until they begin to soften and brown slightly on the edges.

4 Return the meat to the casserole and add the stock, tomato purée, herbs and sugar, at the same time scraping up any sediment that has stuck to the casserole. Heat until the liquid nearly comes to the boil.

5 Cover with a tight-fitting lid and put into the hot oven. Cook for 2–2½ hours, or until the beef is tender.

6 Gently stir in the potatoes and leeks, cover and continue cooking for a further 30 minutes or until the potatoes are tender. Check the seasoning and serve immediately.

Beef Stew Energy 475kcal/1987kJ; Protein 48.4g; Carbohydrate 28.2g, of which sugars 10.8g; Fat 19.4g, of which saturates 7.8g; Cholesterol 116mg; Calcium 73mg; Fibre 4.3g; Sodium 170mg.
Braised Beef Energy 450kcal/1880kJ; Protein 41.3g; Carbohydrate 23.6g, of which sugars 10.3g; Fat 21.7g, of which saturates 7.3g; Cholesterol 97mg; Calcium 63mg; Fibre 3.5g; Sodium 137mg.

Sailor's Steak with Potato and Onion

Also known as seaman's beef, this dish used to be linked with sailors because it requires very few kitchen utensils and just one pot to make it. Cooking the meat, onion and potatoes together gives the dish a delicious stew-like combination of textures and flavours.

Serves 8

8 thin slices entrecôte (sirloin)
   steak, about 600g/1lb 6oz
8 medium potatoes
15g/½oz/1 tbsp butter
4 onions, chopped
1 sprig fresh thyme
2 bay leaves
500ml/17fl oz/generous 2 cups
   dark ale
salt and ground black pepper
15ml/1 tbsp chopped fresh
   parsley, to garnish
pickled beetroot (beet) or pickled
   gherkins, to serve

1 Preheat the oven to 180°C/350°F/Gas 4. Using a rolling pin or heavy wooden mallet, beat the steaks until flattened.

2 Peel the potatoes, cut them in half and then into slices about 1cm/½in thick.

3 Melt the butter in a large flameproof casserole. Add the onions and fry for about 10 minutes, stirring frequently, until golden brown.

4 Push the onions to one side of the dish, add the steaks and fry until sealed on both sides.

5 Add the sliced potatoes to the pan, followed by the thyme and bay leaves. Stir the ingredients until well combined. Season with salt and pepper.

6 Pour the ale over the ingredients in the casserole, cover with a tight-fitting lid and bake in the preheated oven for about 1 hour or until the potatoes are tender.

7 Ladle on to individual plates and sprinkle the chopped parsley over the top to garnish. Serve accompanied by pickled beetroot or pickled gherkins.

Smoked Beef with Potato Pancakes

This tasty and unusual recipe features potato pancakes and fine smoked meats.

Serves 4

500g/1¼lb trimmed beef fillet
oil, for chargrilling
salt and ground black pepper
herb sprigs, to garnish
broccoli florets, white turnip and
   courgettes (zucchini), to serve

For the potato pancakes

250g/9oz potatoes, cooked
50g/2oz/½ cup plain
   (all-purpose) flour

1 egg
freshly grated nutmeg
oil, for frying

For the sauce

4 shallots, finely diced
200ml/7fl oz/scant 1 cup
   chicken stock
120ml/4fl oz/½ cup dry
   white wine
200ml/7fl oz/scant 1 cup double
   (heavy) cream
15ml/1 tbsp chopped fresh herbs,
   such as flat leaf parsley,
   tarragon, chervil and basil
lemon juice, to taste

1 To make the potato pancakes, blend the potatoes with the flour and egg to make a thick paste. Add nutmeg and seasoning to taste. Lightly oil and heat a heavy pan, then use the potato mixture to make eight small pancakes, cooking them on both sides until golden brown. Keep warm.

2 To make the sauce, put the shallots, stock, wine and half the cream into a pan and cook over a medium heat until reduced by two-thirds. Purée the mixture and strain it, then mix in enough of the herbs to turn the sauce green.

3 Season the beef with salt and pepper. In a heavy, preheated pan, seal the meat on all sides over medium heat. Place the meat in a smoker for about 10 minutes until medium-rare. Or, to chargrill the meat, preheat a dry cast-iron ridged pan until very hot. Brush the meat with oil and cook for 3–5 minutes.

4 To serve, whip the remaining cream and fold it into the sauce. Adjust the seasoning and add lemon juice if required. Divide the sauce between four warm plates. Cut the beef into eight slices and place two on each plate. Add the pancakes and garnish with herbs. Serve with the broccoli, turnip and courgettes.

Sailor's Steak Energy 279kcal/1170kJ; Protein 19.4g; Carbohydrate 29.9g, of which sugars 9.7g; Fat 6.6g, of which saturates 3.2g; Cholesterol 50mg; Calcium 38mg; Fibre 2.3g; Sodium 70mg.
Smoked Beef Energy 683kcal/2834kJ; Protein 32.9g; Carbohydrate 23g, of which sugars 3g; Fat 49.5g, of which saturates 27.5g; Cholesterol 219mg; Calcium 82mg; Fibre 1.9g; Sodium 166mg.

Marinated Beef and Potato Salad

The beef steak needs to marinate overnight, but once that is done this dish is quick to assemble. The salad with potato balls makes an interesting side dish.

Serves 6
900g/2lb sirloin steak
3 large white potatoes
½ red (bell) pepper, seeded
 and diced
½ green (bell) pepper, seeded
 and diced
1 small red onion, finely chopped
2 garlic cloves, crushed
4 spring onions (scallions),
 diagonally sliced
1 small cos or romaine lettuce,
 leaves torn
salt and ground black pepper
olive oil, to serve
Parmesan cheese shavings,
 to serve

For the marinade
120ml/4fl oz/½ cup olive oil
120ml/4fl oz/½ cup red
 wine vinegar
90ml/6 tbsp soy sauce

1 Place the beef in a large, non-metallic container. Mix together the ingredients for the marinade. Season with pepper and pour over the meat.

2 Cover the meat and leave to marinate for several hours, or preferably overnight.

3 Drain the marinade from the meat and pat the joint dry. Preheat a frying pan, cut the steak carefully into thin slices and fry for a few minutes until just cooked on each side, but still slightly pink. Set aside to cool.

4 Peel the potatoes. Using a melon baller, carefully scoop out rounds from each potato. Boil in lightly salted water for about 5 minutes or until just tender.

5 Drain the potatoes and transfer to a bowl. Add the peppers, onion, garlic, spring onions and lettuce leaves. Season with salt and pepper and toss together.

6 Transfer the potato and pepper mixture to a plate with the beef. Drizzle with a little extra olive oil and serve topped with Parmesan shavings.

Beef and Grilled Sweet Potatoes

This salad is absolutely delicious with a simple potato salad and some peppery leaves, such as watercress, mizuna or rocket.

Serves 6–8
800g/1¾lb fillet of beef
5ml/1 tsp black
 peppercorns, crushed
10ml/2 tsp chopped fresh thyme
60ml/4 tbsp olive oil
450g/1lb orange-fleshed sweet
 potato, peeled
salt and ground black pepper

For the dressing
1 garlic clove, chopped
15g/½oz flat leaf parsley
30ml/2 tbsp chopped fresh
 coriander (cilantro)
15ml/1 tbsp small salted
 capers, rinsed
½–1 fresh green chilli, seeded
 and chopped
10ml/2 tsp Dijon mustard
10–15ml/2–3 tsp white
 wine vinegar
75ml/5 tbsp extra virgin
 olive oil
2 shallots, finely chopped

1 Roll the beef fillet in the crushed peppercorns and thyme, then set aside to marinate for a few hours. Preheat the oven to 200°C/400°F/Gas 6.

2 Heat half the oil in a frying pan. Add the beef and brown it all over, turning frequently, to seal it. Place on a baking tray and cook in the oven for 10–15 minutes. Remove the beef from the oven and cover with foil, then leave for 10–15 minutes.

3 Meanwhile, preheat the grill (broiler). Cut the sweet potatoes into 1cm/½in slices. Brush with the remaining oil, season to taste, and grill (broil) for 5–6 minutes on each side, until browned. Cut the slices into strips and place in a bowl. Cut the beef into slices or strips and toss with the sweet potato, then set the bowl aside.

4 For the dressing, process the garlic, parsley, coriander, capers, chilli, mustard and 10ml/2 tsp of the vinegar in a food processor or blender. With the motor still running, pour in the oil to make a smooth dressing. Season to taste. Stir in the shallots.

5 Toss the dressing into the sweet potatoes and beef and leave to stand for up to 2 hours before serving.

Marinated Beef Energy 296kcal/1247kJ; Protein 38g; Carbohydrate 20.1g, of which sugars 5g; Fat 7.6g, of which saturates 3.2g; Cholesterol 77mg; Calcium 40mg; Fibre 2.3g; Sodium 120mg.
Beef and Sweet Potatoes Energy 300kcal/1253kJ; Protein 21.9g; Carbohydrate 12g, of which sugars 3.2g; Fat 18.6g, of which saturates 4.6g; Cholesterol 61mg; Calcium 18mg; Fibre 1.4g; Sodium 67mg.

Spicy Corned Beef and Potato Hash

This is real nursery, or comfort, food at its best. Whether you remember Gran's version, or prefer this American-style potato hash, it turns corned beef into a supper fit for any guest.

Serves 4
30ml/2 tbsp vegetable oil
25g/1oz/2 tbsp butter
1 onion, finely chopped
1 green (bell) pepper, diced
2 large firm boiled potatoes, cut into small chunks
350g/12oz can corned beef, cut into small cubes
1.5ml/¼ tsp grated nutmeg
1.5ml/¼ tsp paprika
4 eggs
salt and ground black pepper
deep-fried parsley, to garnish
sweet chilli sauce or tomato sauce, to serve

1 Heat the oil and butter together in a large frying pan. Add the onion and fry for 5–6 minutes until softened.

2 In a bowl, mix together the green pepper, potatoes, corned beef, nutmeg and paprika and season well. Add to the pan and toss gently to distribute the cooked onion. Press down lightly and fry without stirring on a medium heat for about 3–4 minutes until a golden brown crust has formed on the underside.

3 Stir the mixture through to distribute the crust, then repeat the frying twice, until the mixture is well browned.

4 Make four wells in the hash and carefully crack an egg into each. Cover and cook gently for about 4–5 minutes until the egg whites are set.

5 Sprinkle generously with deep-fried parsley and cut into quarters. Serve hot with sweet chilli sauce or tomato sauce.

Cook's Tips
• Chill the can of corned beef for about half an hour before use – it will be easier to cut it into cubes.
• Smoked paprika makes an interesting alternative to the regular variety, offering a mellow smoky flavour.

Beef and Potato Rydberg

The Hotel Rydberg, which overlooked the Royal Palace in Stockholm, Sweden, closed in 1914 but is still remembered for this recipe that was popularly served there at the turn of the century. Using fillet steak (instead of the original kidneys) and potatoes, it is a luxury version of the classic Swedish beef hash.

Serves 6
8 large potatoes
600g/1lb 6oz fillet steak (beef tenderloin)
2 onions
50g/2oz/¼ cup butter
15ml/1 tbsp vegetable oil
salt and ground black pepper
6 very fresh eggs, to serve
Brown sauce, Worcestershire sauce, mustard and tomato ketchup, to serve

1 Peel and cut the potatoes into small cubes measuring about 3mm/⅛in. Cut the steak and onions into cubes the same size as the potatoes.

2 Heat the butter and oil in a frying pan, add the onions and fry for 8–10 minutes until golden brown. Using a slotted spoon, remove from the pan. Add the potatoes, adding more butter if necessary, and fry for about 20 minutes until golden brown. Remove from the pan.

3 Just before serving, so that the steak is not overcooked, add the steak cubes to the pan and fry for less than a minute, until sealed but still rare.

4 Arrange small piles of the fried steak cubes, the fried potatoes and the fried onions on individual serving plates. Break the eggs, one at a time, separating the yolks from the whites, and putting the egg yolks in half the broken shell in the middle of the plates.

5 Serve immediately, accompanied by the brown sauce, Worcestershire sauce, mustard and tomato ketchup so that each person can season the dish at the table according to their own taste. Diners should then mix all the ingredients together themselves and combine them with the raw egg yolk from the shell on their plate.

Beef Hash Energy 421kcal/1758kJ; Protein 30.8g; Carbohydrate 16.9g, of which sugars 5.4g; Fat 26.15g, of which saturates 10.6g; Cholesterol 277mg; Calcium 65mg; Fibre 1.7g; Sodium 870.8mg.
Beef Rydberg Energy 407kcal/1711kJ; Protein 26.4g; Carbohydrate 46.9g, of which sugars 6.3g; Fat 13.9g, of which saturates 7.4g; Cholesterol 79mg; Calcium 34mg; Fibre 3.4g; Sodium 125mg.

Cornish Beef and Potato Pasties

The original portable lunch, pasties made a satisfying midday meal for intrepid Cornish tin miners, who could use the crimped pastry join across the top as a handle when their hands were filthy. These contain the traditional filling of chopped steak, potatoes and other root vegetables.

Makes 6

500–675g/1¼–1½lb
  shortcrust pastry
450g/1lb chuck steak, cubed
1 potato, about 175g/6oz, cubed
175g/6oz swede
  (rutabaga), cubed
1 onion, finely chopped
2.5ml/½ tsp dried mixed herbs
beaten egg, to glaze
salt and ground black pepper

1 Preheat the oven to 220°C/425°F/Gas 7. Divide the pastry into six equal pieces, then roll out each piece to form a rough circle, measuring about 20cm/8in.

2 Mix together the steak, vegetables and herbs. Season with salt and black pepper. Spoon an equal amount of the mixture on to one half of each pastry circle.

3 Brush the edges of the pastry with a little water, then fold the pastry over the filling. Crimp the edges firmly together on the top.

4 Use a metal spatula to transfer the pasties to a non-stick baking sheet, then brush the top of each one with a little beaten egg.

5 Put into the hot oven and cook for 15 minutes, then reduce the oven temperature to 160°C/325°F/Gas 3 and cook for a further 1 hour.

Variation
Swede (rutabaga) is the traditional vegetable in Cornish pasties, along with potatoes, but other vegetables could be used in its place, if you prefer. Turnip, carrot or celery will all be suitable additions to the pasties.

Cottage Pie

This classic dish features minced beef mixed with onion and carrot and then topped with a crispy, golden layer of mashed potato.

Serves 4
50g/2oz/¼ cup butter
1 large onion, finely chopped
1 celery stalk, finely diced
1 large carrot, finely diced

450g/1lb lean minced
  (ground) beef
15ml/1 tbsp plain (all-purpose) flour
250ml/8fl oz/1 cup hot
  beef stock
30ml/2 tbsp chopped fresh parsley
15ml/1 tbsp tomato purée (paste)
900g/2lb floury potatoes, peeled
30–45ml/2–3 tbsp milk
10ml/2 tsp Dijon mustard
salt and ground black pepper

1 Melt ½oz (15g) of the butter in a frying pan over moderate heat. Add the chopped onion, celery and carrot and cook until the onion is soft, stirring occasionally. Add the beef and fry, stirring, until it is brown and crumbly.

2 Sprinkle the flour evenly over the surface, stir it into the meat and vegetables and cook for a minute or two. Gradually add the stock, stirring well. Stir in the parsley and tomato purée. Season with salt and ground black pepper.

3 Bring the mixture to a simmer, then cover with a tight-fitting lid and cook over very low heat, stirring occasionally, for about 45 minutes.

4 Meanwhile, cook the potatoes in boiling salted water for about 10–15 minutes or until they are tender. Drain well.

5 While the potatoes are still warm, place them in a bowl and mash them thoroughly. Add the remaining butter and just enough milk to make a soft fluffy texture. Season to taste with plenty of salt and ground black pepper. Preheat the oven to 200°C/400°F/Gas 6.

6 Stir the mustard into the beef mixture, then turn it into a baking dish. Cover with a neat layer of potatoes and seal to the sides of the dish. Mark a pattern with a fork, if you like. Bake in the oven for 20–25 minutes. Serve hot.

Cornish Pasties Energy 414kcal/1731kJ; Protein 10.4g; Carbohydrate 38.8g, of which sugars 1.4g; Fat 25.3g, of which saturates 9.2g; Cholesterol 51mg; Calcium 93mg; Fibre 1.4g; Sodium 620mg.
Cottage Pie Energy 281kcal/1179kJ; Protein 7.2g; Carbohydrate 34.6g, of which sugars 6.2g; Fat 13.7g, of which saturates 5.1g; Cholesterol 22mg; Calcium 50mg; Fibre 2.9g; Sodium 132mg.

Beef, Lentil and Potato Pie

This microwave dish features lentils and minced meat with a potato and parsnip mash topping.

Serves 4

175g/6oz/1 cup green lentils
1 onion, chopped
2 celery sticks, chopped
1 large carrot, chopped
1 garlic clove, crushed
225g/8oz lean minced
  (ground) beef
400g/14oz can chopped tomatoes
10ml/2 tsp yeast extract
1 bay leaf

For the topping

450g/1lb potatoes, peeled and
  cut into large chunks
450g/1lb parsnips, peeled
  and cut into large chunks
60ml/4 tbsp low-fat natural
  (plain) yogurt
45ml/3 tbsp chopped chives
20ml/4 tsp freshly grated
  Parmesan cheese
2 tomatoes, sliced
25g/1oz/¼ cup pine
  nuts (optional)

1 Place the lentils in a microwave-proof bowl and pour in boiling water to cover. Cover and microwave on HIGH for 6 minutes and set aside. Place the onion, celery, carrot and garlic in a large microwave-proof bowl. Cover, microwave on HIGH for 4 minutes and stir once. Add the mince, stir and microwave on HIGH for 2 minutes. Mix in the tomatoes.

2 Drain the lentils, reserving 250ml/8fl oz/1 cup of the cooking water in a measuring jug (cup). Add the lentils to the meat mixture, then dissolve the yeast extract in the cooking water and stir it in with the bay leaf. Cover loosely, then microwave on HIGH for 12–15 minutes, stirring twice.

3 Make the topping: place the potatoes and parsnips in a microwave-proof bowl with 75ml/5 tbsp water. Cover and microwave on HIGH for 11–13 minutes, stirring once, until tender. Mash together and stir in the yogurt and chives.

4 Remove the bay leaf and place the mixture in a large heatproof dish. Spoon over the potato mixture, sprinkle with Parmesan and garnish with tomato slices. Sprinkle with pine nuts, if using, and grill (broil) until the topping is crisp and golden.

Baked Beef with a Potato Crust

This recipe makes the best of braising beef by marinating it in red wine and topping it with a cheesy grated potato crust that bakes to a golden, crunchy consistency.

Serves 4

675g/1½lb stewing beef, diced
300ml/½ pint/1¼ cups red wine
3 juniper berries, crushed
slice of orange peel
30ml/2 tbsp olive oil
2 onions, cut into chunks
2 carrots, cut into chunks

1 garlic clove, crushed
225g/8oz/3 cups button
  (white) mushrooms
150ml/¼ pint/⅔ cup beef stock
30ml/2 tbsp cornflour
  (cornstarch)
salt and ground black pepper

For the crust

450g/1lb potatoes, grated
15ml/1 tbsp olive oil
30ml/2 tbsp creamed horseradish
50g/2oz/½ cup mature (sharp)
  Cheddar cheese, grated
salt and ground black pepper

1 Place the diced beef in a large, non-metallic bowl. Add the red wine, juniper berries, and orange peel and season with black pepper. Mix the ingredients together until thoroughly combined and then cover and leave to marinate for at least 4 hours or overnight, if possible.

2 Preheat the oven to 160°C/325°F/Gas 3. Drain the beef, making sure to reserve the marinade. Heat the oil in a large flameproof casserole dish and fry the meat in small batches for around 5 minutes until sealed on all sides.

3 Add the onions, carrots and garlic and cook for 5 minutes. Stir in the mushrooms, red wine marinade and beef stock. Simmer. Mix the cornflour with water to make a smooth paste. Stir into the pan. Season, cover and cook for 1½ hours.

4 Make the crust 30 minutes before the end of the cooking time for the beef. Start by blanching the potatoes in boiling water for 5 minutes. Drain and then squeeze out the extra liquid.

5 Stir in the remaining ingredients and then sprinkle over the beef. Increase the oven to 200°C/400°F/Gas 6 and bake for a further 30 minutes so that the top is crisp and browned.

Beef and Lentil Pie Energy 455kcal/1926kJ; Protein 31.7g; Carbohydrate 64g, of which sugars 15.7g; Fat 9.9g, of which saturates 4g; Cholesterol 37mg; Calcium 192mg; Fibre 10.3g; Sodium 293mg.
Baked Beef Energy 641kcal/2678kJ; Protein 45.9g; Carbohydrate 36.6g, of which sugars 10.8g; Fat 29.6g, of which saturates 10.6g; Cholesterol 111mg; Calcium 152mg; Fibre 4.2g; Sodium 306mg.

Potato, Beef and Mushroom Gratin

This medley of potatoes, beef and mushrooms offers an appealing mix of flavours and produces a hearty and rewarding main meal.

Serves 4

30ml/2 tbsp vegetable oil
1 small onion, chopped
15ml/1 tbsp plain
    (all-purpose) flour
150ml/¼ pint/⅔ cup
    vegetable stock
225g/8oz cooked beetroot (beets),
    drained well and chopped
15ml/1 tbsp creamed horseradish
15ml/1 tbsp caraway seeds
3 shallots, or 1 onion, chopped
450g/1lb frying steak, cut into
    thin strips
225g/8oz assorted wild or
    cultivated mushrooms, sliced
10–15ml/2–3 tsp hot mustard
60ml/4 tbsp sour cream
45ml/3 tbsp chopped fresh parsley

For the potato border

900g/2lb floury potatoes, cooked
150ml/¼ pint/⅔ cup milk
25g/1oz/2 tbsp butter
15ml/1 tbsp chopped fresh dill
salt and ground black pepper

1 Preheat the oven to 190°C/375°F/Gas 5. Lightly oil a gratin dish. Heat 15ml/1 tbsp of the oil in a large pan, add the onion and fry until softened. Stir in the flour and gradually add the stock, stirring until blended and thickened. Add the beetroot (reserving a little for the topping), horseradish and caraway seeds. Mix gently, then set aside.

2 Mash the cooked potatoes with the milk and butter. Add the chopped dill, if using, and season to taste. Spoon the potatoes into the prepared dish and push well up the sides, making a large hollow in the middle. Spoon the beetroot mixture into the well, evening it out with the back of a spoon, and set aside.

3 Heat the remaining oil in a frying pan, add the shallots or onion and fry until softened. Add the steak and stir-fry quickly until browned. Add the mushrooms and fry quickly for about 2–3 minutes. Gently stir in the mustard, sour cream, seasoning to taste and half the parsley until well blended.

4 Spoon the steak mixture over the beetroot mixture in the dish, sprinkling the reserved beetroot on top, then cover and bake for 30 minutes. Sprinkle with the remaining parsley and serve.

Meatball and Potato Pie

The breadcrumb and potato crust of this pie hides a delicious and surprising filling of beef and pork meatballs in a Madeira wine gravy.

Serves 4

250g/9oz minced (ground) beef
250g/9oz minced (ground) pork
1 large egg, lightly beaten
25g/1oz/½ cup crushed rusks or
    dry breadcrumbs
2.5ml/½ tsp freshly ground nutmeg
30ml/2 tbsp mild paprika
40g/1½oz/3 tbsp butter
1 onion, chopped
150g/5oz mushrooms
40g/1½oz/⅓ cup plain
    (all-purpose) flour
50ml/2fl oz/¼ cup Madeira
480g/17oz can browned beans,
    drained and rinsed
30 ml/2 tbsp finely chopped
    fresh parsley
800g/1¾lb waxy potatoes

For the topping

25g/1oz/2 tbsp butter, melted
30ml/2 tbsp crushed rusks or
    breadcrumbs

1 Put the meat in a bowl with the egg, rusks, nutmeg, ½ tsp black pepper and salt. Knead until combined. Form the mixture into about 30 small balls then roll the meatballs in the paprika.

2 Melt the butter in a large frying pan, add the meatballs and cook over a high heat, turning frequently, for about 8 minutes, until evenly browned. Add the onion and mushrooms and cook, stirring frequently, for 2–3 minutes. Sprinkle in the flour and cook, stirring constantly, for 2 minutes, until it is lightly coloured.

3 Gradually stir in 400ml/14fl oz/1⅔ cups water, then stir in the Madeira. Lower the heat, cover and simmer for 10 minutes. Add the beans and transfer the mixture to an ovenproof dish. Sprinkle with parsley. Preheat the oven to 200°C/400°F/Gas 6.

4 Par-boil the potatoes in salted boiling water for 5–7 minutes, then drain. Evenly slice the potatoes and arrange the slices, overlapping slightly, on top of the pie. Drizzle with the melted butter and sprinkle with the rusks or breadcrumbs.

5 Bake for around 40–45 minutes until golden brown on top. Serve immediately with brussel sprouts sprinkled with toasted almonds and apple sauce.

Potato Gratin Energy 560kcal/2346kJ; Protein 34.1g; Carbohydrate 49.5g, of which sugars 12g; Fat 26.4g, of which saturates 10.8g; Cholesterol 91mg; Calcium 111mg; Fibre 4.6g; Sodium 354mg.
Meatball Pie Energy 774kcal/3247kJ; Protein 42.4g; Carbohydrate 77g, of which sugars 9.4g; Fat 33.9g, of which saturates 16g; Cholesterol 161mg; Calcium 185mg; Fibre 11.1g; Sodium 813mg.

Beef and Sweet Potato Stew

The tender beef cooked in red wine balances the sweetness of the peaches, pumpkin and sweet potatoes.

Serves 8

1 large pumpkin, about 5kg/11lb
60ml/4 tbsp olive oil
1kg/2¼lb braising steak, cut into 2.5cm/1in cubes
1 large onion, finely chopped
3 fresh red chillies, chopped
2 garlic cloves, crushed
1 large tomato, roughly chopped
2 fresh bay leaves
600ml/1 pint/2½ cups beef stock
350ml/12fl oz/1½ cups red wine
500g/1¼lb potatoes, peeled and cut into 2cm/¾in cubes
500g/1¼lb sweet potatoes, peeled and cut into 2cm/¾in cubes
1 corn cob, cut widthways into 6 slices
3 peaches, peeled, stoned (pitted) and cut into thick wedges
salt and ground black pepper

1 Cut a slice off the top of the pumpkin, 6cm/2½in from the stem, to make a lid. Scoop out the seeds and stringy fibres and discard. Scoop out some of the flesh, leaving a shell about 2cm/¾in thick. Dice the removed flesh into 1cm/½in pieces. Brush the inside and the flesh of the lid with oil and season. Place pumpkin and lid on a baking sheet, flesh side up. Set aside.

2 Preheat the oven to 200°C/400°F/Gas 6. Heat half the remaining oil in a pan over a high heat. Add the beef, season and cook until browned. Set aside. Lower the heat and add the remaining oil to the pan. Stir in the onion and chillies, and cook for 5 minutes. Add the garlic and tomato for 2 minutes.

3 Return the meat to the pan and add the bay leaves, stock and red wine. Bring to the boil, then lower the heat to a gentle simmer. Cook for 1 hour or until the meat is tender.

4 Bake the pumpkin and lid in the oven for 30 minutes. Add the potatoes, sweet potatoes, pumpkin pieces and corn to the stew. Bring to the boil, then simmer, covered, for 15 minutes.

5 Finally add the peach wedges and season to taste. Spoon the stew into the partially cooked pumpkin, cover with the lid and bake for 15 minutes or until tender. To serve, ladle the stew on to plates, then cut the empty pumpkin into eight wedges.

Mussaman Beef and Potato Curry

This delicious meat and potato curry is traditionally based on beef, but chicken, lamb or tofu can be used instead, if you prefer.

Serves 4–6

675g/1½lb stewing steak
600ml/1 pint/2½ cups coconut milk
250ml/8fl oz/1 cup coconut cream
45ml/3 tbsp Mussaman curry paste
30ml/2 tbsp Thai fish sauce
15ml/1 tbsp palm sugar (jaggery) or light muscovado (brown) sugar
60ml/4 tbsp tamarind juice, made by soaking tamarind paste in warm water
6 green cardamom pods
1 cinnamon stick
1 large potato, about 225g/8oz, cut into even chunks
1 onion, cut into wedges
50g/2oz/½ cup roasted peanuts

1 Trim off any excess fat from the stewing steak, then, using a sharp knife, cut it into 2.5cm/1in chunks.

2 Pour the coconut milk into a large, heavy pan and bring to the boil over a medium heat. Add the chunks of beef, reduce the heat to low, partially cover the pan and simmer gently for about 40 minutes, or until tender.

3 Pour the coconut cream into a separate pan. Cook over a medium heat, stirring constantly, for about 5 minutes, or until it separates. Stir in the Mussaman curry paste and cook rapidly for 2–3 minutes, until fragrant and thoroughly blended.

4 Add the coconut cream and curry paste mixture to the pan with the beef and stir until thoroughly blended. Simmer for a further 4–5 minutes, stirring occasionally.

5 Stir the fish sauce, sugar, tamarind juice, cardamom pods, cinnamon stick, potato chunks and onion wedges into the beef curry. Continue to simmer for a further 15–20 minutes, or until the potato is cooked and tender.

6 Add the roasted peanuts to the pan and mix well to combine. Cook for about 5 minutes more, then transfer to warmed individual serving bowls and serve immediately.

Beef Stew Energy 380kcal/1600kJ; Protein 31.4g; Carbohydrate 28.9g, of which sugars 14.9g; Fat 13.1g, of which saturates 3.8g; Cholesterol 0mg; Calcium 133mg; Fibre 6.2g; Sodium 65mg.
Mussaman Curry Energy 626kcal/2610kJ; Protein 44.6g; Carbohydrate 24.8g, of which sugars 15.4g; Fat 39.3g, of which saturates 22.7g; Cholesterol 98mg; Calcium 74mg; Fibre 1.6g; Sodium 288mg.

Tex-Mex Baked Potatoes with Chilli

Classic chilli beef tops crisp, floury-centred baked potatoes. Easy to prepare and great for a simple yet substantial family supper.

Serves 4

2 large baking potatoes
15ml/1 tbsp vegetable oil, plus
    more for brushing
1 garlic clove, crushed
1 small onion, chopped
1/2 red (bell) pepper, chopped
225g/8oz lean minced
    (ground) beef
1/2 small fresh red chilli, seeded
    and chopped
5ml/1 tsp ground cumin
pinch of cayenne pepper
200g/7oz can chopped tomatoes
30ml/2 tbsp tomato
    purée (paste)
2.5ml/1/2 tsp fresh oregano
2.5ml/1/2 tsp fresh marjoram
200g/7oz can red kidney
    beans, drained
15ml/1 tbsp chopped fresh
    coriander (cilantro)
salt and ground black pepper
chopped fresh marjoram,
    to garnish
lettuce leaves, to serve
60ml/4 tbsp sour cream,
    to serve

1 Preheat the oven to 220°C/425°F/Gas 7. Brush or rub the potatoes with a little of the oil and then pierce them with skewers. Place the potatoes on the top shelf of the oven and bake them for 30 minutes before beginning to cook the chilli.

2 Heat the oil in a large heavy pan and add the garlic, onion and pepper. Fry gently for 4–5 minutes until softened.

3 Add the beef and fry until browned, then stir in the chilli, cumin, cayenne pepper, tomatoes, tomato purée, 60ml/4 tbsp water and the herbs. Bring to a boil, then reduce the heat, cover and simmer for about 25 minutes, stirring occasionally.

4 Stir in the kidney beans and cook, uncovered, for 5 minutes. Remove from the heat and stir in the chopped coriander. Season well and set aside.

5 Cut the baked potatoes in half and place them in serving bowls. Top with the chilli mixture and a dollop of sour cream. Garnish with chopped fresh marjoram and serve hot accompanied by a few lettuce leaves.

Beef and Potatoes in Peanut Sauce

This slow-cooked stew has a uniquely Asian flavour. Potatoes, rice and peanuts are used to thicken the juices, yielding a rich and glossy sauce.

Serves 4–6

900g/2lb braising steak
30ml/2 tbsp vegetable oil
15ml/1 tbsp annatto seeds
2 medium onions, chopped
275g/10oz celeriac,
    roughly chopped
2 garlic cloves, crushed
475ml/16fl oz/2 cups
    beef stock
375g/12oz new potatoes, peeled
    and cut into large dice
15ml/1 tbsp fish sauce
30ml/2 tbsp tamarind sauce
10ml/2 tsp sugar
1 bay leaf
1 fresh thyme sprig
45ml/3 tbsp long grain rice
30ml/2 tbsp peanut butter
15ml/1 tbsp white wine vinegar
salt and ground black pepper

1 Cut the beef into 2.5cm/1in cubes and set aside. Heat the oil in a flameproof casserole, add the annatto seeds and stir until the oil is dark red in colour. Remove the seeds with a slotted spoon and discard.

2 Add the onions, celeriac and garlic to the casserole and fry for 3–5 minutes, until softened but not coloured. Add the beef and fry until lightly and evenly browned.

3 Add the stock, potatoes, fish sauce, tamarind sauce, sugar, bay leaf and thyme to the stew. Bring to a simmer, cover with a tight-fitting lid and cook for 2 hours.

4 Meanwhile, soak the rice in cold water for 30 minutes. Drain the rice and grind with the peanut butter in a mortar with a pestle or in a food processor.

5 When the beef is tender, add 60ml/4 tbsp of the cooking liquid to the rice and nut mixture. Blend until smooth, then stir into the casserole.

6 Simmer gently, uncovered, for about 15–20 minutes, until thickened. Stir in the wine vinegar, and spoon into warmed bowls. Serve immediately.

Beef in Peanut Sauce Energy 365kcal/1529kJ; Protein 30.8g; Carbohydrate 17.5g, of which sugars 16.4g; Fat 19.6g, of which saturates 6.2g; Cholesterol 65mg; Calcium 64mg; Fibre 1.2g; Sodium 238mg.
Tex-mex Potatoes Energy 327kcal/1369kJ; Protein 17.7g; Carbohydrate 30.6g, of which sugars 8.2g; Fat 15.7g, of which saturates 6.4g; Cholesterol 43mg; Calcium 71mg; Fibre 5.2g; Sodium 277mg.

Spicy Meat and Potato Fritters

These tasty meat and potato balls are spiced with coriander and cumin seeds and then lightly fried. Serve simply with a dipping sauce or chutney as a snack or with rice and salad for a more substantial meal.

Makes 30

450g/1lb floury potatoes, such as Maris Piper or King Edward
450g/1lb lean minced (ground) beef
1 onion, quartered
1 bunch spring onions (scallions), chopped
3 garlic cloves, crushed
5ml/1 tsp ground nutmeg
15ml/1 tbsp coriander seeds, dry-fried and ground
10ml/2 tsp cumin seeds, dry-fried and ground
4 eggs, beaten
oil for shallow-frying
salt and ground black pepper

1 Cook the potatoes in a large pan of boiling salted water for 15–20 minutes, or until tender, then drain well and leave to one side to cool slightly.

2 While the potatoes are still warm, mash them in the pan until they are well broken up. Add to the minced beef and mix well together.

3 Finely chop the onion, spring onions and garlic. Add to the meat and potato mixture with the ground nutmeg, coriander and cumin. Stir in enough of the beaten egg to give a soft consistency that can be formed into fritters. Season to taste with salt and ground black pepper.

4 Heat enough oil in a large frying pan for shallow-frying. Using a dessertspoon, scoop out 6–8 oval-shaped fritters and drop them into the hot oil. Leave to cook without turning so that they keep their shape (this will take about 3–5 minutes) and then turn over and cook for a further minute until they are evenly browned all over.

5 Drain the fritters well on kitchen paper and keep warm while cooking the remaining fritters. When the mixture is used up, transfer the fritters to a large platter and serve hot.

Beef Tagine with Sweet Potatoes

This warming dish of tender beef and succulent sweet potatoes is eaten during the winter in Morocco, where it can get surprisingly cold.

Serves 4

675–900g/1½–2lb braising or stewing beef
30ml/2 tbsp sunflower oil
a good pinch of ground turmeric
1 large onion, chopped
1 red or green chilli, seeded and chopped
7.5ml/1½ tsp paprika
a good pinch of cayenne pepper
2.5ml/½ tsp ground cumin
450g/1lb sweet potatoes
15ml/1 tbsp chopped fresh parsley
15ml/1 tbsp chopped fresh coriander (cilantro)
15g/½ oz/1 tbsp butter
salt and ground black pepper

1 Cube the beef. Heat the oil in a flameproof casserole and fry the meat, with the turmeric and seasoning, for 3–4 minutes until evenly brown, stirring frequently.

2 Cover the pan with a tight-fitting lid and cook for 15 minutes over a fairly gentle heat, without lifting the lid. Preheat the oven to 180°C/350°F/Gas 4.

3 Add the onion, chilli, paprika, cayenne pepper and cumin to the casserole, with just enough water to cover the meat. Cover tightly and cook in the oven for 1–1½ hours until the meat is very tender, checking occasionally and adding a little extra water to keep the stew moist.

4 Meanwhile, peel the sweet potatoes and slice them straight into a bowl of salted water. Transfer to a pan, bring to the boil and simmer for 3 minutes until just tender. Drain.

5 Stir the herbs into the meat. Arrange the potato slices over the top of the meat and dot with the butter. Cover and bake for 10 minutes more.

6 Increase the oven temperature to 200°C/400°F/Gas 6 or heat the grill (broiler). Remove the lid of the casserole and cook in the oven or under the grill for a further 5–10 minutes until the potatoes are golden.

Spicy Meat Fritters Energy 83kcal/346kJ; Protein 4.1g; Carbohydrate 2.9g, of which sugars 0.4g; Fat 6.3g, of which saturates 1.6g; Cholesterol 35mg; Calcium 10mg; Fibre 0.2g; Sodium 24mg.
Beef Tagine Energy 301kcal/1254kJ; Protein 21.9g; Carbohydrate 12g, of which sugars 3.2g; Fat 18.7g, of which saturates 4.6g; Cholesterol 61mg; Calcium 18mg; Fibre 1.4g; Sodium 67mg.

Roast Pork and Glazed Potatoes

For this pork and potato recipe, select a bone-in pork loin with the skin left on for the crackling.

Serves 8–10

2.25kg/5lb bone-in pork loin,
10ml/2 tsp mustard powder
15 whole cloves
2 bay leaves
900ml/1½ pints/3¾ cups water
175ml/6fl oz/¾ cup single (light)
   cream (optional)
salt and white pepper
braised red cabbage, to serve

For the glazed potatoes

900g/2lb small potatoes
50g/2oz/¼ cup caster
   (superfine) sugar
65g/2½ oz/5 tbsp butter

For the apples with redcurrant jelly

750ml/1¼ pints/3 cups water
115g/4oz/generous ½ cup soft
   light brown sugar
5ml/1 tsp lemon juice
4–5 tart apples, peeled, cored
   and halved
60–75ml/4–5 tbsp redcurrant jelly

1 Preheat the oven to 200°C/400°F/Gas 6. Score the pork skin and rub with the salt, pepper and mustard powder. Push the cloves and bay leaves into the skin. Place the pork, skin side up, on a rack in a roasting pan and cook for 1 hour, until the skin is crisp. Pour the water into the pan and cook for 30 minutes.

2 Boil the potatoes in salted water for 15–20 minutes, or until soft. Drain, peel and keep warm. Melt the sugar in a frying pan over a low heat until it turns light brown. Add the potatoes and butter and cook for 6–8 minutes. Keep warm.

3 Bring the water for the apples to the boil in a pan and stir in sugar, lemon juice and apple halves. Lower the heat and simmer until the apples are just tender. Remove the apples and spoon 7.5ml/1½ tsp jelly into the hollow of each half. Keep warm.

4 Transfer the pork to a serving dish and rest in a warm place for 15 minutes before carving. Meanwhile, make the gravy: pour the roasting pan juices into a pan and reduce over a medium heat. Whisk in a little cream if you wish, and season to taste.

5 Remove the crackling from the pork. Serve the pork with the gravy, potatoes, poached apple halves and crackling.

Pork and Potato Hotpot

Making this dish in the slow cooker makes the pork chops meltingly tender and allows the potato slices to soak up all the delicious juices from the meat.

Serves 4

25g/1oz/2 tbsp butter
15ml/1 tbsp oil
1 large onion, very thinly sliced
1 garlic clove, crushed
225g/8oz/generous 3 cups button
   (white) mushrooms, sliced
1.5ml/¼ tsp dried mixed herbs
900g/2lb potatoes, thinly sliced
4 thick pork chops
750ml/1¼ pints/3 cups vegetable
   or chicken stock
salt and ground black pepper

1 Use 15g/½oz/1 tbsp of the butter to grease the base and halfway up the sides of the ceramic cooking pot.

2 Heat the oil in a frying pan, add the sliced onion and cook gently for about 5 minutes, until softened and translucent. Add the garlic and mushrooms to the pan and cook for a further 5 minutes until softened. Remove the pan from the heat and stir in the mixed herbs.

3 Spoon half the mushroom mixture into the base of the ceramic cooking pot, then arrange half the potato slices on top and season with salt and ground black pepper.

4 Using a sharp knife, trim as much fat as possible from the pork chops, then place them on top of the potatoes in a single layer. Pour about half the stock over the top to cover the potatoes and prevent them discolouring.

5 Continue to layer the mushroom mixture and the sliced potatoes, finishing with a layer of neatly overlapping potatoes. Pour over the remaining stock; it should just cover the top layer of potatoes, so use a little more or less if necessary. Dot the remaining butter on top of the potatoes and cover with the lid.

6 Cook the stew on high for 4–5 hours, or until the potatoes and meat are tender when pierced with a thin skewer. If you like, place the hotpot under a medium grill (broiler) for 5–10 minutes to brown before serving.

Roast Pork Energy 654kcal/2735kJ; Protein 36.9g; Carbohydrate 39.5g, of which sugars 26.2g; Fat 39.9g, of which saturates 16.1g; Cholesterol 124mg; Calcium 36mg; Fibre 1.5g; Sodium 152mg.
Pork Hotpot Energy 511kcal/2132kJ; Protein 17.9g; Carbohydrate 41.5g, of which sugars 6.5g; Fat 31.5g, of which saturates 12.1g; Cholesterol 67mg; Calcium 40mg; Fibre 3.7g; Sodium 529mg.

Oven-cooked Potatoes with Bacon

This traditional Welsh potato dish is often called Miser's Feast, referring to the fact that it could have been cooked over a log fire and eaten over several days. This is delicious served with a crisp salad or stir-fried vegetables, or as an ideal accompaniment to grilled sausages.

Serves 4
15ml/1 tbsp oil
25g/1oz/2 tbsp butter
8 thick rindless bacon rashers
    (strips), chopped
2 onions, thinly sliced
1kg/2¼lb potatoes, thinly sliced
600ml/1 pint/2½ cups chicken or
    vegetable stock
ground black pepper
chopped fresh parsley, to garnish

1 Preheat the oven to 190°C/375°F/Gas 5. Heat the oil and butter in a wide flameproof casserole, add the bacon rashers and cook over a medium heat, stirring occasionally, until the bacon is just beginning to brown at the edges.

2 Add the thinly sliced onions and the cooked bacon to the casserole. Cook for between 5–10 minutes, making sure to stir occasionally, until the onions have slightly softened and turned a rich golden brown.

3 Add the potatoes and stir well. Pour in the stock and level the surface, pushing the potatoes and onions into the liquid. Season with black pepper.

4 Bring to the boil, cover and put into the hot oven. Cook for 30–40 minutes or until the vegetables are soft.

5 Remove the cover. Raise the oven temperature to 220°C/425°F/Gas 7 and cook for a further 15–20 minutes, until the top is crisp and golden brown. Garnish with some chopped parsley.

> **Variation**
> Try adding a little chopped fresh sage, shredded wild garlic or leeks, or some grated mature cheese in step four.

Prosciutto with Potato Rémoulade

Rémoulade is a classic piquant dressing based on mayonnaise. The traditional French version is flavoured with mustard, gherkins, capers and herbs, but simpler variations are seasoned only with mustard. This recipe pairs this tasty cream-enriched dressing with matchstick potatoes and delicate prosciutto for a light and elegant main course.

150ml/¼ pint/⅔ cup mayonnaise
150ml/¼ pint/⅔ cup double
    (heavy) cream
5–10ml/1–2 tsp Dijon mustard
juice of ½ lime
30ml/2 tbsp olive oil
12 prosciutto slices
450g/1lb asparagus
    spears, halved
salt and ground black pepper
25g/1oz wild rocket (arugula),
    to garnish
extra virgin olive oil, to serve

Serves 4
2 potatoes, each weighing about
    175g/6oz, quartered lengthways

1 Put the potatoes in a large pan. Add water to cover and bring to the boil. Add salt, then simmer for about 15 minutes, or until the potatoes are tender, but do not let them get too soft. Drain thoroughly and leave to cool and then cut into long, thin strips.

2 Beat together the mayonnaise, cream, mustard, lime juice and seasoning in a large bowl. Add the potatoes and stir carefully to coat them with the dressing.

3 Heat the oil in a griddle or frying pan and cook the prosciutto in batches until crisp and golden. Use a slotted spoon to remove the ham, draining each piece well.

4 Add the asparagus to the pan and cook in the fat remaining in the pan for about 3 minutes, or until just tender and golden.

5 Put a generous spoonful of potato rémoulade on each plate and top with several slices of prosciutto. Add the asparagus and garnish with rocket. Serve immediately, offering olive oil to drizzle over.

Potatoes with Bacon Energy 396kcal/1659kJ; Protein 42.7g; Carbohydrate 19.2g, of which sugars 4.4g; Fat 16.9g, of which saturates 6.7g; Cholesterol 177mg; Calcium 29mg; Fibre 1.5g; Sodium 310mg.
Rémoulade Energy 612kcal/2530kJ; Protein 13.1g; Carbohydrate 18.6g, of which sugars 5.4g; Fat 56.5g, of which saturates 16.8g; Cholesterol 99mg; Calcium 74mg; Fibre 3.1g; Sodium 693mg.

Potato, Pancetta and Parmesan Galette

This richly flavoured, potato-topped 'pie' is a perfect winter warmer. A mandolin will make quick work of the potatoes, slicing them thinly, but be careful of your fingers because the blade is sharp.

Serves 4

30ml/2 tbsp garlic-infused olive oil
450g/1lb waxy potatoes, peeled and very thinly sliced
6 pancetta slices
50g/2oz/²⁄₃ cup freshly grated Parmesan cheese
salt and ground black pepper

1 Preheat the oven to 180°C/350°F/Gas 4. Brush a 20cm/8in ovenproof dish with some of the oil.

2 Arrange one-third of the sliced potatoes in the bottom of the ovenproof dish, season with salt and pepper and lay three slices of pancetta over the top. Sprinkle over a little cheese and arrange another layer of potatoes on the top.

3 Lay the remaining pancetta on top of the potatoes, sprinkle with a little more of the Parmesan and season with more salt and pepper.

4 Top with the remaining potatoes, season with salt and pepper and drizzle over the remaining olive oil. Press the potatoes down firmly and cover the tin with foil.

5 Bake for 30–35 minutes, then uncover and sprinkle with the remaining Parmesan. Bake for a further 15–20 minutes, or until golden brown on top.

6 Leave to rest for about 10–15 minutes, then cut into wedges and serve immediately.

Cook's Tip
Flavouring olive oil with garlic is very simple, it is ready to use in 2 weeks and it can be stored in a cool, dry place for 3–6 months.

Shropshire Bacon and Potato Pie

This classic combination of potatoes, onions, apples and bacon is packed inside a pastry crust and would have been typical of the thrifty and filling food that was fed to farm workers at the end of a long hard day in the fields.

Serves 4–5

75g/3oz plain (all-purpose) flour
75g/3oz plain wholemeal (whole-wheat) flour
pinch of salt
40g/1½oz/3 tbsp lard, diced
40g/1½oz/3 tbsp butter, diced
15ml/1 tbsp oil
225g/8oz lean bacon or gammon (smoked or cured ham), cut into small strips
2 medium onions, thinly sliced
450g/1lb potatoes, thinly sliced
10ml/2 tsp sugar
2 medium cooking apples, peeled cored and sliced
4 fresh sage leaves, finely chopped
salt and ground black pepper
300ml/½ pint/1¼ cups vegetable stock or medium dry (hard) cider
beaten egg or milk, to glaze

1 Sift the two flours and salt into a bowl and rub in the fats until the mixture resembles fine crumbs. Mix in enough cold water to bind the mixture, gathering it into a ball of dough. Chill for 30 minutes.

2 Preheat the oven to 180°C/350°F/Gas 4. Heat the oil in a pan and cook the bacon until crisp. Transfer to a mixing bowl.

3 Add the onions, potatoes and sugar to the hot pan and brown until beginning to soften. Add to the bowl.

4 Add the apple slices to the bowl. Stir in the sage, season with salt and pepper and mix well. Transfer the mixture into a 1.5 litre/2½ pint/6¼ cup pie dish, level the surface and pour the stock or cider over.

5 Roll out the pastry on a lightly floured surface to a shape large enough to cover the dish. Brush the edges of the dish with milk or beaten egg. Lay the pastry lid over the top, trim the edges and make a slit in the centre. Brush with beaten egg or milk.

6 Put into the hot oven and cook for about 1 hour, until the crust is golden brown and the filling is cooked through.

Potato Galette Energy 286kcal/1191kJ; Protein 9.8g; Carbohydrate 18.1g, of which sugars 1.5g; Fat 19.9g, of which saturates 5.8g; Cholesterol 25mg; Calcium 158mg; Fibre 1.1g; Sodium 385mg.
Shropshire Pie Energy 436kcal/1824kJ; Protein 12.7g; Carbohydrate 42.7g, of which sugars 8.2g; Fat 25g, of which saturates 10.7g; Cholesterol 48mg; Calcium 43mg; Fibre 4g; Sodium 754mg.

Pork Escalopes with Potato Rösti

The juices from the pork cook into the apples and potatoes, giving them a wonderful flavour as well as making a delicious sauce.

Serves 4

2 large potatoes, finely grated
1 medium Bramley apple, grated
2 garlic cloves, crushed
1 egg, beaten
butter, for greasing
15ml/1 tbsp olive oil
4 large slices prosciutto
4 pork escalopes, about
   175g/6oz each
4 sage leaves
1 medium Bramley apple,
   cut into thin wedges
25g/1oz/2 tbsp unsalted
   butter, diced
salt and ground black pepper
caramelized apple wedges,
   to serve

1 Preheat the oven to 200°C/400°F/Gas 6. Squeeze out all the excess liquid from the grated potatoes and apple. Mix the grated ingredients together with the garlic, egg and seasoning.

2 Divide the potatoes into four portions and spoon each quarter on to a baking sheet that has been lined with foil and greased. Form a circle with the potatoes and flatten out slightly with the back of a spoon. Drizzle with a little olive oil. Bake for 10 minutes.

3 Meanwhile, lay the prosciutto on a clean surface and place a pork escalope on top. Lay a sage leaf and a quarter of the apple wedges over each escalope and top each piece with the butter. Wrap the prosciutto around each piece of meat, making sure it is covered completely.

4 Remove the potatoes from the oven, place each pork parcel on top and return to the oven for 20 minutes. Carefully lift the pork and potatoes off the foil and serve with caramelized wedges of apple and any cooking juices on the side.

> **Cook's Tips**
> • Be careful not to overcook the pork as it will start to dry out.
> • Do not grate the potato until just before it is needed: if left for a prolonged period it will take on an unappetizing grey hue.

Bacon and Herb Potato Rösti

This version of the traditional potato dish from Switzerland is enhanced by the addition of bacon and plenty of fresh herbs.

Serves 4

450g/1lb potatoes, left whole
   and unpeeled
30ml/2 tbsp olive oil
1 red onion, finely chopped
4 lean back bacon rashers
   (strips), rinded and diced
15ml/1 tbsp potato flour
30ml/2 tbsp chopped fresh
   mixed herbs
salt and ground black pepper
fresh parsley sprigs, to garnish

1 Lightly grease a baking sheet. Par-boil the potatoes in a pan of lightly salted, boiling water for about 6 minutes. Drain the potatoes and set aside to cool slightly.

2 Once cool enough to handle, peel the potatoes and coarsely grate them into a bowl. Set aside.

3 Heat 15ml/1 tbsp of the oil in a frying pan, add the onion and bacon and cook gently for 5 minutes, stirring occasionally. Preheat the oven to 220°C/425°F/Gas 7.

4 Remove the pan from the heat. Stir the onion mixture, remaining oil, potato flour, herbs and seasoning into the grated potatoes and mix well.

5 Divide the mixture into eight small piles and spoon them on to the prepared baking sheet, leaving a little space between each pile of the mixture.

6 Bake in the oven for about 20–25 minutes until the rösti are crisp and golden brown. Serve immediately, garnished with sprigs of fresh parsley.

> **Variation**
> This dish is also delicious when made with either chopped streaky (fatty) bacon or cooked ham in place of the lean back bacon, if you prefer.

Pork Escalopes Energy 396kcal/1659kJ; Protein 42.7g; Carbohydrate 19.2g, of which sugars 4.4g; Fat 16.9g, of which saturates 6.7g; Cholesterol 177mg; Calcium 29mg; Fibre 1.5g; Sodium 310mg.
Bacon Rösti Energy 245kcal/1025kJ; Protein 10.7g; Carbohydrate 23.6g, of which sugars 1.8g; Fat 12.6g, of which saturates 2.9g; Cholesterol 146mg; Calcium 32mg; Fibre 2.6g; Sodium 572mg.

Mushroom, Bacon and Potato Rösti

Dried ceps or porcini mushrooms have a wonderful woody, earthy aroma and taste. With salty bacon lardons, they turn potato rösti into a memorable supper.

Serves 4
675g/1½lb floury potatoes
10g/¼oz dried ceps or
   porcini mushrooms
225g/8oz very thick smoked
   bacon, cut into lardons or
   thin strips
2 fresh thyme sprigs, chopped
30ml/2 tbsp chopped
   fresh parsley
30ml/2 tbsp vegetable oil
4 large eggs, to serve
1 bunch watercress, to garnish
crushed black peppercorns,
   to garnish

1 Cook the potatoes in a pan of boiling salted water for 5 minutes and no longer, as they need to remain firm enough to grate at the next stage.

2 Meanwhile, cover the mushrooms with boiling water and leave to soften for 5–10 minutes. Drain and chop.

3 Fry the bacon gently in a non-stick pan until all the fat has run out. Remove the bacon using a slotted spoon and reserve the fat for later.

4 Drain the potatoes and leave to cool. When they are cool enough to handle, grate them coarsely, then pat dry thoroughly on kitchen paper to remove all moisture. Place them in a large bowl and add the mushrooms, thyme, parsley and bacon. Mix together well.

5 Heat the bacon fat with a little of the oil in the frying pan until it is really hot. Spoon in the rösti mixture in heaps and flatten out. Fry in small batches for about 6 minutes until crisp and golden on both sides, turning once. Drain of excess oil on kitchen paper and keep warm in a low oven.

6 Heat the remaining oil in the hot pan and fry the eggs as you like them. Serve the rösti immediately with the eggs, watercress and crushed peppercorns.

Chorizo Sausage, Potato and Spring Onion Hash

This moreishly spicy dish is really easy to make and is a great way to use up any leftover boiled potatoes, if you have them. The potatoes will absorb some of the delicious spicy flavours of the chorizo.

Serves 4
450g/1lb fresh chorizo sausages
15ml/1 tbsp olive oil
450g/1lb cooked potatoes, cut
   into small chunks
1 bunch of spring onions
   (scallions), sliced
salt and ground black pepper

1 Heat a large frying pan over a medium heat and add the chorizo sausages. Cook for around 8–10 minutes, turning occasionally, until cooked through. Remove the sausages from the pan and set aside.

2 Add the olive oil to the sausage fat in the pan and when hot add the chunks of potato. Cook them over a low heat for between 5–8 minutes, turning occasionally until golden brown and coated in the chorizo juices.

3 Meanwhile, cut the chorizo sausages into bitesize chunks and add to the pan with the potatoes.

4 Add the spring onions to the pan and cook for a couple more minutes, until they are piping hot. Season with salt and pepper, and serve immediately.

> **Cook's Tips**
> • Fresh chorizo sausages are available from good butchers or from Spanish delicatessens and larger supermarkets. They often come in different varieties, with some being hotter and spicier than others – choose those that match your taste.
> • If you don't have any leftover cooked potatoes then simply boil some from scratch in plenty of salted water until tender. Leave them aside to cool completely before cutting into small chunks and adding them to the frying pan, as specified above.

Wild Mushroom Rösti Energy 387kcal/1616kJ; Protein 18.5g; Carbohydrate 27.2g, of which sugars 2.2g; Fat 23.6g, of which saturates 6.4g; Cholesterol 220mg; Calcium 42mg; Fibre 1.7g; Sodium 955mg.
Chorizo Hash Energy 522kcal/2172kJ; Protein 14.4g; Carbohydrate 29.6g, of which sugars 3.8g; Fat 39.3g, of which saturates 14.3g; Cholesterol 53mg; Calcium 63mg; Fibre 2.1g; Sodium 869mg.

Eggs Baked in Ham and Potato Hash

This dish is based on the traditional hash, but with ham replacing the more common corned beef. It is a great way to use up any leftover meat or potatoes.

Serves 6
50g/2oz/2 tbsp butter
1 large onion, chopped
350g/12oz cooked ham, diced
450g/1lb cooked potatoes, diced
115g/4oz mature (sharp) Cheddar cheese, grated
30ml/2 tbsp tomato ketchup
15–30ml/1–2 tbsp Worcestershire sauce
6 eggs
few drops of Tabasco sauce
salt and ground black pepper
15ml/1 tbsp chopped fresh parsley, to garnish

1 Preheat the oven to 325°F/170°C/Gas 3. Melt half of the butter in a frying pan. Cook the onion until soft, stirring occasionally.

2 Place the onion in a mixing bowl. Add the ham, potatoes, cheese, ketchup and Worcestershire sauce. Season with salt and pepper. Stir the mixture to combine.

3 Spread the hash in a lightly greased baking dish in a layer about 2.5cm/1in deep. Bake for 10 minutes.

4 Make six hollows in the hash. Break an egg into each hollow.

5 Melt the remaining butter in a small pan. Season with a few drops of Tabasco sauce to taste. Drizzle the seasoned butter over the eggs and hash.

6 Bake for 15–20 minutes or until the eggs are set and cooked to your taste. Serve immediately, in the dish, garnished with the chopped parsley.

> **Cook's Tip**
> *If you prefer your food a little spicier then simply add a little more of the Tabasco sauce into the butter.*

Swedish Pork and Potato Hash

This Swedish potato hash was originally introduced as an economy dish made with leftovers. Its popularity has meant that it is invariably now made using only fresh ingredients.

Serves 3–4
4 large potatoes
about 25g/1oz/2 tbsp butter
15ml/1 tbsp vegetable oil
1 large onion, finely chopped
150g/5oz gammon (smoked or cured ham) or bacon, finely chopped
100g/4oz smoked frankfurters, finely chopped
500g/1¼lb cold cooked lamb or beef, cubed
salt and ground black pepper
3–4 very fresh eggs, to serve
Worcestershire sauce, to serve
chopped fresh parsley, to garnish

1 Peel and cut the potatoes into small cubes measuring about 3mm/⅛in. Heat the butter and oil in a large frying pan, add the potato cubes and fry for about 20 minutes, stirring frequently, until golden brown. Remove from the pan with a slotted spoon, put in a bowl and keep warm.

2 Put the onion in the pan, adding more butter if necessary, and fry until golden brown. Remove from the pan and add to the potatoes. Add the gammon or bacon and the frankfurter sausages, fry until cooked and put them in the bowl.

3 Fry the beef or lamb until heated through and add to the other fried ingredients. Season the mixture with salt and pepper to taste and mix together.

4 Serve the mixture on warmed, individual plates. Break the eggs, one at a time, separating the yolks from the whites, and putting an egg yolk in half its shell in the centre of each plate. Garnish with parsley and serve with Worcestershire sauce.

> **Cook's Tip**
> *Make sure that the eggs are fresh and, because the recipe contains raw egg yolks, do not serve the dish to infants, the elderly, pregnant women, and convalescents.*

Egg Hash Energy 305kcal/1275kJ; Protein 19.7g; Carbohydrate 18.2g, of which sugars 5.9g; Fat 17.2g, of which saturates 9.9g; Cholesterol 135mg; Calcium 180mg; Fibre 1.5g; Sodium 1020mg.
Swedish Hash Energy 930kcal/3866kJ; Protein 55.9g; Carbohydrate 18.7g, of which sugars 3.6g; Fat 70.9g, of which saturates 28.8g; Cholesterol 427mg; Calcium 68mg; Fibre 1.3g; Sodium 1992mg.

Pork and Leek Sausages with Mustard Mashed Potato and Gravy

Tangy mustard, mashed potato and rich onion gravy are the perfect partners to delicious grilled sausages.

Serves 4

12 pork and leek sausages
salt and ground black pepper

For the onion gravy
30ml/2 tbsp olive oil
25g/1oz/2 tbsp butter
8 onions, sliced
5ml/1 tsp caster (superfine) sugar
15ml/1 tbsp plain (all-purpose) flour
300ml/½ pint/1¼ cups beef stock

For the mash
1.5kg/3¼lb potatoes
50g/2oz/¼ cup butter
150ml/¼ pint/⅔ cup double (heavy) cream
15ml/1 tbsp wholegrain mustard

1 Heat the oil and butter in a large pan until foaming. Add the onions and mix well to coat them in the fat. Cover and cook gently for about 30 minutes, stirring frequently. Add the sugar and cook for a further 5 minutes, or until the onions are softened, reduced and caramelized.

2 Remove the pan from the heat and stir in the flour, then gradually stir in the stock. Return the pan to the heat. Bring to the boil, stirring, then simmer for 3 minutes, or until thickened. Season.

3 Meanwhile, cook the potatoes in a pan of boiling salted water for 20 minutes, or until tender.

4 While the potatoes are cooking, preheat the grill (broiler) to medium. Arrange the sausages in a single layer in the grill pan and cook, turning occasionally, for around 15–20 minutes, or until cooked and evenly brown.

5 Drain the potatoes well and mash them with the butter, double cream and wholegrain mustard. Season with salt and pepper to taste.

6 Serve the sausages with the creamy mustard mash and plenty of onion gravy.

Potato and Sausage Casserole

You will find numerous variations of this delicious supper dish throughout Britain, but the basic ingredients are the same wherever you go – potatoes, sausages and bacon. It is a great dish to feed the family.

Serves 4
15ml/1 tbsp vegetable oil
4 bacon rashers (strips), cut into 2.5cm/1in pieces
2 large onions, chopped
2 garlic cloves, crushed
8 large pork sausages
4 large baking potatoes, thinly sliced
1.5ml/¼ tsp fresh sage
300ml/½ pint/1¼ cups vegetable stock
salt and ground black pepper
soda bread, to serve

1 Preheat the oven to 180°C/350°F/Gas 4. Grease a large ovenproof dish and set aside.

2 Heat the oil in a frying pan. Add the bacon and fry for 2 minutes. Add the onions and fry for 5–6 minutes until golden. Add the garlic and fry for 1 minute, making sure that it doesn't burn, then remove the mixture from the pan and set aside.

3 Add the sausages to the empty pan and fry for 5–6 minutes until golden brown.

4 Arrange the potatoes in the base of the prepared dish. Spoon the bacon and onion mixture on top. Season with the salt and pepper and sprinkle with the fresh sage.

5 Pour on the stock and top with the sausages. Cover and bake for 1 hour. Serve hot with fresh soda bread.

Cook's Tip
The success of this dish will depend on the quality of the sausages you use. Try to use the best you can find – a local butcher will usually make their own, which will often be of better quality than those from a supermarket.

Pork Sausages Energy 939kcal/3913kJ; Protein 19.9g; Carbohydrate 85g, of which sugars 16.7g; Fat 60g, of which saturates 28.6g; Cholesterol 133mg; Calcium 179mg; Fibre 6.6g; Sodium 942mg.
Sausage Casserole Energy 553kcal/2305kJ; Protein 17.4g; Carbohydrate 48.7g, of which sugars 10g; Fat 33.4g, of which saturates 11.8g; Cholesterol 51mg; Calcium 74mg; Fibre 4g; Sodium 1019mg.

Pork and Garlic Sausage Casserole with Potatoes and Apple

This hearty and filling slow-cooked casserole contains a variety of pork cuts along with flavoursome onion, sauerkraut and potatoes. The light ale helps to tenderize the meat, and adds a robust flavour to the sauce.

Serves 6

45ml/3 tbsp sunflower oil
225g/8oz lean, smoked bacon, rinded and diced
450g/1lb lean shoulder of pork, trimmed and cut into 2.5cm/1in cubes
1 large onion, sliced
900g/2lb potatoes, thickly sliced
250ml/8fl oz/1 cup light ale
225g/8oz/2 cups German garlic sausage, skinned and sliced
500g/1¼lb/2¼ cups sauerkraut, drained
2 red eating apples, cored and sliced
5ml/1 tsp caraway seeds
salt and ground black pepper

1 Preheat the oven to 180°C/350°F/Gas 4. Heat 30ml/2 tbsp of the sunflower oil in a flameproof casserole. Fry the bacon for 2–3 minutes, stirring frequently, until beginning to colour.

2 Add the cubes of pork and cook for 4–5 minutes until lightly browned on all sides. Remove the bacon and pork cubes from the pan and set aside.

3 Add the remaining oil to the pan and gently cook the onion for 6–8 minutes, until soft. Return the meat to the pan and add the sliced potatoes, stirring to mix.

4 Pour the ale into the pan and stir gently to mix. Bring the mixture to the boil, then reduce the heat. Cover the pan with a tight-fitting lid and cook in the preheated oven for 45 minutes.

5 Stir the garlic sausage, drained sauerkraut, sliced apple and caraway seeds into the pan. Season with salt and ground black pepper to taste.

6 Return the casserole to the oven and cook for a further 30 minutes, or until the meat is tender. Serve immediately.

Dublin Potato and Sausage Coddle

This truly Irish dish combines bacon and sausages, two foods known since the earliest Irish literature, and is said to have been the favourite meal of Jonathan Swift, the 18th-century Irish author of *Gulliver's Travels*. Leeks and oatmeal were originally used but potatoes and onion are popular nowadays. As with very simple dishes, the success of coddle lies in the superiority of the ingredients selected.

Makes 4 large or 8 small portions

8 x 8mm/⅓in thick ham or dry-cured bacon slices
8 best-quality lean pork sausages
4 large onions, thinly sliced
900g/2lb potatoes, peeled and sliced
90ml/6 tbsp chopped fresh parsley
salt and ground black pepper

1 Cut the ham or bacon into large chunks and cook with the sausages in 1.2 litres/2 pints/5 cups boiling water for about 5 minutes. Drain, but reserve the cooking liquor.

2 Put the meat and sausages into a pan or ovenproof dish with the sliced onions, potatoes and the chopped parsley. Season with salt and ground black pepper, and add just enough of the reserved cooking liquor to cover. Cover with a tight-fitting lid; lay a piece of buttered foil or baking parchment on top before putting on the lid.

3 Simmer gently over a low heat for about 1 hour, or until the liquid is reduced by half and all the ingredients are cooked but not too mushy. Serve immediately with the vegetables on top, with the traditional accompaniments of fresh soda bread and a glass of stout, if you like.

> **Cook's Tip**
> *The traditional accompaniments to this dish are fresh soda bread and glasses of stout, but a crisp green vegetable, such as lightly cooked Brussels sprouts or purple sprouting broccoli, makes a nice contrast.*

Garlic Sausage Energy 472kcal/1976kJ; Protein 32g; Carbohydrate 37.7g, of which sugars 11.7g; Fat 21.6g, of which saturates 6.2g; Cholesterol 110mg; Calcium 91mg; Fibre 5.3g; Sodium 1449mg.
Dublin Coddle Energy 432kcal/1809kJ; Protein 20.6g; Carbohydrate 52g, of which sugars 10.2g; Fat 17.2g, of which saturates 6.1g; Cholesterol 45mg; Calcium 83mg; Fibre 5.7g; Sodium 1.27g.

Chorizo with Garlic Potatoes

A classic tapas recipe, this simple dish can be served in small quantities as a snack or, as here, in slightly larger proportions for a lunch. The bitesized chunks of potato are the perfect foil to the spicy chorizo and soak up all the delicious smoky flavours of the sausage.

Serves 4

450g/1lb potatoes
3 eggs, hard-boiled and quartered
175g/6oz chorizo sausage, sliced
150ml/¼ pint/⅔ cup mayonnaise
150ml/¼ pint/⅔ cup sour cream
2 garlic cloves, crushed
salt and ground black pepper
30ml/2 tbsp chopped fresh coriander (cilantro), to garnish

1 Cook the potatoes in a pan of boiling salted water for about 15–20 minutes, or until tender. Drain them well and set aside to cool slightly.

2 Cut the potatoes into bitesize pieces. Place them in a large serving dish with the eggs and chorizo sausage, and season to taste with salt and pepper.

3 In a small bowl, mix together the mayonnaise, sour cream and garlic until well combined. Season to taste with salt and ground black pepper.

4 Spoon the sour cream and mayonnaise mixture over the potato and chorizo mixture in the serving dish.

5 Toss the salad gently to thoroughly coat all the ingredients with the sour cream and mayonnaise dressing, then sprinkle over some chopped coriander to garnish. Divide between four plates and serve immediately.

Variation
To give this dish a more piquant flavour, add about 15ml/ 1 tbsp finely chopped cornichons and 4 finely chopped anchovy fillets. If coriander isn't available, then use 15ml/1 tbsp fresh marjoram instead.

Spicy Spanish Potato, Chorizo and Cheese Tortilla

The classic Spanish tortilla contains only onions and potatoes, gently stewed in olive oil then stirred into eggs to make a thick cake-like omelette fried in a pan, then baked in the oven. Here, the combination of sliced potatoes with chilli and chorizo makes a potato cake with a real kick to it.

Serves 4

15ml/1 tbsp vegetable oil
½ onion, sliced
1 small green (bell) pepper, cut into rings
1 garlic clove, finely chopped
1 tomato, chopped
6 pitted black olives, chopped
275g/10oz cooked firm, waxy potatoes, sliced
225g/8oz sliced chorizo, in strips
1 fresh green chilli, chopped
50g/2oz/½ cup Cheddar cheese, grated
6 eggs
45ml/3 tbsp milk
1.5ml/¼ tsp ground cumin
1.5ml/¼ tsp dried oregano
1.5ml/¼ tsp paprika
salt and ground black pepper
rocket (arugula) leaves, to garnish

1 Preheat the oven to 190°C/375°F/Gas 5. Line the base of a 23cm/9in round cake tin (pan) with baking parchment.

2 Heat the oil in a large non-stick frying pan. Add the onion, green pepper and garlic and cook over a medium heat for 5–8 minutes until softened.

3 Spoon the onion mixture into the prepared tin with the tomato, olives, potatoes, chorizo and chilli. Mix the ingredients together until well combined and sprinkle the grated cheese over the top.

4 In a small bowl, whisk together the eggs and milk until frothy. Add the cumin, oregano, paprika and salt and pepper to taste. Pour the mixture on to the vegetables, tilting the tin so that the egg mixture spreads evenly.

5 Bake for 30 minutes until set and lightly golden. Serve in wedges, hot or cold, with rocket leaves.

Chorizo with Potatoes Energy 631kcal/2613kJ; Protein 12.7g; Carbohydrate 24.3g, of which sugars 4g; Fat 54.4g, of which saturates 15.5g; Cholesterol 214mg; Calcium 84mg; Fibre 1.4g; Sodium 582mg.
Spanish Tortilla Energy 439kcal/1824kJ; Protein 23.6g; Carbohydrate 13.1g, of which sugars 1.8g; Fat 32.4g, of which saturates 9.5g; Cholesterol 328mg; Calcium 285mg; Fibre 2.4g; Sodium 669mg.

Spring Onion, Potato and Pepperoni Tortilla

Cooked potatoes are delicious with spicy pepperoni in this thick Spanish-style omelette. Salad and crusty bread are excellent accompaniments.

Serves 4

30ml/2 tbsp olive oil
75g/3oz pepperoni, sliced
225g/8oz potatoes, cooked and
    cut into cubes
3 spring onions (scallions), sliced
115g/4oz Fontina cheese, cut
    into cubes
115g/4oz/1 cup frozen
    peas, thawed
6 eggs
30ml/2 tbsp chopped parsley
salt and ground black pepper

1 Heat the oil in a non-stick frying pan and add the potatoes, pepperoni and spring onions. Cook over a high heat for about 5 minutes, stirring occasionally, until the pepperoni releases some of its fat and the onions have softened. Add the cheese and peas, and stir to combine.

2 In a medium bowl, beat the eggs with the parsley and seasoning, then pour the mixture over the ingredients in the frying pan. Stir well to evenly distribute the egg mixture around the ingredients. Cook gently, without stirring, for about 10 minutes, or until the egg mixture is golden underneath.

3 When the mixture has almost set, cover the pan with a large plate and carefully invert the pan and its cover to turn out the tortilla. Slide the tortilla back into the pan and continue cooking for a further 10 minutes, or until browned underneath.

4 Carefully turn out the tortilla on to a large, flat serving platter and serve hot or warm, cut into slices.

> **Cook's Tip**
> If you do not have the confidence to invert the tortilla and replace it in the pan, simply finish cooking it under a preheated grill (broiler) for 5–8 minutes, or until just set.

Heaven and Earth Potatoes

This dish from Germany, whose name translates as 'heaven and earth', combines apples 'from heaven' and potatoes 'from the earth', and is served with slices of black pudding and crisp onion rings.

Serves 4

450g/1lb floury potatoes, peeled
    and quartered
350g/12oz cooking apples, cored,
    peeled and chopped
50g/2oz/¼ cup butter
2 cloves
pinch of nutmeg
30ml/2 tbsp sunflower oil
350g/12oz blutwurst or black
    pudding (blood sausage), cut
    into 1cm/½in slices
1 onion, sliced into rings
salt and ground black pepper

1 Put the potatoes in a large pan. Add water to cover and bring to the boil. Add salt, then simmer for about 15 minutes, or until the potatoes are tender, but do not let them get too soft. Drain thoroughly and leave to cool.

2 Meanwhile, put the chopped apples and 15g/½oz/1 tbsp of the butter in a small pan along with the cloves. Heat gently and simmer for about 10 minutes, until they are just soft but do not let them get too mushy. Leave to cool slightly.

3 Discard the cloves, then add the cooked apple to the pan with the cooked potato. Add the remaining butter, nutmeg and a little salt and ground black pepper.

4 Mash the mixture until smooth and creamy with a potato masher or pass it all through a food mill. Pile on to a serving plate and keep warm.

5 Meanwhile, heat the oil in a heavy frying pan and cook the slices of blutwurst or black pudding for 5 minutes, or until crisp. Remove from the pan with a slotted spoon and arrange to one side of the purée.

6 Add the onion rings to the pan and fry for 12–15 minutes, until lightly browned and crispy. Pile on top of the purée and serve immediately.

Potato Tortilla Energy 443kcal/1848kJ; Protein 16g; Carbohydrate 32.4g, of which sugars 3.6g; Fat 28.1g, of which saturates 12.3g; Cholesterol 49mg; Calcium 226mg; Fibre 1.9g; Sodium 728mg.
Heaven and Earth Energy 281kcal/1180kJ; Protein 15.6g; Carbohydrate 29.5g, of which sugars 4.5g; Fat 12g, of which saturates 6.1g; Cholesterol 25mg; Calcium 80mg; Fibre 1.7g; Sodium 1050mg.

Chicken with Summer Vegetables and Tarragon

This is an all-in-the-pot dish, with the chicken cooking liquid providing the stock for the potatoes and other vegetables as well as the sauce.

Serves 4
1.8kg/4lb boiling fowl (stewing chicken)
1 onion, peeled, studded with 6 cloves
1 bay leaf
a sprig each of thyme and parsley
10 black peppercorns
12 small potatoes, washed
8 small shallots, peeled
vegetables of your choice, such as carrots, courgettes (zucchini), broad (fava) beans and peas, mangetouts (snowpeas)
25g/1oz/2 tbsp butter
30ml/2 tbsp plain (all-purpose) flour
60ml/4 tbsp chopped fresh tarragon

1 Wash the chicken and dry with kitchen paper. Place in a large pan with the onion, bay leaf, thyme, parsley and peppercorns, with water to cover. Bring to the boil, then reduce the heat and simmer gently for 1½ hours.

2 Remove the chicken from the pan and keep warm. Remove all the seasonings, either with a slotted spoon or by straining the mixture, then bring the cooking liquid back to the boil, skimming off any fat that may have appeared on the top.

3 Cook the vegetables in the liquid, putting the potatoes in first for a few minutes, then adding the shallots and carrots, if using, and finally any green vegetables that take no time at all. When the vegetables are cooked, place the chicken on a serving dish and surround with all the vegetables.

4 In a small pan, melt the butter, add the flour and stir to create a roux. Slowly add some liquor from the large pan until a sauce is created – about 600ml/1 pint/2½ cups – and allow to simmer for a few minutes to reduce down and strengthen the flavour. At the last moment stir in the chopped fresh tarragon, then ladle the sauce over the chicken and vegetables. Serve immediately.

Roast Chicken with Potatoes and Lemon

This is a lovely, easy dish for a family meal. As with other roasts, everything is baked together so that the potatoes absorb all the different flavours, especially that of the lemon.

Serves 4
1.6kg/3½lb chicken
2 garlic cloves, peeled, but left whole
15ml/1 tbsp chopped fresh thyme or oregano, or 5ml/1 tsp dried, plus 2–3 fresh sprigs of thyme or oregano
800g/1¾lb potatoes
juice of 1 lemon
60ml/4 tbsp extra virgin olive oil
300ml/½ pint/1¼ cups hot water
salt and ground black pepper

1 Preheat the oven to 200°C/400°F/Gas 6. Place the chicken, breast side down, in a large roasting pan, then tuck the garlic cloves and the thyme or oregano sprigs inside the bird.

2 Peel the potatoes and quarter them lengthways. If they are very large, slice them lengthways into thinner pieces. Arrange the potatoes around the chicken, then pour the lemon juice over the chicken and potatoes. Season with salt and pepper, drizzle the olive oil over the top and add about three-quarters of the chopped fresh or dried thyme or oregano. Pour the hot water into the roasting pan.

3 Roast the chicken and potatoes for 30 minutes, then remove the roasting pan from the oven and turn the chicken over.

4 Season the bird with a little more salt and pepper, sprinkle over the remaining fresh or dried herbs, and add a little more hot water, if needed. Reduce the oven temperature to 190°C/375°F/Gas 5.

5 Return the chicken and potatoes to the oven and roast them for another hour, or slightly longer, by which time both the chicken and the potatoes will be a golden colour. Serve with a crisp leafy salad.

Chicken and Tarragon Energy 713kcal/2973kJ; Protein 51.2g; Carbohydrate 39.3g, of which sugars 13g; Fat 40g, of which saturates 12.9g; Cholesterol 261mg; Calcium 103mg; Fibre 5.4g; Sodium 251mg.
Roast Chicken Energy 767kcal/3,195kJ; Protein 53.3g; Carbohydrate 32.5g, of which sugars 2.9g; Fat 47.7g, of which saturates 11.8g; Cholesterol 264mg; Calcium 51mg; Fibre 2.6g; Sodium 206mg.

Roast Lime Chicken with Sweet Potatoes

This chicken, delicately flavoured with garlic, turmeric and coriander, would traditionally be spit-roasted. However, it works very well as a conventional roast, and, cooked this way, it can be accompanied by the succulent addition of sweet potatoes flavoured with the delicious juices from the chicken.

Serves 4

4 garlic cloves, 2 finely chopped
    and 2 bruised but left whole
small bunch coriander (cilantro),
    with roots, coarsely chopped
10ml/2 tsp salt
5ml/1 tsp ground turmeric
5cm/2in piece fresh turmeric
1 roasting chicken, about
    1.5kg/3¼lb
1 lime, cut in half
4 medium/large sweet potatoes,
    peeled and cut into
    thick wedges
300ml/½ pint/1¼ cups chicken
    or vegetable stock
30ml/2 tbsp soy sauce
salt and ground black pepper

1 Preheat the oven to 190°C/375°F/Gas 5. Calculate the cooking time for the chicken, allowing 20 minutes per 500g/1¼lb, plus 20 minutes. Using a mortar and pestle or food processor, grind the chopped garlic, coriander, salt and turmeric to a paste.

2 Place the chicken in a roasting pan and smear it with the herb and spice paste. Squeeze the lime juice over and place the lime halves and garlic cloves in the cavity. Cover with foil and roast in the oven.

3 Meanwhile, bring a pan of water to the boil and par-boil the sweet potatoes for 10–15 minutes, until just tender. Drain well and place them around the chicken in the roasting pan. Baste with the cooking juices and sprinkle with salt and pepper. Replace the foil and return the chicken to the oven.

4 About 20 minutes before the end of the cooking time, remove the foil and baste the chicken with the juices. Turn the sweet potatoes over.

5 At the end of the calculated roasting time, check that the chicken is cooked. Lift it out of the roasting pan, tip it so that all the juices collected in the cavity drain into the pan, then place the bird on a carving board. Cover it with tented foil and leave it to rest before carving. Transfer the sweet potatoes to a serving dish and keep them hot in the oven while you make the gravy.

6 Pour away the oil from the roasting pan but retain the meat juices. Place the roasting pan on top of the stove and heat it until the juices are bubbling. Pour in the stock. Bring the mixture to the boil, stirring constantly with a wooden spoon and scraping the base of the pan to incorporate the residue.

7 Stir in the soy sauce and check the seasoning before straining the gravy into a jug (pitcher). Serve it with the carved chicken and the sweet potatoes.

Escalopes of Chicken with Baby Vegetables

This is a quick and light dish – ideal for summer, when it is too hot to slave over the stove for hours or to eat heavy meals. Flattening the chicken breast fillets thins and tenderizes the meat and also speeds up the cooking process. The fresh tomato mayonnaise brings out the sweet flavour of the potatoes.

Serves 4

4 skinless chicken breast fillets,
    each weighing 175g/6oz
juice of 1 lime
120ml/4fl oz/½ cup olive oil
675g/1½lb mixed baby potatoes,
    carrots, fennel (sliced if large),
    asparagus and peas
sea salt and ground black pepper
fresh flat leaf parsley sprigs,
    to garnish

For the tomato mayonnaise
150ml/¼ pint/⅔ cup mayonnaise
15ml/1 tbsp sun-dried
    tomato paste

1 Lay the chicken portions between two sheets of clear film (plastic wrap) or baking parchment and beat them flat with a rolling pin. Season the chicken with salt and pepper and sprinkle with the lime juice.

2 Heat 45ml/3 tbsp of the oil in a frying pan or griddle pan and fry the chicken for 10 minutes on each side, or until cooked.

3 Meanwhile, put the potatoes and carrots in a pan with the remaining oil and season with sea salt. Cover and cook over a medium heat for 10–15 minutes, stirring frequently. Add the fennel and cook for a further 5 minutes, stirring frequently. Finally, add the asparagus and peas and cook for 5 minutes more, or until all the vegetables are tender.

4 To make the sauce, mix together the mayonnaise and sun-dried tomato paste in a small bowl. Spoon the vegetables on to a warmed large serving platter or individual plates and arrange the chicken on top. Serve the tomato mayonnaise with the chicken and vegetables. Garnish with sprigs of flat leaf parsley.

Roast Lime Chicken Energy 620kcal/2581kJ; Protein 47g; Carbohydrate 21.3g, of which sugars 5.7g; Fat 38.9g, of which saturates 11.4g; Cholesterol 240mg; Calcium 43mg; Fibre 2.4g; Sodium 228mg.
Escalopes of Chicken Energy 513kcal/2143kJ; Protein 44g; Carbohydrate 18.9g, of which sugars 9g; Fat 29.6g, of which saturates 4.7g; Cholesterol 141mg; Calcium 41mg; Fibre 3.2g; Sodium 251mg.

Chicken and Vegetable Pot Au Feu

A lovely wine and herb-scented stock contains tender morsels of chicken and baby vegetables in this light and aromatic seasonal version of the French casserole.

Serves 4
1 chicken, about 2.25kg/5lb
1 parsley sprig
15ml/1 tbsp black peppercorns
1 bay leaf
300g/11oz baby carrots, washed and left whole
175g/6oz baby leeks, washed and left whole
25g/1oz/2 tbsp butter
15ml/1 tbsp olive oil
300g/11oz large shallots, halved
200ml/7fl oz/scant 1 cup dry white wine
800g/1¾lb baby new potatoes, scrubbed
120ml/4fl oz/½ cup double (heavy) cream
salt and ground black pepper
small bunch parsley or tarragon, chopped, to garnish

1 Joint the chicken into eight pieces and place the carcass in a large stockpot. Add the parsley sprig, peppercorns, bay leaf and the carrot and leek trimmings. Cover with cold water and bring to the boil. Simmer for about 45 minutes, then strain, reserving the stock for later.

2 Meanwhile, melt the butter with the olive oil in a frying pan, then add the chicken pieces. Add seasoning, and brown the chicken all over.

3 Transfer the chicken pieces to a plate and add the shallots to the pan. Cook over a low heat for 20 minutes, stirring occasionally, until softened, but not browned.

4 Return the chicken pieces to the pan and pour over the white wine. Scoop up any juices from the base of the pan with a wooden spoon.

5 Add the carrots, leeks and potatoes to the pan. Pour in enough stock to just cover the ingredients. Bring the mixture to the boil, then cover the pan and simmer for 20 minutes.

6 Stir the cream into the casserole. Transfer to a serving dish and garnish with the herbs. Serve immediately.

Chicken and Mushroom Potato Bake

This rich, creamy dish is simple to make in the slow cooker and is a hearty supper on a cold winter's day. The sauce combines with juices from the mushrooms and chicken during cooking to make a well-flavoured gravy that is soaked up by the potatoes.

Serves 4
4 large skinless chicken breast fillets, cut into chunks
15ml/1 tbsp olive oil
40g/1½oz/3 tbsp butter
1 leek, finely sliced into rings
25g/1oz/¼ cup plain (all-purpose) flour
550ml/18fl oz/2½ cups milk
5ml/1 tsp Worcestershire sauce (optional)
5ml/1 tsp wholegrain mustard
1 carrot, finely diced
225g/8oz/3 cups button (white) mushrooms, thinly sliced
900g/2lb potatoes, thinly sliced
salt and ground black pepper

1 Heat the olive oil in a large pan. Add the chicken and fry gently until beginning to brown. Remove the chicken from the pan using a slotted spoon, leaving any juices behind. Set aside.

2 Add 25g/1oz/2 tbsp of the butter to the pan and heat gently until melted. Stir in the leeks and fry gently for about 5 minutes. Sprinkle the flour over the leeks, then turn off the heat and gradually blend in the milk until smooth. Slowly bring the mixture to the boil, stirring all the time, until thickened.

3 Remove the pan from the heat and stir in the Worcestershire sauce, if using, mustard, diced carrot, mushrooms and chicken. Season generously.

4 Arrange enough potato slices to cover the base of the ceramic cooking pot. Spoon one-third of the chicken mixture over the top, then cover with another layer of potatoes. Repeat layering, finishing with a layer of potatoes. Dot the remaining butter on top.

5 Cover and cook on high for 4 hours, or until the potatoes are cooked and tender when pierced with a skewer. If you like, place the dish under a moderate grill (broiler) for 5 minutes to brown, then serve immediately.

Chicken Pot Au Feu Energy 613kcal/2563kJ; Protein 53.1g; Carbohydrate 36.4g, of which sugars 17.9g; Fat 25g, of which saturates 11.1g; Cholesterol 196mg; Calcium 128mg; Fibre 5.3g; Sodium 396mg.
Chicken and Potato Bake Energy 359kcal/1511kJ; Protein 31g; Carbohydrate 33.6g, of which sugars 7.8g; Fat 12.1g, of which saturates 6g; Cholesterol 92mg; Calcium 130mg; Fibre 3.1g; Sodium 193mg.

Stoved Chicken and Potatoes

'Stovies' were originally potatoes slowly cooked on the stove, with onions and dripping or butter, until falling to pieces. This version includes a delicious layer of bacon and chicken hidden in the middle of the vegetables.

Serves 4

butter, for greasing
1kg/2¼lb baking potatoes, cut
    into 5mm/¼in slices
2 large onions, thinly sliced
15ml/1 tbsp chopped fresh thyme
25g/1oz/2 tbsp butter
15ml/1 tbsp vegetable oil
2 large bacon slices, chopped
4 large chicken joints, halved
600ml/1 pint/2½ cups
    chicken stock
1 bay leaf
salt and ground black pepper

1 Preheat the oven to 150°C/300°F/Gas 2. Arrange a thick layer of half the potato slices in the bottom of a large, lightly greased heavy casserole, then cover with half the onions. Sprinkle with half of the thyme, and season with salt and pepper to taste.

2 Heat the butter and oil in a large heavy frying pan, add the bacon and chicken, stirring frequently, and brown on all sides. Using a slotted spoon, transfer the chicken and bacon to the casserole. Reserve the fat in the pan.

3 Sprinkle the remaining thyme over the chicken, season with salt and pepper, then cover with the remaining onion slices, followed by a neat layer of overlapping potato slices. Season the dish well with salt and pepper.

4 Pour the stock into the casserole, add the bay leaf and brush the potatoes with the reserved fat. Cover the pan with a tight-fitting lid and bake in the oven for about 2 hours until the chicken is very tender.

5 Preheat the grill (broiler). Take the cover off the casserole and place it under the grill until the slices of potato are beginning to turn golden brown and crisp. Remove the bay leaf and serve hot.

Spinach and Potato Stuffed Chicken

This dish consists of large chicken breasts, filled with a herby spinach and potato mixture, then topped with butter and baked until mouth-wateringly tender.

Serves 6

115g/4oz floury potatoes, diced
115g/4oz spinach leaves,
    finely chopped
1 egg, beaten
30ml/2 tbsp chopped fresh
    coriander (cilantro)
4 large skinless chicken
    breast fillets
50g/2oz/¼ cup butter

For the sauce

400g/14oz can
    chopped tomatoes
1 garlic clove, crushed
150ml/¼ pint/⅔ cup hot
    chicken stock
30ml/2 tbsp chopped
    fresh coriander
salt and ground black pepper
fried mushrooms, to serve

1 Preheat the oven to 180°C/350°F/Gas 4. Boil the potatoes in a large pan of boiling water for 15 minutes or until tender. Drain the potatoes, place them in a large bowl and roughly mash with a fork. Stir the spinach into the potato with the egg and coriander. Season with salt and pepper to taste.

2 Cut almost all the way through the chicken breast fillets and open out to form a pocket in each. Spoon the filling into the centre and fold the chicken back over again. Secure with cocktail sticks (toothpicks) and place in a roasting pan.

3 Dot with butter and cover with foil. Bake for 25 minutes. Remove the foil and cook for a further 10 minutes until the chicken is golden.

4 Meanwhile, to make the sauce, heat the tomatoes, garlic and stock in a pan and cook for 10 minutes. Season and stir in the coriander. Serve the chicken with the sauce and fried mushrooms.

Cook's Tip
Young spinach leaves have a sweeter flavour and are ideal for using in this dish.

Stoved Chicken Energy 630kcal/2653kJ; Protein 69.2g; Carbohydrate 48.2g, of which sugars 8.9g; Fat 19.2g, of which saturates 7.2g; Cholesterol 195mg; Calcium 56mg; Fibre 3.9g; Sodium 574mg.
Spinach and Potato Energy 212kcal/888kJ; Protein 26.6g; Carbohydrate 5.7g, of which sugars 2.8g; Fat 9.4g, of which saturates 5g; Cholesterol 119mg; Calcium 60mg; Fibre 1.5g; Sodium 159mg.

Chicken with Potato Dumplings

Slowly poaching chicken pieces in a creamy sauce topped with light herb and potato dumplings makes a delicate yet hearty and warming meal.

Serves 6
1 onion, chopped
300ml/½ pint/1¼ cups vegetable stock
120ml/4fl oz/½ cup white wine
4 large chicken breast fillets
300ml/½ pint/1¼ cups single (light) cream

15ml/1 tbsp chopped fresh tarragon
salt and ground black pepper

For the dumplings
225g/8oz maincrop potatoes, boiled and mashed
175g/6oz/1¼ cups suet
115g/4oz/1 cup self-raising (self-rising) flour
50ml/2fl oz/¼ cup water
30ml/2 tbsp chopped mixed fresh herbs
salt and ground black pepper

1 Place the onion, stock and wine in a deep-sided frying pan. Add the chicken and simmer, covered, for 20 minutes.

2 Remove the chicken from the stock, cut it into chunks and set aside. Strain the stock and discard the onion. Return the stock to the pan and boil until reduced by one-third. Stir in the single cream and tarragon, and simmer until just thickened. Stir in the chicken and season with salt and ground black pepper.

3 Spoon the mixture into a 900ml/1½ pint/3¾ cup ovenproof dish. Preheat the oven to 190°C/375°F/Gas 5.

4 Mix together the dumpling ingredients to make a soft dough. Divide into six and shape into balls with floured hands.

5 Place the dumplings on top of the chicken mixture and bake uncovered for 30 minutes until cooked. Serve immediately.

Cook's Tip
Make sure that you do not reduce the sauce too much before cooking in the oven as the dumplings absorb quite a lot of liquid.

Chicken and Pesto Jacket Potatoes

Although it is usually served with pasta, pesto also gives a wonderful lift to rice, bread and potato dishes – all good starchy carbohydrates. Here, it is combined with chicken and yogurt to make a tasty topping for jacket potatoes.

Serves 4
4 baking potatoes
2 chicken breast fillets, skin on
15ml/1 tbsp pesto sauce
250ml/8fl oz/1 cup plain (natural) yogurt
fresh basil sprigs, to garnish

1 Preheat the oven to 200°C/400°F/Gas 6. Prick the potatoes all over with a fork and bake in the oven for about 1¼ hours until soft.

2 About 20 minutes before the end of the cooking time for the potatoes, place the chicken fillets in an ovenproof dish and bake in the oven until cooked through.

3 Meanwhile, place the pesto sauce into a bowl. Add the natural yogurt and stir well until the ingredients are thoroughly combined.

4 Skin and slice the chicken fillets. Cut the potatoes open and fill with the chicken slices. Top with the pesto-flavoured yogurt and garnish with basil sprigs.

Cook's Tips
• The chicken fillets and potatoes can be cooked in the microwave, if you like. Microwave the chicken fillets on HIGH for 3–4 minutes, turning over halfway through cooking. Microwave the potatoes on HIGH for 12–15 minutes, turning over once halfway during cooking. Leave to stand for 3–4 minutes.
• A good technique for ensuring that the insides of the jacket potatoes are particularly fluffy is to place a dish towel over them and break them open by stamping them with the palm of the hand. This opens them up quicker than cutting with a knife, which means the air escapes faster, resulting in beautifully light and airy potato inside.

Chicken with Dumplings Energy 552kcal/2300kJ; Protein 28.2g; Carbohydrate 26.5g, of which sugars 2.6g; Fat 37.4g, of which saturates 21g; Cholesterol 121mg; Calcium 83mg; Fibre 1.3g; Sodium 80mg.
Chicken and Pesto Energy 272kcal/1151kJ; Protein 26.1g; Carbohydrate 36.9g, of which sugars 7.3g; Fat 3.3g, of which saturates 1.5g; Cholesterol 57mg; Calcium 180mg; Fibre 2g; Sodium 160mg.

Rice with Chilli Chicken and Potatoes

This Indian dish is so tasty that it is generally reserved for special occasions.

Serves 4 to 6

1.3kg/3lb skinless chicken breast fillet, cut into large pieces
60ml/4 tbsp biryani masala paste
2 green chillies, chopped
15ml/1 tbsp crushed fresh root ginger
15ml/1 tbsp crushed garlic
50g/2oz coriander (cilantro) leaves, chopped
6–8 mint leaves, chopped
150ml/¹/₂ pint/²/₃ cup natural (plain) yogurt, beaten
30ml/2 tbsp tomato purée (paste)
4 onions, finely sliced, deep-fried and crushed
salt, to taste
450g/1lb basmati rice, washed

5ml/1 tsp black cumin seeds
5cm/2in cinnamon stick
4 green cardamoms
2 black cardamoms
vegetable oil, for shallow-frying
4 large potatoes, peeled and quartered
175ml/6fl oz/³/₄ cup milk, mixed with 75ml/2¹/₂fl oz/ ¹/₃ cup water
1 sachet saffron powder, mixed with 90ml/6 tbsp milk
30ml/2 tbsp ghee or unsalted (sweet) butter

For the garnish

ghee or unsalted (sweet) butter, for shallow-frying
50g/2oz cashew nuts
50g/2oz sultanas (golden raisins)
2 hard-boiled eggs, quartered
deep-fried onion slices

1 Mix the chicken with the next 10 ingredients and marinate for 2 hours. Place in a pan and cook for 10 minutes. Set aside. Boil a pan of water and soak the rice with the cumin seeds, cinnamon stick and cardamoms for 5 minutes. Drain well. Heat the oil for frying. Cook the potatoes until browned. Set aside.

2 Place half the rice on top of the chicken, then an even layer of potatoes. Add the remaining rice on the potatoes. Sprinkle the milky water all over the rice. Make a few holes through the rice and pour in a little saffron milk. Dot the surface with ghee or butter, cover and cook over a low heat for 35–45 minutes.

3 Make the garnish. Heat the ghee or butter and fry the nuts and sultanas until they swell. Set aside. When the rice is ready, gently toss the layers together. Garnish with the nut mixture, eggs and onion slices and serve immediately.

Devil's Chicken and Potato Curry

Every Eurasian household in Malaysia has its own version of this devilishly hot chicken and potato curry. Served as a meal on its own with bread to mop up the sauce, it is often eaten at family celebration meals.

Serves 6

4–6 skinless chicken breast fillets, cut into chunks
60ml/4 tbsp vegetable oil
1 onion, halved and sliced
25g/1oz fresh root ginger, peeled and cut into julienne strips
4 garlic cloves, cut into strips
30–45ml/2–3 tbsp vinegar
10ml/2 tsp sugar
3 medium potatoes, cut into bitesize pieces
2 courgettes (zucchini), halved lengthways, seeded and sliced
8 Chinese leaves (Chinese cabbage), cut into squares

10ml/2 tsp brown mustard seeds, ground and mixed to a paste with a little water
salt
fresh crusty bread, to serve

For the spice paste

10 dried chillies, soaked in warm water, seeded and patted dry
6 fresh red chillies, seeded and chopped
8 shallots, chopped
6 garlic cloves, chopped
25g/1oz fresh root ginger, peeled and chopped
6 candlenuts or macadamia nuts
10ml/2 tsp ground turmeric

For the marinade

15ml/1 tbsp light soy sauce
15ml/1 tbsp dark soy sauce
10ml/2 tsp rice or white wine vinegar
10ml/2 tsp caster (superfine) sugar

1 Mix together the ingredients for the marinade and rub it into the chicken pieces. Leave to marinate for 30 minutes. Using a mortar and pestle or food processor, grind the chillies, shallots, garlic, ginger and nuts to a paste. Stir in the turmeric.

2 Heat the oil in a wok or heavy pan. Stir in the onion, ginger and garlic and fry until golden. Add the spice paste, stir, toss in the chicken and stir until it browns. Pour in water to cover.

3 Bring up to the boil, then add the vinegar, sugar and potatoes. Reduce to a simmer and cook until the potatoes are just tender. Add the sliced courgettes and cabbage and cook for 2 minutes. Stir in the mustard paste, season with salt and serve immediately.

Chicken and Rice Energy 940kcal/3944kJ; Protein 66g; Carbohydrate 107.1g, of which sugars 15.5g; Fat 28.4g, of which saturates 5.9g; Cholesterol 153mg; Calcium 166mg; Fibre 4.9g; Sodium 195mg.
Devil's Curry Energy 270kcal/1136kJ; Protein 32.5g; Carbohydrate 15.4g, of which sugars 4.6g; Fat 9.1g, of which saturates 1.3g; Cholesterol 88mg; Calcium 36mg; Fibre 1.8g; Sodium 441mg.

Japanese Chicken and Vegetables

As well as potatoes, this authentic Japanese dish features konnyaku, a black or white yam cake that is available from good Japanese supermarkets.

Serves 4

2 chicken thighs, about 200g/7oz, boned, with skin remaining
1 large carrot, trimmed
1 konnyaku

300g/11oz new potatoes
500g/1¼lb canned bamboo shoots, drained
30ml/2 tbsp vegetable oil
300ml/½ pint/1¼ cups dashi stock
salt

For the seasonings

75ml/5 tbsp shoyu
30ml/2 tbsp sake
30ml/2 tbsp caster (superfine) sugar
30ml/2 tbsp mirin

1 Cut the chicken into bitesize pieces. Chop the carrot into 2cm/¾in triangles. To do this, cut the carrot slightly diagonally and turn it 90 degrees each time you cut.

2 Boil the konnyaku in boiling water for 1 minute and drain under cold running water. Cool and slice it crossways into 5mm/¼in thick rectangular strips. Cut a 4cm/1½in slit down the centre of a strip without cutting the ends. Push the top of the strip through the slit to make a decorative tie. Repeat with all the konnyaku strips.

3 Peel and halve the new potatoes. Halve the canned bamboo shoots, then cut into the same shape as the carrot.

4 In a medium pan, heat the oil and stir-fry the chicken until the meat turns white. Add the carrot, konnyaku ties, potatoes and bamboo shoots. Stir well each time you add a new ingredient.

5 Add the dashi stock and bring to the boil. Cook on a high heat for 3 minutes, then reduce to medium-low. Add the shoyu, sake, caster sugar and mirin, cover the pan, then simmer for 15 minutes.

6 When the potatoes are soft, transfer the cooked chicken and vegetables to a large serving bowl. Serve immediately.

Chicken and Sweet Potato Curry with Coconut and Caramel Sauce

This typical South-east Asian chicken and sweet potato curry is simple to make and delicious to eat. Serve this curry with crusty baguettes for mopping up the sauce, or steamed fragrant rice or noodles.

Serves 4

45ml/3 tbsp Indian curry powder or garam masala
15ml/1 tbsp ground turmeric
500g/1¼lb skinless chicken thighs or chicken breast portions
25ml/1½ tbsp raw cane sugar

30ml/2 tbsp sesame oil
2 shallots, chopped
2 garlic cloves, chopped
4cm/1½in galangal, peeled and chopped
2 lemon grass stalks, chopped
10ml/2 tsp chilli paste or dried chilli flakes
1–2 medium sweet potatoes, peeled and cubed
45ml/3 tbsp Thai fish sauce
600ml/1 pint can coconut milk
1 small bunch each of fresh basil and coriander (cilantro), stalks removed
salt and ground black pepper

1 In a small bowl, mix together the curry powder or garam masala and the turmeric. Put the chicken thighs in a bowl and coat with half of the spice. Set aside.

2 To make the caramel sauce, heat the sugar in a small pan with 7.5ml/1½ tsp water, until the sugar dissolves and the syrup turns golden. Remove from the heat and set aside.

3 Heat a wok or wide heavy pan and add the oil. Stir-fry the shallots, garlic, galangal and lemon grass until they begin to smell fragrant. Stir in the rest of the turmeric and curry powder with the chilli paste or chilli flakes, followed by the chicken, moving it around the wok for 2–3 minutes.

4 Add the sweet potatoes, then the fish sauce, caramel sauce, coconut milk and 150ml/¼ pint/⅔ cup water, stirring well to combine the flavours. Bring the liquid to the boil, reduce the heat and cook for about 15 minutes or until the chicken is tender. Season with salt and pepper and stir half the basil and coriander through the curry. Garnish with the remaining herbs.

Japanese Chicken Energy 168kcal/705kJ; Protein 12.7g; Carbohydrate 15.8g, of which sugars 4.4g; Fat 6.4g, of which saturates 0.9g; Cholesterol 31mg; Calcium 46mg; Fibre 2.2g; Sodium 976mg.
Chicken and Coconut Curry Energy 387kcal/1632kJ; Protein 31g; Carbohydrate 38g, of which sugars 19g; Fat 14g, of which saturates 3g; Cholesterol 131mg; Calcium 1.8mg; Fibre 1g; Sodium 1g.

Chicken and Sweet Potato Curry with Rice Vermicelli

Lemon grass, garlic and sweet potatoes give this South-east Asian curry a wonderful aromatic flavour.

Serves 4

1 chicken, about 1.3–1.6kg/3–3½lb
225g/8oz sweet potatoes
60ml/4 tbsp vegetable oil
1 onion, finely sliced
3 garlic cloves, crushed
30–45ml/2–3 tbsp Thai
  curry powder
5ml/1 tsp sugar
10ml/2 tsp Thai fish sauce

600ml/1 pint/2½ cups
  coconut milk
1 lemon grass stalk, cut in half
350g/12oz rice vermicelli, soaked
  in hot water until soft
1 lemon, cut into wedges,
  to serve

For the garnish
115g/4oz beansprouts
2 spring onions (scallions), finely
  sliced diagonally
2 red chillies, seeded and
  finely sliced
8–10 mint leaves

1 Skin the chicken. Cut the flesh into small pieces and set aside. Peel the sweet potatoes and cut them into large chunks, about the same size as the chicken pieces.

2 Heat half the oil in a large heavy pan. Add the onion and garlic and fry until the onion softens.

3 Add the chicken pieces and stir-fry until they change colour. Stir in the curry powder. Season with salt and sugar and mix thoroughly, then stir in the fish sauce. Pour in the coconut milk and add the lemon grass. Cook over a low heat for 15 minutes.

4 Meanwhile, heat the remaining oil in a large frying pan. Fry the sweet potatoes until lightly golden. Using a slotted spoon, add them to the chicken. Cook for 10–15 minutes more, or until both the chicken and sweet potatoes are tender.

5 Drain the rice vermicelli and cook it in a pan of boiling water for 3–5 minutes. Drain well. Place in shallow bowls, with the chicken curry. Garnish with beansprouts, spring onions, chillies and mint leaves and serve with lemon wedges.

Chicken and Potato Ghiveci

This superb dish, with its colourful medley of sweet and crunchy vegetables, is one of the best potted chicken soups around. The secret of its success is when to add the vegetables so that they are cooked to perfection. For the best results, it is important to use fresh herbs rather than dried, although a mixture of fresh and dried herbs would not compromise the flavour too much.

Serves 6

60ml/4 tbsp vegetable oil, melted
  lard or white cooking fat
1 mild onion, thinly sliced
2 garlic cloves, crushed

2 red (bell) peppers, seeded
  and sliced
about 1.6kg/3½lb chicken, jointed
  into six pieces
90ml/6 tbsp tomato
  purée (paste)
3 potatoes, diced
5ml/1 tsp chopped
  fresh rosemary
5ml/1 tsp chopped
  fresh marjoram
5ml/1 tsp chopped fresh thyme
3 carrots, cut into chunks
½ small celeriac, cut
  into chunks
120ml/4fl oz/½ cup dry
  white wine
2 courgettes (zucchini), sliced
salt and ground black pepper
chopped fresh rosemary and
  marjoram, to garnish

1 Heat the oil in a large flameproof casserole. Add the onion and garlic and cook for 1–2 minutes until softened.

2 Add the peppers to the casserole and cook, stirring occasionally, for a further 2 minutes.

3 Place the chicken in the casserole and brown over the hob for about 15 minutes.

4 Add the tomato purée, potatoes, herbs, carrots, celeriac and white wine to the casserole, and season to taste with salt and pepper. Cook over a gentle heat, covered, for a further 40–50 minutes.

5 At 5 minutes before the end of cooking, add the courgettes. Adjust the seasoning to taste. Garnish with the herbs and serve with rye bread, if you like, or with herb bread or crusty rolls.

Chicken Vermicelli Curry Energy 763kcal/3199kJ; Protein 51.6g; Carbohydrate 92g, of which sugars 11.6g; Fat 21.3g, of which saturates 4.1g; Cholesterol 109mg; Calcium 170mg; Fibre 4g; Sodium 545mg.
Chicken Ghiveci Energy 430kcal/1807kJ; Protein 49.6g; Carbohydrate 28.5g, of which sugars 12.9g; Fat 12.3g, of which saturates 2.3g; Cholesterol 175mg; Calcium 61mg; Fibre 4.4g; Sodium 202mg.

Chicken, Pork and Potatoes in Peanut Sauce

This traditional Peruvian dish is made with dried potatoes, which break up when cooked to thicken the sauce. The same effect is achieved here by using floury potatoes.

Serves 6
75g/3oz/³⁄₄ cup unsalted peanuts
60ml/4 tbsp olive oil
3 chicken breast portions, halved
500g/1¼lb boneless pork loin, cut into 2cm/³⁄₄in pieces
1 large onion, chopped
30–45ml/2–3 tbsp water

3 garlic cloves, crushed
5ml/1 tsp paprika
5ml/1 tsp ground cumin
500g/1¼lb floury potatoes, peeled and thickly sliced
550ml/18fl oz/scant 2½ cups vegetable stock
salt and ground black pepper
cooked rice, to serve

For the garnish
2 hard-boiled eggs, sliced
50g/2oz/½ cup pitted black olives
chopped fresh flat leaf parsley

1 Place the peanuts in a large dry frying pan over a low heat. Toast for 2–3 minutes, until golden. Leave to cool, then process in a food processor until finely ground.

2 Heat half the oil in a heavy pan. Add the chicken pieces, season and cook for 10 minutes, until golden brown all over. Transfer the pieces of chicken to a plate, using a slotted spoon. Heat the remaining oil and cook the pork for 3–4 minutes, until brown. Transfer to the plate with the chicken pieces.

3 Lower the heat, add the onion and fry for 5 minutes. Add the garlic, paprika and cumin and fry for 1 minute. Stir in the sliced potatoes, cover the pan and cook for a further 3 minutes. Mix in the peanuts and stock. Simmer for 30 minutes.

4 Return the meat to the pan and bring to the boil. Lower the heat, replace the lid and simmer for 6–8 minutes.

5 Garnish the stew with the egg slices, black olives and chopped parsley. Serve with the rice.

Turkey Croquette Potatoes

These deliciously crisp patties of smoked turkey mixed with mashed potato and spring onions will be a firm family favourite.

Serves 4
450g/1lb potatoes, diced
3 eggs
30ml/2 tbsp milk
175g/6oz smoked turkey rashers (strips), finely chopped
2 spring onions (scallions), sliced

115g/4oz/2 cups fresh white breadcrumbs
vegetable oil, for deep fat frying

For the sauce
15ml/1 tbsp olive oil
1 onion, finely chopped
400g/14oz can tomatoes, drained
30ml/2 tbsp tomato purée (paste)
15ml/1 tbsp chopped fresh parsley
salt and ground black pepper

1 Boil the potatoes for 20 minutes or until tender. Drain and then return the pan to a low heat to evaporate the excess water.

2 Mash the potatoes with two eggs and the milk. Season well with salt and pepper. Stir in the turkey and spring onions. Chill for 1 hour.

3 Meanwhile, to make the sauce, heat the oil in a frying pan and fry the onion for 5 minutes until softened. Add the tomatoes and purée, stir and simmer for 10 minutes. Stir in the parsley, season to taste and keep the sauce warm until needed.

4 Remove the potato mixture from the refrigerator and divide into eight pieces. Shape each piece into a sausage shape and dip in the remaining beaten egg and then the breadcrumbs.

5 Heat the vegetable oil in a deep-fat fryer to 175°C/330°F and deep fry the croquettes for 5 minutes, or until golden and crisp. Serve immediately, accompanied with the sauce.

Cook's Tip
Test the oil temperature by dropping a cube of bread into it. If it sinks, rises and sizzles in 10 seconds, the oil is ready to use.

Chicken in Peanut Sauce Energy 394kcal/1651kJ; Protein 39.3g; Carbohydrate 16.7g, of which sugars 2.4g; Fat 19.4g, of which saturates 4.1g; Cholesterol 85mg; Calcium 33mg; Fibre 1.8g; Sodium 123mg.
Turkey Croquettes Energy 404kcal/1698kJ; Protein 19.4g; Carbohydrate 47g, of which sugars 7.7g; Fat 16.7g, of which saturates 2.4g; Cholesterol 73mg; Calcium 93mg; Fibre 3.3g; Sodium 315mg.

Poussins and New Potato Pot roast

Pot roasts are traditionally associated with the colder months, but this delicious version is a simple summer dish that makes the most of new season potatoes.

Serves 4
2 poussins, about
  500g/1¼lb each
25g/1oz/2 tbsp butter

15ml/1 tbsp clear honey
500g/1¼lb small
  new potatoes
1 red onion, halved lengthwise
  and cut into thin wedges
4–5 small rosemary sprigs
2 bay leaves
1 lemon, cut into wedges
450ml/¾ pint/scant 2 cups hot
  chicken stock
salt and ground black pepper

1 Soak a clay chicken brick in cold water for 20 minutes, then drain. Cut the poussins in half, along the breast bone.

2 Melt the butter, mix it together with the honey and brush over the poussins. Season with salt and pepper.

3 Place the small new potatoes and onion wedges in the base of the chicken brick. Tuck the rosemary sprigs, bay leaves and lemon wedges in among the vegetables. Pour over the hot chicken stock (see Cook's Tip).

4 Place the halved poussins on top of the vegetables. Cover the chicken brick and place it in an unheated oven. Set the oven to 200°C/400°F/Gas 6 and cook for 55–60 minutes, or until the poussin juices run clear and the vegetables are tender. Uncover the chicken brick for the last 10 minutes of cooking to add more colour to the poussins, if necessary. Serve hot.

> **Cook's Tips**
> • Make sure the stock is hot, but not boiling, when it is added to the chicken brick, otherwise the chicken brick may crack.
> • A poussin is a baby chicken – usually around 4–6 weeks old. Poussins can be cooked by grilling (broiling), roasting or pot-roasting, but are especially tender and moist cooked in a chicken brick.

Roasted Duckling on a Bed of Honeyed Potatoes

The rich flavour of duck combined with these sweetened potatoes glazed with honey makes an excellent treat for a dinner party or special occasion.

Serves 4
1 duckling, giblets removed
60ml/4 tbsp light soy sauce

150ml/¼ pint/⅔ cup fresh
  orange juice
3 large floury potatoes, cut
  into chunks
30ml/2 tbsp clear honey
15ml/1 tbsp sesame seeds
salt and ground black pepper

1 Preheat the oven to 200°C/400°F/Gas 6. Place the duckling in a roasting pan. Prick the skin well.

2 Mix the soy sauce and orange juice together and pour over the duck. Cook in the oven for 20 minutes.

3 Place the potato chunks in a bowl and stir in the honey, toss to mix well. Remove the duckling from the oven and spoon the potatoes all around and under the duckling.

4 Roast for 35 minutes and remove from the oven. Toss the potatoes in the duck's juices so that they cook evenly, and turn the duckling over. Return the roasting pan to the oven and cook for a further 30 minutes.

5 Remove the duckling from the oven and carefully scoop off the excess fat, leaving the juices behind.

6 Sprinkle the sesame seeds over the potatoes, season and turn the duckling back over, breast side up, and cook for a further 10 minutes. Remove the duckling and potatoes from the oven and keep warm, allowing the duckling to stand for a few minutes.

7 Pour off the excess fat and simmer the juices on the hob for a few minutes. Serve the juices with the carved duckling and the potatoes.

Roasted Duckling Energy 806kcal/3341kJ; Protein 20.8g; Carbohydrate 32.3g, of which sugars 6.4g; Fat 66.8g, of which saturates 17.9g; Cholesterol 0mg; Calcium 53mg; Fibre 2.1g; Sodium 403mg.
Poussins Energy 443kcal/1852kJ; Protein 30.1g; Carbohydrate 24.2g, of which sugars 5.4g; Fat 25.8g, of which saturates 8.9g; Cholesterol 158mg; Calcium 23mg; Fibre 1.5g; Sodium 153mg.

Cheese and Potato Truffade

Baked until meltingly soft, this warming cheese and potato supper is the perfect slow bake to come home to. In France, where it originated, it would be made with a Tomme or Cantal cheese, which are now readily available.

Serves 4–6

1 large onion, thinly sliced
675g/1½lb baking potatoes, very thinly sliced
150g/5oz/1¼ cups grated hard cheese, such as Tomme, Cantal or mature (sharp) Cheddar
freshly grated nutmeg
salt and ground black pepper
mixed salad leaves, to serve
a little sunflower oil or melted butter

1 Preheat the oven to 180°C/350°F/Gas 4. Lightly grease the base of a shallow baking dish or roasting pan with the oil or melted butter.

2 Arrange the onions over the bottom of the dish and then add a layer of potatoes over them, and a sprinkling of cheese. Finish with another layer of potatoes.

3 Brush the top layer of potatoes with oil or melted butter and season with nutmeg, salt and pepper.

4 Top the dish with a layer of the grated cheese. Bake in the preheated oven for about 1 hour until the vegetables are tender and the top is golden brown.

5 Leave the dish to stand for about 5 minutes, then serve in wedges with mixed salad leaves.

Variation
In France, they make a non-vegetarian version of this dish, which is cooked with diced streaky (fatty) bacon and the cheese is chopped, not grated. The ingredients are mixed and cooked slowly in a little lard in a pan on top of the stove.

Potatoes Baked with Tomatoes

This simple, hearty dish from the south of Italy is best when potatoes and tomatoes are in season and bursting with flavour, but it can also be made with canned plum tomatoes.

Serves 6

2 large red or yellow onions, thinly sliced
1kg/2¼lb baking potatoes, thinly sliced
450g/1lb tomatoes, fresh or canned, sliced, with their juice
90ml/6 tbsp olive oil
115g/4oz/1 cup Parmesan or Cheddar cheese, freshly grated
a few fresh basil leaves
50ml/2fl oz/¼ cup water
salt and ground black pepper

1 Preheat the oven to 180°C/350°F/Gas 4. Brush a large baking dish generously with oil.

2 Arrange a layer of onions in the base of the dish, followed by layers of potatoes and tomatoes, alternating them to make the dish look colourful.

3 Pour a little of the olive oil over the surface, and sprinkle with some of the grated cheese. Season with salt and ground black pepper.

4 Continue to layer the vegetables in the dish until they are all used up. Finish with a decorative top layer of overlapping potatoes and tomatoes.

5 Tear the basil leaves into small pieces, and add them here and there among the vegetables, saving a few for garnish. Sprinkle the top with the remaining grated cheese and oil.

6 Pour the water over the dish. Bake in the oven for 1 hour until the vegetables are tender.

7 Check the potato dish towards the end of cooking, and if the top begins to brown too much, place a sheet of foil or baking parchment, or a flat baking tray, on top of the dish. Garnish the dish with the remaining fresh basil leaves, once it is cooked, and serve immediately.

Truffade Energy 117kcal/494kJ; Protein 3.2g; Carbohydrate 20.8g, of which sugars 3.4g; Fat 2.9g, of which saturates 1.7g; Cholesterol 7mg; Calcium 40mg; Fibre 1.6g; Sodium 48mg.
Potatoes with Tomatoes Energy 309kcal/1290kJ; Protein 9.8g; Carbohydrate 31.7g, of which sugars 8g; Fat 16.7g, of which saturates 4.9g; Cholesterol 15mg; Calcium 211mg; Fibre 3.2g; Sodium 189mg.

Courgette and Potato Bake

Cook this delicious potato dish, known as briami in Greece, in early autumn, and the aromas spilling from the kitchen will recall the rich summer tastes and colours just past. In Greece, this would constitute a hearty main meal, with a salad, some olives and cheese.

Serves 4 as a main course; 6 as a first course

675g/1½lb courgettes (zucchini)
450g/1lb potatoes, peeled and
    cut into chunks
1 onion, finely sliced
3 garlic cloves, chopped
1 large red (bell) pepper, seeded
    and cubed
400g/14oz can chopped tomatoes
150ml/¼ pint/⅔ cup extra virgin
    olive oil
150ml/¼ pint/⅔ cup hot water
5ml/1 tsp dried oregano
45ml/3 tbsp chopped fresh flat
    leaf parsley, plus a few extra
    sprigs, to garnish
salt and ground black pepper

1 Preheat the oven to 190°C/375°F/Gas 5. Scrape the courgettes lightly under running water to dislodge any grit and then slice them into thin rounds.

2 Put them in a large baking dish and add the chopped potatoes, onion, garlic, red pepper and tomatoes. Mix well, then stir in the olive oil, hot water and dried oregano.

3 Spread the mixture evenly, then season with salt and ground black pepper. Bake for 30 minutes, then stir in the parsley and a little more water.

4 Return to the oven and cook for 1 hour, increasing the temperature to 200°C/400°F/Gas 6 for the remaining 10–15 minutes, so that the potatoes brown. Serve hot or cold.

Variation

Other vegetables can be used in this dish, if you like. Substitute half the courgettes with aubergine (eggplant), or add in a handful of pitted black olives.

Vegetable Gratin with Indian Spices

Subtly spiced with curry powder, turmeric, coriander and mild chilli powder, this rich potato gratin is substantial enough to serve on its own for lunch or supper. It also makes a good side dish to a larger meal.

Serves 4

175g/6oz celeriac
2 large potatoes, total weight
    about 450g/1lb
2 sweet potatoes, total weight
    about 275g/10oz
15ml/1 tbsp unsalted butter
5ml/1 tsp curry powder
5ml/1 tsp ground turmeric
2.5ml/½ tsp ground coriander
5ml/1 tsp mild chilli powder
3 shallots, chopped
150ml/¼ pint/⅔ cup single
    (light) cream
150ml/¼ pint/⅔ cup milk
salt and ground black pepper
chopped fresh flat leaf parsley,
    to garnish

1 Thinly slice the celeriac, potatoes and sweet potatoes, using a sharp knife or the slicing attachment on a food processor. Immediately place the vegetables in a bowl of cold water to prevent them from discolouring.

2 Preheat the oven to 180°C/350°F/Gas 4. Heat half the butter in a heavy pan, add the curry powder, turmeric and coriander and half of the chilli powder. Cook for 2 minutes, then leave to cool slightly. Drain the vegetables, then pat dry with kitchen paper. Place in a bowl, add the spice mixture and the shallots, and mix well.

3 Arrange the vegetables in a gratin dish, seasoning with salt and pepper between the layers. Mix together the cream and milk, pour the mixture over the vegetables, then sprinkle the remaining chilli powder on top.

4 Cover the dish with baking parchment and bake in the preheated oven for about 45 minutes.

5 Remove the baking parchment, dot the surface of the gratin with the remaining butter and bake for a further 50 minutes, until it is golden and bubbling. Serve immediately, garnished with the chopped fresh parsley.

Courgette Bake Energy 374kcal/1,554kJ; Protein 6.6g; Carbohydrate 28.6g, of which sugars 11.2g; Fat 26.7g, of which saturates 4g; Cholesterol 0mg; Calcium 86mg; Fibre 5.1g; Sodium 29mg.
Vegetable Gratin Energy 268kcal/1129kJ; Protein 5.8g; Carbohydrate 37.7g, of which sugars 9.8g; Fat 11.6g, of which saturates 7.1g; Cholesterol 31mg; Calcium 127mg; Fibre 3.6g; Sodium 117mg.

Greek Tomato and Potato Bake

This is an adaptation of a classic Greek potato dish, which is usually cooked on the hob. This recipe has a richer flavour because it is stove-cooked first and then baked in the oven.

Serves 4
120ml/4fl oz/½ cup olive oil
1 large onion, finely chopped
3 garlic cloves, crushed
4 large ripe tomatoes, peeled, deseeded and chopped
1kg/2¼lb waxy new or salad potatoes
salt and ground black pepper
15ml/1 tbsp chopped fresh flat leaf parsley, to garnish

1 Preheat the oven to 180°C/350°F/Gas 4. Heat the oil in a flameproof casserole. Fry the onion and garlic for 5 minutes until softened and just starting to brown.

2 Add the tomatoes to the pan, season with salt and ground black pepper and cook for 1 minute.

3 Cut the potatoes into even wedges. Add to the pan and cook for about 10 minutes. Season again and cover the pan with a tight-fitting lid.

4 Place the covered casserole on the middle shelf of the preheated oven and cook for 45–60 minutes until the potatoes are tender. Garnish with flat leaf parsley and serve.

Variation
To add to the Greek theme of this dish you could add a handful of pitted and chopped black olives. Look out for the superior kalamata olives in delicatessens and supermarkets.

Cook's Tip
Make sure that the potatoes are completely coated in the oil so that they cook evenly.

Potato, Leek and Tomato Bake

This simple potato dish is delicious for lunch or supper – a real winner with all the family. It is made in the microwave to make it even more convenient. Select the best tomatoes you can for a deliciously sweet flavour; if this means using small fruit, then add one or two extra.

Serves 4
675g/1½lb potatoes
2 leeks, trimmed and sliced
3 large tomatoes, sliced
a few fresh rosemary sprigs, crushed
1 garlic clove, crushed
300ml/½ pint/1¼ cups hot vegetable stock
15ml/1 tbsp olive oil
salt and ground black pepper

1 Scrub and thinly slice the potatoes. Layer them with the sliced leeks and tomatoes in a 1.2 litre/2 pint/5 cup microwave-proof dish that is also suitable for grilling (broiling). Sprinkle some of the crushed rosemary sprigs in between each layer and finish with a final layer of sliced potatoes on the top.

2 Add the crushed garlic to the vegetable stock, stir in the salt and ground black pepper to taste and pour over the dish of layered vegetables, ensuring that the mixture seeps down between every layer. Brush the top layer of sliced potatoes with the olive oil.

3 Cover and microwave on HIGH for 15–18 minutes or until the potatoes are tender.

4 Leave the dish to stand for around 5 minutes, then remove the cover. Cook under a preheated hot grill (broiler), if you like, until the top is crisp and brown all over. Serve immediately, straight from the dish at the table.

Cook's Tip
This recipe is also suitable for cooking in a combination microwave. Follow the oven manufacturer's timing guide for the best results.

Greek Bake Energy 399kcal/1670kJ; Protein 5.9g; Carbohydrate 49.3g, of which sugars 10.6g; Fat 21.2g, of which saturates 3.2g; Cholesterol 0mg; Calcium 41mg; Fibre 4.6g; Sodium 39mg.
Potato, Leek and Tomato Bake Energy 178kcal/752kJ; Protein 5g; Carbohydrate 32.4g, of which sugars 6.7g; Fat 4g, of which saturates 0.6g; Cholesterol 0mg; Calcium 39mg; Fibre 4.6g; Sodium 27mg.

Potato and Parsnip Dauphinois

Layers of potatoes and parsnips are baked slowly in creamy milk with a melted cheese topping. This is an ideal special side dish or light supper dish.

Serves 4–6
1kg/2lb potatoes, thinly sliced
1 onion, thinly sliced

450g/1lb parsnips, thinly sliced
2 garlic cloves, crushed
50g/2oz/4 tbsp butter
125g/4oz Gruyère or Cheddar
  cheese, grated
fresh nutmeg, grated
salt and ground black pepper
300ml/½ pint/1¼ cups single
  (light) cream
300ml/½ pint/1¼ cups milk

1 Lightly grease a large shallow ovenproof dish. Preheat the oven to 180°C/350°F/Gas 4.

2 Layer the potatoes in the dish with the onion and parsnips. In between each layer, dot the vegetables with pieces of garlic and butter.

3 Finish with a layer of potatoes and sprinkle over most of the grated cheese. Sprinkle with the fresh nutmeg and season well with salt and ground black pepper.

4 Heat the cream and milk together in a small pan until the mixture is hot but not boiling. Slowly pour the creamy milk over the vegetables in the dish. Shake the pan a little to make sure the sauce seeps underneath the vegetable layers.

5 Sprinkle the remaining cheese over the top of the vegetables and grate a little more nutmeg on top. Bake for about an hour or so until the potatoes are tender and the cheese topping is bubbling and golden. Serve immediately.

Cook's Tip
For this dish you can use either waxy new potatoes, which will hold their shape better after cooking, or the floury variety, which will disintegrate a little bit. Either variety will absorb the delicious creamy garlic flavours of this dish.

Baked Leek, Potato and Brie Gratin

Potatoes baked in a creamy cheese sauce make the ultimate comfort dish, whether served as an accompaniment to pork or fish dishes or, as here, with plenty of leeks and melted cheese as a main course. When preparing leeks, separate the leaves and rinse them thoroughly under cold running water, as soil and grit often get caught between the layers.

Serves 4–6
900g/2lb medium potatoes,
  thinly sliced
2 large leeks, trimmed
200g/7oz ripe Brie or Camembert
  cheese, sliced
450ml/¾ pint/scant 2 cups single
  (light) cream
salt and ground black pepper

1 Preheat the oven to 180°C/350°F/Gas 4. Cook the potatoes in plenty of lightly salted, boiling water for 3 minutes, until slightly softened, then drain.

2 Cut the leeks into 1cm/½in slices and blanch them in a pan of boiling water for 1–2 minutes, until softened, then drain them thoroughly.

3 Place half the potatoes into a lightly greased, shallow, ovenproof dish and spread them out to the edge. Cover the potatoes with about two-thirds of the leeks, then add the remaining potatoes on top.

4 Tuck the cheese and the remaining leeks in among the potatoes. Season with salt and pepper and pour the cream over.

5 Bake for 1 hour, until tender and golden. Cover with foil if the top starts to overbrown before the potatoes are tender.

Variation
This dish can be made with vegetable stock in place of the cream if you are concerned about calories.

Potato Dauphinois Energy 438kcal/1833kJ; Protein 12.6g; Carbohydrate 41.6g, of which sugars 11.6g; Fat 25.4g, of which saturates 15.8g; Cholesterol 70mg; Calcium 304mg; Fibre 5.3g; Sodium 291mg.
Leek Gratin Energy 383kcal/1597kJ; Protein 13.1g; Carbohydrate 28.2g, of which sugars 5.4g; Fat 24.2g, of which saturates 15.4g; Cholesterol 72mg; Calcium 181mg; Fibre 3.3g; Sodium 225mg.

Layered Vegetable Terrine

A combination of vegetables and herbs layered and baked in a spinach-lined loaf tin. Delicious served hot or warm with a simple leafy salad garnish.

Serves 6

3 red (bell) peppers, halved

450g/1lb waxy potatoes
115g/4oz spinach leaves, trimmed
25g/1oz/2 tbsp butter
pinch grated nutmeg
115g/4oz/1 cup vegetarian
    Cheddar cheese, grated
1 medium courgette (zucchini),
    sliced lengthways and blanched
salt and ground black pepper

1 Preheat the oven to 180°C/350°F/Gas 4. Place the peppers in a roasting pan and roast, cores in place, for 30–45 minutes until charred.

2 Remove the peppers from the oven. Place in a plastic bag to cool. Peel the skins and remove the cores. Halve the potatoes and boil in lightly salted water for 10–15 minutes.

3 Blanch the spinach for a few seconds in boiling water. Drain and pat dry on kitchen paper. Line the base and sides of a 900g/2lb loaf tin (pan), making sure the leaves overlap the edges of the tin slightly.

4 Slice the potatoes thinly and lay one-third of the potatoes over the base, dot with a little of the butter and season with salt, pepper and nutmeg. Sprinkle a little cheese over.

5 Arrange three of the peeled pepper halves on top. Sprinkle a little cheese over and then a layer of courgettes. Lay another one-third of the potatoes on top with the remaining peppers and some more cheese, seasoning as you go. Lay the final layer of potato on top and sprinkle over any remaining cheese. Fold the spinach leaves over. Cover with foil.

6 Place the loaf tin in a roasting pan and pour boiling water around the outside, making sure the water comes halfway up the sides of the tin. Bake in the oven for 45–60 minutes. Remove from the oven and turn the loaf out. Serve sliced with lettuce and tomatoes.

Layered Potato Bake with Cheese

This family-sized potato bake is substantial enough for a main course.

Serves 6

105ml/7 tbsp olive oil
1 large onion, chopped
2 garlic cloves, crushed
5ml/1 tsp crushed dried chillies
130g/4½oz/generous 1 cup
    walnut halves

130g/4½oz/generous ½ cup
    fresh cheese, such as ricotta
105ml/7 tbsp warm water
3 eggs
450g/1lb large potatoes, peeled
butter, for greasing
65g/2½oz/scant ¾ cup pitted
    black olives
4 pimientos, cut into strips
salt

1 Heat 30ml/2 tbsp of the oil in a small pan over a low heat. Add the onion and sauté gently for 5 minutes, until soft. Stir in the garlic and dried chillies and cook for a further 2 minutes.

2 Put the walnuts in a blender or food processor. Blend until smooth, then add the cooked onion mixture, with the cheese and remaining olive oil. Season generously with salt and pour in the warm water. Blend to make a smooth paste. Set aside.

3 Put the eggs in a small pan of cold water. Bring to the boil, then lower the heat to a simmer. Cook for 10 minutes, then cool in a bowl of cold water.

4 Add the potatoes to a pan of salted water and cover. Bring to the boil, then simmer for 10 minutes. Drain and refresh under cold water. Drain again and cut into 1cm/½in slices. Shell the eggs and cut them into slices.

5 Preheat the oven to 180°C/350°F/Gas 4. Lightly grease a 28 × 18cm/11 × 7in baking dish with butter. Arrange a layer of potatoes in the dish and generously spread with the prepared paste. Top with egg slices and a sprinkling of olives and pimiento strips. Continue layering until all the ingredients have been used, finishing with olives and pimientos.

6 Bake for 30 minutes, until the potatoes are very tender. Leave to cool for 5 minutes before serving.

Layered Terrine Energy 205kcal/854kJ; Protein 8.3g; Carbohydrate 19.2g, of which sugars 7.7g; Fat 10.6g, of which saturates 6.6g; Cholesterol 27mg; Calcium 196mg; Fibre 3g; Sodium 203mg.
Layered Bake Energy 572kcal/2363kJ; Protein 8.9g; Carbohydrate 16.7g, of which sugars 4.3g; Fat 52.7g, of which saturates 12.3g; Cholesterol 117mg; Calcium 75mg; Fibre 2.2g; Sodium 116mg.

Potato and Parsnip Amandine

Shells of baked potatoes are filled with a spicy parsnip and crunchy almond mix. They make an unusual and delicious alternative to plain jacket potatoes.

Serves 4

4 large baking potatoes
olive oil, for greasing
225g/8oz parsnips, diced
25g/1oz/2 tbsp butter
5ml/1 tsp cumin seeds
5ml/1 tsp ground coriander
30ml/2 tbsp single (light) cream
  or natural (plain) yogurt
salt and ground black pepper
115g/4oz Gruyère or Cheddar
  cheese, grated
1 egg, beaten
50g/2oz/1/4 cup flaked
  (sliced) almonds

1 Preheat the oven to 200°C/400°F/Gas 6. Rub the potatoes all over with the olive oil, score each lightly around its width, then bake in the oven for about 1 hour, until cooked.

2 Meanwhile, boil the parsnips until tender, then drain well, mash them and mix with the butter, spices and cream or natural yogurt.

3 When the potatoes are cooked, leave them to cool slightly, then cut them in half and scoop out the flesh with a spoon. Mash the flesh, then combine with the parsnip mash and season well with salt and black pepper.

4 Stir the cheese, egg and three-quarters of the almonds into the potato and parsnip mash. Fill the hollow potato shells with the mixture and sprinkle over the remaining almonds.

5 Return the filled potatoes to the oven and bake for about 15–20 minutes until golden brown and the filling has set lightly. Serve immediately with a side salad.

> **Cook's Tip**
> *This dish works just as well with single (light) cream or natural (plain) yogurt. Which one you use is a matter of preference and may be influenced by the kind of diet you tend to follow.*

Baked Scalloped Potatoes with Feta

Thinly sliced potatoes are cooked with Greek feta cheese and black and green olives in olive oil. This dish is a good one to serve with toasted pitta bread.

Serves 4

900g/2lb maincrop potatoes
150ml/1/4 pint/2/3 cup olive oil
1 sprig rosemary
275g/10oz/2 1/2 cups feta
  cheese, crumbled
115g/4oz/1 cup pitted black
  and green olives, halved
300ml/1/2 pint/1 1/4 cups hot
  vegetable stock
salt and ground black pepper

1 Preheat the oven to 200°C/400°F/Gas 6. Cook the potatoes in plenty of boiling water for 15 minutes. Drain and cool slightly.

2 When the potatoes are cool enough to handle, peel them and cut into thin slices.

3 Lightly grease the base and sides of a 1.5 litre/2 1/2 pint/ 6 1/4 cup rectangular ovenproof dish with a little of the olive oil.

4 Layer the potatoes in the base of the dish. Break up the rosemary sprig and sprinkle over the potatoes along with the feta cheese and olives.

5 Drizzle with the remaining olive oil and pour over the stock. Season with salt and plenty of ground black pepper.

6 Bake in the oven for about 35 minutes, covering with foil to prevent the potatoes from getting too brown. Serve hot, straight from the dish.

> **Cook's Tips**
> • *Make sure you choose good-quality Greek feta cheese, which has a different texture to the feta cheese that is produced in other countries.*
> • *Try to find fresh olives for this dish, which should be available from the deli counter of your local supermarket, as olives that are canned in brine will be too salty for this dish.*

Potato Amandine Energy 452kcal/1888kJ; Protein 16.2g; Carbohydrate 40.4g, of which sugars 6.7g; Fat 25.5g, of which saturates 11.8g; Cholesterol 94mg; Calcium 293mg; Fibre 5.5g; Sodium 305mg.
Scalloped Potatoes Energy 584kcal/2429kJ; Protein 14.8g; Carbohydrate 37.3g, of which sugars 4g; Fat 42.7g, of which saturates 13.7g; Cholesterol 48mg; Calcium 279mg; Fibre 3.1g; Sodium 1662mg.

Root Vegetable Casserole with Courgette and Caraway Dumplings

Light courgette dumplings spiced with caraway complete this warming slow-cooker dish.

Serves 3

300ml/½ pint/1¼ cups dry (hard) cider
175ml/6fl oz/¾ cup boiling vegetable stock
2 leeks, cut into 2cm/¾in slices
2 carrots, cut into chunks
2 parsnips, cut into chunks
225g/8oz potatoes, cut into chunks
1 sweet potato, cut into chunks
1 bay leaf
7.5ml/1½ tsp cornflour (cornstarch)
115g/4oz full-fat soft cheese with garlic and herbs
salt and ground black pepper

For the dumplings

115g/4oz/1 cup self-raising (self-rising) flour
5ml/1 tsp caraway seeds
50g/2oz/½ cup shredded vegetable suet (chilled, grated shortening)
1 courgette (zucchini), grated
about 75ml/5 tbsp cold water

1 Reserve 15ml/1 tbsp of the cider and pour the rest into the ceramic cooking pot with the stock. Cover and switch to high. Add the vegetables to the ceramic cooking pot with the bay leaf. Cover with the lid and cook for 3 hours.

2 In a small bowl, blend the cornflour with the reserved cider. Add the cheese and mix together until combined, then gradually blend in a few spoonfuls of the cooking liquid. Pour over the vegetables and stir until thoroughly mixed. Season with salt and black pepper. Cover and cook for a further 1–2 hours, or until the vegetables are almost tender.

3 Towards the end of the cooking time, make the dumplings. Sift the flour into a bowl and stir in the caraway seeds, suet, courgettes, salt and black pepper. Stir in the water, adding a little more if necessary, to make a soft dough. With floured hands, shape the mixture into 12 dumplings, about the size of walnuts.

4 Carefully place the dumplings on top of the casserole, cover and cook for a further hour, or until the vegetables and dumplings are cooked. Serve in warmed deep soup plates.

Winter Vegetable Casserole with Herb Dumplings

When the cold weather sets in, make this warming potato casserole with some hearty old-fashioned dumplings.

Serves 6

2 potatoes
2 carrots
1 small fennel bulb
1 small swede (rutabaga)
2 leeks
2 courgettes (zucchini)
50g/2oz/½ cup butter or margarine
30ml/2 tbsp plain (all-purpose) flour
1 x 425g/15oz can butter (lima) beans, with liquid
600ml/1 pint/2½ cups stock
30ml/2 tbsp tomato purée (paste)
1 cinnamon stick
10ml/2 tsp ground coriander
2.5ml/½ tsp ground ginger
2 bay leaves
salt and ground black pepper

For the dumplings

200g/7oz/1¾ cups plain (all-purpose) flour
115g/4oz vegetable suet (US chilled, grated shortening), or chilled butter, grated
5ml/1 tsp dried thyme
5ml/1 tsp salt
120ml/4 fl oz/½ cup milk

1 Cut all the vegetables into even, bitesize chunks, then fry gently in the butter or margarine for about 10 minutes. Stir in the flour, then the liquor from the beans, the stock, tomato purée, spices, bay leaves and seasoning. Bring to the boil, stirring. Cover and simmer for 10 minutes, then add the beans and cook for a further 5 minutes.

2 Meanwhile, make the dumplings. Mix the flour, suet or butter, thyme and salt to a firm but moist dough with the milk and knead with your hands until it is smooth. Divide the dough into 12 pieces, rolling each one into a ball with your fingers. Uncover the simmering stew and then add the dumplings, allowing space between each one for expansion.

3 Replace the lid and cook on a gentle simmer for a further 15 minutes. Do not remove the lid or you will let out all the steam. Be careful not to cook dumplings too fast, or they will break up. Remove the cinnamon stick and bay leaves before you serve this dish, steaming hot.

Vegetable Casserole Energy 616kcal/2584kJ; Protein 11.9g; Carbohydrate 74.9g, of which sugars 17.1g; Fat 28.9g, of which saturates 15.9g; Cholesterol 35mg; Calcium 256mg; Fibre 9.5g; Sodium 369mg.
Winter Casserole Energy 510kcal/2132kJ; Protein 12.5g; Carbohydrate 59.7g, of which sugars 9.9g; Fat 26.2g, of which saturates 13.7g; Cholesterol 20mg; Calcium 160mg; Fibre 8.3g; Sodium 358mg.

Creamy Beetroot and Potato Gratin with Wild Mushrooms

This delicious dish of mashed potato with beetroot and wild mushrooms captures the true spirit of autumn.

Serves 4
30ml/2 tbsp vegetable oil
1 medium onion, chopped
45ml/3 tbsp plain
   (all-purpose) flour
300ml/½ pint/1¼ cups
   vegetable broth
675g/1½lb cooked beetroot
   (beets), peeled and chopped
75ml/5 tbsp single (light) cream
30ml/2 tbsp horseradish sauce
5ml/1 tsp hot mustard
15ml/1 tbsp wine vinegar

5ml/1 tsp caraway seeds
30ml/2 tbsp unsalted butter
1 shallot, chopped
225g/8oz/3 cups assorted wild
   and cultivated mushrooms, such
   as ceps, chanterelles, oyster,
   shiitake and field (portabello)
   mushrooms, trimmed
   and sliced
45ml/3 tbsp chopped
   fresh parsley

For the potato border
900g/2lb floury potatoes, peeled
150ml/¼ pint/⅔ cup milk
15ml/1 tbsp chopped fresh
   dill (optional)
salt and ground black pepper

1 Preheat the oven to 190°C/375°F/Gas 5. Oil a 23cm/9in round baking dish. Heat the oil in a large pan, add the onion and sauté until soft. Stir in the flour, then remove from the heat and gradually stir in the broth. Return to the heat and add the beetroot, cream, horseradish, mustard, vinegar and caraway seeds.

2 Bring the potatoes to a boil in salted water and cook for 20 minutes. Drain well and mash with the milk. Add the dill, if using, and season to taste with salt and pepper. Spoon the potatoes into the prepared dish and make a well in the centre. Spoon the beetroot mixture into the well and set aside.

3 Melt the butter in a large frying pan and cook the shallot until soft, but not browned. Add the mushrooms and cook, stirring, until their juices run. Increase the heat and boil off the moisture. When dry, season and stir in the chopped parsley. Spread the mushrooms over the beetroot mixture, cover and bake for 30 minutes. Serve hot.

Tomato and Rich Mediterranean Vegetable Hotpot

Here's a one-dish meal that's suitable for feeding large numbers of people. It's lightly spiced and has plenty of garlic – who could refuse?

Serves 4
60ml/4 tbsp extra virgin olive oil
   or sunflower oil
1 large onion, chopped
2 small or medium aubergines
   (eggplants), cut into small cubes
4 courgettes (zucchini), cut into
   small chunks
2 red, yellow or green (bell)
   peppers, seeded and chopped
115g/4oz/1 cup fresh or
   frozen peas

115g/4oz green beans
200g/7oz can flageolet (small
   cannellini) beans, rinsed
   and drained
450g/1lb new or salad potatoes,
   peeled and cubed
2.5ml/½ tsp ground cinnamon
2.5ml/½ tsp ground cumin
5ml/1 tsp paprika
4–5 tomatoes, peeled
400g/14oz can chopped tomatoes
30ml/2 tbsp chopped fresh parsley
3–4 garlic cloves, crushed
350ml/12fl oz/1½ cups
   vegetable stock
salt and ground black pepper
black olives and fresh parsley,
   to garnish

1 Preheat the oven to 190°C/375°F/ Gas 5. Heat 45ml/ 3 tbsp of the oil in a heavy pan, and cook the onion until golden. Add the aubergines, sauté for 3 minutes, then add the courgettes, peppers, peas, beans and potatoes, and stir in the spices and seasoning. Cook for 3 minutes, stirring constantly.

2 Cut the peeled tomatoes in half and scoop out the seeds. Finely chop the tomatoes and place them in a bowl. Stir in the canned tomatoes with the chopped fresh parsley, crushed garlic and the remaining olive oil. Spoon the cooked vegetable mixture into a shallow ovenproof dish and level the surface.

3 Pour the stock over the aubergine mixture and then spoon over the prepared tomato mixture.

4 Cover the dish with foil and bake for 30–45 minutes, until the vegetables are tender. Serve hot, garnished with black olives and parsley.

Creamy Beetroot Energy 445kcal/1874kJ; Protein 11.1g; Carbohydrate 64.4g, of which sugars 20.5g; Fat 17.8g, of which saturates 7.6g; Cholesterol 31mg; Calcium 140mg; Fibre 7g; Sodium 295mg.
Vegetable Hotpot Energy 365kcal/1529kJ; Protein 14.3g; Carbohydrate 48.2g, of which sugars 20.1g; Fat 14.1g, of which saturates 2.3g; Cholesterol 0mg; Calcium 141mg; Fibre 12.8g; Sodium 224mg.

Cowboy's Vegetable Hotpot

A great dish to serve as a children's main meal, which adults will enjoy too – if they are allowed to join the posse. You can use any vegetable mixture you like – just remember that potatoes and baked beans are a must for every self-respecting cowboy.

Serves 4–6

45ml/3 tbsp sunflower oil
1 onion, sliced
1 red (bell) pepper, sliced
1 sweet potato or 2 carrots, cut into chunks
115g/4oz green beans, chopped
1 x 400g/14oz can baked beans
1 x 200g/7oz can corn
15ml/1 tbsp tomato purée (paste)
5ml/1 tsp barbecue spice seasoning
115g/4oz cheese (preferably smoked), cubed
450g/1lb potatoes, thinly sliced
25g/1oz/2 tbsp butter, melted
salt and ground black pepper

1 Heat the sunflower oil in a large, heavy frying pan. Add the sliced onion, red pepper and sweet potato or carrots to the frying pan and cook gently for about 5 minutes, until softened but not browned.

2 Add the green beans, baked beans, corn (including the liquid from the can of corn), tomato purée and barbecue spice seasoning. Stir well to combine all of the ingredients and then bring the mixture to a boil. Reduce the heat and simmer gently for about 10 minutes.

3 Transfer the vegetables to a shallow ovenproof dish, spreading them out into an even layer. Sprinkle the cubed cheese over the top of the vegetables.

4 Preheat the oven to 190°C/375°F/Gas 5. Layer the sliced potatoes over the vegetable and cheese mixture and brush with the melted butter. Season generously with salt and ground black pepper.

5 Place the hotpot in the preheated oven and bake for about 30–40 minutes until it is golden brown on top and the potato slices are just tender. Serve immediately.

Three Vegetable Kugel

Grated seasonal vegetables are baked until crisp on top and creamy and tender inside. This version of the classic Jewish casserole combines the traditional flavours and method but uses a more contemporary combination of vegetables.

Serves 4

2 courgettes (zucchini), coarsely grated
2 carrots, coarsely grated
2 potatoes, peeled and coarsely grated
1 onion, grated
3 eggs, lightly beaten
3 garlic cloves, chopped
pinch of sugar
15ml/1 tbsp finely chopped fresh parsley
2–3 pinches of dried basil
30–45ml/2–3 tbsp matzo meal
105ml/7 tbsp olive oil or vegetable oil
salt and ground black pepper

1 Preheat the oven to 180°C/350°F/Gas 4. Put the courgettes, carrots, potatoes, onion, eggs, garlic, sugar, parsley, basil, salt and pepper in a bowl and combine.

2 Add the matzo meal to the bowl and stir together until the mixture forms a thick batter.

3 Pour half the olive or vegetable oil into an ovenproof dish. Spoon in the vegetable mixture, then evenly pour over the remaining oil.

4 Bake in the preheated oven for 40–60 minutes, or until the vegetables are tender and the kugel top is golden brown. Serve immediately.

Cook's Tip
Matzo is a brittle unleavened bread, rather like a cracker. It is made with plain (all-purpose) flour and water, although some have additional flavourings, such as onion. Matzo is traditionally eaten during the Jewish Passover festival in place of leavened bread, which cannot be eaten at that time. Matzo meal is made by grinding matzos, and comes in fine or medium texture.

Cowboy Hotpot pot Energy 351kcal/1470kJ; Protein 12g; Carbohydrate 40.1g, of which sugars 11.1g; Fat 16.6g, of which saturates 7.3g; Cholesterol 27mg; Calcium 199mg; Fibre 5.7g; Sodium 503mg.
Vegetable Kugel Energy 358kcal/1488kJ; Protein 9.2g; Carbohydrate 26.6g, of which sugars 5.7g; Fat 24.5g, of which saturates 4.2g; Cholesterol 143mg; Calcium 63mg; Fibre 2.9g; Sodium 71mg.

Grated Potato Casserole

This recipe comes from Satakunta, a south-western region of Finland. Floury, maincrop potatoes will produce the best results.

Serves 4
a small knob (pat) of butter
2 eggs

250ml/8floz/1 cup full-fat (whole) milk
30ml/2 tbsp plain (all-purpose) flour
5ml/1 tsp salt
2 potatoes
15ml/1 tbsp chopped fresh parsley, to garnish (optional)

1 Preheat the oven to 180°C/350°F/Gas 4. Melt the butter gently in a pan and use it to grease an ovenproof dish.

2 Beat the eggs together in a large mixing bowl, then add the milk and mix together.

3 Add the flour and salt to the eggs and milk and mix with your hands until the mixture forms a smooth batter.

4 Peel the potatoes, then grate them using a hand grater and add them to the batter.

5 Transfer the potato mixture to the prepared dish, then bake in the oven for about 50 minutes, until the potatoes are cooked. Serve hot, sprinkled with chopped parsley, if using.

Cook's Tip
Fresh parsley is simple to grow yourself. Buy a plant and keep it on a sunny windowsill in your kitchen. Ensure it is kept moist but don't over-water it and pull off the leaves as and when you need them. They will regrow in a matter of days.

Variation
To make a richer, creamier version, substitute half the milk with single (light) cream.

Casserole with Harvest Vegetables

In autumn, thoughts turn to hearty, satisfying food. This sustaining, yet low-fat dish is the ideal choice.

Serves 6
15ml/1 tbsp sunflower oil
2 leeks, sliced
1 garlic clove, crushed
4 celery sticks, chopped
2 carrots, sliced
2 parsnips, diced
1 sweet potato, diced
225g/8oz swede (rutabaga), diced

175g/6oz/3/4 cup whole brown or green lentils
450g/1lb tomatoes, peeled, seeded and chopped
15ml/1 tbsp chopped fresh thyme
15ml/1 tbsp chopped fresh marjoram
900ml/1 1/2 pints/3 3/4 cups vegetable stock
15ml/1 tbsp cornflour (cornstarch)
45ml/3 tbsp water
salt and ground black pepper
fresh thyme sprigs, to garnish

1 Preheat the oven to 180°C/350°F/Gas 4. Heat the oil in a large, flameproof casserole. Add the leeks, garlic and celery and cook over a low heat, stirring occasionally, for 3 minutes, until the leeks begin to soften.

2 Add the carrots, parsnips, sweet potato, swede, lentils, tomatoes, herbs and stock. Stir well and season with salt and ground black pepper to taste. Bring to the boil, stirring the mixture occasionally.

3 Cover the casserole, put it in the oven and bake for about 50 minutes, until the vegetables and lentils are tender, stirring the vegetable mixture once or twice.

4 Remove the casserole from the oven. Blend the cornflour with the water in a small bowl until it forms a smooth paste.

5 Stir the cornflour mixture into the casserole and heat it gently on top of the stove, stirring constantly, until the mixture boils and thickens. Lower the heat and simmer gently for 2 minutes, stirring.

6 Spoon on to warmed serving plates or into bowls, garnish with the thyme sprigs and serve.

Grated Potato Casserole Energy 215kcal/894kJ; Protein 8.7g; Carbohydrate 13g, of which sugars 3.3g; Fat 14.7g, of which saturates 7.7g; Cholesterol 123mg; Calcium 277mg; Fibre 3g; Sodium 297mg.
Harvest Casserole Energy 202kcal/857kJ; Protein 9.4g; Carbohydrate 36.2g, of which sugars 10.3g; Fat 3.2g, of which saturates 0.5g; Cholesterol 0mg; Calcium 70mg; Fibre 6.4g; Sodium 60mg.

Winter Vegetable Hotpot

Making this in the microwave and then finishing it under a grill results in a richly flavoured and substantial one-pot meal. To accompany the potatoes in this recipe, use whatever other seasonal vegetables you have to hand.

Serves 4
2 onions, sliced
4 carrots, sliced
1 small swede (rutabaga), sliced
2 parsnips, sliced
3 small turnips, sliced
½ celeriac, cut into matchsticks
2 leeks, thinly sliced
1 garlic clove, chopped
1 bay leaf, crumbled
30ml/2 tbsp chopped fresh mixed
 herbs, such as parsley
 and thyme
300ml/½ pint/1¼ cups
 vegetable stock
15ml/1 tbsp plain
 (all-purpose) flour
675g/1½lb red-skinned potatoes,
 scrubbed and thinly sliced
50g/2oz/4 tbsp butter
salt and ground black pepper

1 Arrange all the vegetables, except the potatoes, in layers in a large microwave-proof dish with a tight-fitting lid.

2 Season the vegetable layers lightly with salt and pepper, and sprinkle them with chopped garlic, crumbled bay leaf and chopped herbs.

3 Blend the stock into the flour and pour over the vegetables. Carefully arrange the potatoes in overlapping layers on top. Dot with butter and cover tightly.

4 Microwave on HIGH for 10 minutes. Reduce the power setting to MEDIUM and microwave for a further 25–30 minutes or until the vegetables are tender. Remove the lid and cook under a preheated hot grill (broiler) until the potato top is golden and crisp. Serve hot.

Cook's Tip
This recipe is also suitable for cooking in a combination microwave. Follow the oven manufacturer's timing guide for the best results.

Mixed-bean and Potato Hotpot

This slow-cooker dish, topped with sliced potatoes, is incredibly easy, making the most of dried and canned ingredients from the kitchen.

Serves 6
40g/1½oz/3 tbsp butter
4 shallots, peeled and
 finely chopped
40g/1½oz/⅓ cup plain
 (all-purpose) or wholemeal
 (whole-wheat) flour
300ml/½ pint/1¼ cups passata
 (bottled strained tomatoes)
120ml/4fl oz/½ cup unsweetened
 apple juice
60ml/4 tbsp soft light brown sugar
60ml/4 tbsp tomato ketchup
60ml/4 tbsp dry sherry
60ml/4 tbsp cider vinegar
60ml/4 tbsp light soy sauce
400g/14oz can butter (lima) beans
400g/14oz can flageolet (small
 cannellini) beans
400g/14oz can chickpeas
175g/6oz green beans, cut into
 2.5cm/1in lengths
225g/8oz/3 cups mushrooms, sliced
450g/1lb unpeeled potatoes,
 thinly sliced
15ml/1 tbsp olive oil
15ml/1 tbsp chopped fresh thyme
15ml/1 tbsp fresh marjoram
salt and ground black pepper
fresh herbs, to garnish

1 Melt the butter in a pan, add the shallots and fry gently for 5–6 minutes, until soft. Add the flour and cook for 1 minute, stirring, then gradually stir in the passata. Add the apple juice, sugar, tomato ketchup, sherry, vinegar and light soy sauce to the pan and stir in. Bring to the boil, stirring constantly until it thickens.

2 Rinse the beans and chickpeas and drain. Place them in the slow cooker pot with the green beans and mushrooms and pour in the sauce. Stir, then cover and cook on high for 3 hours.

3 Meanwhile, par-boil the potatoes for 4 minutes. Drain well, then toss them in the oil so that they are lightly coated all over.

4 Stir the herbs into the vegetable mixture and season. Arrange the potato slices on top, overlapping them slightly so that they completely cover them. Cover the pot and cook for a further 2 hours, or until the potatoes are tender.

5 Place the cooking pot under a medium grill (broiler) and cook for 4–5 minutes to brown. Serve garnished with herbs.

Bean Hotpot Energy 483kcal/2042kJ; Protein 18.5g; Carbohydrate 73.3g, of which sugars 24.8g; Fat 13.8g, of which saturates 4.5g; Cholesterol 14mg; Calcium 134mg; Fibre 10.9g; Sodium 826mg.
Winter Hotpot Energy 367kcal/1542kJ; Protein 8.5g; Carbohydrate 58.2g, of which sugars 24.5g; Fat 12.8g, of which saturates 7g; Cholesterol 27mg; Calcium 203mg; Fibre 13.1g; Sodium 178mg.

Middle-eastern Vegetable Stew

A spiced dish of mixed
vegetables makes a delicious
and filling vegetarian main
course in this microwave
recipe. Children may prefer
less chilli.

Serves 4–6

45ml/3 tbsp vegetable stock
1 green (bell) pepper, seeded
  and sliced
2 courgettes (zucchini), sliced
2 carrots, sliced
2 celery sticks, sliced
2 potatoes, diced
400g/14oz can chopped tomatoes
5ml/1 tsp chilli powder
30ml/2 tbsp chopped fresh mint
400g/14oz can chickpeas, drained
15ml/1 tbsp ground cumin
salt and ground black pepper
mint sprigs, to garnish

1 Place the vegetable stock in a large microwave-proof
casserole with the sliced pepper, courgettes, carrots and celery.
Cover and microwave on HIGH for 2 minutes.

2 Add the potatoes, tomatoes, chilli powder, fresh mint,
chickpeas and ground cumin to the vegetable dish and stir well.
Cover the dish and microwave on HIGH for 15–20 minutes,
remembering to stir twice during the cooking time.

3 Leave to stand, covered, for 5 minutes, until all the vegetables
are tender. Season to taste with salt and pepper and serve hot,
garnished with mint leaves.

Cook's Tip
*Chickpeas are a traditional ingredient in this type of Middle-
Eastern dish. If you prefer, you can use dried ones rather than
canned. They will need soaking for a few hours, or overnight,
before being boiled until tender.*

Variation
*Other vegetables can be substituted for those in the recipe, just
use whatever you have to hand – try swede (rutabaga), sweet
potato or parsnips.*

Braised Barley and Vegetables

One of the oldest of
cultivated cereals, pot barley
has a nutty flavour and
slightly chewy texture. It
makes a warming and filling
dish when combined with
root vegetables.

Serves 4

225g/8oz/1 cup pearl or
  pot barley
30ml/2 tbsp sunflower oil
1 large onion, chopped
2 celery sticks, sliced
2 carrots, halved lengthways
  and sliced
225g/8oz swede (rutabaga)
  or turnip, cut into
  2cm/¾in cubes
225g/8oz potatoes, cut into
  2cm/¾in cubes
475ml/16fl oz/2 cups
  vegetable stock
salt and ground black pepper
celery leaves, to garnish

1 Put the pearl or pot barley in a measuring jug (cup) and add
enough cold water to reach the 600ml/1 pint/2½ cup mark.
Leave to soak in a cool place for at least 4 hours, or overnight
if time permits.

2 Heat the oil in a large frying pan or flameproof casserole and
fry the onion for about 5 minutes until beginning to soften.

3 Add the sliced celery and carrots to the pan and cook,
stirring occasionally, for 3–4 minutes, or until the onion is
starting to brown.

4 Add the barley and its soaking liquid to the pan. Then add
the swede or turnip, potato and stock to the barley, stirring to
ensure the ingredients are well combined. Season with salt and
ground black pepper.

5 Bring the mixture slowly to the boil, then reduce the heat
and cover the pan with a tight-fitting lid.

6 Simmer for about 40 minutes, or until most of the stock has
been absorbed and the barley is tender. Stir the mixture
occasionally towards the end of the cooking time to prevent
the barley from sticking to the base of the pan. Serve, garnished
with celery leaves.

Middle-Eastern Stew Energy 149kcal/630kJ; Protein 7.8g; Carbohydrate 24.9g, of which sugars 6.8g; Fat 2.7g, of which saturates 0.4g; Cholesterol 0mg; Calcium 66mg; Fibre 5.7g; Sodium 172mg.
Braised Vegetables Energy 333kcal/1407kJ; Protein 6.6g; Carbohydrate 65g, of which sugars 8.3g; Fat 7g, of which saturates 0.8g; Cholesterol 0mg; Calcium 69mg; Fibre 3.1g; Sodium 33mg.

Potato, Leek and Apple Pie

Apples are the unusual ingredient used to flavour this warming potato dish. A perfect meal on a cold winter evening.

Serves 6
1.5kg/3lb potatoes
3 leeks, sliced
60ml/4 tbsp olive oil
3 onions, roughly chopped
small head of celery, chopped

2 large cooking apples
50g/2oz potato flour or
    cornflour (cornstarch)
450ml/¾ pint/scant 2 cups milk
    or soya milk
75g/3oz pumpkin seeds, partially
    pulverized in a food processor
15ml/1 tbsp sesame seeds
salt and ground black pepper

1 Preheat the oven to 180°C/350°F/Gas 4. Scrub the potatoes or sweet potatoes well and cut into thin slices. Par-cook them, with the leeks, in a steamer or microwave for about 10 minutes or until softened.

2 Lightly grease a shallow, ovenproof dish. Arrange half of the potatoes and all of the leeks in a layer at the base of the dish.

3 Peel, core and dice the apples. Heat 45ml/3 tbsp of the oil in a pan and cook the onions, celery and apples until soft.

4 Add the potato or cornflour, stir well, then add the milk and continue to cook until the sauce thickens. Spoon over the potatoes and leeks, then cover with the remaining potato slices.

5 Brush the top of the potatoes with the remaining 15ml/1 tbsp oil. Season, then sprinkle over the pumpkin and sesame seeds.

6 Bake for 20–30 minutes or until the dish is well heated through and the potatoes on top are lightly browned. Serve immediately.

> **Cook's Tip**
> If you have trouble slicing the potatoes or sweet potatoes, cook them whole and slice them when cooked.

Shepherdess Pie

A no-meat version of the timeless potato-topped classic, this dish also has no dairy products in it, so it is suitable for those on a vegan diet. However, you can serve it with confidence to anyone wanting a hearty and delicious meal.

Serves 6–8
1kg/2lb potatoes
45ml/3 tbsp extra virgin olive oil
salt and ground black pepper
1 large onion, chopped

1 green (bell) pepper, chopped
2 carrots, coarsely grated
2 garlic cloves
45ml/3 tbsp sunflower oil
    or margarine
115g/4oz mushrooms, chopped
2 x 400g/14oz cans aduki
    beans, drained
600ml/1 pint/2½ cups stock
5ml/1 tsp vegetable
    yeast extract
2 bay leaves
5ml/1 tsp dried mixed herbs
dried breadcrumbs or chopped
    nuts, to sprinkle

1 Put the potatoes in a large pan. Add water to cover and bring to the boil. Add salt, then simmer for about 15 minutes, or until the potatoes are tender, but do not let them get too soft. Drain thoroughly and leave to cool.

2 Peel the potatoes (potatoes are easier to peel when boiled in their skins. This also helps preserve more of the vitamins). Mash the peeled potatoes well, mixing in the olive oil and seasoning until you have a smooth purée.

3 In a frying pan, gently fry the onion, pepper, carrots and garlic in the sunflower oil or margarine for about 5–7 minutes until they are soft.

4 Stir in the mushrooms and beans and cook for a further 2 minutes, then add the stock, yeast extract, bay leaves and mixed herbs. Simmer for 15 minutes. Meanwhile, preheat the grill (broiler).

5 Remove the bay leaves and empty the vegetables into a shallow ovenproof dish. Spoon on the potatoes in dollops and sprinkle over the crumbs or nuts. Cook under the grill until golden brown. Serve immediately.

Potato and Apple Pie Energy 446kcal/1837kJ; Protein 12.4g; Carbohydrate 69.1g, of which sugars 16.2g; Fat 15.1g, of which saturates 7.1g; Cholesterol 118mg; Calcium 58mg; Fibre 6.6g; Sodium 69.7mg.
Shepherdess Pie Energy 305kcal/1285kJ; Protein 11.9g; Carbohydrate 46.7g, of which sugars 7.6g; Fat 9.1g, of which saturates 1.3g; Cholesterol 0mg; Calcium 63mg; Fibre 7.7g; Sodium 74mg.

Potato and Leek Filo Pie

This filo pastry pie makes an attractive and unusual centrepiece for a vegetarian buffet. Serve it cool, with a choice of salads.

Serves 8

800g/1¾lb new potatoes, sliced
75g/3oz/6 tbsp butter
400g/14oz leeks, thinly sliced
15g/½oz parsley, finely chopped
60ml/4 tbsp chopped mixed fresh herbs (such as chervil, chives, a little tarragon and basil)
12 sheets filo pastry
150g/5oz Cheshire, Lancashire or Cantal cheese, sliced
2 garlic cloves, finely chopped
250ml/8floz/1 cup double (heavy) cream
2 large egg yolks
salt and ground black pepper

1 Preheat the oven to 190°C/375°F/Gas 5. Cook the potatoes in boiling, salted water for 3–4 minutes. Drain and set aside.

2 Melt 25g/1oz/2 tbsp of the butter in a frying pan and fry the leeks gently, stirring, until softened. Remove from the heat, season and stir in half the parsley and half the mixed herbs.

3 Melt the remaining butter. Line a 23cm/9in loose-based metal cake tin (pan) with 6–7 sheets of filo pastry, brushing each layer with butter. Let the edges overhang the tin. Layer the potatoes, leeks and cheese in the tin, sprinkling a few herbs and the garlic between the layers. Season.

4 Flip the overhanging pastry over the filling and cover with two sheets of filo, tucking in the sides to fit and brushing with melted butter as before. Cover the pie loosely with foil and bake for 35 minutes. (Keep the remaining pastry covered.)

5 Meanwhile, beat the cream, egg yolks and remaining herbs together. Make a hole in the centre of the pie and gradually pour in the eggs and cream.

6 Arrange the remaining pastry on top, teasing it into swirls and folds, then brush with melted butter. Reduce the oven temperature to 180°C/350°F/Gas 4 and bake the pie for another 25–30 minutes, until the top is golden and crisp. Allow to cool before serving.

Vegetarian Moussaka

This tasty dish of layered aubergines, potatoes and courgettes is ideal for a dinner party as it can be made ahead of time, and then reheated when needed.

Serves 8

150ml/¼ pint/⅔ cup olive oil, plus extra if required
2 large aubergines (eggplants), thinly sliced
6 courgettes (zucchini), diced
675g/1½lb potatoes, thinly sliced
2 onions, sliced
3 garlic cloves, crushed
150ml/¼ pint/⅔ cup white wine
2 x 400g/14oz cans chopped tomatoes
30ml/2 tbsp tomato purée (paste)
1 x 430g/15oz can green lentils
10ml/2 tsp dried oregano
60ml/4 tbsp fresh parsley, chopped
225g/8oz/2 cups feta cheese, diced
salt and ground black pepper

For the béchamel sauce

40g/1½oz/3 tbsp butter
40g/1½oz/4 tbsp plain (all-purpose) flour
600ml/1 pint/2½ cups milk
2 eggs, beaten
115g/4oz Parmesan cheese
nutmeg, freshly grated

1 Heat the oil in a frying pan and cook the aubergines and courgettes. Drain on a kitchen paper towel. Brown the potato slices, remove and pat dry. Add the onion and garlic to the pan with a little extra oil, if required, and cook until softened.

2 Pour in the wine and cook until reduced down, then add the tomatoes and lentils plus the liquid from the can. Stir in the herbs and season well. Cover and simmer for 15 minutes.

3 In an ovenproof dish, layer the vegetables, adding the sauce in between and sprinkling with feta. Top with a layer of aubergine. Cover with foil and bake at 190°C/375°F/Gas 5 for 25 minutes.

4 Meanwhile, for the béchamel sauce, put the butter, flour and milk into a pan all together and bring slowly to a boil, stirring until thickened and smooth. Season and add the nutmeg. Remove the sauce from the heat, then beat in the eggs. Pour over the aubergines and sprinkle with the Parmesan.

5 To finish, return to the oven, uncovered, and bake for a further 25–30 minutes until golden and bubbling hot.

Potato and Leek Pie Energy 468kcal/1948kJ; Protein 10.7g; Carbohydrate 33g, of which sugars 3.5g; Fat 33.1g, of which saturates 20g; Cholesterol 137mg; Calcium 225mg; Fibre 3.2g; Sodium 218mg.
Moussaka Energy 588kcal/2445kJ; Protein 37.9g; Carbohydrate 14.8g, of which sugars 3.7g; Fat 40.9g, of which saturates 18.2g; Cholesterol 206mg; Calcium 379mg; Fibre 2.4g; Sodium 506mg.

Spicy Potato Strudel

Wrap up a tasty mixture of vegetables in a spicy, creamy sauce with crisp filo pastry. Serve with a good selection of chutneys or a spicy yogurt sauce.

Serves 4

1 onion, chopped
2 carrots, coarsely grated
1 courgette (zucchini), chopped
350g/12oz firm potatoes, finely chopped
65g/2½ oz/5 tbsp butter
10ml/2 tsp mild curry paste
2.5ml/½ tsp dried thyme
150ml/¼ pint/⅔ cup water
1 egg, beaten
30ml/2 tbsp single (light) cream
50g/2oz/¼ cup Cheddar cheese, grated
8 sheets filo pastry, thawed if frozen
sesame seeds, for sprinkling
salt and ground black pepper

1 In a large frying pan, cook the onion, carrots, courgette and potatoes in about 25g/1oz/2 tbsp of the butter for 5 minutes, tossing frequently so they cook evenly. Add the curry paste and stir in. Continue to cook the vegetables for a further minute.

2 Add the thyme, water and seasoning. Gradually bring to the boil, then reduce the heat and simmer for about 10 minutes until tender, stirring occasionally.

3 Remove from the heat and leave to cool. Transfer the mixture into a large bowl and then mix in the egg, cream and cheese. Chill until ready to fill the filo pastry.

4 Melt the remaining butter and lay out four sheets of filo pastry, slightly overlapping them to form a fairly large rectangle. Brush with some melted butter and fit the other sheets on top. Brush again.

5 Preheat the oven to 190°C/375°F/Gas 5. Spoon the filling along one long side, then roll up the pastry. Form it into a circle and set on a baking sheet. Brush again with the last of the butter and sprinkle over the sesame seeds.

6 Bake the strudel in the oven for about 25 minutes until golden and crisp. Leave to stand for 5 minutes before cutting.

Baked Potatoes and Three Fillings

Potatoes baked in their skins make an excellent and nourishing meal on their own. For an even better treat, add one of these three delicious and easy toppings.

Serves 4

4 medium baking potatoes
olive oil
sea salt
filling of your choice (see below)

Stir-fry vegetables

45ml/3 tbsp groundnut or sunflower oil
2 leeks, thinly sliced
2 carrots, cut into sticks
1 courgette (zucchini), thinly sliced
115g/4oz baby corn, halved
115g/4oz/1½ cup button (white) mushrooms, sliced
45ml/3 tbsp soy sauce
30ml/2 tbsp dry sherry or vermouth
15ml/1 tbsp sesame oil
sesame seeds, to garnish

Red bean chilli sauce

425g/15oz can red kidney beans, drained
200g/7oz/scant 1 cup low-fat cottage or cream cheese
30ml/2 tbsp mild chilli sauce
5ml/1 tsp ground cumin

Cheese and creamy corn

425g/15oz can creamed corn
115g/4oz/1⅓ cups hard cheese, grated
5ml/1 tsp mixed dried herbs
fresh parsley sprigs, to garnish

1 Preheat the oven to 200°C/400°F/Gas 6. Score the potatoes with a cross and rub all over with the oil. Bake for 45 minutes to 1 hour until tender. Cut the potatoes open along the score lines and push up the flesh. Season and top with a filling.

2 For the vegetables, heat the oil in a wok or frying pan until bubbling. Add the leeks, carrots, courgette and baby corn and stir-fry for about 2 minutes, then add the mushrooms and stir-fry for 1 minute. Add the soy sauce, sherry or vermouth and sesame oil. Heat through until bubbling and sprinkle with sesame seeds.

3 For the red beans, heat the beans in a pan and stir in the cottage or cream cheese, chilli sauce and cumin.

4 For the creamy corn, heat the corn gently in a pan with the cheese and herbs. Garnish with the parsley sprigs.

Spicy Strudel Energy 362kcal/1512kJ; Protein 9.8g; Carbohydrate 34.8g, of which sugars 6.5g; Fat 21.1g, of which saturates 12.7g; Cholesterol 98mg; Calcium 169mg; Fibre 3g; Sodium 227mg.
Baked Potatoes Energy 223kcal/941kJ; Protein 7.3g; Carbohydrate 38.6g, of which sugars 8.3g; Fat 4.5g, of which saturates 0.8g; Cholesterol 0mg; Calcium 55mg; Fibre 5.4g; Sodium 1150mg.

Peppers Filled with Vegetables

Nigella seeds have a mild, slightly nutty flavour and are best toasted for a few seconds in a dry frying pan before being used in a recipe. This helps to bring out their flavour.

Serves 6

6 large evenly shaped red or
   yellow (bell) peppers
500g/1¼lb waxy potatoes
1 small onion, chopped
4 or 5 garlic cloves, chopped
5cm/2in piece fresh root
   ginger, chopped
1 or 2 fresh green chillies,
   seeded and chopped
105ml/7 tbsp water
90–105ml/6–7 tbsp vegetable oil
1 aubergine (eggplant), diced
10ml/2 tsp cumin seeds
5ml/1 tsp nigella seeds
2.5ml/½ tsp ground turmeric
5ml/1 tsp ground coriander
5ml/1 tsp ground toasted
   cumin seeds
cayenne pepper
about 30ml/2 tbsp lemon juice
sea salt and ground black pepper
30ml/2 tbsp chopped fresh
   coriander (cilantro), to garnish

1 Cut the tops off the red or yellow peppers, then remove and discard the seeds. Cut a thin slice off the base of any wobbly peppers so that they stand upright. Bring a large pan of lightly salted water to the boil. Add the peppers to the water and cook for 5–6 minutes. Remove from the pan and leave them upside down in a colander to drain thoroughly.

2 Cook the potatoes in lightly salted, boiling water for 10–12 minutes until just tender. Drain, cool and peel, then cut into 1cm/½in dice.

3 Put the onion, garlic, ginger and green chillies in a food processor or blender with 60ml/4 tbsp of the water and process to a purée.

4 Heat 45ml/3 tbsp of the vegetable oil in a large, deep frying pan and cook the aubergine, stirring occasionally, until it is evenly browned. Remove the aubergine from the pan using a slotted spoon and set aside to cool. Add another 30ml/2 tbsp of the vegetable oil to the pan, then add the potatoes and cook until lightly browned. Remove the potatoes from the pan and set aside.

5 If necessary, add another 15ml/1 tbsp sunflower oil to the pan, then add the cumin and nigella seeds. Fry briefly until the seeds darken, then add the turmeric, coriander and ground cumin. Cook for 15 seconds. Stir in the onion and garlic purée and fry, scraping the pan with a spatula, until the onions begin to brown.

6 Return the potatoes and aubergine to the pan, season with salt, ground black pepper and one or two pinches of cayenne. Add the remaining water and 15ml/1 tbsp lemon juice and then cook, stirring, until the liquid evaporates. Preheat the oven to 190°C/375°F/Gas 5.

7 Fill the peppers with the spiced vegetable mixture and place on a lightly greased baking tray. Brush the peppers with a little oil and bake for 30–35 minutes until they are cooked. Leave to cool a little, then sprinkle with a little more lemon juice. Garnish with the coriander and serve.

Vegetables in Ashes with Salsa

Use a double layer of coals to start the barbecue so they will be deep enough to make a bed for the foil-wrapped vegetables.

Serves 4–6

2 small whole heads of garlic
2 butternut squash, halved
   lengthways and seeded
4–6 onions, with a cross cut in
   the top of each
4–6 baking potatoes
4–6 sweet potatoes
45ml/3 tbsp olive oil
fresh thyme, bay leaf and
   rosemary sprigs
salt and ground black pepper
2 handfuls of hickory wood chips
   soaked in cold water for at
   least 30 minutes

For the tomato salsa
500g/1¼lb tomatoes, quartered
   and seeded
2.5ml/½ tsp sugar
a pinch of chilli flakes
1.5ml/¼ tsp smoky
   chilli powder
30ml/2 tbsp tomato chutney

1 Prepare a barbecue with plenty of coals. Wrap the garlic, squash and onions separately in a double layer of foil, but do not seal. Wrap the potatoes in pairs, with one sweet and one ordinary potato. Drizzle olive oil over each packet, season and add a herb sprig. Spray with a little water and seal the parcels.

2 Once the flames have died down and the coals are hot, or with a light coating of ash, place the parcels on top of them. The garlic will take 20 minutes to cook, the squash 30 minutes, the onions 45 minutes and the potatoes 1 hour. As each vegetable cooks, remove the parcel and wrap in an extra layer of foil to keep warm. Set aside. Shortly before serving, loosen the tops of all the parcels, except the garlic, and put them all back on the coals so the vegetables dry out a little before serving.

3 Meanwhile, make the salsa. Heat an oiled grill rack. Sprinkle the tomatoes with sugar, chilli flakes and seasoning. Place them on the rack and cook, covered, for 5 minutes. Drain the hickory chips and place a handful on the coals, replace the cover and leave to smoke for 5 minutes. Add some more wood chips and grill for 10 minutes. Spoon the tomato flesh from the charred skins into a bowl, crush with a fork and mix in the other ingredients. Serve with the vegetables.

Filled Peppers Energy 222kcal/926kJ; Protein 3.6g; Carbohydrate 26.1g, of which sugars 13g; Fat 12.1g, of which saturates 2.5g; Cholesterol 0mg; Calcium 25mg; Fibre 4.4g; Sodium 17mg.
Vegetables in Ashes Energy 439kcal/1860kJ; Protein 9.5g; Carbohydrate 89.6g, of which sugars 21.5g; Fat 7.3g, of which saturates 1.3g; Cholesterol 0mg; Calcium 114mg; Fibre 9.6g; Sodium 118mg.

Grilled Vegetables with Bagna Cauda

Bagna cauda means 'warm bath' and this rich dip is the traditional Piedmontese accompaniment to raw or cooked vegetables. It is kept warm in an earthenware dish over a candle heater, but the edge of a waning barbecue is also ideal.

Serves 4–6
675g/1½lb sweet potatoes
375g/13oz carrots
400g/14oz parsnips

400g/14oz raw beetroot (beets)
450g/1lb asparagus, trimmed
60ml/4 tbsp extra virgin olive oil
salt and ground black pepper

For the bagna cauda
3–4 garlic cloves, crushed
50–65g/2–2½oz drained
  anchovy fillets, chopped
25g/1oz/2 tbsp unsalted
  butter, melted
200ml/7fl oz/scant 1 cup extra
  virgin olive oil

1 Prepare the barbecue. Cutting lengthways, slice each sweet potato and carrot into eight pieces, each parsnip into seven and each beetroot into ten. Toss all the vegetables except the beetroot in most of the oil on a big tray. Put the beetroot on a separate tray as it might otherwise stain the other vegetables. Gently toss the beetroot in the remaining oil and season all the vegetables well.

2 Make the bagna cauda. Place the garlic, anchovies and butter, with a little pepper, into a food processor. Pour in 30ml/2 tbsp of the oil and whizz to a purée. With the motor running, add the remaining oil. Transfer into a heatproof bowl or pan and warm very gently at the edge of the barbecue, or over a pan of simmering water, when ready to serve.

3 Once the flames have died down, position a lightly oiled grill rack over the coals to heat. When the coals are medium-hot, or with a moderate coating of ash, arrange the vegetables over the grill rack.

4 Lightly grill the vegetables for about 3 minutes on each side, or until tender and branded with dark golden grill lines. Remove them as they cook and serve hot or warm with the heated bagna cauda.

Polish Potato Pierogi

These Polish dumplings of spicy mashed potato, served with melted butter and sour cream, are hearty enough to ward off the rigours of a cold winter.

Serves 4–6
675g/1½lb baking potatoes,
  peeled and cut into chunks

50–75g/2–3oz/4–5 tbsp unsalted
  butter, plus extra melted
  butter to serve
3 onions, finely chopped
2 eggs, lightly beaten
1 250g/9oz packet
  wonton wrappers
salt and ground black pepper
chopped parsley, to garnish
sour cream, to serve

1 Cook the potatoes in a large pan of salted boiling water until tender. Drain well. Meanwhile, melt the butter in a frying pan, add the onions and fry over a medium heat for about 10 minutes, or until browned.

2 Mash the potatoes, then stir in the fried onions and leave them to cool. When cool, add the eggs and mix together. Season with salt and pepper to taste.

3 Brush the edges of the wonton wrappers with a little water. Place 15–30ml/1–2 tbsp of the potato filling in the centre of each wrapper, then top with another sheet. Press the edges together and pinch with your fingers. Set aside to allow the edges to dry out and seal firmly.

4 Bring a pan of salted water to the boil, then lower the heat to a simmer. Carefully slip the dumplings into the water, keeping it simmering gently, and cook for about 2 minutes, until tender.

5 Using a slotted spoon, remove the potato dumplings from the water and drain. Serve the dumplings on plates or in bowls. Drizzle with butter and sour cream and garnish with parsley.

> **Variation**
> *Add a generous sprinkling of chopped spring onions (scallions) to the filling.*

Grilled Vegetables Energy 571kcal/2378kJ; Protein 8.9g; Carbohydrate 44.9g, of which sugars 21g; Fat 40.9g, of which saturates 7.4g; Cholesterol 10mg; Calcium 131mg; Fibre 10.1g; Sodium 471mg.
Polish Dumplings Energy 364kcal/1532kJ; Protein 10.3g; Carbohydrate 55.9g, of which sugars 7.9g; Fat 12.7g, of which saturates 5.9g; Cholesterol 94mg; Calcium 55mg; Fibre 3.7g; Sodium 164mg.

Bavarian Potato Dumplings

The cuisines of Germany and Central Europe are unimaginable without potato dumplings, consumed in all shapes and sizes. In this version, crunchy croûtons are placed in the centre.

Serves 6
1.5kg/3lb potatoes, peeled
115g/4oz/²/₃ cup semolina
115g/4oz/1 cup wholemeal (whole-wheat) flour
5ml/1 tsp salt
1.5ml/¹/₄ tsp nutmeg
30ml/2 tbsp sunflower oil
2 thin white bread slices, crusts removed, cubed
1.5 litres/2¹/₂ pints/6¹/₄ cups beef or vegetable stock
ground black pepper
chopped fresh flat leaf parsley, crispy bacon (optional) and onion slices, to garnish
melted butter, to serve

1 Put the potatoes in a large pan. Add water to cover and bring to the boil. Add salt, then simmer for about 15 minutes, or until the potatoes are tender.

2 Drain well, mash roughly with a potato masher and then press through a sieve (strainer) with a large spoon into a bowl. Add the semolina, flour, salt, a little pepper and the nutmeg, and mix well.

3 Heat the oil in a heavy frying pan and fry the cubes of bread, stirring frequently, until light golden brown. Drain the croûtons on kitchen paper.

4 Divide the potato mixture into 24 balls. Press a few of the fried croûtons firmly into each dumpling.

5 Bring the beef or vegetable stock to the boil in a large pan, add the dumplings, in batches if necessary, and cook gently for 5 minutes, turning once.

6 Remove the dumplings from the pan with a slotted spoon and arrange on a warmed serving dish. Keep warm while you finish cooking the remainder if cooking in batches. Sprinkle with chopped parsley, crispy bacon (if using) and fried onion slices and serve with a warmed sauce boat of melted butter.

Spiced Stuffed Vegetables

The vegetarian filling of these oven-roasted vegetables is mildly spiced and has the delicious tang of lemon juice. They are also excellent cold and are good served as an appetizer as well as a main course.

Serves 4
4 potatoes, peeled
4 onions, skinned
4 courgettes (zucchini), halved widthways
2–4 garlic cloves, chopped
45–60ml/3–4 tbsp olive oil
45–60ml/3–4 tbsp tomato purée (paste)
1.5ml/¹/₄ tsp ras al hanout or curry powder
large pinch of ground allspice
seeds of 2–3 cardamom pods
juice of ¹/₂ lemon
30–45ml/2–3 tbsp chopped fresh parsley
90–120ml/6–8 tbsp vegetable stock
salt and ground black pepper
salad, to serve (optional)

1 Bring a large pan of salted water to the boil. Starting with the potatoes, then the onions and finally the courgettes, add to the boiling water and cook until they become almost tender but not cooked through. Allow about 10 minutes for the potatoes, 8 minutes for the onions and 4–6 minutes for the courgettes. Remove the vegetables from the pan and set aside to cool.

2 When the vegetables are cool enough to handle, hollow them out using a knife and spoon. Preheat the oven to 190°C/375°F/Gas 5.

3 Finely chop the cut-out vegetable flesh and put it in a bowl. Add the garlic, half of the olive oil, the tomato purée, ras al hanout or curry powder, allspice, cardamom seeds, lemon juice, chopped parsley, salt and pepper, and mix until thoroughly combined. Spoon the stuffing mixture into the hollowed vegetables, filling to just over the top.

4 Arrange the stuffed vegetables in a roasting pan and drizzle with the vegetable stock and the remaining oil. Roast for about 35–40 minutes, or until they are golden brown. Serve warm with a salad, if you like.

Bavarian Dumplings Energy 356kcal/1509kJ; Protein 9.5g; Carbohydrate 71.8g, of which sugars 3.9g; Fat 5.4g, of which saturates 0.8g; Cholesterol 0mg; Calcium 36mg; Fibre 4.8g; Sodium 405mg.
Stuffed Vegetables Energy 347kcal/1452kJ; Protein 10.2g; Carbohydrate 56.7g, of which sugars 22.1g; Fat 10.3g, of which saturates 1.6g; Cholesterol 0mg; Calcium 135mg; Fibre 8.2g; Sodium 62mg.

Potato, Cabbage and Cheddar Cheese Rissoles

Originally made on Mondays with leftover potatoes and cabbage from the Sunday lunch, these rissoles are quick to make and great for any light meal. Make them for brunch teamed with fried eggs, grilled tomatoes and mushrooms.

Serves 4
450g/1lb potatoes
225g/8oz steamed or boiled cabbage or kale, shredded
1 egg, beaten
115g/4oz/1 cup Cheddar cheese, grated
freshly grated nutmeg
plain (all-purpose) flour, for coating
vegetable oil, for frying
salt and ground black pepper
lemon wedges, to serve

1 Put the potatoes in a large pan. Add water to cover and bring to the boil. Add salt, then reduce the heat to a simmer for about 15 minutes, or until the potatoes are tender, but do not let them get too soft. Drain and leave to cool.

2 Mix the mashed potato with the cabbage or kale, egg, cheese, nutmeg and seasoning. Shape into eight small burgers.

3 Chill for an hour or so, if possible, as this enables the rissoles to become firm and makes them easier to fry. Dredge them in the flour, shaking off the excess.

4 Heat a 1cm/½in layer of oil in a frying pan until it is really hot. Carefully slide the rissoles into the oil and fry in batches on each side for about 3 minutes until golden and crisp.

5 Remove the rissoles from the pan and drain on kitchen paper. Serve piping hot with wedges of freshly cut lemon.

> **Cook's Tip**
> *You can flavour the rissoles with a stronger tasting cheese, if you prefer. Try using Stilton or Shropshire Blue in place of Cheddar.*

Cabbage and Potato Charlotte

This cabbage and potato dish takes its name from the container with heart-shaped handles in which it is cooked. Any straight-sided dish, such as a soufflé dish, will do.

Serves 6
450g/1lb green or Savoy cabbage
30g/1oz/2 tbsp butter
1 medium onion, chopped
500g/1¼lb potatoes, peeled and quartered
1 large (US extra large) egg, beaten
15–30ml/1–2 tbsp milk, if needed
salt and ground black pepper

1 Preheat the oven to 190°C/375°F/ Gas 5. Lightly butter a 1.2 litre/2 pint/5 cup charlotte mould. Line the base with baking parchment and butter again.

2 Bring a pan of salted water to the boil. Remove 5–6 large leaves from the cabbage and add to the pan. Cook the leaves for 2 minutes until softened and bright green, then plunge them into cold water. Chop the remaining cabbage.

3 Melt the butter in a frying pan and cook the onion for 2–3 minutes until just soft. Stir in the chopped cabbage and cook, covered, over a medium heat for 10–15 minutes until tender.

4 Put the potatoes in a large pan of cold, salted water to cover and bring to the boil. Cook until the potatoes are tender, then drain. Mash with the egg and a little milk, if needed, until smooth, then stir in the cabbage mixture. Season to taste.

5 Dry the cabbage leaves and cut out the thickest part of the centre vein. Use the cabbage leaves to line the mould, saving one leaf for the top. Spoon the potato mixture into the dish, smoothing it evenly, then cover with the remaining cabbage leaf. Cover tightly with foil. Put the mould in a shallow roasting pan or a baking dish and pour in boiling water to come halfway up the side of the mould. Bake for 40 minutes.

6 To serve, remove the foil and place a serving plate over the mould. Holding the plate tightly against the mould, turn over together. Lift off the mould and peel off the paper.

Potato Rissoles Energy 423kcal/1762kJ; Protein 12.8g; Carbohydrate 30.7g, of which sugars 4.4g; Fat 27.9g, of which saturates 8.5g; Cholesterol 75mg; Calcium 272mg; Fibre 2.7g; Sodium 242mg.
Cabbage Charlotte Energy 131kcal/551kJ; Protein 3.7g; Carbohydrate 18g, of which sugars 5.3g; Fat 5.4g, of which saturates 3.1g; Cholesterol 43mg; Calcium 50mg; Fibre 2.6g; Sodium 64mg.

Mushroom Tart with Potato Pastry

Potato and cheese pastry combines well with a mushroom and broccoli filling to ensure this savoury flan is a favourite.

Serves 8

115g/4oz small broccoli florets
15ml/1 tbsp olive oil
3 shallots, finely chopped
175g/6oz mixed wild mushrooms, such as ceps, shiitake mushrooms and oyster mushrooms, sliced
2 eggs
200ml/7fl oz/scant 1 cup semi-skimmed (low-fat) milk
15ml/1 tbsp chopped fresh tarragon
50g/2oz/¼ cup grated Cheddar cheese
salt and ground black pepper
fresh herb sprigs, to garnish

For the pastry

75g/3oz/¾ cup brown rice flour
75g/3oz/¾ cup cornmeal
pinch of salt
75g/3oz/6 tbsp soft margarine
115g/4oz cold mashed potatoes
50g/2oz/½ cup grated Cheddar cheese

1 First make the pastry. Place the rice flour, cornmeal and salt in a mixing bowl and stir to mix. Lightly rub in the margarine with your fingertips until the mixture resembles breadcrumbs. Stir in the mashed potatoes and cheese and mix to form a smooth, soft dough. Wrap in a plastic bag and chill for 30 minutes.

2 Roll out the pastry between two sheets of baking parchment and use to line a 24cm/9½in loose-bottomed flan tin (pan), gently pressing the pastry into the sides of the tin. Carefully trim around the top edge of the pastry case with a sharp knife. Cover the pastry, and chill while making the filling.

3 Preheat the oven to 200°C/400°F/ Gas 6. Cook the broccoli florets in a pan of lightly salted, boiling water for 3 minutes. Drain and set aside. Heat the oil in a pan and cook the shallots for 3 minutes. Add the mushrooms and cook for 2 minutes.

4 Spoon into the pastry case (pie shell) and top with broccoli. Beat the eggs, milk, tarragon and seasoning together and pour over the vegetables. Top with cheese. Bake for 10 minutes, reduce the oven to 180°C/350°F/Gas 4 and bake for 30 minutes until lightly set. Serve warm or cold, garnished with fresh herbs.

Wild Mushroom Gratin with Beaufort Cheese, New Potatoes and Walnuts

This is one of the simplest and most delicious ways of cooking mushrooms. Serve this dish as the Swiss do, with new potatoes and gherkins.

Serves 4

900g/2lb small new or salad potatoes
50g/2oz/4 tbsp unsalted butter or 60ml/4 tbsp olive oil
350g/12oz/5 cups assorted wild and cultivated mushrooms, thinly sliced
175g/6oz Beaufort or Fontina cheese, thinly sliced
50g/2oz/½ cup broken walnuts, toasted
salt and ground black pepper
12 gherkins and mixed green salad leaves, to serve

1 Put the potatoes in a large pan. Add water to cover and bring to the boil. Add a little salt, then simmer for around 15 minutes, or until the potatoes are tender, but do not let them get too soft.

2 Drain the potatoes thoroughly and return them to the pan. Add a knob (pat) of butter or a splash of olive oil and cover to keep warm.

3 Heat the remaining butter or the olive oil in a large frying pan over a medium-high heat. Add the mushrooms and fry until their juices appear.

4 Increase the heat under the pan and cook the mushrooms briskly until most of their juices have cooked away. Season with salt and black pepper.

5 Meanwhile, preheat the grill (broiler). Arrange the cheese on top of the mushroom slices, place the pan under the grill and cook until bubbly and golden brown.

6 Sprinkle the gratin with the broken walnuts and serve immediately with the buttered potatoes and sliced gherkins. Serve a side dish of mixed green salad, if you like, to complete this meal.

Mushroom Tart Energy 253kcal/1051kJ; Protein 8.4g; Carbohydrate 19g, of which sugars 2.2g; Fat 15.6g, of which saturates 3.6g; Cholesterol 61mg; Calcium 145mg; Fibre 1.3g; Sodium 201mg.
Mushroom Gratin Energy 529kcal/2207kJ; Protein 18.4g; Carbohydrate 37g, of which sugars 3.5g; Fat 34.2g, of which saturates 17.3g; Cholesterol 71mg; Calcium 356mg; Fibre 3.7g; Sodium 440mg.

Potato and Onion Cakes with Beetroot Relish

These grated potato cakes are utterly irresistible. They are especially delicious with a sweet-sharp beetroot relish and sour cream.

Serves 4
500g/1¼lb potatoes (such as King Edward, Estima or Desirée)
1 small cooking apple, peeled, cored and coarsely grated
1 small onion, finely chopped
50g/2oz/½ cup plain (all-purpose) flour
2 large eggs, beaten
30ml/2 tbsp chopped chives
vegetable oil, for shallow frying
salt and ground black pepper
250ml/8fl oz/1 cup sour cream or crème fraîche
fresh dill sprigs and fresh chives or chive flowers, to garnish

For the beetroot relish
250g/9oz beetroot (beets), cooked, peeled and diced
1 large dessert apple, cored and finely diced
15ml/1 tbsp finely chopped red onion
15–30ml/1–2 tbsp tarragon vinegar
15ml/1 tbsp chopped fresh dill
15–30ml/1–2 tbsp light olive oil
pinch of caster (superfine) sugar (optional)

1 To make the relish, mix the beetroot with the apple and onion. Add 15ml/1 tbsp of the vinegar, the dill and 15ml/1 tbsp of oil. Season, adding more vinegar and oil if necessary, and a pinch of sugar to taste.

2 Coarsely grate the potatoes, then rinse, drain and dry them on a clean dish towel. Mix the potatoes, apple and onion in a bowl. Stir in the flour, eggs and chives. Season and mix again.

3 Heat about 5mm/¼in depth of oil in a frying pan and fry spoonfuls of the mixture. Flatten them to make pancakes 7.5–10cm/3–4in across and cook for 3–4 minutes on each side, until browned. Drain on kitchen paper and keep warm until the mixture is used up.

4 Serve a stack of cakes with spoonfuls of sour cream or crème fraîche, and relish. Garnish with dill sprigs and chives or chive flowers and season with black pepper just before serving.

Potato Cakes with Goat's Cheese

Goat's cheese makes a tangy, bubbling topping for these herby potato cakes. They are particularly delicious served with a flavoursome salad.

Serves 2–4
450g/1lb floury potatoes
10ml/2 tsp chopped fresh thyme
1 garlic clove, crushed
2 spring onions (scallions) (including the green parts), finely chopped
30ml/2 tbsp olive oil
50g/2oz/¼ cup unsalted butter
2 x 65g/2½oz firm goat's cheese
salt and ground black pepper
salad leaves, such as curly endive, radicchio and lamb's lettuce, tossed in walnut dressing, to serve
thyme sprigs, to garnish

1 Coarsely grate the potatoes. Using your hands, squeeze out as much of the thick starchy liquid as possible, then gently combine with the chopped thyme, garlic and spring onions. Season with salt and black pepper.

2 Heat half the oil and butter in a non-stick frying pan. Add two large spoonfuls of the potato mixture, spacing them well apart, and press firmly down with a spatula. Cook for 3–4 minutes on each side until golden.

3 Drain the potato cakes on kitchen paper and keep warm in a low oven. Heat the remaining oil and butter and fry two more potato cakes in the same way with the remaining mixture. Meanwhile preheat the grill (broiler).

4 Cut the cheese in half horizontally and place one half, cut side up, on each potato cake. Grill (broil) for 2–3 minutes until lightly golden. Serve on plates and arrange the salad leaves around them. Garnish with thyme sprigs.

Cook's Tip
These potato cakes make great party snacks. Make them half the size and serve warm on a large platter.

Beetroot Potato Cakes Energy 471kcal/1964kJ; Protein 10.3g; Carbohydrate 42.1g, of which sugars 13.4g; Fat 30.2g, of which saturates 10.6g; Cholesterol 152mg; Calcium 118mg; Fibre 3.7g; Sodium 125mg.
Goat's Cheese Cakes Energy 310kcal/1290kJ; Protein 7.9g; Carbohydrate 18.6g, of which sugars 2g; Fat 23.2g, of which saturates 12.6g; Cholesterol 54mg; Calcium 48mg; Fibre 1.3g; Sodium 272mg.

Potato, Smoked Mozzarella and Garlic Pizza

New potatoes, smoked mozzarella and garlic make this pizza unique.

Serves 2–3
350g/12oz small new or
  salad potatoes
45ml/3 tbsp olive oil
2 garlic cloves, crushed
1 pizza base, about 25–30cm/
  10–12in diameter

1 red onion, thinly sliced
150g/5oz/1¼ cups smoked
  mozzarella cheese, grated
10ml/2 tsp chopped fresh
  rosemary or sage
salt and ground black pepper
30ml/2 tbsp freshly grated
  Parmesan cheese, to garnish

1 Preheat the oven to 220°C/425°F/Gas 7. Put the potatoes in a large pan. Add water to cover and bring to the boil. Add salt, then simmer for about 5 minutes, or until the potatoes are just becoming tender. Drain thoroughly and leave to cool.

2 When the potatoes are cool enough to handle, peel and slice them thinly.

3 Heat 30ml/2 tbsp of the oil in a frying pan. Add the sliced potatoes and garlic and fry for 5–8 minutes, turning frequently until tender.

4 Brush the pizza base with the remaining oil. Sprinkle the onion over, then arrange the potatoes on top.

5 Sprinkle over the mozzarella and rosemary or sage and plenty of black pepper. Bake for 15–20 minutes until golden. Remove from the oven, sprinkle with Parmesan and more ground black pepper.

Variation
For non-vegetarians, you could add sliced smoked pork sausage or pastrami to the pizza to make it even more substantial.

Raclette with New Potatoes

Traditional to both Switzerland and France, raclette melts to a velvety creaminess and warm golden colour and has a savoury taste with a hint of sweetness, perfect with delicate new potatoes.

Serves 4
For the pickle
2 red onions, sliced

5ml/1 tsp sugar
90ml/6 tbsp red wine vinegar
2.5ml/½ tsp salt
generous pinch of dried dill

For the potatoes
500g/1¼lb new or salad
  potatoes, halved if large
250g/9oz raclette cheese slices
salt and ground black pepper

1 To make the pickle, spread out the sliced onions in a glass dish, pour over enough boiling water to cover them, and set aside until cold.

2 Meanwhile, mix the sugar, red wine vinegar, salt and dill in a small pan. Heat gently, stirring, until the sugar has dissolved, then set aside to cool.

3 Drain the onions and return them to the dish, pour the vinegar mixture over, cover and leave for at least 1 hour, preferably overnight.

4 Cook the potatoes in their skins in boiling water until tender, then drain and place in a roasting tin (pan). Preheat the grill (broiler). Season the potatoes and arrange the raclette on top.

5 Place the pan under the grill until the cheese has melted. Serve hot. Drain the excess vinegar from the red onion pickle and serve the pickle with the potatoes.

Cook's Tip
To speed up the process, look for ready-sliced raclette for this dish. It is available from most large supermarkets and specialist cheese shops.

Raclette Energy 327kcal/1366kJ; Protein 19.3g; Carbohydrate 27.1g, of which sugars 6.9g; Fat 15.9g, of which saturates 10.1g; Cholesterol 50mg; Calcium 508mg; Fibre 2.3g; Sodium 899mg.
Potato Pizza Energy 413kcal/1727kJ; Protein 14.1g; Carbohydrate 39.5g, of which sugars 3.7g; Fat 23.1g, of which saturates 8.5g; Cholesterol 29mg; Calcium 222mg; Fibre 2.1g; Sodium 302mg.

Herby Potatoes Baked with Tomatoes, Olives and Feta

This tasty potato dish comes from western Anatolia. Traditionally baked in an earthenware dish, it makes a fabulous accompaniment to meat, poultry or fish. Or serve it on its own as a main course with a squeeze of lemon or a dollop of yogurt, and a green salad.

Serves 4–6
675g/1½lb organic new potatoes
15ml/1 tbsp butter
45ml/3 tbsp olive oil, plus extra
 for drizzling
3–4 garlic cloves, chopped

2 red onions, cut in half lengthways,
 in half again crossways, and
 sliced along the grain
5–10ml/1–2 tsp cumin
 seeds, crushed
5–10ml/1–2 tsp Turkish red
 pepper, or 1 fresh red chilli,
 seeded and chopped
10ml/2 tsp dried oregano
10ml/2 tsp sugar
15ml/1 tbsp white wine vinegar
400g/14oz can chopped
 tomatoes, drained of juice
12–16 black olives
115g/4oz feta cheese, crumbled
salt and ground black pepper
1 lemon, cut into wedges

1 Preheat the oven to 200°C/400°F/ Gas 6. Cook the potatoes for 15–20 minutes, until just tender. Drain and refresh in cold water. Peel and cut the potatoes into thick slices or bitesize wedges.

2 Heat the butter and 30ml/2 tbsp of the oil in a heavy pan, add the garlic and onions and cook until soft. Add the cumin seeds, red pepper or chilli and most of the oregano, then add the sugar, vinegar and tomatoes. Season generously with salt and pepper.

3 Put the sliced potatoes and olives into a baking dish and spoon over the tomato mixture. Crumble the feta cheese evenly over the top and sprinkle with the remaining oregano. Generously drizzle with the remaining olive oil, then bake in the preheated oven for 25–30 minutes.

4 Serve hot, straight from the oven, with lemon wedges to squeeze over.

Potatoes with Blue Cheese and Walnuts

Firm small potatoes, served in a creamy blue cheese sauce with the crunch of walnuts, make a great side dish to a simple roast meal. For a change, serve it as a lunch dish or a light supper with a green salad.

Serves 4
450g/1lb small new or
 salad potatoes

1 small head of celery, sliced
1 small red onion, sliced
115g/4oz/1 cup blue
 cheese, mashed
150ml/¼ pint/⅔ cup single
 (light) cream
50g/2oz/½ cup walnut pieces
30ml/2 tbsp chopped
 fresh parsley
salt and ground black pepper

1 Cook the potatoes in their skins in a large pan with plenty of boiling water for about 15 minutes or until tender, adding the sliced celery and onion to the pan for the last 5 minutes or so of cooking.

2 Drain the vegetables well through a colander and put them into a shallow serving dish.

3 In a small pan, slowly melt the cheese in the cream, stirring occasionally. Do not allow the mixture to boil but heat it until it is simmering.

4 Check the sauce and season to taste with salt and ground black pepper. Pour it evenly over the vegetables in the dish and sprinkle over the walnut pieces and chopped fresh parsley. Serve hot, straight from the dish.

Cook's Tip
Use a combination of blue cheeses, such as Dolcelatte and Roquefort, or go for the distinctive flavour of Stilton on its own. If walnuts are not available, blue cheeses marry equally well with hazelnuts.

Herby Potatoes Energy 243kcal/1016kJ; Protein 6.3g; Carbohydrate 27.5g, of which sugars 9.3g; Fat 12.8g, of which saturates 5g; Cholesterol 19mg; Calcium 102mg; Fibre 2.9g; Sodium 447mg.
Potatoes with Walnuts Energy 350kcal/1459kJ; Protein 11.2g; Carbohydrate 21.9g, of which sugars 4.8g; Fat 24.8g, of which saturates 10.6g; Cholesterol 42mg; Calcium 236mg; Fibre 2.7g; Sodium 427mg.

Grilled Halloumi and Bean Salad with Skewered Potatoes

Halloumi, the hard, white salty goat's milk cheese that squeaks when you bite it, grills really well and is the perfect complement to fresh-tasting vegetables.

Serves 4
20 baby new potatoes, total weight about 300g/11oz
200g/7oz extra-fine green beans, trimmed
675g/1½lb broad (fava) beans, shelled weight 225g/8oz
200g/7oz halloumi cheese, cut into 5mm/¼in slices
1 garlic clove, crushed to a paste with a large pinch of salt
90ml/6 tbsp olive oil
5ml/1 tsp cider vinegar or white wine vinegar
15g/½oz/½ cup fresh basil leaves, shredded
45ml/3 tbsp chopped fresh savory
2 spring onions (scallions), finely sliced
salt and ground black pepper

1 Thread five potatoes on to each skewer, and cook in a large pan of salted boiling water for about 7 minutes or until almost tender. Add the green beans and cook for 3 minutes more. Add the broad beans and cook for just 2 minutes. Drain all the vegetables in a large colander.

2 Refresh the cooked broad beans under cold water. Pop each broad bean out of its skin to reveal the bright green inner bean. Place in a bowl, cover and set aside.

3 Preheat a grill (broiler) or griddle. Place the halloumi slices and the potato skewers in a wide dish. Whisk the garlic and oil together with a generous grinding of black pepper. Add to the dish and toss the halloumi and potato skewers until thoroughly coated in the mixture.

4 Cook the cheese and potato skewers under the grill or on the griddle for about 2 minutes on each side.

5 Add the vinegar to the oil and garlic remaining in the dish and whisk to mix. Toss in the beans, herbs and spring onions, with the cooked halloumi. Serve with the potato skewers.

Potato Gnocchi with Simple Tomato and Butter Sauce

Potato gnocchi make a substantial and tasty alternative to pasta. In this dish they are served with a very simple, but delicious, fresh tomato sauce.

Serves 4
675g/1½lb floury potatoes
2 egg yolks
75g/3oz/¾ cup plain (all-purpose) flour
60ml/4 tbsp finely chopped fresh parsley, to garnish

For the sauce
25g/1oz/2 tbsp butter, melted
450g/1lb plum tomatoes, peeled, seeded and chopped
salt

1 Preheat the oven to 200°C/400°F/ Gas 6. Scrub the potatoes, then bake them in their skins in the oven for 1 hour or until the flesh feels soft when pricked with a fork.

2 While the potatoes are still warm, cut them in half and gently squeeze the flesh into a bowl, or use a spoon to scrape the flesh out of the shells. Mash the potato well, then season with a little salt. Add the egg yolks and mix lightly with a fork or spoon.

3 Add the flour and mix to a rough dough. Place on a floured work surface and knead for around 5 minutes until the dough is smooth and elastic. Shape the dough into small thumb-sized shapes by making long rolls and cutting them into evenly sized segments. Press each of these with the back of a fork to give a ridged effect. Place the gnocchi on a floured work surface.

4 Preheat the oven to 140°C/275°F/Gas 1. Cook the gnocchi in small batches in barely simmering, slightly salted water for about 10 minutes. Remove with a slotted spoon, drain well and transfer to a dish. Cover and keep hot in the oven.

5 To make the sauce, heat the butter in a small pan for 1 minute, then add the tomatoes and cook over a low heat until the juice starts to run. Sprinkle the gnocchi with chopped parsley and serve with the sauce.

Halloumi and Bean Energy 393kcal/1635kJ; Protein 16.5g; Carbohydrate 20.8g, of which sugars 3.4g; Fat 27.7g, of which saturates 9.4g; Cholesterol 29mg; Calcium 263mg; Fibre 6.3g; Sodium 215mg.
Gnocchi with Sauce Energy 278kcal/1174kJ; Protein 6.9g; Carbohydrate 45.3g, of which sugars 6g; Fat 9g, of which saturates 4.4g; Cholesterol 114mg; Calcium 57mg; Fibre 3.4g; Sodium 72mg.

Potato Gnocchi

Gnocchi are little Italian dumplings made either with mashed potato and flour, or with semolina. To ensure that they are light and fluffy, take care not to overmix the dough.

Serves 4–6

1kg/2¼lb waxy potatoes

250–300g/9–11oz/2¼–2¾ cups
    plain (all-purpose) flour, plus
    more if necessary
1 egg
pinch of freshly grated nutmeg
25g/1oz/2 tbsp butter
salt
fresh basil leaves, to garnish
Parmesan cheese cut in shavings,
    to garnish

1 Cook the potatoes in their skins in a large pan of boiling, salted water until tender but not falling apart. Drain and peel while the potatoes are still hot.

2 Spread a layer of flour on a work surface. Pass the hot potatoes through a food mill, dropping them directly on to the flour. Sprinkle with about half of the remaining flour and mix in very lightly. Break the egg into the mixture.

3 Finally, add the nutmeg to the dough and knead lightly, adding more flour if the mixture is too loose. When the dough is light to the touch and no longer moist it is ready to be rolled. Divide the dough into four pieces. On a lightly floured surface, form each into a roll about 2cm/¾in diameter. Cut the rolls crossways into even pieces of about 2cm/¾in in length.

4 Hold an ordinary table fork with tines sideways, leaning on the board. Then one by one, press and roll the gnocchi lightly along the tines of the fork towards the points, making ridges on one side, and a depression from your thumb on the other.

5 Bring a large pan of salted water to the boil, then drop in about half the gnocchi. When they rise to the surface, after 3–4 minutes, they are done. Lift them out with a slotted spoon, drain well, and place in a warmed serving bowl. Dot with butter. Cover to keep warm while cooking the remainder. As soon as they are cooked, toss the gnocchi with the butter, garnish with Parmesan and basil leaves, and serve immediately.

Potato Gnocchi with Gorgonzola

Potato gnocchi are prepared all over Italy with different ingredients used in different regions. These are delicious with a creamy cheese sauce.

Serves 4

450g/1lb potatoes, unpeeled
1 large (US extra large) egg
115g/4oz/1 cup plain
    (all-purpose) flour

fresh thyme sprigs, to garnish
salt and ground black pepper

For the sauce

115g/4oz Gorgonzola cheese
60ml/4 tbsp double
    (heavy) cream
15ml/1 tbsp fresh
    thyme, chopped
60 ml/4 tbsp freshly grated
    Parmesan cheese, to serve

1 Cook the potatoes in boiling, salted water for 20 minutes until they are tender. Drain and, when cool, remove the skins.

2 Force the potatoes through a sieve (strainer) into a mixing bowl. Season and then beat in the egg until combined. Add the flour a little at a time, stirring well with a wooden spoon after each addition until you have a smooth dough.

3 Turn the dough out on to a floured surface and knead for about 3 minutes, adding more flour if necessary, until it is smooth and soft and not sticky to the touch.

4 Divide the dough into six equal pieces. Flour your hands and gently roll each piece into a log shape measuring 15–20cm/ 6–8in long and 2.5cm/1in around. Cut each log into six to eight pieces, about 2.5cm/1in long, then gently roll each piece in the flour. Form into gnocchi by gently pressing on to the floured surface with the tines of a fork to leave clear ridges in the dough.

5 To cook, drop the gnocchi into a pan of boiling water about 12 at a time. Once they rise to the surface, after about 2 minutes, cook for 4–5 minutes more. Remove and drain.

6 Place the Gorgonzola, cream and thyme in a large frying pan and heat gently until the cheese melts to form a thick, creamy consistency. Add the drained gnocchi and toss well to combine. Serve with Parmesan and garnish with thyme.

Potato Gnocchi Energy 296kcal/1254kJ; Protein 7.8g; Carbohydrate 59.2g, of which sugars 2.8g; Fat 4.7g, of which saturates 2.3g; Cholesterol 39mg; Calcium 74mg; Fibre 3g; Sodium 52mg.
Gorgonzola Gnocchi Energy 430kcal/1801kJ; Protein 18.1g; Carbohydrate 40.9g, of which sugars 2.3g; Fat 23.6g, of which saturates 13.5g; Cholesterol 104mg; Calcium 386mg; Fibre 2g; Sodium 562mg.

Spiced Pumpkin and Potato Gnocchi

Pumpkin adds a sweetness to these potato gnocchi, which are superb on their own or served with meat.

Serves 4
450g/1lb pumpkin, peeled, seeded and chopped
450g/1lb potatoes, boiled
2 egg yolks
200g/7oz/1¾ cups plain (all-purpose) flour, plus more if necessary
pinch of ground allspice
1.5ml/¼ tsp cinnamon
pinch of freshly grated nutmeg
finely grated rind of ½ orange
salt and ground pepper

For the sauce
30ml/2 tbsp olive oil
1 shallot, finely chopped
175g/6oz/2½ cups fresh chanterelles, sliced, or 15g/½oz/½ cup dried, soaked in warm water for 20 minutes, then drained
10ml/2 tsp almond butter
150ml/¼ pint/⅔ cup crème fraîche
a little milk or water
75ml/5 tbsp chopped fresh parsley
50g/2oz/½ cup Parmesan cheese, freshly grated

1 Wrap the pumpkin in foil and bake at 180°C/350°F/Gas 4 for 30 minutes. Pass the pumpkin and cooked potatoes through a food mill into a bowl. Add the egg yolks, flour, spices, orange rind and seasoning and mix well to make a soft dough. If the mixture is too loose, add a little flour to stiffen it.

2 To make the sauce, heat the oil in a pan and fry the shallot until soft. Add the chanterelles and cook briefly, then add the almond butter. Stir to melt and stir in the crème fraîche. Simmer briefly, add the parsley and season to taste. Keep hot.

3 Flour a work surface. Spoon the gnocchi dough into a piping (pastry) bag fitted with a 1cm/½in plain nozzle. Pipe on to the flour to make a 15cm/6in sausage. Roll in flour and cut crossways into 2.5cm/1in pieces. Repeat. Mark each piece lightly with a fork and drop into a pan of fast boiling, salted water.

4 The gnocchi are done when they rise to the surface, after 3–4 minutes. Drain and turn into bowls. Spoon the sauce over, sprinkle with Parmesan, and serve immediately.

Orecchiette with Potatoes and Rocket

This hearty potato dish is from the south-east of Italy. Serve it as a main course with country bread. Some delicatessens and supermarkets sell a farmhouse-style Italian loaf called pugliese, which would be most appropriate.

Serves 4–6
45ml/3 tbsp olive oil
1 small onion, finely chopped
300g/11oz canned chopped Italian plum tomatoes or passata (bottled strained tomatoes)
2.5ml/½ tsp dried oregano
pinch of chilli powder or cayenne pepper
about 30ml/2 tbsp red or white wine (optional)
2 potatoes, total weight about 200g/7oz, diced
300g/11oz/2¾ cups dried orecchiette
2 garlic cloves, finely chopped
150g/5oz rocket (arugula) leaves, stalks removed, shredded
90g/3½oz/scant ½ cup ricotta cheese
salt and ground black pepper
freshly grated Pecorino cheese, to serve

1 Heat 15ml/1 tbsp of the olive oil in a medium pan, add half the finely chopped onion and cook gently, stirring frequently, for about 5 minutes until softened. Add the canned tomatoes or passata, oregano and chilli powder or cayenne pepper to the onion. Pour the wine over, if using, and add a little salt and pepper to taste. Cover and simmer for about 15 minutes.

2 Bring a large pan of salted water to the boil. Add the potatoes and pasta. Stir well and let the water return to the boil. Lower the heat and simmer for 15 minutes, or according to the packet instructions, until the pasta is cooked.

3 Heat the remaining oil in a large frying pan, add the rest of the onion and the garlic and fry for 2–3 minutes, stirring occasionally. Add the rocket, toss over the heat for about 2 minutes until wilted, then stir in the tomato sauce and the ricotta. Mix well.

4 Drain the pasta and potatoes, add both to the pan of sauce and toss to mix. Taste for seasoning and serve immediately in warmed bowls, with grated Pecorino handed separately.

Pumpkin Gnocchi Energy 553kcal/2317kJ; Protein 15.6g; Carbohydrate 61.7g, of which sugars 5.9g; Fat 28.8g, of which saturates 14.7g; Cholesterol 156mg; Calcium 299mg; Fibre 4.5g; Sodium 166mg.
Orecchiette Energy 584kcal/2451kJ; Protein 18.9g; Carbohydrate 65.4g, of which sugars 3.5g; Fat 29.2g, of which saturates 7.1g; Cholesterol 19mg; Calcium 311mg; Fibre 3.3g; Sodium 260mg.

Roasted Red Pepper Tortilla

This comforting and delicious recipe relies on only a few basic ingredients, but the mixture of eggs, potatoes and silky red peppers is always a winner. This is perfect when served with a seasonal salad for a tasty and sophisticated lunchtime treat.

Serves 2

450g/1lb potatoes, peeled and
  cut into small chunks
50ml/2fl oz/¼ cup olive oil
1 large onion, finely sliced
2 red (bell) peppers, halved
  and seeded
4 eggs
salt and ground black pepper

1 Season the potatoes well with salt and pepper. Heat half the oil in a non-stick frying pan and cook the potatoes over a medium heat for 15 minutes until starting to brown. Make sure to keep the potatoes moving so that they do not stick to the bottom of the pan.

2 Meanwhile, in another pan, heat half the remaining oil and fry the onion slices for about 20 minutes until really soft.

3 Grill (broil) the peppers for 10 minutes until charred on the outside. Put in a plastic bag, seal, and leave for around 10 minutes to steam.

4 Beat the eggs in a bowl, add the potatoes and onions and stir well. Season to taste.

5 Peel the skins off the peppers, roughly chop the flesh and add to the egg, potato and onion mixture.

6 Heat the remaining oil in the non-stick frying pan and pour in the egg and potato mixture. Cook over a low heat for around 10 minutes, until beginning to set.

7 Invert a large plate or lid over the pan and carefully turn the omelette over on to it. Slide the omelette back into the pan and cook on the other side for a further 3–4 minutes until set.

8 Serve hot from the pan, cut into wedges and accompanied by a light, seasonal salad.

Pasta with Pesto and Potatoes

This is one of the traditional ways to serve pesto in Liguria. Although the mix of pasta and potatoes may seem odd, it is delicious with the rich pesto sauce.

Serves 4

50g/2oz/½ cup pine nuts
2 large garlic cloves, chopped
90g/3½oz fresh basil leaves
90ml/6 tbsp extra virgin olive oil
50g/2oz/⅔ cup Parmesan cheese
40g/1½oz/½ cup freshly grated
  Pecorino cheese

For the pasta mixture

275g/10oz waxy potatoes, thickly
  sliced or cut into
  1cm/½in cubes
200g/7oz fine green beans
350g/12oz dried trenette,
  linguine, tagliatelle
  or tagliarini
salt and ground black pepper

To serve

extra virgin olive oil
pine nuts, toasted
Parmesan Cheese
basil leaves, to garnish

1 Toast the pine nuts in a dry frying pan until golden. Place in a mortar with the garlic and a pinch of salt, and crush with a pestle. Add the basil and add a little oil as you work the mixture to a paste. Add the Parmesan and Pecorino and the remaining oil.

2 Bring a pan of lightly salted water to the boil and add the potatoes. Cook for 10–12 minutes, until tender. Add the green beans to the pan for the last 5–6 minutes of cooking.

3 Meanwhile, cook the pasta in boiling salted water for 8–12 minutes, or according to the packet instructions, until just tender. Times vary according to the pasta shapes.

4 Drain the pasta, potatoes and beans. Place in a large bowl and toss with two-thirds of the pesto. Season with pepper and sprinkle basil leaves over the top. Serve with the rest of the pesto, extra olive oil, pine nuts and grated Parmesan.

Cook's Tip
*To freeze pesto, make it without the cheeses, then freeze.
To use, simply thaw, then stir in the cheeses.*

Pasta with Pesto Energy 658kcal/2760kJ; Protein 20g; Carbohydrate 78.6g, of which sugars 5.9g; Fat 31.5g, of which saturates 5.8g; Cholesterol 13mg; Calcium 240mg; Fibre 5.7g; Sodium 154mg.
Pepper Tortilla Energy 515kcal/2130kJ; Protein 22.6g; Carbohydrate 38.6g, of which sugars 5.6g; Fat 40.7g, of which saturates 14.2g; Cholesterol 47.3mg; Calcium 281mg; Fibre 3.5g; Sodium 68mg.

Potato and Onion Tortilla

This deep-set omelette with sliced potatoes and onions is the best-known Spanish tortilla and makes a deliciously simple meal when served with a leafy salad and crusty bread. Use waxy potatoes rather than the floury variety as they will hold their shape better when cooked.

Serves 6
800g/1¾lb medium potatoes
100ml/3½fl oz/scant ½ cup
    extra virgin olive oil
2 onions, thinly sliced
salt and ground black pepper
6 eggs

1 Thinly slice the potatoes. Heat 75ml/5 tbsp of the oil in a frying pan and cook the potatoes, turning frequently, for about 10 minutes.

2 Add the onions to the pan, and continue to cook gently for a further 10 minutes, until the vegetables are tender. Season with salt and ground black pepper.

3 Meanwhile, beat the eggs in a large bowl with a little salt and black pepper. Transfer the potatoes and onions into the eggs and mix gently. Leave to stand for 10 minutes.

4 Wipe out the pan with kitchen paper and heat the remaining oil in it. Pour the egg mixture into the pan and spread it out in an even layer.

5 Cover the pan and cook over a very gentle heat for about 20 minutes, until the eggs are just set. Serve immediately, cut into wedges, or leave to cool completely before serving.

Variation
Tortilla are often made with a variety of other ingredients – chopped red or yellow (bell) peppers, cooked peas, pitted olives, corn, or grated Cheddar or Gruyère cheese can all be added to the mixture in step 3, if you like.

Potato Tortilla

The classic tortilla can be found in every tapas bar in Spain. The inclusion of potatoes makes it dense and very satisfying. It can be eaten in wedges with a fork – a meal in itself with salad – or cut up into chunks and speared, to be enjoyed as a snack with drinks.

Serves 6
450g/1lb small waxy
    potatoes, peeled
1 Spanish (Bermuda) onion
45ml/3 tbsp vegetable oil
4 large eggs
salt and ground black pepper
fresh flat leaf parsley or tomato
    wedges, to garnish

1 Using a sharp knife, cut the potatoes into thin slices and slice the onion into thin rings. Heat 30ml/2 tbsp of the oil in a 20cm/8in heavy frying pan.

2 Add the potatoes and the onions to the pan and cook over a low heat for 20 minutes, or until the potato slices are just tender. Stir from time to time to prevent the potatoes sticking. Remove from the heat.

3 In a large bowl, beat together the eggs with a little salt and pepper. When the cooked potatoes and onion have cooled a little, stir them into the eggs.

4 Clean the frying pan with kitchen paper then heat the remaining oil and pour in the potato mixture. Cook very gently for 5–8 minutes until set underneath. During cooking, lift the edges of the tortilla with a spatula, and allow any uncooked egg to run underneath. Shake the pan from side to side, to prevent sticking.

5 Place a large heatproof plate upside down over the pan, invert the tortilla on to the plate and then slide it back into the pan. Cook for 2–3 minutes more, until the underside of the tortilla is golden brown.

6 Cut the tortilla into wedges and serve immediately or leave until warm or cold. Serve garnished with fresh flat leaf parsley or tomato wedges.

Potato and Onion Tortilla Energy 443kcal/1848kJ; Protein 16g; Carbohydrate 32.4g, of which sugars 3.6g; Fat 28.1g, of which saturates 12.3g; Cholesterol 49mg; Calcium 226mg; Fibre 1.9g; Sodium 728mg.
Potato Tortilla Energy 163kcal/681kJ; Protein 5.8g; Carbohydrate 14.7g, of which sugars 2.9g; Fat 9.5g, of which saturates 1.9g; Cholesterol 127mg; Calcium 32mg; Fibre 1.2g; Sodium 56mg.

Pepper and Potato Tortilla

Tortilla is traditionally a Spanish egg and potato dish like a thick omelette, best eaten cold in chunky wedges. Use a hard Spanish cheese, like Mahón, or a goat's cheese, although sharp Cheddar makes a good substitute.

Serves 4

2 medium waxy potatoes

45ml/3 tbsp olive oil, plus more
   if necessary
1 large onion, thinly sliced
2 garlic cloves, crushed
2 (bell) peppers, one green
   and one red, seeded and
   thinly sliced
6 eggs, beaten
115g/4oz/1 cup mature (sharp)
   cheese, grated
salt and ground black pepper

1 Par-boil the potatoes in boiling water for about 10 minutes. Drain and leave to cool slightly. Slice them thickly. Preheat the grill (broiler).

2 In a large non-stick or well-seasoned frying pan, heat the oil over a medium heat. Add the onion, garlic and peppers and cook for 5 minutes until softened. Add the potatoes and cook, stirring occasionally, until the potatoes are tender.

3 Pour in half the beaten eggs, sprinkle half the cheese over this and then the remainder of the egg. Season with salt and pepper. Finish with a layer of cheese. Reduce the heat to low and continue to cook without stirring, half covering the pan with a lid to help set the eggs.

4 When the tortilla is firm, place the pan under the hot grill to seal the top just lightly. Leave the tortilla in the pan to cool. Serve at room temperature, cut into wedges.

> **Variation**
> You can add any sliced and lightly cooked vegetable, such as mushrooms, courgette (zucchini) or broccoli, to this tortilla instead of the green and red (bell) peppers. Cooked pasta or brown rice are both excellent alternatives to the potatoes.

Courgette and Potato Tortilla

Microwaves can be an incredibly convenient tool in the kitchen of a busy household. This delicious, chunky, omelette-style potato tortilla can be made in next to no time in the microwave. All it needs is a little browning under a hot grill at the end of cooking.

Serves 4

30ml/2 tbsp chopped
   fresh tarragon

4 eggs, beaten
30ml/2 tbsp olive oil
1 onion, finely chopped
450g/1lb potatoes, cut into
   small dice
1 garlic clove, crushed
2 courgettes (zucchini),
   thinly sliced
salt and ground black pepper
mixed leafy salad and crusty
   bread, to serve

1 Stir the tarragon into the eggs and season with salt and ground black pepper. Set aside.

2 Place the oil and onion in a large, shallow microwave-proof dish which is suitable for putting under the grill (broiler). Cover and microwave on HIGH for 3 minutes. Add the diced potatoes, garlic and sliced courgettes, cover again and microwave on HIGH for 10 minutes, stirring twice during the cooking process.

3 Pour the eggs over the vegetables, cover and microwave on HIGH for about 3–5 minutes, rotating the dish twice, until the eggs are beginning to set slightly. Meanwhile, preheat the grill.

4 Place the tortilla under the grill and cook for a few minutes until the top has set and is tinged golden. Cut into wedges and serve from the dish with a mixed salad and crusty bread.

> **Cook's Tip**
> This recipe is also suitable for cooking in a combination microwave. Follow the oven manufacturer's timing guide for the best results.

Pepper Tortilla Energy 321kcal/1333kJ; Protein 13.1g; Carbohydrate 19.6g, of which sugars 10.2g; Fat 21.1g, of which saturates 8.3g; Cholesterol 123mg; Calcium 256mg; Fibre 3g; Sodium 254mg.
Courgette Tortilla Energy 221kcal/923kJ; Protein 9.7g; Carbohydrate 20.7g, of which sugars 3.6g; Fat 11.7g, of which saturates 2.5g; Cholesterol 190mg; Calcium 58mg; Fibre 2g; Sodium 84mg.

Spanish Potato Omelette

The traditional Spanish omelette consists simply of potatoes, onions and eggs. This one has other vegetables too, and makes a substantial vegetarian meal.

Serves 6

30ml/2 tbsp olive oil, plus extra
  for drizzling
1 Spanish onion, chopped
1 small red pepper, seeded
  and diced
2 celery sticks, chopped
225g/8oz potatoes, peeled, diced
  and cooked
400g/14oz can cannellini
  beans, drained
8 eggs
salt and ground black pepper

1 Heat the olive oil in a 30cm/12in frying pan or paella pan. Add the chopped onion, red pepper and celery, and cook over a medium heat for between 3–5 minutes until the vegetables are soft, but not coloured.

2 Add the potatoes and beans, and cook for several minutes to heat through.

3 In a small bowl, beat the eggs with a fork, then season well and pour over the ingredients in the pan.

4 Stir the egg mixture with a wooden spatula until it begins to thicken, then allow it to cook over a low heat for about 8 minutes. The omelette should be firm, but still slightly moist in the middle. Cool slightly, then very carefully invert on to a large serving plate.

5 Cut the omelette into thick wedges. Serve warm or cool with a green salad and olives and a little olive oil.

> **Cook's Tip**
> *In Spain, this omelette is often served as a tapas dish or appetizer. It is delicious served cold, cut into bitesize pieces and accompanied with a chilli sauce or mayonnaise for dipping. Other sliced seasonal vegetables, baby artichoke hearts and chickpeas can also be used in this recipe.*

Potato, Pepper and Mint Frittata

This fresh-tasting Italian version of the ever-popular omelette is filled with potatoes and plenty of fresh herbs. Try to use fresh mint in preference to the dried variety if you can find it. It is delicious served either hot or cold.

Serves 3–4

450g/1lb small new or
  salad potatoes
6 eggs
30ml/2 tbsp chopped fresh mint
30ml/2 tbsp olive oil
1 onion, chopped
2 garlic cloves, crushed
2 red (bell) peppers, seeded and
  roughly chopped
salt and ground black pepper
mint sprigs, to garnish

1 Cook the potatoes in their skins in boiling salted water until just tender. Drain and leave to cool slightly. When cool enough to handle, cut them into thick slices.

2 Whisk together the eggs and mint in a bowl. Season with salt and ground black pepper, then set aside. Heat the oil in a large frying pan.

3 Add the onion, garlic, peppers and potatoes to the pan and cook, stirring occasionally, for about 5–7 minutes, until the onion and peppers are soft but not browned.

4 Pour the beaten egg mixture over the vegetables in the frying pan and stir gently to distribute the egg evenly.

5 Push the mixture towards the centre of the pan as it cooks to allow any liquid egg to run on to the base and cook through. Meanwhile, preheat the grill (broiler).

6 When the frittata is lightly set on the bottom, place the pan under the hot grill for 2–3 minutes until the top is a light golden brown colour.

7 Serve hot or cold, cut into wedges piled high on a serving dish and garnished with sprigs of mint.

Potato Frittata Energy 267kcal/1115kJ; Protein 12.2g; Carbohydrate 23.7g, of which sugars 6.8g; Fat 14.5g, of which saturates 3.3g; Cholesterol 285mg; Calcium 57mg; Fibre 2.5g; Sodium 121mg.
Spanish Omelette Energy 374kcal/1563kJ; Protein 16.7g; Carbohydrate 34.9g, of which sugars 11.3g; Fat 19.4g, of which saturates 4.5g; Cholesterol 381mg; Calcium 87mg; Fibre 3.9g; Sodium 162mg.

Potato and Onion Tortilla with Broad Beans

Adding chopped herbs and a few skinned broad beans to the classic potato tortilla makes this a very summery dish to enjoy at lunch, or cut it into small pieces and serve as an appetizer.

Serves 2

45ml/3 tbsp olive oil
2 Spanish (Bermuda) onions, thinly sliced
300g/11oz waxy potatoes, cut into 1cm/½in dice
250g/9oz/1¾ cups shelled broad (fava) beans
5ml/1 tsp chopped fresh thyme or summer savory
6 large eggs
45ml/3 tbsp mixed chopped chives and chopped flat leaf parsley
salt and ground black pepper

1 Heat 30ml/2 tbsp of the oil in a 23cm/9in deep non-stick frying pan. Add the onions and potatoes and stir to coat. Cover and cook gently, stirring frequently, for 20–25 minutes until the potatoes are tender. Do not let the mixture brown.

2 Meanwhile, cook the beans in boiling salted water for 5 minutes. Drain well and set aside to cool.

3 When the beans are cool enough to handle, peel off the grey outer skins. Add the beans to the frying pan, together with the thyme or summer savory, and season with salt and pepper to taste. Stir well to mix and cook for a further 2–3 minutes.

4 Beat the eggs with salt and pepper to taste and the mixed herbs, then pour over the potatoes and onions and increase the heat slightly. Cook gently until the egg on the bottom sets and browns, gently pulling the omelette away from the sides of the pan and tilting it to allow the uncooked egg to run underneath.

5 Invert the tortilla on to a plate. Add the remaining oil to the pan and heat until hot. Slip the tortilla back into the pan, uncooked side down, and cook for another 3–5 minutes to allow the underneath to brown. Slide the tortilla out on to a plate. Divide as wished, and serve warm rather than piping hot.

Chilli Cheese and Potato Tortilla with Fresh Tomato Salsa

Good warm or cold, this is like a sliced potato quiche without the pastry base, spiked with chilli. The salsa can be made without the chilli, if you prefer. Use a firm but not hard cheese, such as Double Gloucester, Monterey Jack or Manchego.

Serves 4

45ml/3 tbsp sunflower or olive oil
1 small onion, thinly sliced
2–3 fresh green jalapeño chillies, seeded and sliced
200g/7oz cold cooked potato, thinly sliced
120g/4¼oz/generous 1 cup cheese, grated
6 eggs, beaten
salt and ground black pepper
fresh herbs, to garnish

For the salsa
500g/1¼lb fresh flavoursome tomatoes, peeled, seeded and finely chopped
1 fresh mild green chilli, seeded and finely chopped
2 garlic cloves, crushed
45ml/3 tbsp chopped fresh coriander (cilantro)
juice of 1 lime
2.5ml/½ tsp salt

1 To make the salsa, put the tomatoes in a bowl and add the chopped chilli, garlic, coriander, lime juice and salt. Mix well and set aside.

2 Heat 15ml/1 tbsp of the oil in a large omelette pan and gently fry the onion and jalapeños for 5 minutes, stirring until softened. Add the potato and cook for another 5 minutes until lightly browned, keeping the slices whole.

3 Using a slotted spoon, transfer the vegetables to a warm plate. Wipe the pan with kitchen paper, then add the remaining oil and heat until really hot. Return the vegetables to the pan. Sprinkle the cheese over the top. Season.

4 Pour in the beaten eggs, making sure that they seep under the vegetables. Cook the tortilla over a low heat, without stirring, until set. Serve hot or cold, cut into wedges, garnished with fresh herbs and with the salsa on the side.

Potato Tortilla Energy 673kcal/2812kJ; Protein 34.9g; Carbohydrate 59.2g, of which sugars 18.1g; Fat 35.2g, of which saturates 7.3g; Cholesterol 571mg; Calcium 272mg; Fibre 14.3g; Sodium 252mg.
Cheese Tortilla Energy 375kcal/1563kJ; Protein 19.3g; Carbohydrate 13.5g, of which sugars 5.7g; Fat 27.1g, of which saturates 10g; Cholesterol 315mg; Calcium 305mg; Fibre 2.6g; Sodium 589mg.

Potato, Red Onion and Feta Frittata

This Italian omelette is cooked with vegetables and crumbly feta cheese, and is given real substance by the addition of golden new potatoes. Cut it into generous wedges and serve with crusty bread and a tasty tomato salad.

Serves 2–4
25ml/1½ tbsp olive oil
1 red onion, sliced
350g/12oz cooked new potatoes,
    halved or quartered, if large
6 eggs, lightly beaten
115g/4oz/1 cup feta
    cheese, diced
salt and ground black pepper

1 Heat the oil in a large heavy, flameproof frying pan. Add the onion and cook for 5 minutes until softened, stirring occasionally.

2 Add the potatoes and cook for a further 5 minutes until golden, stirring to prevent them sticking. Spread the mixture evenly over the base of the pan.

3 Preheat the grill (broiler) to high. Season the beaten eggs, then pour them over the onion and potatoes. Sprinkle the cheese on top and cook over a moderate heat for 5–6 minutes until the eggs are set and the base of the frittata is lightly golden.

4 Place the pan under the preheated grill (protect the pan handle with a double layer of foil if it is not flameproof) and cook the top of the omelette for about 3 minutes until it is set and golden. Serve the frittata warm or cold, cut into wedges.

Cook's Tip

Eggs are an important source of vitamin B12, which is vital for the nervous system and the development of red blood cells. They also supply other B vitamins, zinc and selenium and a useful amount of iron. It is beneficial to eat a food rich in vitamin C at the same time in order to help the absorption of iron. Do not eat too many eggs, though – try not to exceed a maximum of three per week.

Indian Spiced Potato, Corn and Pea Omelette

This delicately spiced Indian potato omelette is a delicious and intriguing twist on the traditional Spanish tortilla. The distinctive warming aroma of cumin and the bulk given by the corn, potatoes and peas make this a truly memorable dish.

Serves 4–6
30ml/2 tbsp vegetable oil
1 onion, finely chopped
2.5ml/½ tsp ground cumin
1 garlic clove, crushed

1 or 2 fresh green chillies,
    finely chopped
a few coriander (cilantro)
    sprigs, chopped, plus extra,
    to garnish
1 firm tomato, chopped
1 small potato, cubed
    and boiled
25g/1oz/¼ cup cooked peas
25g/1oz/¼ cup cooked corn,
    or drained canned corn
2 eggs, beaten
25g/1oz/¼ cup grated Cheddar
    cheese or Monterey Jack
salt and ground black pepper

1 Heat the oil in a wok or omelette pan, add the onion, cumin, garlic, chillies, coriander, tomato, potato, peas and corn. Mix well.

2 Cook over a medium heat, stirring, for 5 minutes, until the potato and tomato are almost tender. Season well with salt and ground black pepper.

3 Preheat the grill (broiler) to high. Increase the heat under the pan and pour in the beaten eggs. Reduce the heat to medium, cover and cook until the bottom layer is brown. Turn the omelette over, then sprinkle with the grated cheese. Place under the hot grill and cook until the egg sets and the cheese has melted.

4 Garnish the omelette with sprigs of coriander and serve with salad for a light lunch, or on its own as a wholesome breakfast.

Variation

You can use any vegetable with the potatoes. Try thickly sliced button (white) mushrooms, which can be added in step 1.

Potato and Feta Frittata Energy 289kcal/1207kJ; Protein 15.5g; Carbohydrate 15.7g, of which sugars 2.4g; Fat 18.9g, of which saturates 7g; Cholesterol 306mg; Calcium 155mg; Fibre 1.1g; Sodium 529mg.
Spicy Omelette Energy 93kcal/388kJ; Protein 4g; Carbohydrate 3.7g, of which sugars 1.2g; Fat 7.1g, of which saturates 1.9g; Cholesterol 67mg; Calcium 46mg; Fibre 0.6g; Sodium 104mg.

Pan Haggerty

This traditional dish from Northumberland in northern England works best with firm-fleshed potatoes such as Cara, Desirée or Maris Piper. Serve it cut into even wedges or spoon it straight out of the pan.

Serves 4
60ml/4 tbsp oil
450g/1lb firm potatoes, thinly sliced
1 large onion, thinly sliced
115g/4oz/1 cup grated mature (sharp) Cheddar cheese
salt and ground black pepper

1 Heat the oil in a large, heavy frying pan. Remove the pan from the heat and add alternate layers of potato, onion slices and grated cheese, starting and ending with potatoes. Season each layer as you go with salt and plenty of ground black pepper. Replace the pan over a low heat.

2 Cook over a medium heat for about 30 minutes, until the potatoes are soft and tender and the underside has browned. Meanwhile, preheat the grill (broiler).

3 Place the pan under the grill for about 5–10 minutes to brown the top of the potatoes. Slide the potatoes on to a warmed plate to serve.

Cook's Tip
Slice the vegetables for this dish as thin as you can. A mandolin is an ideal kitchen tool for this job, although be careful when using as they have very sharp blades.

Variations
• Add in some chopped bacon between the layers of potato for non-vegetarians, if you like.
• A central layer of thin apple slices will add a delicious sweet note to the dish.
• A crushed clove of garlic will add a pungent spicy sweetness to this dish, but be careful, a little goes a long way.

Chicken of the Woods with Potatoes

This hash brown dinner is a very special treat. As well as potatoes it calls for the intriguing chicken of the woods, a wild mushroom which looks, tastes and has the texture of chicken.

Serves 4
900g/2lb potatoes, peeled
60ml/4 tbsp unsalted butter
2 medium onions, sliced
1 celery stalk, sliced
1 small carrot, peeled and cut into small slices
225g/8oz/3 cups chicken of the woods, trimmed and sliced
45ml/3 tbsp medium sherry
45ml/3 tbsp chopped fresh parsley
15ml/1 tbsp chopped fresh chives
grated rind of 1/2 lemon
salt and ground black pepper
frisée and spinach leaves, to serve

1 Put the potatoes in a large pan. Add water to cover and bring to the boil. Add salt, then simmer for about 15 minutes, or until the potatoes are tender, but do not let them get too soft. Drain thoroughly and leave to cool.

2 Melt the butter in a large non-stick frying pan, add the onions, celery and carrot and cook for 5–7 minutes until softened and lightly browned.

3 Add the chicken of the woods and the sherry to the pan, then simmer gently until the liquid has reduced and the alcohol has evaporated.

4 Add the potatoes, herbs and lemon rind to the pan. Season with salt and ground black pepper and toss and fry together until crispy brown. Serve with a salad of frisée and young spinach leaves.

Cook's Tips
• The best hash browns are made from late season floury potatoes that are inclined to fall apart when cooked. This quality helps the mixture to form a more solid mass in the pan.
• Do not harvest wild mushrooms yourself without expert guidance. Some mushroom websites offer a mail order service.

Pan Haggerty Energy 271kcal/1128kJ; Protein 9.8g; Carbohydrate 21.1g, of which sugars 3.6g; Fat 16.9g, of which saturates 7.5g; Cholesterol 30mg; Calcium 215mg; Fibre 1.7g; Sodium 206mg.
Hash Brown Energy 307kcal/1287kJ; Protein 5.7g; Carbohydrate 40.1g, of which sugars 6.2g; Fat 13.5g, of which saturates 8.4g; Cholesterol 35mg; Calcium 56mg; Fibre 4.3g; Sodium 156mg.

Vegetable Fried Noodles

Tofu adds food value to this deliciously satisfying hot and spicy noodle dish that will become a firm favourite with young and old alike.

Serves 4
2 eggs
5ml/1 tsp chilli powder
5ml/1 tsp ground turmeric
60ml/4 tbsp vegetable oil
1 large onion, finely sliced
2 red chillies, seeded and
   finely sliced

15ml/1 tbsp soy sauce
2 large cooked potatoes, cut into
   small cubes
6 pieces fried tofu, sliced
225g/8oz/4 cups beansprouts
115g/4oz/³⁄₄ cup green
   beans, blanched
350g/12oz fresh thick
   egg noodles
salt and ground black pepper
sliced spring onions (scallions),
   to garnish

1 Beat the eggs lightly, then strain them into a bowl. Heat a lightly greased omelette pan. Pour in half of the egg to cover the base of the pan thinly. When the egg is just set, turn the omelette over and cook the other side briefly. Slide on to a plate, blot with kitchen paper, roll up and cut into narrow strips. Make a second omelette in the same way and slice. Set the omelette strips aside for the garnish.

2 In a cup, mix together the chilli powder and turmeric. Form a paste by stirring in a little water.

3 Heat the oil in a wok or large frying pan. Cook the onion until soft, reduce the heat and add the chilli paste, sliced chillies and soy sauce. Stir-fry for 2–3 minutes.

4 Add the potatoes and stir-fry for about 2 minutes, mixing well with the chillies. Add the tofu, then the beansprouts, green beans and noodles.

5 Gently stir-fry until the noodles are evenly coated in the sauce and heated through. Take care not to break up the potatoes or the tofu. Season to taste with salt and ground black pepper. Serve immediately, garnished with the reserved omelette strips and the sliced spring onion.

Potato Rösti and Tofu

Although this potato and tofu dish features various different components, it is not difficult to make. Allow enough time to marinate the tofu for at least an hour before you start to cook it, to allow it to absorb the flavours of the ginger, garlic and tamari.

Serves 4
425g/15oz/3³⁄₄ cups tofu, cut
   into 1cm/¹⁄₂in cubes
4 large potatoes, about 900g/2lb
   total weight, peeled
sunflower oil, for frying

salt and ground black pepper
30ml/2 tbsp sesame
   seeds, toasted

For the marinade
30ml/2 tbsp tamari or dark
   soy sauce
15ml/1 tbsp clear honey
2 garlic cloves, crushed
4cm/1¹⁄₂in piece fresh root
   ginger, grated
5ml/1 tsp toasted sesame oil

For the sauce
15ml/1 tbsp olive oil
8 tomatoes, halved, seeded
   and chopped

1 Mix all the marinade ingredients in a bowl and add the tofu. Leave to marinate in the refrigerator for at least 1 hour, turning the tofu occasionally to allow the flavours to infuse.

2 To make the rösti, par-boil the potatoes for 10–15 minutes until almost tender. Leave to cool, then grate coarsely. Season well. Preheat the oven to 200°C/400°F/Gas 6. Drain the tofu, reserving the marinade, and spread out on a baking tray. Bake for 20 minutes, turning occasionally, until golden and crisp.

3 Meanwhile, to make the sauce, heat the oil in a pan, add the marinade and tomatoes and bring to the boil. Reduce the heat and simmer, covered, for 10 minutes. Pass through a sieve (strainer) to make smooth and keep warm.

4 Form the potato mixture into four cakes. Heat a frying pan with enough oil to cover the base. Place the cakes in the frying pan, flattening them slightly with a spatula. Cook until golden and crisp, then flip over to cook the other side. To serve, place on four serving plates. Scatter the tofu on top, spoon over the tomato sauce and sprinkle with sesame seeds.

Vegetable Noodles Energy 696kcal/2923kJ; Protein 28.3g; Carbohydrate 83g, of which sugars 8.2g; Fat 30.3g, of which saturates 4.2g; Cholesterol 121mg; Calcium 813mg; Fibre 5g; Sodium 476mg.
Potato Rösti Energy 433kcal/1811kJ; Protein 15g; Carbohydrate 42.3g, of which sugars 8.6g; Fat 23.7g, of which saturates 3.3g; Cholesterol 0mg; Calcium 618mg; Fibre 4.6g; Sodium 46mg.

Sweet Vegetable Couscous

A wonderful combination of sweet vegetables and spices in this microwave recipe makes a substantial and convenient winter dish.

Serves 4–6

1 generous pinch of
    saffron threads
45ml/3 tbsp boiling water
15ml/1 tbsp olive oil
1 red onion, sliced
2 garlic cloves, crushed
1–2 fresh red chillies, seeded and
    finely chopped
2.5ml/½ tsp ground ginger
2.5ml/½ tsp ground cinnamon
400g/14oz can chopped tomatoes

300ml/½ pint/1¼ cups hot
    vegetable stock or water
4 carrots, peeled and cut into
    5mm/¼in slices
2 turnips, peeled and cut into
    2cm/¾in cubes
450g/1lb sweet potatoes, peeled
    and cut into 2cm/¾in cubes
75g/3oz/⅓ cup raisins
2 courgettes (zucchini), cut into
    5mm/¼in slices
400g/14oz can chickpeas,
    drained and rinsed
45ml/3 tbsp chopped
    fresh parsley
45ml/3 tbsp chopped fresh
    coriander (cilantro) leaves
450g/1lb quick-cook couscous

1 Sprinkle the saffron into the boiling water in a bowl and set this aside to soak.

2 Place the oil in a large microwave-proof bowl. Add the onion, garlic and chillies. Microwave on HIGH for 2 minutes, stirring halfway through cooking.

3 Add the ground ginger and cinnamon and microwave on HIGH for 1 minute.

4 Stir in the tomatoes, stock or water, the saffron and liquid, carrots, turnips, sweet potatoes and raisins. Cover and microwave on HIGH for 15 minutes, stirring twice during cooking.

5 Add the courgettes, chickpeas, parsley and coriander, cover and microwave on HIGH for 5–8 minutes, stirring once, until the vegetables are tender.

6 Meanwhile, prepare the couscous following the packet instructions and serve it with the vegetables.

Spicy Vegetable Couscous

The cuisine of Morocco and Tunisia has many wonderful dishes using the wheat grain couscous, which is steamed over simmering spicy stews. Bulked out with potatoes, this makes a nutritious and filling main course.

Serves 4–6

450g/1lb couscous grains
60ml/4 tbsp olive oil
1 onion, cut in chunks
2 carrots, cut in thick slices
4 baby turnips, halved
8 small new potatoes, halved
1 green (bell) pepper, cut
    into chunks

115g/4oz green beans, halved
1 small fennel bulb,
    sliced thickly
2.5cm/1in cube fresh root
    ginger, grated
2 garlic cloves, crushed
5ml/1 tsp ground turmeric
15ml/1 tbsp ground coriander
5ml/1 tsp cumin seeds
5ml/1 tsp ground cinnamon
45ml/3 tbsp red lentils
1 x 400g/14oz can
    chopped tomatoes
1 litre/1¾ pints/4½ cups stock
60ml/4 tbsp raisins
rind and juice of 1 lemon
salt and ground black pepper
harissa paste, to serve (optional)

1 Cover the couscous with cold water and soak for 10 minutes. Drain and spread out on a tray for 20 minutes, stirring it occasionally with your fingers.

2 Meanwhile, in a large pan, heat the oil and fry the vegetables for about 10 minutes, stirring from time to time. Add the ginger, garlic and spices, stir well and cook for 2 minutes. Pour in the lentils, tomatoes, stock and raisins, and add seasoning.

3 Bring to a boil, then turn down to a simmer. By this time the couscous should be ready for steaming. Place in a steamer and fit this on top of the stew.

4 Cover and steam gently for about 20 minutes. The grains should be swollen and soft. Fork through and season well. Spoon into a serving dish.

5 Add the lemon rind and juice to the stew and check the seasoning. If you like, add harissa paste to taste. Spoon the couscous on to a plate and ladle the stew on top.

Spicy Couscous Energy 225kcal/948kJ; Protein 22.5g; Carbohydrate 16.5g, of which sugars 8g; Fat 8.3g, of which saturates 1.2g; Cholesterol 15mg; Calcium 67mg; Fibre 4.4g; Sodium 345mg.
Sweet Couscous Energy 300kcal/1261kJ; Protein 31.3g; Carbohydrate 24.1g, of which sugars 10.9g; Fat 9.4g, of which saturates 1.5g; Cholesterol 70mg; Calcium 88mg; Fibre 7.2g; Sodium 600mg.

Turnip and Sweet Potato Cobbler

This tasty and attractive dish is ideal as a midweek meal for the whole family. Use a star-shape cutter to create the attractive savoury scone topping.

Serves 4–6

1 onion, sliced
2 carrots, chopped
3 medium size turnips, chopped
1 small sweet potato or swede (rutabaga), chopped
2 celery sticks, sliced thinly
45ml/3 tbsp sunflower oil
2.5ml/½ tsp ground coriander
2.5ml/½ tsp dried mixed herbs
1 x 425g/15oz can chopped tomatoes
1 x 400g/14oz can chickpeas
1 vegetable stock (bouillon) cube
salt and ground black pepper

For the topping

225g/8oz/2 cups self-raising (self-rising) flour
5ml/1 tsp baking powder
50g/2oz/4 tbsp margarine
45ml/3 tbsp sunflower seeds
30ml/2 tbsp Parmesan cheese, grated
150ml/¼ pint/⅔ cup milk

1 Heat the oil in a large, heavy frying pan and cook all the vegetables for about 10 minutes until they are soft. Add the coriander, herbs, tomatoes, chickpeas with their liquor and stock cube. Season well and simmer for 20 minutes.

2 Pour all the cooked vegetables into a shallow casserole dish while you make the topping. Preheat the oven to 190°C/375°F/Gas 5.

3 Mix together the flour and baking powder, then rub in the margarine until it resembles fine crumbs. Stir in the sunflower seeds and Parmesan cheese. Add the milk and mix to a firm dough.

4 Lightly roll out the topping on a floured surface to a thickness of 1cm/½in and stamp out star shapes or rounds, or simply cut it into small squares.

5 Place the shapes on top of the vegetable mixture in the casserole and brush with a little extra milk. Bake in the oven for 12–15 minutes until the topping is risen and golden brown. Serve hot with green, leafy vegetables.

Sweet Potato Roulade

Sweet potato works particularly well as the base for this roulade. Serve in thin slices for a truly impressive dinner party dish.

Serves 6

225g/8oz/1 cup low-fat soft cheese
75ml/5 tbsp low-fat natural (plain) yogurt
6–8 spring onions (scallions), finely sliced
30ml/2 tbsp chopped brazil nuts, roasted
450g/1lb sweet potatoes, peeled and cubed
12 allspice berries, crushed
4 eggs, separated
50g/2oz/¼ cup Edam cheese, finely grated
salt and ground black pepper
15ml/1 tbsp sesame seeds

1 Preheat the oven to 200°C/400°F/ Gas 6. Grease and line a 33 × 25cm/13 × 10in Swiss roll tin (jelly roll pan) with baking parchment, snipping the corners with scissors to fit.

2 In a small bowl, mix together the soft cheese, yogurt, spring onions and brazil nuts. Set aside.

3 Boil or steam the sweet potato until tender. Drain well. Place in a food processor with the allspice and blend until smooth. Spoon into a bowl and stir in the egg yolks and Edam. Season to taste with salt and pepper.

4 Whisk the egg whites until stiff but not dry. Fold ⅓ of the egg whites into the sweet potatoes to lighten the mixture before gently folding in the rest.

5 Pour into the prepared tin, tipping it to get the mixture right into the corners. Smooth gently with a palette knife and cook in the oven for 10–15 minutes.

6 Meanwhile, lay a large sheet of baking parchment on a clean dish towel and sprinkle with the sesame seeds. When the roulade is cooked, transfer it on to the paper, trim the edges and roll it up. Leave to cool. When cool, carefully unroll, spread with the filling and roll up again. Cut into slices to serve.

Turnip Cobbler Energy 449kcal/1885kJ; Protein 13.9g; Carbohydrate 55.8g, of which sugars 9.9g; Fat 20.5g, of which saturates 2.7g; Cholesterol 6mg; Calcium 217mg; Fibre 7.2g; Sodium 319mg.
Sweet Potato Roulade Energy 250kcal/1045kJ; Protein 14.8g; Carbohydrate 18.7g, of which sugars 6.9g; Fat 14g, of which saturates 5.5g; Cholesterol 143mg; Calcium 195mg; Fibre 2.4g; Sodium 336mg.

Sweet Potatoes with Gorgonzola

The contrast of colours in this dish looks stunning and the mixture of flavours tastes wonderful with the sharp, spicy tones of the cheese mingling deliciously with the sweet potato.

Serves 4
4 large sweet potatoes, scrubbed
30ml/2 tbsp olive oil
2 large leeks, washed and sliced
115g/4oz Gorgonzola cheese, thinly sliced
salt and ground black pepper

1 Preheat the oven to 190°C/375°F/Gas 5. Dry the sweet potatoes with kitchen paper and rub them all over with about 15ml/1 tbsp of the oil. Place them on a baking sheet and sprinkle with salt. Bake in the oven for about 45 minutes to 1 hour, or until tender.

2 Meanwhile, heat the remaining oil in a frying pan and add the sliced leeks. Cook for 3–4 minutes, or until softened and just beginning to turn golden.

3 Cut the potatoes in half lengthways and place them cut side up on the baking sheet. Top with the cooked leeks and season.

4 Lay the cheese slices on top and grill (broil) under a hot grill (broiler) for 2–3 minutes, until bubbling. Serve immediately.

Cook's Tip
Ensure that the potatoes are completely cooked by inserting a sharp knife or a metal skewer into the centre of the potato.

Variations
• Use other cheeses if you like. Mature (sharp) Cheddar would work well, or go for another blue cheese, such as Stilton or Dolcelatte, if you prefer.
• The sweetness of the potato is key to the success of this recipe, but delicately flavoured chunks of sweet pumpkin or butternut squash would work just as well.

Aubergine and Sweet Potato Stew

Inspired by Thai cooking, this aubergine and sweet potato stew cooked in a coconut sauce is scented with fragrant lemon grass, ginger and lots of garlic.

Serves 6
60ml/4 tbsp groundnut (peanut) oil
2 aubergines (eggplants), cut into chunks
225g/8oz Thai red shallots or other shallots
5ml/1 tsp fennel seeds, lightly crushed
4–5 garlic cloves, thinly sliced
25ml/1½ tbsp finely chopped fresh root ginger
475ml/16fl oz/2 cups vegetable stock
2 stems lemon grass, outer layers discarded, finely chopped
15g/½oz fresh coriander (cilantro), stalks and leaves chopped separately
3 kaffir lime leaves, lightly bruised
2–3 small red chillies
45–60ml/3–4 tbsp Thai green curry paste
675g/1½lb sweet potatoes, cut into thick chunks
400ml/14fl oz/1⅔ cups coconut milk
2.5–5ml/½–1 tsp light muscovado (brown) sugar
250g/9oz mushrooms, sliced
juice of 1 lime, to taste
salt and ground black pepper
18 fresh Thai basil leaves or ordinary basil, to garnish

1 Heat half the oil in a lidded frying pan. Add the aubergines and cook over a medium heat, stirring occasionally, until lightly browned on all sides. Remove from the pan and set aside.

2 Slice 4–5 of the shallots and set aside. Fry the remaining whole shallots in the pan, adding more oil if necessary, until browned. Set aside. Add the remaining oil to the pan and cook the sliced shallots, fennel, garlic and ginger until soft but not browned. Add the vegetable stock, lemon grass, coriander stalks, lime leaves and whole chillies. Cover and simmer for 5 minutes.

3 Stir in 30ml/2 tbsp of the curry paste and the sweet potatoes. Simmer for 10 minutes, return the aubergines and shallots to the pan and cook for a further 5 minutes. Stir in the coconut milk and sugar. Season to taste, then add the mushrooms and simmer for 5 minutes. Stir in more curry paste and lime juice to taste, followed by the chopped coriander leaves. Sprinkle with basil and serve.

Baked Sweet Potatoes Energy 338kcal/1425kJ; Protein 9.5g; Carbohydrate 44.8g, of which sugars 13.1g; Fat 14.8g, of which saturates 6.6g; Cholesterol 22mg; Calcium 206mg; Fibre 6.5g; Sodium 432mg.
Aubergine Stew Energy 234kcal/986kJ; Protein 3.5g; Carbohydrate 30.1g, of which sugars 12.3g; Fat 12.1g, of which saturates 2.3g; Cholesterol 0mg; Calcium 65mg; Fibre 5g; Sodium 126mg.

Sweet Potato and Pumpkin Curry

A hearty, soothing curry that is perfect for autumn or winter evenings. The cheerful colour of the sweet potato alone will brighten you up – and it tastes terrific.

Serves 4

30ml/2 tbsp vegetable oil
4 garlic cloves, crushed
4 shallots, finely chopped
30ml/2 tbsp yellow
 curry paste
600ml/1 pint/2½ cups
 vegetable stock
2 kaffir lime leaves, torn
15ml/1 tbsp chopped
 fresh galangal
450g/1lb pumpkin, peeled,
 seeded and diced
225g/8oz sweet potatoes, diced
90g/3½oz/scant 1 cup peanuts,
 roasted and chopped
300ml/½ pint/1¼ cups
 coconut milk
90g/3½oz/1½ cups chestnut
 mushrooms, sliced
15ml/1 tbsp soy sauce
30ml/2 tbsp mushroom ketchup
50g/2oz/⅓ cup pumpkin seeds,
 toasted, and fresh green chilli
 flowers, to garnish

1 Heat the oil in a large pan. Add the garlic and shallots and cook over a medium heat, stirring occasionally, for 10 minutes, until softened and golden. Do not let them burn.

2 Add the yellow curry paste and stir-fry over a medium heat for 30 seconds, until fragrant, then add the stock, lime leaves, galangal, pumpkin and sweet potatoes. Bring to the boil, stirring frequently, then reduce the heat to low and simmer gently for 15 minutes.

3 Add the peanuts, coconut milk and mushrooms to the pan. Stir in the soy sauce and mushroom ketchup and simmer for 5 minutes more. Spoon into warmed individual serving bowls, garnish with the pumpkin seeds and chillies and serve.

Cook's Tip
The well-drained vegetables from any of these curries would make a very tasty filling to be used in a pastry or pie. This may not be the most Eastern tradition, but it is a good example of modern fusion food.

Mixed Vegetables in Coconut Sauce

A vegetable dish is an essential part of an Indian meal, even for a simple occasion, where one or two vegetable dishes may be served with a lentil dhal, a raita, and bread or boiled rice. There are many ways to make a vegetable curry, but this recipe, in which the potatoes and other vegetables are simmered in coconut milk, is typical of South India.

Serves 4

225g/8oz potatoes, cut into
 5cm/2in cubes
115g/4oz green beans
150g/5oz carrots, scraped and
 cut into 5cm/2in cubes
500ml/17fl oz/2¼ cups
 hot water
1 small aubergine (eggplant),
 about 225g/8oz, quartered
 lengthways
75g/3oz coconut milk powder
5ml/1 tsp salt
30ml/2 tbsp vegetable oil
6–8 fresh or 8–10 curry leaves
1 or 2 dried red chillies,
 chopped into small pieces
5ml/1 tsp ground cumin
5ml/1 tsp ground coriander
2.5ml/½ tsp ground turmeric
rice, dhal or Indian bread, to serve

1 Put the cubed potatoes, green beans and carrots in a large pan, add 300ml/½ pint/1¼ cups of the hot water and bring to the boil. Reduce the heat a little, cover the pan and continue to cook for 5 minutes.

2 Cut the aubergine quarters into 5cm/2in pieces. Rinse and then add to the pan.

3 Blend the coconut milk powder with the remaining hot water and add to the vegetables, with the salt. Bring to a slow simmer, cover and cook for 6–7 minutes.

4 In a small pan, heat the oil over a medium heat and add the curry leaves and the dried red chillies. Immediately follow with the ground cumin, coriander and turmeric.

5 Stir-fry the spices together for 15–20 seconds and pour the entire contents of the pan over the vegetables. Stir to distribute the spices evenly and remove the pan from the heat. Serve the mixed vegetables with rice, dhal or any Indian bread.

Pumpkin Curry Energy 337kcal/1404kJ; Protein 10.3g; Carbohydrate 21.7g, of which sugars 10.8g; Fat 23.8g, of which saturates 4g; Cholesterol 0mg; Calcium 168mg; Fibre 5.1g; Sodium 554mg.
Mixed Vegetables Energy 80kcal/335kJ; Protein 1.2g; Carbohydrate 5.6g, of which sugars 5.3g; Fat 6.1g, of which saturates 0.9g; Cholesterol 0mg; Calcium 29mg; Fibre 2.3g; Sodium 71mg.

Potato Curry with Yogurt

Variations of this simple Indian potato curry are popular in Singapore, where fusion dishes like this one cater for a community that includes people from all over Asia, as well as from Europe and the Americas.

Serves 4

6 garlic cloves, chopped
25g/1oz fresh root ginger, peeled and chopped
30ml/2 tbsp ghee, or 15ml/1 tbsp oil and 15g/1/2oz/1 tbsp butter
6 shallots, halved lengthways and sliced along the grain
2 fresh green chillies, seeded and finely sliced
10ml/2 tsp sugar
a handful of fresh or dried curry leaves
2 cinnamon sticks
5–10ml/1–2 tsp ground turmeric
15ml/1 tbsp garam masala
500g/1 1/4lb waxy potatoes, cut into bitesize pieces
2 tomatoes, peeled, seeded and quartered
250ml/8fl oz/1 cup Greek (US strained plain) yogurt
salt and ground black pepper
5ml/1 tsp red chilli powder, and fresh coriander (cilantro) and mint leaves, finely chopped, to garnish
1 lemon, quartered, to serve

1 Using a mortar and pestle or a food processor, grind the garlic and ginger to a coarse paste. Heat the ghee in a heavy pan and stir in the shallots and chillies, until soft and fragrant.

2 Add the garlic and ginger paste with the sugar, and stir until the mixture begins to colour. Stir in the curry leaves, cinnamon sticks, turmeric and garam masala, and toss in the cubed potatoes, making sure that they are thoroughly coated in the ground spice mixture.

3 Pour in just enough cold water to cover the potatoes. Bring to the boil, then reduce the heat and simmer until the potatoes are just cooked – they should still have a bite to them.

4 Season with salt and ground black pepper to taste. Gently toss in the tomatoes to heat them through. Fold in the yogurt so that it is streaky. Sprinkle with the chilli powder, coriander and mint. Serve immediately from the pan, with lemon to squeeze over.

Potato and Cauliflower Curry

This is a hot and spicy vegetable curry, loaded with potatoes, cauliflower and broad beans, and is especially tasty when served with cooked rice, a few poppadums and a cooling cucumber raita.

Serves 4

2 garlic cloves, chopped
2.5cm/1in piece fresh root ginger
1 fresh green chilli, seeded and chopped
30ml/2 tbsp oil
1 onion, sliced
1 large potato, chopped
15ml/1 tbsp curry powder, mild or hot
1 cauliflower, cut into small florets
600ml/1 pint/2 1/2 cups vegetable stock
275g/10oz can broad (fava) beans
juice of 1/2 lemon (optional)
salt and ground black pepper
fresh coriander (cilantro) sprig, to garnish
plain rice, to serve

1 Blend the chopped garlic, ginger, chopped chilli with 15ml/ 1 tbsp of the oil in a food processor or blender until the mixture forms a smooth paste.

2 In a large, heavy pan, fry the sliced onion and chopped potato in the remaining oil for 5 minutes, until the onion is soft and the potato is starting to brown, then stir in the spice paste and curry powder. Cook for another minute.

3 Add the cauliflower florets to the onion and potato and stir well until they are thoroughly combined with the spicy mixture, then pour in the stock and bring to the boil over medium to high heat.

4 Season well, cover and simmer for 10 minutes. Add the beans with the liquid from the can and cook, uncovered, for a further 10 minutes.

5 Check the seasoning and adjust if necessary. Add a good squeeze of lemon juice and give the curry a final stir.

6 Serve immediately, on preheated plates, garnished with fresh coriander sprigs and accompanied by plain boiled rice.

Potato Curry Energy 231kcal/967kJ; Protein 6.7g; Carbohydrate 26.2g, of which sugars 7.4g; Fat 12.4g, of which saturates 4.1g; Cholesterol 0mg; Calcium 110mg; Fibre 2g; Sodium 63mg.
Broad Bean Curry Energy 194kcal/813kJ; Protein 11.5g; Carbohydrate 20.9g, of which sugars 4.8g; Fat 7.7g, of which saturates 1g; Cholesterol 0mg; Calcium 96mg; Fibre 8.1g; Sodium 40mg.

Black-eyed Bean and Potato Curry

Nutty-flavoured black-eyed beans make a nutritious supper dish, especially when mixed with potatoes. This hot and spicy combination will be ideal for an autumn or winter evening.

Serves 4–6
2 potatoes
225g/8oz/1¼ cups black-eyed beans (peas), soaked overnight and drained
1.5ml/¼ tsp bicarbonate of soda (baking soda)
5ml/1 tsp five-spice powder
1.5ml/¼ tsp asafoetida
2 onions, finely chopped
2.5cm/1in piece fresh root ginger, crushed
a few fresh mint leaves
450ml/¾ pint/scant 2 cups water
60ml/4 tbsp vegetable oil
2.5ml/½ tsp each ground cumin, ground coriander, ground turmeric and chilli powder
4 fresh green chillies, chopped
75ml/5 tbsp tamarind juice
115g/4oz/4 cups fresh coriander (cilantro), chopped
2 firm tomatoes, chopped
salt

1 Cut the potatoes into cubes and boil in lightly salted water until tender.

2 Place the drained black-eyed beans in a heavy pan and add the bicarbonate of soda, five-spice powder and asafoetida. Add the chopped onions, crushed root ginger, mint leaves and the measured water. Simmer until the beans are soft. Remove any excess water and reserve.

3 Heat the oil in a frying pan. Gently fry the ground cumin and coriander, the turmeric and chilli powder with the green chillies and tamarind juice, until they are well blended and releasing their fragrances.

4 Pour the spice mixture over the black-eyed beans and mix well.

5 Add the potatoes, fresh coriander, tomatoes and salt. Mix well, and, if necessary, thin with a little reserved water. Reheat and serve.

Vegetable and Coconut Milk Curry

Fragrant jasmine rice is the perfect accompaniment for this spicy and flavoursome vegetable curry.

Serves 4
10ml/2 tsp vegetable oil
400ml/14fl oz/1⅔ cups coconut milk
300ml/½ pint/1¼ cups vegetable stock
225g/8oz new potatoes, halved
8 baby corn cobs
5ml/1 tsp sugar
185g/6½oz/1¼ cups broccoli florets
1 red (bell) pepper, seeded and sliced lengthways
115g/4oz spinach, tough stalks removed, leaves shredded
30ml/2 tbsp chopped fresh coriander (cilantro)
salt and ground black pepper
cooked fragrant jasmine rice, to serve

For the spice paste
1 fresh red chilli, seeded and chopped
3 fresh green chillies, seeded and chopped
1 lemon grass stalk, outer leaves removed and lower 5cm/2in finely chopped
2 shallots, chopped
finely grated rind of 1 lime
2 garlic cloves, chopped
5ml/1 tsp ground coriander
2.5ml/½ tsp ground cumin
1cm/½in piece fresh galangal, finely chopped, or 2.5ml/½ tsp dried galangal (optional)
30ml/2 tbsp chopped fresh coriander (cilantro)

1 Make the spice paste. Place all the ingredients in a food processor and process until you have a coarse paste. Heat the oil in a large, heavy pan. Add the spice paste and stir-fry for 1–2 minutes. Pour in the coconut milk and vegetable stock. Boil, then add the potatoes and simmer gently for about 15 minutes, until almost tender.

2 Add the baby corn cobs to the potatoes, season with salt and pepper to taste, then cook for 2 minutes. Stir in the sugar, broccoli and red pepper, and cook for 2 minutes more, until the vegetables are tender.

3 Stir in the shredded spinach and half the fresh coriander. Cook for 2 minutes, then spoon into a serving dish and garnish with the remaining fresh coriander. Serve immediately with the jasmine rice.

Black-eyed Bean Curry Energy 266kcal/1118kJ; Protein 11.8g; Carbohydrate 36.8g, of which sugars 8.5g; Fat 9g, of which saturates 1.1g; Cholesterol 0mg; Calcium 110mg; Fibre 8.8g; Sodium 28mg.
Vegetable Curry Energy 198kcal/827kJ; Protein 3.4g; Carbohydrate 19.2g, of which sugars 18.7g; Fat 12.6g, of which saturates 1.8g; Cholesterol 0mg; Calcium 191mg; Fibre 6.4g; Sodium 312mg.

Vegetable Korma

Here the aim is to produce a subtle, aromatic curry rather than an assault on the senses.

Serves 4

50g/2oz/¼ cup butter
2 onions, sliced
2 garlic cloves, crushed
2.5cm/1in piece fresh root ginger, grated
5ml/1 tsp ground cumin
15ml/1 tbsp ground coriander
6 cardamom pods
5cm/2in piece of cinnamon stick
5ml/1 tsp ground turmeric
1 fresh red chilli, seeded and finely chopped
1 potato, peeled and cut into 2.5cm/1in cubes
1 small aubergine (eggplant), chopped
115g/4oz/1½ cups mushrooms, thickly sliced
175ml/6fl oz/¾ cup water
115g/4oz green beans, cut into 2.5cm/1in lengths
60ml/4 tbsp natural (plain) yogurt
150ml/¼ pint/⅔ cup double (heavy) cream
5ml/1 tsp garam masala
salt and ground black pepper
fresh coriander (cilantro) sprigs, to garnish
boiled rice and poppadums, to serve

1 Melt the butter in a heavy pan. Add the onions and cook for 5 minutes until soft.

2 Add the garlic and ginger and cook for 2 minutes, then stir in the cumin, coriander, cardamom pods, cinnamon stick, turmeric and finely chopped chilli. Cook, stirring, for 1–2 minutes.

3 Add the potato cubes, aubergine and mushrooms and the water. Cover the pan, bring to the boil, then lower the heat and simmer for 15 minutes.

4 Add the beans and cook, uncovered, for 5 minutes. With a slotted spoon, remove the vegetables to a warmed serving dish and keep hot.

5 Allow the cooking liquid to bubble up until it has reduced a little. Season with salt and pepper to taste, then stir in the yogurt, double cream and garam masala. Pour the sauce over the vegetables and garnish with fresh coriander. Serve with boiled rice and poppadums.

Madras Sambal

There are many variations of this popular dish but it is regularly cooked in one form or another in almost every south-Indian home. You can use any combination of vegetables that are in season.

Serves 4

225g/8oz/1 cup tuvar dhal or red split lentils
600ml/1 pint/2½ cups water
2.5ml/½ tsp ground turmeric
2 large potatoes, cut into 2.5cm/1in chunks
30ml/2 tbsp oil
2.5ml/½ tsp black mustard seeds
1.5ml/¼ tsp fenugreek seeds
4 curry leaves
1 onion, thinly sliced
115g/4oz green beans, cut into 2.5cm/1in lengths
5ml/1 tsp salt
2.5ml/½ tsp chilli powder
15ml/1 tbsp lemon juice
toasted coconut, to garnish
fresh coriander relish, to serve

1 Wash the tuvar dhal or lentils in several changes of water. Place in a heavy pan with the measured water and the turmeric. Bring to the boil, then reduce the heat, cover the pan with a tight-fitting lid and simmer for 30–35 minutes until the lentils are soft.

2 Par-boil the potatoes in a large pan of boiling water for 10 minutes. Drain well and set aside.

3 Heat the oil in a large frying pan and fry the mustard and fenugreek seeds and the curry leaves for 2–3 minutes until the seeds begin to splutter.

4 Add the sliced onion and the green beans to the pan and stir-fry for around 7–8 minutes. Add the par-boiled potatoes to the pan and cook for a further 2 minutes.

5 Drain the lentils. Stir them into the spiced potato mixture with the salt, chilli powder and lemon juice. Simmer for around 2 minutes or until everything is heated through. Garnish with the toasted coconut and serve with a freshly made coriander relish.

Vegetable Korma Energy 381kcal/1577kJ; Protein 5.1g; Carbohydrate 20.9g, of which sugars 9.9g; Fat 31.4g, of which saturates 19.3g; Cholesterol 78mg; Calcium 95mg; Fibre 3.9g; Sodium 108mg.
Madras Sambal Energy 401kcal/1687kJ; Protein 16.7g; Carbohydrate 50.8g, of which sugars 5.1g; Fat 16g, of which saturates 8.9g; Cholesterol 0mg; Calcium 52mg; Fibre 6.7g; Sodium 36mg.

Karahi Potatoes with Whole Spices

The potato is transformed into something quite exotic when it is cooked like this.

Serves 4

15ml/1 tbsp oil
5ml/1 tsp cumin seeds
3 curry leaves
5ml/1 tsp crushed dried red chillies
2.5ml/½ tsp mixed onion, mustard and fenugreek seeds

2.5ml/½ tsp fennel seeds
3 garlic cloves, sliced
2.5cm/1in piece fresh root ginger, grated
2 onions, sliced
6 new potatoes, thinly sliced
15ml/1 tbsp chopped fresh coriander (cilantro)
1 fresh red chilli, seeded and sliced
1 fresh green chilli, seeded and sliced

1 Heat the oil in a karahi, wok or heavy pan. Lower the heat slightly and add the cumin seeds, curry leaves, dried red chillies, mixed onion, mustard and fenugreek seeds, fennel seeds, garlic slices and ginger. Fry for 1 minute.

2 Add the onions and fry for a further 5 minutes, or until the onions are golden brown.

3 Add the potatoes, fresh coriander and sliced fresh red and green chillies and mix well. Cover the pan tightly with a lid or foil; if using foil, make sure that it does not touch the food. Cook over a very low heat for about 7 minutes or until the potatoes are tender.

4 Remove the pan from the heat, and take off the lid or foil cover. Serve hot straight from the pan.

Cook's Tip
Try and choose a waxy variety of new potato for this fairly spicy vegetable dish; if you use a very soft potato, it will crumble and not be possible to cut it into thin slices without it breaking up. Suitable varieties are often labelled 'salad potatoes' when sold at supermarkets. Leave the skin on for an even tastier result.

Indian Mee Goreng

This is a truly international noodle dish combining Indian, Chinese and Western ingredients. It is a delicious treat for lunch or supper, or any time of day.

Serves 4

450g/1lb fresh yellow egg noodles
60–90ml/4–6 tbsp vegetable oil
115g/4oz fried tofu or 150g/5oz firm tofu
2 eggs

30ml/2 tbsp water
salt and ground black pepper
1 onion, sliced
1 garlic clove, crushed
15ml/1 tbsp light soy sauce
30–45ml/2–3 tbsp tomato ketchup
15ml/1 tbsp chilli sauce
1 large cooked potato, evenly diced
4 spring onions (scallions), shredded
1–2 fresh green chillies, seeded and thinly sliced (optional)

1 Bring a large pan of water to the boil, add the fresh egg noodles and cook for just 2 minutes. Drain the noodles, rinse under cold water, drain again and set aside.

2 If using fried tofu, cut each cube in half, refresh it in a pan of boiling water, then drain well and set aside. Heat 30ml/ 2 tbsp of the oil in a large frying pan. If using plain tofu, cube it, fry until brown, then set aside.

3 Beat the eggs with 30ml/2 tbsp water and seasoning. Add to the frying pan and cook, without stirring, until set. Flip over, cook the other side, then slide it out of the pan, roll up and slice thinly.

4 Heat the remaining oil in a wok and fry the onion and garlic for 2–3 minutes. Add the drained noodles, soy sauce, ketchup and chilli sauce. Toss well over medium heat for 2 minutes, then add the diced potato. Reserve a few spring onion shreds for garnish and stir the rest into the noodles with the chilli, if using, and the tofu.

5 When hot, stir in the omelette slices. Serve on a hot platter, garnished with the remaining spring onion.

Karahi Potatoes Energy 152kcal/641kJ; Protein 3.8g; Carbohydrate 27.5g, of which sugars 6g; Fat 3.9g, of which saturates 0.5g; Cholesterol 0mg; Calcium 46mg; Fibre 2.6g; Sodium 19mg.
Mee Goreng Energy 478kcal/2010kJ; Protein 16.8g; Carbohydrate 64.2g, of which sugars 5.1g; Fat 18.9g, of which saturates 3.2g; Cholesterol 86mg; Calcium 323mg; Fibre 2.9g; Sodium 466mg.

Potatoes in a Fiery Red Sauce

This piquant potato dish should be hot and sour but, if you prefer a little less fire, you can reduce the chillies and add extra tomato purée instead. Likewise if you like your food with a kick, you can increase the number of dried chillies used.

Serves 4 to 6
450g/1lb small new potatoes, washed and dried
25g/1oz whole dried red chillies, preferably kashmiri
5ml/1½ tsp cumin seeds
4 garlic cloves
90ml/6 tbsp vegetable oil
60ml/4 tbsp thick tamarind juice
30ml/2 tbsp tomato purée (paste)
4 curry leaves
5ml/1 tsp sugar
1.5ml/¼ tsp asafoetida
salt
coriander (cilantro) leaves and lemon wedges, to garnish

1 Put the potatoes in a large pan. Add water to cover and bring to the boil. Add salt, then simmer for about 15 minutes, or until the potatoes are tender, but do not let them get too soft. To test, insert a thin sharp knife into the potatoes. It should slip off cleanly when the potatoes are fully cooked through. Drain thoroughly and leave to cool.

2 Soak the chillies for 5 minutes in a bowl of warm water. Drain well and grind them with the cumin seeds and garlic cloves to a coarse paste using a mortar and pestle. Alternatively, purée the ingredients in a blender or food processor.

3 Fry the paste, tamarind juice, tomato purée, curry leaves, salt, sugar and asafoetida until the oil separates. Add the potatoes. Reduce the heat, cover and simmer for about 10 minutes. Garnish with coriander and lemon wedges and serve immediately.

Cook's Tip
Asafoetida is a pungent spice and can seem overpowering in its raw state, but once it has been added to a dish and cooked, it imparts a deep oniony flavour.

Mung Beans with Potatoes

Small mung beans are one of the quicker-cooking pulses. They do not require soaking and are easy and convenient to use. In this recipe they are cooked with potatoes and Indian spices to give a tasty and nutritious dish.

Serves 4
175g/6oz/1 cup mung beans
750ml/1¼ pints/3 cups water
225g/8oz potatoes, cut into 2cm/¾in chunks
30ml/2 tbsp oil
2.5ml/½ tsp cumin seeds
1 fresh green chilli, finely chopped
1 garlic clove, crushed
2.5cm/1in piece fresh root ginger, finely chopped
1.5ml/¼ tsp ground turmeric
2.5ml/½ tsp chilli powder
5ml/1 tsp salt
5ml/1 tsp sugar
4 curry leaves
5 tomatoes, peeled and finely chopped
15ml/1 tbsp tomato purée (paste)
curry leaves, to garnish
plain rice, to serve

1 Wash the beans. Pour the water into a pan, add the beans and bring to the boil. Boil hard for 15 minutes, then reduce the heat, cover the pan and simmer until soft, about 30 minutes cooking time. Drain.

2 In a separate pan, par-boil the chunks of potato in boiling water for about 10 minutes, until just tender, then drain well and put aside.

3 Heat the oil in a heavy pan and fry the cumin seeds until they splutter. Add the chilli, garlic and ginger, and fry for 3–4 minutes.

4 Add the turmeric, chilli powder, salt and sugar, and cook for 2 minutes, stirring to prevent the mixture from sticking to the pan.

5 Add the four curry leaves, chopped tomatoes and tomato purée, and simmer for about 5 minutes until the sauce has thickened. Mix the tomato sauce and the potatoes with the mung beans and heat through. Garnish with the extra curry leaves and serve with plain boiled rice.

Mung Beans Energy 265kcal/1118kJ; Protein 13.8g; Carbohydrate 37.4g, of which sugars 5.7g; Fat 7.9g, of which saturates 1.1g; Cholesterol 0mg; Calcium 58mg; Fibre 5.8g; Sodium 34mg.
Potatoes in a Fiery Sauce Energy 156kcal/650kJ; Protein 1.7g; Carbohydrate 12.8g, of which sugars 1.7g; Fat 11.3g, of which saturates 1.4g; Cholesterol 0mg; Calcium 8mg; Fibre 0.9g; Sodium 21mg.

Stuffed Baby Vegetables

The combination of potatoes and aubergines is popular in Indian cooking.

Serves 4

12 small potatoes
8 baby aubergines (eggplants)

For the stuffing

15ml/1 tbsp sesame seeds
30ml/2 tbsp ground coriander
30ml/2 tbsp ground cumin
2.5ml/ $^1\!/_2$ tsp salt
1.5ml/ $^1\!/_4$ tsp chilli powder
2.5ml/ $^1\!/_2$ tsp ground turmeric
10ml/2 tsp sugar

1.5ml/ $^1\!/_4$ tsp garam masala
15ml/1 tbsp gram flour
2 garlic cloves, crushed
15ml/1 tbsp lemon juice
30ml/2 tbsp chopped fresh
   coriander (cilantro)

For the sauce

15ml/1 tbsp oil
2.5ml/ $^1\!/_2$ tsp black
   mustard seeds
400g/14oz can
   chopped tomatoes
30ml/2 tbsp chopped fresh
   coriander (cilantro)
150ml/ $^1\!/_4$ pint/ $^2\!/_3$ cup water

1 Preheat the oven to 200°C/400°F/Gas 6. Make deep slits in the potatoes and aubergines to hold the stuffing, ensuring that you do not cut right through.

2 Mix all the ingredients for the stuffing together in a large mixing bowl.

3 Carefully spoon the spicy stuffing mixture into each of the slits in the potatoes and aubergines.

4 Arrange the stuffed potatoes and aubergines in a greased ovenproof dish, filling side up.

5 For the sauce, heat the oil in a heavy pan and fry the mustard seeds for 2 minutes until they begin to splutter, then add the canned tomatoes, chopped coriander and any leftover stuffing. Stir in the water. Bring to the boil and simmer for 5 minutes until the sauce thickens.

6 Pour the tomato sauce over the potatoes and aubergines. Cover and bake in the oven for 25–30 minutes until the potatoes and aubergines are soft.

Lentils and Rice with Potatoes

Here, lentils are cooked with whole and ground spices, potato, rice and onion to produce a tasty and nutritious meal.

Serves 4

150g/5oz/ $^3\!/_4$ cup tuvar dhal or
   red split lentils

115g/4oz/ $^1\!/_2$ cup basmati rice
1 large potato
1 large onion
30ml/2 tbsp oil
4 whole cloves
1.5ml/ $^1\!/_4$ tsp cumin seeds
1.5ml/ $^1\!/_4$ tsp ground turmeric
10ml/2 tsp salt
300ml/ $^1\!/_2$ pint/1 $^1\!/_4$ cups water

1 Wash the tuvar dhal or red split lentils and rice in several changes of cold water. Put into a bowl and cover with water. Leave to soak for 15 minutes, then transfer to a strainer and drain well.

2 Peel the potato, then cut it into 2.5cm/1in chunks. Using a sharp knife, thinly slice the onion and set aside for later.

3 Heat the oil in a heavy pan and fry the cloves and cumin seeds for 2 minutes until the seeds are beginning to splutter.

4 Add the onion and potato chunks and fry for 5 minutes. Stir in the lentils, rice, turmeric and salt and cook for a further 3 minutes.

5 Add the water. Bring to the boil, cover and simmer gently for 15–20 minutes until all the water has been absorbed and the potato chunks are tender. Leave to stand, covered, for about 10 minutes before serving.

> **Cook's Tip**
> Red split lentils are very economical and are widely available in most supermarkets. Before cooking they are salmon-coloured and they turn a pale, dull yellow during cooking. They have a mild, pleasant, nutty flavour. Soaking them in water overnight rehydrates the lentils and speeds up the cooking process but is not strictly necessary.

Stuffed Baby Vegetables Energy 222kcal/938kJ; Protein 6.5g; Carbohydrate 35.3g, of which sugars 6.6g; Fat 7.3g, of which saturates 1.2g; Cholesterol 0mg; Calcium 72mg; Fibre 4.4g; Sodium 31mg.
Lentils and Rice Energy 364kcal/1529kJ; Protein 13.3g; Carbohydrate 57.8g, of which sugars 4.4g; Fat 9.8g, of which saturates 1.4g; Cholesterol 0mg; Calcium 49mg; Fibre 3g; Sodium 22mg.

Malay Vegetable Curry with Cumin and Turmeric

Originally from southern India, this delicious spicy dish is substantial and flexible – although delicious with sweet potato, feel free to choose your own assortment of vegetables, such as pumpkin, butternut squash, winter melon, yams, aubergines or beans.

Serves 4

2–3 green chillies, seeded and chopped
25g/1oz fresh root ginger, peeled and chopped
5–10ml/1–2 tsp roasted cumin seeds
10ml/2 tsp sugar
5–10ml/1–2 tsp ground turmeric
1 cinnamon stick
5ml/1 tsp salt
2 carrots, cut into bitesize sticks
2 sweet potatoes, cut into bitesize sticks
2 courgettes (zucchini), partially peeled in strips, seeded and cut into bitesize sticks
1 green plantain, peeled and cut into bitesize sticks
small coil of long (snake) beans or a handful of green beans, cut into bitesize sticks
handful fresh curry leaves
1 fresh coconut, grated
250ml/8fl oz/1 cup natural (plain) yogurt
salt and ground black pepper

1 Using a mortar and pestle or a food processor, grind the chillies, ginger, roasted cumin seeds and sugar to a paste.

2 In a heavy pan, bring 450ml/15fl oz/scant 2 cups water to the boil. Stir in the turmeric, cinnamon stick and salt. Add the carrots and cook for 1 minute. Add the sweet potatoes and cook for 2 minutes. Add the courgettes, plantain and beans and cook for a further 2 minutes. Reduce the heat, stir in the spice paste and curry leaves, and cook gently for 4–5 minutes, or until the vegetables are tender but not soft and mushy, and the liquid has greatly reduced.

3 Gently stir in half the coconut. Take the pan off the heat and fold in the yogurt. Season to taste with salt and pepper. Quickly roast the remaining coconut in a heavy pan over a high heat, until nicely browned. Sprinkle a little over the vegetables, and serve the rest separately.

Cauliflower and Potatoes Chilli-style

Cauliflower and potatoes are encrusted with Indian spices in this delicious recipe. It is a popular side dish or can be served as a main course with other dishes such as a salad, dhal or simply with Indian breads.

Serves 4

450g/1lb potatoes, cut into 2.5 cm/1 in chunks
30ml/2 tbsp oil
5ml/1 tsp cumin seeds
1 green chilli, finely chopped
450g/1lb cauliflower, broken into florets
5ml/1 tsp ground coriander
5ml/1 tsp ground cumin
1.5ml/¼ tsp chilli powder
2.5ml/½ tsp ground turmeric
2.5ml/½ tsp salt
chopped fresh coriander (cilantro), to garnish
tomato and onion salad and pickle, to serve

1 Par-boil the potatoes in a large pan of boiling water for 10 minutes. Drain well and set aside.

2 Heat the oil in a wok or large frying pan and fry the cumin seeds for about 2 minutes until they begin to splutter and release their fragrance. Add the chilli to the pan and fry, stirring constantly, for a further 1 minute.

3 Add the cauliflower florets to the pan and fry, stirring constantly, for 5 minutes.

4 Add the potatoes and the ground spices and salt and cook for 7–10 minutes, or until both the vegetables are tender.

5 Garnish with fresh coriander and serve with a tomato and onion salad and pickle.

> **Variation**
> *Try using sweet potatoes instead of ordinary potatoes for an alternative curry with a sweeter flavour. The cauliflower could also be replaced with the same amount of broccoli.*

Malay Curry Energy 419kcal/1753kJ; Protein 9.9g; Carbohydrate 47.7g, of which sugars 19.4g; Fat 23g, of which saturates 16.9g; Cholesterol 0mg; Calcium 176mg; Fibre 9g; Sodium 104mg.
Cauliflower Chilli-style Energy 181kcal/759kJ; Protein 6.7g; Carbohydrate 23.2g, of which sugars 4.3g; Fat 7.5g, of which saturates 1.1g; Cholesterol 0mg; Calcium 40mg; Fibre 3.2g; Sodium 24mg.

Chinese Potatoes with Chilli Beans

East meets West in this American-style dish with a distinctly Chinese flavour – the sauce is very tasty. Try it as a quick supper when you fancy a potato recipe with a little zing.

Serves 4

4 medium firm or waxy potatoes, cut into thick chunks
30ml/2 tbsp sunflower or groundnut (peanut) oil
3 spring onions (scallions), sliced
1 large fresh chilli, seeded and sliced
2 garlic cloves, crushed
400g/14oz can red kidney beans, drained
30ml/2 tbsp soy sauce
15ml/1 tbsp sesame oil
salt and ground black pepper
15ml/1 tbsp sesame seeds, to garnish
chopped fresh coriander (cilantro) or parsley, to garnish

1 Cook the potatoes in boiling water until they are just tender. Take care not to overcook them. Drain and reserve.

2 Heat the oil in a large frying pan or wok over a medium-high heat. Add the spring onions and chilli to the pan and stir-fry for about 1 minute, then add the garlic and stir-fry for a few seconds longer.

3 Add the potatoes, stirring well, then the beans and finally the soy sauce and sesame oil.

4 Season to taste with salt and ground black pepper and continue to cook the vegetables until they are well heated through. Sprinkle with the sesame seeds and the coriander or parsley and serve hot.

> **Cook's Tip**
> If you prefer your food with a little more heat, then simply add in an extra chopped chilli pepper. Alternatively, replace the sunflower or groundnut (peanut) oil with some oil that has been flavoured with chillies.

Curried Spinach and Potato with Mixed Chillies

This delicious spinach and potato curry, suitable for vegetarians, is mildly spiced with a warming flavour from the fresh and dried chillies.

Serves 4 to 6

60ml/4 tbsp vegetable oil
225g/8oz potato
2.5cm/1in piece fresh root ginger, crushed
4 garlic cloves, crushed
1 onion, coarsely chopped
2 green chillies, chopped
2 whole dried red chillies, coarsely broken
5ml/1 tsp cumin seeds
225g/8oz fresh spinach, trimmed, washed and chopped or 225g/8oz frozen spinach, thawed and drained
salt
2 firm tomatoes, coarsely chopped, to garnish

1 Wash the potatoes and cut into quarters. If using small new potatoes, leave them whole. Heat the oil in a frying pan and fry the potatoes until brown on all sides. Remove and set aside.

2 Remove the excess oil leaving 15ml/1 tbsp in the pan. Fry the ginger, garlic, onion, green chillies, dried chillies and cumin seeds until the onion is golden brown.

3 Add the potatoes and salt to the pan and stir well. Cover the pan and cook gently until the potatoes are tender and can be easily pierced with a sharp knife.

4 Add the spinach and stir well. Cook with the pan uncovered until the spinach is tender and all the excess fluids in the pan have evaporated. Transfer the curry to a serving plate, garnish with the chopped tomatoes and serve immediately.

> **Cook's Tip**
> India is blessed with over 18 varieties of spinach. If you have access to an Indian or Chinese grocer, look out for some of the more unusual varieties.

Curried Spinach Energy 135kcal/560kJ; Protein 3g; Carbohydrate 13.5g, of which sugars 5.9g; Fat 8g, of which saturates 1g; Cholesterol 0mg; Calcium 86mg; Fibre 2.6g; Sodium 62mg.
Chinese Potatoes Energy 272kcal/1141kJ; Protein 9.7g; Carbohydrate 34.8g, of which sugars 5.7g; Fat 11.4g, of which saturates 1.6g; Cholesterol 0mg; Calcium 107mg; Fibre 7.6g; Sodium 936mg.

Baked Jacket Potatoes

Once the potato, one of England's staple foods, is cooked in its skin in the oven it is transformed into the ultimate comfort food. The deliciously crispy skin masks a moreishly soft and fluffy interior. It can be served split and laced with butter or sour cream, or with a filling of grated cheese.

Serves 4

4 large floury potatoes of even
    size, such as King Edward
    or Maris Piper
a little oil
salt (optional)
butter or sour cream,
    to serve
chopped fresh parsley or chives,
    to serve

1 Preheat the oven to 200°C/400°F/Gas 6. Scrub and dry the potatoes, and prick the skins with a fork to prevent them bursting during cooking.

2 Rub the skins all over with a little oil and sprinkle with a little salt, if using.

3 Put the potatoes in the hot oven, either on a baking sheet or straight on to the oven shelf. Cook for about 1 hour or until soft throughout.

4 Leave the cooked potatoes to stand for 5 minutes before splitting them open. Be careful of the escaping steam.

5 Serve with a dollop of butter on top, or sour cream and a sprinkling of parsley or chives.

Cook's Tips
• Cooking potatoes in the microwave is quicker and easier, but the results will be nowhere near as good. If you have the time to prepare baked potatoes as laid out above it is well worth the effort.
• Ensure that the potatoes are completely cooked by inserting a sharp knife or a metal skewer into the centre of the potato. You will be able to tell if they need cooking a bit longer because there will be a little resistance.

Roast Potatoes

For crisp roasties with fluffy interiors, cook them in a single layer. Cooking potatoes in goose fat may seem decadent, but the results will be well worth the expense.

Serves 4

1.3kg/3lb floury potatoes
90ml/6 tbsp oil, lard, white
    cooking fat or goose fat
salt

1 Preheat the oven to 200°C/400°F/Gas 6. Peel the potatoes and cut into chunks. Boil in salted water for 5 minutes, drain, return to the pan, and shake them to roughen the surfaces.

2 Put the fat into a large roasting pan and put into the hot oven to heat the fat. Add the potatoes, coating them in the fat. Return to the oven and roast for 40–50 minutes, turning once or twice, until crisp, golden and cooked through.

Chips

Chips, or French fries, are the ultimate potato classic. Fry these twice – once to cook them, and the second time to crisp them.

Serves 4

sunflower or vegetable oil, for
    deep frying
675g/1½lb potatoes
salt

1 Heat the oil to 150°C/300°F. Peel the potatoes and cut them into chips (French fries) about 1cm/½in thick. Rinse and dry.

2 Lower a batch of chips into the hot oil and cook for about 5 minutes or until tender but not browned. Lift out on to kitchen paper and leave to cool.

3 Just before serving, increase the temperature of the oil to 190°C/375°F. Add the par-cooked chips, in batches. Cook until crisp and golden.

4 Lift out of the fryer and drain on kitchen paper. Sprinkle the cooked chips with salt and serve immediately.

Baked Jacket Potatoes Energy 182kcal/772kJ; Protein 3.8g; Carbohydrate 36.2g, of which sugars 2.9g; Fat 3.4g, of which saturates 0.6g; Cholesterol 0mg; Calcium 14mg; Fibre 2.3g; Sodium 25mg.
Roast Potatoes Energy 484kcal/2048kJ; Protein 9.4g; Carbohydrate 84.2g, of which sugars 2g; Fat 14.6g, of which saturates 5.9g; Cholesterol 13mg; Calcium 26mg; Fibre 5.9g; Sodium 29mg.
Chips Energy 403kcal/1689kJ; Protein 5.4g; Carbohydrate 51.5g, of which sugars 2.9g; Fat 14.5g, of which saturates 6.1g; Cholesterol 0mg; Calcium 19mg; Fibre 3.7g; Sodium 59mg.

Hasselback Potatoes

This dish is named after the Stockholm restaurant that created it, and is a method of cooking rather than a recipe. Choose similar-sized potatoes so that they cook uniformly, and the essential thing is to cut the potatoes most of the way, but not completely, through. It is a good idea to thread a skewer through the potato three-quarters of the way down before cutting, so that your knife travels just to the point you want it to reach and no farther.

Serves 4
4 large potatoes
75g/3oz/6 tbsp butter
45ml/3 tbsp olive oil
50g/2oz/1 cup fine fresh
  breadcrumbs
50g/2oz/²⁄₃ cup grated
  Parmesan cheese
salt and ground black pepper

1 Preheat the oven to 200°C/400°F/Gas 6. Peel the potatoes, then – and this is the crucial part – cut them widthways, not lengthways, down to three-quarters of their depth at 3mm/⅛in intervals, preferably at a slight angle.

2 Wash the potatoes in cold water, then arrange, cut sides uppermost, in a deep, ovenproof dish.

3 Melt the butter in a small pan, then add the olive oil and mix together. Brush the mixture over the potatoes, then season well with salt and black pepper. Sprinkle over the breadcrumbs and the grated cheese.

4 Roast the potatoes in the preheated oven for about 1 hour, depending on their size, until golden brown and fanned apart along the cut lines. Serve hot.

> **Cook's Tip**
> *If the potatoes are to be served as an accompaniment to a roast joint of meat, you can use the cooking juices from the meat to baste them during cooking. Don't move them around while they roast, because they won't crisp up properly.*

Griddle Potatoes

This dish makes a tasty accompaniment to grilled meat or fish.

Serves 4–6
2 onions, peeled and chopped
450–675g/1lb–1½lb whole cooked potatoes, boiled in their skins
a mixture of butter and oil, for shallow frying
salt and ground black pepper

1 Put the onions in a large pan and scald them briefly in boiling water. Refresh under cold water and drain well. Peel and slice the potatoes.

2 Put a mixture of butter and oil into a large, heavy frying pan and heat well. When the fat is hot, fry the onion until tender. Add the potato slices and brown them together, turning the potato slices to brown as evenly as possible on both sides. Transfer to a warmed serving dish and season with salt and pepper. Serve very hot.

Garlicky Roasties

Potatoes roasted in their skins retain a deep, earthy taste while the garlic mellows on cooking.

Serves 4
1kg/2¼lb small floury potatoes
60–75ml/4–5 tbsp sunflower oil
10ml/2 tsp walnut oil
2 whole garlic bulbs, unpeeled
salt

1 Preheat the oven to 240°C/475°F/Gas 9. Place the potatoes in a pan of cold water and bring to the boil. Drain.

2 Combine the oils in a roasting pan and place in the oven to get really hot. Add the potatoes and garlic and coat in oil.

3 Sprinkle with salt and roast for 10 minutes. Reduce the heat to 200°C/400°F/Gas 6. Continue roasting, basting occasionally, for 40 minutes. Serve with several cloves of garlic per portion.

Hasselback Potatoes Energy 380kcal/1593kJ; Protein 9.9g; Carbohydrate 42g, of which sugars 3.1g; Fat 20.4g, of which saturates 12.5g; Cholesterol 52mg; Calcium 182mg; Fibre 2.3g; Sodium 367mg.
Griddle Potatoes Energy 163kcal/681kJ; Protein 3.4g; Carbohydrate 26.4g, of which sugars 5g; Fat 5.5g, of which saturates 3.3g; Cholesterol 13mg; Calcium 26mg; Fibre 2.6g; Sodium 49mg.
Garlicky Roasties Energy 312kcal/1310kJ; Protein 6.2g; Carbohydrate 44.3g, of which sugars 3.7g; Fat 13.4g, of which saturates 1.7g; Cholesterol 0mg; Calcium 20mg; Fibre 3.5g; Sodium 29mg.

Chilli Fried Potatoes

These make the perfect accompaniment for eggs and bacon, and also go very well with chorizo.

Serves 4
6 fresh jalapeño chillies
60ml/4 tbsp vegetable oil
1 onion, finely chopped
450g/1lb waxy potatoes, scrubbed and cut in 1cm/½ in cubes
few sprigs of fresh oregano, chopped, plus extra sprigs, to garnish
75g/3oz/1 cup freshly grated Parmesan cheese (optional)

1 Dry roast the jalapeños in a griddle pan, turning them frequently so that the skins blacken but do not burn. Place them in a strong plastic bag and tie the top to keep the steam in. Set aside for 20 minutes.

2 Remove the jalapeños from the bag, peel off their skins and remove any stems. Cut them in half, carefully scrape out the seeds, then chop the flesh finely.

3 Meanwhile, heat half the oil in a large heavy frying pan which has a lid. Add the onion and fry, stirring occasionally, for about 3–4 minutes, until translucent, then add the potato cubes.

4 Stir to coat the potato cubes in oil, then cover the pan and cook over a moderate heat for 20–25 minutes, until the potatoes are tender. Shake the pan occasionally to stop them from sticking to the bottom.

5 When the potatoes are tender, push them to the side of the frying pan, then add the remaining oil.

6 When the oil is hot, spread out the potatoes again and add the chopped jalapeños. Cook over a high heat for 5–10 minutes, stirring carefully so that the potatoes turn golden brown all over but do not break up.

7 Add the chopped oregano, with the grated Parmesan, if using. Mix gently, spoon on to a heated serving dish and garnish with extra oregano sprigs. Serve as part of a cooked breakfast or brunch.

Oven Chip Roasties

This easy alternative to deep-fried chips (French fries) tastes just as good and is much easier to cook, as well as being healthier for you.

Serves 4–6
150ml/¼ pint/⅔ cup olive oil
4 medium to large baking potatoes
5ml/1 tsp mixed dried herbs (optional)
sea salt flakes
mayonnaise, to serve

1 Preheat the oven to the highest temperature, which is generally 240°C/475°F/Gas 9. Lightly oil a large shallow roasting pan and place it in the oven to get really hot while you prepare the potatoes.

2 Cut the potatoes in half lengthways, then into long thin wedges, or thicker ones, if you prefer. Brush each side lightly with olive oil.

3 When the oven is really hot, remove the pan carefully and sprinkle the potato wedges over it, spreading them out in a single layer over the hot oil.

4 Sprinkle the potato wedges with the herbs and salt and roast for about 20 minutes, or longer if they are thicker, until they are golden brown, crisp and lightly puffy. Remove from the oven and serve with a dollop of mayonnaise.

Cook's Tip
Oven chip roasties make great mid-week suppers served with fried eggs, mushrooms and tomatoes.

Variation
Sweet potatoes also make fine oven chips. Prepare and roast in the same way as above, although you may find they do not take as long to cook.

Chilli Potatoes Energy 186kcal/775kJ; Protein 2.5g; Carbohydrate 19.4g, of which sugars 2.4g; Fat 11.4g, of which saturates 1.4g; Cholesterol 0mg; Calcium 14mg; Fibre 1.3g; Sodium 14mg.
Oven Chip Roasties Energy 200kcal/838kJ; Protein 3.2g; Carbohydrate 28g, of which sugars 2.2g; Fat 9.1g, of which saturates 1.4g; Cholesterol 0mg; Calcium 15mg; Fibre 1.7g; Sodium 19mg.

Rosemary and Garlic New Potatoes

These new potatoes, flavoured with fresh rosemary and lots of garlic, are an ideal accompaniment to vegetable stews.

5 garlic cloves, peeled and bruised
3 sprigs of rosemary
30ml/2 tbsp olive oil
sea salt and ground black pepper

Serves 4
800g/1¾lb small new potatoes

1 Preheat the oven to 200°C/400°F/Gas 6. Put the potatoes, garlic and rosemary in a roasting pan. Drizzle with the olive oil, and toss to coat the ingredients evenly in the oil. Season well with salt and pepper.

2 Bake the potatoes in the preheated oven for about 40–45 minutes until the potatoes are crisp on the outside and soft in the centre. Remove the pan from the oven halfway through cooking and give it a shake to turn the potatoes and coat them in oil.

3 Test the potatoes are done by inserting the tip of a knife or a metal skewer into the centre of a couple of potatoes. Discard the rosemary and garlic, if you wish, and serve hot.

> **Variations**
> • Shallots can be roasted in the same way. Cook for 35 minutes or until tender. Roast a pan of shallots on their own or add a handful in with the potatoes.
> • Add a handful of sweet vine-ripened cherry tomatoes to the roasting pan before baking for a delicious Mediterranean twist.

> **Cook's Tip**
> So much can be said about the healing power of garlic. It is particularly valued for its ability to boost the immune system, helping to protect us against disease.

Kailkenny Cabbage and Potatoes

This cabbage and potato dish is ideal alongside any meat main course.

50g/2oz/¼ cup butter
50ml/2fl oz/¼ cup milk
450g/1lb cabbage, finely shredded
30ml/2 tbsp olive oil
50ml/2fl oz/¼ cup double (heavy) cream
salt and ground black pepper

Serves 4
450g/1lb potatoes, peeled and chopped

1 Boil the potatoes for 15–20 minutes. Drain, replace on the heat for a few minutes, then mash. Heat the butter and milk in a pan and then mix into the mashed potatoes. Season to taste.

2 Heat the olive oil in a large frying pan, add the shredded cabbage and fry for a few minutes. Season to taste. Add the potato, mix well, then stir in the cream. Serve immediately.

Easy Mashed Potatoes

These fluffy mashed potatoes are the traditional accompaniment to sausages.

about 150ml/¼pint/⅔ cup milk
115g/4oz/½ cup soft butter
salt
freshly grated nutmeg (optional)

Serves 4
1kg/2¼lb floury potatoes, such as Maris Piper

1 Peel the potatoes and cook them whole in a large pan of boiling water for about 20 minutes or until soft throughout. Drain. Warm the milk and butter in a large pan.

2 Push the warm potatoes through a ricer, pass them through a mouli, or mash with a potato masher or fork.

3 Add the mashed potato to the milk and beat with a wooden spoon, adding extra milk if necessary to achieve the desired consistency. Season to taste with salt and a little grated nutmeg, if using. Serve immediately.

Rosemary and Garlic Potatoes Energy 171kcal/721kJ; Protein 3.9g; Carbohydrate 31.8g, of which sugars 2.9g; Fat 3.9g, of which saturates 0.7g; Cholesterol 0mg; Calcium 41mg; Fibre 2.8g; Sodium 26mg.
Kailkenny Energy 183kcal/766kJ; Protein 3.9g; Carbohydrate 24g, of which sugars 7.3g; Fat 8.5g, of which saturates 2.4g; Cholesterol 7mg; Calcium 73mg; Fibre 3.5g; Sodium 24mg.
Easy Mashed Potatoes Energy 338kcal/1424kJ; Protein 5.9g; Carbohydrate 50.4g, of which sugars 3.3g; Fat 14g, of which saturates 9.1g; Cholesterol 39mg; Calcium 42mg; Fibre 3.6g; Sodium 140mg.

Celeriac and Potato Purée

Celeriac is a most delicious vegetable which is ignored too often. This is sad as it is so good grated raw with mayonnaise and served with smoked salmon.
Here it is mixed with potato in a delicious purée that goes very well with game, poultry or roast pork or boar.

Serves 4
1 celeriac bulb, cut into chunks
1 lemon
2 potatoes, cut into chunks
300ml/½ pint/1¼ cups double (heavy) cream
salt and ground black pepper
chopped chives, to garnish

1 Place the celeriac in a pan. Cut the lemon in half and squeeze it into the pan, dropping the two halves in too.

2 Add the potatoes to the pan and just cover with cold water. Place a disc of baking parchment over the vegetables. Bring to the boil, reduce the heat and simmer until the potatoes are tender, about 20 minutes.

3 Remove the lemon halves and drain through a colander. Return to the pan and allow to steam dry for a few minutes over a low heat.

4 Remove from the heat and purée in a food processor. Put this mixture aside until you need it, it can be kept in the refrigerator for a few days, covered with clear film (plastic wrap).

5 When ready to use, pour the cream into a pan and bring almost to the boil. Add the celeriac mixture and stir to heat through. Season with salt and ground black pepper, garnish wth chopped chives and serve.

Cook's Tip
This recipe makes a very light, creamy purée. Use less cream to achieve a firmer purée, more for a softer purée. Be sure the cream is almost boiling or it will cool the mixture. Keep the purée warm in a bowl over simmering water.

Fennel, Potato and Garlic Mash

This flavoursome mash of potato, fennel and garlic goes particularly well with fish or chicken. It is also extremely delicious with roast pork.

Serves 4
1 head of garlic, separated into cloves
800g/1¾lb boiling potatoes, cut into chunks
2 large fennel bulbs
65g/2½oz/5 tbsp butter or 90ml/6 tbsp extra virgin olive oil
120–150ml/4–5fl oz/½–⅔ cup milk or single (light) cream
freshly grated nutmeg
salt and ground black pepper

1 If using a food mill to mash the potato, leave the garlic unpeeled, otherwise peel it. Boil the garlic and potatoes in salted water for 20 minutes.

2 Meanwhile, trim and roughly chop the fennel, reserving any feathery tops. Chop the tops and set them aside.

3 Heat 25g/1oz/2 tbsp of the butter or 30ml/2 tbsp of the oil in a heavy pan. Add the fennel, cover and cook over a low heat for 20–30 minutes, until soft but not browned.

4 Drain and mash the potatoes and garlic. Purée the fennel in a food mill or blender and beat it into the potato with the remaining butter or olive oil.

5 Warm the milk or cream and beat into the potato and fennel to make a creamy mixture. Season and add a little grated nutmeg.

6 Reheat gently, then beat in the reserved chopped fennel tops. Transfer to a warmed dish and serve immediately.

Cook's Tip
A food mill is good for mashing potatoes as it ensures a smooth texture. Never mash potatoes in a food processor or blender as this releases the starch, giving a result that resembles wallpaper paste.

Garlic Mashed Potatoes

These creamy mashed potatoes are delicious with all kinds of roast or sautéed meats as well as vegetarian main dishes.

Serves 6–8

3 whole garlic bulbs, separated
   into cloves, unpeeled
115g/4oz/8 tbsp unsalted butter
1.5kg/3lb baking
   potatoes, quartered
about 120–175ml/4–6fl oz/
   ½–¾ cup milk
salt and ground white pepper

1 Bring a small pan of water to the boil over a high heat. Add two-thirds of the garlic cloves and boil for 2 minutes. Drain the pan and then peel the boiled garlic cloves.

2 Place the remaining garlic cloves in a roasting pan and bake in a preheated oven at 200°C/400°F/Gas 6 for 30–40 minutes.

3 In a heavy frying pan, melt 50g/2oz/4 tbsp of the butter over a low heat. Add the blanched garlic cloves, then cover and cook gently for 20–25 minutes until very tender and just golden, shaking the pan and stirring occasionally. Do not allow the garlic to scorch or brown.

4 Remove the pan from the heat and cool. Spoon the garlic and melted butter into a blender or a food processor fitted with the metal blade and process until smooth. Transfer into a bowl, press clear film (plastic wrap) on to the surface to prevent a skin forming and set aside.

5 Cook the potatoes in boiling salted water until tender, then drain and pass through a food mill or press through a sieve (strainer) back into the pan. Return the pan to a medium heat and, using a wooden spoon, stir the potatoes for 1–2 minutes to dry out completely. Remove the pan from the heat.

6 Warm the milk over a medium-high heat until bubbles form around the edge. Gradually beat the milk, remaining butter and garlic purée into the potatoes. Season with salt, if needed, and white pepper, and serve hot, with the roasted garlic cloves.

Potato and Spring Onion Champ

Simple but unbelievably tasty, this traditional Irish way with mashed potatoes makes an excellent companion for a hearty stew of lamb or beef.

Serves 4

900g/2lb floury potatoes
1 small bunch spring onions
   (scallions), finely chopped
150ml/¼ pint/⅔ cup milk
50g/2oz/¼ cup butter
salt and ground black pepper

1 Cut the potatoes up into large chunks and put them in a large pan. Add water to cover and bring to the boil. Add salt, then simmer for about 15 minutes, or until the potatoes are tender, but do not let them get too soft. Drain thoroughly and leave to cool.

2 Meanwhile, put the spring onions into a small pan with the milk. Bring the mixture gently to the boil, then reduce the heat to low and simmer very gently until the spring onions are just tender.

3 When the potatoes are cool enough to handle, peel and return to the pan. Place the pan back on the heat and, using a wooden spoon, stir gently and constantly for about 1 minute until any excess moisture has evaporated. Remove the pan from the heat.

4 Mash the potatoes thoroughly with the milk and spring onions and season with salt and ground black pepper. Serve hot with a pool of melted butter in each portion.

Cook's Tips
• *If you make too much mashed potato, don't worry. It will keep well in the refrigerator if covered, and then it simply needs re-heating before using.*
• *Evaporating the excess moisture from the potatoes before mashing ensures that you get light and airy mash.*

Garlic Mashed Potatoes Energy 261kcal/1093kJ; Protein 5g; Carbohydrate 33.3g, of which sugars 3.8g; Fat 12.8g, of which saturates 7.9g; Cholesterol 32mg; Calcium 43mg; Fibre 2.4g; Sodium 118mg.
Champ Energy 186kcal/790kJ; Protein 7.4g; Carbohydrate 37.2g, of which sugars 5.9g; Fat 2g, of which saturates 0.9g; Cholesterol 5mg; Calcium 121mg; Fibre 2.9g; Sodium 51mg.

Biarritz Potatoes

A combination of classic mashed potatoes with finely diced ham and peppers.

Serves 4
900g/2lb floury potatoes, diced
50g/2oz/¼ cup butter

90ml/6 tbsp milk
50g/2oz cooked ham, finely diced
1 red (bell) pepper, seeded and
    finely diced
15ml/1tbsp chopped fresh parsley
sea salt and ground black pepper

1 Boil the potatoes in lightly salted water for 20 minutes or until very tender. Drain and return the potatoes to the pan and allow the steam to dry off over a low heat.

2 Mash the potatoes or pass them through a potato ricer. Add the butter and milk and stir in the cooked ham, peppers and parsley. Season and serve.

Perfect Creamed Potatoes

These potatoes are the perfect comfort food and are easy to make.

Serves 4
900g/2lb firm but not waxy
    potatoes, diced
45ml/3 tbsp extra virgin olive oil

150ml/¼ pint/⅔ cup hot milk
freshly grated nutmeg
fresh basil leaves or parsley
    sprigs, chopped
salt and ground black pepper
basil leaves, to garnish
fried bacon, to serve

1 Cook the potatoes in boiling water until just tender but not too mushy. Drain thoroughly. Press the potatoes through a potato ricer (which looks like a large garlic press) or mash them with a potato masher. Beat in olive oil and enough hot milk to make a smooth, thick purée.

2 Flavour to taste with the nutmeg, salt and black pepper, then stir in the chopped fresh herbs. Spoon into a warm serving dish and serve immediately, garnished with basil leaves and pieces of fried bacon.

Root Vegetable Clapshot

This root vegetable dish is an excellent accompaniment to haggis or used on top of a shepherd's pie in place of simple mashed potato. Turnips give a delicious earthy flavour, and swede introduces a sweet accent. It is also slightly less heavy than mashed potato, which makes it good for a lighter meal or supper.

Serves 4
450g/1lb potatoes
450g/1lb turnips or
    swede (rutabaga)
50g/2oz/¼ cup butter
50ml/2fl oz/¼ cup milk
5ml/1 tsp freshly grated nutmeg
30ml/2 tbsp chopped
    fresh parsley
salt and ground black pepper

1 Peel the potatoes and turnips or swede, then cut them into small, even chunks. You will need a large sharp knife for the turnips.

2 Place the chopped vegetables in a pan and cover with cold water. Bring to the boil over a medium heat, then reduce the heat and simmer until both vegetables are cooked, which will take about 15–20 minutes. Test the vegetables by pushing the point of a sharp knife into one of the cubes; if it goes in easily and the cube begins to break apart, then it is cooked.

3 Drain the vegetables through a colander. Return to the pan and allow them to dry out for a few minutes over a low heat, stirring occasionally to prevent any from sticking to the base of the pan.

4 Place the butter and the milk in a small pan over a low heat. Gently heat until the butter has melted, stirring constantly to combine it with the milk.

5 Mash the dry potato and turnip or swede mixture with a potato masher, then add the milk mixture.

6 Grate in the nutmeg, add the chopped parsley, mix thoroughly and season to taste with salt and pepper. Serve immediately with roast meat or game.

Biarritz Potatoes Energy 289kcal/1214kJ; Protein 7.5g; Carbohydrate 40.4g, of which sugars 6.9g; Fat 11.9g, of which saturates 7.4g; Cholesterol 37mg; Calcium 54mg; Fibre 3.2g; Sodium 284mg.
Perfect Creamed Potatoes Energy 249kcal/1049kJ; Protein 5.1g; Carbohydrate 38.1g, of which sugars 4.8g; Fat 9.6g, of which saturates 1.8g; Cholesterol 2mg; Calcium 59mg; Fibre 2.3g; Sodium 46mg.
Clapshot Energy 204kcal/852kJ; Protein 3.4g; Carbohydrate 24.1g, of which sugars 7.2g; Fat 11.2g, of which saturates 6.8g; Cholesterol 27mg; Calcium 78mg; Fibre 3.8g; Sodium 111mg.

Garlic Sweet Potato Mash

Delicious mashed with garlicky butter, orange-fleshed sweet potatoes not only look good, they're packed with vitamins.

40g/1½oz/3 tbsp unsalted butter
3 garlic cloves, crushed
salt and ground black pepper

Serves 4
4 large sweet potatoes, total
    weight about 900g/2lb, cubed

1 Put the sweet potatoes in a large pan. Add enough water to cover and bring to the boil. Add a little salt, then simmer for about 15 minutes, or until the potatoes are tender, but do not let them get too soft. Drain thoroughly in a colander and then return them to the pan.

2 Melt the butter in a heavy frying pan, then cook the garlic over a low to medium heat for about 1–2 minutes until it turns light golden. Stir the garlic frequently to prevent it from burning, otherwise it will taste bitter.

3 Pour the garlic butter over the sweet potatoes, season with salt and plenty of black pepper, and mash thoroughly until smooth and creamy. Serve immediately.

Variation
Add some chopped fresh herbs, such as parsley or coriander, if you wish.

Cook's Tips
• If the sweet potatoes seem to be on the dry side when you are mashing them, add a little milk.
• Orange-fleshed sweet potatoes are rich in beta carotene and vitamins C and E, which are believed to be linked with lowering the risk of cancer, heart disease and strokes.

Spiced Potato Purée

A flavoursome and fragrant addition to a festive dining table, this delicately spiced potato purée, originating from Holland, is the perfect accompaniment to any roast dinner and is especially delicious when served alongside game.

Serves 4
750g/1lb 10oz peeled floury
    potatoes, cut into quarters
½ tsp salt
½ tsp paprika
½ tsp nutmeg
½ tsp black pepper
2 egg yolks
knob (pat) of butter
milk

1 Preheat the oven to 220°C/425°F/Gas 7. Grease an ovenproof dish with butter or line a baking sheet with baking parchment.

2 Put the potatoes in a pan, add water to cover, bring to the boil and cook for about 15 minutes, or until tender. Drain well.

3 While still warm, pass the potatoes through a potato ricer or alternatively, mash with a hand-held electric mixer, but take care as a mixer can produce a purée that is too sticky.

4 Stir in the salt, spices, egg yolks and butter. Add some milk if the purée seems too thick.

5 While still warm, pipe or spread the purée with a fork into the prepared dish. Alternatively, pipe rosettes on to the baking sheet lined with baking parchment.

6 Bake the purée in the oven for 20 minutes. When cooked, if unpiped, transfer the hot purée into a serving dish and place on the dining table. Allow people to serve themselves.

Variation
This traditional side dish makes a warming and decadent meal in its own right if smothered in a rich cheese sauce and baked for around 20 minutes, until golden.

Potato Purée Energy 174kcal/732kJ; Protein 4.5g; Carbohydrate 28.4g, of which sugars 2.3g; Fat 5.4g, of which saturates 2.3g; Cholesterol 106mg; Calcium 24mg; Fibre 1.8g; Sodium 236mg.
Sweet Potato Mash Energy 586kcal/2477kJ; Protein 16.3g; Carbohydrate 101.4g, of which sugars 52.1g; Fat 15.8g, of which saturates 7.1g; Cholesterol 240mg; Calcium 182mg; Fibre 2.8g; Sodium 968mg.

Masala Mashed Potatoes

This delightfully simple variation on the popular Western side dish can be used as an accompaniment to just about any main course dish, not just Indian food. There are easily obtainable alternatives to mango powder if you cannot get hold of any (see Cook's Tip).

15ml/1 tbsp chopped fresh mint and coriander (cilantro), mixed
5ml/1 tsp mango powder (amchur)
5ml/1 tsp salt
5ml/1 tsp crushed black peppercorns
1 fresh red chilli, chopped
1 fresh green chilli, chopped
50g/2oz/¼ cup butter

Serves 4
3 medium potatoes

1 Put the potatoes in a large pan. Add water to cover and bring to the boil. Add salt, then simmer for about 15 minutes, or until the potatoes are tender, but do not let them get too soft.

2 Drain thoroughly and leave to cool slightly, then mash them down using a masher or potato ricer.

3 Stir all the remaining ingredients together in a small mixing bowl until well combined.

4 Stir the spice mixture into the mashed potatoes. Mix together thoroughly with a fork and serve warm.

Cook's Tip
Mango powder, also known as amchur, is the unripe green fruit of the mango tree ground to a powder. The sour mangoes are sliced and dried in the sun, turning a light brown, before they are ground. Mango powder adds a fruity sharpness and a slightly resinous bouquet to a dish. It is widely used with vegetables and is usually added towards the end of the cooking time. If mango powder is unavailable, the nearest substitute is lemon or lime juice, in double or treble quantity.

Potato and Endive Mash

This unusual and nutritious variant of mashed potato is made with raw endive and flavoured with the mild smoky tastes of either bacon or Gouda cheese.

Serves 4
1kg/2¼lb potatoes, peeled and cut into even chunks

200g/7oz/generous 1 cup diced lean smoked bacon or
200g/7oz/1¾ cups diced mild Gouda cheese
1kg/2¼lb frisée lettuce, cut into thin strips
25g/1oz/2 tbsp butter
100ml/3½ fl oz/scant ½ cup milk
salt
butter or gravy, to serve

1 Cook the potatoes in lightly salted boiling water for about 20 minutes, until tender.

2 Meanwhile, cook the bacon, if using, in a dry frying pan over a low heat, turning occasionally, for about 8 minutes, until light brown and crisp. Remove from the pan and crumble.

3 Drain the potatoes, return to the pan and mash with the butter and enough of the milk to make a smooth but not thin purée. Stir in the lettuce and bacon, if using. Alternatively, stir in the cheese and cook in the microwave for ten seconds.

4 Serve immediately. All mash is eaten with a well in the centre for a knob (pat) of butter or a spoonful of gravy.

Cook's Tip
Firm-textured potatoes such as Desirée, Pentland Dell and Estima are perfect for this dish. If you can't locate Gouda cheese, look out for a medium Cheddar or use Monterey Jack.

Variation
As an alternative to endive, turnip tops (greens), nettles, spinach, purslane, watercress or rocket (arugula) can also be served in this way.

Endive Mash Energy 368kcal/1543kJ; Protein 14.6g; Carbohydrate 48.5g, of which sugars 6.2g; Fat 16g, of which saturates 7.4g; Cholesterol 41.2mg; Calcium 101.2mg; Fibre 4.7g; Sodium 848.7mg.
Masala Mashed Potatoes Energy 219kcal/919kJ; Protein 3.1g; Carbohydrate 28.9g, of which sugars 3g; Fat 10.9g, of which saturates 6.7g; Cholesterol 27mg; Calcium 13mg; Fibre 1.8g; Sodium 600mg.

Mashed Potato Dumplings

These soft little mashed potato dumplings, which are similar to Italian gnocchi, are served here with a breadcrumb topping, which adds colour and texture. These are especially tasty served as an accompaniment to braised meats.

Serves 4-6
5 potatoes, unpeeled
225g/8oz/2 cups plain
  (all-purpose) flour
1 egg, beaten
2.5ml/½ tsp salt
45ml/3 tbsp butter
45ml/3 tbsp fresh white
  breadcrumbs

1 Cut the potatoes into quarters. Place in a pan of boiling water and cook for 10–15 minutes, or until just tender. Remove from the heat, drain and leave to cool.

2 Push the potatoes through a ricer, or mash to a paste with a potato masher. Add the flour, egg and salt, and knead to combine.

3 Transfer the dough to a lightly floured surface and, with damp hands, shape into walnut-sized balls. Flatten the balls slightly and make a small indentation in the centre.

4 Bring a large pan of lightly salted water to the boil, then drop in the dumplings and cook for 5 minutes, or until they are cooked through and firm to the touch.

5 Meanwhile, melt the butter in a frying pan, add the breadcrumbs and fry for about 3 minutes, or until they are golden brown.

6 Drain the dumplings and arrange on a serving dish. Sprinkle the browned breadcrumbs over the top, and serve immediately.

Hot Lightning Potatoes

The unlikely combination of creamy mashed potatoes, sweet, piping hot apple purée and rich black pudding combine to produce the unique and delicious flavour and intriguing dark and light visual contrast that give this traditional Dutch dish its unusual name.

Serves 4
1kg/2¼lb potatoes, peeled
500g/1¼lb eating apples, peeled,
  cored and cut into large chunks
250g/9oz cooking apples, peeled,
  cored and cut into large chunks
40g/1½oz/3 tbsp butter
salt and ground black pepper
fried black pudding (blood
  sausage) or smoked bacon and
  butter, to serve

1 Chop the potatoes into even chunks and place in a large pan. Half cover the potatoes with cold, salted water, then pile both varieties of apple on top and add 25g/1oz/2 tbsp of the butter.

2 Slowly bring the pan up to the boil, lower the heat, cover and simmer for about 30 minutes, until the potatoes are tender.

3 Drain well, reserving the cooking liquid. Mash the potatoes and apples until smooth, adding some of the retained cooking liquid if necessary.

4 Season the dish with salt and pepper and serve, hot, with either fried black pudding or bacon and butter.

> **Variation**
> *The fried breadcrumb topping adds a deliciously moreish crunch to these little dumplings, but a topping of fried onions or leeks, crispy bacon lardons or even grated Cheddar cheese would work equally well.*

> **Variations**
> • *This dish makes a delicious light supper or decadent afternoon snack. If you would like a more substantial meal, omit the black sausage or bacon and serve with grilled pork sausages in a sweet onion gravy, accompanied by buttered Savoy cabbage.*
> • *Try experimenting with the quantity and variety of apples that you use: for a tarter dish, use a higher proportion of cooking apples; for a sweeter dish, use more eating apples or even a quantity of pears.*

Hot Lightning Energy 315kcal/1334kJ; Protein 4.8g; Carbohydrate 57g, of which sugars 20g; Fat 9.1g, of which saturates 5.4g; Cholesterol 21.2mg; Calcium 24.2mg; Fibre 5.5g; Sodium 91.7mg.
Mashed Dumplings Energy 313kcal/1321kJ; Protein 10.3g; Carbohydrate 65.6g, of which sugars 3.7g; Fat 41.1g, of which saturates 16.2g; Cholesterol 130mg; Calcium 71mg; Fibre 3.5g; Sodium 64mg.

Grated Potato Dumplings

These dumplings contain a mixture of mashed and grated potato, which gives them an interesting texture. They make an ideal accompaniment to many casseroled or braised dishes and are tasty served with fried cubes of pork fat.

Serves 4
1kg/2¼ lb potatoes, peeled
2 eggs, beaten
pinch of salt
115g/4oz plain (all-purpose) flour, plus extra for dusting
15ml/1 tbsp potato flour
150g/5oz pork fat, cut into 1cm/½ in cubes

1 Chop half the potatoes into chunks, then add to a pan of lightly salted, boiling water. Cook for 10 minutes, or until soft. Drain the potatoes, then mash in a large bowl.

2 Grate the remaining potatoes and squeeze in a sieve (strainer) to remove the excess liquid. Add to the mashed potato.

3 Add the eggs, a pinch of salt and both the flours to the bowl, and knead thoroughly to form a dough. Using floured hands, roll spoonfuls of the dough into balls.

4 Bring a large pan of lightly salted water to the boil, then add the dumplings. Cook for 4–5 minutes, or until the dumplings float on the surface of the water.

5 Meanwhile, fry the cubes of pork fat for about 4 minutes, or until golden brown all over.

6 Transfer the cooked dumplings to a serving plate and spoon over the fried pork fat cubes.

Variation

Delicious served as a quick snack or floating in a robust casserole, these dumplings can also be transformed into a substantial and delicious meal in their own right. Try smothering with a rich cheese sauce and baking at 200°C/400°F/Gas 6 for 20–25 minutes until beautifully golden and bubbling.

Potato and Cheese Pierogi

These traditional Polish dumplings, stuffed with potato and curd cheese, are made from simple, cheap ingredients and are deceptively easy to make. They are a wonderful side dish or, by being creative with the stuffing, a substantial meal in their own right.

Serves 4-6
500g/1¼lb plain (all-purpose) flour, plus extra for dusting

2.5ml/½tsp salt
2 eggs, beaten
45ml/3 tbsp vegetable oil
250ml/8fl oz/1 cup warm water
chopped fresh parsley, to garnish
thick sour cream, to serve

For the filling
15g/½oz/1 tbsp butter
½ large onion, finely chopped
250g/9oz peeled, cooked potatoes
250g/9oz/1¼ cups curd cheese
1 egg, beaten
salt and black pepper, to taste

1 For the filling, heat the butter in a small pan, add the onion and cook for about 5 minutes. Push the cooked potatoes through a ricer, add the cheese and stir thoroughly. Add the egg, onion and seasoning to the potato mixture and mix well.

2 For the dough, sift the flour into a bowl, then add the salt and eggs. Pour in the oil and water, and mix to form a loose dough.

3 Turn out on to a floured surface and knead well for about 10 minutes, or until the dough is pliant and does not stick to the work surface. Divide the dough into four pieces, then roll each one out thinly with a floured rolling pin. Cut the dough into 5–6cm/2–2½in circles using a pastry (cookie) cutter.

4 Place a heaped teaspoonful of the potato filling mixture in the centre of each of the circles of dough, then fold over the dough and press to seal the edges. The dumplings should be neat and well filled, but not bursting.

5 Bring a large pan of lightly salted water to the boil, add the dumplings and cook for about 4–5 minutes, or until they rise up to float on the surface. Cook for a further two minutes once they have risen, then remove to a serving dish. Garnish with chopped parsley and serve with thick sour cream.

Potato Dumplings Energy 658kcal/2746kJ; Protein 10.3g; Carbohydrate 65.6g, of which sugars 3.7g; Fat 41.1g, of which saturates 16.2g; Cholesterol 130mg; Calcium 71mg; Fibre 3.5g; Sodium 64mg.
Pierogi Energy 419kcal/1768kJ; Protein 11.7g; Carbohydrate 71.6g, of which sugars 2.3g; Fat 11.5g, of which saturates 2.9g; Cholesterol 100mg; Calcium 136mg; Fibre 3.1g; Sodium 57mg.

Marquis Potatoes

These crispy potato treats are finished with a deliciously tangy tomato mixture set in the centre of the potato nest.

Serves 6

900g/2lb floury potatoes
450g/1lb ripe tomatoes
15ml/1tbsp olive oil
2 shallots, finely chopped
25g/1oz/2 tbsp butter
3 egg yolks
60ml/4 tbsp milk
chopped fresh parsley, to garnish
sea salt and ground black pepper

1 Peel and cut the potatoes into small chunks, then boil in a pan of lightly salted water for about 15–20 minutes or until they are very tender.

2 Meanwhile, cut a small cross into each tomato, blanch them in boiling water and then plunge into a bowl of cold water. Peel the skins and scoop the seeds out. Chop the tomato flesh.

3 Heat the olive oil in a large frying pan and fry the shallots for 2 minutes, stirring constantly.

4 Add the chopped tomatoes to the pan and fry for a further 10 minutes until the moisture has evaporated. Set aside.

5 Drain the potatoes through a colander, return them to the pan and allow the steam to dry them off. Set the potatoes aside to cool slightly.

6 Mash the potatoes thoroughly with the butter and two of the egg yolks and the milk. Season with plenty of salt and ground black pepper.

7 Grease a baking sheet. Spoon the potato into a piping (pastry) bag fitted with a medium star nozzle. Pipe six oval nests on to the baking sheet. Beat the remaining egg with a little water and carefully brush over the potato. Grill for 5 minutes or until golden.

8 Spoon the tomato mixture inside the nests and top with a little parsley. Serve them immediately.

Swiss Soufflé Potatoes

A fabulous combination of rich and satisfying ingredients – cheese, eggs, cream, butter and potatoes. This is perfect for cold-weather eating.

Serves 4

4 floury baking potatoes
115g/4oz/1 cup Gruyère cheese, grated
115g/4oz/8 tbsp herb-flavoured butter
60ml/4 tbsp double (heavy) cream
2 eggs, separated
salt and ground black pepper

1 Preheat the oven to 220°C/425°F/Gas 7. Prick the potatoes all over with a fork. Bake in the oven for 1–1½ hours until tender. Remove them from the oven and reduce the temperature to 180°C/350°F/Gas 4.

2 Cut each potato in half and scoop out the flesh into a bowl. Return the shells to the oven to crisp them up while making the filling.

3 Mash the potato flesh using a fork, then add the Gruyère, herb-flavoured butter, cream, egg yolks and seasoning. Beat well until smooth.

4 Whisk the egg whites in a separate bowl until they hold stiff but not dry peaks, then carefully fold into the potato mixture.

5 Pile the mixture back into the potato shells and place on a baking sheet. Bake in the oven for 20–25 minutes until risen and golden brown.

6 Serve the potatoes hot, sprinkled with fresh, chopped chives, if wished, and a bowl of mayonnaise on the side.

> **Variation**
> Use other cheeses, if you like. Mature (sharp) Cheddar would work well, or go for another blue cheese such as Stilton or Dolcelatte, if you prefer.

Marquis Potatoes Energy 136kcal/571kJ; Protein 3.3g; Carbohydrate 18.5g, of which sugars 3.6g; Fat 5.9g, of which saturates 2.4g; Cholesterol 74mg; Calcium 27mg; Fibre 1.6g; Sodium 43mg.
Swiss Potatoes Energy 576kcal/2394kJ; Protein 14.2g; Carbohydrate 32.6g, of which sugars 3g; Fat 44.3g, of which saturates 27.2g; Cholesterol 209mg; Calcium 251mg; Fibre 2g; Sodium 486mg.

Yorkshire Potato Puffs

Mini Yorkshire puddings with a soft centre of herby potato mash will be delicious with the Sunday roast, or serve them for a weekday supper with sausages.

Makes 6
275g/10oz floury potatoes
creamy milk and butter,
    for mashing
5ml/1 tsp chopped fresh parsley
5ml/1 tsp chopped fresh tarragon
75g/3oz/²/₃ cup plain
    (all-purpose) flour
1 egg
120ml/4fl oz/½ cup milk
vegetable oil or sunflower fat,
    for baking
salt and ground black pepper

1 Cook the potatoes in a large pan of boiling water until tender, then mash with a little creamy milk and butter. Stir in the chopped parsley and tarragon and season well to taste. Preheat the oven to 200°C/400°F/Gas 6.

2 Process the flour, egg, milk and a little salt in a food processor fitted with the metal blade, or a blender, to make a smooth batter.

3 Place about 2.5ml/½ tsp of oil or a small knob (pat) of sunflower fat in each of six ramekin dishes and place in the oven on a baking tray for 2–3 minutes until the oil or fat is very hot.

4 Working quickly, pour a small amount of batter (about 20ml/4 tsp) into each ramekin dish. Add a heaped tablespoon of the mashed potatoes and then pour an equal amount of the remaining batter in each dish. Bake for around 15–20 minutes until the puddings are puffy and golden brown.

5 Using a metal spatula, ease the puddings out of the ramekin dishes and arrange on a large serving dish. Serve immediately.

Cook's Tip
Cook and mash the potatoes the day before to save time, making a quick supper dish, or to prepare for a dinner party in advance.

Sautéed Potatoes with Rosemary

These rosemary-scented, crisp golden potatoes are a firm favourite in many households. They make a great alternative to chips or roast potatoes to partner grilled or roasted meats.

Serves 6
1.5kg/3lb firm baking potatoes
60–90ml/4–6 tbsp oil, bacon
    dripping or clarified butter
2 fresh rosemary sprigs,
    leaves chopped
salt and ground black pepper

1 Using a vegetable peeler or sharp knife, peel the potatoes and then cut into 2.5cm/1in slices.

2 Place the slices in a bowl of cold water and soak for 10 minutes. Drain, rinse and then drain thoroughly. Pat dry with kitchen paper.

3 In a large frying pan, heat 60ml/4 tbsp of the oil, dripping or butter over a medium-high heat until hot, but not smoking. Add the potatoes to the pan and cook for 2 minutes without stirring so that they seal completely and brown on one side.

4 Shake the pan and toss the potatoes to brown on another side. Continue to shake the pan until the potatoes are browned on all sides. Season with plenty of salt and ground black pepper.

5 Add a little more oil, dripping or butter to the frying pan, reduce the heat to medium-low to low, and continue cooking the potatoes for about 20–25 minutes until tender, stirring and shaking the pan frequently. Test them by piercing with the tip of a knife or metal skewer.

6 About 5 minutes before the end of the cooking time, generously sprinkle the potatoes with chopped fresh rosemary. Serve immediately.

Cook's Tip
Try to cut the slices of potato as uniformly as possible: this will ensure that the slices are evenly cooked and beautifully golden.

Potatoes with Roasted Poppy Seeds

Poppy seeds are used in Indian cooking as thickening agents, and to lend a nutty taste to sauces.

Serves 4

45ml/3 tbsp white poppy seeds
45–60ml/3–4 tbsp vegetable oil
675g/1½lb potatoes, peeled and cut into 1cm/½in cubes
2.5ml/½ tsp black mustard seeds
2.5ml/½ tsp onion seeds
2.5ml/½ tsp cumin seeds
2.5ml/½ tsp fennel seeds
1 or 2 dried red chillies, chopped or broken into small pieces
2.5ml/½ tsp ground turmeric
2.5ml/½ tsp salt
150ml/¼ pint/⅔ cup warm water
fresh coriander (cilantro) sprigs, to garnish
pooris and natural (plain) yogurt, to serve

1 Preheat a karahi, wok or large pan over a medium setting. When the pan is hot, reduce the heat slightly and add the poppy seeds. Stir them around in the pan until they are just a shade darker. Remove from the pan and leave to cool.

2 In the pan, heat the vegetable oil over a medium heat and fry the cubes of potato until they are light brown. Remove them with a slotted spoon and drain on kitchen paper.

3 To the same oil, add the mustard seeds. As soon as they begin to pop, add the onion, cumin and fennel seeds and the chillies. Let the chillies blacken, but remove them from the pan before they burn.

4 Stir in the turmeric and follow quickly with the fried potatoes and salt. Stir well and add the warm water. Cover the pan with the lid and reduce the heat to low. Cook for 8–10 minutes, or until the potatoes are tender.

5 Grind the poppy seeds in a mortar and pestle or spice grinder. Stir the ground seeds into the potatoes. This should form a thick paste which should cling firmly to the potatoes. If there is too much liquid, continue to stir over a medium heat until you have the right consistency. Transfer to a serving dish. Garnish with coriander and serve with pooris and natural yogurt.

Berrichonne Potatoes

A potato dish with a difference. The top of the potatoes will be crispy with a soft base cooked in the stock, onions and bacon.

Serves 4

900g/2lb maincrop potatoes
25g/1oz/2 tbsp butter
1 onion, finely chopped
115g/4oz unsmoked streaky (fatty) bacon rashers (strips), rinds removed
350ml/12fl oz /1½ cups vegetable stock
chopped fresh parsley, to garnish
sea salt and ground black pepper

1 Preheat the oven to 200°C/400°F/Gas 6. Peel the potatoes and trim them into barrel shapes. Leave the potatoes to stand in a bowl of cold water.

2 Melt the butter in a heavy frying pan. Add the chopped onions, stir to coat in the butter and cover the pan with a tight-fitting lid. Cook gently for 5–7 minutes, until they have softened but not turned brown.

3 Chop the streaky bacon rashers and add to the onions in the pan. Stir to combine, cover the pan again and cook for a further 2–3 minutes.

4 Spoon the onion mixture into the base of a 1.5 litre/ 2½ pint/6¼ cup rectangular shallow ovenproof dish. Lay the potatoes over the onion mixture and pour the stock over, making sure that it comes halfway up the sides.

5 Season with salt and pepper and bake in the preheated oven for about 1 hour until crisp and beautifully golden brown on top. Garnish with chopped parsley and serve.

> **Cook's Tip**
> *This dish makes an ideal accompaniment to more neutral dishes as it is very tasty and quite salty. Serve with white, meaty fish fillets that have been simply fried in butter, or with roast pork or pork chops.*

Potatoes with Seeds Energy 260kcal/1091kJ; Protein 6.2g; Carbohydrate 30.2g, of which sugars 4.7g; Fat 6.9g, of which saturates 0.9g; Cholesterol 0mg; Calcium 205mg; Fibre 4.3g; Sodium 668mg.
Berrichonne Potatoes Energy 289kcal/1213kJ; Protein 8.6g; Carbohydrate 37.5g, of which sugars 3.8g; Fat 12.6g, of which saturates 5.9g; Cholesterol 32mg; Calcium 20mg; Fibre 2.5g; Sodium 425mg.

Deep-fried New Potatoes with Saffron Aioli

Serve these crispy little golden potatoes dipped into a wickedly garlicky mayonnaise – then watch them disappear in a matter of minutes. They make an ideal accompaniment to most dishes or are equally tasty as a snack.

Serves 4

1 egg yolk
2.5ml/½ tsp Dijon mustard
300ml/½ pint/1¼ cups extra
 virgin olive oil
15–30ml/1–2 tbsp lemon juice
1 garlic clove, crushed
2.5ml/½ tsp saffron strands
20 baby, new or salad potatoes
vegetable oil, for deep frying
salt and ground black pepper

1 For the aioli, put the egg yolk in a small mixing bowl with the mustard and a pinch of salt. Mix until combined. Beat in the olive oil very slowly, drop by drop, then in a thin stream. Add the lemon juice.

2 Season the aioli with salt and ground black pepper, then add the crushed garlic and beat the mixture thoroughly until well combined.

3 Place the saffron in a small bowl and add 10ml/2 tsp of hot water. Press the saffron firmly, using the back of a teaspoon, to extract the colour and flavour, and leave to infuse (steep) for around 5 minutes. Beat the saffron and the infused liquid into the aioli.

4 Cook the potatoes in their skins in boiling salted water for 5 minutes, then turn off the heat. Cover the pan and leave for about 15 minutes. Drain the potatoes, then dry them thoroughly in a clean dish towel.

5 Heat a 1cm/½in layer of vegetable oil in a deep pan. When the oil is very hot, add the potatoes and fry them quickly, turning them occasionally until they are crisp and golden brown all over. Drain them thoroughly on kitchen paper and serve hot with the saffron aioli.

Potatoes, Peppers and Shallots Roasted with Rosemary

These potatoes soak up both the taste and wonderful aromas of the shallots and the fresh rosemary sprigs. Serve this as an accompaniment to grilled or cold meats.

12 shallots
2 sweet yellow (bell) peppers
olive oil
2 rosemary sprigs
salt and ground black pepper
olive oil
crushed peppercorns, to garnish

Serves 4

500g/1¼lb waxy potatoes

1 Preheat the oven to 200°C/400°F/Gas 6. Par-boil the potatoes in their skins in boiling salted water for 5 minutes. Drain, and when they are cool, peel them and halve lengthways.

2 Peel the shallots, allowing them to fall into their natural segments. Cut each sweet pepper lengthways into eight strips, discarding seeds and pith.

3 Oil a shallow ovenproof dish thoroughly with olive oil. Arrange the potatoes and peppers in alternating rows and stud with the shallots.

4 Cut the rosemary sprigs into 5cm/2in lengths and tuck among the vegetables. Season the vegetables generously with salt and pepper, then toss in the olive oil.

5 Roast, uncovered, in the oven for 30–40 minutes until all the vegetables are tender. Turn the vegetables occasionally to cook and brown evenly. Serve hot or at room temperature, with crushed peppercorns.

Cook's Tip
Liven up a simple dish of roast or grilled (broiled) lamb or chicken with these delicious and easy potatoes.

Deep-fried Potatoes Energy 795kcal/3282kJ; Protein 2.9g; Carbohydrate 20.1g, of which sugars 1.6g; Fat 78.7g, of which saturates 10.5g; Cholesterol 50mg; Calcium 13mg; Fibre 1.3g; Sodium 16mg.
Potatoes with Rosemary Energy 176kcal/742kJ; Protein 4.2g; Carbohydrate 33.6g, of which sugars 12.6g; Fat 3.7g, of which saturates 0.6g; Cholesterol 0mg; Calcium 40mg; Fibre 4.1g; Sodium 20mg.

Roasted Root Vegetables with Whole Spice Seeds

These spiced vegetables can be roasted alongside a joint of meat or a whole chicken. They will virtually look after themselves and make a delicious side dish.

Serves 4

3 parsnips, peeled
3 potatoes, peeled
3 carrots, peeled
3 sweet potatoes, peeled
60ml/4 tbsp olive oil
8 shallots, peeled
2 garlic cloves, sliced
10ml/2 tsp white
  mustard seeds
10ml/2 tsp coriander seeds,
  lightly crushed
5ml/1 tsp cumin seeds
2 bay leaves
salt and ground black pepper

1 Preheat the oven to 190°C/375°F/Gas 5. Bring a pan of lightly salted water to the boil. Cut the parsnips, potatoes, carrots and sweet potatoes into chunks. Add them to the pan and bring the water back to the boil. Boil for 2 minutes, then drain the vegetables thoroughly.

2 Pour the olive oil into a large, heavy roasting pan and place over a moderate heat. When the oil is hot, add the drained vegetables, together with the whole shallots and garlic. Fry, tossing the vegetables over the heat, until they are pale golden at the edges.

3 Add the mustard, coriander and cumin seeds and the bay leaves. Cook for 1 minute, then season with salt and pepper.

4 Transfer the roasting pan to the oven and roast for about 45 minutes, turning the vegetables occasionally, until they are crisp and golden and cooked through.

Variation
Vary the selection of vegetables according to what is available. Try using swede (rutabaga) or pumpkin instead of, or as well as, the vegetables suggested.

Roasted Potatoes with Red Onions

These mouthwatering potatoes are a great accompaniment to just about anything. The key is to use small firm potatoes; the smaller they are cut, the less time they will take to cook.

25 g/1oz/2 tbsp butter
30ml/2 tbsp olive oil
2 red onions, cut into chunks
8 garlic cloves, unpeeled
30ml/2 tbsp chopped
  fresh rosemary
salt and ground black pepper

Serves 4

675 g/1½lb small firm potatoes

1 Preheat the oven to 230°C/450°F/Gas 8. Peel and quarter the potatoes, rinse them well and pat thoroughly dry on kitchen paper.

2 Place the butter and olive oil in a roasting pan and place in the oven to heat.

3 When the butter has melted and is foaming, add the potatoes, red onions, garlic and rosemary. Toss well, then spread out in one layer.

4 Place the pan in the oven and roast for about 25 minutes until the potatoes are golden and tender when tested with a fork. Shake the pan from time to time whilst cooking to redistribute the potatoes. When cooked, season with salt and ground black pepper before serving.

Cook's Tip
To ensure that the potatoes are crisp, make sure they are completely dry before cooking. Resist the urge to turn the potatoes too often. Allow them to brown on one side before turning. Do not salt the potatoes until the end of cooking – salting beforehand encourages them to give up their liquid, making them limp.

Root Vegetables Energy 290kcal/1213kJ; Protein 11.5g; Carbohydrate 32.5g, of which sugars 13.3g; Fat 13.6g, of which saturates 1.6g; Cholesterol 0mg; Calcium 175mg; Fibre 9.1g; Sodium 271mg.
Roasted Potatoes Energy 254kcal/1063kJ; Protein 4.5g; Carbohydrate 35.4g, of which sugars 8.1g; Fat 11.5g, of which saturates 4.2g; Cholesterol 13mg; Calcium 59mg; Fibre 3.7g; Sodium 63mg.

Potato-stuffed Aubergines

This typical Ligurian dish is spiked with paprika and allspice, a legacy from the days when spices imported from the East came into northern Italy via the port of Genoa.

Serves 4
2 aubergines, about 225g/8oz
  each, stalks removed
275g/10oz potatoes, peeled
  and diced

30ml/2 tbsp olive oil
1 small onion, finely chopped
1 garlic clove, finely chopped
good pinch of ground allspice
  and paprika
1 egg, beaten
40g/1½oz/½ cup grated
  Parmesan cheese
15ml/1 tbsp fresh
  white breadcrumbs
salt and ground black pepper
fresh mint sprigs, to garnish
salad leaves, to serve

1 Bring a large pan of lightly salted water to the boil. Add the whole aubergines and cook for 5 minutes, turning frequently. Remove with a slotted spoon and set aside. Add the potatoes to the pan and cook for 20 minutes until soft.

2 Meanwhile, cut the aubergines in half lengthways and gently scoop out the flesh with a small sharp knife and a spoon, leaving 5mm/¼in of the shell intact. Select a baking dish that will hold the aubergines snugly in a single layer. Brush it lightly with oil. Put the shells in the baking dish and chop the aubergine flesh roughly.

3 Heat the oil in a frying pan, add the onion and cook gently, stirring frequently, until softened. Add the chopped aubergine flesh and the garlic. Cook, stirring frequently, for 6–8 minutes. Tip into a bowl. Preheat the oven to 190°C/375°F/Gas 5.

4 Drain and mash the potatoes. Add to the aubergine mixture with the spices and egg. Set aside 15ml/1 tbsp of the Parmesan and add the rest to the aubergine mixture. Season to taste.

5 Spoon the mixture into the aubergine shells. Mix together the breadcrumbs with the reserved Parmesan cheese and sprinkle the mixture over the aubergines. Bake for around 40–45 minutes until the topping is crisp. Garnish with mint and serve with salad.

Baked Anglesey Eggs and Potatoes

This creamy dish of potatoes, leeks, eggs and cheese sauce makes a perfect warming winter lunch and is equally delicious when served as part of an evening meal.

Serves 4
500g/1lb 2oz potatoes, peeled

3 leeks, sliced
6 eggs
600ml/1 pint/2½ cups milk
50g/2oz/½ cup plain
  (all-purpose) flour
100g/3½oz/1 cup Caerphilly
  cheese, grated
25g/1oz fresh root ginger, peeled
  and grated
salt and ground black pepper

1 Cook the potatoes in boiling water for about 15 minutes or until soft. Meanwhile, cook the leeks in a little water for about 10 minutes until soft. Hard-boil the eggs, drain and put under cold running water to cool them.

2 Preheat the oven to 200°C/400°F/Gas 6. Drain and mash the potatoes.

3 Drain the leeks and stir into the potatoes with a little black pepper. Remove the shells from the eggs and cut into quarters.

4 Pour the milk into a pan and add the butter and flour. Stirring constantly with a whisk, bring slowly to the boil and bubble gently for 2 minutes, until thickened, smooth and glossy. Remove from the heat, stir in half of the Caerphilly cheese and season to taste.

5 Arrange the eggs in four shallow ovenproof dishes. Spoon the potato and leek mixture into the dishes. Pour the cheese sauce over the top with the remaining cheese. Put into the hot oven and cook for 15–20 minutes, until bubbling and golden brown. Serve immediately.

> **Cook's Tip**
> *The leeks could be cooked in the microwave in a covered dish: there is no need to add water. Stir once or twice during cooking.*

Stuffed Aubergines Energy 193kcal/809kJ; Protein 8g; Carbohydrate 17.6g, of which sugars 4.1g; Fat 10.6g, of which saturates 3.3g; Cholesterol 48mg; Calcium 150mg; Fibre 3.2g; Sodium 162mg.
Anglesey Eggs Energy 540kcal/2259kJ; Protein 26.6g; Carbohydrate 41.3g, of which sugars 12.3g; Fat 30.6g, of which saturates 16.2g; Cholesterol 345mg; Calcium 471mg; Fibre 5g; Sodium 443mg.

Potato and Pumpkin Pudding

Serve this savoury pumpkin and potato pudding with any rich meat dish or simply with a mixed salad.

Serves 4

45ml/3 tbsp olive oil
1 garlic clove, sliced
675g/1½lb pumpkin flesh, cut
    into 2cm/¾ in chunks
350g/12oz potatoes
25g/1oz/2 tbsp butter
90g/3½oz/scant ½ cup
    ricotta cheese
50g/2oz/⅔ cup grated
    Parmesan cheese
pinch grated nutmeg
4 eggs, separated
salt and ground black pepper
chopped fresh parsley, to garnish

1 Preheat the oven to 200°C/400°F/Gas 6. Grease a 1.75 litre/3 pint/7½ cup shallow, oval baking dish.

2 Heat the oil in a large shallow pan, add the garlic and pumpkin and cook, stirring often to prevent sticking, for 15–20 minutes or until the pumpkin is tender.

3 Meanwhile, cook the potatoes in boiling salted water for 20 minutes until tender. Drain, leave until cool enough to handle, then peel off the skins. Place the potatoes and pumpkin in a large bowl and mash well with the butter.

4 Mash the ricotta with a fork until smooth and add to the potato and pumpkin mixture, mixing well. Stir the Parmesan, nutmeg and seasoning into the mixture – it should be smooth and creamy. Mix in the egg yolks one at a time.

5 Whisk the egg whites with an electric whisk until they form stiff peaks, then fold gently into the mixture. Spoon into the prepared baking dish and bake for 30 minutes until golden and firm. Serve hot, garnished with parsley.

Cook's Tip
You may process the vegetables in a food processor for a few seconds, but be careful not to overprocess, as they will become very gluey.

Boulangère Potatoes

This tasty dish features layers of potato and onions cooked in butter and stock. This is a delicious savoury potato dish that makes a great accompaniment to both meat and fish.

Serves 6
butter for greasing

450g/1lb maincrop potatoes, very
    finely sliced
2 onions, finely sliced into rings
2 garlic cloves, crushed
50g/2oz/¼ cup butter, diced
300ml/½ pint/1¼ cups chicken
    or vegetable stock
chopped parsley
sea salt and ground black pepper

1 Preheat the oven to 180°C/350°F/Gas 4. Grease the base and sides of a 1.5 litre/2½ pint/6¼ cup shallow ovenproof dish.

2 Line the dish with some of the sliced potatoes. Sprinkle some onions and garlic on top. Layer up the remaining potatoes and onions. Season between each layer with salt and black pepper.

3 Push the vegetables down into the dish and dot the top with the butter. Pour the stock over and bake in the preheated oven for about 1½ hours.

4 After 1 hour, if the top starts to brown too much, then cover with a piece of foil. Serve with parsley and plenty of salt and pepper sprinkled over the top.

Cook's Tip
Slice the potatoes for this dish as thin as you can. A mandolin is an ideal kitchen tool for this job, although be careful when using as they have very sharp blades.

Variation
If you want to make this dish more substantial, add some grated cheese, sprinkled over the top just before you bake it.

Potato Pudding Energy 434kcal/1801kJ; Protein 14.7g; Carbohydrate 18g, of which sugars 4g; Fat 34.3g, of which saturates 15.6g; Cholesterol 239mg; Calcium 256mg; Fibre 2.6g; Sodium 330mg.
Boulangère Potatoes Energy 118kcal/494kJ; Protein 1.5g; Carbohydrate 12.9g, of which sugars 1.6g; Fat 7.1g, of which saturates 4.4g; Cholesterol 18mg; Calcium 9mg; Fibre 0.9g; Sodium 59mg.

Potato Pan Gratin

Potatoes, layered with mustard butter and baked until golden, are perfect to serve with a green salad for supper, or as an accompaniment to a vegetable or nut roast.

Serves 4

4 large potatoes, total weight about 900g/2lb
25g/1oz/2 tbsp butter
15ml/1 tbsp olive oil
2 large garlic cloves, crushed
30ml/2 tbsp Dijon mustard
15ml/1 tbsp lemon juice
15ml/1 tbsp fresh thyme leaves, plus extra to garnish
50ml/2fl oz/¼ cup vegetable stock
salt and ground black pepper

1 Thinly slice the potatoes using a knife or a slicing attachment on a food processor. Place in a bowl of cold water to prevent them discolouring.

2 Preheat the oven to 200°C/400°F/Gas 6. Heat the butter and oil in a deep, flameproof frying pan. Add the garlic and cook gently for 3 minutes until light golden, stirring constantly. Stir in the mustard, lemon juice and thyme. Remove from the heat and pour the mixture into a jug (pitcher).

3 Drain the potatoes and pat dry with kitchen paper. Place a layer of potatoes in the frying pan, season and pour over one-third of the butter mixture. Place another layer of potatoes on top, season, and pour over another third of the butter mixture. Arrange a final layer of potatoes on top, pour over the rest of the butter mixture and then the stock. Season and sprinkle with the reserved thyme.

4 Cover the top with baking parchment and bake for 1 hour, then remove the paper and cook for a further 15 minutes or until golden. Serve immediately.

> **Variation**
> Any root vegetables can be used in this dish: try celeriac, parsnips, swede (rutabaga) or turnips.

Potatoes Baked with Fennel, Onions, Garlic and Saffron

Potatoes, fennel and onions infused with garlic, saffron and spices make a sophisticated and attractive accompaniment for fish or chicken or an egg-based main course dish.

Serves 4–6

500g/1¼lb small waxy potatoes, cut into chunks or wedges
good pinch of saffron strands (12–15 strands)
1 head of garlic, separated into cloves
12 small red or yellow onions, peeled but left whole
3 fennel bulbs, cut into wedges, feathery tops reserved
4–6 fresh bay leaves
6–9 fresh thyme sprigs
175ml/6fl oz/¾ cup fish, chicken or vegetable stock
30ml/2 tbsp sherry vinegar
2.5ml/½ tsp sugar
5ml/1 tsp fennel seeds, lightly crushed
2.5ml/½ tsp paprika
45ml/3 tbsp olive oil
salt and ground black pepper

1 Put the potatoes in a large pan. Add water to cover and bring to the boil. Add salt, then simmer for about 8–10 minutes, or until the potatoes are just tender. Drain thoroughly.

2 Preheat the oven to 190°C/375°F/Gas 5. Place the saffron strands in a bowl with 30ml/2 tbsp warm water and leave to infuse (steep) for 10 minutes.

3 Peel and finely chop two garlic cloves. Place the potatoes, onions, the remaining unpeeled garlic cloves, fennel wedges, bay leaves and thyme sprigs in a roasting pan.

4 Mix together the stock, saffron and its soaking liquid, vinegar and sugar, then pour over the vegetables. Stir in the fennel seeds, paprika, chopped garlic and olive oil, and season with salt and pepper.

5 Place the pan in the oven and bake for 1–1¼ hours, stirring occasionally, until the vegetables are tender. Chop the reserved feathery tops of the fennel, sprinkle over the vegetables and serve immediately.

Potato Pan Gratin Energy 238kcal/1002kJ; Protein 3.9g; Carbohydrate 36.3g, of which sugars 3g; Fat 9.6g, of which saturates 4.5g; Cholesterol 16mg; Calcium 15mg; Fibre 2.3g; Sodium 70mg.
Potatoes Baked with Fennel Energy 162kcal/676kJ; Protein 4.4g; Carbohydrate 23.6g, of which sugars 7.1g; Fat 6.2g, of which saturates 0.9g; Cholesterol 0mg; Calcium 49mg; Fibre 4.9g; Sodium 23mg.

Herby Potato Bake

This dish features wonderfully creamy potatoes that are well flavoured with lots of fresh herbs, and sprinkled with cheese to make a golden, crunchy topping. Serve as an accompaniment to grilled fish or meat.

Serves 4

butter, for greasing
675g/1½lb waxy potatoes
25g/1oz/2 tbsp butter
1 onion, finely chopped
1 garlic clove, crushed
2 eggs
300ml/½ pint/1¼ cups crème fraîche or double (heavy) cream
115g/4oz/1 cup Gruyère cheese, grated
60ml/4 tbsp chopped mixed fresh herbs, such as chervil, thyme, chives and parsley
freshly grated nutmeg
salt and ground black pepper

1 Place a baking sheet in the oven and preheat to 190°C/375°F/Gas 5. Butter an ovenproof dish.

2 Peel the potatoes and cut them into matchsticks. Set aside while you make up the sauce mixture.

3 Start by melting the butter in a heavy pan and cook the onion and garlic for 5–7 minutes until softened. Remove from the heat to cool slightly.

4 In a large mixing bowl, whisk together the eggs, crème fraîche or double cream and about half of the grated Gruyère cheese. Whisk thoroughly until all the ingredients are well combined.

5 Stir the onion mixture, mixed herbs and potatoes into the creamy egg mixture. Season with plenty of salt and ground black pepper, and sprinkle with the grated nutmeg. Spoon the mixture into the prepared dish and top with a sprinkling of the remaining cheese.

6 Place the dish in the oven on the hot baking sheet and bake for 50 minutes to 1 hour until the top is golden brown and the potato is tender. Serve immediately, straight from the dish, as this will ensure that the potatoes stay really hot.

Potatoes and Parsnips with Garlic and Cream

For the best results, cut the potatoes and parsnips very thinly – use a mandolin if you have one. As an alternative this method is also ideal for cooking sweet potatoes, which will produce a sweeter candied, but equally delicious, result.

Serves 4–6

3 large potatoes, total weight about 675g/1½lb
2 garlic cloves, crushed
350g/12oz small to medium parsnips
200ml/7fl oz/scant 1 cup single (light) cream
100ml/3½fl oz/scant ½ cup milk
butter, for greasing
about 5ml/1 tsp freshly grated nutmeg
75g/3oz/¾ cup coarsely grated Cheddar or Red Leicester cheese
salt and ground black pepper

1 Peel the potatoes and parsnips and cut them into thin slices. Cook in a large pan of salted boiling water for around 5 minutes. Drain and cool slightly.

2 Meanwhile, pour the cream and milk into a heavy pan and add the crushed garlic. Bring to the boil over a medium heat, then remove from the heat and leave to stand for about 10 minutes.

3 Preheat the oven to 180°C/350°F/Gas 4 and lightly butter the bottom and sides of a shallow ovenproof dish. Arrange the potatoes and parsnips in the dish, sprinkling each layer with a little freshly grated nutmeg, salt and ground black pepper.

4 Pour the liquid into the dish and press the potatoes and parsnips down into it. Cover with lightly buttered foil and cook in the hot oven for 45 minutes.

5 Remove the foil and sprinkle the cheese over the vegetables. Return the dish to the oven and continue cooking, uncovered, for a further 20–30 minutes, or until the potatoes and parsnips are tender and the top is golden brown.

Herby Potato Bake Energy 614kcal/2550kJ; Protein 15.6g; Carbohydrate 30.6g, of which sugars 5g; Fat 48g, of which saturates 30.8g; Cholesterol 221mg; Calcium 310mg; Fibre 2.5g; Sodium 321mg.
Potatoes and Parsnips Energy 241kcal/1012kJ; Protein 7.8g; Carbohydrate 27.2g, of which sugars 6.4g; Fat 11.7g, of which saturates 7.2g; Cholesterol 31mg; Calcium 173mg; Fibre 3.9g; Sodium 126mg.

Colcannon

This traditional Irish potato dish is especially associated with Hallowe'en, when it is likely to be made with curly kale and would have a ring hidden in it - predicting marriage during the coming year for the person who found it. However, it is also served throughout the winter, when green cabbage is more often used.

Serves 3–4 as a main dish, or 6–8 as a side dish
450g/1lb potatoes, peeled and boiled
450g/1lb curly kale or cabbage, cooked
milk, if necessary
50g/2oz/2 tbsp butter, plus extra for serving
1 large onion, finely chopped
salt and ground black pepper

1 Mash the potatoes. Chop the curly kale or cabbage, add it to the potatoes and mix to combine. Stir in a little milk if the mash is too stiff.

2 Melt a little butter in a frying pan over a medium heat and add the onion, Cook until softened, but not browned. Remove from the heat and mix well with the mashed potato and kale or cabbage mixture.

3 Add the remainder of the butter to the hot pan. When very hot, turn the potato mixture on to the pan and spread it out. Fry until golden brown and crispy.

4 Cut the colcannon into roughly sized pieces and continue frying until they are crisp and brown on all sides, taking care not to burn.

5 Serve in warmed bowls, or as a side dish to roasted or braised meats with plenty of butter.

> **Variation**
> Try varying the dish, by adding cooked swede (rutabaga) or turnip before mashing, or mixing in some freshly chopped mixed herbs with the kale or cabbage.

Potato, Onion and Garlic Gratin

This is a simple but delicious way of cooking potatoes and onions together. Choose stock to complement the main dish that it is accompanying. Alternatively, use water and add some bacon to give flavour. This gratin also makes a good base on which to bake fish.

Serves 4–6
40g/1½oz/3 tbsp butter or bacon fat or 45ml/3 tbsp olive oil
2–4 garlic cloves, finely chopped
900g/2lb waxy potatoes, thinly sliced
450g/1lb onions, thinly sliced
450ml/¾ pint/scant 2 cups fish, chicken, beef or lamb stock
salt and ground black pepper

1 Use half the butter, fat or oil to grease a 1.5 litre/2½ pint/6¼ cup gratin dish. Preheat the oven to 180°C/350°F/Gas 4.

2 Sprinkle a little of the chopped garlic over the base of the dish and then layer the potatoes and onions in the dish, seasoning each layer with a little salt and pepper and adding the remaining garlic. Finish with a layer of overlapping potato slices on top.

3 Bring the stock to the boil in a pan and pour it over the gratin. Dot the top with the remaining butter or bacon fat cut into small pieces, or drizzle over the reserved oil. Cover tightly with foil and bake for 1½ hours.

4 Increase the oven temperature to 200°C/400°F/Gas 6. Uncover the gratin and then cook for a further 35–50 minutes, until the potatoes are completely cooked and the top layer is browned and crusty. Serve immediately.

> **Variation**
> Layer 175g/6oz thinly sliced cheese with the potatoes. About 15–20 minutes before the end of cooking time, sprinkle the gratin with another 50g/2oz/½ cup grated cheese, dot with more butter and finish baking. This version is also good made with leeks.

Potato Gratin Energy 181kcal/762kJ; Protein 3.5g; Carbohydrate 30.1g, of which sugars 6.2g; Fat 6.1g, of which saturates 3.8g; Cholesterol 15mg; Calcium 29mg; Fibre 2.6g; Sodium 69mg.
Colcannon Energy 306kcal/1281kJ; Protein 5.4g; Carbohydrate 40.6g, of which sugars 13.6g; Fat 14.6g, of which saturates 8.8g; Cholesterol 36mg; Calcium 104mg; Fibre 5.9g; Sodium 127mg.

Potato and Spinach Gratin

Pine nuts add a satisfying crunch to this gratin of wafer-thin potato slices and spinach in a wonderfully creamy cheese sauce.

Serves 2

450g/1lb potatoes
1 garlic clove, crushed
3 spring onions (scallions), thinly sliced

150ml/¼ pint/⅔ cup single (light) cream
250ml/8fl oz/1 cup milk
225g/8oz frozen chopped spinach, thawed
115g/4oz/1 cup grated mature (sharp) Cheddar cheese
25g/1oz/¼ cup pine nuts
salt and ground black pepper
lettuce and tomato salad, to serve

1 Peel the potatoes and cut them carefully into wafer-thin slices. This is most easily done with a mandoline or the slicing attachment of a food processor. Spread the slices out in a large, heavy, non-stick frying pan.

2 Sprinkle the crushed garlic and sliced spring onions evenly over the potatoes.

3 Mix together the cream and milk in a jug (pitcher) and pour the mixture over the potatoes. Place the pan over low heat, cover with a tight-fitting lid and cook for 8 minutes, or until the potatoes are tender.

4 Drain the spinach thoroughly, then, using both hands, squeeze it as dry as possible. Add the spinach to the potatoes, mixing lightly. Cover the pan with a tight-fitting lid and cook for 2 minutes more.

5 Season to taste with salt and pepper, then spoon the mixture into a gratin dish. Preheat the grill (broiler).

6 Sprinkle the grated cheese and pine nuts evenly over the potato and spinach mixture. Lightly toast under the grill for around 2–3 minutes, until the cheese has melted and the topping is bubbling and golden brown. Serve the gratin immediately as a side dish, or for a light meal with a lettuce and tomato salad.

Lacy Potato Pancakes

These pretty, lacy potato pancakes should be served as an accompaniment to a fish dish or smoked salmon. Small pancakes make attractive and delicious canapés at parties.

Serves 6

6 large potatoes
1 leek, finely sliced
1 carrot, grated (optional)
15g/½oz/1 tbsp butter
15ml/1 tbsp vegetable oil
salt and ground black pepper

1 Peel and grate the potatoes. Put in a bowl, add the leek and carrot, if using, and mix them all together.

2 Heat the butter and oil in a frying pan and when smoking, add spoonfuls of the potato mixture to make 7.5cm/3in pancakes. Fry the pancakes, turning once, until golden brown on both sides. Season with salt and pepper and serve hot.

Byron Potatoes

A meal in itself, this dish is based on baked potatoes with a creamy cheese filling.

Serves 6

3 baking potatoes

115g/4oz/1 cup mature (sharp) Cheddar cheese, grated
90ml/6 tbsp single (light) cream
sea salt and ground black pepper

1 Preheat the oven to 200°C/400°F/Gas 6. Scrub the potatoes and pat dry. Prick each one with a fork and cook directly on the middle shelf for 1 hour 20 minutes.

2 Remove the potatoes from the oven and halve. Place the halves on a baking sheet and make shallow dips in the centre of each potato, raising the potato up at the edges.

3 Mix the cheese and cream together and divide evenly between the potatoes. Grill (broil) for 5 minutes until the cheese has melted and started to bubble. Serve hot, sprinkled with salt and pepper.

Potato Gratin Energy 248kcal/1037kJ; Protein 3.6g; Carbohydrate 30.7g, of which sugars 6.6g; Fat 13.2g, of which saturates 3.4g; Cholesterol 10mg; Calcium 31mg; Fibre 2.7g; Sodium 50mg.
Lacy Pancakes Energy 182kcal/767kJ; Protein 3.9g; Carbohydrate 33.1g, of which sugars 3.3g; Fat 4.6g, of which saturates 1.8g; Cholesterol 5mg; Calcium 20mg; Fibre 2.7g; Sodium 38mg.
Byron Potatoes Energy 180kcal/751kJ; Protein 7g; Carbohydrate 16.7g, of which sugars 1.9g; Fat 9.4g, of which saturates 6g; Cholesterol 27mg; Calcium 161mg; Fibre 1g; Sodium 157mg.

Potato Latkes

Latkes are traditional Jewish potato pancakes, fried until golden and crisp and served with hot salt beef or apple sauce and sour cream.

Serves 4
2 medium floury potatoes

1 onion
1 large egg, beaten
30ml/2 tbsp medium-ground matzo meal
vegetable oil, for frying
salt and ground black pepper
sour cream, to serve

1 Coarsely grate the potatoes and the onion. Put them in a large colander but don't rinse them. Press them down, squeezing out as much of the thick starchy liquid as possible. Transfer the potato mixture to a bowl.

2 Immediately stir the beaten egg into the potatoes. Add the matzo meal, stirring gently to mix. Season with salt and plenty of black pepper.

3 Heat a 1cm/½in layer of oil in a heavy frying pan for a few minutes (test it by throwing in a small piece of bread – it should sizzle). Take a spoonful of the potato mixture and lower it carefully into the oil. Continue adding spoonfuls, leaving space between each one.

4 Flatten the pancakes slightly with the back of a spoon. Fry for a few minutes until the latkes are golden brown on the underside, carefully turn them over and continue frying until golden brown.

5 Drain the latkes on kitchen paper, then transfer to an ovenproof serving dish and keep warm in a low oven while frying the remainder. Serve hot, topped with sour cream.

Variation
Try using equal quantities of potatoes and Jerusalem artichokes for a really distinct flavour.

Straw Potato Cake

This dish gets its name from its interesting straw-like appearance. Serve cut into wedges alongside roast meats as a change from the usual potato dishes.

Serves 4
450g/1lb firm baking potatoes
25ml/1½ tbsp butter, melted
15ml/1 tbsp vegetable oil
salt and ground black pepper

1 Peel and grate the potatoes, then toss with melted butter and season with salt and pepper.

2 Heat the oil in a large heavy frying pan. Add the potato and press down to form an even layer that covers the base of the pan. Cook over a medium heat for 7–10 minutes until the base is well browned.

3 Loosen the cake if it has stuck to the bottom by shaking the pan or running a knife under it. To turn the cake, invert a large baking tray over the frying pan and, holding it tightly against the pan, turn them both over together. Lift off the frying pan, return it to the heat and add a little more oil if it looks dry.

4 Slide the potato cake back into the frying pan, browned side uppermost, and continue cooking until the underside is crisp and golden. Serve the cake hot, cut into individual wedges.

Cook's Tip
Use the bigger side of a manual grater or a large blade on the food processor for the potatoes. They will then hold their shape better while being cooked than if you grate them finely.

Variation
Another nice way to serve this dish is to make several small cakes instead of a large one. They will not take quite so long to cook, so follow the method as for the large cake, but adjust the cooking time accordingly.

Potato Latkes Energy 221kcal/929kJ; Protein 4.3g; Carbohydrate 37.6g, of which sugars 20g; Fat 6.8g, of which saturates 1g; Cholesterol 43mg; Calcium 33mg; Fibre 2.7g; Sodium 28mg.
Straw Potato Cake Energy 146kcal/610kJ; Protein 2g; Carbohydrate 18.2g, of which sugars 1.5g; Fat 7.7g, of which saturates 3.4g; Cholesterol 12mg; Calcium 8mg; Fibre 1.1g; Sodium 47mg.

Cheese Bubble and Squeak

This London potato breakfast dish was originally made on Mondays with leftover vegetables from the previous Sunday's lunch.

Serves 4
about 450g/1lb/3 cups mashed potatoes
about 225g/8oz/4 cups shredded cooked cabbage or kale
1 egg, lightly beaten
115g/4oz/1 cup grated Cheddar cheese
pinch of freshly grated nutmeg
salt and ground black pepper
plain (all-purpose) flour, for coating
vegetable oil, for frying

1 Mix together the mashed potatoes, cabbage or kale, egg, cheese and nutmeg in a bowl and season with salt and pepper. Divide the mixture into eight pieces and shape into patties.

2 Place the patties on a large plate, cover with clear film (plastic wrap) and chill in the refrigerator for 1 hour or more, if possible, as this helps firm up the mixture.

3 Gently toss the patties in the flour to coat lightly. Heat about 1cm/½in oil in a frying pan until it is quite hot.

4 Carefully slide the patties into the oil and cook in the oil for about 3 minutes on each side, until golden and crisp. Remove with a slotted spatula, drain on kitchen paper and serve immediately.

> **Variation**
> For a more traditional version of bubble and squeak, heat 30ml/2 tbsp vegetable oil in a frying pan. Add 1 finely chopped onion and cook over low heat, stirring occasionally, for about 5 minutes, until softened but not coloured. Using a slotted spoon, transfer the onion to a bowl and mix with the other ingredients in step 1, omitting the cheese and using finely chopped cooked cabbage or Brussels sprouts. Use the same frying pan, with additional oil, for cooking the patties in step 4.

Bubble and Squeak

Whether you have leftovers, or cook this old-fashioned potato classic from fresh, be sure to give it a really good 'squeak' (fry) in the pan so it turns a rich honey brown as all the flavours caramelize together. It is known as colcannon in Ireland, where it is turned in chunks or sections, producing a creamy brown and white cake.

Serves 4
60ml/4 tbsp beef dripping, bacon fat or vegetable oil
1 onion, finely chopped
450g/1lb floury potatoes, cooked and mashed
225g/8oz cooked cabbage or Brussels sprouts, finely chopped
salt and ground black pepper

1 Heat 30ml/2 tbsp of the dripping, fat or oil in a heavy frying pan. Add the onion and cook, stirring frequently, until softened but not browned.

2 In a large bowl, mix together the potatoes and cooked cabbage or sprouts and season with salt and plenty of ground pepper to taste. Add the vegetables to the pan with the onions, stir well, then press the mixture into a large, even cake.

3 Cook over a medium heat for about 15 minutes until the cake is browned underneath.

4 Invert a large plate over the pan, and, holding it tightly against the pan, turn them both over together. Lift off the frying pan, return it to the heat and add the remaining dripping, fat or oil. When hot, slide the cake back into the pan, browned side up.

5 Cook over a medium heat for 10 minutes or until the underside is golden brown. Serve hot, in wedges.

> **Cook's Tip**
> If you don't have leftover cooked cabbage or Brussels sprouts, shred raw cabbage and cook in boiling salted water until tender. Drain, then chop.

Cheese Bubble and Squeak Energy 181kcal/762kJ; Protein 8.5g; Carbohydrate 21g, of which sugars 2.4g; Fat 7.7g, of which saturates 4.5g; Cholesterol 68mg; Calcium 130mg; Fibre 1.6g; Sodium 447mg.
Bubble and Squeak Energy 219kcal/908kJ; Protein 2.5g; Carbohydrate 17.2g, of which sugars 2.5g; Fat 15.9g, of which saturates 1.9g; Cholesterol 0mg; Calcium 33mg; Fibre 2.6g; Sodium 14mg.

Potato Pampushki

When these crunchy Russian potato dumplings are split open, a tasty, creamy curd cheese and chive filling is revealed.

Serves 4
225g/8oz potatoes, peeled and diced

675g/1½lb potatoes, peeled and left whole
2.5ml/½ tsp salt
75g/3oz/scant ½ cup curd cheese
30ml/2 tbsp chopped fresh chives
ground black pepper
oil, for deep frying

1 Put the diced potatoes in a large pan. Add water to cover and bring to the boil. Add salt, then simmer for about 10 minutes, or until the potatoes are tender, but do not let them get too soft. Drain thoroughly and then return to the pan and mash thoroughly. Set aside.

2 Coarsely grate the whole potatoes and squeeze out as much water as possible. Put them in a bowl with the mashed potato, salt and black pepper. Mix together. In another bowl, mix the curd cheese and chives together.

3 Using a spoon and your fingers, scoop up a portion of the potato mixture, slightly smaller than an egg, and then flatten to a circle. Put 5ml/1 tsp of the cheese filling into the middle, then fold over the edges and pinch to seal. Repeat with remaining potato and cheese mixtures, to make about 12 dumplings.

4 Heat the oil to 170°C/340°F in a heavy pan or deep-fat fryer. Deep-fry the dumplings for about 10 minutes, or until deep brown and crisp on the outide. Drain well on kitchen paper and serve immediately.

Cook's Tip
Pampushki are traditionally cooked in stock or water and served with soup. If you prefer to poach them, add 15ml/ 1 tbsp plain (all-purpose) flour and 1 beaten egg to the mixture and poach the dumplings for 20 minutes.

Hash Browns

Crispy golden wedges of potato, 'hashed' up with a little onion, are a favourite American breakfast dish, but they will satisfy your potato cravings and taste delicious at any time of the day.

Serves 4
450g/1lb medium potatoes
60ml/4 tbsp sunflower or olive oil
1 small onion, chopped
salt and ground black pepper
chives, to garnish
tomato sauce, to serve

1 Put the potatoes in a large pan. Add water to cover and slowly bring to the boil. Add salt, then simmer for about 15 minutes, or until the potatoes are just tender, but do be careful not let them get too soft. Drain thoroughly and leave aside to cool.

2 When cool, peel the potatoes and grate them or chop into small even chunks.

3 Heat the oil in a large heavy frying pan until very hot. Add the potatoes in a single layer. Sprinkle the onion on top and season well with salt and pepper.

4 Cook on a medium heat, pressing down on the potatoes with a spoon or spatula to squash them together.

5 When the potatoes are nicely browned underneath, turn them over in sections with a spatula and fry until the other side is also golden brown and lightly crisp, pressing them down firmly again.

6 Serve immediately with a garnish of chopped chives and tomato sauce alongside.

Variation
Turn this side dish into a main meal by adding other ingredients to the potatoes in the pan, such as cooked diced meat, sliced sausages or even corned beef for a northern English corned beef hash supper.

Pampushki Energy 201kcal/852kJ; Protein 6.7g; Carbohydrate 36.6g, of which sugars 3.4g; Fat 4.4g, of which saturates 2.7g; Cholesterol 11mg; Calcium 39mg; Fibre 2.3g; Sodium 125mg.
Hash Browns Energy 183kcal/764kJ; Protein 2.1g; Carbohydrate 19.3g, of which sugars 2.3g; Fat 11.4g, of which saturates 1.4g; Cholesterol 0mg; Calcium 11mg; Fibre 1.3g; Sodium 13mg.

Lyonnaise Potatoes

Two simple ingredients are prepared separately and then tossed together to create the perfect combination. These potatoes go very well with a simple meat dish, such as steak or pork chops. Serve with a bowl of French beans, tossed in butter.

Serves 6
900g/2lb floury potatoes
vegetable oil for shallow frying
25g/1oz/2 tbsp butter
15ml/1 tbsp olive oil
2 medium onions,
  sliced into rings
sea salt
15ml/1 tbsp chopped
  fresh parsley

1 Scrub the potatoes clean and put them in a large pan. Add water to cover and bring to the boil. Add salt, then simmer for about 15 minutes, or until the potatoes are tender, but do not let them get too soft.

2 Drain the potatoes through a colander and leave to cool slightly. When the potatoes are cool enough to handle, peel and finely slice them.

3 Heat the vegetable oil in a large, heavy frying pan and shallow fry the potatoes in two batches for about 10 minutes until crisp, turning occasionally.

4 Meanwhile, melt the butter with the oil in a separate frying pan and fry the onions for 10 minutes until golden, stirring frequently. Drain the cooked onions thoroughly on pieces of kitchen paper.

5 Remove the potatoes with a slotted spoon and drain on kitchen paper. Toss with sea salt and carefully mix with the onions. Sprinkle with the parsley and serve.

> **Variation**
> *For a more substantial version of this dish, ham or bacon can be added. Use about 50g/2oz chopped roast ham or bacon and fry with the onions until cooked through.*

Potato Kugel

This traditional Jewish potato accompaniment can be prepared with butter but this recipe uses vegetable oil, which gives a much lighter, healthier result. Perfect served with roasted meat or game.

2 eggs, lightly beaten
120–180ml/8–12 tbsp medium
  matzo meal
10ml/2 tsp salt
3–4 onions, grated
120ml/4fl oz/½ cup vegetable oil
ground black pepper

Serves 6–8
2kg/4½lb potatoes

1 Preheat the oven to 200°C/400°F/Gas 6. Peel the potatoes and grate them finely. Place the grated potatoes in a large mixing bowl and add the beaten eggs, matzo meal, salt and ground black pepper. Mix together until thoroughly combined. Stir in the grated onions, then add 90ml/6 tbsp of the vegetable oil.

2 Pour the remaining 30ml/2 tbsp oil into an ovenproof dish that is large enough to spread the potato mixture out to a thickness of no more than 4–5cm/1½–2in. Heat the dish in the oven for about 5 minutes, or until the oil is very hot.

3 Carefully remove the dish from the oven. Spoon the potato mixture into the dish, letting the hot oil bubble up around the sides and on to the top a little. (The sizzling oil helps to crisp the kugel as it cooks.)

4 Bake the kugel in the oven for about 45–60 minutes, or until tender and golden brown and crisp on top. Serve immediately, cut into wedges.

> **Cook's Tip**
> *Don't be tempted to grate the onions in the food processor as the action of the knife creates a bitter flavour by breaking down the cells of the onion flesh.*

Potato Kugel Energy 361kcal/1516kJ; Protein 8g; Carbohydrate 56.2g, of which sugars 6.8g; Fat 12.8g, of which saturates 1.8g; Cholesterol 48mg; Calcium 38mg; Fibre 3.7g; Sodium 538mg.
Lyonnaise Potatoes Energy 248kcal/1037kJ; Protein 3.6g; Carbohydrate 30.7g, of which sugars 6.6g; Fat 13.2g, of which saturates 3.4g; Cholesterol 10mg; Calcium 31mg; Fibre 2.7g; Sodium 50mg.

SIDE DISHES

Grilled Potatoes with Chive Flower Dressing

There is something very enjoyable about using edible plants and herbs from the garden. Chive flowers and champagne vinegar are used here as a dressing to grilled potatoes, and the result is a truly special dish. This is ideal served with simple grilled fish or meat, and also makes a sophisticated potato salad at a barbecue.

Serves 4–6

900g/2lb salad potatoes, such as
    Charlottes, Jersey royals or
    French ratte
15ml/1 tbsp champagne
    vinegar
105ml/7 tbsp olive oil
45ml/3 tbsp chopped chives
about 10 chive flowers
4–6 small bunches yellow cherry
    tomatoes on the vine
salt and ground black pepper

1 Light the barbecue and leave until the flames have died down. Boil the potatoes in a large pan of lightly salted water for about 10 minutes, or until just tender.

2 Meanwhile, make the dressing by whisking the vinegar with 75ml/5 tbsp of the oil, then stirring in the chives and flowers. Drain the potatoes and cut them in half horizontally. Season to taste with salt and pepper.

3 Once the barbecue flames have died down, position a grill rack directly over the coals to heat. When the coals are medium-hot, or with a moderate coating of ash, toss the potatoes in the remaining oil and lay them on the grill rack, with the cut side facing down. Leave over the heat for about 5 minutes, then press down a little so that they are imprinted with the marks of the grill.

4 Turn the potatoes over and cook the second side for about 3 minutes. Place the potatoes in a bowl, pour over the dressing and toss lightly to mix.

5 Grill the tomatoes for 3 minutes, or until they are just beginning to blister. Serve with the potatoes, which can be hot, warm or cold.

New Potatoes with Thyme and Lemon

These potatoes are cooked in a clay pot and are the perfect accompaniment to meat or poultry. You can even use old potatoes, cut into chunks, if you prefer. These make an ideal alternative to traditional roast potatoes.

Serves 4

675g/1½lb small new potatoes
4 garlic cloves, sliced
8 thyme sprigs
4 strips finely pared lemon rind
75ml/5 tbsp olive oil
coarsely ground black pepper
coarse sea salt

1 Soak a clay potato pot in cold water for 20 minutes, then drain. Scrub the new potatoes and rinse thoroughly in cold running water. Place the potatoes in the pot.

2 Add the garlic, thyme sprigs and pared lemon rind to the pot, tucking them in among the potatoes. Sprinkle over plenty of coarsely ground black pepper and coarse sea salt.

3 Drizzle over the olive oil. Cover with the lid and place in an unheated oven. Set the oven to 200°C/400°F/Gas 6 and cook for 1 hour, or until just tender.

4 If you wish, remove the lid and bake for a further 15–20 minutes, until slightly golden. If you prefer to keep the skins soft, remove the potatoes from the oven and leave to stand for about 10 minutes before serving.

Cook's Tips
• Thyme is an aromatic, woody herb that goes particularly well with lemon. It has a strong aroma and pungent flavour and grows wild in most warm climates. Thyme is often associated with dishes from the Mediterranean.
• You could easily make this dish with older potatoes – simply peel them, if you like, then cut them into even chunks or wedges before adding them to the pot.

Summer Squash and Baby New Potatoes in Warm Dill Sour Cream

Fresh vegetables and fragrant dill are delicious tossed in a simple sour cream or yogurt sauce. Choose small squash with bright skins that are free from blemishes and bruises. To make a simpler potato salad, pour the dill sour cream over warm cooked potatoes. Serve either version of the potato salad with poached salmon or chargrilled chicken.

Serves 4
400g/14oz mixed squash, such as yellow and green courgettes (zucchini), and pale green patty pan
400g/14oz tiny baby new potatoes
1 large handful mixed fresh dill and chives, finely chopped
300ml/½ pint/1¼ cups sour cream or Greek (US strained plain) yogurt

1 Cut the squash into pieces about the same size as the potatoes. Put the potatoes in a pan and add water to cover and a pinch of salt. Bring to the boil, then simmer for about 10 minutes, until almost tender.

2 Add the squash to the pan with the potatoes. Bring back to the boil and then reduce the heat and continue to simmer gently until the vegetables are just tender, then drain.

3 Transfer the vegetables into a wide, shallow pan and gently stir in the finely chopped fresh dill and chives.

4 Remove the pan from the heat and stir in the sour cream or yogurt. Return to the heat and heat gently until warm. Season with salt and pepper and serve.

> **Cook's Tip**
> *This dish is equally delicious if served cold. If you chill it in the refrigerator, allow it to come to room temperature and stir well before serving.*

Glazed Sweet Potatoes with Smoked Bacon

Smoky bacon is the perfect addition to these melt-in-the-mouth, sugar-topped potatoes. They taste great as a change from roast potatoes, with roast duck or chicken.

Serves 4–6
butter, for greasing
900g/2lb sweet potatoes
115g/4oz/½ cup soft light brown sugar
30ml/2 tbsp lemon juice
45ml/3 tbsp butter
4 strips smoked lean bacon, cut into matchsticks
salt and ground black pepper
1 flat leaf parsley sprig, chopped, to garnish

1 Preheat the oven to 190°C/375°F/Gas 5 and lightly butter a shallow ovenproof dish. Cut each unpeeled sweet potato crossways into three and cook in boiling water, covered, for about 25 minutes until just tender.

2 Drain thoroughly in a colander and leave to cool. When cool enough to handle, peel and slice thickly. Arrange in a single layer, overlapping the slices, in the prepared dish.

3 Sprinkle the sugar and lemon juice on the potato slices and dot the surface with butter.

4 Top with the bacon and season well with salt and black pepper. Bake in the oven, uncovered, for about 35–40 minutes, basting once or twice.

5 The potatoes are ready once they are tender – test them with a knife or metal skewer to make sure. Remove from the oven once they are cooked.

6 Preheat the grill (broiler) to a high heat. Sprinkle the potatoes with the chopped flat leaf parsley. Place the pan under the grill for about 2–3 minutes until the sweet potatoes are evenly browned and the pieces of bacon have turned crispy. Serve immediately.

Summer Squash Energy 317kcal/1317kJ; Protein 5.8g; Carbohydrate 21g, of which sugars 6.1g; Fat 23.9g, of which saturates 14.8g; Cholesterol 66mg; Calcium 105mg; Fibre 2g; Sodium 104mg.
Glazed Potatoes Energy 387kcal/1627kJ; Protein 7.2g; Carbohydrate 49.5g, of which sugars 26.1g; Fat 19.3g, of which saturates 9.8g; Cholesterol 50mg; Calcium 49mg; Fibre 3.6g; Sodium 562mg.

Colombian Cheesy Potatoes

Tender new potatoes are coated in a creamy cheese and tomato sauce.

Serves 6
1kg/2¼lb new or salad potatoes
25g/1oz/2 tbsp butter
4 spring onions (scallions), sliced
2 large tomatoes, peeled, seeded and chopped
200ml/7fl oz/scant 1 cup double (heavy) cream
90g/3½oz/1 cup grated mozzarella
salt and ground black pepper

1 Place the potatoes in a large pan of salted cold water. Cover and bring to the boil, then simmer for 18–20 minutes, until tender.

2 Meanwhile, melt the butter in a frying pan, add the spring onions and cook gently for 5 minutes, until softened. Stir in the tomatoes and cook for a further 2–3 minutes, stirring occasionally, until the tomatoes break up.

3 Drain the potatoes and put them in a warmed serving bowl. Add the cream to the onion and tomato mixture, bring to the boil, then add the cheese, stirring until it melts. Season to taste. Pour the hot sauce over the potatoes and serve immediately.

Creamed Sweet Potatoes

This dish uses white sweet potatoes rather than the orange variety.

Serves 4
900g/2lb sweet potatoes
50g/2oz/¼ cup butter
45ml/3 tbsp single (light) cream
freshly grated nutmeg
15ml/1 tbsp chopped fresh chives
salt and ground black pepper

1 Peel the sweet potatoes, cut them into large chunks and place in a pan of water. Boil for 20–30 minutes until tender.

2 Drain the potatoes and return them to the pan. Add the butter, cream, nutmeg, chives and seasoning. Mash with a potato masher and serve warm.

Glazed Sweet Potatoes with Ginger and Allspice

Fried sweet potatoes acquire a candied coating when cooked with ginger, syrup and allspice. The addition of cayenne pepper cuts through the sweetness and prevents the dish from becoming cloying.

Serves 4
900g/2lb sweet potatoes
50g/2oz/¼ cup butter
45ml/3 tbsp vegetable oil
2 garlic cloves, crushed
2 pieces preserved stem ginger, drained and finely chopped
10ml/2 tsp ground allspice
15ml/1 tbsp syrup from the preserved ginger jar
salt and cayenne pepper
10ml/2 tsp chopped fresh thyme, plus a few thyme sprigs, to garnish

1 Peel the sweet potatoes and cut them into 1cm/½in cubes. Melt the butter with the oil in a large frying pan. Add the sweet potato cubes and fry, stirring frequently, for about 10 minutes, until they are just soft.

2 Stir in the garlic, chopped ginger and allspice. Cook, stirring constantly, for 5 minutes more. Stir in the preserved ginger syrup. Season with salt and a generous pinch of cayenne pepper and add the chopped thyme. Stir for 1–2 minutes more, then serve, sprinkled with thyme sprigs.

Variation
For a less sweet, unglazed version of this dish, use a 2.5cm/1in piece of fresh ginger, finely chopped, instead of the preserved ginger and omit the syrup.

Cook's Tip
Some sweet potatoes have white flesh and some have yellow. Although they taste similar, the yellow-fleshed variety look particularly colourful and attractive.

Cheesy Potatoes Energy 343kcal/1430kJ; Protein 6.6g; Carbohydrate 29g, of which sugars 4.3g; Fat 25g, of which saturates 14.5g; Cholesterol 62mg; Calcium 87mg; Fibre 2.1g; Sodium 125mg.
Creamed Sweet Potatoes Energy 310kcal/1308kJ; Protein 3.1g; Carbohydrate 48.4g, of which sugars 13.3g; Fat 13g, of which saturates 8.3g; Cholesterol 35mg; Calcium 66mg; Fibre 5.4g; Sodium 189mg.
Glazed Potatoes Energy 387kcal/1627kJ; Protein 7.2g; Carbohydrate 49.5g, of which sugars 26.1g; Fat 19.3g, of which saturates 9.8g; Cholesterol 50mg; Calcium 49mg; Fibre 3.6g; Sodium 562mg.

Orange and Maple Syrup Candied Sweet Potatoes

A true taste of America, no Thanksgiving or Christmas table is complete unless sweet potatoes are on the menu. Serve with extra orange segments to make it really special.

Serves 8
900g/2lb sweet potatoes

250ml/8 fl oz/1 cup orange juice
50ml/2fl oz/¼ cup maple syrup
5ml/1 tsp freshly grated ginger
7.5ml/1½ tsp ground cinnamon
6.5ml/1¼ tsp ground cardamom
7.5ml/1½ tsp salt
ground black pepper
ground cinnamon, to garnish
orange segments, to serve

1 Preheat the oven to 180°C/350°F/Gas 4. Peel and dice the potatoes. Put the chunks into a large pan. Add water to cover and bring to the boil. Add salt, then simmer for about 5–8 minutes, or until the potatoes are tender, but do not let them get too soft.

2 Meanwhile, stir all the remaining ingredients together in a large mixing bowl. Spread out on to a non-stick shallow ovenproof dish.

3 Drain the diced sweet potatoes thoroughly and sprinkle over the other ingredients in the dish.

4 Place the dish in the preheated oven and bake for about 1 hour, stirring the potatoes every 15 minutes until they are tender and well coated. Serve as a accompaniment to a main dish, with orange segments and ground cinnamon.

Variation
Butternut squash would also work well in this recipe. Replace about half the quantity of the sweet potato with the squash and cut into similar-sized pieces. Boil with the sweet potato in the pan and cook for the same length of time in the oven, mixed together with the potato in the ovenproof dish.

Sweet Potato Salsa

Eye-catchingly colourful and delightfully sweet, this delicious salsa makes the perfect accompaniment to hot, spicy Mexican dishes.

Serves 4
675g/1½lb sweet potatoes
juice of 1 small orange
5ml/1 tsp crushed dried jalapeño chillies
4 small spring onions (scallions)
juice of 1 small lime (optional)
salt

1 Peel the sweet potatoes and dice the flesh finely. Bring a pan of water to the boil. Add the sweet potato and cook for 8–10 minutes, until just soft.

2 Drain off and discard the cooking water from the sweet potato, cover the pan and put it back on the hob, having first turned off the heat. Leave the sweet potato for about 5 minutes until the excess liquid has evaporated, then transfer to a bowl and set aside to cool.

3 Mix the orange juice and crushed dried chillies in a bowl. Chop the spring onions finely and add them to the orange juice and chilli mixture.

4 When the sweet potato is cool, add the orange juice mixture and toss carefully until all the pieces are coated.

5 Cover the bowl and chill for at least 1 hour, then taste and season with salt. Stir in the lime juice if you prefer a fresher taste to the salsa.

Cook's Tips
• This fresh and tasty salsa is also very good served with a simple grilled salmon fillet or other fish dishes, and makes a delicious accompaniment to veal escalopes or grilled (broiled) chicken.
• The salsa will keep for 2–3 days in a covered bowl in the refrigerator. Leaving the salsa to stand in this way will also help the flavours to develop.

Candied Sweet Potatoes Energy 124kcal/529kJ; Protein 1g; Carbohydrate 31.6g, of which sugars 26.1g; Fat 0.2g, of which saturates 0g; Cholesterol 0mg; Calcium 22mg; Fibre 0.9g; Sodium 461mg.
Sweet Potato Salsa Energy 153kcal/653kJ; Protein 2.4g; Carbohydrate 36.7g, of which sugars 9.9g; Fat 0.7g, of which saturates 0.2g; Cholesterol 0mg; Calcium 47mg; Fibre 4.2g; Sodium 69mg.

Sweet Potatoes, Onions and Beetroot in Coconut and Ginger Paste

Sweet potatoes and beetroot take on a wonderful sweetness when roasted.

Serves 4

30ml/2 tbsp groundnut (peanut) oil or mild olive oil
450g/1lb sweet potatoes, peeled and cut into thick strips or chunks
4 beetroot (beets), cooked, peeled and cut into wedges
450g/1lb small red or yellow onions, halved
5ml/1 tsp coriander seeds, lightly crushed
3–4 small whole fresh red chillies
salt and ground black pepper

chopped fresh coriander (cilantro), to garnish

For the paste

2 large garlic cloves, chopped
1–2 green chillies, seeded and chopped
15ml/1 tbsp chopped fresh root ginger
45ml/3 tbsp chopped fresh coriander (cilantro)
75ml/5 tbsp coconut milk
30ml/2 tbsp groundnut oil or mild olive oil
grated rind of 1/2 lime
2.5ml/1/2 tsp light muscovado (brown) sugar

1 First make the paste. Process the garlic, chillies, ginger, coriander and coconut milk in a food processor, blender or coffee grinder.

2 Turn the paste into a small bowl and beat in the oil, lime rind and muscovado sugar. Preheat the oven to 200°C/400°F/Gas 6.

3 Heat the oil in a roasting tin (pan) in the oven for 5 minutes. Add the sweet potatoes, beetroot, onions and coriander seeds, tossing them in the hot oil. Roast for 10 minutes.

4 Stir in the paste and the whole red chillies. Season well and toss the vegetables to coat them thoroughly with the paste.

5 Roast the vegetables for a further 25–35 minutes, or until the sweet potatoes and onions are fully cooked and tender. Stir two or three times to prevent the paste from sticking to the pan. Serve immediately, sprinkled with chopped coriander.

Bombay Potatoes

This authentic dish is most closely linked to the Gujarati, a totally vegetarian people and the largest population group in the city of Mumbai.

Serves 4–6

2 onions
2 fresh green chillies
50g/2oz/2 cups fresh coriander (cilantro)

450g/1lb new potatoes
5ml/1 tsp turmeric
60ml/4 tbsp vegetable oil
2 dried red chillies
6–8 curry leaves
1.5ml/1/4 tsp asafoetida
2.5ml/1/2 tsp each cumin, mustard, onion, fennel and nigella seeds
lemon juice, to taste
salt

1 Chop the onions and chillies finely, and coarsely chop the coriander.

2 Scrub the potatoes under cold running water and cut them into small pieces.

3 Boil the potatoes in water with a little salt and 2.5ml/1/2 tsp of the turmeric for 10–15 minutes, or until tender. Drain the potatoes well, then mash them and set aside.

4 Heat the oil in a frying pan and fry the dried chillies and curry leaves until the chillies are nearly burnt.

5 Add the sliced onions, green chillies, fresh coriander and remaining turmeric to the pan and fry for two minutes, until the onions are starting to soften.

6 Add the asafoetida, cumin, mustard, onion, fennel and nigella seeds. Cook, stirring occasionally, until the onions are soft.

7 Fold in the potatoes and add a few drops of water. Cook over a low heat for about 10 minutes, stirring well to ensure the spices are evenly mixed.

8 Stir the lemon juice to taste into the potatoes, and serve immediately.

Sweet Potato Energy 272kcal/1143kJ; Protein 4.4g; Carbohydrate 39.8g, of which sugars 19.2g; Fat 11.8g, of which saturates 1.7g; Cholesterol 0mg; Calcium 98mg; Fibre 6.3g; Sodium 122mg.
Bombay Potatoes Energy 143kcal/595kJ; Protein 2.1g; Carbohydrate 17.4g, of which sugars 4.7g; Fat 7.7g, of which saturates 0.9g; Cholesterol 0mg; Calcium 21mg; Fibre 1.7g; Sodium 10mg.

Patatas Bravas

The name of this Spanish tapas dish, patatas bravas, means fiercely hot potatoes, but luckily tapas are usually only eaten in small quantities.

Serves 4
900g/2lb small new or
  salad potatoes
60ml/4 tbsp olive oil
1 onion, finely chopped
2 garlic cloves, crushed
15ml/1 tbsp tomato purée (paste)
200g/7oz can chopped tomatoes
15ml/1 tbsp red wine vinegar
2–3 small dried red chillies,
  seeded and finely chopped, or
  5–10ml/1–2 tsp hot
  chilli powder
5ml/1 tsp paprika
salt and ground black pepper
1 flat leaf parsley sprig, to garnish
chopped fresh red chillies,
  to garnish (optional)

1 Put the potatoes in a large pan. Add water to cover and bring to the boil. Add salt, then simmer for about 15 minutes, or until the potatoes are tender, but do not let them get too soft. Drain thoroughly and leave to cool slightly, then cut in half and set aside.

2 Heat the oil in a large pan and add the onion and garlic. Fry them gently for 5–6 minutes until just softened. Stir in the tomato purée, tomatoes, vinegar, chillies or chilli powder and paprika and simmer for about 5 minutes.

3 Stir the potatoes into the sauce mixture until they are well coated. Cover and simmer gently for 8–10 minutes until the potatoes are tender.

4 Season the potatoes well and transfer to a warmed serving dish. Serve immediately, garnished with a sprig of flat leaf parsley. To make the dish even hotter, add a garnish of chopped fresh red chillies.

Cook's Tip
If you don't like your potatoes to be too fiery, simply reduce the amount of chilli to taste. Conversely, if you prefer a little more heat then increase the quantity used.

Fiery Spanish-style Chilli and Potatoes with Peppers

The most important thing with this potato dish is the spicing, which is made hotter still by adding vinegar. This version is made with fresh tomato sauce flavoured with garlic and chilli, and is a variation of traditional patatas bravas. The name implies that the potatoes are so hot that it is manly to eat them. Patatas bravas often appear on tapas menus and are good with drinks.

Serves 4
675g/1½lb small new potatoes
75ml/5 tbsp olive oil
2 garlic cloves, sliced
3 dried chillies, seeded
  and chopped
2.5ml/½ tsp ground cumin
10ml/2 tsp paprika
30ml/2 tbsp red or white
  wine vinegar
1 red or green (bell) pepper,
  seeded and sliced
coarse sea salt, for sprinkling
  (optional)

1 Scrub the potatoes and put them into a pan of lightly salted water. Bring to the boil and cook for 10 minutes, or until almost tender. Drain and leave to cool slightly. Peel, if you like, then cut the potatoes in half.

2 Heat the oil in a large frying or sauté pan and fry the potatoes, turning them frequently, until golden.

3 Meanwhile, crush together the garlic, chillies and cumin using a mortar and pestle. Mix the paste with the paprika and red or white wine vinegar, then add to the potatoes with the sliced pepper and cook, stirring, for 2 minutes. Scatter with salt, if using, then serve hot as a tapas dish or cold as a side dish.

Variation
Patatas bravas means fierce potatoes. They are meant to be fiery but the flavour can be moderated by reducing the amount of chilli. Although classically vegetarian, they are often served with chorizo or with chunks of roast pork. Try making them with sweet potatoes for a tasty change.

Patatas Bravas Energy 384kcal/1605kJ; Protein 5g; Carbohydrate 45g, of which sugars 7.3g; Fat 21.6g, of which saturates 3.3g; Cholesterol 0mg; Calcium 21mg; Fibre 3.6g; Sodium 31mg.
Spanish Potatoes Energy 256kcal/1070kJ; Protein 3.3g; Carbohydrate 30g, of which sugars 4.9g; Fat 14.4g, of which saturates 2.2g; Cholesterol 0mg; Calcium 14mg; Fibre 2.4g; Sodium 20mg.

Cumin and Fennel Spiced Potatoes

If you like chillies, you'll love these potatoes. However, if you're not a fan of very fiery flavours, simply leave out the chilli seeds, from both the dried and fresh chillies, and use the flesh by itself.

Serves 4

12–14 small new or salad
   potatoes, halved
30ml/2 tbsp vegetable oil
2.5ml/½ tsp dried red
   chillies, crushed
2.5ml/½ tsp white cumin seeds
2.5ml/½ tsp fennel seeds
2.5ml/½ tsp crushed
   coriander seeds
5ml/1 tsp salt
1 onion, sliced
1–4 fresh red chillies, chopped
15ml/1 tbsp chopped fresh
   coriander (cilantro), plus extra
   to garnish

1 Cook the potatoes in boiling salted water until tender but still firm. Remove from the heat and drain off the water. Set aside until needed.

2 In a deep frying pan, heat the oil over a medium-high heat, then reduce the heat to medium. Add the crushed chillies, cumin, fennel and coriander seeds and salt and fry, stirring, for 30–40 seconds.

3 Add the sliced onion and fry until softened and golden brown. Then add the potatoes, red chillies and chopped fresh coriander and stir well.

4 Reduce the heat to very low, then cover and cook for 5–7 minutes. Serve the potatoes hot, garnished with more fresh coriander.

Cook's Tips
• To prepare fresh chillies, trim the stalk end, slit down one side and scrape out the seeds, unless you want a really hot dish. Finely slice or chop the flesh.
• Wear rubber gloves if you have very sensitive skin and wash your hands thoroughly after handling chillies. Avoid touching your eyes if you have any trace of chilli on your fingers.

New Potatoes in Dashi Stock

As the stock evaporates in this delicious dish, the onion becomes meltingly soft and caramelized, making a wonderful sauce that coats the potatoes.

Serves 4

15ml/1 tbsp vegetable oil
15ml/1 tbsp toasted sesame oil
1 small onion, thinly sliced
1kg/2¼lb baby new or salad
   potatoes, unpeeled
200ml/7fl oz/scant 1 cup water
   with 5ml/1 tsp instant
   dashi powder
45ml/3 tbsp shoyu, dark soy
   sauce or kecap manis

1 Heat the vegetable and sesame oils in a wok or large frying pan until very hot. Add the onion slices and stir-fry for about 30 seconds, then add the potatoes. Stir constantly, until all the potatoes are well coated in the sesame oil, and have begun to sizzle.

2 Pour on the dashi stock and shoyu, dark soy sauce or kecap manis, and reduce the heat to the lowest setting. Cover the wok or pan and cook for 15 minutes, using a slotted spoon to turn the potatoes every 5 minutes to prevent sticking and to ensure that they cook evenly.

3 Uncover the wok or pan for a further 5 minutes to reduce the liquid. If there is already very little liquid remaining, remove the wok or pan from the heat, cover and leave to stand for 5 minutes. Check that the potatoes are cooked, then remove from the heat.

4 Transfer the potatoes and onions to a deep, warmed serving bowl. Pour the sauce over the top and serve immediately.

Cook's Tip
Toasted sesame oil is recommended because of its distinctive aroma, but mixing it with vegetable oil not only moderates the flavour, it also lessens the likelihood of the oil burning when heated in the pan.

Cumin Potatoes Energy 260kcal/1091kJ; Protein 4.8g; Carbohydrate 35.2g, of which sugars 2.8g; Fat 12.1g, of which saturates 1.5g; Cholesterol 0mg; Calcium 39mg; Fibre 3.4g; Sodium 40mg.
Potatoes in Dashi Stock Energy 210kcal/890kJ; Protein 4.8g; Carbohydrate 42.4g, of which sugars 4.9g; Fat 3.5g, of which saturates 0.7g; Cholesterol 0mg; Calcium 21mg; Fibre 2.7g; Sodium 829mg.

Spicy Potato Cakes

Quick and easy to make, these piquant potato cakes are very popular. Try serving them with salsa as a light meal, or as an accompaniment to roasted or pan-fried meats.

Makes 10
600g/1lb 6oz potatoes
115g/4oz/1 cup grated
  Cheddar cheese
2.5ml/½ tsp salt
50g/2oz/⅓ cup drained pickled
  jalapeño chilli slices, finely
  chopped (optional)
1 egg, beaten
small bunch of fresh coriander
  (cilantro), finely chopped
plain (all-purpose) flour,
  for shaping
oil, for shallow frying
fresh citrus salsa, to serve

1 Peel the potatoes and halve them if large. Put them in a large pan. Add water to cover and bring to the boil. Add salt, then simmer for about 15 minutes, or until the potatoes are tender, but do not let them get too soft.

2 Drain the potatoes thoroughly and return to the pan and mash. Don't overdo this step as the mashed potato should not be too smooth.

3 Scrape the potato into a bowl and stir in the grated cheese, with the salt and the chopped jalapeños, if using. Stir in the beaten egg and most of the chopped fresh coriander and mix to a dough.

4 When the dough is cool enough to handle, put it on to a lightly floured board. With floured hands, divide it into ten pieces of equal size. Shape each piece into a ball, then flatten to a cake.

5 Heat the oil in a large frying pan. Fry the potato cakes, in batches if necessary, for about 2–3 minutes over a moderate heat until golden brown on the underside.

6 Turn them over and cook until both sides are evenly golden. Pile on a platter, sprinkle with salt and the remaining chopped coriander and serve with salsa.

Potatoes in Chilli Tamarind Sauce

In this favourite potato dish from India, the combination of chilli and tamarind awakens the taste buds immediately. This version adapts the traditional recipe slightly, to reduce the customary pungency and enhance the fiery appearance of this delicious combination.

Serves 4–6
450g/1lb small new potatoes,
  washed and dried
25g/1oz whole dried red chillies,
  preferably Kashmiri
7.5ml/1½ tsp cumin seeds
4 garlic cloves, chopped
90ml/6 tbsp vegetable oil
60ml/4 tbsp thick tamarind juice
30ml/2 tbsp tomato
  purée (paste)
4 curry leaves
5ml/1 tsp sugar
1.5ml/¼ tsp asafoetida
salt
coriander (cilantro) sprigs and
  lemon wedges, to garnish

1 Boil the new potatoes until they are fully cooked, ensuring they do not break. To test, insert a thin sharp knife into the potatoes. It should come out clean when they are fully cooked. Drain and cool the potatoes in iced water to prevent them from cooking further.

2 Soak the chillies for 5 minutes in warm water. Drain and grind with the cumin seeds and garlic to a coarse paste, either using a mortar and pestle or in a food processor.

3 Heat the oil and fry the paste, tamarind juice, tomato purée, curry leaves, sugar, asafoetida and salt until the oil can be seen to have separated from the spice paste.

4 Add the potatoes and stir to coat thoroughly in the sauce. Reduce the heat, cover the pan and simmer for 5 minutes. Garnish and serve immediately.

Variation
Chunks of large potatoes can be used as an alternative to new potatoes. Alternatively, try this dish with sweet potatoes. The spicy sweet-and-sour taste works very well in this variation.

Potato Cakes Energy 149kcal/621kJ; Protein 4.8g; Carbohydrate 9.8g; of which sugars 0.9g; Fat 10.1g; of which saturates 3.4g; Cholesterol 30mg; Calcium 101mg; Fibre 0.8g; Sodium 197mg.
Potatoes in Chilli Sauce Energy 90kcal/379kJ; Protein 2.7g; Carbohydrate 19.5g; of which sugars 5.7g; Fat 0.7g; of which saturates 0.1g; Cholesterol 0mg; Calcium 30mg; Fibre 1.9g; Sodium 12mg.

Indonesian Potatoes with Onions and Chilli Sauce

This dish gives another dimension to potato chips, with the addition of crisp onions and a spicy chilli dressing. Eat these hot, warm or cold, as a tasty snack.

Serves 6

3 large potatoes, about 225g/8oz each, peeled and cut into chips (French fries)

sunflower or groundnut (peanut) oil for deep-frying
2 onions, finely sliced
salt

For the dressing

1–2 fresh red chillies, seeded and ground, or 2.5ml/½ tsp chilli sambal
45ml/3 tbsp dark soy sauce

1 Rinse the potato chips and then pat dry very well with kitchen paper.

2 Heat the oil in a large pan. Deep-fry the chips, until they are golden brown in colour and evenly crisp.

3 Drain the chips on kitchen paper and then transfer to a dish, sprinkle with salt and keep warm.

4 Fry the onion slices in the hot oil until they are similarly crisp and golden brown. Drain well on kitchen paper and then add to the potato chips.

5 Mix the ground chillies or chilli sambal with the soy sauce and heat gently.

6 Pour over the potato and onion mixture and serve immediately if you want them hot or leave to cool before serving.

Variation
Alternatively, you could boil the potatoes in their skins. Drain, cool and slice them and then shallow-fry until golden. Cook the onions and pour over the dressing, as above.

Curried Spinach and Potatoes

Traditional Indian spices – mustard seed, ginger and chilli – give a really good kick to potatoes and spinach in this delicious and authentic curry.

Serves 4

450g/1lb spinach
30ml/2 tbsp vegetable oil

5ml/1 tsp black mustard seeds
1 onion, thinly sliced
2 garlic cloves, crushed
2.5cm/1in piece root ginger, finely chopped
675g/1½lb firm potatoes, cut into 2.5cm/1in chunks
5ml/1 tsp chilli powder
5ml/1 tsp salt
120ml/4fl oz/½ cup water

1 Wash the spinach in several changes of water, then blanch it in a little boiling water for 3–4 minutes.

2 Drain the spinach thoroughly and leave to cool. When it is cool enough to handle, use your hands to squeeze out any remaining liquid.

3 Heat the oil in a large pan and fry the mustard seeds for 2 minutes, stirring, until they begin to splutter.

4 Add the onion, garlic and ginger to the pan and fry for 5 minutes, stirring.

5 Stir in the potatoes, chilli powder, salt and water and cook for about 8 minutes, stirring occasionally.

6 Finally, add the spinach to the pan. Cover and simmer for 10–15 minutes until the spinach is very soft and the potatoes are tender. Serve hot.

Cook's Tip
To make certain that the spinach is dry before adding it to the potatoes, put it in a clean dish towel, roll up tightly and squeeze gently to remove any excess liquid. Choose a firm waxy variety of potato or a salad potato so the pieces do not break up during cooking.

Indonesian Potatoes Energy 194kcal/815kJ; Protein 2.9g; Carbohydrate 25.6g, of which sugars 3.1g; Fat 9.6g, of which saturates 1.3g; Cholesterol 0mg; Calcium 13mg; Fibre 1.6g; Sodium 551mg.
Curried Spinach Energy 201kcal/845kJ; Protein 6.2g; Carbohydrate 30.2g, of which sugars 4.7g; Fat 6.9g, of which saturates 0.9g; Cholesterol 0mg; Calcium 205mg; Fibre 4.3g; Sodium 668mg.

Potatoes with Chorizo and Green Chillies

Mexicans make their own chorizo sausage, sometimes using it fresh, but also putting it into casings to dry, when it resembles the Spanish version which is now popular the world over. This recipe makes a delicious brunch dish. Typical of peasant food, it is based on the combination of plenty of potato mixed with strongly flavoured meat to help it go further.

Serves 4–6

900g/2lb potatoes, peeled and diced
30ml/2 tbsp vegetable oil
2 garlic cloves, crushed
4 spring onions (scallions), chopped
2 fresh jalapeño chillies, seeded and diced
300g/11oz chorizo sausage, skinned
150g/5oz/1¼ cups grated Monterey Jack or Cheddar cheese
salt (optional)

1 Bring a large pan of water to the boil and add the potatoes. When the water returns to the boil, lower the heat and simmer the potatoes gently for about 5 minutes. Transfer the potatoes into a colander and drain thoroughly.

2 Heat the oil in a large frying pan, add the garlic, spring onions and chillies and cook for 3–4 minutes. Add the diced potato and cook until the cubes begin to brown a little.

3 Cut the chorizo into small cubes and add these to the pan. Cook the mixture for 5 minutes more, until the sausage has heated through. Season with salt if necessary, then add the cheese. Mix carefully, trying not to break up the cubes of potato. Serve immediately, while the cheese is still melting.

Cook's Tip
Use firm-textured potatoes such as Desirée, Pentland Dell and Estima for this dish. If you can't locate Monterey Jack, look out for a mature Gouda, or use a medium mature Cheddar.

Potatoes in Spicy Yogurt Sauce

Tiny potatoes cooked with their skins on are delicious in this fairly spicy yet tangy yogurt sauce. Serve with any meat or fish dish or just with hot chapatis.

Serves 4

12 small new or salad potatoes, halved
275g/10oz/1¼ cups natural (plain) low-fat yogurt
300ml/½ pint/1¼ cups water
1.5ml/¼ tsp turmeric
5ml/1 tsp chilli powder
5ml/1 tsp ground coriander
2.5ml/½ tsp ground cumin
5ml/1 tsp salt
5ml/1 tsp soft brown sugar
30ml/2 tbsp vegetable oil
5ml/1 tsp white cumin seeds
15ml/1 tbsp chopped fresh coriander (cilantro)
2 fresh green chillies, sliced
1 coriander (cilantro) sprig, to garnish (optional)

1 Cook the potatoes in their skins in boiling salted water until just tender, then drain and set aside.

2 Mix together the yogurt, water, turmeric, chilli powder, ground coriander, ground cumin, salt and sugar in a bowl. Set aside.

3 Heat the oil in a medium pan over a medium-high heat and stir in the white cumin seeds.

4 Reduce the heat to medium, and stir in the yogurt mixture. Cook the sauce, stirring constantly, for about 3 minutes.

5 Add the fresh coriander, green chillies and potatoes to the sauce. Mix well and cook for 5–7 minutes, stirring occasionally.

6 Transfer to a serving dish, garnish with the coriander sprig, if you like, and serve hot.

Cook's Tip
If new potatoes are unavailable, use 450g/1lb large potatoes instead, but choose a waxy not a floury variety. Peel them and cut into large chunks, then cook as described above.

Potatoes with Chorizo Energy 443kcal/1847kJ; Protein 16g; Carbohydrate 32.4g, of which sugars 3.6g; Fat 28.1g, of which saturates 12.3g; Cholesterol 49mg; Calcium 226mg; Fibre 1.9g; Sodium 728mg.
Potatoes in Yogurt Sauce Energy 161kcal/677kJ; Protein 5.9g; Carbohydrate 24.7g, of which sugars 7g; Fat 5.1g, of which saturates 1g; Cholesterol 1mg; Calcium 154mg; Fibre 1.1g; Sodium 73mg.

Balti Baby Vegetables

There is a wide and wonderful selection of baby vegetables available in supermarkets these days, and this simple recipe does full justice to their delicate flavour and attractive appearance. Serve as part of a main meal or even as a light appetizer.

Serves 4–6
10 new potatoes, halved
12–14 baby carrots
12–14 baby courgettes (zucchini)

30ml/2 tbsp corn oil
15 baby onions
30ml/2 tbsp chilli sauce
5ml/1 tsp crushed garlic
5ml/1 tsp grated fresh
   root ginger
5ml/1 tsp salt
400g/14oz/scant 3 cups drained
   canned chickpeas
10 cherry tomatoes
5ml/1 tsp crushed dried
   red chillies
30ml/2 tbsp sesame seeds

1 Bring a medium pan of salted water to the boil and add the new potatoes and baby carrots. Cook for 12–15 minutes, then add the courgettes, and boil for a further 5 minutes or until all the vegetables are just tender. Take care not to overcook them, as they will be given a brief additional cooking time later.

2 Drain the vegetables well and put them in a bowl. Set aside.

3 Heat the oil in a karahi, wok or deep pan and add the baby onions. Fry until the onions turn golden brown. Lower the heat and add the chilli sauce, garlic, ginger and salt to the pan, taking care not to burn the mixture.

4 Stir in the chickpeas and stir-fry over a medium heat until the moisture has been absorbed.

5 Add the cooked vegetables and cherry tomatoes, and stir constantly over the heat with a slotted spoon for about 2 minutes until everything is heated through.

6 Sprinkle the crushed red chillies and sesame seeds evenly over the vegetable mixture and serve.

Crisp Deep-fried Vegetables

Stir-fried, steamed or deep-fried vegetables served with a dipping sauce are common fare throughout Asia, and often appear among the delightful 'no-name' dishes popular in Thai tourist fare.

Serves 4–6
6 eggs
1 long aubergine (eggplant), peeled, halved lengthways and sliced into half moons
1 long sweet potato, peeled and sliced into rounds

1 small butternut squash, peeled, seeded, halved lengthways and sliced into half moons
salt and ground black pepper
vegetable oil, for deep-frying
chilli sambal or hot chilli sauce for dipping

1 Beat the eggs in a wide bowl. Season with salt and pepper. Toss the vegetables in the egg to coat thoroughly.

2 Heat enough oil for deep-frying in a large wok. Cook the vegetables in small batches, making sure there is plenty of egg coating each piece.

3 When they turn golden, lift them out of the oil with a slotted spoon and drain on kitchen paper.

4 Keep the vegetables hot while successive batches are being fried. Serve warm with chilli sambal, hot chilli sauce or a dipping sauce of your choice.

Cook's Tips
• To encourage the beaten egg coating to adhere to the pieces of aubergine (eggplant), sweet potatoes and butternut squash, toss them in flour or cornflour (cornstarch) before coating with the egg.
• Courgettes (zucchini), angled loofah, taro root or pumpkin could also be used.

Deep-fried Vegetables Energy 280kcal/1164kJ; Protein 8; Carbohydrate 11.9g, of which sugars 5.7g; Fat 23g, of which saturates 4g; Cholesterol 190mg; Calcium 90mg; Fibre 3.5g; Sodium 84mg
Balti Baby Vegetables Energy 311kcal/1306kJ; Protein 12.3g; Carbohydrate 48.7g, of which sugars 15.2g; Fat 8.5g, of which saturates 1.3g; Cholesterol 0mg; Fibre 8.4g; Sodium 230mg.

Spiced Potatoes & Carrots Parisienne

Ready-prepared 'parisienne' vegetables have recently become available in many supermarkets. These are simply root vegetables that have been peeled and cut into perfectly spherical shapes. This dish looks very fresh and appetizing and is delicious. If you can't locate 'parisienne' vegetables, you can simply dice the potatoes and carrots yourself, or cut them into batons.

Serves 4

175g/6oz carrots parisienne
175g/6oz potatoes parisienne
115g/4oz green
   beans, sliced
75g/3oz/6 tbsp butter
15ml/1 tbsp vegetable oil
1.5ml/¼ tsp onion seeds
1.5ml/¼ tsp fenugreek seeds
4 dried red chillies
2.5ml/½ tsp mustard seeds
6 curry leaves
1 medium onion, sliced
5ml/1 tsp salt
4 garlic cloves, sliced
4 fresh red chillies
15ml/1 tbsp chopped fresh
   coriander (cilantro)
15ml/1 tbsp chopped fresh
   mint, plus 1 mint sprig
   to garnish

1 Drop the carrots, potatoes and green beans into a pan of boiling water, and cook for about 7 minutes, or until they are just tender but not overcooked. Drain in a colander, then refresh under cold water to arrest the cooking process. Drain again and set to one side.

2 Heat the butter and oil in a deep frying pan or a large karahi and add the onion seeds, fenugreek seeds, dried red chillies, mustard seeds and curry leaves.

3 When the seeds have sizzled for a few seconds and are starting to pop, add the onion and fry for 3–5 minutes, until the onion is soft, stirring the mixture occasionally.

4 Add the salt, sliced garlic cloves and fresh chillies, followed by the cooked vegetables, and stir gently and constantly for around 5 minutes, over a medium heat.

5 Add the fresh coriander and mint, and serve hot, garnished with a sprig of mint.

Roasted Vegetables and Spicy Sauce

Served as a vegetable side dish or as a main course, a selection of roasted vegetables in a peanut sauce, enhanced by chillies and soy sauce, is a favourite throughout South-east Asia.

Serves 4

1 aubergine (eggplant), partially
   peeled and cut into long strips
2 courgettes (zucchini), partially
   peeled and cut into long strips
1 thick, long sweet potato, cut into
   long strips
2 leeks, trimmed, halved
   and sliced
2 garlic cloves, chopped
25g/1oz fresh root ginger, peeled
   and chopped
60ml/4 tbsp vegetable or oil
salt
45ml/3 tbsp roasted peanuts,
   ground, to garnish
fresh crusty bread, to serve

For the sauce

4 garlic cloves, chopped
2–3 red chillies, seeded
   and chopped
5ml/1 tsp shrimp paste
115g/4oz/1 cup roasted
   peanuts, crushed
15–30ml/1–2 tbsp dark soy sauce
juice of 1 lime
5–10ml/1–2 tsp Chinese
   rice vinegar
10ml/2 tsp palm sugar (jaggery)
   or honey
salt and ground black pepper

1 Preheat the oven to 200°C/400°F/Gas 6. Arrange the vegetables in a roasting pan. Using a mortar and pestle or food processor, grind the garlic and ginger to a paste, and smear it over the vegetables. Sprinkle with salt and pour over the oil.

2 Place the pan in the oven for about 45 minutes, until the vegetables are lightly browned, tossing halfway through cooking.

3 Meanwhile, make the sauce. Using a mortar and pestle or a food processor, grind the garlic and chillies to a paste. Beat in the shrimp paste and peanuts. Stir in the soy sauce, lime juice, vinegar and sugar or honey, and blend with a little water so that the sauce is the consistency of pouring cream. Season with salt and pepper and adjust the balance of sweet and sour to taste.

4 Arrange the roasted vegetables on a plate. Drizzle the sauce over them, or serve it separately in a bowl. Sprinkle over the ground peanuts and serve with bread.

Spiced Potatoes Energy 186kcal/790kJ; Protein 7.4g; Carbohydrate 37.2g, of which sugars 5.9g; Fat 2g, of which saturates 0.9g; Cholesterol 5mg; Calcium 121mg; Fibre 2.9g; Sodium 51mg.
Roasted Vegetables Energy 361kcal/1502kJ; Protein 11.9g; Carbohydrate 22.7g, of which sugars 11.1g; Fat 25.4g, of which saturates 4.1g; Cholesterol 0mg; Calcium 76mg; Fibre 6.9g; Sodium 292mg.

Pumpkin, Sweet Potato and Banana in Coconut Milk

This dish of sweet potato and pumpkin cooked with bananas in coconut milk is a Malaysian favourite. Traditionally served as a sweet snack, or for breakfast, it is both nourishing and warming. The recipe can be adapted by alternating the sweet vegetable; try gourds such as yam, butternut squash and winter melon.

Serves 4–6

900ml/1 ½ pints/3¾ cups coconut milk
½ small pumpkin, seeded and cut into bitesize cubes
2 sweet potatoes, cut into bitesize pieces
1 pandanus (screwpine) leaf
150g/5oz/¾ cup palm sugar (jaggery)
2.5ml/½ tsp salt
3 bananas, cut into thick diagonal slices

1 Pour the coconut milk into a heavy pan and slowly bring it to the boil, taking care not to scald the bottom of the pan.

2 Stir the pumpkin, sweet potatoes and pandanus leaf into the pan of coconut milk. Continue to boil for 1 minute, then reduce the heat and simmer for about 15 minutes, until the pumpkin and sweet potato are tender but not too soft.

3 Using a slotted spoon, lift the pumpkin and sweet potato pieces out of the coconut milk and put them on a plate.

4 Add the sugar and salt to the coconut milk and stir until the sugar has dissolved.

5 Return the pan to the heat and bring the sweetened coconut milk to the boil, then reduce the heat and simmer for 5 minutes.

6 Add the bananas to the sweetened coconut milk and simmer for 4 minutes.

7 Put the pumpkin and sweet potato back into the pan and gently mix all the ingredients together. Remove the pandanus leaf and serve warm.

Pratie Potato and Apple Cake

This farmhouse classic is the perfect indulgent recipe for high tea, especially when using home-grown apples in autumn. The mashed potato dough is filled with deliciously sweet apples dredged in sugar, butter and lemon juice. A truly comforting tea-time treat.

Makes 2 farls; Serves 4–6

450g/1lb cooked potatoes in their skins, preferably still warm
pinch of salt
25g/1oz/2 tbsp butter, melted
about 115g/4oz/1 cup plain (all-purpose) flour

For the filling
3 large or 4 small cooking apples, such as Bramley's Seedlings
a little lemon juice (optional)
about 50g/2oz/¼ cup butter in thin slices
50–115g/2–4oz/¼ – generous ½ cup caster (superfine) sugar, or to taste

1 Preheat the oven to 200°C/400°F/Gas 6. Peel the potatoes and mash them in a large heavy pan until very smooth. Season to taste with the salt, and drizzle the melted butter over. Knead in as much plain flour as necessary to make a pliable dough. The dough should be elastic enough to roll out, but do not knead more than necessary.

2 Roll the potato mixture out on a lightly floured surface into a large circle and cut into four farls (triangular pieces).

3 To make the filling, peel, core and slice the apples and pile slices of the raw apple on to two of the farls. Sprinkle the apple with a little lemon juice, if you like. Dampen the edges of the farls with water or melted butter, place the other two on top, and press with your fingers around the edges to seal them together. For a less rustic finish, press round the edges, with a fork. Cook the farls in the preheated oven for about 15–20 minutes until browned.

4 Slit each cake around the side and turn the top back. Lay thin slices of butter over the apples, until they are almost covered, and then sweeten with sugar. Replace the top and return to the oven until the butter and sugar have melted to make a sauce. Cut each farl into pieces and serve.

Pumpkin in Coconut Energy 249kcal/1063kJ; Protein 2.6g; Carbohydrate 61.4g, of which sugars 51.7g; Fat 1g, of which saturates 0.5g; Cholesterol 0mg; Calcium 97mg; Fibre 2.8g; Sodium 187mg.
Pratie Apple Cake Energy 786kcal/3307kJ; Protein 9.5g; Carbohydrate 121.9g, of which sugars 40.5g; Fat 32.4g, of which saturates 19.9g; Cholesterol 80mg; Calcium 117mg; Fibre 6.1g; Sodium 253mg.

Steamed Cake with Sweet Potatoes

This soft steamed cake, known as mushi-kasutera in Japan, is not too sweet, and can be eaten almost like bread. The secret is a little miso, which adds a delicious and subtle saltiness to the cake.

Serves 4

200g/7oz/scant 2 cups plain (all-purpose) flour
140g/4³/₄oz/scant ³/₄ cup caster (superfine) sugar
45ml/3 tbsp sweetened condensed milk
4 eggs, beaten
40g/1¹/₂oz shiro miso
150g/5oz sweet potatoes
10ml/2 tsp cream of tartar
2.5ml/¹/₂ tsp bicarbonate of soda (baking soda)
30ml/2 tbsp melted butter

1 Sift the flour and the sugar together into a large mixing bowl. In a separate bowl, beat the condensed milk, eggs and shiro miso together to make a smooth cream.

2 Add the cream mixture to the flour and mix until well combined. Cover the bowl with clear film (plastic wrap) and leave to rest for 1 hour.

3 Trim the hard end of the sweet potatoes and thinly peel, then cut into 2cm/³/₄in dice. Cover with water to prevent discolouring. Drain just before using. Preheat the steamer, and line with muslin (cheesecloth).

4 In a bowl, mix the cream of tartar and bicarbonate of soda with 15ml/1 tbsp water. Add the mixture to the cake mixture along with the melted butter and two-thirds of the diced sweet potato.

5 Carefully pour the cake mixture into the steamer, then push the rest of the sweet potato on to the surface of the cake.

6 Steam the cake for 30 minutes, or until risen to a dome shape. Remove from the heat and cool a little. Serve warm or cold, cut into wedges.

Chocolate Potato Cake

Mashed potato makes this cake moist and delicious.

Makes one 23cm/9in cake

200g/7oz/1 cup sugar
250g/9oz/1 cup and 2 tbsp butter
4 eggs, separated
275g/10oz dark (bittersweet) chocolate
75g/3oz/³/₄ cup ground almonds
165g/5¹/₂oz mashed potato
225g/8oz/2 cups self-raising (self-rising) flour
5ml/1 tsp cinnamon
45ml/3 tbsp milk
white and dark (bittersweet) chocolate shavings, to garnish
whipped cream, to serve

1 Preheat the oven to 180°C/350°F/Gas 4. Grease and line a 23cm/9in round cake tin (pan) with baking parchment.

2 In a bowl, cream together the sugar and 225g/8oz/1 cup of the butter until light and fluffy. Then beat the egg yolks into the creamed mixture one at a time until it is smooth and creamy.

3 Finely chop or grate 175g/6oz of the chocolate and stir it into the creamed mixture with the ground almonds. Pass the mashed potato through a sieve (strainer) or ricer and stir it into the creamed chocolate mixture. Sift together the flour and cinnamon and fold into the mixture with the milk.

4 Whisk the egg whites until they hold stiff but not dry peaks, and fold into the cake mixture.

5 Spoon into the tin (pan) and smooth the top, but make a slight hollow in the middle to keep the surface of the cake level while cooking. Bake in the oven for 1¼ hours, until a skewer inserted in the centre comes out clean. Allow the cake to cool slightly in the tin, then turn out and cool on a wire rack.

6 Break up the remaining chocolate into a heatproof bowl over a pan of hot water. Add the remaining butter in small pieces and stir until the mixture is smooth and glossy.

7 Peel off the lining paper and trim the top of the cake so it is level. Smooth over the chocolate icing. When set, decorate with the chocolate shavings and serve with whipped cream.

Chocolate Cake Energy 5749kcal/24,034kJ; Protein 87.1g; Carbohydrate 590.9g, of which sugars 391.8g; Fat 354.8g, of which saturates 188.1g; Cholesterol 1465mg; Calcium 1408mg; Fibre 21.5g; Sodium 2731mg.
Steamed Cake Energy 512kcal/2165kJ; Protein 12.9g; Carbohydrate 90.5g, of which sugars 46.5g; Fat 13.6g, of which saturates 6.3g; Cholesterol 210mg; Calcium 162mg; Fibre 2.5g; Sodium 862mg.

Mung Bean and Potato Dumplings

These sweet and savoury rice and potato dumplings are often served with jasmine tea.

Serves 6
100g/3½oz/scant ½ cup split
  mung beans, soaked for
  6 hours and drained
50g/2oz/½ cup rice flour
115g/4oz/generous ½ cup caster
  (superfine) sugar
300g/10½oz/scant 3 cups
  glutinous rice flour
1 medium potato, boiled in its
  skin, peeled and mashed
75g/3oz/6 tbsp sesame seeds
vegetable oil, for deep-frying

1 Put the mung beans in a large pan with half the caster sugar and pour in 450ml/¾ pint/scant 2 cups water. Bring to the boil, stirring constantly until all the sugar has dissolved. Reduce the heat and simmer gently for 15–20 minutes until the mung beans are soft. You may need to add more water if the beans are becoming dry, otherwise they may burn.

2 Once the mung beans are soft and all the water has been absorbed, reduce the beans to a smooth paste in a mortar and pestle, or use a blender or food processor, and set aside the paste to cool.

3 In a large bowl, beat the flours and remaining sugar into the mashed potato. Add about 200ml/7fl oz/scant 1 cup water to bind the mixture into a moist dough. Divide the dough into 24 pieces, roll each one into a small ball, then flatten with the heel of your hand to make a disc and lay out on a lightly floured board.

4 Divide the mung bean paste into 24 small portions. Place one portion of the paste in the centre of a dough disc. Fold over the edges of the dough and then shape into a ball. Repeat for the remaining dumplings.

5 Spread the sesame seeds on a plate and roll the dumplings in them until evenly coated. Heat enough oil for deep-frying in a wok or heavy pan. Fry the balls in batches until crisp and golden. Drain on kitchen paper and serve warm.

Bean Paste, Sweet Potato and Chestnut Candies

It is customary in Japan to offer special bean paste candies with tea. These sweet potato and chestnut candies tend to be very sweet by themselves, but contrast well with Japanese green teas; in particular, large-leaf Sencha and Bancha.

Makes 18
450g/1lb sweet potato, peeled
  and roughly chopped
1.5ml/¼ tsp salt
2 egg yolks
200g/7oz sugar
60ml/4 tbsp water
75g/5 tbsp rice flour or plain
  (all-purpose) wheat flour
5ml/1 tsp orange flower water or
  rose water (optional)
200g/7oz canned chestnuts in
  syrup, drained
caster (superfine) sugar,
  for dusting
2 strips candied angelica
10ml/2 tsp plum or
  apricot preserve
3–4 drops red food colouring

1 Place the sweet potatoes in a heavy pan, cover with cold water and add the salt. Bring to the boil and simmer until tender, about 20–25 minutes.

2 Drain well and return to the pan. Mash the sweet potatoes well, or rub through a fine strainer. Place the egg yolks, sugar and water in a small bowl, then combine the flour and orange flower or rose water (if using). Add to the purée and stir over a gentle heat to thicken for about 3–4 minutes. Turn the paste out on to a tray and cool.

3 To shape the sweet potato paste, place 10ml/2 tsp of the mixture into the centre of a wet cotton napkin. Enclose the paste in the cotton and twist into a nut shape. If the mixture sticks a litte, ensure that the fabric is kept properly wet.

4 To prepare the chestnuts, rinse away the syrup and dry well. Roll the chestnuts in caster sugar and decorate with strips of angelica. To finish the candies, colour the plum or apricot preserve with red colouring and decorate each one with a spot of colour. Serve in a Japanese lacquer box or on a plate or tray.

Mung Bean Dumplings Energy 321kcal/1346kJ; Protein 7g; Carbohydrate 40g, of which sugars 21g; Fat 16g, of which saturates 2g; Cholesterol 0mg; Calcium 104mg; Fibre 3.1g; Sodium 0mg.
Bean Paste Candies Energy 300kcal/1278kJ; Protein 10.5g; Carbohydrate 66.5g, of which sugars 22.1g; Fat 1g, of which saturates 0.2g; Cholesterol 0mg; Calcium 94mg; Fibre 7.8g; Sodium 24mg.

Sweet Potato, Apple and Bean Paste Cakes

A mixture of mashed sweet potato and a hint of apple is shaped into cubes, covered in batter and then seared in a hot pan to seal in the natural moisture. Aduki bean paste is also made into cakes by the same method.

Serves 3 (makes 6)

about 250g/9oz canned neri-an (Japanese soft aduki bean paste), divided into 3 pieces

For the batter
90ml/6 tbsp plain (all-purpose) flour
pinch of sugar
75ml/5 tbsp water

For the stuffing
150g/5oz sweet potato, peeled
¼ red eating apple, cored and peeled
200ml/7fl oz/scant 1 cup water
50g/2oz/¼ cup sugar
¼ lemon

1 Put all the ingredients for the batter in a bowl and mix well until smooth. Pour the batter into a large, shallow dish.

2 Dice the sweet potato and soak it in plenty of cold water for 5 minutes to remove any bitterness, then drain well.

3 Coarsely chop the apple and place in a pan. Add the water and sweet potato. Sprinkle in 7.5ml/1½ tsp sugar and cook over a moderate heat until the apple and potato are softened.

4 Add the lemon juice and remove the pan from the heat. Then drain the sweet potato and apple and crush them to a coarse paste with the remaining sugar in a bowl.

5 Using your hands, shape the mixture into three cubes.

6 Heat a non-stick frying pan. Coat a cube of mixture in batter, then, taking great care not to burn your fingers, sear each side of the cube on the hot pan until the batter has set and cooked.

7 Repeat this procedure with the remaining mixture and with the neri-an, shaped into similar-sized cubes. Arrange one of each type of cake on a small plate and serve hot or cold.

Fruit and Sweet Potato Syrup

Arrope is an old Arab recipe whose name means 'syrup'. This version of it comes from the Pyrenees. It starts as a lovely fruit compote and becomes a syrupy jam, perfect with soft bread.

Serves 10

3 firm peaches
1kg/2¼lb/5 cups sugar

3 large eating apples
finely grated rind of 1 lemon
3 firm pears
finely grated rind of 1 orange
1 small sweet potato, 150g/5oz prepared weight
200g/7oz butternut squash, peeled, prepared weight
250ml/8fl oz/1 cup dark rum
30ml/2 tbsp clear honey

1 Cut the peaches into eighths, without peeling, and place in a large flameproof casserole. Sprinkle with 15ml/1 tbsp of the sugar. Peel and core the apples and cut into 16 segments, then arrange on top of the peaches. Sprinkle with the lemon rind and 15ml/1 tbsp of the sugar. Prepare the pears in the same way, place in the casserole, then sprinkle over the orange rind, followed by 15ml/1 tbsp of the sugar.

2 Slice the sweet potato into small pieces and spread over the top, followed by the sliced squash. Sprinkle with 15ml/1 tbsp of the sugar. Cover with a plate that fits inside the rim, weight it and leave for 2–12 hours for juice to form.

3 Put the casserole over a fairly low heat and bring to a simmer. Cook for 20 minutes, stirring once or twice. Add the remaining sugar, in three or four batches, stirring to dissolve each time. Bring the mixture up to a rolling boil and boil very steadily for 45 minutes. Stir and lift off any scum.

4 Test the reduced syrup by pouring a spoonful on a plate: it should wrinkle when a spoon is pulled across it. Off the heat, stir in the rum and honey. Return the casserole to a moderate heat and cook for a further 10 minutes, stirring frequently to prevent the fruit sticking. The colour will deepen to russet brown. Remove the pan from the heat and set aside to cool. If the resulting compote is a little too stiff, stir in some more rum before serving.

Sweet Potato Paste Cakes Energy 65kcal/275kJ; Protein 1.2g; Carbohydrate 13.6g, of which sugars 3.7g; Fat 1g, of which saturates 0.3g; Cholesterol 22mg; Calcium 19mg; Fibre 1.1g; Sodium 16mg.
Syrup Energy 308kcal/1291kJ; Protein 11g; Carbohydrate 38.1g, of which sugars 28.6g; Fat 13.2g, of which saturates 2.4g; Cholesterol 9mg; Calcium 246mg; Fibre 2.4g; Sodium 69mg.

Sweet Potato and Almond Panellets

The Catalan name for these nutty festival cakes means 'little bread', but they are, in fact, much closer to marzipan, with a slightly soft centre that is produced by their secret ingredient – sweet potato. Patisserie shops make hundreds of these little cakes for All Saints' Day, I November, when families take flowers to the graveyards of their relatives.

Makes about 24
115g/4oz sweet potato
butter, for greasing
1 large (US extra large)
 egg, separated
225g/8oz/2 cups ground almonds
200g/7oz/1 cup caster (superfine)
 sugar, plus extra for sprinkling
finely grated rind of
 1 small lemon
7.5ml/1½ tsp vanilla extract
60ml/4 tbsp pine nuts
60ml/4 tbsp pistachio
 nuts, chopped

1 Peel and dice the sweet potato and cook it in a pan of boiling water for about 15 minutes, until soft but not falling apart. Drain well and leave to cool.

2 Preheat the oven to 200°C/400°F/Gas 6. Line one or two baking sheets with foil and grease well with butter.

3 Put the cooled sweet potato into a food processor and process to a smooth purée. Gradually work in the egg yolk, ground almonds, caster sugar, lemon rind and vanilla extract, processing to make a soft dough. Transfer the dough to a bowl, cover with clear film (plastic wrap) and chill in the refrigerator for 30 minutes.

4 Spoon walnut-size balls of dough on to the prepared baking sheets, spacing them about 2.5cm/1in apart, then flatten them out slightly.

5 Lightly beat the egg white and brush over the cookies. Sprinkle half with pine nuts, slightly less than 5ml/1 tsp each, and half with pistachio nuts. Sprinkle lightly with sugar. Bake for 10 minutes, or until lightly browned.

6 Leave to cool on the foil, then lift off with a metal spatula.

Potato and Caraway Biscuits

These savoury potato biscuits are delicious warm or cold.

Makes 30
115g/4oz/8 tbsp butter, softened

115g/4oz/1⅓ cups mashed potato
150g/5oz/1¼ cups plain
 (all-purpose) flour
2.5ml/½ tsp salt
1 egg, beaten
30ml/2 tbsp caraway seeds

1 Preheat the oven to 220°C/425°F/Gas 7. Put the butter and mashed potato in a large bowl. Sift the flour and salt into the bowl, then mix to a soft dough. Knead the dough on a lightly floured surface until smooth. Cover and chill for 30 minutes.

2 Roll out the potato dough on a lightly floured surface until 8mm/⅓in thick. Brush with beaten egg, then cut into strips 2 × 7.5cm/¾ × 3 in. Transfer to an oiled baking sheet and sprinkle with caraway seeds. Bake for 12 minutes, or until lightly browned. Transfer to a wire rack and leave to cool.

Sweet Potato Muffins with Raisins

These muffins have the great colour of sweet potatoes.

Makes 12
1 large sweet potato, cooked,
 peeled and mashed
350g/12oz/3 cups plain
 (all-purpose) flour
15ml/1 tbsp baking powder

1 egg, beaten
225g/8oz/1 cup butter, melted
250ml/8fl oz/1 cup milk
50g/2oz/scant ½ cup raisins
50g/2oz/¼ cup caster
 (superfine) sugar
salt
12 paper muffin cases
icing (confectioners') sugar, to dust

1 Preheat the oven to 220°C/425°F/Gas 7. Sift the flour and baking powder over the mashed potatoes with a pinch of salt and beat in the egg. Stir the butter and milk together and pour into the bowl. Add the raisins and sugar and mix to combine.

2 Spoon the mixture into muffin cases. Bake for 25 minutes until golden. Dust with icing sugar and serve warm.

Panellets Energy 130kcal/541kJ; Protein 3.1g; Carbohydrate 10.7g, of which sugars 9.6g; Fat 8.6g, of which saturates 0.8g; Cholesterol 8mg; Calcium 32mg; Fibre 1g; Sodium 20mg.
Caraway Biscuits Energy 51kcal/212kJ; Protein 0.8g; Carbohydrate 4.6g, of which sugars 0.1g; Fat 3.4g, of which saturates 2.1g; Cholesterol 15mg; Calcium 9mg; Fibre 0.2g; Sodium 26mg.
Sweet Potato Muffins Energy 293kcal/1227kJ; Protein 4.1g; Carbohydrate 34.2g, of which sugars 9.3g; Fat 16.5g, of which saturates 10.1g; Cholesterol 57mg; Calcium 70mg; Fibre 1.4g; Sodium 135mg.

Sweet Potato Pie

Sweet potatoes make a wonderful pie filling and are available all year round. This spicy dessert, scented with cinnamon, ginger and nutmeg, is the perfect end to a summer barbecue or will make a deliciously warming end to a decadent winter feast.

Serves 6–8

675g/1½lb sweet
  potatoes, unpeeled
170g/6oz/1 cup light
  brown sugar
2 large (US extra large)
  eggs, separated
pinch of salt
5ml/1 tsp ground cinnamon
2.5ml/½ tsp ground ginger
1.25ml/¼ tsp grated nutmeg
175ml/6fl oz/¾ cup
  whipping cream
pinch of cream of tartar
  (if needed)
23cm/9in pie shell made from
  plain pastry

1 Put the sweet potatoes in a pan of boiling water. Simmer for 20–25 minutes, until tender. Drain and let cool. When the sweet potatoes are cool enough to handle, peel them.

2 Pureé the sweet potatoes in a blender or food processor; there should be 350ml/12fl oz/1½ cups of pureé. Preheat the oven to 190°C/375°F/Gas 5.

3 Combine the pureé, sugar, egg yolks, salt and spices in a bowl. Stir well to dissolve the sugar. Add the cream and stir to mix.

4 In another bowl, completely clean and grease free, beat the egg whites until they hold a soft peak. Add the cream of tartar when the whites are frothy.

5 Stir one quarter of the whites into the potato mixture to lighten it. Fold in the remaining whites with a metal spoon or rubber spatula.

6 Pour the filling into the pie shell and spread it out evenly. Bake for about 40–45 minutes, until the filling is set and lightly golden brown and the pastry is golden. The filling will rise during baking but will fall again when the pie cools. Serve warm or at room temperature with cream or ice cream.

Sweet Potato Scones

These are scones with a difference. A sweet potato gives them a pale orange colour and they are meltingly soft in the centre, just waiting for a knob of butter.

Makes about 24

150g/5oz sweet potatoes, peeled
  and cut into large chunks
butter, for greasing
150g/5oz/1¼ cups plain
  (all-purpose) flour
20ml/4 tsp baking powder
5ml/1 tsp salt
15g/½oz/1 tbsp soft light
  brown sugar
150ml/¼ pint/⅔ cup milk
50g/2oz/4 tbsp butter or
  margarine, melted

1 Put the sweet potatoes in a large pan. Add water to cover and bring to the boil, then simmer for about 8–10 minutes, or until the potatoes are tender.

2 Drain the potatoes thoroughly and leave to cool slightly, then mash and set aside.

3 Preheat the oven to 230°C/450°F/Gas 8. Grease a baking sheet. Sift together the flour, baking powder and salt into a bowl. Mix in the sugar.

4 In a separate bowl, mix the mashed sweet potatoes with the milk and melted butter or margarine. Beat until the ingredients are well blended.

5 Add the flour to the sweet potato mixture and stir until a smooth dough forms.

6 Turn out the dough on to a lightly floured surface and knead until soft and pliable.

7 Roll or pat out the dough to a 1cm/½in thickness. Cut into rounds using a 4cm/1½in cutter.

8 Arrange the rounds on the baking sheet. Bake for about 15 minutes until risen and lightly golden. Serve warm.

Sweet Potato Pie Energy 416Kcal/1736kJ; Protein 5.3g; Carbohydrate 38.2g, of which sugars 18.6g; Fat 28g, of which saturates 16.9g; Cholesterol 114mg; Calcium 98mg; Fibre 1.9g; Sodium 360mg.
Sweet Potato Scones Energy 48kcal/200kJ; Protein 0.9g; Carbohydrate 7.1g, of which sugars 1.4g; Fat 1.9g, of which saturates 1.2g; Cholesterol 5mg; Calcium 18mg; Fibre 0.3g; Sodium 18mg.

Savoury Potato Drop Scones

A light scone with a mild mustard and cheese flavour, these make a delicious breakfast dish served with scrambled eggs and juicy grilled tomatoes.

Makes 16
175g/6oz floury potatoes, diced
5ml/1 tsp mustard powder
115g/4oz/1 cup self-raising
  (self-rising) flour
1 egg, beaten
25g/1oz/¼ cup Cheddar
  cheese, grated
150ml/¼ pint/⅔ cup milk
oil, for frying and greasing
salt and ground black pepper
butter, to serve

1 Put the potato in a large pan. Add water to cover and bring to the boil, then simmer for about 15 minutes, or until the potatoes are tender, but do not let them get too soft.

2 Drain the potatoes thoroughly and then return to the pan. Mash with a potato masher or pass through a potato ricer or food mill into the pan.

3 Spoon the mashed potato from the pan into a large mixing bowl and then add the mustard powder, flour, egg, grated cheese and milk.

4 Beat well until the mixture comes together. Season with salt and ground black pepper.

5 Heat a griddle pan and brush lightly with oil. Drop generous tablespoonfuls of the mixture on to the griddle and cook for 1–2 minutes until browned on the underside. Flip the scones over and cook the second side. Repeat to make 16 scones. Serve warm with butter.

> **Cook's Tip**
> It is best to use a flat griddle rather than one with ridges for this recipe as the scones are quite small and thin. If you don't have a griddle, then a frying pan with a heavy base will work just as well.

Dill and Potato Scones

Potato scones flavoured with dill are quite scrumptious and can be served warm just with butter. Or if you want to make them substantial enough for a light supper, serve them topped with flaked salmon, kipper or mackerel.

oil, for greasing
225g/8oz/2 cups self-raising
  (self-rising) flour
40g/1½oz/3 tbsp butter, softened
pinch of salt
15ml/1 tbsp finely chopped
  fresh dill
30–45ml/2–3 tbsp milk

Makes about 10
175g/6oz potato, peeled and cut
  into chunks

1 Put the potato in a large pan. Add water to cover and bring to the boil, then simmer for about 15 minutes, or until the potatoes are tender, but do not let them get too soft. Drain thoroughly and then mash with a potato masher or pass through a potato ricer and set aside.

2 Preheat the oven to 230°C/450°F/Gas 8. Grease a baking sheet. Sift the flour into a bowl, and rub in the butter with your fingertips. Add the salt and dill and stir.

3 Add the mashed potato to the mixture and enough milk to make a soft, pliable dough.

4 Turn out the dough on to a well-floured surface and roll out until it is fairly thin. Cut into rounds using a 7.5cm/3in cutter.

5 Place the scones on the prepared baking sheet, leaving space between each one, and bake for 20–25 minutes until risen and golden. Serve warm.

> **Cook's Tip**
> If you don't have any dill you can replace it with the herb of your choice. Try fresh parsley or basil as an alternative.

Irish Griddle Potato Scones

These are also called potato cakes or griddle cakes, but whatever you call them they are delicious served hot with butter and jam, or with bacon for a hearty and sustaining breakfast.

Makes 6

225g/8oz floury potatoes, cut into
 uniform chunks

115g/4oz/1 cup plain
 (all-purpose) flour
2.5ml/½ tsp salt
2.5ml/½ tsp baking powder
50g/2oz/4 tbsp butter, diced
25ml/1½ tbsp milk
bacon rashers (strips), to serve
butter, for greasing

1 Cook the potatoes in a pan of boiling water until tender.

2 Drain the potatoes and return them to the pan over a high heat. Using a wooden spoon, stir the potatoes for 1 minute until all traces of moisture have evaporated. Remove from the heat. Mash well, making sure there are no lumps.

3 Sift together the flour, salt and baking powder into a bowl. Rub in the butter with your fingertips until it has the consistency of fine breadcrumbs.

4 Add the mashed potatoes and mix thoroughly with a fork. Make a well in the centre and pour in the milk. Mix to form a smooth dough.

5 Turn out on to a lightly floured surface and knead gently for about 5 minutes until soft and pliable. Roll out to a round about 5mm/¼in thick. Cut in half, then cut each half into three wedges.

6 Before you cook the scones, fry a batch of bacon rashers to serve with them. Keep warm in a low oven, until the scones are ready.

7 Grease a griddle or frying pan with a little butter and heat until very hot. Add the cakes and fry for 3–4 minutes until golden brown on both sides, turning once. Serve hot with the bacon rashers.

Chive and Potato Scones

These little potato scones should be fairly thin, soft and crisp on the outside. Serve them for breakfast.

Makes 20

450g/1lb potatoes

115g/4oz/1 cup plain
 (all-purpose) flour, sifted
30ml/2 tbsp olive oil
30ml/2 tbsp chopped chives
salt and freshly ground black pepper
low fat spread, for
 topping (optional)

1 Put the potatoes in a large pan. Add water to cover and bring to the boil. Add salt, then simmer for about 15 minutes, or until the potatoes are tender. Drain the potatoes thoroughly in a colander.

2 Return the potatoes to the clean pan and mash them with a masher or pass through a potato ricer. Preheat a griddle or heavy frying pan.

3 Add the flour, olive oil and chopped chives with a little salt and black pepper to the hot mashed potato in the pan. Mix to a soft dough.

4 Roll out the dough on a well-floured surface to a thickness of 5 mm/¼ in and stamp out rounds with a 5cm/2in plain pastry (cookie) cutter. Lightly grease the griddle or frying pan with a little oil.

5 Cook the scones, in batches, on the hot griddle or frying pan for about 10 minutes, turning once, until they are golden brown on both sides. Keep the heat low.

6 Top the scones with a little low-fat spread, if you like, and serve immediately.

> **Cook's Tip**
> *Cooking the scones over a low heat ensures that the outsides do not become burnt before the insides of the scones are cooked through.*

Irish Griddle Scones Energy 155kcal/650kJ; Protein 2.6g; Carbohydrate 21.1g, of which sugars 1g; Fat 7.2g, of which saturates 4.6g; Cholesterol 19mg; Calcium 35mg; Fibre 1g; Sodium 70mg.
Chive and Potato Scones Energy 45kcal/191kJ; Protein 0.9g; Carbohydrate 8.1g, of which sugars 0.4g; Fat 1.2g, of which saturates 0.2g; Cholesterol 0mg; Calcium 9mg; Fibre 0.4g; Sodium 3mg.

Three Herb Potato Scones

These flavoursome scones are perfect served warm and split in two with hand-carved ham and Parmesan shavings as a filling.

Makes 12

225g/8oz/2 cups self-raising (self-rising) flour
5ml/1 tsp baking powder
pinch of salt
50g/2oz/4 tbsp butter, diced
25g/1oz potato flakes
15ml/1 tbsp chopped fresh parsley
15ml/1 tbsp chopped fresh basil
15ml/1 tbsp chopped fresh oregano
150ml/¼ pint/⅔ cup milk
oil, for greasing

1 Preheat the oven to 180°C/350°F/Gas 4. Sift the flour into a bowl with the baking powder. Add a pinch of salt. Rub in the butter with your fingertips to form crumbs. Place the potato flakes in a bowl and pour over 200ml/7fl oz/scant 1 cup boiling water. Beat well and cool slightly.

2 Stir the potatoes into the dry ingredients in the bowl with the herbs and milk.

3 Bring the mixture together to form a soft dough. Turn out on to a floured surface and knead the dough very gently for a few minutes, until soft and pliable.

4 Roll the dough out on a floured surface to about 4cm/1½in thickness and stamp out rounds using a 7.5cm/3in cutter. Reshape any remaining dough and re-roll for more scones. Place the scones on to a greased baking dish and brush the surfaces with a little more milk.

5 Cook for 15–20 minutes and serve warm. They can be eaten plain, or with a filling.

> **Cook's Tip**
> *Don't be tempted to season the mixture too much, as once cooked the baking powder can also increase the salty flavour of the finished scone and this can overpower the taste of the herbs.*

Oven-baked Potato Cakes

Potato cakes are widely made in Ireland and come in a variety of forms, but they're all at their best if made with freshly cooked potatoes, preferably while still warm. Serve straight from the oven, split open and buttered while hot.

Makes about 12

175g/6oz potatoes, peeled and cut into chunks
225g/8oz/2 cups self-raising (self-rising) flour
2.5ml/½ tsp baking powder
50g/2oz/¼ cup butter, diced
a pinch of salt
15ml/1 tbsp chopped fresh chives
200ml/7fl oz/scant 1 cup buttermilk

1 Put the potatoes in a large pan. Add water to cover and bring to the boil, then simmer for about 15 minutes, or until the potatoes are tender, but do not let them get too soft. Drain thoroughly and then mash and set aside.

2 Preheat the oven to 220°C/425°F/Gas 7 and lightly grease a baking tray with butter.

3 Sift the flour and the baking powder into a bowl and rub in the butter. Season with salt.

4 Add the mashed potato and chives to the bowl. Mix well, and then incorporate enough of the buttermilk until a soft dough forms.

5 Turn the dough on to a lightly floured work surface, knead lightly into shape then quickly roll out.

6 Cut into squares with a sharp floured knife or stamp out into rounds with a 5cm/2in cutter.

7 Place the rounds on the baking tray and bake in the preheated oven for about 20 minutes or until well risen and golden brown and crisp. Transfer to a wire rack to cool slightly. Serve warm or cold.

Herb Potato Scones Energy 46kcal/193kJ; Protein 1g; Carbohydrate 8.1g, of which sugars 0.4g; Fat 1.3g, of which saturates 0.2g; Cholesterol 0mg; Calcium 12mg; Fibre 0.5g; Sodium 3mg.
Oven-baked Potato Cakes Energy 108kcal/455kJ; Protein 2g; Carbohydrate 16.5g, of which sugars 0.4g; Fat 4.3g, of which saturates 2.6g; Cholesterol 11mg; Calcium 68mg; Fibre 0.7g; Sodium 99mg.

Cheese and Potato Scones

The unusual addition of creamy mashed potato gives these wholemeal scones a light moist crumb and a crisp crust. A sprinkling of mature Cheddar and sesame seeds adds the finishing touch.

Makes 9
115g/4oz/1 cup wholemeal
  (whole-wheat) flour
2.5ml/½ tsp salt
20ml/4 tsp baking powder
40g/1½oz/3 tbsp unsalted butter,
  plus extra for greasing
2 free-range eggs, beaten
50ml/2fl oz/¼ cup semi-skimmed
  (low-fat) milk or buttermilk
115g/4oz/1⅓ cups cooked,
  mashed potato
45ml/3 tbsp chopped fresh sage
50g/2oz/½ cup grated
  mature Cheddar
sesame seeds, for sprinkling

1 Preheat the oven to 220°C/425°F/Gas 7. Grease a baking sheet.

2 Sift the flour, salt and baking powder into a bowl. Rub in the butter using your fingers until the mixture resembles fine breadcrumbs, then mix in half the beaten eggs and all the milk or buttermilk.

3 Add the mashed potato, sage and half the Cheddar, and mix to a soft dough with your hands.

4 Turn out the dough on to a floured surface and knead lightly until smooth. Roll out the dough to 2cm/¾in thick, then stamp out nine scones using a 6cm/2½in fluted cutter.

5 Place the scones on the prepared baking sheet and brush the tops with the remaining half of the beaten egg. Sprinkle the rest of the cheese and the sesame seeds on top and bake for 15 minutes until golden. Transfer to a wire rack and leave to cool.

> **Variations**
> • Use unbleached self-raising (self-rising) flour instead of wholemeal (whole-wheat) flour and baking powder, if you wish.
> • Fresh rosemary, basil or thyme can all be used in place of the sage, with equally delicious results.

Sweet Potato and Honey Bread Rolls

These sweet potato rolls taste delicious served with jams or with a savoury soup.

Makes 12
1 large sweet potato
225g/8oz/2 cups strong white
  bread flour
5ml/1 tsp easy-blend (rapid-rise)
  dried yeast
pinch ground nutmeg
pinch cumin seeds
5ml/1 tsp runny honey
200ml/7fl oz/scant 1 cup
  lukewarm milk
oil, for greasing

1 Cook the potato in plenty of boiling water for 45 minutes or until very tender. Preheat the oven to 220°C/425°F/Gas 7.

2 Meanwhile, sift the flour into a large bowl, add the yeast, ground nutmeg and cumin seeds. Give the ingredients a good stir.

3 Mix the honey and milk together. Drain the potato and peel the skin. Mash the potato flesh and mix into the flour mixture with the liquid.

4 Bring the mixture together and knead for 5 minutes on a floured surface. Place the dough in a bowl and cover with a damp cloth. Leave to rise for 30 minutes.

5 Turn the dough out and knock back to remove any air bubbles. Divide the dough into 12 pieces and shape each one into a round.

6 Place the rolls on a greased baking sheet. Cover with a damp cloth and leave to rise in a warm place for 30 minutes or until doubled in size.

7 Bake for 10 minutes. Remove from the oven and drizzle with more honey and cumin seeds before serving.

> **Cook's Tip**
> This dough is quite sticky, so use plenty of flour on the surface when you are kneading and rolling it.

Cheese and Potato Scones Energy 124kcal/519kJ; Protein 4.8g; Carbohydrate 10.7g, of which sugars 0.7g; Fat 7.1g, of which saturates 4.1g; Cholesterol 58mg; Calcium 60mg; Fibre 1.3g; Sodium 94mg.
Sweet Potato Rolls Energy 87kcal/372kJ; Protein 2.5g; Carbohydrate 19.3g, of which sugars 2.4g; Fat 0.6g, of which saturates 0.2g; Cholesterol 1mg; Calcium 50mg; Fibre 1g; Sodium 16mg.

Cheese and Potato Bread Twists

A complete Ploughman's lunch, with the cheese and potato cooked right in the bread. This makes an excellent base for a filling of smoked salmon.

Makes 8
225g/8oz floury
  potatoes, diced

225g/8oz/2 cups strong white
  bread flour
5ml/1 tsp easy-blend (rapid-rise)
  dried yeast
150ml/¼ pint/⅔ cup
  lukewarm water
175g/6oz/1½ cups red Leicester
  cheese, finely grated
10ml/2 tsp olive oil, for greasing
salt

1 Cook the potatoes in a large pan with plenty of lightly salted boiling water for 20 minutes or until tender. Drain through a colander and return to the pan. Mash until smooth and set aside to cool.

2 Meanwhile, sift the flour into a large bowl and add the yeast and a good pinch of salt. Stir in the potatoes and rub with your fingers to form a crumb consistency.

3 Make a well in the centre and pour in the water. Start by bringing the mixture together with a round-bladed knife, then use your hands. Knead for 5 minutes on a well-floured surface. Return the dough to the bowl. Cover with a damp cloth and leave to rise in a warm place for 1 hour or until doubled in size.

4 Turn the dough out and knock back the air bubbles. Knead it again for a few seconds. Divide the dough into 12 pieces and shape into rounds.

5 Sprinkle the cheese over a baking sheet. Take each ball of dough and roll it in the cheese. Roll each cheese-covered roll on a dry surface to a long sausage shape. Fold the two ends together and twist the bread. Lay the bread twists on an oiled baking sheet.

6 Cover with a damp cloth and leave the bread to rise in a warm place for 30 minutes. Preheat the oven to 220°C/425°F/Gas 7. Bake the bread for 10–15 minutes. Serve hot or cold.

Potato Bread with Onions

This potato bread is utterly delicious served warm with a simple vegetable soup.

Makes a 900g/2lb loaf
450g/1lb/4 cups strong white
  bread flour
5ml/1 tsp easy-blend (rapid-rise)
  dried yeast
a pinch of salt, for the dough

15g/½oz/1 tbsp butter
325ml/11fl oz/1⅓ cups
  warmed milk
15ml/1 tbsp olive oil
2 medium onions, sliced into rings
115g/4oz maincrop
  potatoes, grated
1 sprig rosemary, chopped
2.5ml/½ tsp sea salt
oil, for greasing and to serve

1 Sift the flour into a large bowl. Make a well in the centre and stir in the yeast and a pinch of salt. Rub in the butter until the mixture resembles fine breadcrumbs. Gradually pour in the milk. Incorporate the ingredients with a round-bladed knife and then bring together with your fingers.

2 Turn the dough out and knead on a floured surface until it is smooth and elastic. Return the bread to a clean bowl and cover with a damp cloth. Leave to rise in a warm place for 45 minutes or until the dough has doubled in size.

3 Meanwhile, heat the oil in a pan and add the onions, stir over a low heat and cook for about 20 minutes until the onions are golden brown and very soft. Set aside. Boil the grated potatoes in lightly salted water for 5 minutes or until just tender.

4 Turn the dough out of the bowl and knock back (punch down). Roll out on a lightly floured surface. Drain the potatoes and sprinkle half over the surface with a little rosemary and half the onions. Carefully roll the dough up into a sausage shape.

5 Lift the dough into an oiled 23 × 23cm/9 × 9in flan tin (pan). Using the palms of your hands, flatten the dough out. Sprinkle with the remaining potatoes, onions, salt and rosemary. Cover again with a damp cloth and leave to rise for 20 minutes.

6 Meanwhile, preheat the oven to 220°C/425°F/Gas 7. Bake for 15–20 minutes. Serve warm drizzled with a little oil.

Cheese Twists Energy 231kcal/971kJ; Protein 8.7g; Carbohydrate 26.4g, of which sugars 0.8g; Fat 10.4g, of which saturates 5.2g; Cholesterol 21mg; Calcium 203mg; Fibre 1.2g; Sodium 162mg.
Potato Bread Energy 2154kcal/9113kJ; Protein 61.1g; Carbohydrate 423.9g, of which sugars 52.5g; Fat 36g, of which saturates 13.9g; Cholesterol 54mg; Calcium 1154mg; Fibre 22.1g; Sodium 332mg.

Thin Potato Bread

This is a traditional bread from Norway, known as lefse. The many types of lefse are all very thin, slightly soft potato breads. They can be eaten buttered and sprinkled with sugar or served with honey or cloudberry jam. Lefse can also be wrapped around a hotdog or filled with meat and a salad.

Makes about 35
1kg/2¼lb potatoes
40g/1½oz/3 tbsp butter
120ml/4fl oz/½ cup single (light) cream
450–600g/1–1⅓lb/4–5 cups plain (all-purpose) flour
salt

1 Put the potatoes in a large pan. Add water to cover and bring to the boil, then simmer for about 15 minutes, or until the potatoes are tender, but do not let them get too soft.

2 Drain the potatoes thoroughly in a colander and then return to the pan. Mash with a potato masher or pass through a potato ricer or food mill into the pan and set aside. Add the butter, single cream and about 5ml/1 tsp of salt and beat together. Set aside to cool.

3 When the potatoes are cool enough to handle, add enough flour to form a firm dough. On a lightly floured surface, knead the dough until smooth.

4 Divide the dough into pieces about the size of a large egg, roll into balls and put on a baking tray. Chill in the refrigerator for 30 minutes.

5 On a lightly floured surface, roll out each ball of dough until very thin. Heat a large ungreased frying pan or flat griddle until hot.

6 Cook the breads in batches over a medium heat, one at a time, until brown spots appear on the upper surface. Turn them over with a metal spatula and cook the second side. Put the breads between two dish towels to stop them from drying out. Serve immediately.

German Potato Bread

This is an adaptation of the classic German-style bread. This version is made with strong white flour and floury potatoes.

Makes a 450g/1lb loaf
175g/6oz potatoes, peeled and cut into chunks
butter, for greasing
225g/8oz/2 cups strong white bread flour
10ml/2 tsp baking powder
5ml/1 tsp salt
15ml/1 tbsp vegetable oil
paprika, for dusting
mustard-flavoured butter, to serve

1 Put the potatoes in a large pan. Add water to cover and bring to the boil, then simmer for about 15 minutes, or until the potatoes are tender, but do not let them get too soft.

2 Drain the potatoes thoroughly in a colander and then return to the pan. Mash with a potato masher or pass through a potato ricer or food mill into the pan and set aside.

3 Preheat the oven to 230°C/450°F/Gas 8. Grease and line a 450g/1lb loaf tin (pan).

4 Sift the flour into a large bowl and mix together with baking powder and the salt.

5 Rub the mashed potato into the dry ingredients making sure you achieve an even mixture.

6 Stir in the oil and 200ml/7fl oz/scant 1 cup lukewarm water. Turn the dough into the tin and dust with the paprika.

7 Bake in the oven for 25 minutes. Turn out on to a wire rack to cool. Cut the bread into thick chunks and serve with mustard-flavoured butter.

Cook's Tip
This bread is best eaten while still warm, with lashings of the mustard-flavoured butter.

German Bread Energy 989kcal/4191kJ; Protein 24.1g; Carbohydrate 203g, of which sugars 5.7g; Fat 14.4g, of which saturates 1.8g; Cholesterol 0mg; Calcium 326mg; Fibre 8.7g; Sodium 1991mg.
Thin Potato Bread Energy 71kcal/301kJ; Protein 1.8g; Carbohydrate 14.7g, of which sugars 0.6g; Fat 1g, of which saturates 0.5g; Cholesterol 2mg; Calcium 23mg; Fibre 0.7g; Sodium 5mg.

Savoury Cranberry and Potato Bread Slice

An interesting combination of cranberries with bacon and potatoes.

Makes a 450g/1lb loaf
450g/1lb/4 cups strong white
  bread flour
5ml/1 tsp easy-blend (rapid-rise)
  dried yeast
5ml/1 tsp salt
25g/1oz/2 tbsp butter, diced

325ml/11fl oz/1⅓ cups
  lukewarm water
75g/3oz/¾ cup fresh or frozen
  cranberries, thawed
oil, for greasing
225g/8oz floury potatoes, halved
6 rashers (strips) rindless streaky
  (fatty) bacon, chopped
30ml/2 tbsp runny honey
salt and ground black pepper

1 Sift the flour into a bowl, stir in the yeast and 5ml/1 tsp salt. Rub in the butter to form breadcrumbs. Make a well in the centre and stir in the water.

2 Bring the mixture together with a round-bladed knife and then turn out on to a floured surface. Knead for 5 minutes. Place the dough in a bowl and cover with a damp cloth. Leave to rise for 1 hour or until doubled in size.

3 Turn the dough out and knock back (punch down) to remove the air bubbles. Knead for a few minutes. Carefully knead the cranberries into the bread. Roll the dough out to a rectangle and place in an oiled 23 × 23cm/9 × 9in flan tin (pan). Push the dough into the corners and cover with a damp cloth. Leave to rise in a warm place for 30 minutes.

4 Preheat the oven to 220°C/425°F/Gas 7. Meanwhile, boil the potatoes in plenty of salted water for 15 minutes or until just tender. Drain and when cool enough to handle, slice thinly.

5 Sprinkle the potatoes and bacon over the risen bread dough, season, then drizzle with the honey and bake for 25 minutes, covering the bread loosely with foil after 20 minutes to prevent burning. Remove the bread from the oven, transfer to a wire rack and leave to cool.

Russian Potato Bread

This lovely, moist potato loaf is delicious just served with butter. This easy-to-make bread also keeps really well.

Makes 1 loaf
butter, for greasing
225g/8oz floury potatoes, diced
6g/¼oz sachet easy-blend
  (rapid-rise) dried yeast

350g/12oz/3 cups unbleached
  white bread flour
115g/4oz/1 cup wholemeal
  (whole-wheat) bread flour, plus
  extra for sprinkling
2.5ml/½ tsp caraway
  seeds, crushed
10ml/2 tsp salt
25g/1oz/2 tbsp butter, diced

1 Lightly grease a baking sheet. Cook the potatoes in boiling water until tender. Drain well, reserving 150ml/¼ pint/⅔ cup of the cooking water. Mash the potatoes and leave to cool.

2 Mix together the yeast, white bread flour, wholemeal bread flour, caraway seeds and salt in a large bowl. Add the butter, cut into small pieces and rub in to form a breadcrumb consistency.

3 Mix together the reserved potato water and sieved potatoes. Gradually work this mixture into the flour mixture to form a soft dough. Turn out on to a lightly floured surface and knead for 8–10 minutes until smooth and elastic.

4 Place the dough in a large, lightly oiled bowl, cover with lightly oiled clear film (plastic wrap) and leave to rise, in a warm place, for about 1 hour, or until it has doubled in size.

5 Turn out on to a floured surface and knead gently. Shape into a plump oval loaf about 18cm/7in long. Place on the prepared baking sheet and sprinkle with a little wholemeal flour. Cover with lightly oiled clear film and leave to rise, in a warm place, for 30 minutes, or until doubled in size.

6 Meanwhile, preheat the oven to 200°C/400°F/Gas 6. Using a sharp knife, slash the top with 3–4 diagonal cuts to make a criss-cross effect. Bake for 30–35 minutes until golden and hollow sounding when tapped on the base. Transfer to a wire rack to cool.

Cranberry Bread Energy 2196kcal/9292kJ; Protein 58.4g; Carbohydrate 415.5g, of which sugars 39.3g; Fat 44.7g, of which saturates 20.8g; Cholesterol 106mg; Calcium 657mg; Fibre 17.4g; Sodium 3141mg.
Russian Bread Energy 1893kcal/8026kJ; Protein 51.5g; Carbohydrate 381.8g, of which sugars 10.7g; Fat 28.3g, of which saturates 14.3g; Cholesterol 53mg; Calcium 553mg; Fibre 23.4g; Sodium 4120mg.

Sweet Potato Bread with Cinnamon and Walnuts

A wonderful sweet potato brunch dish, completely delicious served with crispy bacon for a hearty breakfast.

Makes a 900g/2lb loaf
1 medium sweet potato
5ml/1 tsp ground cinnamon
450g/1lb/4 cups strong white
    bread flour
5ml/1 tsp easy-blend (rapid-rise)
    dried yeast
50g/2oz/³⁄₂ cup walnut pieces
300ml/¹⁄₂ pint/1¹⁄₄ cups
    warmed milk
salt and ground black pepper
oil, for greasing

1 Boil the whole potato in its skin in a pan of lightly salted water for 20–30 minutes or until tender.

2 Meanwhile, sift the cinnamon and flour together into a large bowl. Stir in the dried yeast.

3 Drain the potato and cool in cold water, then peel the skin. Mash the potato with a fork and mix into the dry ingredients with the nuts. Make a well in the centre and pour in the milk. Bring the mixture together with a round-bladed knife, place on a floured surface and knead for 5 minutes.

4 Return the dough to a bowl and cover with a damp cloth. Leave to rise for 1 hour or until doubled in size.

5 Turn the dough out and knock back (punch down) to remove any air bubbles. Knead again for a few minutes. If the dough feels sticky, add more flour to the mixture.

6 Shape the dough into a ball and place the bread in an oiled and lined 900g/2lb loaf tin (pan). Cover with a damp cloth and leave to rise in a warm place for 1 hour or until doubled in size.

7 Preheat the oven to 200°C/400°F/Gas 6. Bake on the middle shelf of the oven for 25 minutes. Turn out and tap the base; if it sounds hollow the bread is cooked. Cool on a wire rack.

Cheese and Onion Potato Bread

A braided potato and olive loaf with a crisp cheese and onion topping.

Makes a 900g/2lb loaf
225g/8oz floury potatoes
350g/12oz/3 cups strong white
    bread flour
7.5ml/1¹⁄₂ tsp easy-blend
    (rapid-rise) dried yeast
25g/1oz/2 tbsp butter, diced
50g/2oz/¹⁄₂ cup pitted green or
    black olives

For the topping
30ml/2 tbsp olive oil
1 onion, sliced into rings
50g/2oz/¹⁄₂ cup mature (sharp)
    Cheddar cheese, grated
salt and ground black pepper

1 Chop the potatoes and cook in a large pan with plenty of salted boiling water for 15–20 minutes or until tender.

2 Meanwhile, sift the flour into a bowl, add the yeast and a little salt. Rub in the butter to form fine crumbs. Drain the potatoes and mash well. Add to the dry ingredients with 300ml/¹⁄₂ pint/1¹⁄₄ cups lukewarm water.

3 Bring the mixture together with a round-bladed knife and then turn out on to a floured surface. Knead for about 5 minutes. Return the dough to the bowl and cover with a damp cloth. Leave to rise for 1 hour or until doubled in size. Turn the dough out on to a floured surface and knock back (punch down) to remove any air bubbles. Carefully knead in the olives. Cut the dough into three even pieces.

4 Roll each piece out to a long thick sausage. Twist the sausages over each other to form a plait. Lift on to a greased baking sheet. Cover with a damp cloth and leave to rise for 30 minutes or until doubled in size.

5 Preheat the oven to 220°C/425°F/Gas 7. Heat the oil in a pan and fry the onions for 10 minutes, stirring occasionally, until golden. Remove the onions from the pan and drain well on kitchen paper.

6 Sprinkle the onions and grated cheese over the bread and bake for 20 minutes until golden. Serve warm or cold.

Sweet Potato Bread Energy 87kcal/372kJ; Protein 2.5g; Carbohydrate 19.3g, of which sugars 2.4g; Fat 0.6g, of which saturates 0.2g; Cholesterol 1mg; Calcium 50mg; Fibre 1g; Sodium 16mg.
Cheese Potato Bread Energy 231kcal/971kJ; Protein 8.7g; Carbohydrate 26.4g, of which sugars 0.8g; Fat 10.4g, of which saturates 5.2g; Cholesterol 21mg; Calcium 203mg; Fibre 1.2g; Sodium 162mg.

252 Index